# OUR LÁTIN HERITÁGE

**THIRD EDITION**

**BOOK**

# I

**LILLIAN M. HINES, Author**

**EDWARD J. WELCH, Consultant**

**Harcourt Brace Jovanovich, Publishers**

Orlando   New York   Chicago   San Diego   Atlanta   Dallas

LILLIAN M. HINES, widely known as a Latin teacher, has taught in schools in Massachusetts, Ohio, Maryland, Connecticut, and California. Prior to the Chinese-Japanese War, she taught in China and studied Chinese. She obtained her A.B. at Xavier University, Ohio, and received her master's degree in Latin from Stanford University. She has studied the classics on the graduate level in various universities in the United States. In preparation for the revision of *Our Latin Heritage,* she spent some time in Rome doing archaeological research.

Among her writings are numerous articles on Latin, on the art of teaching Latin, and on related subjects. She is also author of the book *Vocabulary Building by the Cluster Method.*

We gratefully acknowledge the assistance of the following scholars in the preparation of this revision: Professor Rita M. Fleischer, Brooklyn College of the City University of New York; Professor Robert J. Penella, Fordham University; Ms. Stephanie Russell, New York University; Professor Robert Stieglitz, Rutgers University—Newark.

PHOTO CREDITS—KEY: top (t); bottom (b); left (l); right (r)

COVER: Vivian Peevers/Peter Arnold, Inc.

Insert A-1: Eric Carle/Shostal; A-2: J. Alex Langley/DPI; A-3: (tl) EPA; (tr) The Granger Collection; (b) Ray Manley/Shostal; A-4: (t) F.H.C. Birch/Bruce Coleman; (b) Scala/EPA; A-5: (t) Carl Purcell/Photo Researchers; (bl, br) Herschel Levit; A-6: (t,b) Herschel Levit; A-7: Scala/EPA; A-8: Walter S. Clark; B-1: Yan/Rapho/Photo Researchers; B-2: Scala/EPA; B-3: (l) Scala/EPA; (r) The Bettmann Archive; B-4: (t) The Metropolitan Museum of Art, Rogers Fund, 1909; (b) EPA; B-5: Hirmer Foto Archive; B-6: Scala/EPA; B-7: (t) The Bettmann Archive; (b) EPA; B-8: (t) German Archaeological Institute, Rome; (b) The Metropolitan Museum of Art, Harris Brisbane Dick Fund, 1940; C-1: The Metropolitan Museum of Art Purchase, 1953, Joseph Pulitzer Bequest; C-2: Herschel Levit; C-3: (t) Steve Vidler/Leo de Wys; (b) Victor Englebert/Photo Researchers; C-4: The Metropolitan Museum of Art, Bequest of Walter C. Baker, 1972; C-5: (t) Nigel Cameron/Photo Researchers; (b) The Metropolitan Museum of Art, Rogers Fund, 1906; C-6: Corning Museum of Glass; C-7: The Metropolitan Museum of Art, Rogers Fund, 1903; C-8: Scala/EPA; D-1: Herschel Levit; D-2: Herschel Levit; D-3: (t) Scala/EPA; (b) Herschel Levit; D-4: (t) Jan Lukas/Photo Researchers; (b) EPA; D-5: E. A. Weber/Photo Researchers; D-6: Leonard von Matt/Rapho/Photo Researchers; D-7: Fritz Henle/Photo Researchers; D-8: EPA

ILLUSTRATIONS: Marilyn Miller

ISBN 0-15-389465-2

# *Preface*

The immediate objective of *Our Latin Heritage: Book I* is to develop the student's ability to read and comprehend Latin. The method used is based upon the conviction that there is no incompatibility between the functional and the formal approaches to the teaching of Latin. Indeed, one is auxiliary to the other.

Ability to read Latin with easy and accurate comprehension depends upon the automatic recognition of the meanings of words and the functions of forms in phrase and sentence patterns. Achievement of this automatic recognition demands the use of all the pedagogical devices proper to learning to read any language. Therefore, in each of the sixty Units of this book we find the following:

**1. Provision for audio-lingual work.** Although training to speak Latin for its own sake is not one of our aims, the practice of precise and pure pronunciation is. Students cannot learn forms and functions accurately if their audio image of Latin words is vague and uncertain. They should hear and pronounce new words before attempting to read or write them. The simple Conversations in each Unit serve as a device to fix patterns and develop style, as well as to create an awareness of Latin as a *living* language. These Conversations are also a means of introducing functionally new vocabulary and syntax, and of reviewing in a fresh and lively manner material previously taught. Since they may be dramatized, they offer opportunity for class participation, group activity, and audience situation.

Over and over again in the course of an hour a teacher may repeat the same commands, and give the same directions in exactly the same way. These recurring phrases in classroom procedure can be given in Latin from the start. At the end of the first year a considerable number of words and expressions are learned independently of the textbook without overloading the memory. Such a practice serves the purpose of loosening the tongue and making Latin live. A list of classroom vocabulary and expressions may be found in the Appendix, pages 360–361.

**2. Provision for mastery of forms and syntax.** The second essential in learning to read a language is accurate and concise knowledge of the forms and the syntax of the language. If students are to develop facility in comprehending Latin, the declensions and conjugations and the rules of grammar must be learned thoroughly. Only then will a required form or function come to mind as needed.

In our method we assume no knowledge on the part of the student of either the facts or the terminology of basic grammar, English or Latin. In the Discussion sections each new form and each new principle of syntax are explained thoroughly but clearly in relation to both languages. Identical principles in both languages are noted; differences are stressed.

In Latin there is a closer relationship between form and function than in English since the inflections signal function. In this text the structural signals of Latin are called case indicators, person indicators, and tense indicators. Students master form and function through repetition of practice in using these indicators. In the presentation of declensions and conjugations, students are given a formula by which they can build up or break down any verb, noun, or adjective form. Always they proceed from the known to the unknown.

The short and easy Practice Patterns and Sentence Patterns in each Unit provide the student with ample practice in using new forms and syntax in conjunction with new vocabulary. The devices for building various patterns on each sentence may be found in the *Teacher's Handbook*.

To insure further mastery of form and function, there is a Comprehensive Review after every five Units. Usually the teacher can tell when reviews are needed and what they should include; but a uniform plan of testing achievement is very useful in the first year of a language for diagnostic purposes and for its contribution to the learning process.

The tenses of the subjunctive are presented, but the use of the subjunctive in the first year of Latin is optional. This subject matter is repeated in the second book of the series where it may be used for review or taught for the first time.

**3. Provision for the acquisition of vocabulary.** Acquiring vocabulary is at times the most tedious task in learning a new language. In this text the basic vocabulary has been selected for its surrender value in both English and Latin, as well as for its importance in the progressive development of power to read and understand primarily classical Latin.

Twelve new words are presented in the Words to Master section in each Unit. Many of these words are first introduced functionally in the opening Conversation. They are all used in the Practice Patterns and Sentence Patterns as a preparation for their recognition in the Latin reading at the end of the immediate lesson. Unfamiliar words are never used in the practice exercises. The Latin readings occasionally contain new words which closely resemble their English derivatives. Every word in the Words to Master is covered again in the appropriate Comprehensive Review.

In each Unit there is a section entitled Building Word Power, which is devoted to training students thoroughly in word-building techniques. Fundamental principles are presented simply and progressively. Abundant practice is offered to develop habits of word analysis in both Latin and English. All the ordinary prefixes and suffixes are explained in orderly sequence and used in practical drills.

**4. Provision of content leading to cultural objectives.** The words of a language belong to the culture in which they are uttered. Without a knowledge of that culture, the meanings of words can never be fully understood or appreciated; the study of the language becomes empty and colorless. In this text, therefore, content leading to cultural objectives is an integral part of the Latin readings and the English essays entitled Roman Life, Roman History, and Living Mythology.

It is important to give the students an understanding of the role played by Latin culture in shaping our own Western culture in literature, art, law, and the basic principles of social and political organization. Thus, many of the cultural sections deal with the social life of the Romans, early Roman history, and prominent leaders of ancient Roman times.

An acquaintance with the heroes and the deeds of Roman legend and history is valuable, but a knowledge of mythology is even more so. The many allusions to mythical characters and episodes in the works of English and American authors are a constant source of difficulty to students who have not studied Latin or taken a course in mythology. For these reasons an attempt has been made to tell in very simple English some of the best-known stories from Latin and Greek mythology.

**5. Provision for reading in Latin.** We have already stated the immediate objective of the *Our Latin Heritage* series. Every Section in each Unit has been polarized in this direction, to develop the student's ability to read and comprehend Latin. The best way to learn to read any language is by much reading in that language. In *Book I* there are sixty Latin readings, exclusive of the twelve Sight Translations in the Comprehensive Reviews and the sixty Conversations. This reading material has been very carefully graded in vocabulary and syntax so as to make it possible for the students to develop progressive ability to read Latin with ease and enjoyment.

As soon as the vocabulary becomes adequate, the consecutive story is told of Rome and its founders, from the causes of the Trojan War to the reign of Augustus. This sequence is interrupted occasionally by the introduction in Latin of myths, of stories identifying the Roman gods, and of descriptions of the games and parades in the Circus and the Colosseum. The story of the Helvetian War is narrated in simple form to be used as optional reading matter for the more advanced students.

The aim in the Latin readings has been to give the student the opportunity to read connected stories of cultural value. Many of the Latin selections are adaptations from classical authors. Where advisable, exact quotations from the Latin originals have been used.

**Conclusion.** There is an ever-increasing demand for more foreign language learning in the United States. This learning seems essential not merely for progress and a position of leadership in world affairs but also for national self-preservation. Latin is the ideal language for beginning foreign language learning. It is the mother language of most of the tongues of Western Europe and of their offspring in North and South America and other large areas of the world. Latin, as an inflected language, is the best possible preparation for the learning of other inflected languages. A knowledge of the structure, inflections, and terminology of Latin renders the study of German and Russian much easier than they would otherwise be. The same is true of the languages of the entire Indo-European family.

Students of Latin can achieve a number of valuable benefits incidental to the learning of Latin, such as an awareness of linguistic form and grammatical structure; better mastery of English language and literature; increased ability

*v*

to learn other languages; considerable firsthand acquaintance with the ancient Greek and Roman culture; training of the mind to logical thinking with possible transfer of skills, methods, and ideals learned through the study of Latin to other fields of intellectual endeavor. The student who conscientiously follows the plan of study in *Our Latin Heritage: Book I* will not only learn the fundamental principles of Latin but will be well on his way to enjoying the advantages derived from a study of this language.

# Contents

*ix*

# Introduction

## Monuments More Lasting than Bronze

As far back as Caesar Augustus' time, two thousand years ago, people spoke of an Eternal City. A thousand years before the Christian era, the earliest form of that city was only a small settlement of shepherds, farmers, and traders who had built their huts on or near the Palatine. This was the most inviting and convenient of the seven hills that sloped upward from the marshes near the Tiber River about sixteen miles from the sea. In time this settlement united with others on the neighboring hills, and out of this union grew the mighty city-state that eventually spread its power over most of the civilized world.

Although Rome today is neither a great commercial hive nor an industrial center nor a thriving port, it remains the world's most famous city, the capital of a great modern nation, the capital of a world-wide Christian Church, and the capital, in its ruins, of the ancient world. It is good for us to know all that we can about a city and a people that remained the greatest power in the world for a longer period than any other nation before or since. We are interested, however, in learning the language, the history, and the culture of Rome because our life today is an extension of the life of the ancient Romans.

Rome transmitted to the nations of the modern world not only her singular achievements but also those of the civilizations preceding hers. Every country that Rome conquered gave as well as received much that made for human progress. Rome took what each had to give, used and developed it, and passed it on to the medieval and modern world. The civilization which she spread and we received included the learning of the Greeks, the skills of the Phoenicians, the religious concepts of the Hebrews, and the best in the culture of Mesopotamia and Egypt.

Rome's greatest direct contribution to the world's civilization was her splendid system of government and law. Rome did more than conquer the peoples of the ancient world; she organized them. She succeeded in making peoples of diverse interests and ideas live together in harmony. Instead of allowing them to fight among themselves and bring about their own destruction, she forced them to accept the Roman rule, to merge their nationality with that of the Romans, and to become Roman citizens. Usually she allowed them to keep their own culture, religion, customs, and what was good in local government.

A large part of the civilized world of today derives its legal system directly from the Romans. Roman law is still in operation in Italy, France, Spain, Latin America, and other lands colonized by these and other European countries. It is, to a great extent, the basis of International Law and Canon Law, used in the Roman Catholic Church. Even in the United States, throughout the British Commonwealth, and in Mohammedan countries, its influence is extensive and profound.

Rome's second most important contribution to world civilization was engineering. The most spectacular of her engineering feats were her roads, her bridges, her aqueducts and sewers, and her great public buildings. After two thousand years some of these are still in use in Europe, Asia, and Africa. The secrets of their survival are the durability of their concrete and cement, and the structural strength of the Roman arch.

Roman roads gave the world its best system of land communication until the establishment of the railroads. Rivers were spanned by massive bridges, marshes and valleys by viaducts. The entire Roman empire was covered with a network of broad, straight roads, all leading to Rome, for the use of armies, traders, couriers, and government officials. Elevated channels, lined with cement, were used for aqueducts. Some are still in use in Rome and in other countries of Europe. An underground network of vaulted sewers matched the aqueducts as feats of engineering.

The combination of arch and column, as well as the use of the dome, made possible the erection of colossal buildings. Domes such as are found in magnificent temples like the Pantheon, now a Christian church, are made of cement, hardened into a single solid unit. Rows of arches and columns were placed in tiers one above the other as in the Colosseum, an amphitheater with a seating capacity of fifty thousand.

Latin, the language of the Romans, spread throughout the Roman world displacing the local languages, which gradually died out. After the decay of the Empire, Latin survived and was transformed into Italian, Spanish, Portuguese, French, and Rumanian, which are known as the Romance languages. About eighty per cent of the English vocabulary used by educated Americans is derived, directly or indirectly, from the Latin language. Throughout the Middle Ages, Latin was an international language. Until almost modern times it was the language of schools and scholars. Even in our day no person can claim to be fully educated without some knowledge of Latin culture.

*Rem tene; verba sequenter.*
Grasp the subject; the words will follow.
—Marcus Porcius Cato, the Elder, 234–149 B.C.

# *Unit* I

## CONVERSATION

Salvē'te, pu'erī et puel'lae! — Good morning, boys and girls!
  Sal've, magis'ter (magis'tra)! — Good morning, teacher!
Quid a'gitis ho'diē? — How are you today?
  Be'ne, grā'tiās ti'bi a'gimus. — Well, thank you.
Cōnsī'dite, sī pla'cet. Le'ō! — Sit down, please. Leo!
  Ad'sum, magister. — I am present, teacher.
U'bi est Pau'la? — Where is Paula?
  Adsum, magister. — I am present, teacher.
Ubi est Pau'lus? — Where is Paul?
  Paulus ab'est, magister. — Paul is absent, teacher.
Sur'gite, disci'pulī (disci'pulae)! — Stand up, pupils!
  *Discipulī surgunt.* — *The pupils stand.*
Cantā'te: "Al'ma Mā'ter!" — Sing: "Alma Māter!"
  *Discipulī cantant.* — *The pupils sing.*
Bene! Nunc valē'te, discipulī. — Good! Now good-by, pupils.
  Va'lē, magister. — Good-by, teacher.

▶ WHAT IS YOUR LATIN NAME?

Many American boys and girls have Latin names. Can you find the equivalent of yours among them?

| | | | | |
|---|---|---|---|---|
| Albertus | Ferdinandus | Joannes | Mārcus | Robertus |
| Antōnius | Francīscus | Jōsēphus | Martīnus | Rūfus |
| Bernardus | Frederīcus | Jūlius | Michael | Silvester |
| Carolus | Gregōrius | Jūstīnus | Patricius | Simon |
| Chrīstophorus | Gulielmus | Laurentius | Paulus | Stephanos |
| Cornelius | Henrıcus | Leo | Petrus | Thomas |
| Dominicus | Īgnātius | Leonardus | Philippus | Tīmotheus |
| Eduardus | Jacōbus | Ludovīcus | Raymundus | Victor |

| | | | | |
|---|---|---|---|---|
| Aemilia | Caecilia | Jūlia | Patricia | Teresia |
| Agatha | Catharīna | Jūliāna | Paula | Ursula |
| Agnes | Chrīstīna | Lūcia | Paulīna | Vēra |
| Alma | Clāra | Magdalēna | Rēgīna | Vēronica |
| Anastasia | Deana | Margarīta | Roberta | Victōria |
| Angela | Dorothēa | Marīa | Rosa | Viōla |
| Anna | Flōra | Martha | Stella | Virginia |
| Barbara | Flōrentia | Monica | Susanna | Vīviāna |

▶ DISCUSSION

The pronunciation of Latin will not be difficult because nearly every sound in Latin has an equivalent English sound. All consonants have only one sound; each vowel has two sounds, one long and one short. The long vowels have a line, called a macron, over them.

You will learn correct pronunciation of Latin by imitating your teacher, but the sounds of the Latin letters and the rules for the accent and the syllabication of Latin words are given for reference in the Appendix, page 357.

▶ PRACTICE PATTERNS

Here are some words that have the same spelling and the same, or almost the same, meaning in both English and Latin:

| radius | creātor | splendor | vacuum | stadium | superior |
|--------|---------|----------|--------|---------|----------|
| error | stimulus | candelābrum | cēnsus | specimen | dictātor |

A. Divide the above words into syllables, using virgules between the syllables, as: *fōr/mu/la*. The Latin word *virgula* means *little rod*.

B. Mark *U* over the ultima (last syllable), *P* over the penult (second-to-last syllable), and *A* over the antepenult (third-to-last syllable) of each of the above words if there are three syllables in the word.

C. Mark the accent, as: *fōr'/mu/la*. Pronounce these words in Latin, then in English.

*Let Us Sing in Latin*

Singing is a good way to practice Latin pronunciation and accent. The following inspiring song was written to serve as a school anthem. Repeat the words after your teacher. The anthem may be sung to the melody of "Maryland, My Maryland."

Alma Māter

Al/ma Mā/ter, au/dī/nōs  Al/ma Mā/ter, om/ni/a,
Om/nēs tē lau/dan/tēs,  Nō/bīs quae de/dis/tī,
Cor/di/bus lae/tis/si/mōs  Pul/chra sunt et op/ti/ma;
Om/nēs tē a/man/tēs.  Be/ne do/cu/is/tī
Glō/ri/am vel māx/i/mam  Ar/tēs et sci/en/ti/am,
Ti/bi et per/pe/tu/am  Vē/ri/tā/tem in/te/gram,
Nōs red/dē/mus grā/ti/am,  Fi/dem vel sānc/tis/si/mam,
Al/ma Mā/ter cā/ra.  Al/ma Mā/ter cā/ra.

2

# SECTION 2 Comparison Between English and Latin

▶ DISCUSSION

Latin and English are closely related in grammar. The likenesses between English and Latin, as well as the differences, will be stressed throughout this book. An understanding of the grammar of both languages will be made clearer by constant comparison.

### SOME SIMILARITIES

1. Can you name and define the parts of speech in English grammar? The same names and definitions are used in Latin grammar.

2. You have learned the terms *sentence, subject, predicate, person, number, gender, case* from your study of English grammar. These terms are used in the same way in Latin.

### SOME DIFFERENCES

1. There is no article in Latin. *Via* may mean *street, a street, the street.*

2. Adjectives in Latin, as in English, are used in two ways: to modify nouns or pronouns, and to complete the verb as predicate adjectives. In English, adjectives do not change their form; but adjectives in Latin agree in gender, number, and case with the nouns they modify.

3. The relation of words in a Latin sentence is shown by their endings and not by their position in the sentence as in English.

4. Many nouns that in English are neuter, because they do not represent living things, are masculine or feminine in Latin.


# SECTION 3 Nominative Case

▶ DISCUSSION

The main divisions of a sentence are the subject and the predicate. The *predicate* is composed of the verb and all its dependent words and phrases. The *subject* is the noun or pronoun about which the predicate states or asks something.

In Latin as in English: (1) The subject of a finite verb is in the *nominative* case. (2) A noun used in the predicate after a linking verb such as *is* and *are* is in the *nominative* case. This is called the *predicate nominative.*

> **Amērica est patria nostra.** *America is our country.*

**Amērica** is the *subject;* **patria** is the *predicate nominative.*

An adjective in Latin agrees with the word it modifies in gender, number, and case.

**Patria *nostra* est Amērica.**  *Our* country is America.

*Nostra* is an adjective modifying *patria* and is in the nominative case, singular number, feminine gender, agreeing with *patria.*

An adjective used in the predicate after a linking verb is a *predicate adjective.*

**Amērica est *lībera*.**  America is *free.*

The predicate adjective describes the subject of the verb *est* and is in the *nominative* case.

# SECTION 4 Case Indicators

▶ DISCUSSION

In Latin each case of the noun or adjective has its own *signal* by which it may be recognized. The final letters signal each case of the Latin noun or adjective and are called *case indicators*. The *case indicators* not only end the word, but they indicate a particular meaning or use of the word.

*Case indicators* for the nominative case, singular and plural, of nouns and adjectives of the first declension are: *−a, −ae.*

| SINGULAR: −a | | PLURAL: −ae | |
|---|---|---|---|
| puell**a** | = *girl* | puell**ae** | = *girls* |
| parv**a** puell**a** | = *small girl* | parv**ae** puell**ae** | = *small girls* |

▶ PRACTICE PATTERNS

A. Read aloud and translate into English:

| | | |
|---|---|---|
| māgna villa | pulchra puella | multae viae |
| lāta via | antīqua lingua | antīquae villae |
| māgnae villae | pulchrae viae | multae puellae |

B. Write in Latin:

| | | |
|---|---|---|
| a pretty girl | the broad streets | many farmhouses |
| an ancient language | beautiful roads | ancient languages |
| a country house | large farms | the wide roads |

*A Note About Words to Master*

You will meet in the reading lessons many words whose meanings you will readily recognize because of their likeness to English derivatives. If these words do not appear in the lists of Words to Master, they may be found in the Latin-English vocabulary at the end of the book.

*4*

antī'qua, *adj.*, ancient, old (*antique*)

et, *conj.*, and; et . . . et, both . . . and

lā'ta, *adj.*, broad, wide (*latitude*)

lin'gua, –ae, *f.*, tongue, language (*linguist*)

māg'na, *adj.*, large, great (*magnitude*)

mul'ta, *adj.*, much; *pl.*, many (*multitude*)

nōn, *adv.*, not (*nonentity*)

puel'la, –ae, *f.*, girl

pul'chra, *adj.*, pretty, beautiful (*pulchritude*)

sed, *conj.*, but

vi'a, –ae, *f.*, road, street, way (*viaduct*)

vil'la, –ae, *f.*, farmhouse, country house, farm (*villa*)

## BUILDING WORD POWER

Each unit in this book contains a section designed to help you build your word power, both in Latin and in English. You will notice that a large number of English words have the same or almost the same meaning and spelling in Latin. You will learn how to find the true meaning of words by breaking them up into their component parts: prefix, root, and suffix.

The most important part of a word is its root. A *root* is the simplest element that appears in a word or in several related words; it always expresses the same general meaning. Ordinarily it is monosyllabic; that is, it consists of one syllable. **Dūc–** is a root from which we have *adduce, induce, reduce, produce, duct, conduct, introduction,* and many other words, all of which have the idea of leading, because in Latin the verb *dūcere* means *to lead*.

A *prefix* gives a particular shade of meaning to the root. A *suffix* may modify not only the meaning but also the part of speech. In the word *incredible, in–* is the prefix, meaning *not; cred–* is the root meaning *believe; –ble* is the suffix meaning *able*. Therefore,

*incredible* = not able to be believed, unbelievable

All words do not have all three component parts, but a large number of our apparently difficult words do. By learning a few of the prefixes, roots, and suffixes, you will have the clue to the accurate meanings of thousands of Latin words and of the English words derived from them. You will then be well on your way to that superior vocabulary that is so essential to success in school and in adult life.

## SENTENCE PATTERNS

A. Read aloud and translate into English:

1. Via est (*is*) via Rōmāna (*Roman*).
2. Via Rōmāna nōn est lāta.

**5**

3. Via Rōmāna nōn est lāta sed est pulchra.
4. Viae Rōmānae sunt (*are*) pulchrae sed sunt antīquae.
5. Multae villae Rōmānae sunt māgnae et pulchrae.
6. Lingua Rōmāna est antīqua et pulchra.
7. Viae et villae et puellae Rōmānae sunt pulchrae.

B. Translate into Latin and read aloud:
1. The farmhouse is a Roman farmhouse.
2. The Roman farmhouse is large and beautiful.
3. Many farmhouses are broad and large.
4. The Roman language is ancient, but it is (*est*) beautiful.
5. The streets are not wide, but they are pretty.

Atlas supporting the world
on his shoulders.

## Why Do We Study Myths?

**A**ges ago when the world was new, before we had discovered the scientific reasons for natural phenomena, people feared and worshiped the forces of nature. What caused the thunder to roar, the lightning to flash, the ocean waves to roll and swell, the sun to rise and set? Surely, people thought, there exist some powerful supernatural beings who control these actions so far beyond our mortal power!

Thus they devised myths, fictitious stories that seemed to explain the real or imaginary mysteries. Soon names of supernatural beings and of their habitations and adventures were invented. For long ages these myths were not written but were handed down by tradition from one generation to another. In the telling they were often greatly altered, but when poets like the Greek Homer included their native myths in their poems, the stories became more or less fixed.

A myth, then, may be defined as a traditional story of unknown authorship, serving usually to explain some natural occurrence, human origin, or the customs, institutions, and religious rites of a people. In general they are pure fancy — tales that abound in marvelous incidents, extraordinary characters, and descriptions of the virtues and the vices of human nature as portrayed by gods and demigods. Often the myth, chiefly concerned with the gods, and the saga, concerned with human beings and based upon some actual historical event, are blended with invented stories told for amusement, as in the stories of the Argonauts, of Ulysses, and of Hercules.

We, of course, do not believe in the myths, but we study them because they have had a deep influence on literature, music, and art. We cannot fully understand world literature without a knowledge of the myths of ancient Greece and Rome. Some of our finest musical compositions have been inspired by characters whose stories are related in myths. The same is true of works of art.

Mythological figures are also found in trade-marks, advertisements of business products, and on postage stamps. Scientists have used mythological names for plants and animals, constellations, and chemical elements. Missiles, satellites, and atomic-powered submarines bear such names as *Jupiter*, *Atlas*, *Midas*, and *Triton*.

▶ STUDY HELPS

Read the following story orally in Latin, sentence by sentence, until you have grasped the thought. Many words are so similar to the English that you will recognize their meaning at once. The words to be mastered will be found on page 5. When you are sure of the meaning of the story in Latin, write out a translation in good English. Notice that **Rōmae** can mean both *of Rome* and *at Rome*.

### Eternal Rome

Māgna est glōria, māgna est fāma Rōmae (*of Rome*). Rōma est antīqua, sed Rōma est pulchra. Rōma est in Ītaliā; Ītalia est in Eurōpā.

Ītalia est longa sed nōn lāta. Ītalia est paenīnsula. In Ītaliā sunt multae viae. In Ītaliā sunt villae, māgnae et pulchrae. Ītalia est pulchra.

Antīquae viae Rōmānae nōn sunt lātae sed sunt longae. Rōmae (*At Rome*) est māgna arēna. Arēna est et lāta et longa. Rōmae sunt multae statuae. Statuae sunt et māgnae et pulchrae.

7

Antīqua lingua Rōmāna est Latīna. Est (*It is*) lingua pulchra. Māgna est fāma linguae Rōmānae (*of the Roman language*). In Americā lingua nōn est Latīna. Rōma nōn est in Americā; Rōma in Ītaliā est. Lingua Rōmāna antīqua est. Māgna est fāma, māgna est glōria et Rōmae et linguae Rōmānae.

There is nothing so easy but that it becomes difficult when you do it with reluctance.
—Terence, 185–159 B.C.

# *Unit* II

## CONVERSATION

MAGISTRA: Salvēte, discipulae. Quid agitis ho'diē (*today*)?
DISCIPULAE: Salvē, magistra. Quid agis?
MAGISTRA (*holds a piece of chalk*): Crēta est. Quid est (*What is it*), Prīma?
PRĪMA: Crēta est, magistra.
MAGISTRA (*holds a piece of paper*): Charta (KAR'TA) est. Quid est, Secunda?
SECUNDA: Charta est, magistra.
MAGISTRA: Arca est. Quid est, Tertia?
TERTIA: Arca est, magistra.

| Names of Pupils | | Names of Articles in Classroom | | | |
|---|---|---|---|---|---|
| **Prī'ma** | *First (pupil)* | **ar'ca** | *box* | **pictū'ra** | *picture* |
| **Secun'da** | *Second* | **ca'mera** | *room* | **pi'la** | *ball* |
| **Ter'tia** | *Third* | **cor'bula** | *basket* | **rē'gula** | *ruler* |
| **Quār'ta** | *Fourth* | **ērāsū'ra** | *eraser* | **ro'sa** | *rose* |
| **Quīn'ta** | *Fifth* | **fenes'tra** | *window* | **sel'la** | *chair* |
| **Sex'ta** | *Sixth* | **jā'nua** | *door* | **sta'tua** | *statue* |
| **Sep'tima** | *Seventh* | **mēn'sa** | *table* | **ta'bula** | *tablet* |
| **Octā'va** | *Eighth* | **pen'na** | *pen* | **tabula ni'gra** | *blackboard* |

For further classroom expressions in Latin, see page 360.

▶ THE FLAG SALUTE

E'go vexil'lō Ūnītō'rum Sta'tuum Amē'ricae ac Re'ī Pūb'licae quam dēsīg'nat, fidēlitā'tem spon'deō: Ū'nī Natiō'nī sub De'ō indīvīsi'bilī cum lībertā'te at'que jūsti'tiā om'nibus!

# SECTION 1 Genitive Case

▶ DISCUSSION

In English, possession or ownership is indicated by the letter –s, used either as –'s or –s':

the farmer's cottage  the farmers' cottage

The same meaning may be expressed by a phrase introduced by *of:*

the cottage of the farmer  the cottage of the farmers

In Latin, the possessive case is called the *genitive case. Case indicators* for the genitive, singular and plural, of first declension nouns and adjectives are: *–ae, –ārum.*

|  | SINGULAR: **–ae** | PLURAL: **–ārum** | USE |
|---|---|---|---|
| Nominative | puell**a** = *girl* | puell**ae** = *girls* | Subject |
| Genitive | puell**ae** = *girl's, of the girl* | puell**ārum** = *girls', of the girls* | Possession |

▶ STUDY HELPS

1. The first declension case indicators of the genitive singular and the nominative plural of the first declension are the same.

2. The genitive usually follows the noun it possesses.

3. **Mea,** *my;* **tua,** *your* (sing.); **nostra,** *our;* **vestra,** *your* (pl.) are possessive adjectives and usually follow the nouns they modify. These words are used only when the meaning is not clear without them.

▶ PRACTICE PATTERNS

A. Read aloud and translate into English:

| | | |
|---|---|---|
| incolae īnsulārum | puellae Ītaliae | fēminae Americae |
| patria puellae | fēminae patria | servae multārum terrārum |

B. Write in Latin:

| | | |
|---|---|---|
| my country | land of the queen | your (sing.) queen |
| our fatherland | queen of the land | your (pl.) mistress |
| of the slaves | the girls' fatherland | your (sing.) slaves |

# SECTION 2 Vocative Case and Apposition

▶ DISCUSSION

1. In Latin the case of direct address is called the *vocative case.* In the first declension the *vocative* of the noun has the same form as the

nominative. Unless emphatic, the *vocative* does not stand first in the sentence.

> **Salvē, *parva puella.*** Good morning, *little girl.*

2. In Latin as in English, when two nouns stand side by side, one identifying the other, they are in the same case and are said to be *in apposition.* An appositive is often separated from the rest of the sentence by commas.

> Helena, the good *slave*, is an inhabitant of Sicily, a Roman *province.*

*Slave* identifies *Helena*, the subject of the sentence and, therefore, is in the nominative case. *Province* identifies *Sicily* and is in the genitive case because it is in apposition to Sicily, a genitive.

> **Helena, bona *serva*, est incola Siciliae, *prōvinciae* Rōmānae.**

## SECTION 3 Person, Number, and Gender

▶ DISCUSSION

1. The word *person* has an interesting history. The Latin word **persōna** originally meant a *mask.* The sound (**sonus**) came through (**per**) the mask, which all characters in ancient plays — comedies and tragedies — wore. From meaning mask, it came to mean the character who wore the mask. Eventually the one who spoke and referred to himself as *I* was called the *first* person (pl., *we*). The person spoken to and addressed as *you* was called the *second* person (pl., *you*). The person or thing spoken about, as *he*, *she*, or *it*, was called the *third* person (pl., *they*).

2. Nouns and pronouns in both English and Latin have two numbers, *singular* and *plural.* Ordinarily in English we add –*s* to a singular noun to make it plural. In Latin each case has its own characteristic *indicator* in both singular and plural.

3. In Latin, as in English, there are three genders, *masculine, feminine,* and *neuter.* Nouns indicating male beings are masculine, and those indicating female beings are feminine. Nouns that are neuter in English are classified in Latin as masculine or feminine or neuter, generally on the basis of the nominative singular ending. This is known as *grammatical* gender to distinguish it from *natural* gender. The gender and the genitive case indicator of each noun will be given after the noun in the section Words to Master.

4. Ordinarily adjectives accompany nouns and modify or limit them in

size, color, appearance, or other characteristics. In Latin, adjectives are declined like nouns, and agree with the nouns they modify in gender, number, and case.

## WORDS TO MASTER

do'mina, –ae, f., mistress, lady
fē'mina, –ae, f., woman (feminine)
in'cola, –ae, m. & f., inhabitant (colony)
īn'sula, –ae, f., island (insulate)
lī'bera, adj., free (liberate)
pae'ne, adv., almost; paenīn'sula, –ae, f., peninsula
par'va, adj., small, little

pa'tria, –ae, f., fatherland, country, native land (repatriate)
–que, conj., enclitic attached to the second of two connected words, and
rēgī'na, –ae, f., queen
ser'va, –ae, f., female slave, handmaid (servile)
ter'ra, –ae, f., earth, land, country (territory)

## BUILDING WORD POWER

There was a time in history when, through the conquests of great military leaders, the Romans were masters not only of all Italy, but also of northern Africa, the western part of Asia, Spain, France (**Gallia**), Germany, and sections of England. This conquest is still reflected in the modern names of these countries.

What are the modern names for **Britannia, Germania, Italia, Graecia, Crēta, Sardinia, Corsica?** Name the continents.

Although they never conquered the Irish, the Romans knew that there was such a place as Ireland. Julius Caesar is the first person on record to have called the island west of Britain **Hibernia.** One Roman writer thought it was part of Britain and not an island at all.

Many Latin words of the first declension that end in –ia became English nouns ending in –y. What are the English words for: **colōnia, familia, furia, historia, glōria, industria, infāmia, injūria, memoria, miseria, perfidia, victōria?**

## SENTENCE PATTERNS

A. Translate into English. Pick out the nouns and the adjectives in the nominative and genitive cases.

1. Amērica, patria nostra, est terra lībera māgnaque.
2. Hibernia, terra lībera, est īnsula parva sed pulchra.
3. Īnsula tua, Ō Rēgīna, est pulchra et lībera!
4. Domina est incola Ītaliae, māgnae paenīnsulae.
5. Patria mea est paenīnsula; patria tua nōn est paenīnsula.

B. Translate into Latin:

1. The inhabitants of America are free.
2. Beautiful Italy is almost an island.
3. Greece, a country of Europe, is a small peninsula.
4. The women of our native land are beautiful.
5. O Lady, your slaves are small; my slaves are large.

## Our Native Land

In Eurōpā, Āsiā, Āfricā sunt multae terrae et multae īnsulae. Gallia (*France*), Germānia, Ītalia, Graecia sunt in Eurōpā. Britannia, Hibernia, Sardinia, Corsica, Sicilia sunt māgnae īnsulae Eurōpae. Multae īnsulae Americae sunt parvae sed pulchrae.

Hibernia, īnsula pulchra, est prope (*near*) Britanniam. Scōtia (*Scotland*) est pulchra sed īnsula nōn est. Ītalia est paene īnsula. Ītalia est paenīnsula, longa sed nōn lāta. Hispānia et Graecia sunt (*are*) paenīnsulae. Hispānia est māgna, sed Graecia est parva. Et Hispānia et Graecia pulchrae sunt.

América est patria tua et patria mea. Patria nostra est terra et pulchra et lībera, sed América nōn est in Eurōpā. Patria nostra nōn est īnsula; paenīnsula nōn est. Patria nostra América nōn est antīqua sed est māgna pulchraque. América est lībera terra. Est patria nostra.

Happy he who knows the country of the gods—
Pan and old Sylvanus and the sisterhood of the nymphs.
—Vergil, 70–19 B.C.
*Georgics*

# *Unit* III

## CONVERSATION

PRĪMA:     E'go (*points to self*) sum Américāna. Familia mea est Américāna.

SECUNDA:   Tū (*points to Prīma*) es Américāna. Familia tua *est* Américāna, sed ego sum Britannica.

TERTIA:    Secunda est Britannica. Ego nōn sum Britannica. Ego sum Américāna, sed familia mea est Hibernica.

QUĀRTA:    Ego et Quīnta *sumus* Américānae. Familiae nostrae quoque *sunt* Américānae. América, patria nostra, est pulchra terra.

QUĪNTA:    América est patria nostra. Patria nostra est pulchra.

SEXTA:  Nōn Amērīcāna ego sum sed Ītalica. Ītalia est patria mea.
SEPTIMA:  Ītalia pulchra terra est, sed Amērica, Britannia, Hibernia
quoque sunt terrae pulchrae.
OCTĀVA:  Patriae vestrae, Secunda et Sexta, terrae līberae sunt. Vōs
quoque līberae *estis.*
PRĪMA:  Ego *sum* Amērīcāna, tū *es* Britannica, Sexta *est* Ītalica.
Nōs *sumus* līberae, vōs *estis* līberae, multae puellae *sunt*
līberae.

# SECTION 1 Verbs

▶ DISCUSSION

1. A verb is the most important word of the sentence. It tells what
the subject does or what is done to the subject.

The boy *shouts.*     The man *is called.*

In the first sentence the boy *does* something; in the second, something
*is done* to the man.

2. Some verbs do not express feeling or action. They merely show
existence or connection. Verbs that link the subject with a noun or
adjective in the predicate are called *linking* verbs. Forms of the verb
*to be* in both English and Latin may show existence or connection.

**Est īnsula.**     *There is* an island.     An island *exists.* (Existence)
**Īnsula *est* māgna.**     The island *is* large.     (Connection)

3. In Latin as in English, a finite verb agrees with its subject in person
and number. There are three persons: first, second, and third, and
two numbers: singular and plural.

4. In English we use pronouns as separate words to indicate different
persons. In Latin the person and the number of a verb are indicated
by the last one, two, or three letters of the verb form. For example,
*sunt* means *they are.* The *–nt* indicates that the subject of *sunt* is
the third person plural, expressed in English by *they.*

Because these person indicators are included in the Latin verb form,
it is not necessary to express the pronoun subject of a Latin verb, although sometimes it is expressed for emphasis.

The *person indicators* (*P.I.*), used for all tenses of the active voice,
except the perfect, are given here. They must be memorized.

|  | SINGULAR P.I. | PLURAL P.I. |
|---|---|---|
| First Person | **–ō** or **–m** = *I* | **–mus** = *we* |
| Second Person | **–s**     = *you* | **–tis**  = *you* |
| Third Person | **–t**     = *he, she, it* | **–nt**  = *they* |

*13*

1. In English the pronoun *you* may be either singular or plural. In Latin, *–s* indicates the singular, *–tis* the plural, of *you.*

2. Throughout this book, *P.I.* stands for *person indicator* in the paradigms of verbs, that is, the models of the conjugations of verbs.


## SECTION 2 Conjugation of the Verb *sum*

▶ DISCUSSION

Changing the form of a word to indicate a change in meaning or use is called inflection. The inflection of a verb is called conjugation.

As the English verb *to be* is irregular, so is the Latin verb **sum,** which is conjugated in the present tense as follows:

| Person | P.I. | Form | Translation | P.I. | Form | Translation |
|--------|------|------|-------------|------|------|-------------|
| | | | SINGULAR | | | PLURAL |
| First | –m | sum | *I am* | –mus | sumus | *we are* |
| Second | –s | es | *you are* | –tis | estis | *you are* |
| Third | –t | est | *he, she, it is, there is* | –nt | sunt | *they are, there are* |

▶ STUDY HELPS

1. When third person forms of a verb begin a sentence, they may be translated with the expletive *there.* Do not confuse the expletive *there* with the adverb *there,* **ibi.** The expletive *there* is an introductory word included in the Latin verb; the adverb *there,* **ibi,** refers to a definite place.

**Est** = There is    **Ibi est.** = *There he is.*

2. Any form of the verb **sum** may be used to link the predicate noun or adjective with the subject. The *predicate nominative* agrees with the subject in case, and usually in gender and number. The *predicate adjective* agrees with the subject in gender, number, and case.

3. The present infinitive of the verb **sum** is **esse,** *to be.*


▶ PRACTICE PATTERNS

A. Supply the proper case indicator, and translate the sentence:

1. Ītalia est paenīnsul___.
2. Eurōpa et Amērica sunt māgn___.
3. Hibernia et Britannia sunt īnsul___.
4. Patria nostr___ est terr___ līber___.
5. Vīt___ mea in silv___ māgnā est lībera.

6. Nōn sum puell___ parv___.
7. Estis amīcae nostr___.
8. Sum fīli___ laeta agricol___.
9. Es quoque amīc___ naut___.
10. In cas___ sunt multae serv___.

*14*

B. Use the correct form of *sum* in the following:

1. The queen is beautiful.
2. You are not little girls.
3. We are farmers.
4. I am happy in my hut.
5. It is not a peninsula.

6. Italy is a beautiful country.
7. There are many large islands.
8. We are not slaves but free.
9. You (sing.) are happy in your hut.
10. It is a large hut in the forest.

# SECTION 3 Ablative Case; Ablative of Place Where

## ▶ DISCUSSION

1. Latin nouns have a case to which no English case is exactly equivalent. This case, called the *ablative*, expresses many ideas that are expressed in English by adverbial prepositional phrases. Sometimes the Romans used Latin prepositions with nouns in the ablative case.

2. Nouns ending in *–a* in the nominative singular change the short *–a* to long *–ā* to form the ablative singular, and to long *–īs* to form the ablative plural.

|  | SINGULAR –ā |  | PLURAL –īs |  | USE |
|---|---|---|---|---|---|
| Nominative | puella | *girl* | puellae | *girls* | Subject |
| Ablative | puellā | *from, by, with the girl* | puellīs | *from, by, with the girls* | Adverbial |

3. When a noun in the ablative case is used with the preposition *in,* we call this construction the *ablative of place where:*

**in Graeciā** = *in Greece*    **in viā** = *on the street*

The names of *cities* or *small islands* and a *few other words* expressing place do not need a preposition to show *place in which*. A special case called the *locative* is used. If these nouns belong to the first declension, they end in *–ae* in the singular, *–īs* in the plural.

**Rōmae** = *at* or *in Rome*    **Athēnīs** = *at* or *in Athens*

## ▶ PRACTICE PATTERNS

A. Translate into English:

1. In Āmēricā vīta est laeta.
2. Rōmae sunt multae viae.
3. Agricolae in silvīs nōn sunt.

4. In īnsulā fēminae pulchrae multaeque sunt.
5. Athēnīs sunt servae.
6. Amīca mea est in casā.

B. Translate into Latin the italicized phrases:

1. The girls are *in the cottage.*
2. Athens is *in Greece.*
3. *On the island* are many sailors.

4. They live *in Athens.*
5. The women are *in the forest.*
6. My friends live *in Rome.*

**15**

## WORDS TO MASTER

**agri′cola,** –ae, *m.*, farmer (*agriculture*)
**amī′ca,** –ae, *f.*, friend (*amicable*)
**ca′sa,** –ae, *f.*, cottage, hut (*casino*)
**cum,** *prep. with abl.*, with, together with
**fī′lia,** –ae, *f.*, daughter; *dat. and abl.*, **fīliābus** (*filial*)
**in,** *prep. with abl.*, in, on; *with acc.*, into, to, against

**lae′ta,** *adj.*, happy, glad, joyful
**laeti′tia,** –ae, *f.*, joy
**nau′ta,** –ae, *m.*, sailor (*nautical*)
**prōvin′cia,** –ae, *f.*, province (*provincial*)
**quo′que,** *conj.*, also (*never stands first in clause*)
**sil′va,** –ae, *f.*, forest, woods (*sylvan*)
**vī′ta,** –ae, *f.*, life (*vital*)

## BUILDING WORD POWER

What happens to our final *t*'s and *d*'s in English when we are not careful about proper enunciation? What do you think happened to the final unaccented syllables in Latin words used in ordinary everyday speech? When the final *-a* dropped from the following Latin words, what English words were left? *Caverna, fōrma, palma, ūrna, vīpera, ancora, herba, taberna* (*-b* became *-v*).

Some first declension Latin nouns lost the sound of the final *-a*, but in English they end in silent or mute *-e*. Give the English form and meaning of these Latin words: *fāma, fortūna, disciplīna, spīna, cūra, plūma.* If *picture* is derived from the Latin *pictūra*, what are the Latin words for: *nature, scripture, culture, stature, pressure, fracture, tincture, puncture, juncture, stricture?*

Many English words that end in *-ture* or *-sure* came originally from first declension nouns; but the word *sure* has the same derivation as *secure.* Both words are derived from *sē + cūra* and mean *free from care.*

## SENTENCE PATTERNS

A. Translate into English:

1. Sum fīlia nautae, et Sicilia, māgna īnsula, est patria mea.
2. Vīta agricolae est laeta, sed vīta nautae quoque est laeta.
3. Sumus incolae Hispāniae, terrae pulchrae.
4. In Galliā silvae sunt māgnae, sed in Siciliā silvae sunt parvae.
5. Britannia est prōvincia Rōmāna; Hibernia nōn est prōvincia Rōmāna.
6. Galba est incola Sardiniae; Sulla est incola Ītaliae.
7. In Americā estis, sed casa vestra est parva.
8. Amīcae tuae in silvā cum fēminīs sunt.
9. In Eurōpā sunt multae prōvinciae Rōmānae.
10. Es laeta, Helena, sed amīca tua nōn est laeta.

B. Translate into Latin:

1. We are inhabitants of a beautiful and happy country.
2. The sailor's daughter is in Sicily, a large island.
3. We are farmers; our cottages are not large.
4. Girls, you are happy, but your slaves are not happy.
5. In America there are large forests and small islands.

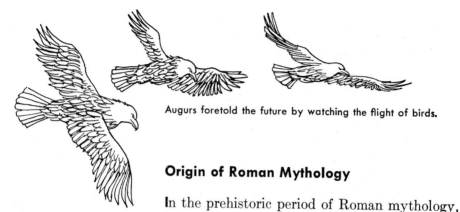

Augurs foretold the future by watching the flight of birds.

## Origin of Roman Mythology

In the prehistoric period of Roman mythology, belief and worship were of the simplest character. To all forces of nature the people attributed spirits, called *numina.* Some spirits were regarded as strong, others as weak. Some were kind and helpful, others unkind and destructive. The sun with its beneficial effects was a good spirit, the storm with its devastating effects, a bad spirit.

Every tree, rock, or animal was a potential friend or enemy. At all costs these numina must be wooed or pacified, since all things were under their direct supervision. Each spirit had its own sphere of activity — a door, a hearth, a boundary, a field. They were believed to direct and permeate all the little things of daily life. Even babies were attended by at least forty numina, who watched over all their actions.

The earliest attempts at religious worship, consisting largely of ceremonies, began during the earlier and middle ages of the Roman kingdom. The people fashioned crude images, imagining perhaps that good spirits would be happy to live in them. Eventually worship of the images became more and more complicated. A priesthood was established, as well as a detailed system of regulations for worship. The king himself directed all rites.

Since these kings were Etruscan, the Romans borrowed many of their ideas about religion from the Etruscans, especially an elaborate system of omens, by which all future events, good or evil, could be foretold. Augurs watched the flights of birds with studied care; haruspices examined the entrails of animals in order to interpret the omens.

## Roman Provinces

Multae terrae Eurōpae, Āsiae, Āfricae sunt prōvinciae Rōmānae. Ītalia, māgna paenīnsula Eurōpae, est prōvincia Rōmāna. In Ītaliā est Rōma pulchra, domina prōvinciārum.

Sunt in prōvinciīs villae multae pulchraeque. Galba est agricola. Patria Galbae est Ītalia, sed māgnae villae Galbae sunt in Galliā (*Gaul*). Pulchrae sunt Galbae villae. Pulchrae sunt Marcella et Angela, fīliae Galbae. Cum Galbā in Galliā sunt.

Vīta fīliārum Galbae laeta est et in Ītaliā et in Galliā. In parvīs casīs villārum sunt mēnsae sellaeque. Statua Diānae in casā Līviae est. Statua cum rosīs est in mēnsā. Līvia est amīca cāra (*dear*) fīliārum Galbae. Fīlia Sullae nautae est. Patria Līviae est Sicilia, prōvincia Rōmāna, sed in Galliā cum amīcīs nunc (*now*) est.

Fīliae agricolae et fīlia nautae sunt amīcae. Amīcae laetae sunt. Līvia cum Marcellā et Angelā in silvīs Galliae ambulat (*walks*). Sicilia et Gallia prōvinciae Rōmānae sunt. Rōma est domina multārum prōvinciārum.

Freedom has a thousand charms to show,
That slaves, howe'er contented, never know.
    —William Cowper, 1731–1800

# *Unit* IV

## CONVERSATION

PAULUS:      Pictūram ego *spectō*. Quid tū *spectās?*
PAULA:      Fenestram ego spectō. Quid Cornēlius *spectat?*
CORNĒLIUS:      Jānuam ego spectō. Quid Cornēlia spectat?
CORNĒLIA:      Ego et Anna mēnsam *spectāmus*. Quid nōs spectāmus?
JŪLIUS:      Mēnsam vōs *spectātis*. Quid Stella et Clāra *spectant?*
JŪLIA:      Sellam spectant. Quid, Alma et Rosa, vōs spectātis?
ALMA:      Mēnsam magistrae nōs spectāmus. Quid Jūlius portat?
JŪLIUS:      Pictūram puellārum portō. Quid Robertus et Roberta portant?

ROBERTUS: Rosās in casam portāmus. Quid Lūcius et Lūcia in casam portant?

ROBERTA: Statuam in casam portant. Quid, Anna et Marīa, amātis?

MARĪA: Rosās amāmus. Quid Petrus et Paulus amant?

PETRUS: Māgnam cameram amāmus. Quid puellae in cameram portant?

PAULUS: Rosās et statuās in cameram portant. Quid, Jūstīna, laudās?

JŪSTĪNA: Linguam Latīnam laudō. Magistram quoque laudō.

JŪSTĪNUS: Magistra puellās vocat. Ad scholam ambulāmus.

# SECTION 1 Voice, Mood, and Tense

▶ DISCUSSION

1. In English we inflect, or conjugate, a verb partly by changing its form, partly by using personal pronouns and auxiliary verbs. In Latin we conjugate a verb mainly by changing the form of the verb itself.

2. In both languages, when we conjugate a verb, we must know its voice, mood, and tense. These terms have, in general, the same meanings in both languages. *Voice* is the way of speaking that shows whether the subject performs the action of the verb (*active*) or receives the action of the verb (*passive*).

3. *Mood* is the manner of expressing the action of the verb as a fact (*indicative*), command (*imperative*), or wish (*subjunctive*), etc. For the present, all verbs in the sentences will be in the active voice and the indicative mood, which is used in making statements or asking questions.

4. *Tense* tells time. Each form of the verb tells its own time — past, present, or future. In both English and Latin there are six tenses in the indicative mood. A verb that asserts action or state of being as occurring at the present time or as occurring regularly is in the *present tense*.

5. In English, if we wish to express present time, we have three ways to do so; Latin has only one. Note the following.

|  | ENGLISH |  | LATIN |
|---|---|---|---|
| (1) Simple present | *I call* | = | **vocō** |
| (2) Progressive present | *I am calling* | = | **vocō** |
| (3) Emphatic present | *I do call* | = | **vocō** |

▶ STUDY HELPS

There is no Latin word for *do* or *am* when these words are used as auxiliary, or helping, verbs.

**19**

# SECTION 2 Formation of the Present Indicative

▶ DISCUSSION

You frequently use such verb forms as *to call, to carry, to walk.*

I tried *to walk* quickly.

Such verb forms are called infinitives. The word *infinitive* means *not limited.* It simply gives the basic idea of the verb; its form is not limited by person and number, though it is limited by tense and voice. The sign of the infinitive is usually *to,* but it is sometimes omitted.

Let me *go.*    Hear him *talk.*

In Latin the present active infinitive of all regular verbs ends in *–re:*

**vocāre** = to call

Regular verbs of the *first conjugation* are characterized by the infinitive ending *–āre.* In the Words to Master the figure (1) after the verb indicates a verb of the first conjugation. There are four conjugations in Latin.

The present stem of a regular verb is found by dropping the *–re* of the present infinitive. The present stem of *vocāre* is *vocā/.* To conjugate the verb in the present tense, add the *person indicators.*

PRESENT INDICATIVE ACTIVE, FIRST CONJUGATION

*Formula: Present Stem + Person Indicator = Form*

| Person | Pres. Stem + P.I. = | Form | Translation |
|---|---|---|---|
| | | SINGULAR | |
| First | **vocā** + **ō** = | **vocō** | *I call, am calling, do call* |
| Second | **vocā** + **s** = | **vocās** | *you call, are calling, do call* |
| Third | **vocā** + **t** = | **vocat** | *he, she, it calls, is calling, does call* |
| | | PLURAL | |
| First | **vocā** + **mus** = | **vocāmus** | *we call, are calling, do call* |
| Second | **vocā** + **tis** = | **vocātis** | *you call, are calling, do call* |
| Third | **vocā** + **nt** = | **vocant** | *they call, are calling, do call* |

▶ STUDY HELPS

1. The inflection vowel, or long *–ā,* of the stem drops out before *–ō* in the first person singular and changes to short *–a* before *–t* and *–nt.*

2. When the subject of a Latin verb is not expressed by a separate word, it is included in the verb, which must be translated backwards:

**–mus + vocā–** = **vocāmus** = *we call*

▶ PRACTICE PATTERNS

A. Write the present infinitive, the present stem, and conjugate in the present indicative, translating each form in three ways: laudō, spectō, amō.

**20**

B. Write in Latin:

| | | |
|---|---|---|
| I am | we are walking | the farmer watches |
| I am praising | you (pl.) are | the slaves care for |
| you (sing.) are | you (pl.) are carrying | the woman likes |
| you (sing.) are looking | they are | the mistress does call |
| he is | they are calling | the sailors do praise |
| he is praising | the lady lives | we care for |
| we are | the girls walk | the slave carries |

C. Write the person indicators for the present tense in Latin, and translate into English.

# SECTION 3 Accusative Case

▶ DISCUSSION

1. Verbs are either transitive or intransitive. A *transitive* verb requires a direct object to complete its meaning. An *intransitive* verb admits of no direct object to complete its meaning. The person or thing directly affected by the action of the verb is called the *direct object*.

2. In English the direct object of a transitive verb or of a preposition is in the objective case. In Latin this case is called the *accusative*. Most Latin prepositions govern the accusative case; a few govern the ablative.

3. In English the object has the same form as the subject, except some pronouns, such as *me, him, whom*. In Latin, nouns ending in –*a* in the nominative singular change the –*a* to –*am* to form the *accusative singular,* and change the –*a* to –*ās* to form the *accusative plural*.

| | SINGULAR –am | | PLURAL –ās | | USE |
|---|---|---|---|---|---|
| Nominative | puella | *girl* | puellae | *girls* | Subject |
| Accusative | pucllam | *girl* | puellās | *girls* | Object |

▶ STUDY HELPS

The Latin accusative is generally placed before the verb in the sentence.

▶ PRACTICE PATTERNS

Write in Latin the nominative and accusative case, singular and plural, of:

| | | | | | | |
|---|---|---|---|---|---|---|
| girl | life | house | island | slave | forest | inhabitant |
| villa | care | friend | street | queen | province | fatherland |
| lady | land | farmer | sailor | woman | daughter | language |

---

**ad,** *prep. with acc.*, to, toward, near
**am'bulō** (1), walk, march (*perambula-tor*)
**a'mō** (1), love, like (*amiable*)
**bo'na,** *adj.*, good (*bonus*)
**be'ne,** *adv.*, well (*benefactor*)
**cū'ra,** –ae, *f.*, care (*cure*)
**cū'ro** (1), take care of (*curator*)

**ha'bitō** (1), live, dwell (*habitation*)
**lau'dō** (1), praise (*laud*)
**mi'sera,** *adj.*, wretched, unhappy, un-fortunate (*miserable*)
**por'tō** (1), carry (*portable*)
**sae'pe,** *adv.*, often
**spec'tō** (1), look at, watch (*spectator*)
**vo'cō** (1), call, summon (*vocation*)

## BUILDING WORD POWER

A large number of Latin words of the first declension end in *–tia.* The English derivatives end in *–ce.* Our word *justice* is only slightly changed in spelling from its Latin original, **jūstitia.** What are the Latin originals for: *malice, avarice, notice, grace?* Notice that these are abstract nouns, names of qualities.

Many Latin words end in *–ntia* and retain the *–n* in English, as *science* does, deriving from **scientia,** *knowledge.* Write the Latin for the following: *patience, innocence, temperance, diligence, absence, adolescence, audience, providence, violence, sentence.* Sometimes these words end in *–y* in English, as *infancy* from **īnfantia.** What is the Latin for *constancy?*

Do you know that *infant* literally means *not talking?* In olden days young boys were attendants of knights, and they took care of the equipment and armor of the knights. Since they were not of age and were not permitted to speak for themselves, they were called **īnfanteria,** which eventually became *infantry* in English.

## SENTENCE PATTERNS

A. Translate into English. Account for the case of each noun, and the person and number of each verb.

1. Incolae īnsulae silvās pulchrās amant.
2. Servae in casīs miserīs habitant.
3. Ad villam dominae ambulāmus.
4. Agricolae terram bonam saepe laudant.
5. Vīta servārum Rōmānārum nōn est laeta.
6. Agricolās et nautās spectātis.
7. Serva bona parvam fīliam dominae saepe cūrat.
8. Domina pulchra servās vocat.
9. Rosās in casam portās. Laetitia dominae est māgna.
10. Fēminās bonās amō et laudō.

B. Translate into Latin. Account for the case of each noun and adjective.

1. You live in a cottage, but we live in a villa.
2. The inhabitants of the islands like the small forests.
3. The farmers are looking at and praising the good earth.
4. You (sing.) walk to the woods with your friend.
5. They are calling the unhappy slaves into the cottage.

### Roman Slaves

In Ītaliā et in multīs prōvinciīs Rōmānīs sunt multae servae. Jūlia, domina Rōmāna, in villā māgnā pulchrāque cum servīs habitat. Servae dominam bonam amant et laudant. Jūlia servās bonās quoque amat et laudat.

Vīta multārum servārum Rōmānārum est misera. Multae dominae nōn sunt benīgnae (*kind*), sed Jūlia est benīgna. Servae Jūliae sunt laetae. Ad dominam benīgnam rosās portant. In silvā cum Jūliā saepe ambulant.

Galba et Sulla sunt agricolae. In casīs parvīs habitant, et in terrā bene labōrant. Servae Jūliae agricolās saepe spectant et laudant. Patria agricolārum est Āfrica, sed patria servārum Jūliae nōn est Āfrica. Patria multārum servārum Jūliae est Gallia. Āfrica et Gallia sunt prōvinciae Rōmānae. Agricolae et servae Ītaliam nōn amant.

Helena, serva Jūliae, Rōmāna nōn est. Patria Helenae est Graecia pulchra. Helena Graeciam, parvam sed pulchram paenīnsulam, amat. Serva benīgna Annam, parvam fīliam Jūliae, cūrat.

How happy is the blameless vestal's lot!
The world forgetting, by the world forgot.
—Alexander Pope, 1688–1744

# *Unit* V

## CONVERSATION

PRĪMA: Helena *serva* bona est.
SECUNDA: Domina *servae* cārae Līvia est.
TERTIA: Līvia *servae* pulchrae rosam dat.
QUĀRTA: Līvia *servam* laetam amat.
QUĪNTA: Līvia cum *servā* parvā ambulat.

SEXTA: Helena et Syra *servae* bonae sunt.
SEPTIMA: Domina *servārum* cārārum Līvia est.
OCTĀVA: Līvia *servīs* pulchrīs rosās dat.
NŌNA: Līvia *servās* laetās amat.
DECIMA: Līvia cum *servīs* parvīs ambulat.
PRĪMA: Nōminātīvus singulāris, *serva;* plūrālis, *servae.*
SECUNDA: Genitīvus singulāris, *servae;* plūrālis, *servārum.*
TERTIA: Datīvus singulāris, *servae;* plūrālis, *servīs.*
QUĀRTA: Accūsātīvus singulāris, *servam;* plūrālis, *servās.*
QUĪNTA: Ablātīvus singulāris, *servā;* plūrālis, *servīs.*
MAGISTRA: Bene, discipulae. Discipulīs bonīs fābulam narrābō (*will tell*).

## SECTION 1 Dative Case

▶ DISCUSSION

In English the indirect object may be expressed in two ways:
The lady gives a rose *to the slave.*
The lady gives *the slave* a rose.

In Latin there is only one way of expressing the indirect object. The noun or pronoun to whom or for whom something is given, shown, said, or the like, is in the dative case.

**Domina *servae* rosam dat.**

| | SINGULAR –ae | PLURAL –īs | USE |
|---|---|---|---|
| Nominative | puell**a** = *girl* | puell**ae** = *girls* | Subject |
| Dative | puell**ae** = *to, for the girl* | puell**īs** = *to, for the girls* | Indirect Object |

▶ STUDY HELPS

1. The case indicator *–ae* is used for the genitive and dative singular and for the nominative plural.
2. The case indicator *–īs* is used for the dative and ablative plural.
3. The word *to* in English has three different uses: (1) with the infinitive, *to call* (**vocāre**); (2) with the indirect object, *to the slave* (**servae**); (3) after verbs of motion toward, *to the hut* (**ad casam**).

▶ PRACTICE PATTERNS

A. Write in Latin and translate the dative case singular of:
nauta    poēta    amīca    agricola    fēmina    incola    domina

B. Write in Latin the dative plural of:
land    care    island    life    slave    cottage    villa

▶ DISCUSSION

1. Inflection, or change in form, of nouns and adjectives is called *declension*. To decline is to give the case forms in regular order.

2. The simple formula for declining a noun or an adjective is to add the case indicators to the base. The *base* is that part of a noun or adjective that is unchanged in inflection. The base of a noun is found by dropping the case indicator of the genitive singular, which is always given in the vocabulary. The *base of most adjectives* is found by dropping the case indicator of the nominative feminine singular.

3. In Latin there are five declensions, each having its own set of case indicators and its own special inflection vowel. Nouns with the case indicator (C.I.) *–a* in the nominative and *–ae* in the genitive belong to the *first declension*. The inflection vowel for this declension is *–ā*.

FIRST DECLENSION

| Base + C.I. | | = Case Form | Translation | Use |
|---|---|---|---|---|
| | | SINGULAR | | |
| Nom. | puell/ + **a** | = puella | *the girl* | Subject, Pred. Nom. |
| Gen. | puell/ + **ae** | = puellae | *of the girl* | Possessive |
| Dat. | puell/ + **ae** | = puellae | *to, for the girl* | Indirect Object |
| Acc. | puell/ + **am** | = puellam | *the girl* | Direct Object |
| Abl. | puell/ + **ā** | = puellā | *from, by, with the girl* | Adverbial |
| | | PLURAL | | |
| Nom. | puell/ + **ae** | = puellae | *the girls* | Subject, Pred. Nom. |
| Gen. | puell/ + **ārum** | = puellārum | *of the girls* | Possessive |
| Dat. | puell/ + **īs** | = puellīs | *to, for the girls* | Indirect Object |
| Acc. | puell/ + **ās** | = puellās | *the girls* | Direct Object |
| Abl. | puell/ + **īs** | = puellīs | *from, by, with the girls* | Adverbial |

▶ STUDY HELPS

1. Nouns of the first declension are feminine with very few exceptions. The initial letters of the few exceptions spell *PAIN:* **P̲oēta, A̲gricola, I̲ncola, N̲auta.**

2. **Fīlia,** *daughter,* and **dea,** *goddess,* have the dative and ablative plural in *–ābus:* **fīliābus, deābus.**

3. Adjectives of the first declension are declined like nouns of the first declension and are feminine. They frequently follow the nouns they modify, unless they show emphasis or refer to quantity or size.

*25*

**4.** *Modify* means to limit or restrict one word by means of another. The noun *rose*, by itself, gives a general idea. The addition of the adjective *white* limits the word *rose* so that only a specific group of roses is meant. All other colors are excluded.

▶ PRACTICE PATTERNS

A. Decline: domina bona. Give the English translation of each form and the use of each case.

B. Fill each blank with a form of nauta. Give the reason for your choice. Translate the sentences into Latin.

1. We call ___.
2. I watch ___.
3. I walk with ___.
4. The ___ tell stories.
5. The huts ___ are large.
6. The island is dear ___.
7. The poet is near the ___.
8. I am giving the ___ money.
9. We are sailing near___.

## WORDS TO MASTER

**al'ba,** *adj.,* white (*album*)
**cā'ra,** *adj.,* dear (*caress*)
**dē,** *prep. with abl.,* down from, concerning, about
**dō** (1), *irreg.,* give (*data*)
**ē, ex,** *prep. with abl.,* out of, from
**fā'bula, –ae,** *f.,* story, tale (*fable*)
**nar'rō** (1), tell, narrate (*narrator*)
**nā'vigō** (1), sail, sail over (*navigate*)

**pecū'nia, –ae,** *f.,* money (*pecuniary*)
**poē'ta, –ae,** *m.,* poet
**pro'pe,** *prep. with acc.,* near; *adv.,* nearly, almost
**propin'qua,** *adj.,* near, nearby; *with dat.,* near to (*propinquity*)
**ro'gō** (1), *with two accusatives,* ask, ask for, inquire (*rogation*)

## BUILDING WORD POWER

About four out of every five difficult words in your English reading are derived from Latin. These words came into English either directly from the Latin or indirectly via the Romance languages, particularly from the Norman French.

In the eleventh century a French Duke, William of Normandy, conquered England, and French-speaking nobles became the ruling class in the conquered country. They spoke Norman-French, a language that had been derived *by ear* from vulgar, or spoken, Latin, the Latin of the ordinary people who could neither read nor write. In those days very few people, except the clergy and a few educated nobles, were literate.

Although eventually French ceased to be the language even of the overlords, large numbers of French words of Latin origin were adopted into English. Because they were learned *by ear*, there were many irregularities in spelling and frequent changes in meaning. Therefore, it is usually difficult to recognize in most of these words the original Latin from which they were derived. It would take a vivid imagination to trace the word *kerchief* back to the original **cooperīre,** *to cover,* and **caput,** *head;* or the word *chauffeur* back to **calēre,** *to warm,* and **facere,** *to make.* Evidently a chauffeur was formerly a stoker.

## SENTENCE PATTERNS

A. Translate into English. Tell the reason for the case of each noun.

1. In Siciliā casās parvās et albās spectāmus.
2. Domina bona servae miserae pecūniam dat.
3. Poētae fābulās dē īnsulā antīquā narrant.
4. Ad Ītaliam nautae saepe nāvigant.
5. Prope villam māgnam pulchramque habitāmus.
6. Saepe agricolae fīliābus fābulās bonās narrant.
7. Puellae laetae ē casā ad silvam ambulant.
8. Villa dominae est propinqua casīs servārum.
9. Rēgīna pulchra est cāra parvīs fīliābus.
10. Servae miserae pecūniam rogant, sed domina servīs pecūniam nōn dat.

B. Translate into Latin:

1. The lady is walking out of the villa with the slaves.
2. The daughters of the sailors give roses to the good lady.
3. The farmer tells stories to the dear little girl.
4. We often walk to the forest.
5. You (pl.) are sailing near the large and beautiful island.

The Temple of Vesta, in which the city fire was kept continuously burning.

## Origin of Roman Mythology (*continued*)

The mythology of the later years of the kingdom and the era of the Republic was marked by the introduction of foreign divinities and ceremonies, chiefly from the Greeks. Under the Republic a Pontifex Maximus took over the direction of all religious affairs and appointed priests for each duty and function.

Temples were built and supported by state money. Augurs and haruspices were consulted before all important state events. Vestal Virgins were state-elected and state-controlled. Worship of the *lares*, *penates*, and *manes* become important features of the Roman religion.

Vesta was the goddess of the hearth. In the home the hearth fire was tended by the daughters of the household; in the Temple of Vesta, the city fire was kept continuous by the Vestal Virgins.

The Lares were deified spirits of departed ancestors who continued to hover over the places that they had once inhabited. Only the spirits of good men were honored as lares. The *lar familiaris* was looked upon as the founder of the family.

The penates were the household gods whose duty it was to attend to the welfare and prosperity of the family. Images of the lares and penates, small human figures, were to be found at the hearth of every home. There were also public lares and penates who did for the city what the others did for the family.

The manes were the spirits in Hades of those who had lived good lives while on earth. The Romans were always very careful to see that their dead received proper burial, for they believed that otherwise their manes could not gain admittance to the Underworld and would return to haunt them. Sometimes the manes were regarded as divine and were worshiped.

### Sicily

Sicilia, prīma prōvincia Rōmāna, est māgna īnsula propinqua paenīnsulae Ītaliae. Incolae Siciliae antīquae sunt et agricolae et nautae. Agricolae terram cūrant, et nautae in aquā nāvigant.

Patria multārum incolārum Siciliae antīquae est Graecia. Nautae ē Siciliā ad Graeciam saepe nāvigant. Pictūrās et statuās ē Graeciā in Siciliam portant. Fīliābus pulchrīs multās fābulās dē Graeciā narrant. Poētae quoque fābulās dē Graeciā narrant.

Claudia, fīlia Sullae nautae, rogat: "Quid in Graeciā spectās?" Sulla fīliae cārae respondet (*answers*), "Multās silvās, rosās pulchrās, casās parvās albāsque spectāmus. Servae miserae terram et villās cūrant. Dominae servīs bonīs pecūniam saepe dant. Prope Graeciam sunt multae et parvae īnsulae. Lingua incolārum Graeciae est lingua Graeca. Lingua incolārum Siciliae saepe est Graeca. Lingua Latīna quoque lingua incolārum Siciliae est."

"Linguam Latīnam et linguam Graecam," inquit (*says*) Claudia, "laudāmus. Statuās pictūrāsque Graecās quoque laudāmus, sed Siciliam, patriam nostram, amāmus."

# Comprehensive Review: Units I–V

A. Write in Latin the nominative singular, genitive singular, and base of these nouns:

| | | | | | | |
|---|---|---|---|---|---|---|
| girl | poet | woman | money | sailor | cottage | peninsula |
| care | life | story | street | island | daughter | farmhouse |
| lady | earth | queen | forest | farmer | language | inhabitant |
| land | farm | slave | tongue | friend | province | fatherland |

B. Translate these verbs into the specified English form:

SIMPLE: habitās, vocant, datis, rogō
PROGRESSIVE: portat, laudāmus, ambulās, amō
EMPHATIC: nāvigat, spectātis, narrant, cūrāmus

C. Write in Latin:

| | | | |
|---|---|---|---|
| I am | I do tell | he does call | you (sing.) ask |
| I love | he watches | I am walking | they do praise |
| they are | we care for | you (pl.) live | they are giving |
| there are | we do carry | you (sing.) are | you (sing.) are sailing |

D. Decline in the singular and plural: amīca cāra. Give the name and use of each case. Mark the long vowels in the case indicators.

E. Conjugate in the present tense: narrō, sum. Translate.

F. Write in Latin the specified forms:

1. accusative singular: road, life
2. ablative plural: queen, island
3. dative singular: mistress, daughter
4. accusative plural: inhabitant, hut
5. genitive singular: money, land
6. nominative plural: care, province
7. accusative singular: sailor, farmer
8. dative plural: friend, slave
9. genitive plural: joy, forest
10. ablative singular: tongue, story

G. Write the meanings of the following adjectives:

| | | | | | | | |
|---|---|---|---|---|---|---|---|
| tua | lāta | bona | māgna | lībera | nostra | parva | pulchra |
| mea | cāra | laeta | multa | misera | vestra | antīqua | propinqua |

H. Write in Latin:

| | | |
|---|---|---|
| not | and (enclitic) | often |
| but | with | down from |
| and | in | out from |
| both . . . and | also | near (prep. and adv.) |
| almost | to (prep.) | near (adj.) |

I. Answer the following questions:

1. Which syllable in a Latin word is never accented?
2. In a two-syllable word, which syllable receives the accent?
3. What are the names of the last three syllables of a Latin word?
4. How is the base of a noun found? the present stem of a verb?
5. What is the inflection vowel of a first declension noun? of a first conjugation verb?
6. Name the case indicators of first declension nouns, the person indicators of the present tense in the indicative mood.

## SENTENCE PATTERNS

A. Translate into English:

1. Patria nostra nōn est Ītalia.
2. Graecia paene īnsula est.
3. Ē Siciliā in Graeciam nāvigātis.
4. Puellīs multam pecūniam damus.
5. Fēminās Amēricae laudant.
6. Linguam Latīnam amāmus et laudāmus.
7. Rōmae sunt multae servae.
8. In Ītaliā habitant agricolae nautaeque.
9. Domina cum amīcā in silvam ambulat.
10. Fēminae fīliābus fābulās dē Galliā narrant.

B. Translate into Latin:

1. Italy is the fatherland of poets.
2. The poets of America like and praise our beautiful country.
3. In Sicily there are many small but beautiful forests.
4. The sailors tell many good stories about the islands of our country.
5. Both the women and the girls are watching the wretched slaves.

## SIGHT TRANSLATION: A ROMAN VILLA

Galba et Sulla sunt agricolae. In Ītaliā habitant. Māgnam villam cūrant. Jūlia est parva fīlia Galbae; Cornēlia est parva fīlia Sullae. Jūlia et Cornēlia sunt amīcae. Ad villam pulchram saepe ambulant, et gallīnās (*hens*) et columbās (*doves*) spectant. Servae gallīnās et columbās cūrant.

Lūcia, serva bona, rosās cūrat. Parvae puellae rosās pulchrās amant. Lūcia Jūliam et Cornēliam vocat et puellīs laetīs multās rosās dat. Et Jūlia et Cornēlia rosās albās amant. Gallīnās columbāsque quoque amant. Amīcae bonae gallīnīs et columbīs frūmentum (*grain*) dant, sed rosās ad casās portant.

*Unit* VI

## CONVERSATION

| | |
|---|---|
| PAULUS: | Salvē, Paula. Quid tū vidēs? |
| PAULA: | Mēnsam magistrae ego videō. Quem (*Whom?*) tū vidēs? |
| JŪLIUS: | Magistram ego videō. Quid magistrae dās? |
| JŪLIA: | Ego magistrae chartam dō. Quid habet magistra? |
| CORNĒLIUS: | Magistra chartam et multās pennās habet. Quid magistra docet? |
| CORNĒLIA: | Linguam Latīnam magistra docet. Quem magistra docet? |
| ROBERTUS: | Puellam magistra nunc docet. Quem puella timet? |
| ROBERTA: | Magistram puella nōn timet. Quem magistra monet? |
| MĀRCUS: | Puellās magistra monet. Quid puellae habent? |
| MĀRCELLA: | Pilam puellae habent. Quid rogat magistra nunc? |
| LŪCIUS: | Magistra rogat: "Ubi est Rōma?" Quid respondent puellae? |
| LŪCIA: | Respondent: "Rōma in Ītaliā est." Quid magistra nunc videt? |
| ALBERTUS: | Pilam magistra videt. Ubi nunc est pila? |
| ALBERTA: | Ibi in magistrae mensā est pila. Quis puellās monet? |
| VICTOR: | Hodiē magistra puellās monet sed puellīs pilam dat. |
| VICTŌRIA: | Puellae cum laetitiā magistrae respondent: "Grātiās tibi agimus." |

# SECTION 1 Second Conjugation Verbs, Present Tense

▶ DISCUSSION

In Latin, verbs are classified in four groups: first, second, third, and fourth conjugation. Each conjugation has its own inflection vowel. You have already seen that verbs of the first conjugation have –*ā* for their inflection vowel. Verbs of the second conjugation have –*ē* for their inflection vowel.

**moneō, monēre** = *warn*

**monē/** = present stem

PRESENT INDICATIVE ACTIVE, SECOND CONJUGATION

*Formula: Present Stem + Person Indicator = Form*

| *Person* | *Pres. Stem* | *+ P.I. =* | *Form* | *Translation* |
|----------|--------------|------------|--------|---------------|
| | | SINGULAR | | |
| First | monē | + ō | = moneō | *I warn, am warning, do warn* |
| Second | monē | + s | = monēs | *you warn, are warning, do warn* |
| Third | monē | + t | = monet | *he, she, it warns, is warning, does warn* |
| | | PLURAL | | |
| First | monē | + mus | = monēmus | *we warn, are warning, do warn* |
| Second | monē | + tis | = monētis | *you warn, are warning, do warn* |
| Third | monē | + nt | = monent | *they warn, are warning, do warn* |

▶ STUDY HELPS

1. The present tense of the second conjugation differs from the first in the inflection vowel and in the first person singular. In the first person singular of **moneō**, the long –*ē* of the stem has become short before another vowel, while in **vocō** the long –*ā* of the stem is dropped entirely.

2. In both conjugations the inflection vowels become short before –*t* and –*nt.*

▶ PRACTICE PATTERNS

A. Write the present infinitive and present stem, and conjugate in the present indicative: doceō, laudō, habeō. Translate each form three ways.

B. Write in Latin:

| | | | |
|---|---|---|---|
| he fears | I do love | you (sing.) fear | you (sing.) praise |
| we see | they look at | she does love | they are teaching |
| they tell | you (pl.) have | he is warning | we are carrying |
| I ask | we do care | you (pl.) walk | they are sailing |
| we answer | he does have | she is afraid | you (sing.) live |

# SECTION 2 Latin Word Order

▶ DISCUSSION

Regardless of their positions, the words in a Latin sentence show their relationship to one another by means of end signals or indicators. The more or less normal order in a declarative sentence is: (1) the subject and its modifiers; (2) the ablative; (3) the dative, indirect object; (4) the direct object; (5) the verb and its modifiers. As regards the position of different parts of speech, great freedom is allowed, but the following tendencies may be noted:

1. Adjectives and genitive modifiers usually follow their nouns, but adjectives denoting quantity and size precede their nouns.

2. Appositives stand immediately after the nouns they limit.

3. The vocative does not usually stand first in the sentence.

4. Forms of the verb **sum** may stand between the subject and predicate nominative or at the end of the sentence.

5. In questions and commands the verb often stands at or near the beginning of the sentence.

6. Special emphasis is secured by placing any word or phrase where it does not normally stand. In general, Latin differs from English in having more freedom in the arrangement of words to express the relative importance of ideas.

## WORDS TO MASTER

**a'qua, –ae,** *f.,* water (*aquatic*)
**do'ceō** (2), *with two accusatives,* teach (*docile*)
**ha'beō** (2), have, hold (*habit*)
**ho'diē,** *adv.,* today
**i'bi,** *adv.,* there
**mo'neō** (2), warn, advise (*admonition*)

**nunc,** *adv.,* now
**per,** *prep.,* through
**respon'deō** (2), answer (*respond*)
**ti'meō** (2), fear, be afraid (*timid*)
**u'bi,** *adv. and conj.,* where, when (*ubiquitous*)
**vi'deō** (2), see (*vision*)

## BUILDING WORD POWER

About the fifteenth century there was a revival of interest in the ancient Latin and Greek classics in the schools and universities. As a result, many words came into English directly from the Latin. These we may call *eye-Latin* because they are pure Latin and resemble their originals closely in spelling, and frequently in meaning. You have already used some of these eye-Latin words in previous units.

Can you give English words that resemble these Latin words: *adōrō, labōrō, respondeō, moveō, exspectō, cōnfīrmō, vīsitō, columna, fōrma, tunica, nōrma, nātūra, herba, doctrīna?*

Most of our word study will be from eye-Latin, but because Latin words come into English through two channels, one direct (eye-Latin), the other indirect (ear-Latin), we frequently have two, sometimes three, words from the identical Latin original. We call these pairs *doublets. Regal* and *royal,* from **rēx,** *king; legal* and *loyal,* from **lēx,** *law; pair* and *peer,* from **pār,** *equal; sure* and *secure,* from **sē + cūra,** are doublets.

**33**

**SENTENCE PATTERNS**

A. Translate into English:

1. Nautae cum fīliābus prope aquam ambulant.
2. Ubi hodiē sunt agricolae? Ubi habitant agricolae?
3. Agricolae in casīs propinquīs silvīs habitant.
4. Serva aquam ex villā portat et agricolīs aquam dat.
5. Fēmina parvam puellam vocat, sed puella fēminae bonae nōn respondet.
6. Ubi est domina nunc? Ibi est.
7. Magistra bona puellās linguam Latīnam docet.
8. Nautam videō sed nōn timeō.
9. Poētae fābulās dē Rōmā saepe narrant.
10. Agricolae et nautae nunc multam pecūniam nōn habent.

B. Translate into Latin:

1. We often walk through the woods.
2. They do not have much money, but they are happy.
3. The lady warns the little girl, but she does not answer the lady.
4. Where do you see the white house? There it is.
5. We are now watching the daughters of the sailors.

## A Visit from the Pirates

In īnsulā Corsicā antīquā et agricolae et nautae habitant. Tullia est fīlia pulchra Sullae nautae; Lūcia est fīlia cāra Galbae agricolae. Incolae īnsulae fābulās dē terrā et dē aquā amant. Sulla Tulliae fābulās dē aquā, et Galba Lūciae fābulās dē silvīs saepe narrat.

Sed hodiē Sulla puellīs fābulam dē pīrātīs narrat. Pīrātae albās casās propinquās aquae saepe vīsitant. Ibi et agricolae et nautae pīrātās timent et pīrātīs pecūniam et gemmās (*gems*) dant. Pīrātae māgnās arcās pecūniae et gemmārum saepe habent.

Hodiē arcās pecūniae per aquam ad terram portant. Sulla et Tullia ubi pīrātās vident incolās monent. Agricolae et nautae pīrātās nunc spectant. Ubi pīrātae arcās in silvīs celant (*hide*), nautae pīrātās necant (*kill*), et agricolae arcās ad casās portant.

Ibi et agricolae et nautae Sullam fīliamque laudant, et Sullae multam pecūniam dant. Fīlia pulchra Sullae pīrātās nōn laudat. Fābulās dē pīrātīs et dē arcīs pecūniae gemmārumque nōn amat. Et Lūcia et Tullia fābulās dē agricolīs nautīsque laudant et amant.

To the gods alone
Belongs it never to be old or die,
But all things else melt with all-powerful Time.
—Sophocles, 496?–406 B.C.

# *Unit* VII

## CONVERSATION

| | |
|---|---|
| JŪLIUS: | Quis (*Who*) erat Sulla, Jūlia? |
| JŪLIA: | Sulla erat nauta. Ōlim in Corsicā habitābat. |
| LŪCIUS: | Cūjus (*Whose*) fīlia erat Tullia? |
| LŪCIA: | Tullia erat fīlia Sullae nautae. |
| PAULUS: | Cui (*To whom*) Sulla fābulās narrābat? |
| PAULA: | Sulla fīliae Tulliae fābulās narrābat. |
| VICTOR: | Quem (*Whom*) Tullia timēbat? |
| VICTŌRIA: | Pīrātam Tullia timēbat. |
| JŪLIUS: | Quōcum (*With whom?*) Sulla ambulābat? |
| JŪLIA: | Sulla cum Tulliā in īnsulā ambulābat. |
| LŪCIUS: | Cūr Sulla et Tullia agricolam et fīliam monēbant? |
| LŪCIA: | Pīrātae prope terram nāvigābant. Incolās īnsulae terrēbant. |
| PAULUS: | Quid pīrātae habēbant? |
| PAULA: | Pecūniam et gemmās pīrātae habēbant. |
| VICTOR: | Agricolae et nautae prō patriā labōrābant. Agricolae terram arābant. Nautae in aquā nāvigābant. Pīrātās timēbant. |

## Imperfect Tense

▶ DISCUSSION

The word *imperfect* means *not finished* or *incomplete*. It indicates a past action or state that is incomplete, continuous, customary, or going on at the same time as another.

In English four forms are used to cover the idea expressed by the *Latin imperfect indicative:*

**ambulābam** = *I was walking, I kept on walking, I used to walk, I walked*

The translation into English often will depend on the context, but sometimes the imperfect is translated into English by the simple past, *I walked.* In translating into Latin, the imperfect should not be used unless the reason for doing so is expressed clearly in English. The imperfect is not used for an action that occurred once and was completed in the past.

**35**

The imperfect tense is formed by adding to the present stem the *tense indicator* (*T.I.*), **-bā-**, and the *person indicators* (*P.I.*).

IMPERFECT INDICATIVE ACTIVE, FIRST CONJUGATION

*Formula: Present Stem + Tense Indicator + Person Indicator = Form*

| Person | Pres. Stem | + T.I. | + P.I. | = Form | Translation |
|--------|-----------|--------|--------|--------|-------------|
| | | | SINGULAR | | |
| First | vocā | + bā | + m | = vocābam | *I was calling, called, did call* |
| Second | vocā | + bā | + s | = vocābās | *you were calling, called, did call* |
| Third | vocā | + bā | + t | = vocābat | *he was calling, called, did call* |
| | | | PLURAL | | |
| First | vocā | + bā | + mus | = vocābāmus | *we were calling, called, did call* |
| Second | vocā | + bā | + tis | = vocābātis | *you were calling, called, did call* |
| Third | vocā | + bā | + nt | = vocābant | *they were calling, called, did call* |

The imperfect of the second conjugation is formed like that of the first conjugation.

**monē + bā + m = monēbam** = *I was warning, I warned*
**monēbās, monēbat, monēbāmus, monēbātis, monēbant**

IMPERFECT INDICATIVE OF SUM

| Person | SINGULAR | | | PLURAL | |
|--------|----------|--|--|--------|--|
| First | **eram** | *I was* | | **erāmus** | *we were* |
| Second | **erās** | *you were* | | **erātis** | *you were* |
| Third | **erat** | *he, she, it was* | | **erant** | *they were* |

▶ STUDY HELPS

1. *Was* and *were* in the translations of **vocābam** and **monēbam** are auxiliary verbs of the imperfect tense in English and must not be translated into Latin by forms of **sum.**

2. In the imperfect indicative, **-m,** not **-ō,** is the person indicator of the first person singular. The **-a** is short before **-m.**

3. Compounds of **sum,** as **absum** and **adsum,** are conjugated in all tenses like **sum:**

**aberam** = *I was absent*
**aderam** = *I was present*

▶ PRACTICE PATTERNS

A. Conjugate in the imperfect tense and translate in the progressive form: nāvigō, respondeō.

B. Conjugate in the imperfect tense and translate: sum, absum, adsum.

*36*

### C. Translate into Latin:

| | | |
|---|---|---|
| he is absent | you (sing.) were present | they are hastening |
| you (pl.) were afraid | I was preparing | they used to labor |
| he was absent | he is frightening | I plowed (every day) |
| they are present | they were present | he was frightening |

## WORDS TO MASTER

**ab′sum,** *irreg.,* be absent (*absent*)
**ad′sum,** *irreg.,* be present
**a′rō** (1), plow (*arable*)
**cūr,** *adv.,* why? wherefore?
**fā′ma, −ae, f.,** report, fame (*famous*)
**glō′ria, −ae, f.,** glory (*glorious*)
**labō′rō** (1), work, labor, suffer (*labor*)

**ō′lim,** *adv.,* once upon a time, formerly
**pa′rō** (1), prepare, get ready (*preparation*)
**prō,** *prep. with abl.,* for, in front of, in behalf of
**pro′perō** (1), hasten, hurry
**ter′reō** (2), frighten, terrify (*terror*)

## BUILDING WORD POWER

A knowledge of Latin will help you not only to learn and remember the meanings of a very large number of English words, but also to distinguish shades of meanings rarely perceived by one ignorant of Latin.

Our English words *pecuniary,* *peculiar,* and *peculate* have interesting life stories that can be traced back to a common origin. You have already learned that the Latin word **pecūnia** means *money.* It seems that the wealth of the ancients consisted of cattle. The word for cattle in Latin is **pecus.** When people found it no longer convenient to barter with cattle, they used coins, and the word **pecūnia,** derived from **pecus,** came to mean *money.* The addition of the suffix **−ārius** gave us our English word *pecuniary.*

**Pecūlium,** also from **pecus,** was property that was one's own. From this word we have **pecūliāris,** *peculiar,* which eventually developed into the meaning *strange* or *odd,* since what is one's own sometimes seems strange to one's neighbor. To *peculate* means to *steal,* not cattle, but the special property one is supposed to guard. Another word for *peculator* is *embezzler.*

## SENTENCE PATTERNS

A. Complete and translate into English:

1. Fīliae fēminārum ad vill____properāba____et agricol____spectābant.
2. Cūr nautae ex Itali____ ad prōvinci____ nāvigāba____?
3. Domina bon____ servās nōn terrēba____.
4. Servae in casīs vill____ pulchrae labōrāba____.

5. Māgn____ erant fām____ et glōri____ Rōmae.
6. Agricol____ terram arābat, et servae cas____ cūrābant.
7. Puellae adera____, sed fēmin____ aberant.
8. Nautae et agricolae pro patriā labōrāba____.
9. Ōlim naut____ ex Ītali____ ad Graeci____ nāvigābant.
10. Agricolae terram bonam parāba____ et arābant.

B. Translate into Latin:

1. Once upon a time Rome was mistress of many provinces.
2. The maidservants were working in the house, but the daughters of the farmer were walking in the woods.
3. Why were the girls absent? Why were they not present?
4. The women were hastening to the water and were watching the sailors.
5. The fame and the glory of our fatherland were great.

Mt. Olympus.

## The Celestial Hierarchy

As we have already learned, the Romans had almost no mythology of their own. They did not regard their *numina*, who watched over almost every act of their lives, as persons since they were powers without bodily shape or form. However, long before they had subjected Greece to Roman power in 146 B.C., they had gradually absorbed the Greek myths and identified them as nearly as possible with their most popular numina.

The Greeks had very definite ideas about their deities. In Greece, separating the regions of Macedonia and Thessaly, is a long and high mountain range, at the end of which stand the snowy peaks of Mt. Olympus. Here, according to the natives, lived the gods, magnified human beings to whom the Greeks attributed superhuman powers.

In a magnificent palace on Mt. Olympus, they lived merrily, enjoying ambrosia and nectar for daily sustenance. They wore clothing similar to that of human beings. At night they slept just as mortals do. They were born, grew up, and married, but they did not die. They experienced the joys and sorrows of human living, but they could perform feats far beyond the powers of ordinary mortals. Their chief interest was in the affairs of human beings, in which they frequently played an active part.

Greek literature was saturated with invented fables about these deities. The country of Greece was filled with magnificent temples in their honor. Worship of the gods was an important duty in the daily life of the people. We must remember, however, that the thoughtful Greek of historical times did not share this blind faith of the ordinary people.

### Fabiola at Her Country Estate

Ōlim in Ītaliā et in prōvinciīs erant villae māgnae pulchraeque. Fāma et glōria villārum Rōmānārum erant māgnae. Saepe ruīnās et pictūrās ruīnārum vidēmus.

Fabiola, domina villae, Rōmae habitābat et multās servās habēbat. Agricolae terram arābant; servae in parvīs casīs villae labōrābant. Servae multās camerās cūrābant et in culīnā (*kitchen*) cēnam (*dinner*) parābant. In māgnīs camerīs erant multae columnae et statuae quoque Diānae, deae silvae. Servae dominae rosās dabant quod (*because*) rosās amābat.

Syra erat serva bona pulchraque Fabiolae. Cum dominā saepe erat. Fabiola, domina superba (*proud*), nōn semper (*always*) erat benīgna (*kind*). Ubi domina nōn erat benīgna, Syra erat serēna et tranquilla.

"Cūr, Syra, es semper serēna et tranquilla?" rogābat Fabiola.

"Ego semper serēna et tranquilla nōn sum, sed tū, domina, benīgna saepe es. Pulchram dominam meam amō, et in villā māgnā dominae meae habitō. Nōn semper in villā pulchra habitābam. Ōlim in casā miserā et parvā habitābam. Casa prope silvam lātam erat. Ibi lībera eram, et in silvīs antīquīs saepe ambulābam. Nunc lībera nōn sum; ego sum serva et prō dominā labōrō, sed sum laeta quod dominam meam amō."

Posteā (*Later*) Fabiola in perīculō (*danger*) erat, et Syra, serva bona, vītam prō dominā dedit (*gave*). Mox (*Soon*) servae līberae erant et cum dominā Rōmānā in villā pulchrā habitābant. Domina et servae erant semper laetae et benīgnae.

## CONVERSATION

MAGISTER: Salvēte, puerī et puellae. Cōnsīdite, sī placet.
PRĪMUS: Salvē, magister. Quid agis hodiē?
MAGISTER: Bene, grātiās tibi agō. Ubi est Sextus?
PRĪMA: Sextus abest. In Viā Sacrā ambulābat.
SECUNDA: Ad villam properābat. Sextum ego vidēbam.
MAGISTER: Quōcum Sextus ambulābat?
SECUNDUS: Cum māgnō virō ambulābat. Māgnum virum nōs vidēbāmus.
MAGISTER: Quis erat māgnus vir?
TERTIUS: Māgnus vir erat dominus villae et multōrum servōrum.
TERTIA: Sextus ad villam cum dominō saepe ambulat.
MAGISTER: Cūr parvus puer ad villam hodiē properābat?
QUĀRTUS: Agrōs et agricolās dominī Sextus amat.
QUĀRTA: Servōs fīdōs dominī quoque amat.
QUĪNTUS: Dominus tubā servōs semper vocat. Sextus tubam amat.
MAGISTER: Sextus puer malus (*bad*) est quod hodiē abest. Vōs bonī discipulī estis quod vōs in scholā adestis. Nunc valēte.

## SECTION 1 Second Declension Masculine Nouns

▶ DISCUSSION

1. Nouns of the second declension are of two types: *masculine,* with the nominative singular usually in *–us;* and *neuter,* with the nominative singular in *–um.* The case indicator of the genitive singular is *–ī.*

2. All second declension masculine nouns, except those that end in *–ius,* are declined like the nouns in the following paradigms.

| | servus, servī *m.* slave | puer, puerī *m.* boy | ager, agrī *m.* field | vir, virī *m.* man | |
|---|---|---|---|---|---|
| BASE: | serv/ | puer/ | agr/ | vir/ | |
| | | SINGULAR | | | C.I. |
| Nom. | serv**us** | puer | ager | vir | **–us** (**–er**, **–ir**) |
| Gen. | serv**ī** | puer**ī** | agr**ī** | vir**ī** | **–ī** |
| Dat. | serv**ō** | puer**ō** | agr**ō** | vir**ō** | **–ō** |
| Acc. | serv**um** | puer**um** | agr**um** | vir**um** | **–um** |
| Abl. | serv**ō** | puer**ō** | agr**ō** | vir**ō** | **–ō** |

**40**

| Nom. | servī | puerī | agrī | virī | -ī |
| Gen. | servōrum | puerōrum | agrōrum | virōrum | -ōrum |
| Dat. | servīs | puerīs | agrīs | virīs | -īs |
| Acc. | servōs | puerōs | agrōs | virōs | -ōs |
| Abl. | servīs | puerīs | agrīs | virīs | -īs |

## ▶ STUDY HELPS

1. Nouns in –er in the second declension are rare, and **vir** is the only second declension noun that ends in –ir.

2. Some nouns whose nominative ends in –er keep the –e in cases other than the nominative singular; others do not. In the vocabulary form, the genitive will be given in such a way as to show whether the given noun retains or drops the –e.

English derivatives from these words can also serve as guides: *puerile* (**puer**), *library* (**liber**), *agriculture* (**ager**), *magistrate* (**magister**). Do not confuse **liber**, *book* (*library*), with **līber**, *free* (*liberty*).

## ▶ PRACTICE PATTERNS

A. Decline and give English meanings: dominus, magister.

B. Write in Latin the specified forms:

1. genitive singular: puer, dominus, magister, amīca, vir
2. dative singular: ager, servus, magistra, tuba, puer
3. genitive plural: servus, vir, glōria, dominus, tuba

C. Write in Latin the specified forms:

1. nominative plural: field, slave, boy, man, teacher
2. ablative plural: master, girl, field, poet, money
3. accusative plural: friend, teacher, sailor, farmer, forest

# SECTION 2 Masculine Adjectives

## ▶ DISCUSSION

1. When adjectives modify masculine nouns, they must have a masculine form. These adjectives are declined like **servus**; a few are declined like **puer** and **ager**.

The feminine nominative singular shows whether the –e has been retained or dropped: **pulcher, pulchra,** masculine and feminine for *beautiful;* **līber, lībera** for *free*. Again, as with the nouns, the English derivatives will serve as guides; *pulchritude* (**pulchr–**), liberty (**liber–**), misery (**miser–**).

Masculine adjectives must be used with masculine nouns of the first declension: **Poēta, Agricola, Incola, Nauta.** Remember the word *PAIN*.

▶ PRACTICE PATTERNS

A. Decline in Latin and translate each case: a faithful slave (m.).

B. Write the masculine form of:

| | | | | | |
|---|---|---|---|---|---|
| fīda | lībera | bona | antīqua | māgna | parva |
| cāra | nostra | laeta | multa | lāta | misera |
| tua | mea | vestra | propinqua | alba | pulchra |

## SECTION 3 Ablative of Means

▶ DISCUSSION

The ablative is used *without* a preposition to express the means or instrument with which some act is done.

**Dominus *tubā* servum vocābat.**   The master was calling the servant *with (by means of) a trumpet.*

This ablative is called the *ablative of means* and is translated into English thus: *by, by means of, with.* It always answers the question: With what? By means of what? The noun in the ablative of means is usually a concrete noun, never a person.

**WORDS TO MASTER**

**a′ger, a′grī,** *m.*, field, territory, land (*agriculture*)
**do′minus, –ī,** *m.*, master (*domino*)
**fī′dus, –a, –um,** *adj.*, faithful (*fidelity*)
**lī′ber, –era, –erum,** *adj.*, free (*liberal*); **lī′berī, –ōrum,** *m. pl.*, children
**magis′ter, –trī,** *m.*, teacher (*master*); **magis′tra, –ae,** *f.*, teacher

**nātū′ra, –ae,** *f.*, nature (*natural*)
**pu′er, pu′erī,** *m.*, boy (*puerile*)
**quod,** *conj.*, because
**sem′per,** *adv.*, always
**ser′vus, –ī,** *m.*, slave (*servile*)
**tu′ba, –ae,** *f.*, trumpet (*tuba*)
**vir, vi′rī,** *m.*, man, hero, husband (*virile*)

**BUILDING WORD POWER**

You already know a large number of masculine nouns of the second declension. Often they came directly into English with no change in spelling and sometimes with little or no change in meaning. Use the

*42*

following words in sentences, and check with the dictionary for ancient and modern meanings. Notice particularly *focus, bacillus,* and *virus.*

| radius | genius | focus | campus | terminus | circus | stimulus |
| nucleus | virus | humus | animus | bacillus | discus | alumnus |

A few of these words retain their Latin plural endings in English. Pronounce: *alumni, stimuli, radii.* Notice that in English the final –*i* rhymes with the pronoun *I*.

Many boys' names in English are of Latin origin and are from the second declension. What names are derived from these? ***Antōnius*** *(inestimable),* ***Augustus*** *(majestic),* ***Calvīnus*** *(bald),* ***Petrus*** *(rock),* ***Paulus*** *(small),* ***Jūstīnus*** *(just),* ***Patricius*** *(noble),* ***Claudus*** *(lame),* ***Laurentius*** *(crowned with laurel),* ***Rūfus*** *(red).*

## SENTENCE PATTERNS

A. Translate into English:
1. Rōmānī agrōs et agricolās semper laudabant.
2. Poëtae Rōmānī dē silvīs et de agris fābulās narrābant.
3. Virī cum puerīs Rōmānīs terram arābant.
4. Cūr in Ītaliā antīquā erant multī servī et servae?
5. Cincinnatus erat dominus bonus, et cum servīs in agrīs saepe labōrābat.
6. Magister puerōs fābulās docēbat.
7. Agricola tubā servōs semper vocābat.
8. Servī fīdī ex agrīs properābant.
9. Poëtae fābulās de nātūrā narrābant quod nātūram amābant.
10. Servae līberōs dominī cūrābant quod servae erant nōn līberae.

B. Translate into Latin:
1. The man was calling the boys with a trumpet.
2. The farmer used to praise the faithful men and boys.
3. Many men of ancient Italy worked in the fields with the slaves.
4. The slaves were unhappy because they were not free.
5. The Roman poets praised Rome by their stories.

## Britain's Brave Queen

Ōlim in īnsulā Britanniā rēgīna pulchra bonaque habitābat. Incolae Britanniae erant et agricolae et nautae. Agricolae bonī agrōs arābant, et līberī agricolārum in agrīs labōrābant. Nautae prope ōram maritimam (*seacoast*) nāvigābant. Līberī nautārum cum nautīs saepe nāvigābant. Vīta et agricolārum et nautārum erat laeta. Puerī puellaeque quoque erant laetī.

Boadicea erat rēgīna Britannōrum. Britanniam amābat. Agricolās fīdōs et nautās bonōs amābat et laudābat. Incolae īnsulae, virī, fēminae, puerī puellaeque rēgīnam Boadiceam amābant et laudābant, quod rēgīna erat bona et pulchra.

Britannī erant līberī. Subitō (*Suddenly*) Rōmānī prope ōram maritimam īnsulae pulchrae nāvigābant. Britannī Rōmānōs vidēbant et ad rēgīnam properābant. Rēgīna cum virīs, fēminīs līberīsque prope aquam stābat (*stood*) et Rōmānōs spectābat. Rōmānōs nōn timēbant. Britannī erant līberī; nōn erant servī.

Britannī cum Rōmānīs pūgnābant (*fought*). Prō patriā vītam dedērunt (*gave*). Sed Rōmānī Britannōs superābant (*conquered*) quod Britannī multa tēla (*weapons*) nōn habēbant. Post (*After*) victōriam Rōmānōrum Britannia erat prōvincia Rōmāna, et multī incolae īnsulae pulchrae erant servī. Rōmānī erant dominī. Sed pulchra rēgīna Boadicea semper erat lībera. Numquam (*Never*) erat serva Rōmānōrum.

Chaos often breeds life when order breeds habit.
—Henry Brooks Adams, 1838–1918

# *Unit* IX

## CONVERSATION

MAGISTER: Salvē, Paula. Ubi sunt puerī puellaeque?

PAULA: In viīs vīcī erant, sed ad scholam nunc properant.

PUELLAE: Salvē, magister. Nunc adsumus, sed puerī absunt.

PUERĪ: Salvē, magister. Sumus tardī (*late*). Servōs spectābāmus.

MAGISTER: Salvēte, puerī. Cūjus servōs spectābātis?

JŪLIUS: Servī dominī Rōmānī multum frūmentum ē prōvinciīs in oppida Ītaliae portābant.

CORNĒLIUS: Multī servī miserī viās parābant et aedificābant.

PAULA: Unde servī sunt? Erantne semper servī?

MAGISTER: Ōlim cūnctī (*all*) Rōmānī erant agricolae. Servōs nōn habēbant.

PAULA: Quandō Rōmānī antīquī servōs superābant?

CORNĒLIUS: Nōnne incolae Rōmae antīquae erant bellicōsī (*warlike*)?

MAGISTER: Bellicōsī erant quod fīnitimōs bellicōsōs habēbant.

PAULUS: Num Rōmānī fīnitimōs semper superābant?

MAGISTER:   Rōmānīs Fortūna multās victōriās dabat.   Post bella multōs servōs habēbant.   Posteā servī bonam terram Ītaliae
arābant.   Multī agricolae ad oppida migrābant quod agrōs
nōn habēbant.

# SECTION 1 Second Declension Neuter Nouns and Adjectives

▶ DISCUSSION

Nouns and adjectives of the second declension that terminate in
–*um* in the nominative case are *neuter*.   The *case indicators* of the
neuter noun and the neuter adjective are always identical in the second
declension.

|  | **oppidum, oppidī** | **māgnum, māgnī** |  |
|---|---|---|---|
|  | *n.* town | *adj.* large |  |
| BASE: | **oppid/** | **māgn/** |  |

|  |  | SINGULAR | C.I. |
|---|---|---|---|
| Nom. | māgn**um** oppid**um** | *a large town* | **–um** |
| Gen. | māgnī oppidī | *of a large town, a large town's* | **–ī** |
| Dat. | māgnō oppidō | *to, for a large town* | **–ō** |
| Acc. | māgn**um** oppid**um** | *a large town* | **–um** |
| Abl. | māgnō oppidō | *from, by, with a large town* | **–ō** |

|  |  | PLURAL |  |
|---|---|---|---|
| Nom. | māgn**a** oppid**a** | *large towns* | **–a** |
| Gen. | māgn**ōrum** oppid**ōrum** | *of large towns, large towns'* | **–ōrum** |
| Dat. | māgnīs oppidīs | *to, for large towns* | **–īs** |
| Acc. | māgn**a** oppid**a** | *large towns* | **–a** |
| Abl. | māgnīs oppidīs | *from, by, with large towns* | **–īs** |

▶ STUDY HELPS

1. The case indicators of neuter nouns and adjectives differ from those
of the masculine gender of this declension only in the nominative singular, nominative plural, and accusative plural.

2. The dative and ablative plural for all nouns and adjectives of the
first and second declensions have the case indicator –*īs*.   *Dea* and *fīlia*
(*deābus* and *fīliābus*) are the only exceptions.

3. Neuter nouns and adjectives are always identical in the nominative
and the accusative cases, singular and plural.   This case indicator is
always short –*a*.

A. Write in Latin the neuter form, singular and plural nominative, for the adjectives:

alba  cāra  māgna  nostra  antīqua  lāta  bona  parva  misera  pulchra

B. Decline in Latin and give English meanings: small kingdom.

C. Write in Latin the specified forms:

1. accusative plural:   ancient war, good word, small village, little girl
2. genitive singular:   unhappy kingdom, beautiful sky, wide fields
3. dative plural:   many dangers, free towns, ancient town, dear friend
4. dative singular:   small grain, wide sky, our town, your village
5. ablative plural:   our words, many wars, unhappy slave

# SECTION 2 Questions and Answers

▶ DISCUSSION

There are two kinds of questions: (1) those introduced by an interrogative pronoun, adjective, or adverb; (2) those that seek the answer *yes* or *no* to the whole question.

The use of interrogative words is the same in both English and Latin. In the Conversations, you have used forms of the interrogative pronoun **quis, quid** and the interrogative adverbs **ubi** and **cūr.**

In English, *yes* and *no* questions are usually distinguished from *statements* by the *order of words.* In Latin, questions are never indicated by word order alone but by special question signs: **–ne, nōnne, num.**

1. The syllable **–ne,** called an enclitic, is attached to the first word of the sentence, usually the verb or the emphatic word. A question introduced by **–ne** merely seeks information and may be answered by *yes* or *no.*

**Timēbatne dominum?**   *Did he fear the master?*

**Multōsne servōs habēbat?**   *Did he have many slaves?*

2. In a question expecting only the answer *yes,* **nōnne (nōn + ne)** is placed first in the sentence.

**Nōnne dominum timēbat?**   *Did he not fear the master?*
   *He feared the master, didn't he?*

3. In a question expecting the answer *no,* **num** is placed first in the sentence.

**Num dominum timēbat?**   *He did not fear the master, did he?*

Sometimes in English the meaning of this kind of question is expressed by the tone of voice.

*Answers* to Latin questions are not usually made by single words meaning *yes* or *no*. If the answer is *yes*, the verb or some other emphatic word is repeated; if the answer is *no*, the verb with **nōn** or a similar negative is repeated. The Romans sometimes used words like *ita* or *sīc, so,* **certē,** *certainly,* **minimē,** *not at all.*

| | | | |
|---|---|---|---|
| **Timēbatne dominum?** | *Yes.* | **Timēbat.** | **(Certē.)** |
| **Num timēbat dominum?** | *No.* | **Nōn timēbat.** | **(Minimē.)** |

▶ STUDY HELPS

These interrogative words will be used in the Sentence Patterns, Conversations, and stories. Memorize them.

| | | | |
|---|---|---|---|
| **Ubi?** | = Where? When? | **Unde?** | = Where from? Whence? |
| **Quō?** | = Where to? | **Cūr?** | = Why? |
| **Quālis?** | = What kind of? | **Quandō?** | = When? |

**Ubi, unde, quō, cūr, quandō** are interrogative adverbs. **Quālis** is an interrogative adjective.

▶ PRACTICE PATTERNS

A. Translate into English:

1. Ubi est puer?
2. Quō puer properat?
3. Unde puer est?
4. Quid est verbum?
5. Quis est vir?

6. Quandō puer ad oppidum ambulābat?
7. Ambulābatne puer ad oppidum?
8. Nōnne puer ad oppidum ambulābat?
9. Num puer ad oppidum ambulābat?
10. Cūr puer ad oppidum ambulābat?

B. Answer in Latin the questions in A.

C. Translate into Latin:

1. Where are you?
2. Where is he from?
3. Where is he hurrying?
4. When did he walk to town?
5. Did he hasten to the villa?

6. He did not hurry, did he?
7. He hurried, didn't he?
8. What kind of man is he?
9. Is he sailing?
10. Whence did he sail?

**WORDS TO MASTER**

**aedi'ficō** (1), build (*edify*)
**bel'lum, -ī,** *n.,* war (*bellicose*)
**cae'lum, -ī,** *n.,* heavens, sky (*celestial*)
**fīnitimus,-a,-um,** *adj.,* neighboring; **fīnitimī, -ōrum,** *m. pl.,* neighbors
**frūmen'tum, -ī,** *n.,* grain (*frumentaceous*)
**op'pidum, -ī,** *n.,* town
**perī'culum, -ī,** *n.,* danger (*peril*)

**post,** *adv. and prep. with acc.,* after, behind (*posterity*)
**posteā,** *adv.,* afterward
**rēg'num, -ī,** *n.,* royal power, kingdom (*regnancy*)
**su'perō** (1), conquer, surpass, overcome (*superable*)
**ver'bum, -ī,** *n.,* word (*verbose*)
**vī'cus, -ī,** *m.,* village (*vicinity*)

## BUILDING WORD POWER

Some second declension neuter nouns that have come into our language unchanged are neuter forms of adjectives: *album, medium, maximum, minimum, sanctum, vacuum.* **Album,** besides meaning *white,* came to mean *a white tablet* on which the Pontifex Maximus of Rome published the events of the year.

The neuter noun **forum** originally meant *a market place* in a Roman town. In Rome there were many forums, such as the cattle market, the fish market, and the vegetable market. But to a Roman *the* Forum was the **Forum Rōmānum.** Rows of shops were erected, and temples were built. Games were held in the central open space.

From the stage in the Forum, orators addressed their fellow citizens. This platform was called the **Rōstra,** plural of **rōstrum,** which originally meant *beak* and was derived from **rōdere,** *to gnaw.* The prows of ships in those days resembled birds' beaks. When the Romans won a naval battle, they brought home the **rōstrum** of the ship to prove the victory and, you may be sure, to boast about it. The first of these **rōstra** were taken from the Antians in 337 B.C.

We use the word *rostrum* to designate a speaker's platform, but the Romans always called their platform **Rōstra.**

## SENTENCE PATTERNS

A. Complete and translate into English:

1. Nōnne oppida Ītaliae pulchr_____ sunt? Certē.
2. Num Rōma semper erat oppid_____ māgnum? Minimē.
3. Habitābantne agricolae prope vīc_____ fīnitim_____?
4. Rōmānīne perīcul_____ bellī timēbant?
5. Ubi servī miserī parv_____ oppida aedificāba_____?
6. Cūr agricolae bonī frūmentum ad vīcōs portāba_____?
7. Quandō Rōmānī fīnitim_____ superāba_____?
8. Quō agricolae Rōmān_____ post bella properābant?
9. Unde erant servī miser_____? Ē prōvinciīs era_____.
10. Poēta rēgnum pulchrum caelī multīs verbīs laudāba_____.

B. Translate into Latin:

1. Why were there many slaves after the wars?
2. The master liked the good grain, didn't he?
3. The Romans did not always conquer their neighbors, did they?
4. When did the boys and men build the large towns?
5. Did the queen give money to the slaves of her kingdom?

Prometheus bringing fire to earth
from Mt. Olympus.

## Origin of the Universe

At the beginning of time, according to the myths taken over by
the Romans, there was Chaos, a vast, seething disorder. Gradually, after a long time, Chaos ceased to be darkness and con-
fusion, and there came into being two deities of great majesty,
called Gaea, or Mother Earth, and Uranus, god of heaven.

The children of Gaea and Uranus were divided into two groups.
Twelve were very beautiful, of great size and strength. These
were the *Titans.* The others were monsters, such as the *Cyclopes,*
giants who had only one eye, and the *Hecatoncheires,* who had
a hundred hands.

Uranus hated all his children, particularly the monsters whom
he imprisoned in the Underworld, a place called Tartarus.
Mother Earth, enraged at the imprisonment of six of her children, called upon the Titans to help her against their unnatural
father. Cronus was the only Titan to respond to this plea.
He slew his father, and from the blood of Uranus sprang the
Giants and the Furies, who had writhing serpents for hair.

Cronus married Rhea and divided the empire among his
fellow Titans; but later, fearing his own children, Cronus tried
to destroy them. By an artifice of Rhea, Jupiter was saved,
and he in turn saved his two brothers, Pluto and Neptune, and·
his three sisters, Vesta, Ceres, and Juno.

Jupiter fought against his father, Cronus, in a war that lasted
for ages. The old gods were on the side of Cronus, but the
younger gods and the gods Jupiter had released from Tartarus
were all on his side. At last Jupiter triumphed. Most of the
Titans were confined to Tartarus. Atlas, the son of one of them,
was forced to bear the world on his shoulders forever. Only
Prometheus refused to take arms against Jupiter.

In the meantime several human races had come into being on
the face of the earth. As the Golden, Silver, Bronze, and Iron
Ages succeeded each other, conditions of living for human beings

became harder and harder. Prometheus, whose name meant *foresight,* recognized that each generation was weaker than the preceding one. He begged Jupiter to give humans the gift of fire so that they could warm themselves and make tools and weapons with which to till the soil and defend themselves against wild beasts.

Jupiter feared that if he gave this boon to mortals, they would think themselves the equals of the gods, and he refused. So Prometheus left Olympus, carrying with him a reed in which fire was concealed. Jupiter became very angry. For helping mortals with the gift of fire, Prometheus was bound to a crag on a high mountain. There each day an eagle came and consumed part of his body, which each night grew whole again. Never, however, would Prometheus yield to Jupiter or give up his devotion to humanity.

## The Good Earth

CLĀRA: Nōnne agrī propinquī Rōmae sunt pulchrī? Erantne incolae Rōmae antīquae agricolae?

MĀRCUS: Incolae Rōmae antīquae erant agricolae bonī, Clāra.

CLĀRA: Num Rōma semper erat oppidum māgnum lātumque?

MĀRCUS: Incolae Rōmae in casīs parvīs miserīsque habitābant, ubi Palātīnus nunc est. Agrī erant parvī sed terra erat bona. Agricolae Rōmānī terram bonam semper amābant.

CLĀRA: Erantne casae agricolārum propinquae agrīs?

MĀRCUS: Casae agricolārum erant in vīcīs. Ē vīcīs ad agrōs cotīdiē (*daily*) properābant, et terram bonam arābant. Sed semper erat bellum.

CLĀRA: Cūr semper erat bellum? Erantne Rōmānī bellicōsī?

MĀRCUS: Rōmānī erant bellicōsī. Perīcula bellī nōn timēbant.

CLĀRA: Superābantne Rōmānī semper fīnitimōs?

MĀRCUS: Fortūna populī (*people*) Rōmānī nōn erat semper bona, sed multae erant victōriae Rōmānōrum. In bellīs Gallōs et Germānōs et populōs barbarōs superābant, et post victōriās multōs captīvōs habēbant. Posteā captīvī Rōmae erant servī.

CLĀRA: Cūr agricolae post bella in oppidīs habitābant?

MĀRCUS: Post bella nautae Rōmānī ē prōvinciīs in Ītaliam frūmentum portābant. Patriciī (*The nobles*) māgnās terrās et multōs servōs habēbant. Servī villās pulchrās aedificābant. Dominī Rōmānī in māgnīs villīs, servī in parvīs casīs miserīs habitābant.

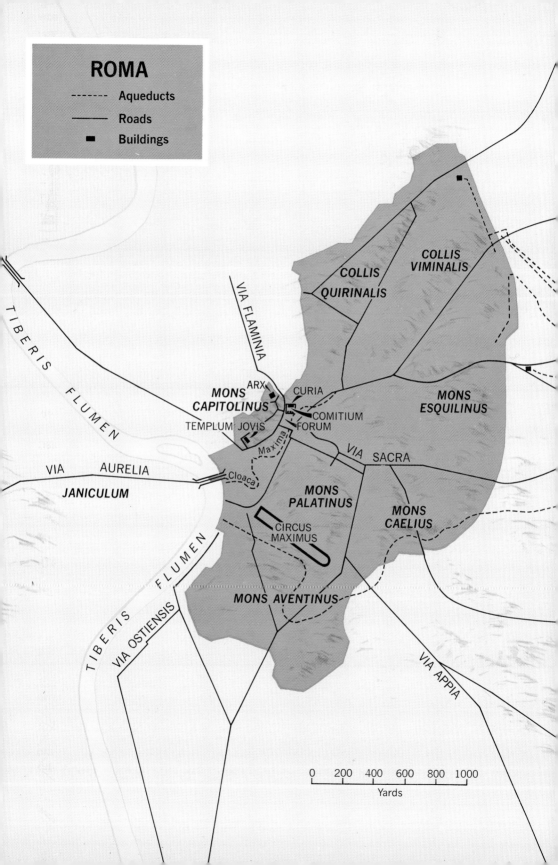

ROMA
- - - - Aqueducts
——— Roads
■ Buildings

COLLIS QUIRINALIS

COLLIS VIMINALIS

VIA FLAMINIA

TIBERIS FLUMEN

ARX
MONS CAPITOLINUS
CURIA
TEMPLUM JOVIS
COMITIUM
FORUM
Maxima
VIA AURELIA
JANICULUM
Cloaca
VIA SACRA

MONS ESQUILINUS

MONS PALATINUS
CIRCUS MAXIMUS

MONS CAELIUS

TIBERIS FLUMEN
VIA OSTIENSIS

MONS AVENTINUS

VIA APPIA

0   200   400   600   800   1000
Yards

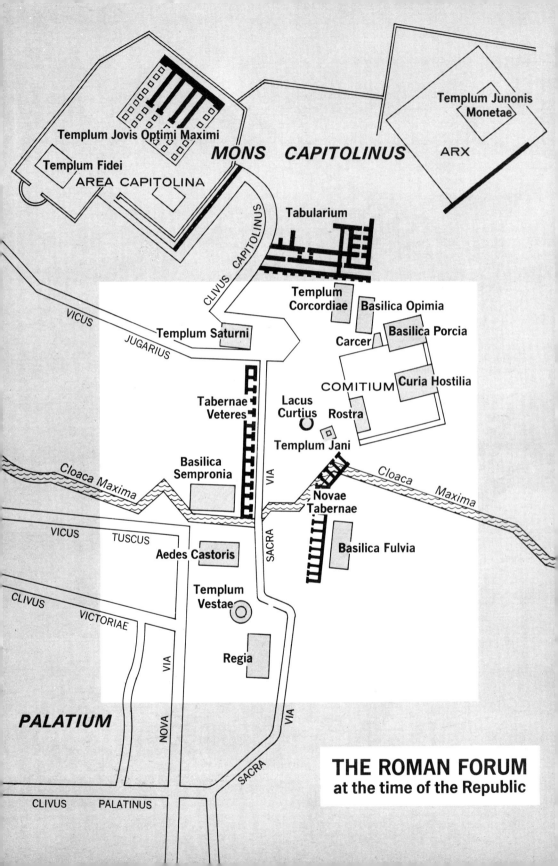

THE ROMAN FORUM
at the time of the Republic

# The Column

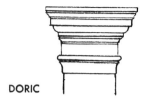

**DORIC**

**IONIC**

**CORINTHIAN**

Columns, the most beautiful of all architectural supports, were adapted by the Romans from the three principal Greek styles, or orders. The Doric is the oldest, the most substantial, and the heaviest. It has no base and a very simple capital, or top. Next in weight is the Ionic, which is furnished with a base and which has a capital decorated with volutes—spiral, scroll-shaped ornaments. The Corinthian is the lightest; it has a base and a deep capital ornamented with acanthus leaves and volutes.

# The Arch

An arch is formed by a series of wedgelike stones supporting one another and all bound firmly together by the pressure of the center stone, or keystone. The Greeks and Egyptians of an earlier period knew and used the arch, but it was the Romans who brought this architectural principle to its perfection in their buildings, monuments, and aqueducts. Pictured at the left is the triumphal arch at Rimini, Italy, as it appears today.

# The Dome

The dome, the most important Roman architectural principle, is best illustrated by the Pantheon, which was designed and constructed by the Emperor Hadrian (*circa* A.D. 118–126). Originally, the Pantheon was a planetarium and temple; it is now a church. The building consists of a cylinder on which rests a dome constructed of horizontal layers of brick laid in thick cement, strengthened by a series of arches coming together and meeting in the crown. The dome is low and rather inconspicuous from the exterior; from the interior, however, it gives a vast and awesome impression of space.

HIBERNIA

BRITANNIA

OCEANUS

ATLANTICUS

GERMANIA

Sequana

Rhenus

GALLIA

HISPANIA

Tagus

CORSICA

Tiberis

MARE ADRIATIC

Roma

ITALI

SARDINIA

MARE
TYRRHENUM

M
A
R
E

SICILIA

MAURETANIA

NUMIDIA

A
F
R
I
C
A

| 0 | 125 | 250 | | 500 |

Miles

# The ROMAN REPUBLIC: 44 B.C.

ROMAN DOMINION
ROMAN ALLIES
PARTHIAN EMPIRE

SARMATIA

DACIA

*Danuvius*

ICUM

*PONTUS EUXINUS*

THRACIA

ARMENIA

BITHYNIA

PONTUS

MACEDONIA

GALATIA

CAPPADOCIA

ASIA

LYCAONIA

*MARE
AEGAEUM*

PAMPHYLIA

CILICIA

GRAECIA

LYCIA

SYRIA

CYPRUS

CRETA

*I N T E R N U M*

CYRENAICA

ARABIA

AEGYPTUS

# The Roman House

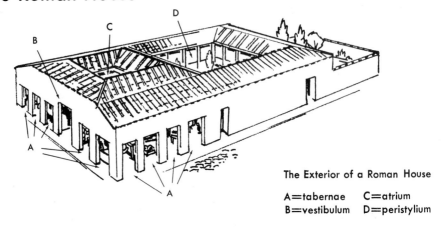

**The Exterior of a Roman House**

A=tabernae    C=atrium
B=vestibulum    D=peristylium

The earliest dwellings of the Latin people were probably mere huts of willow branches daubed with mud hardened by the sun. There was one hut for one family. The hut consisted of one room, which was oval or rectangular, with a door at one side and a hearth facing the door.

In later years, as the population of Rome increased, the huts or houses were built closer together and were made higher. Romans in the lower- and middle-income brackets constructed buildings of several stories. The buildings were not joined by common walls with neighboring houses, but rather, each building was encompassed by streets. The ground floor was usually rented to *tabernae*, or shops; the upper stories were let out in apartments or separate rooms to different families or persons.

Romans in the upper-income bracket, especially in the last century of the Republic (133-27 B.C.), began to build private houses, or *domus*. These buildings had many rooms, most of which were on the ground floor; the reception room and the patio, because they were designed to be open to the sky, did not permit an upper story. It soon became the fashion, especially among these wealthy Romans,

**Floor Plan of a Roman House**

not only to build their *domus* of an immense size but also to adorn them with marble columns, paintings, statues, and costly works of art.

According to Vitruvius, a Roman writer on architecture, the principal parts of a Roman *domus* were: 1 *vestibulum*, 2 *ostium*, 3 *atrium*, 4 *alae*, 5 *tablinum*, 6 *fauces*, and 7 *peristylium*.

The *vestibulum* was, generally speaking, a vacant space before the house, forming a courtyard or entrance court, surrounded on three sides by the house and open on the fourth side to the street.

The *ostium* was the entrance to the house. The word is synonymous with *janua* and *fores*, "the door." A curtain hanging from the lintel or a door on pivots separated the interior of the house from the *vestibulum*.

The *atrium* was a large room or court which had a small opening in the ceiling called the *compluvium*. Toward this hole the roof sloped so as to throw the rainwater into a cistern in the floor called the *impluvium*. The water from the *impluvium* then flowed into an underground well. It must be remembered that,

A Roman Peristyle

before the construction of the aqueducts, the Romans were dependent upon wells for their supply of water.

The *alae* or wings were two small quadrangular apartments or recesses on the left and right sides of the *atrium*. Here the *imagines*, or portrait-masks of deceased members of the family, were kept in the houses of the nobles.

The *tablinum* was, in all probability, a recess or room at the farther end of the *atrium*. It contained the family records and archives.

The *fauces* was a passage by the side of the tablinum, which passed from the *atrium* to the *peristylium* or open court.

The *peristylium* was an open court which was surrounded by columns. It contained a fountain in the center, and flowers, shrubs, and trees formed an attractive, sometimes a symmetrical, garden around it.

The rooms leading out of the *peristylium* were: bedchambers, dining rooms, spacious halls, a picture gallery, a library, a bath, and a kitchen.

**ITALIA**

-- -- -- Roman roads

*ALPES*

VENETIA
Aquileia

Mediolanum
(Milan)
Verona • Patavium
GALLIA • Mantua
CISALPINA
LIGURIA *APPENINUS MONS*
Genua

Ariminum

Luca
Pisae • Faesulae
Arretum UMBRIA • Ancona
*L. Trasimenus* PICENUM
ETRURIA *MARE ADRIATICUM*

Falerii SABINI
SAMNIUM
Roma • Praeneste
Ostia • Alba Longa APULIA
Ardea • Cannae
LATIUM
Capua Beneventum • Venusia
Herculaneum ▲ *M. Vesuvius* Brundisiu
Pompeii CAMPANIA • Tarentum
LUCANIA
*MARE TYRRHENUM* • Heraclea

CORSICA

SARDINIA

CALABRIA

BRUTIUM

Mylae
Messana • Rhegium
Lilybaeum
SICILIA ▲ *M. Aetna*
Agrigentum
Carthago • Syracusae

0    50    100
Miles

*MARE    AFRICUM*

CLĀRA: Post bella agricolae Rōmānī terram bonam nōn habēbant, et nōn erant laetī. Servī terram bonam arāre nōn amābant et nōn erant laetī. Patriciī multam terram bonam habēbant et erant laetī. Num fortūna populī Rōmānī post multa bella erat bona?

When tillage begins, other arts follow. The farmers are therefore the founders of human civilization.
—Daniel Webster, 1782–1852

# Unit X

## CONVERSATION

TULLIUS: Salvē, mī fīlī. Laetus sum, Lūcī, quod tū ades.
LŪCIUS: Salvē, tū quoque. Laetus nōn sum quod ad scholam ego nunc properāre dēbeō.
TULLIUS: Quis fīlium meum historiam Rōmānam docet?
LŪCIUS: Dominus Cornēlius puerōs historiam docet. Multa dē agricolīs et poētīs Rōmānīs narrat.
TULLIUS: Quī (*Who?* pl.) erant Horātius et Vergilius, Lūcī?
LŪCIUS: Clārī poētae Rōmānī erant, et multās fābulās dē glōriā imperiōque Rōmae narrābant. Horātius et Vergilius erant amīcī.
TULLIUS: Num Horātius fābulās dē bellō Trōjānō narrābat?
LŪCIUS: Minimē. Fābulās dē villā Sabīnā narrābat.
TULLIUS: Nōnne Vergilius agrōs et agricolās amābat?
LŪCIUS: Cūnctam (*all*) Nātūram amābat, sed fābulās dē Graeciā et Trōjānīs narrābat. Graecī inimīcī cum Trōjānīs pūgnābant.
TULLIUS: Bene respondēs, mī puer. Nunc negōtia mea cūrāre dēsīderō.
LŪCIUS: Et ego ad scholam properāre dēbeō. Valē.

## SECTION 1 Second Declension Nouns and Adjectives Ending in *–ius* and *–ium*

▶ DISCUSSION

Nouns and adjectives of the second declension ending in *–ius* and *–ium* have a base that terminates in *–i,* to which the regular case

**51**

indicators are added. In this book the genitive singular of nouns is written –ī; that of adjectives is always written –ī͞i.

nūntī industriī   of the industrious messenger

The vocative case for nouns in Latin is the same as the nominative, except for some masculine nouns of the second declension. Nouns and adjectives whose nominative ends in –*us* have the vocative singular in –*e*:

Mārce!  Mark!  Amīce fīde!  O faithful friend!

The noun *fīlius* and proper names in –*ius* form the vocative singular in –*ī.* The vocative of adjectives in –*ius* is –*ie.*

Cornēlī industrie!  O industrious Cornelius!

The vocative singular of **meus,** *my,* is **mī**; the vocative plural of **meus** is **meī.**

Fīlī mī!  O my son!

|  | **fīlius, fīlī**<br>*m.* son | **negōtium, negōtī**<br>*n.* business | **industrius, –a, –um**<br>*adj.* industrious | | |
|---|---|---|---|---|---|
| BASE: | **fīlī/** | **negōtī/** | **industrī/** | | |
| | | SINGULAR | | | |
| Nom. | fīlius | negōtium | industrius | –a | –um |
| Gen. | fīlī | negōtī | industriī | –ae | –ī |
| Dat. | fīliō | negōtiō | industriō | –ae | –ō |
| Acc. | fīlium | negōtium | industrium | –am | –um |
| Abl. | fīliō | negōtiō | industriō | –ā | –ō |
| | | PLURAL | | | |
| Nom. | fīliī | negōtia | industriī | –ae | –a |
| Gen. | fīliōrum | negōtiōrum | industriōrum | –ārum | –ōrum |
| Dat. | fīliīs | negōtiīs | industriīs | –īs | –īs |
| Acc. | fīliōs | negōtia | industriōs | –ās | –a |
| Abl. | fīliīs | negōtiīs | industriīs | –īs | –īs |

▶ STUDY HELPS

The base of nouns in –*ius* and –*ium* is identical with the genitive singular in form. The adjectives, however, are regular in formation.

▶ PRACTICE PATTERNS

A. Decline in Latin and translate each case:

    servus industrius    imperium bonum    socius fidus    amicus clārus

B. Write in Latin:

| for your sons | with famous comrades | of industrious slaves |
|---|---|---|
| with great power | of faithful friends | to (*ad*) a small town |
| by my sons | in unfriendly towns | from a hostile messenger |

▶ DISCUSSION

It is well to review here a typical first and second declension adjective.

**fīdus,** *m.,* **fīda,** *f.,* **fīdum,** *n.,* faithful   BASE: **fīd/**

|  | M. | F. | N. | M. | F. | N. |
|------|--------|--------|--------|------|------|------|
|  | | SINGULAR | | | INDICATORS | |
| Nom. | fīd**us** | fīd**a** | fīd**um** | –us | –a | –um |
| Gen. | fīd**ī** | fīd**ae** | fīd**ī** | –ī | –ae | –ī |
| Dat. | fīd**ō** | fīd**ae** | fīd**ō** | –ō | –ae | –ō |
| Acc. | fīd**um** | fīd**am** | fīd**um** | –um | –am | –um |
| Abl. | fīd**ō** | fīd**ā** | fīd**ō** | –ō | –ā | –ō |
|  | | PLURAL | | | | |
| Nom. | fīd**ī** | fīd**ae** | fīd**a** | –ī | –ae | –a |
| Gen. | fīd**ōrum** | fīd**ārum** | fīd**ōrum** | –ōrum | –ārum | –ōrum |
| Dat. | fīd**īs** | fīd**īs** | fīd**īs** | –īs | –īs | –īs |
| Acc. | fīd**ōs** | fīd**ās** | fīd**a** | –ōs | –ās | –a |
| Abl. | fīd**īs** | fīd**īs** | fīd**īs** | –īs | –īs | –īs |

▶ STUDY HELPS

1. The base of most adjectives is found by dropping the case indicator from the nominative singular of the feminine form:

**fīd/a   līber/a   pulchr/a**

2. An adjective is sometimes used without a noun in Latin as a substitute for a noun. It may be masculine, feminine, or neuter according to the gender of the noun:

**bonī** = *good men*   **bonae** = *good women*   **bona** = *good things, goods, property*

▶ PRACTICE PATTERNS

A. Write the masculine, feminine, and neuter nominative plural of:

clārus   amīcus   antīquus   pulcher   māgnus   līber

B. Write the masculine, feminine, and neuter genitive singular of:

miser   bonus   cārus   lātus   albus   parvus

C. Write in Latin these specified forms:

1. a good business (ablative singular)
2. famous neighbor (genitive plural)
3. small son (nominative plural)
4. unhappy messenger (dative singular)
5. old enemy (accusative plural)
6. small town (dative plural)
7. large man (genitive singular)
8. great danger (ablative plural)

**53**

## WORDS TO MASTER

amī′cus, –a, –um, *adj.*, friendly;
  amī′cus, –ī, *m.*, friend (*amicable*)
clā′rus, –a, –um, *adj.*, clear, famous
  (*clarity*)
dē′beō (2), owe, ought (*debit*)
dēsī′derō (1), long for, desire greatly,
  want, wish for (*desire*)
fī′lius, –ī, *m.*, son (*filial*)
impe′rium, –ī, *n.*, command, power,
  empire, control (*imperious*)

inimī′cus, –a, –um, *adj.*, unfriendly,
  hostile; inimī′cus, –ī, *m.*, personal
  enemy (*inimical*)
ma′neō (2), remain, stay (*mansion*)
negō′tium, –ī, *n.*, business, difficulty
  (*negotiate*)
nūn′tius, –ī, *m.*, messenger, message
  (*annunciation*)
pūg′nō (1), fight (*pugnacious*)
so′cius, –ī, *m.*, ally, comrade (*social*)

### BUILDING WORD POWER

What English words remain if you drop –*um* from the following
Latin words? *Monumentum, ōrnāmentum, sacrāmentum, impedīmentum, complēmentum.* Write the Latin words for: *argument, document, testament.* Notice that the following words end in
–*mōnium: mātrimōnium, testimōnium, patrimōnium, sānctimōnium.* What are their derivatives in English?

Write the English derivatives for these Latin words that end in –*ium: spatium, solātium, aedificium, commercium, collēgium, vestīgium, praemium.*

The suffix –*ōrium* or –*ārium* indicates a neuter noun of place. What
are the English words derived from the following: *sōlārium, audītōrium, grānārium, dormītōrium, factōrium, librārium, observatōrium, aquārium. Apis* means *bee; avis,* bird; *formica,* ant; *columba,* dove. Define: *apiārium, aviārium, formīcārium, columbārium.*

### SENTENCE PATTERNS

A. Translate into English:

1. Dabatne dominus servīs industriīs pecūniam?
2. Nōnne multī Rōmānī clārī erant agricolae?
3. Amīcōs et inimīcōs amāre dēbēmus.
4. Cūr Rōmānī cum fīnitimīs inimīcīs pūgnābant?
5. Num fīnitimōs semper superābant? Minimē.
6. Catō, agricola clārus, multa dē agricultūrā docēbat.
7. Nūntiī ex Ītaliā ad prōvinciās saepe properābant.
8. Cincinnātus cum fīliīs in agrīs semper labōrābat.
9. Vir clārus pecūniam, māgnās terrās, imperium, negōtium nōn dēsīderābat.
10. Sociī imperium Rōmānōrum nōn semper amābant.

54

B. Translate into Latin:

1. The Romans did not always overcome (their) neighbors, did they?
2. The farmers had friendly allies, didn't they?
3. Why did the farmers remain in the towns after the wars?
4. The power of the allies was not great, was it?
5. Did the inhabitants of the village fear (their) hostile neighbors?

### Famous Roman Farmers

Cincinnātus, agricola clārus, Rōmae (458 B.C.) habitābat. Rōmānī cum Aequīs, fīnitimīs inimīcīs, pūgnābant. Aequī fīrmī (*strong*) Rōmānōs superābant. Rōmānī Aequōs timēbant. Nūntiī ad casam Cincinnātī properābant. Cincinnātum esse (*to be*) dictātōrem dēsīderābant. Ibi vir clārus cum fīliīs et servīs industriīs in agrīs arābat. Esse dictātor nōn dēsīderābat, sed Rōmam amābat. Cum nūntiīs ad oppidum properābat.

Cincinnātus cum multīs Rōmānīs, māgnīs et parvīs, in Aequōs pūgnābat. Rōmānī Aequōs terrēbant et superābant. Post bellum, Cincinnātus Rōmae manēre nōn dēsīderābat. Pecūniam et imperium nōn dēsīderābat. Terram bonam amābat, et ad parvum agrum properābat.

Mārcus Porcius Catō quoque agricola Rōmānus erat. Multīs bellīs vir clārus prō patriā Rōmā pūgnābat. Posteā māgnās terrās et multōs servōs habēbat. Rōmānōs multa dē agrīcultūrā docēbat.

Horātius, poēta Rōmānus, parvum agrum Sabīnum amābat. Vergilius, poēta Rōmānus quoque, terram bonam laudābat. Multa bona dē apibus (*about bees*) Rōmānōs docēbat. Varrō et Plinius librōs (*books*) dē agrīs et agricolīs parābant.

Multī Rōmānī villās rusticās et urbānās habēbant. Agricolae nōn erant, sed villās amābant et saepe vīsitābant. Hodiē in Ītaliā et in antīquīs prōvinciīs Rōmānīs ruīnās villārum māgnārum et pulchrārum spectāmus et laudāmus.

# *Comprehensive Review: Units* VI–X

A. Write in Latin the nominative singular and the base of each noun:

| man | word | field | master | trumpet | enemy | message | power |
|-----|------|-------|--------|---------|-------|---------|-------|
| boy | town | slave | friend | command | nature | kingdom | lord |
| son | ally | grain | danger | village | comrade | children | sky |
| war | fame | water | teacher | messenger | business | neighbors | glory |

B. Write in Latin the masculine, feminine, and neuter nominative singular forms of:

| | | | | | | |
|---|---|---|---|---|---|---|
| our | wide | large | much | joyful | ancient | neighboring |
| good | free | small | clear | unhappy | faithful | industrious |
| near | dear | white | your (sing.) | hostile | wretched | beautiful |

C. Write in Latin:

| | | | |
|---|---|---|---|
| why? | after | today | because |
| for | where | always | formerly |
| now | there | through | afterward |

D. Translate these verbs into correct English form:

SIMPLE: manētis, dēsīderō, dēbent, aderam, erant, aberās, properās
PROGRESSIVE: timēbat, docēs, habēbant, monēbāmus, respondet, vidēbam
EMPHATIC: labōrō, aedificābat, terrēbātis, pūgnat, parat, arābam

E. Write in Latin:

| | | |
|---|---|---|
| we were | he ought | you (sing.) were present |
| she remained | they prepared | he was frightening |
| he prepares | I labored | you (pl.) fought |
| he warned | I was absent | you (sing.) overcame |
| they plowed | they were plowing | they were building |

F. Conjugate the imperfect tense of: superō, adsum. Translate.

G. Write in Latin the specified forms:

1. genitive singular: amīcus, nūntius, vir, nātūra, puer, perīculum
2. nominative plural: fīlius, vīcus, verbum, fāma, negōtium, frūmentum
3. ablative singular: inimīcus, socius, caelum, rēgnum, dominus, oppidum
4. accusative plural: magister, servus, bellum, fīnitimī, tuba, imperium

H. Decline in the singular: ager lātus; in the plural: puer industrius. Give the name and use of each case; mark long vowels in case indicators.

I. Answer these questions:

1. What is the tense indicator of the imperfect tense?
2. What are the case indicators for first and second declension nouns and adjectives?
3. Write two masculine nouns of the second declension that do not have -us as the case indicator in the nominative singular.
4. Write the vocative singular of: dominus, fīlius, Jūlius, Jūlia.
5. How is *means* expressed in Latin?

J. Change this sentence into three interrogative sentences, the first expecting the answer *yes;* the second, *no;* the third, *yes* or *no.* Translate each sentence into English.

Servī terram arābant.

A. Translate into English:

1. Vocābatne agricola tubā servōs?
2. Nōnne dominus servās servōsque multōs habēbat?
3. Servī miserī frūmentum ē prōvinciīs in Ītaliam portābant.
4. Num amīcī tuī aderant?  Cūr aberant?
5. Ubi agricola labōrābat?  Ibi labōrābat agricola.
6. Unde nautae erant?  Quō properābant?
7. Quandō virī casam aedificābant?
8. Num fīliī agricolārum industriōrum in agrīs manēbant?
9. Nūntiī per viās saepe properant.
10. Erantne servī bonōrum dominōrum industriī?

B. Translate into Latin:

1. Did you (pl.) give grain to the unfortunate slaves?
2. Did not the famous poets tell stories about the fatherland?
3. They did not always overcome the hostile neighbors, did they?
4. In the streets of Rome were there many dangers?
5. They did not take care of the wretched slaves, did they?

## SIGHT TRANSLATION: ROMAN POETS

In Ītaliā habitābant multī bonīque poētae.  Horātius, clārus poēta, villam Sabīnam saepe laudābat.  Vergilius, poēta Rōmānus, quoque clārus, fābulās dē nātūrā narrābat.  Et agrōs et silvās et īnsulās amābat. Ītalia erat patria poētārum et agricolārum clārōrum.  Poētās, oppida, viās semper laudāmus, sed agricolīs et villīs et vīcīs Ītaliae quoque glōriam dare dēbēmus.

## CONVERSATION

MAGISTER: Salvēte, puerī. Nōlīte stāre! Cōnsīdite, sī placet.
SEXTUS: Ō magister, discipulīs fābulam narrā, sī placet!
MAGISTER: Fābulam narrāre dēbeō quod puerī bonī estis.
CŪNCTĪ: Numquam, magister, malī sumus. Sumusne?
MAGISTER: Cūnctī discipulī meī bonī sunt. Fābulam dē Mārcellō narrābō.
SEXTUS: Quis erat Mārcellus? Unde erat? Ubi habitābat?
QUĪNTUS: Ōlim habitābat Rōmae parvus puer.
SEXTUS: Sed, Quīnte, cūnctī puerī magistrum fābulam narrāre dēsīderant.
MAGISTER: Tacē (*Be quiet*), Quīnte! Mārcellus per viās Rōmae ambulābat. Fēmina bona puerum pulchrum vidēbat. Subitō Mārcellum vocābat et rogābat: "Quō properās, mī puer cāre? Līberōs nōn habeō et parvōs puerōs amō! Vīsitābisne villam meam?"
QUĪNTUS: Sed Mārcellus negōtium prīvātum habēbat. Num villam fēminae bonae vīsitābat, magister?
MAGISTER: Crās, puerī, fābulam narrābō. Quīntus aberit. Valēte!

## SECTION 1 Future Tense

▶ DISCUSSION

In English the auxiliary verbs *shall* and *will* are the signs of the *future tense*. In Latin, instead of a separate word, a future tense indicator, *–bi–*, placed between the present stem of the verb and the person indicator, expresses futurity in verbs of the first and second conjugations.

FUTURE INDICATIVE ACTIVE, FIRST CONJUGATION

*Formula: Present Stem + Tense Indicator + Person Indicator = Form*

| Person | Pres. Stem + | T.I. + | P.I. = | Form | Translation |
|---|---|---|---|---|---|
| | | SINGULAR | | | |
| First | vocā + | bĭ + | ō = | vocābō | *I shall call* |
| Second | vocā + | bi + | s | vocābis | *you will call* |
| Third | vocā + | bi + | t | vocābit | *he, she, it will call* |

| First | vocā | + | bi | + mus | = | vocābimus | *we shall call* |
| Second | vocā | + | bi | + tis | = | vocābitis | *you will call* |
| Third | vocā | + | bi̯(u) + nt | | = | vocābunt | *they will call* |

The future of the second conjugation is formed like that of the first conjugation.

**monēbō, monēbis, monēbit, monēbimus, monēbitis, monēbunt**

▶ STUDY HELPS

1. The *–i* always drops out before *–ō* and changes to *–u* before *–nt* in the future tense of the first and second conjugations.

FUTURE INDICATIVE OF SUM

| | SINGULAR | | | PLURAL | |
| First | erō | *I shall be* | | erimus | *we shall be* |
| Second | eris | *you will be* | | eritis | *you will be* |
| Third | erit | *he, she, it will be* | | erunt | *they will be* |

▶ PRACTICE PATTERNS

A. Conjugate stō and habeō in the future active, and translate.

B. Write in Latin:

| I shall remain | he will be present | you (sing.) will be |
| we shall prepare | you (pl.) will be absent | I shall shout |
| he will plow | they will shout | he will answer |
| they will ask | you (sing.) will answer | she will praise |
| he will sail | you (pl.) will remain | we shall teach |
| you (pl.) will be | I shall not answer | they will not work |

# SECTION 2 Imperative Mood

▶ DISCUSSION

1. Commands are expressed in English and Latin by the *imperative mood*. The form of the Latin verb used in giving a command to one person is the same as that of the present stem, formed by dropping the *–re* of the present active infinitive:

vocā/re: vocā = imperative singular = *call*

monē/re: monē = *warn*

In English the forms for the singular and plural imperative are the same; in Latin *–te* is added to the present stem if the subject understood is plural.

| *Mary, hurry!* | **Properā, Marīa!** |
| *Boys, hurry!* | **Properāte, puerī!** |

2. To give a *negative command* in Latin is very simple. Use *nōlī* with the present infinitive if the subject is singular; *nōlīte*, if plural. Both forms mean *be unwilling* or *don't.*

| | |
|---|---|
| *Don't fear, Mary!* | **Nōlī timēre, Marīa!** |
| *Don't fear, boys!* | **Nōlīte timēre, puerī!** |

▶ STUDY HELPS

1. The tense of the imperative most used is the present; it is always second person, singular or plural.

2. The imperative of the verb *sum* is *es,* singular, and *este,* plural.

| | |
|---|---|
| *Be good, Mary!* | **Es bona, Marīa!** |
| *Be good, boys!* | **Este bonī, puerī!** |

▶ PRACTICE PATTERNS

A. Form the present active imperative, singular and plural. Translate:

stō   clāmō   moveō   respondeō   adsum   dō   laudō   videō   aedificō

B. Write in Latin the present active imperative, singular and plural:

look   prepare   labor   plow   sail   teach   take care of   remain

## SECTION 3 Complementary Infinitive

▶ DISCUSSION

The present infinitive is frequently used in Latin as in English to *complete* the meaning of other verbs. In Latin this is called the *complementary infinitive.* It frequently precedes the main verb. If *nōn* is used, it stands before the main verb.

**Patriam *amāre* dēbēmus.**   We ought *to love* our native land.
**Puerī *clāmāre* nōn dēbent.**   Boys ought not *to shout.*

The *complementary infinitive* may have an *object,* direct or indirect.

**Miserīs auxilium dare dēbēmus.**   We ought to give *help to unfortunate people.*

The predicate adjective after a complementary infinitive agrees with the subject of the main verb.

**Puerī *industriī* esse dēbent.**   Boys ought to be *industrious.*

▶ PRACTICE PATTERNS

A. Translate:

1. Nōlī clāmāre, Jūlī.
2. Nōn dēbēmus esse malī.
3. Virī validī esse amāmus.
4. Virī nāvigāre parābant.
5. Nōlīte manēre in oppidō, virī.
6. Cūnctī virī esse līberī dēbent.
7. Puerī amīcī esse dēsīderābant.
8. Spectāte cōpiās, agricolae.

**60**

## B. Write in Latin:

1. The troops ought to fight again.
2. They will hurry to watch the crowd.
3. We ought to give food to the men.
4. Tomorrow prepare to sail again.
5. Stand, boys and girls.
6. Never be bad, boys.
7. Don't fear the crowd, Clara.
8. Don't shout, troops.

## WORDS TO MASTER

ci′bus, –ī, *m.*, food
clā′mō (1), shout (*clamor*)
cō′pia, –ae, *f.*, supply (*copious*); cō′-
 piae, –ārum, *pl.*, troops, forces
crās, *adv.*, tomorrow (*procrastinate*)
cūnc′tus, –a, –um, *adj.*, all, the whole
i′terum, *adv.*, again (*reiterate*)

ma′lus, –a, –um, *adj.*, bad, evil
 (*malice*)
num′quam, *adv.*, never
stō (1), *irreg.*, stand (*stable*)
su′bitō, *adv.*, suddenly
tur′ba, –ae, *f.*, crowd (*turbulent*)
va′lidus, –a, –um, *adj.*, strong (*valid*)

## BUILDING WORD POWER

The suffixes *–ulum, –bulum, –culum* and *–brum, –crum, –trum*
denote the means or place of an action. The spelling of many of them
is the same in both Latin and English, but others in English end in
*–cle, –ble, –cher.* What words are derived from: *mīrāculum; vehiculum, stābulum, ōrāculum, sepulcrum?*

Sometimes words that remained unchanged in spelling were quite
changed in meaning. Originally *curriculum* meant *running, race;
vinculum, band; spectrum, apparition, vision, specter; fulcrum,
bedpost.* What do these words mean in modern English? The renowned
Greek mathematician Archimedes exclaimed: "Give me a lever and a
fulcrum, and I will lift the world!"

Many English adjectives that end in *–ary* or *–ory* are derived from
Latin adjectives with the suffix *–ārius* or *–ōrius,* which mean *pertaining
to.* Give the English for: *temporārius, voluntārius, exclāmātōrius,
mercenārius, honōrārius, trānsitōrius, audītōrius.* Write the
Latin for: *ordinary, salutary, cursory.*

## SENTENCE PATTERNS

### A. Translate into English:

1. Cūnctī virī līberī esse dēsīderant.
2. Servī validī ad oppida cōpiam cibī crās portābunt.
3. Narrābitne magister puerīs fābulam dē puerō Rōmānō?
4. Māgnae cōpiae et virī clārī in viīs Rōmae ambulāre amābant.
5. Nōlīte manēre in agrīs. Crās properāte in oppidum.

6. Iterum iterumque puerī malī clāmābant: "Quid sub togā portās?"
7. Nōnne puerī validī parvum Mārcellum superābunt?
8. Erunt perīcula multa in viīs Rōmae, sed parvus puer perīcula numquam timēbit.
9. Subitō turba virōrum ad puerōs ambulābat.
10. Cūr, puer mī, properās? Ubi habitās? Nōlī tīmēre!

B. Translate into Latin:

1. Give to the unfortunate, and you will be happy, children!
2. Don't be afraid, little girl!
3. All men ought to be free, my son!
4. The good boy does not wish to fight, does he?
5. Will not the strong man carry the little boy to the cottage?

The hut of Romulus,
the mythical founder of Rome.

## The City of Rome

Rome, situated on the left bank of the Tiber, has often been called the City of Seven Hills. In reality, however, the so-called hills are, for the most part, gently rising elevations of land southeast of the Tiber, about sixteen miles from its mouth. The Palatine Hill is thought to have been settled about a thousand years before Christ. Here was the hut of Romulus, the mythical founder of Rome. The traditional date of the city's founding is 753 B.C.

Closely surrounding the Palatine were the Aventine, Caelian, Esquiline, Viminal, and Quirinal, settled also in prehistoric times. Between the hills and the river, standing by itself, was a seventh hill, the Capitoline, which became the religious center of the city and the location of the Arx, the citadel to which the inhabitants of Rome fled for safety during enemy attacks. On the opposite bank of the Tiber were two more hills, the Janiculum and the Vatican.

The fertile plain called Latium, of which Rome was a part, furnished food for the inhabitants of the city. Before long Rome became a convenient trading center between settlements to the north and south.  Her location and her easily defended city helped Rome to divide her enemies.  She could attack in any direction.

By first conquering her neighbors and then granting them Roman citizenship, Rome was able to blend the city-states and tribes of Italy into a powerful whole.  Before the first Punic War in 264 B.C., Rome was ruling most of Italy.


## A Young Roman Hero

Ōlim parvus puer per viās Rōmae properābat.  Fēmina pulchra puerum Rōmānum spectābat.  "Salvē, mī puer cārē!  Quis es?  Ubi habitās?  Cūr et quō properās?" rogābat fēmina bona.

"Sum Mārcellus," respondēbat puer.  "Rōmae cum amīcīs habitō.  Sed nunc negōtium prīvātum habeō.  Properāre dēbeō.  Valē!"

"Vīsitābisne crās villam meam?  Līberōs nōn habeō."  "Crās," ridēbat (*smiled*) Mārcellus, "villam tuam vīsitābō."

Per viās Rōmae puer properābat.  Multa erant perīcula, sed puer nōn timēbat.  Subitō puerōs māgnōs vidēbat.  "Quō properās, Mārcelle?"  Corvīnus erat puer malus.  "Quid sub togā portās?  Estne epistula?  Dā mihi (*to me*) epistulam."

"Numquam!" respondēbat Mārcellus.  "Negōtium prīvātum habeō et properāre dēsīderō."  "Quid est negotium prīvātum?"  Iterum iterumque Corvīnus validus parvum puerum pulsābat (*beat*).  Mox (*Soon*) turba prope puerōs stābat.  "Puer est amīcus Galbae!" vir clāmābat.  "Epistulam sēcrētam portat!"

"Ēripite (*Seize*) epistulam sēcrētam!" clāmābat turba.  Mārcellus in terrā erat.  Corvīnus puerum miserum calcitrābat (*kept kicking*).  Subitō erat silentium.  Quadrātus, vir validus et Mārcellī amīcus, in viā properābat.

"Ō Quadrāte!  Epistulam sēcrētam ad senātum portābam.  Crās in senātū inimīcus cōnsulem (*consul*) necābit (*kill*).  Galba, amīcus meus, senātum monēre et cōnsulem servāre dēsīderat.  Cōnsul est vir bonus et patriam amat.  Hodiē prō cōnsule et prō patriā vītam dō.  Valē!"

The people who make no roads are ruled out from
intelligent participation in the world's brotherhood.
—Margaret Fairless Barber, 1869–1901

# *Unit* XII

## CONVERSATION

JŪLIA:     Habēbantne Rōmānī bonās viās, Jūlī?

JŪLIUS:    Multās viās lātās ac longās habēbant.

MĀRCELLA:  Ubi erant viae Rōmānae, Mārce?

MĀRCUS:   In Ītaliā, in Galliā, in cūnctīs prōvinciīs Rōmānīs erant
viae Rōmānae multae ac bonae.

PAULA:     Cūr bonās viās Rōmānī aedificābant, Paule?

PAULUS:    Multa bella Rōmānōs validōs saepe vocābant.

MĀRCUS:   Per viās māgnae cōpiae Rōmānae ad bellum cotīdiē properābant.  Gladiōs ac tēla virī portābant.

JŪLIUS:    Captīvī equīs ac carrīs cibum frūmentumque portābant.

PAULUS:    Perīcula et bella Rōmānī nōn timēbant.

MĀRCUS:   Patriam amābant, et prō patriā pūgnābant.

CORNĒLIA:  Nōnne Rōmānī prīmō fīnitimōs inimīcōs Ītaliae superābant?

CORNĒLIUS: Prīmum cūnctam Ītaliam superābant.  Posteā cum incolīs
Eurōpae, Āsiae, Āfricae pūgnābant.

JŪLIA:     Rōmānīs multās victōriās Fortūna dabat.

## SECTION 1 Principal Parts of the Verb

▶ DISCUSSION

Certain forms of the verb have been called its *principal parts* because
from them the verb is conjugated in all its moods and tenses.  In Latin
the regular verb has four principal parts.

1. Present Indicative Active (first person singular)

        **vocō** = *I call*    **moneō** = *I warn*

2. Present Infinitive Active (no person or number)

        **vocāre** = *to call*    **monēre** = *to warn*

3. Perfect Indicative Active (first person singular)

    **vocāvī** = *I have called, I called*    **monuī** = *I have warned, I warned*

4. Perfect Passive Participle (verbal adjective)

        **vocātus, –a, –um** = *(having been) called*

        **monitus, –a, –um** = *(having been) warned*

In the *first conjugation* most verbs form their principal parts according to the same pattern as **vocō, –āre, –āvī, –ātus.** A few exceptions which are used in this book must be carefully noted.

| | | | | |
|---|---|---|---|---|
| **dō** | **dare** | **dedī** | **datus, –a, –um** | *give* |
| **stō** | **stāre** | **stetī** | **stātūrus, –a, –um** | *stand* |
| **(ad)juvō** | **(ad)juvāre** | **(ad)jūvī** | **(ad)jūtus, –a, –um** | *aid* |

▶ STUDY HELPS

1. **Dō,** *give,* is the only first conjugation verb with a short *–a* in the infinitive; all others have a long *–ā.*

2. Intransitive verbs, as **stō,** *stand,* do not have a perfect passive participle; the *future active participle* is substituted in the principal parts.

3. The principal parts of **sum,** *to be,* are: **sum, esse, fuī, futūrus.** See page 376 for the conjugation of **sum.**

▶ PRACTICE PATTERNS

Write in Latin the principal parts of these first conjugation verbs:

amō rogō cūrō laudō portō ambulō spectō nāvigō properō aedificō
arō parō vocō clāmō pūgnō nārrō labōrō habitō superō dēsīderō

# SECTION 2 Principal Parts of Second Conjugation Verbs

▶ DISCUSSION

Verbs of the *second conjugation* do not follow a definite pattern in forming the third and fourth principal parts. The first two parts keep a consistent formation. These second conjugation verbs found in Units I–XII should be memorized.

| *Pres. Ind.* | *Pres. Inf.* | *Perf. Ind.* | *Perf. Pass. Part.* | *Meaning* |
|---|---|---|---|---|
| **habeō** | **habēre** | **habuī** | **habitus, –a, –um** | *have, hold* |
| **dēbeō** | **dēbēre** | **dēbuī** | **dēbitus, –a, –um** | *owe, ought* |
| **moneō** | **monēre** | **monuī** | **monitus, –a, –um** | *warn, advise* |
| **terreō** | **terrēre** | **terruī** | **territus, –a, –um** | *frighten* |
| **timeō** | **timēre** | **timuī** | —— | *fear, be afraid* |
| **doceō** | **docēre** | **docuī** | **doctus, –a, –um** | *teach* |
| **maneō** | **manēre** | **mānsī** | **mānsūrus, –a, –um** | *remain* |
| **videō** | **vidēre** | **vīdī** | **vīsus, –a, –um** | *see* |
| **sedeō** | **sedēre** | **sēdī** | **sessūrus, –a, –um** | *sit* |
| **respondeō** | **respondēre** | **respondī** | **respōnsus, –a, –um** | *answer* |

1. All second conjugation verbs have long *-ē* in the present infinitive.

2. Some verbs, as *timēre,* do not have a fourth principal part.

3. Hereafter the four principal parts and the conjugation number will be given in the vocabularies, except for regular verbs of the first conjugation, which will be indicated by (1)

## WORDS TO MASTER

**angus′tus, –a, –um,** *adj.,* narrow, difficult

**at′que (ac),** *conj.,* and, and also

**captī′vus, –a, –um,** *adj.,* taken, captured; **captī′vus, –ī,** *m.,* captive, prisoner

**car′rus, –ī,** *m.,* cart, wagon (*carriage*)

**cotī′diē,** *adv.,* daily, every day

**e′quus, –ī,** *m.,* horse (*equine*)

**gla′dius, –ī,** *m.,* sword (*gladiator*)

**li′ber, –brī,** *m.,* book (*library*)

**prī′mus, –a, –um,** *adj.,* first (*prime*); **prī′mō,** *adv.,* at first; **prī′mum,** *adv.,* first, first of all

**se′deō, –ēre, sēdī, sessūrus** (2), sit (*sedentary*)

**taber′na, –ae,** *f.,* shop (*tavern*)

**tē′lum, –ī,** *n.,* weapon, dart

## BUILDING WORD POWER

Some adjectives meaning *pertaining to* or *belonging to* were formed by adding the suffix *–icus* or *–ticus* to the stems of some nouns. If the word *aquatic* was derived from the Latin *aquāticus,* what is the Latin for *civic, erratic, lunatic, fanatic, domestic, rustic, nautic, public?* But not all words that terminate in *–ic* are Latin derivatives. Some of them are Greek, and many of them are modern scientific terms.

Another group of adjectives was formed by adding *–idus* to the root of the verb. These adjectives denote a quality expressed in the verb, which frequently belongs to the second conjugation: *tim/ēre + idus = timidus = timid.*

Using the above form as a model, write the adjectives from: *horrēre, frigēre, arēre, acēre, liquēre, humēre, rigēre, torrēre.*

A *solidus* was a gold piece used in the time of the Empire. *Soldārius* was the term used for one serving in the army for money, hence, our word *soldier.* *Solder* and *soldier* are doublets.

## SENTENCE PATTERNS

A. Complete and translate:

1. Prīmō agricolae in vīcīs habitāba____, sed erant laet____.

2. Nōnne viae Rōmae erant angust____?

3. Num servī tēlīs gladiīsque Rōmān____ superāba____?
4. Sedēbantne puerī prope cas____ parvās?
5. Captīvī equīs ac carrīs frūment____ in Ītaliam portābunt.
6. Prīmī incolae Rōmae agricolae valid____ erant.
7. In librīs māgn____ sunt multae fābul____ dē Rōmā.
8. Sedēte ibi, puer____ et puell____. Librōs spectābimus.
9. Prīmum ad tabern____ properābunt.
10. Cūr Rōmānī viās lāt____ aedificāre dēsīderābant?

B. Translate into Latin:
1. Every day the men used to sit in the small shop and tell stories.
2. The teacher does want to give the books to the boys, doesn't he?
3. In Italy and in all the provinces there were broad streets.
4. Men, don't carry the weapons from the town to the master's villa.
5. Did the Romans always overcome their hostile neighbors with swords and weapons?

## The Master Road Builders

Cornēlius et Mārcus erant amīcī bonī. Puerī erant discipulī scholae Rōmānae propinquae Viae Sacrae. Cornēlius in Americā habitābat, sed Mārcus erat incola Rōmae. Amīcī per viās Rōmae cotīdiē ambulābant. Ōlim Mārcus cum Cornēliō in Viā Sacrā ambulābat. Colloquium (*Conversation*) puerōrum erat longum.

CORNĒLIUS: Narrābisne fābulam dē viīs Rōmānīs? Viās Rōmae amō. Nōnne sunt pulchrae?

MĀRCUS: Certē. Fābula est longa. Rōma nōn semper erat domina Ītaliae et Eurōpae. Prīmō erat parvus vīcus. Incolae erant pastōrēs (*shepherds*) et agricolae. In casīs miserīs parvī vīcī habitābant, sed erant bonī et laetī.

CORNĒLIUS: Viāsne pulchrās semper habēbant?

MĀRCUS: Primō viās nōn habēbant, sed agrī erant māgnī. Agricolae terram bonam arābant; pastōrēs ovēs (*sheep*) cūrābant. Posteā cum fīnitimīs inimīcīs pūgnābant. Rōmānī erant validī et fīnitimōs saepe superābant. Cūnctam Ītaliam superābant.

CORNĒLIUS: Quōmodo (*How*) incolās cūnctae Ītaliae superābant?

MĀRCUS: Rōmānī viās lātās solidāsque aedificābant quod necesse (*necessary*) erat per viās arma et gladiōs et tēla ad oppida et vīcōs fīnitimōrum inimīcōrum portāre. Imperātōrēs (*Generals*) Rōmānī cum māgnīs cōpiīs per viās Rōmae et Ītaliae ad Siciliam, ad Graeciam, ad Galliam, ad Hispāniam, ad Britanniam, ad Āfricam, ad Āsiam properābant. Per agrōs et per silvās ad oppida Ītaliae atque ad terrās prōvinciārum servī viās aedificābant. Servī equīs et carrīs cibum et frūmentum ad prōvinciās et ē prōvinciīs portābant. Sed fābulam meam crās narrābō.

"We Romans love fresh water. Rome is a town of baths and fish pools and fountains."
—Claudius in *Claudius the God*
Robert Graves, 1895–

# *Unit* XIII

## CONVERSATION

CORNĒLIA:    Quī clārās viās Rōmānās aedificāvērunt, Cornēlī?
CORNĒLIUS:    Prīmō agricolae Rōmānī, posteā captīvī ac servī viās longās aedificāvērunt.
JŪLIA:    Nōnne Rōmānī māgnam scientiam (*knowledge*) viārum habēbant, Jūlī?
JŪLIUS:    Scientiam, māgnam pecūniam, multōs servōs habēbant.
PAULA:    Ubi servī labōrābant, Paule?
PAULUS:    Cotīdiē servī per agrōs silvāsque viās parābant.
CORNĒLIUS:    Vīta servōrum erat misera, sed dominī Rōmānī bonās viās habēre dēsīderābant.
MĀRCELLA:    Quis Viam Appiam, prīmam viam Rōmānam, aedificāvit, Mārce?
MĀRCUS:    Appius Claudius servīs mandāta dedit. Prīmam viam atque aquaeductum Appiānum aedificāvērunt.
CORNĒLIUS:    Caligula et Claudius aquaeductum Claudiānum parāvērunt.
CORNĒLIA:    Viārum Rōmānārum fāma māgna est.
PAULUS:    Cotīdiē viātōrēs (*travelers*) viās Rōmānās vīsitant. Ruīnās templōrum, sepulchrōrum, monumentōrum spectant.
PAULA:    Americānī viās ac ruīnās antīquās amant et laudant.
JŪLIUS:    Viās et ruinās Ītaliae antīquae vidēre dēsīderō.

## SECTION 1 Perfect Tense

▶ DISCUSSION

1. In English a completed past act may be expressed by the *present perfect*, as: *I have called.* This is usually a single act or event, completed just before present time. Or the completed past act may be expressed

by the *simple past tense,* as *I called.* This is a *single* act, finished at some *definite* time in the past.

In Latin the perfect tense corresponds to both the English present perfect and the simple past tense. The meaning of the whole passage will help you to determine whether to translate a Latin perfect by an English present perfect or by a simple past tense.

2. The third principal part of a Latin verb is the perfect indicative active, first person singular. By dropping the final *–i* from this form, we have the perfect stem: **vocāv/ī; monu/ī.**

▶ STUDY HELPS

1. There is no special tense indicator for the perfect tense.

2. The person indicators of the perfect tense are different from those of the other tenses.

3. The person indicators are the same for the perfect indicative active of all Latin verbs.

PERFECT INDICATIVE ACTIVE, FIRST CONJUGATION

*Perf. Stem +  P.I.   =    Form*

SINGULAR

| First | **vocāv** | + | **ī** | = | **vocāvī** | *I called, have called, did call* |
| Second | **vocāv** | + | **istī** | = | **vocāvistī** | *you called, have called, did call* |
| Third | **vocāv** | + | **it** | = | **vocāvit** | *he called, has called, did call* |

PLURAL

| First | **vocāv** | + | **imus** | = | **vocāvimus** | *we called, have called, did call* |
| Second | **vocāv** | + | **istis** | = | **vocāvistis** | *you called, have called, did call* |
| Third | **vocāv** | + | **ērunt** | = | **vocāvērunt** | *they called, have called, did call* |

▶ STUDY HELPS

1. The perfect tense of the second conjugation is formed like that of the first:

**monuī, monuistī, monuit, monuimus, monuistis, monuērunt**

2. The perfect tense of the verb *sum* is formed regularly:

**fuī, fuistī, fuit, fuimus, fuistis, fuērunt**

▶ PRACTICE PATTERNS

A. Conjugate in the perfect tense and give the English translation of:

rogō   habeō   dō   stō   sum   adsum   absum   maneō

B. Write in Latin:

| he built | we have hurried | she remained | we have been |
| I feared | you (sing.) saw | they watched | he was absent |
| they taught | you (pl.) stood | he did call | I was present |

# SECTION 2 Difference Between Perfect and Imperfect Tenses

▶ **DISCUSSION**

Unlike the imperfect tense, the perfect tense *never* presents action as *going on* or *customary* or *repeated* in the past. The perfect tense is used in Latin much more frequently than the imperfect. Compare the meanings of the perfect and the imperfect tenses in the following sentences:

PERFECT

**Rōmānī Gallōs superāvērunt.**  The Romans *conquered* (*have conquered*) the Gauls.

**Vir tubā fīlium vocāvit.**  The man *called* his son with a trumpet.

IMPERFECT

**Tum Rōmānī Gallōs *superābant*.**  At that time the Romans *were conquering* the Gauls.

**Vir tubā fīlium *vocābat*.**  The man *used to call* his son with a trumpet.

## WORDS TO MASTER

**auxi'lium, –ī,** *n.,* help (*auxiliary*)
**e'tiam,** *adv.,* also, even, still
**he'rī,** *adv.,* yesterday
**impedīmen'tum, –ī,** *n.,* hindrance; **impedīmen'ta, –ōrum,** *pl.,* baggage (*impediment*)
**lon'gus, –a, –um,** *adj.,* long; **lon'gē,** *adv.,* far, by far (*longitude*)

**mandā'tum, –ī,** *n.,* command; *pl.,* instructions, directions (*mandate*)
**mox,** *adv.,* soon, presently
**no'vus, –a, –um,** *adj.,* new (*novice*)
**prae'da, –ae,** *f.,* booty (*predatory*)
**tem'plum, –ī,** *n.,* temple (*templar*)
**tum,** *adv.,* at that time, then
**un'dique,** *adv.,* on all sides

## BUILDING WORD POWER

Hundreds of English adjectives are derived from Latin adjectives. The spelling and meaning are almost the same in both languages. What English adjectives are derived from the following: *dēnsus, mūtus, sōlus, acūtus, largus, rārus, sānus, matūrus, crūdus?* Notice that the English derivatives end in mute *–e.*

What is the English for: *varius, dubius, sērius, industrius, strēnuus, arduus, spurius?*

The suffix *–ōsus* means *full of, endowed with, given to.* What are the

English adjectives from the following: *officiōsus, cōpiōsus, injūriō-sus?* Is a *verbose* person full of words, and a *bellicose* one full of war?

The suffix *–lentus* has almost the same meaning as *–ōsus.* Sometimes it means *disposed to* or *abounding in.* Can you figure out the meaning of: *corpulent* (**corpus,** *body*); *pestilent* (**pestis,** *plague*); **viru-lent** (**vīrus,** *poison*); *opulent* (**ops,** *wealth*); *violent* (**vīs,** *force*).

## SENTENCE PATTERNS

A. Translate into English:

1. Tum captīvī et equī ex prōvinciīs in Ītaliam impedīmenta portāvērunt.
2. Herī templa spectāvimus; crās Rōmae manēbimus.
3. Dominus servīs mandāta dedit, sed auxilium nōn dedit.
4. Perīcula bellōrum novōrum māgna fuērunt.
5. Posteā Rōmānī multōs captīvōs et multam praedam habuērunt.
6. Num Via Sacra erat longa lātaque?
7. Bella numquam amāvī, sed prō patriā meā laetus pūgnābō.
8. Laetī sunt virī quod mox in patriā erunt.
9. Undique captīvī labōrābant et Viam Appiam aedificābant.
10. Fēminae etiam in Viā Sacrā cum amīcīs ambulābant.

B. Translate the italicized words into Latin:

1. *Daily* on the Via Sacra *we saw shops, temples,* and statues.
2. *At that time* the Romans *built new roads* to southern Italy.
3. Messengers *hastened yesterday* to *towns* in northern Italy.
4. *Did not* many beautiful women *also live* near *the shops?*
5. *After the wars* slaves *carried baggage* and *booty from the provinces.*

## Rome's Most Important Public Utility

An elevated aqueduct.

In early days Rome obtained its water from wells, fountains, or rivers. Rain water was collected in cisterns to augment this supply. When these sources became inadequate because of the increase in population, an aqueduct eleven miles long was built in 300 B.C. under the direction of Appius Claudius, the same Censor who constructed the Appian Way. Except for about three hundred feet this aqueduct ran underground.

There were other underground aqueducts, but the first high-level one was built in 140 B.C. in order to bring water to the top of the Capitoline Hill. Eventually there were fourteen aqueducts in operation, the greatest of which was the Aqua Claudia, whose ruined arches may still be seen near Rome. From the hills almost fifty miles away, it brought to the city an abundant supply of pure water through a masonry channel, ten miles of which had to be elevated on enormous arches. Once inside Rome this water was distributed through lead pipes to more than a thousand public reservoirs and fountains. Every house of any size had its own tap but not above the first floor.

Sewage disposal was taken care of by a network of underground channels built of masonry. Some sewers, as the Cloaca Maxima, were so large that a wagon could be driven through them. This water and sewerage system that Rome developed was probably the reason that Rome escaped the terrible epidemics that in later times ravaged many European cities.


## The Master Road Builders: The Via Appia

CORNĒLIUS: Quis Viam Appiam parāvit, Mārce?

MĀRCUS: Appius Claudius, Rōmānus clārus, Viam Appiam parāvit. Rōmae (300 B.C.) habitāvit. Hodiē post MM annōs (*years*), Via Appia etiam est rēgīna viārum Rōmānārum.

CORNĒLIUS: Cūr erat Via Appia rēgīna viārum?

MĀRCUS: Erat prīma māgna via in Ītaliā. Prīmō ad oppidum Capuam, posteā ad oppidum Brundisium pertinēbat (*it extended*). Brundisium est prope aquam, nōn longē ā Graeciā. Multī viātōrēs (*travelers*) ex Ītaliā in Graeciam saepe nāvigābant.

CORNĒLIUS: Cūr Rōmānī Graeciam vīsitāre dēsīderāvērunt?

MĀRCUS: Tum in Graeciā erant multae scholae clārae. Rōmānī scholās bonās Graeciae amābant. Multī virī Rōmānī et puerī in scholīs Graecīs studēbant. Linguam Graecam et templa et statuās et columnās amābant.

CORNĒLIUS: Nōnne servī in Viā Appiā saepe labōrābant?

MĀRCUS: Multī servī in Viā Appiā et in Viā Flāminiā et in Viā

Latīnā labōrābant. Impedīmenta et praedam et frūmentum ex prōvinciīs in Ītaliam portābant. Nūntiī etiam litterās et mandāta ex Ītaliā ad prōvinciās et ē prōvinciīs in Ītaliam portābant. Crās fābulam dē Viā Sacrā narrābō.

<table>
<tr><td>"The Roman road is the greatest monument ever raised to liberty by a noble and generous people."<br>—Claudius in Claudius the God<br>Robert Graves, 1895–</td><td>Unit XIV</td></tr>
</table>

## CONVERSATION

MAGISTER: Hodiē, puerī, verba recitāre dēbēmus. Post magistrum cum dīligentiā recitāte:

In viā *ambulā'veram.*      Ad aedificium *ambulāverā'mus.*
Prope aquam *ambulā'verās.*   Per viās *ambulāverā'tis.*
Ex silvā *ambulā'verat.*     Ā templō *ambulā'verant.*

ROBERTUS: Recitāvimus. Narrābisne puerīs fābulam dē Viā Sacrā?

MAGISTER: Bene, puerī, recitāvistis. Via Sacra est via antīqua.

PAULUS: Ubi est Via Sacra? Estne propinqua Forō?

MAGISTER: Ā Colosseō per Forum Rōmānum ad Capitōlium pertinet (*extends*).

PETRUS: Quālis via est Via Sacra?

MAGISTER: Est angusta, antīqua, tortuōsa (*crooked*), sed Rōmānī Viam Sacram amant.

JŪSTĪNUS: Prope Viam Sacram multae ruīnae nunc sunt. Herī Viam Sacram ac Forum cum amīcīs meīs vīsitāvī.

MAGISTER: Crās ad Viam Sacram māgnō cum studiō ambulābimus ac Forum Rōmānum spectābimus. Valēte, bonī puerī meī.

## SECTION 1 Pluperfect Tense

▶ DISCUSSION

The pluperfect indicative active in Latin is an exact translation of the corresponding tense in English, which is sometimes called the *past perfect tense.* In both languages it expresses an action that was *completed before a definite past time.*

**73**

In English we easily recognize this tense because it is always composed of the auxiliary verb *had* and the past participle of the main verb. In Latin it can be just as easily recognized by the tense indicator –*erā*– attached to the perfect stem.

**Servī viās aedificāv/era/nt.**   The slaves *had built* the roads.

PLUPERFECT INDICATIVE ACTIVE, FIRST CONJUGATION

*Perf. Stem* + *T.I.* + *P.I.* =   *Form*

SINGULAR

| First | vocāv | + erā + | m | = | vocāveram | *I had called* |
| Second | vocāv | + erā + | s | = | vocāverās | *you had called* |
| Third | vocāv | + erā + | t | = | vocāverat | *he, she, it had called* |

PLURAL

| First | vocāv | + erā + | mus | = | vocāverāmus | *we had called* |
| Second | vocāv | + erā + | tis | = | vocāverātis | *you had called* |
| Third | vocāv | + erā + | nt | = | vocāverant | *they had called* |

▶ STUDY HELPS

1. The pluperfect tense of the second conjugation is formed like that of the first:

**monueram, monuerās, monuerat,**
**monuerāmus, monuerātis, monuerant**

2. The pluperfect tense of the verb *sum* is formed regularly:

**fueram, fuerās, fuerat, fuerāmus, fuerātis, fuerant**

3. The verb *had* is also the past tense of *have*, and as such is not an auxiliary verb:

**habent** = *they have*   **habēbant** = *they had*

4. The person indicators of the pluperfect and imperfect tenses are identical.

▶ PRACTICE PATTERNS

A. Conjugate in the pluperfect tense and give the English translation:

clāmō   moveō   dō   stō   adsum   absum   sum   spectō

B. Write in Latin the pluperfect indicative active, third person singular, of:

ask   answer   sail   look at   see   plow   fear   move

# SECTION 2 Ablative of Accompaniment

▶ DISCUSSION

In an earlier lesson you learned that the preposition **cum,** meaning *with*, governs the ablative case. When used with *persons*, and meaning *in company with* or *in conflict with,* this phrase is called the *ablative of accompaniment.*

**Servī *cum agricolīs* labōrāverant.**   The slaves had worked *with the farmers.*
**Incolae *cum fīnitimīs* pūgnāve-** The inhabitants had fought *with neigh-*
**rant.**                                                   *bors.*

This ablative is generally used with *persons,* but it may be used with *things,* if the **cum** means *together with.*

**Gladiī *cum tēlīs* in agrō erant.**   The swords were *with (together with)*
                                                                *the weapons* in the field.

# SECTION 3 Ablative of Manner

▶ DISCUSSION

There is another common use of the ablative with **cum,** which shows the *manner* of an action, that is, *how* the action is done. This is called the *ablative of manner.*

**Servī *cum dīligentiā* labōrāverant.**   The slaves had labored *with diligence.*

**Cum** may be omitted if the noun in the ablative is modified by an adjective.

**Servī *magnā dīligentiā* (*magnā*** The slaves had worked *with great dili-*
***cum dīligentiā*) labōrāverant.**          *gence.*

The ablative of manner is often equivalent to an English adverb. Thus,

cum dīligentiā = *with diligence* = *diligently*
mā̆gnā cum dīligentiā = *with great diligence* = *very diligently*

▶ STUDY HELPS

1. The *ablative of accompaniment* is generally used with *persons,* regularly has **cum,** and is always translated *with.*

The slaves will work *with* farmers in the fields.   (Persons)

2. The *ablative of manner* is generally used with *abstract nouns,* may omit **cum** if an adjective is used with the noun, and may be translated with the word *with,* or as an adverb.

The slaves will work with *diligence* in the fields.   (Abstract noun)

3. The *ablative of means* is generally used with *concrete things,* never has **cum** or any other preposition, and may be translated *with, by, by means of.*

The slaves will work with *plows* in the fields.   (Concrete things)

► PRACTICE PATTERNS

A. Identify the ablatives from this lesson used in the Sentence Patterns on page 77.

B. Identify these ablatives, and translate into Latin:

1. to fight with weapons
2. to work with diligence
3. to move with great care
4. to walk with friends
5. to prepare with industry
6. to fight with enemies
7. to give with great joy
8. to warn with a signal
9. to call with a trumpet
10. to work with slaves
11. to carry grain by cart
12. to walk by the road

## WORDS TO MASTER

**ā (ab),** *prep. with abl.,* away from, from, by

**aedifi′cium,** –ī, *n.,* building (*edifice*)

**an′te,** *adv., and prep. with acc.,* before, in front of (*antique*)

**de′us,** –ī, *m.,* god; **de′a,** –ae, *f.,* goddess (*deity*)

**dīligen′tia,** –ae, *f.,* care, industry (*diligence*)

**mo′veō,** –ēre, **mōvī, mōtus** (2), move (*motion*)

**nu′merus,** –ī, *m.,* number, measure (*numeral*)

**po′pulus,** –ī, *m.,* people, nation, the people, the citizens (*popular*)

**prae′mium,** –ī, *n.,* reward, gift (*premium*)

**scū′tum,** –ī, *n.,* shield (*scutate*)

**sīg′num,** –ī, *n.,* signal, sign, military standard (*sign*)

**stu′dium,** –ī, *n.,* eagerness, zeal (*study*)

## BUILDING WORD POWER

Many Latin adjectives end in *–tīvus* or *–sīvus*. They are formed from the perfect passive participle of a root verb and express the action or quality implied in that verb.

It is easy to translate English adjectives that terminate in *–ive* into Latin and vice versa. Just change the final silent *–e* into *–us,* or *–us* to *–e.* Write the Latin for: *nominative, genitive, dative, accusative, ablative, active, passive.* What is the English for: **nātīvus, fugitīvus, captīvus, dēmōnstrātīvus, imperātīvus, indicātīvus, subjūnctīvus?**

Many adjectives formed from nouns have the suffix *–ānus* with the meaning *pertaining to, belonging to.* These adjectives came into English ending in *–an* or *–ane.* Anything *American* belongs to or pertains to America. What are the Latin words for *Christian, Italian, Roman, African, Asian?* What English words are derived from: **urbānus, silvānus, meridiānus, humānus, mundānus?**

## SENTENCE PATTERNS

### A. Translate into English:

1. Multī servī fuerant magistrī puerōrum Rōmānōrum.
2. Dominus sīgnō servōs monuerat, et cum studiō ex agrīs properāverant.
3. Nōnne captīvī māgnā cum dīligentiā viās lātās aedificāvērunt?
4. In Americā equīs et carrīs impedīmenta ab oppidō ad oppidum saepe nōn movēmus.
5. Virī clārī māgnum numerum templōrum aedificiōrumque laudāvērunt.
6. Populus Rōmānus multōs deōs et multās deās habēbat.
7. Dederatne dominus servīs fīdīs māgna praemia?
8. Rōmānī gladiīs tēlīsque cum incolīs vīcōrum pūgnāvērunt.
9. Ante bella Rōmānī fuerant agricolae; sed post bella servī terram arābant.
10. Tum captīvī scūta et gladiōs ab prōvinciīs in Ītaliam portābant.

### B. Translate into Latin:

1. In the arena men often fought with men before a large number of people.
2. The master gave large rewards to the slaves because they had moved the grain with great care from the fields to the villa.
3. Did the inhabitants of the island fight with swords and weapons?
4. Carefully they carried a small supply of food to the people.
5. Did not the slaves carry the baggage to town by means of carts?

## The Master Road Builders: The Via Sacra

CORNĒLIUS: Salvē, Mārce! Quid agis hodiē? Quō properās?

MĀRCUS: Salvē, Cornēlī! Ad Viam Sacram properō.

CORNĒLIUS: Ubi est Via Sacra? Estne via longa et lāta?

MĀRCUS: Nōn est longa, nōn est lāta. Via antīqua est angusta ac tortuōsa sed est clāra.

CORNĒLIUS: Cūr Via Sacra est clāra, Mārce?

MĀRCUS: Via Sacra ā Colosseō per Forum Rōmānum ad Capitōlium pertinet (*extends*), et per viam ambulābant (*marched*) multae pompae (*parades*). Pompae Rōmānae erant spectācula māgna ac splendida. Legiōnēs Rōmānae cum studiō per Viam Sacram ad bella properābant, et post bella victōrēs per Viam Sacram in pompā ambulābant.

CORNĒLIUS: Amābantne Rōmānī pompās?

MĀRCUS: Rōmānī māgnō cum studiō pompās spectābant. Multī virī, fēminae, līberī in tabernīs, aedificiīs, viīs stābant et clāmābant: "Iō (*Hurrah*) triumphe! Iō triumphe!" In triumphō ambulābant cūnctī virī clārī. Legiōnēs sīgna, servī tēla ac scūta portābant. Multī captīvī quoque in pompā erant.

CORNĒLIUS: Properāvitne pompa per Forum Rōmānum?

MĀRCUS: In Forō Rōmānō pompa stetit, et imperātor (*general*) virīs legiōnum (*of the legions*) Rōmānōrum māgna praemia dedit. Nōnne pompa in Viā Sacrā spectāculum splendidum erat, Cornēlī?

CORNĒLIUS: Ruīnae columnārum et templōrum propinquae Viae Sacrae glōriam Rōmae antīquae in memoriam revocant (*recall*), sed Via Sacra captīvōs miserōs, quī (*who*) in viīs Rōmānīs ad mortem (*death*) saepe ambulāvērunt, quoque in memoriam revocat.

MĀRCUS: Nunc ad Viam Sacram properābimus et Forum Rōmānum vīsitābimus.

Thy Naiad airs have brought me home
 To the glory that was Greece,
And the grandeur that was Rome.
 —Edgar Allan Poe, 1809–1849

# *Unit* XV

## CONVERSATION

ATRICIUS: Laetus nōn sum. Lūdum nōn amō!

ROBERTUS: Lūdum numquam amābam sed lūdōs amō.

MAGISTER: Tacēte, sī placet. (*Be quiet, please.*) Hodiē discipulōx fōrmulam (*rule*) novam docēbō. Habētisne tabellās et pennās (*pens*), puerī et puellae?

PATRICIUS: Tabellam nōn habeō, magister.

ROBERTUS: Pennam nōn habeō, magister.

ANNA: Puerīs tabellam et pennam dabō, magister.

MAGISTER: Grātiās tibi, Anna, sed sī Patricius et Robertus cum dīligentiā nōn labōrāverint, puerīs fābulam nōn narrābō.

JŪLIA: Puerī māgnō cum studiō labōrābunt. Quae est fōrmula?

MAGISTER: In tabellā pennā scrībite (*write*): "Servus fīdus cibum parat. Servus cibum fīdē parat. Agricola industrius labōrat. Agricola industriē labōrat. Cārus, cārē. Clārus, clārē." Fīdē, industriē, cārē, clārē sunt adverbia. Quid est *bene*, Roberte?

ROBERTUS: *Bene* est adverbium, magister.

MAGISTER: Bene respondistī, Roberte. Puerīs fābulam cum laetitiā nunc narrābō.

# SECTION 1 Future Perfect Tense

▶ DISCUSSION

In both English and Latin the future perfect tense represents an act as completed in future time or completed before another future act. "As you *sow*, so shall you reap," really means: As you *shall have sown*, so shall you reap.

The future perfect is much more frequently used in Latin than in English, because Latin is far more exact than English in making a distinction between what is *future action* and what is *action completed* in the future.

In English the *future perfect indicative* is composed of the sign for the future plus the sign for the present perfect plus the past participle:

*shall + have + called = shall have called*

In Latin it is composed of the perfect stem plus the special tense indicator *–eri–* plus the person indicators:

**vocāv + eri + t = vocāverit** = *he will have called*

FUTURE PERFECT INDICATIVE ACTIVE, FIRST CONJUGATION

*Perf. Stem + T.I. + P.I. =      Form*

SINGULAR

| First | **vocāv** | + **eri** + | **ō** | = | **vocāverō** | *I shall have called* |
|-------|-----------|-------------|-------|---|--------------|----------------------|
| Second | **vocāv** | + **eri** + | **s** | = | **vocāveris** | *you will have called* |
| Third | **vocāv** | + **eri** + | **t** | = | **vocāverit** | *he, she, it will have called.* |

PLURAL

| First | **vocāv** | + **eri** + | **mus** | = | **vocāverimus** | *we shall have called* |
|-------|-----------|-------------|---------|---|-----------------|------------------------|
| Second | **vocāv** | + **eri** + | **tis** | = | **vocāveritis** | *you will have called* |
| Third | **vocāv** | + **eri** + | **nt** | = | **vocāverint** | *they will have called* |

▶ STUDY HELPS

1. The future perfect tense of the second conjugation is formed like that of the first:

**monuerō, monueris, monuerit, monuerimus, monueritis, monuerint**

The future perfect of the verb *sum* is formed regularly:

**fuerō, fueris, fuerit, fuerimus, fueritis, fuerint**

2. The future perfect, as well as the simple future, is sometimes translated loosely into the English present. We may call this a false present.

**Māgnum erit praemium vestrum sī miserīs sociīs auxilium *dederitis*.** — Great will be your reward if *you give* (*will have given*) help to your unfortunate companions.

A. Conjugate in the future perfect indicative and translate:

ōrō   adjuvō   maneō   absum   moveō   sum   adsum   sedeō

B. Write in Latin the perfect, pluperfect, and future perfect indicative, third person plural, of:

| | | | |
|---|---|---|---|
| have | pray | give | sit |
| set free | carry | move | remain |

# SECTION 2 Formation of Adverbs

▶ DISCUSSION

In English we have many adverbs formed from adjectives by adding the suffix –ly: adj. *clear* + *–ly* = adv. *clearly*. In Latin many adverbs are formed by adding –**ē** to the base of adjectives of the first and second declensions.

| *Adjective* | *Base* | *+ Indicator =* | *Adverb* |
|---|---|---|---|
| **clārus,** clear | **clār/** | + **ē** | = **clārē,** clearly |
| **līber,** free | **līber/** | + **ē** | = **līberē,** freely |
| **pulcher,** beautiful | **pulchr/** | + **ē** | = **pulchrē,** beautifully |

▶ STUDY HELPS

In Latin we sometimes use an adjective, which is translated into English as an adverb.

**Fēminae *laetae* patriam adjūvērunt.**   The women *gladly* (*glad*) helped their country.

▶ PRACTICE PATTERNS

A. Using the above formula, form adverbs from the following adjectives, and give English meanings.

| | | | | | |
|---|---|---|---|---|---|
| cārus | vērus | laetus | validus | angustus | altus |
| miser | fīdus | līber | inimīcus | industrius | lātus |

B. Review the English meanings of:

| | | | |
|---|---|---|---|
| ibi | ōlim | etiam | posteā |
| tum | crās | paene | quoque |
| cūr | nunc | prope | iterum |
| mox | herī | subitō | cotīdiē |
| nōn | hodiē | quandō | undique |
| ubi | saepe | semper | numquam |

## WORDS TO MASTER

**ad'juvō,–āre,–jūvī,–jūtus** (1), *irreg.*, aid, help (*adjutant*)

**adō'rō** (1), adore (*adoration*)

**aliē'nus, –a, –um,** *adj.*, another's, foreign (*alien*)

**domici'lium, –ī,** *n.*, house, home, dwelling (*domicile*)

**hō'ra, –ae,** *f.*, hour

**in'ter,** *prep. with acc.*, between, among (*interregnum*)

**lī'berō** (1), set free, free (*liberate*)

**lū'dus, –ī,** *m.*, game, sport, school (*ludicrous*)

**ō'rō** (1), beg, ask, pray to (*oration*)

**sī,** *conj.*, if

**sub,** *prep. with abl.*, under, at the foot of; *prep. with acc., with verbs of motion to,* under, close up to

**vē'rus, –a, –um,** *adj.*, true, real (*verity*); **vē'rō,** *adv.*, in truth; **vē'rum,** *adv.*, truly, but; **vē'rē,** *adv.*, truly

## BUILDING WORD POWER

If *pāgus* means *country district*, what is the true meaning of *pāgānus?* Do we call people who live in country districts *pagans?* In ancient Rome peasants (*pāgānī*) lived outside the city. They did not belong to the same religious group as those living in the city, hence the name *pagan* came to have a religious significance. Later, when the Caesars ruled Rome, the term *pāgānus* was used to signify a *civilian,* as opposed to *mīles,* a *soldier.* The Christians called themselves the *soldiers* of Christ, and all who were not Christians were *pagans.*

Today Christians, Moslems, and Jews each use the word in a different sense, but generally a pagan is one who has no religion.

Originally a *villānus* was a *farmhand.* Wealthy men of ancient Rome had fine country homes or *villae.* Those who worked on the farm were called *villānī,* the serfs in the days of feudalism. Before long we find them with a bad reputation. The original farmhand, *villānus* (*villain* in French) is now a scoundrel or criminal.

## SENTENCE PATTERNS

A. Complete each sentence with the correct form of the Latin words that have been omitted; then translate each sentence.

1. Prō patriā (with great eagerness) pūgnāverint.
2. Rōmānī antīquī multōs deōs (used to adore).
3. Laetī ad lūdum properāvērunt quod magister fābulās semper (narrates).
4. Dominus servīs māgnum praemium dabit sī cum dīligentiā (they will have labored.)

5. Māgnā cum cūrā fēminae cibum (had prepared).
6. Inter virōs bonōs amīcī amīcōs fidē (help).
7. Altō in caelō erat domicilium deōrum, sed incolae terrae prō deīs et prō deābus templa (used to build).
8. Populōs miserōs vērē adjuvābunt, sī auxilium (they will have asked).
9. Nōnne Rōmānī in terrīs aliēnīs (did fight)?
10. Ōlim servōs miserōs (we freed), et nunc laetī (we live) in patriā "sub Deō cum lībertāte et jūstitiā cūnctīs."

B. Translate into Latin:

1. Did not the slaves work industriously for foreign masters?
2. The good teacher will aid the boys if they ask (will have asked) for help.
3. Among the ancient peoples there had been many wars.
4. The inhabitants of the town saw the foreign troops clearly.
5. With great diligence they prepared to fight for their homes and fatherland.

The Roman Forum today.

## The Grandeur That Was Rome

For over a thousand years the Roman Forum was the hub of Rome's political and commercial activity. About it cluster more associations of historical importance than about any region of equal size on the globe. In the early city the Forum was the natural and convenient place where people gathered from the seven surrounding hills for barter and for trade. Shops along the sides were still to be found there in the time of Cicero.

Gradually, however, as public business increased and required more room, the Forum developed into a center for the religious, civil, legal, political, and commercial life of the city. Here was the Senate House, here were the courts, here were erected temples in honor of the favorite deities of Rome. Here crowds of people assembled to listen to Cicero and other famous orators.

But it was not only in business hours that the Forum was thronged. In the evenings the people met to talk and to discuss the events of the day, or to find amusement in the soothsayers and fortunetellers and the dealers who hawked their wares. Public amusements were sometimes given in the Forum. Triumphal processions passed up the Sacred Way to the Capitolium and back again to the Forum.

The Forum was the great center for learning the news about a war or the latest expedition or the newest development in politics. Rome had no telephones, no radios, no television sets, no newspapers, but news from all over Italy and the provinces was constantly flowing into the government by special couriers. Announcements were made orally, but from the time of Caesar bulletins were posted containing a summary of the acts of the senate and people, appointments, items of news from the provinces as well as from Italy, notices of festivals and processions, and even sometimes of births, marriages, deaths, and divorces. This news sheet was renewed daily.

Today the ruins of the Forum lie twenty or thirty feet below the modern pavements of Rome. During the Middle Ages the famous buildings were almost completely destroyed. But it is interesting to know that much of the precious marble and other adornments brought by Roman rulers from distant quarries and lands to beautify these buildings is still in Rome in churches and palaces and fountains. Even the high altar in St. Peter's is classical marble taken from the Temple of Minerva. Not the buildings but the marble has proved "more enduring than brass"!

## The Master Road Builders of America

MĀRCUS: Narrā puerīs nunc dē viīs Amērīcānis, sī placet, Roberte.

ROBERTUS: Certē. In Āmericā viae sunt longae, lātae, pūrae (clean), pulchrae. Viās sordidās et angustās et tortuōsās nōn saepe habēmus. In lātīs viīs sunt multae arborēs (trees). Māgnus numerus virōrum et fēminārum cum līberīs in viīs ambulāre amat. Paene cūnctae familiae Āmericānae vehicula mōbilia (autos) habent et per viās ab oppidō ad oppidum properant.

MĀRCUS: Sed Rōmānī prīmī viās fīrmās et solidās aedificāvērunt.

ROBERTUS: Rōmānī viās bene aedificāvērunt. Hodiē viae antīquae sunt in Ītaliā et in prōvinciīs Rōmānīs Eurōpae, Āsiae, Āfricae. Etiam nunc bonae et fīrmae et solidae sunt.

MĀRCUS: Rōmānī multās terrās superāvērunt. Superāvēruntne Āmericānī terrās novās et aliēnās?

ROBERTUS: Amēricānī terrās aliēnās superāre nōn dēsīderant. Terrās
miserās et aliēnās adjuvāre amāmus. Amēricānī sunt benīgnī.
In multīs terrīs sub imperiō Rōmānō multī populī erant servī;
nōn erant laetī; nōn erant līberī. Cibum et domicilia bona nōn
habēbant. Per multās hōrās in agrīs, in viīs, in aedificiīs sub
virīs malīs labōrābant. In arēnā cum sociīs gladiīs pūgnābant.
In Circō virī cum bestiīs pūgnābant. Rōmānī antīquī lūdōs cārē
amābant; servōs, virōs et fēminās et līberōs, cārē nōn amābant.

MĀRCUS: Vērum est. Habēbantne Amēricānī servōs?

ROBERTUS: In Amēricā servōs nunc nōn habēmus. Amēricānī servōs
habēre nōn dēsīderant. In Amēricā cūnctī virī sunt līberī. Populus Amēricānus cibum bonum, māgna domicilia, lātōs agrōs habet.
Līberī ad scholās cotīdiē properant et post hōrās lūdōs habent.
Amēricānī līberōs et domicilia et patriam cārē amant. Sociōs et
fīnitimōs miserōs adjuvant.

Magistrī Amēricānī līberōs docent: "Deus cūnctōs virōs līberōs
et aequālēs creat. Populus prō patriā nōn est (*exist*); patria
prō populō est. Amērica est 'ūna nātiō sub Deō, indīvīsibilis,
cum lībertāte et jūstitiā cūnctīs.'"

# *Comprehensive Review: Units* XI–XV

A. Write in Latin the ablative singular and the base of:

| | | | | | | | |
|---|---|---|---|---|---|---|---|
| food | game | booty | people | number | dwelling | command | wagon |
| sign | shop | crowd | supply | weapon | building | baggage | shield |
| hour | help | horse | temple | troops | industry | captive | reward |
| god | book | sword | school | nation | eagerness | goddess | signal |

B. Write in Latin the feminine and the neuter nominative singular
forms and meanings of:

angustus   novus   aliēnus   vērus   prīmus   longus   malus   cūnctus

C. Write in Latin the adverbs formed on these adjectives, and give
meanings:

| | | | | | | |
|---|---|---|---|---|---|---|
| lātus | cārus | fīdus | laetus | clārus | validus | antīquus |
| līber | vērus | miser | longus | pulcher | inimīcus | industrius |

D. Write in Latin:

| | | | | | |
|---|---|---|---|---|---|
| if | near | daily | almost | tomorrow | every day |
| also | then | still | never | suddenly | yesterday |
| soon | once | truly | again | at first | on all sides |
| now | often | today | always | by far | afterward |

E. Write in Latin the principal parts of these verbs. Indicate the present and perfect stems.

free    sit    move    aid    pray    adore    shout    stand

F. Conjugate in Latin and translate the perfect, pluperfect, and future perfect tenses of: sum, moveō, līberō.

G. Write in Latin the specified forms and translate:
1. genitive plural: equus, scūtum, taberna, auxilium
2. dative singular: dea, populus, sīgnum, captīvus
3. accusative plural: templum, numerus, praeda, imperium
4. ablative singular: dīligentia, studium, gladius, aedificium

H. Translate into Latin the italicized words or phrases:
1. He walked *with a friend.*
2. He worked *with eagerness.*
3. They ran *out of the house.*
4. You remained *in the town.*
5. You lived *at Rome.*
6. He wounded the man *with a sword.*
7. She gave a reward *to the children.*
8. I hurried *into school.*
9. They answered *clearly.*
10. He jumped *down from the horse.*

I. Write in Latin the positive and negative imperatives of these verbs, and translate:

SINGULAR: līberō, moveō, stō, sedeō, adōrō
PLURAL: moneō, ōrō, clāmō, doceō, parō


## SENTENCE PATTERNS

A. Translate into English:
1. Etiam nunc māgna est fāma populī Rōmānī et viārum Rōmānārum.
2. Virī validī praedam et cibum ē prōvinciīs ad oppida Ītaliae carrīs et equīs portāverant.
3. Num captīvī māgnā cum dīligentiā impedīmenta mōvērunt?
4. Properābantne māgnae cōpiae per viās angustās?
5. Date, nūntiī, Rōmānō clārō mandāta et litterās.
6. Imperium Rōmānum bonās viās habēbat quod Rōmānī multōs servōs habēbant.
7. Hodiē in Britanniā, in Galliā, in Ītaliā antīquās viās saepe vidēmus.
8. Litterās quoque nūntiī per viās portāvērunt.
9. Prope māgnum aedificium virī industriē labōrābant.
10. Ubi servī longās viās parāverint, Rōmānī ad bellum properābunt.

B. Translate into Latin:
1. The Roman people often fought with great eagerness.
2. Before the first hour there was a large number of horses and wagons on the street between the temple and the shops.

3. Did not the famous Roman warn the people about the dangers?
4. The farmers had labored industriously with the slaves.
5. With swords and weapons the slaves overcame the masters.

## SIGHT TRANSLATION: APPIUS CLAUDIUS

Cornēlia et puerī in Viā Appiā ambulābant. Cornēlia puerīs fābulās dē aedificiīs pūblicīs et templīs deōrum deārumque narrābat. "Rōma aedificia templaque clāra habēbat, sed Rōma etiam multōs et clārōs virōs semper habēbat. Fābulam dē virō clārō narrābō."

"In Viā Appiā nunc ambulāmus. Quis Viam Appiam aedificāvit?"

"Appius Claudius, Rōmānus clārus, longam et bonam viam ad Capuam, oppidum Ītaliae, aedificāvit. Sunt multae viae in Ītaliā sed Via Appia clārissima (*the most famous*) est."

"Appius Claudius etiam māgnum et longum aquaeductum aedificāvit. Aquaeductus bonam aquam in Rōmam portābat. Via Appia et ruīnae aquaeductūs Appiānī hodiē manent. Ruīnās clārē vidēmus."

What is called eloquence in the forum is
commonly found to be rhetoric in the study.
—Henry David Thoreau, 1817–1862

# *Unit* XVI

## CONVERSATION

HENRĪCUS: Ubi erat Forum Rōmānum, magister?

MAGISTER: Prope Tiberis rīpās et inter Capitōlium et Palātium erat Forum Rōmānum. Prīmō locus negōtī erat.

ROBERTUS: Nōnne multae tabernae prope Forum erant?

MAGISTER: Ōlim Rōmānī parvās tabernās ibi aedificāverant. Posteā virī clārī basilicās et templa et monumenta et aedificia pūblica aedificāvērunt.

ANNA: Undique erant multa simulācra (*images*) deōrum et statuae clārōrum virōrum atque altae columnae.

ROBERTA: In Forō erant Cūria et Templum Concordiae et Rōstra.

MAGISTER: Quis populum Rōmānum in Rōstrīs saepe monēbat?

ROBERTA: Cicerō in Rōstrīs saepe stābat et populum Rōmānum dē māgnīs perīculīs Rōmae monēbat. Catilīna, vir malus, cum multīs sociīs Rōmam ac cūnctam Ītaliam vāstāre dēsīderāvit. Cicerō multīs verbīs Rōmam servāvit.

MAGISTER: Multa verba virī clārī memoriā tenēre dēbēmus.

## SECTION 1 Summary of Tenses

### ▶ DISCUSSION

One of the surest ways to learn a verb accurately is to summarize the similarities and the differences in the formation of the tenses. In the chart given here, you will notice how simple and logical is the formation of the Latin verb.

| STEM | TENSE | TENSE INDICATOR | PERSON INDICATOR | |
|------|-------|-----------------|------------------|---|
| *Present* | Present | (1) long –ā | –ō, –s, –t | –mus, –tis, –nt |
| | | (2) long –ē | –ō, –s, –t | –mus, –tis, –nt |
| | Imperfect | –bā– | –m, –s, –t | –mus, –tis, –nt |
| | Future | –bi– | –ō, –s, –t | –mus, –tis, –nt |
| *Perfect* | Perfect | — | –ī, –istī, –it | –imus, –istis, –ērunt |
| | Pluperfect | –erā– | –m, –s, –t | –mus, –tis, –nt |
| | Fut. Perfect | –eri– | –ō, –s, –t | –mus, –tis, –nt |

The Latin verb really includes: an *action* indicator, a *time* indicator, and a *person* indicator. The stem tells the action; the tense sign is the time indicator; the person indicator tells who or what performed the action.

Note that in the Latin verb action came first, time second, and person last.

**portā/bi /t**
*carry /will/he*

In English we usually reverse this process. It is well to translate a Latin verb in the following order:

Person Indicator → Time Indicator → Action Indicator

▶ PRACTICE PATTERNS

In the following verb forms, separate the stem, the time indicator, and the person indicator: portā/bi/t. Translate into English.

| | | | | |
|---|---|---|---|---|
| **ōrābāmus** | **manēbimus** | **mōverat** | **habuerimus** | **adfuerat** |
| **tenēbat** | **servāvit** | **adfueritis** | **vāstāveris** | **adōrāvimus** |

# SECTION 2 The Meaning of Synopsis

▶ DISCUSSION

A synopsis is an organized plan, which is both short and simple, for remembering the conjugation of a verb. *Synopsis* is a Greek word that means literally *a general view*. A complete synopsis of a verb includes a summary of the forms of a given person and number throughout all voices, moods, and tenses. In this lesson our synopsis will be of the *active voice* and *indicative mood* only.

In writing the synopsis of a verb, it is important that the principal parts should be placed first and the stems indicated. The following is the synopsis of the verb *vocō* in the active voice, indicative mood, third person, singular number.

| | *Pres. Ind.* | *Pres. Inf.* | *Perf. Ind.* | *Perf. Pass. Part.* |
|---|---|---|---|---|
| PRINCIPAL PARTS: | **vocō** | **vocā/re** | **vocāv/ī** | **vocātus, –a, –um** |

| | | |
|---|---|---|
| Present | **vocat** | *he calls, is calling, does call* |
| Imperfect | **vocābat** | *he was calling, used to call, called* |
| Future | **vocābit** | *he will call, will be calling* |
| Perfect | **vocāvit** | *he called, has called, did call* |
| Pluperfect | **vocāverat** | *he had called* |
| Future Perfect | **vocāverit** | *he will have called* |

# SECTION 3 Auxiliary Verbs

▶ **DISCUSSION**

There are *no auxiliary verbs in Latin* for the active voice. However, an accurate knowledge of auxiliary verbs in English is essential for the correct translation of verbs into Latin.

Present:  *am, is, are, do, does*  Perfect:  *have, has, did*
Imperfect: *was, were*  Pluperfect:  *had*
Future:  *shall, will*  Future Perfect: *shall have, will have*

▶ **PRACTICE PATTERNS**

Write the following synopses. Translate into English:

1. third person singular: vāstō
2. first person singular: dō
3. second person plural: pertineō

4. first person plural: teneō
5. third person plural: servō
6. second person singular: sum

## WORDS TO MASTER

**cir′cum,** *prep. with acc.,* around, about (*circumnavigate*)

**con′trā,** *adv., and prep. with acc.,* opposite, against (*contrary*)

**lit′tera, –ae,** *f.,* letter of the alphabet; **litterae, –ārum,** *pl.,* letter, epistle (*literature*)

**lo′cus, –ī,** *m.,* place, region; *pl. regularly* **loca, –ōrum,** *n.* (*local*)

**memo′ria, –ae,** *f.,* memory (*memorial*)

**mū′rus, –ī,** *m.,* wall (*mural*)

**perti′neō, –ēre, –uī, —** (2), extend to, arrive at, relate to (*pertinent*)

**por′ta, –ae,** *f.,* gate, door (portal)

**rī′pa, –ae,** *f.,* bank (*riparian*)

**ser′vō**(1), keep, save, guard (*preserve*)

**te′neō, –ēre, –uī, tentus** (2), hold, keep, occupy (*tenet*); **memoriā tenēre,** remember

**vās′tō** (1), lay waste, ravage, destroy (*devastate*)

## BUILDING WORD POWER

Did you ever hear of anyone having an *aquiline* nose? Where are your *canine* teeth? Why is someone who is sneaky said to have *feline* ways? Have you had an injection of *vaccine* recently? Does *columbine* grow in your garden? Have you ever seen golden poppies intermingled with blue *lupine* on a California hillside? Did you ever preserve specimens in a *saline* solution?

Each italicized word above has a synonym in the following list: *dovelike, eaglelike, doglike, catlike, wolflike, cowlike, salty.* As you probably have already guessed, the suffix **–īnus** has the same meaning as **–ānus,** or, as we sometimes express the idea in English, –*like*. What do the words *divine* and *feminine* mean?

The flower of the *columbine* resembles a group of *doves*, hence its name; but it is difficult to see the relation between the dainty blue *lupine* and the *wolf* after which it is named. Do you know that if you are *capricious* (**caper,** *goat*) in your moods, you are also *hircine*, acting like a *goat* (**hircus**)?

## SENTENCE PATTERNS

A. Complete with the required form and translate:
1. Rōmānī propinqua loca (were ravaging).
2. Virī prope rīpam industriē labōrant et fēminae virōs (are aiding).
3. Fīnitimī inimīcī ubi mūrum circum oppidum (they will have built) contrā Rōmānōs (will fight).
4. Agrōs sociōrum (they had laid waste), sed incolās servāverant.
5. Mūrus Rōmānus multās portās (has), et per portās multī Rōmānī cotīdiē (walked).
6. Nōnne viae longae lātaeque ab Ītaliā ad multās terrās (did extend)?
7. Portābantne (messengers) litterās saepe ad locum?
8. Ōlim (there were) multae tabernae (on all sides), sed posteā virī clārī aedificia pulchra (built).
9. Sī sociī Rōmānōs nōn (will have aided), Rōmānī agrōs sociōrum (will lay waste).
10. Portam bene memoriā teneō. Per portam et circum oppidum saepe (I walked).

B. Translate into Latin the italicized words or phrases.
1. If the Romans *will have built* a wall *around the town*, the inhabitants *will not fear* the enemy.
2. Cicero *with many words warned the Roman people about the great danger* to the fatherland.
3. The Sacra Via *is not far away* from the Rostra, where *the famous Roman is standing*.
4. *On all sides there used to be* many *shops*.
5. *They fought* in many wars *against hostile neighbors*.

## The Glory of Ancient Rome

Paulus et Patricius cum amīcīs ad Forum Rōmānum properābant. Forum, magnum spatium oblongum inter Capitōlium et Palātīnum, in mediō (*middle of*) oppidō prope rīpam Tiberis erat. Prīmō Forum erat locus negōtī, et undique erant parvae tabernae.

Posteā Rōmānī clārī aedificia māgna pulchraque ibi aedificāvērunt. Comitium (*Place of Assembly*) prope tabernās erat. In
aedificiō Mārcī Aemilī, Rōmānī negōtia pūblica cūrābant. Prope
monumentum erat Cūria ubi senātōrēs Rōmānī congregābant.
Nōn longē ā Cūriā erant Āra (*Altar*) deī Vulcānī et Templum deī
Jānī et carcer (*prison*) et Rōstra ubi multī virī clārī ōrātiōnēs
habēbant (*delivered speeches*). Cicerō ibi populum Rōmānum
dē virīs malīs monēbat.

Paulus et Patricius cum amīcīs per templa et circum aedificia
ambulāvērunt. Templum Vestae in Forō erat. Ibi sex puellae,
Virginēs Vestālēs, flammam perpetuam Vestae semper servābant.
Prope Templum Vestae stābat atrium ubi Virginēs habitābant.
Multae statuae Virginum Vestālium clārārum ibi erant.

Puerī Templum Sāturnī, deī agricultūrae, et Templum pulchrum Castoris et Pollūcis amābant. Castor et Pollūx in bellō
Rōmānōs adjūverant et Rōmam servāverant. Multī nūntiī ad
Rōstra litterās ē virīs clārīs et ē prōvinciīs portābant. Senātōrēs
nōbilēs in quadrīgīs (*chariots*), fēminae pulchrae in lectīcīs (*litters*),
agricolae cum equīs et carrīs per Forum cotīdiē properābant.
Puellae et puerī, māgnī et parvī, in viīs et prope aedificia lūdēbant
(*used to play*).

Puerī vērō aedificia splendida amābant et bene memoriā tenēbunt. Sed quid est hodiē in Forō Rōmānō? Tristēs (*sad*) ruīnās
spectāmus. Nōn jam (*No longer*) virī et fēminae in templīs
pulchrīs multōs deōs adōrant. Nōn jam senātōrēs superbī (*proud*)
in Cūriā negōtia pūblica cūrant. Nōn jam Rōmānī clārī ē
Rōstrīs ōrātiōnēs habent. Līberī laetī inter ruīnās lūdunt. Forum
Rōmānum locus desertus est, sed ruīnae pulchrae cūnctīs populīs
glōriam Rōmae antīquae vērē prōclāmant.

"When falls the Coliseum, Rome shall fall;
And when Rome falls—the world."
—Pilgrims, *Childe Harold's Pilgrimage*
George Gordon, Lord Byron, 1788–1824

# *Unit* XVII

## CONVERSATION

MAGISTER: Quī servus contrā dominōs Rōmānōs pūgnāvit, Roberte?
ROBERTUS: Spartacus gladiātor sociōs ad bellum incitāvit et contrā
populum Rōmānum māgnō cum studiō pūgnāvērunt.
MAGISTER: Cūr servus clārus sociōs convocāvit et incitāvit?
ROBERTUS: Spartacus cūnctōs servōs līberāre dēsīderāvit.

| | |
|---|---|
| HENRĪCUS: | Cotīdiē servī cum servīs in arēnā pūgnābant et cotīdiē gladiīs amīcōs ac sociōs necāvērunt. |
| MAGISTER: | Quem Spartacus necāvit, Henrīce? |
| HENRĪCUS: | Mārcum, amīcum cārum, necāvit. Posteā gladiātōrēs ac sociōs convocāvit et contrā Rōmānōs incitāvit. |
| MAGISTER: | Quōrum armīs servī pūgnāvērunt, Roberte? |
| ROBERTUS: | Gladiīs suīs (*their own*) multōs Rōmānōs necāvērunt. |
| MAGISTER: | Quī Spartacum sociōsque superāvērunt ac necāvērunt? |
| ROBERTUS: | Post duōs (*two*) annōs Crassus et Pompējus miserōs servōs superāvērunt. Multōs in proeliō necāvērunt. |
| MAGISTER: | Diū Rōmānī facta Spartacī memoriā tenuērunt. |

## SECTION 1 Interrogative Pronouns

▶ DISCUSSION

In English the interrogative pronouns are *who? whose? whom? which? what?* *Who* is there? *Whose* book is this? *To whom* did you speak? *Whom* did you see? *With whom* did you walk? *Which* is it? *What* is it? *Who? whose? whom?* refer to persons; *what?* to things; *which?* to either persons or things.

In the Conversation at the beginning of each lesson, you have often used the Latin for the above interrogatives, particularly in the singular. You will now learn the entire declension.

In Latin there is but one interrogative pronoun corresponding to the English *who? which?* and *what?*, but it has various forms as it is declined. In English *who? which? what?* may refer to either a singular or plural noun; therefore the translation of the Latin forms into English is the same for both singular and plural. In the singular the same forms are used for the masculine and feminine interrogative pronouns.

SINGULAR

| | M. & F. | | | N. | |
|---|---|---|---|---|---|
| Nom. | **quis?** | *who?* | | **quid?** | *what?* |
| Gen. | **cūjus?** | *whose? of whom?* | | **cūjus?** | *of what?* |
| Dat. | **cui?** | *to, for whom?* | | **cui?** | *to, for what?* |
| Acc. | **quem?** | *whom?* | | **quid?** | *what?* |
| Abl. | **quō?** | *from, by, with whom?* | | **quō?** | *from, by, with what?* |

|      | M.       | F.       |                     | N.       |                     |
|------|----------|----------|---------------------|----------|---------------------|
| Nom. | **quī?** | **quae?** | *who?*             | **quae?** | *what?*            |
| Gen. | **quōrum?** | **quārum?** | *whose? of whom?* | **quōrum?** | *of what?*       |
| Dat. | **quibus?** | **quibus?** | *to, for whom?*  | **quibus?** | *to, for what?*  |
| Acc. | **quōs?** | **quās?** | *whom?*            | **quae?** | *what?*            |
| Abl. | **quibus?** | **quibus?** | *from, by, with whom?* | **quibus?** | *from, by, with what?* |

▶ STUDY HELPS

1. The genitive, dative, and ablative singular, and the dative and ablative plural have the same case forms for all genders.

2. When *quō?* and *quibus?* are used with the preposition *cum, cum* is attached to them, forming single words, *quōcum? quibuscum?*

# SECTION 2 Interrogative Adjectives

▶ DISCUSSION

The interrogative pronoun *who?* cannot be used as an adjective in English. We do not say: *Who* man? but *What* man? *Which* man? *What* or *which*, as interrogative adjectives, may be used with persons or things: *What* woman? *What* book? *Which* woman? *Which* book?

In Latin the interrogative adjectives for the English *which, what* have special forms for each of the genders of the singular. The forms of the *interrogative adjective* in the *plural* are identical with the forms of the *interrogative pronoun* in the *plural*.

|      | SINGULAR | | | | PLURAL | | |
|------|----------|----------|----------|----------------------|----------|----------|----------|
|      | M.       | F.       | N.       |                      | M.       | F.       | N.       |
| Nom. | **quī**  | **quae** | **quod** | *which, what*        | **quī**  | **quae** | **quae** |
| Gen. | **cūjus** | **cūjus** | **cūjus** | *of which, what*   | **quōrum** | **quārum** | **quōrum** |
| Dat. | **cui**  | **cui**  | **cui**  | *to, for which, what* | **quibus** | **quibus** | **quibus** |
| Acc. | **quem** | **quam** | **quod** | *which, what*        | **quōs** | **quās** | **quae** |
| Abl. | **quō**  | **quā**  | **quō**  | *from, by, with which, what* | **quibus** | **quibus** | **quibus** |

▶ STUDY HELPS

1. The English translation is the same for all genders, singular and plural.

2. The *masculine* interrogative *adjective* and *pronoun* differ in the *nominative singular* only; the neuter adjective and pronoun, in the

nominative and accusative singular only; the feminine adjective and pronoun differ in the nominative, accusative, and ablative singular.

PRONOUN

**Quis abest?** *Who* is absent?      **Quid vidēs?** *What* (sing.) do you see?
**Quī absunt?** *Who* are absent?      **Quae vidēs?** *What* (pl.) do you see?

ADJECTIVE

**Quī puer** (**Quae puella**) **abest?**     *What* boy (*What* girl) is absent?
**Quī puerī** (**Quae puellae**) **absunt?** *What* boys (*What* girls) are absent?
**Quod sīgnum vidēs?**            *What* standard do you see?
**Quae sīgna vidēs?**             *What* standards do you see?

▶ PRACTICE PATTERNS

Decline in Latin and translate:
     What man?    What sailor?    Which lady?    What danger?

## WORDS TO MASTER

**ae′quus, –a, –um,** *adj.*, equal, even, fair (*equity*)

**an′nus, –ī,** *m.*, year (*annual*)

**a′pud,** *prep. with acc.*, near, at, among

**ar′ma, –ōrum,** *n. pl.*, arms, weapons (*armament*)

**con′vocō** (1), call together, summon (*convoke*)

**di′ū,** *adv.*, for a long time

**fac′tum, –ī,** *n.*, deed, act (*fact*)

**in′citō** (1), urge on, stir up (*incite*)

**ne′cō** (1), put to death, kill (*internecine*)

**nūn′tiō** (1), announce, report (*pronunciation*)

**offi′cium, –ī,** *n.*, service, duty, employment (*office*)

**proe′lium, –ī,** *n.*, battle

## BUILDING WORD POWER

To *diminish* something means *to make it smaller, to reduce it in size, importance, degree, etc.* When the Romans wanted to indicate something very small, they added a suffix, called a *diminutive* to the noun stem. In Latin this suffix may assume one of several forms: *–culus, –ellus, –olus; –cle, –el, –le* in English.

If **gladius** means *sword*, what is the true meaning of *gladiola?* A **gladiolus** was a *sword lily* in ancient times. Through ear-Latin **avunculus**, *a little grandfather* (**avus**), became *uncle*. **Calx** was a *stone* used as a counter in gaming. What did **calculus** mean? A **calculator** was one who taught arithmetic in a Roman school. What do *calculus* and *calculator* mean in modern times?

A **scrūpus** was a *sharp stone;* a **scrūpulus,** *a little sharp stone,* which

94

might be a source of annoyance if it got into your shoe. Later a *scruple* meant *annoyance of conscience* or a *small weight* used by an apothecary. What do *animalcule, formula, particle, granule, globule, corpuscle* mean?

## SENTENCE PATTERNS

A. Translate into English:

1. Quis erat Spartacus?  Spartacus erat servus clārus.
2. Cūjus amīcus est Mārcus?  Mārcus est amīcus servī clārī.
3. Cui Spartacus fābulam narrāvit?  Quōs Spartacus incitāvit?
4. Quibuscum servī pūgnāverant?  Quī servōs superābunt?
5. Quī servus sociōs incitāverit?  Quārum prōvinciārum Rōmānī erant dominī?
   Quōcum Spartacus in arēnā stābit?
6. Quem servus clārus necāvit?  Quōs Rōmānī necāvērunt?
7. Quae erant officia dominōrum aequōrum?
8. Quōrum arma et scūta servī portāverant?
9. Quae proelia nūntiī populō Rōmānō nūntiāvērunt?
10. Quōs servōs Spartacus convocāvit et incitāvit?

B. Translate into Latin:

1. What evil deeds of the Romans did the slave announce to his friends?
2. In what battle did the masters kill the slaves?
3. Who was urging on his companions for a long time?
4. With whom did the Romans fight?  Whom did they kill?
5. After many years, who freed the slaves?

The Colosseum today.

## Pagan Amusements

If you were to visit Rome today, you would see in the heart of the city the ruins of an immense circular stadium. This in its day was the most famous of the many Roman amphitheaters, the Colosseum. Completed in A.D. 80, it was known as the Flavian amphitheater. There were many such stadiums throughout the Roman Empire, and some of them are still in use, but not for the purposes for which they were built — gladiatorial combats, animal hunts, and other forms of savage amusement.

Gladiators were men who fought with swords in public contests. The word gladiator comes from *gladius*, meaning sword. The gladiatorial combat was borrowed by the Romans from the Etruscans, who celebrated funerals of important people by forcing men to kill one another in sword duels. Eventually these degrading demonstrations developed into the most popular form of entertainment.

The first gladiatorial combat on record in Roman history occurred in 264 B.C. In A.D. 404 the Roman Emperor Honorius suppressed these spectacles in the West by imperial edict. In the interim of 668 years, men were trained to butcher men for the amusement of the Roman people.

The gladiators were slaves, captives, or condemned criminals. They were trained in special schools for single or group combat. Some of these schools were government-supported, with the direct encouragement of the Emperors. As long as the rabble had amusements to occupy their thoughts and free food to satisfy their hunger, there was less danger of revolt against the government.

The gladiatorial contest began with a procession of the gladiators through the arena. As they passed before the magistrate responsible for giving the games, they saluted him with the words: "Nos morituri te salutamus!" *We about to die salute you!*

For the animal hunts and contests, thousands of wild beasts were brought to the amphitheater from all parts of the empire. Sometimes the contests consisted of mock hunts in which specially trained men killed the beasts. Sometimes the struggle was between the animals themselves. But very often the contest was between animals, which had been purposely starved, and armed or unarmed men.

Sometimes, the arena was flooded for mock sea battles. A vast network of water and drainage pipes under the arena floor transformed the amphitheater into a lake in a matter of hours. Sailors on the decks of galleys manned by scores of rowers fought to the death for the pleasure of Roman holiday crowds.


### Hero: Spartacus or Telemachus?

Ōlim Rōmae fuit servus clārus, captīvus Rōmānōrum. Sociōs convocāvit et nūntiāvit: "Ō gladiātōrēs, sumusne virī? Cūr prō dominīs malīs amīcōs sociōsque nostrōs necāmus? Cūr servī

sumus? Nōn semper servī fuimus. Nōn semper servus fuī.
Ōlim fuī līber! Ōlim domicilium pulchrum, agrōs lātōs, patriam,
amīcōs habēbam.

"Tum Rōmānī domicilia, agrōs, patriam vāstāvērunt. Virōs et
puerōs ad Ītaliam portāvērunt. Ego (I) et Mārcus, amīcus meus,
captīvī, servī, gladiātōrēs mox erāmus. Cotīdiē in arēnā contrā
amīcōs et sociōs gladiīs pūgnābāmus. Hodiē in arēnā Mārcum
necāvī. Nunc contrā Rōmānōs gladiō pūgnābō. Rōmānōs
necābō. Līberī erimus! Ad arma! Pro servīs et prō patriā
pūgnāte!"

Sīc Spartacus miser māgnō cum studiō gladiātōrēs incitāvit.
Per duōs annōs servī contrā dominōs Rōmānōs pūgnābant.
Multōs agrōs et multa oppida cūnctae Ītaliae vāstāvērunt. Tum
Crassus et Pompējus servōs miserōs superāvērunt et necāvērunt.
Spartacus servōs, amīcōs et sociōs, nōn līberāverat.

Post multōs annōs Tēlemachus, vir bonus, in amphitheātrō
Rōmānō sedēbat. Gladiātōrēs tristis (sad) spectābat. Servōs
amāvit quod cūnctōs virōs amāvit. Subitō in arēnam dēsiluit
(leaped). Gladiātōrēs īrātī (angered) factum Tēlemachī nōn comprehendērunt (did not understand) et virum necāvērunt. Sed multī
spectātōrēs Rōmānī factum comprehendērunt et laudāvērunt.
Tēlemachus prō servīs vītam dederat. Numquam iterum gladiātōrēs pūgnāvērunt. Mox multī Rōmānī servōs miserōs lībe-
rāvērunt.

Two things only the people anxiously desire— *Unit* XVIII
bread and circuses.
—Juvenal, A.D. 47–138

## CONVERSATION

SEXTUS: Herī in scholā esse nōn poteram. Ad Circum ambulāvī.
MĀRCELLUS: Poterāsne subsellium (seat) idōneum obtinēre?
SEXTUS: Māgnus numerus virōrum puerōrumque paene cūncta sub-
sellia tenēbat, sed prope terminum arēnae sedēbam unde
lūdōs spectāre poteram. Diū exspectābam.
MĀRCELLUS: Quōs gladiātōrēs nōtōs vidistī?
SEXTUS: Herī gladiātōrēs nōn aderant. Equōs et quadrīgās (chari-
ots) et aurīgās (charioteers) spectāvimus.

**97**

| MĀRCELLUS: | Certāmen quadrīgārum (*chariot race*) Rōmānōs semper dēlectat. Quī erant aurīgae notī? |
| SEXTUS: | Pūblius, Syrus, Lydus, Āfer in quadrīgīs aderant. Tunicās ac pilleōs (*caps*) multōrum colōrum habēbant. Propinquī pompae (*of the parade*) portīs sīgnum exspectāvērunt. |
| MĀRCELLUS: | Quem colōrem Pūblius habuit? Eratne grātus populō Rōmānō? |
| SEXTUS: | Pūblius tunicam ac pilleum album habuit. Māgnō cum animō in quadrīgīs stābat. Pūblium populus probāvit. |

## SECTION 1 Conjugation of *possum*

▶ DISCUSSION

The verb **possum** is a compound of the verb **sum** and the adjective **potis** (*able*):

$$\text{potis} + \text{sum} = \text{pot}\!\!\not{s}\text{sum} = \text{possum} = \text{I am able}$$

Notice in the following paradigm that *-t* becomes *-s* before all forms of **sum** beginning with *s-*.

### PRESENT INDICATIVE OF POSSUM

#### SINGULAR

| | | | |
|---|---|---|---|
| po$\not{t}$(s) + sum | = possum | = *I am able, can* |
| pot | + es | = potes | = *you are able, can* |
| pot | + est | = potest | = *he, she, it is able, can* |

#### PLURAL

| | | | |
|---|---|---|---|
| po$\not{t}$(s) + sumus | = possumus | = *we are able, can* |
| pot | + estis | = potestis | = *you are able, can* |
| po$\not{t}$(s) + sunt | = possunt | = *they are able, can* |

### SYNOPSIS OF POSSUM

PRINCIPAL PARTS: **possum, posse, potui, —**, *be able, can*

| | | |
|---|---|---|
| Present | potest | *he, she, it is able, can* |
| Imperfect | poterat | *he, she, it was able, could* |
| Future | poterit | *he, she, it will be able* |
| Perfect | potuit | *he, she, it has been able, could* |
| Pluperfect | potuerat | *he, she, it had been able* |
| Future Perfect | potuerit | *he, she, it will have been able* |

▶ STUDY HELPS

1. **Possum** has no forms in the imperative mood.

2. The imperfect and future tenses are the same as the imperfect and future of **sum** plus the prefix **pot-**: **poteram, poterō**.

98

3. In the formation of the *perfect stem*, the *–f–* drops out after *–t.*

**pot + fuī = potꞁfuī = potuī** = *I have been able, I could*

4. ***Possum*** requires an infinitive to complete its meaning. This use is the same as in English (*see* Complementary Infinitive, p. 60).

5. Do not confuse ***po'terat***, *he was able*, with ***potu'erat***, *he had been able;* nor ***po'terit***, *he will be able*, with ***potu'erit***, *he will have been able*. Note the differences in pronunciation and meaning.

▶ PRACTICE PATTERNS

A. Write a synopsis of possum, third person, plural number. Give the English translation.

B. Write the conjugation of the imperfect, pluperfect, future, and future perfect tenses of possum, and translate. Mark the accent in each form.

# SECTION 2 Dative with Adjectives

▶ DISCUSSION

The dative is used with certain Latin adjectives that in English are followed by a phrase introduced by *to* or *for*. Sometimes the preposition is omitted in English; otherwise the usage is the same in both languages. These adjectives denote likeness, fitness, nearness, friendliness, usefulness, and their opposites.

Examine the following:

1. **praemium** *grātum puerīs*     a reward *pleasing to the boys*
2. **locus** *templō idōneus*     a place *suitable for a temple*
3. **oppidum** *propinquum silvae*     a town *close to the forest*
4. **dominus** *inīquus servīs*     a master *unjust to the slaves*
5. **puer** *inimīcus magistrō*     a boy *unfriendly to the teacher*

## BUILDING WORD POWER

The adjective ***potis*** means *able* or *capable*. ***Potis + sum = possum***, *I am able*. From this combination of two words we have some useful English derivatives. The infinitive ***posse*** became a noun in English and has come to mean a group legally summoned to assist a sheriff.

From the present participle ***potēns*** (*having power over*), we have the words italicized in the following sentences:

1. The *potent* (*powerful*) remedy was used with great caution.
2. The *potency* (*power*) of his reasons settled the argument.
3. The happiness of a people depends much on the type of their *potentate* (*one having power, ruler*).
4. A tightly coiled spring has *potential* (*possible*) energy.
5. The teacher encouraged the boy because he thought the boy had great *potentiality* (*possibility*).

From **posse**, *to be able*, we have also our words *possible* and *possibility* and their negatives.

## WORDS TO MASTER

**a′nimus, –ī,** *m.*, spirit, mind, courage (*animosity*)

**dēlec′tō** (1), please, delight (*delectation*)

**exspec′tō** (1), wait, wait for (*expect*)

**grā′tus, –a, –um,** *adj.*, pleasing, pleasant, acceptable (*gratify*)

**idō′neus, –a, –um,** *adj.*, suitable, fit

**inī′quus, –a, –um,** *adj.*, unequal, unjust (*iniquity*)

**nō′tus, –a, –um,** *adj.*, well-known, familiar (*notable*)

**obti′neō, –ēre, –uī, –tentus** (2), hold fast, hold, acquire, get (*obtain*)

**pro′bō** (1), prove, approve (*probation*)

**ter′minus, –ī,** *m.*, limit, end (*terminal*)

**un′de,** *rel. adv.*, whence, from which; *interrog. adv.*, whence?

**vo′lō** (1), fly, rush (*volatile*)

## SENTENCE PATTERNS

A. Translate into English:

1. Locum altum habēre dēsīderāvī unde equōs clārē vidēre potuī.
2. Nōnne lūdī līberōs laetōs dēlectāvērunt?
3. Saepe Rōmānī virōs validōs bellō obtinēre poterant.
4. Captīvī māgnō cum animō in arēnam ambulāvērunt.
5. Arēna erat locus lūdīs idōneus atque puerīs grātus.
6. Multī Rōmānī servīs erant inīquī, et multī servī Rōmānīs erant inimīcī.
7. Nōtus dominus lūdōrum tubā sīgnum dederat.
8. Nōnne puerī cum studiō equōs exspectābant?
9. Equī circum prīmam portam volāvērunt.
10. Puerī locum propinquum terminō arēnae probāvērunt.

B. Translate into Latin:

1. Were the boys able to obtain suitable places near the end of the arena?
2. The men were urging on the horses with many words.
3. A well-known man was giving the games to the people.
4. When men killed men, the good Romans did not approve the deed.
5. The games delighted the children, but they could not see the horses clearly.

## A Day at the Races

"Cūr properās, Sexte? Quō vadis (*are you going*)?"

"Ad Circum Māximum et ad certāmen quadrigārum (*chariot race*) properō, Fabī. Vinicius, nōtus fīlius cōnsulis, populō lūdōs hodiē dabit, et equōs nigrōs (*black*) vidēbimus, sī properāverimus. Locum altum dēsīderō unde equōs vidēre poterō. Properā, Fabī, sī placet."

"Nunc in arēnā adsumus. Quis Circum Māximum aedificāvit, Sexte?" rogāvit Fabius.

"Tarquinius Prīscus, quīntus rēx (*king*) Rōmānus — ut (*as*) fāma est — Circum Māximum aedificāvit," respondit Sextus. "Vidē! Arēna longa angustaque est equīs et quadrīgīs idōnea. Circus Māximus est similis (*like*) stadiō ubi sunt multa subsellia.'

"Cūr longus mūrus in mediā (*in the middle of*) arēnā est?"

"Spīna est. Nōn est alta, sed arēnam dīvidit. Prope terminōs spīnae sunt mētae (*goals*). Mētae sunt trēs (*three*) altae columnae. Super (*Upon*) spīnam multās statuās aurīgārum et equōrum nōtōrum vidēre potes. Jūdicēs (*Judges*) super spīnam prope mētās stābunt."

"Ubi sunt quadrīgae?" iterum iterumque rogāvit Fabius.

"Mox pompam (*parade*) vidēbimus. Paene semper ante certāmen (*contest*) est pompa," nūntiāvit Sextus.

Tum subitō virī et puerī stābant ac clāmābant: "Iō pompa! Iō pompa!" Per portam ambulābat pompa. In pompā erat Vinicius, cōnsulis fīlius. Populō lūdōs dabat. Post Vinicium dominus lūdōrum et virī clārī prōcēdēbant (*advanced*). Servī simulācra (*images*) deōrum et statuās aurīgārum nōtōrum portābant. (Crās fābulam certāminis narrābō.)

But at my back I always hear
Time's wingèd chariot hurrying near . . .
—Andrew Marvell, 1620–1678

# *Unit* XIX

## CONVERSATION

SEXTUS: Grātum nōn est sīgnum et quadrīgās exspectāre!

FABIUS: Longa est mora. Per duās (*two*) hōrās pompam exspectāvimus.

SEXTUS: Pompa appropinquat. Virī clāmant: "Iō pompa!"

FABIUS: Vidē! Pompa per Forum et Viam Sacram ad Circum ambulat et nunc per Portam Pompae in Circum intrat (*enters*).

SEXTUS: Iō pompa! Equōs atque aurīgās vidēre dēsīderō!
FABIUS: Dominum lūdōrum vidēre temptō! Post Vinicium, cōnsulis fīlium, ambulat. Quadrīgae ad portās appropinquant.
SEXTUS: Nunc quadrīgae prope portās stant! Vir tubā sīgnum dat! Vidē! Dominus lūdōrum mappam (*flag*) albam levāvit!
FABIUS: Quadrīgae ē portīs sine (*without*) morā volāre temptant!
SEXTUS: Āfer paene prīmus est! Nōlī dubitāre, Āfer! Equōs incitā!
FABIUS: Āfer tunicam albam habet. Prīmum locum tenē, Āfer!
SEXTUS: Nunc Lydus rotās Afrī quadrīgārum dēlēre temptat! Pūblius pilleum ac tunicam rubram (*red*) habet! Pūblius prīmus est!
FABIUS: Miser Āfer injūriās, palmam victōriae Pūblius habet.

# More Uses of the Infinitive

▶ DISCUSSION

1. You have already learned that the infinitive in English and Latin may be used to complete the meaning of other verbs. The infinitive has other uses that are almost the same in both languages.

The infinitive is a *verbal noun*. As a verb it may have a subject, an object, and adverbial modifiers. As a noun it is neuter singular, and may be itself a subject, object, or predicate noun in a sentence.

2. The infinitive may be used as the subject of **est, erat, erit,** etc., and of certain impersonal verbs. These verbs are called impersonal because they have no person or thing as subject. They are used only in the third person singular and may have an infinitive as a subject. This construction is common in English, where we regularly use the impersonal pronoun *it* to indicate the subject:

It is pleasant *to walk.* (*To walk* is pleasant.)     **Ambulāre est grātum.**

3. In English and in Latin such verbs as **jubeō,** *order,* **prohibeō,** *keep away,* **doceō,** *teach,* **dēsīderō,** *long for,* **vetō,** *forbid,* may have an infinitive as *object,* with a noun or pronoun in the accusative that may be regarded as the *subject* of the infinitive.

**Agricola *servōs labōrāre* docuit.**     The farmer taught *the slaves to work.* The object of **docuit** consists of the infinitive **labōrāre** with its subject **servōs.**

4. The infinitive may be used as a *predicate nominative* after various forms of **esse,** *to be.*

**Vidēre est crēdere.**     To see is *to believe.* (Seeing is believing.)

**Crēdere** is a predicate nominative after the verb **est.**

102

1. No subject is expressed for the *complementary infinitive* since the subject is the same as the main verb.

> **Vir *labōrāre* dēsīderat.**   The man desires *to work.*

2. An *objective infinitive* always has a subject in the accusative case.

> **Vir *servōs labōrāre* dēsīderat.**   The man desires *the slaves to work.*

3. A *subjective infinitive* may or may not have a subject in the accusative case.

> **Ambulāre est grātum.**   It is pleasant *to walk.*
> **Līberōs ambulāre est grātum.**   It is pleasant *for the children to walk.*

4. A predicate noun or adjective after a complementary infinitive is in the nominative case.

> **Puer *clārus* esse dēsīderat.**   The boy desires to be *famous.*

5. A predicate noun or adjective after an objective infinitive is in the accusative case.

> **Puer amīcum *clārum* esse dēsīderat.**   The boy desires his friend to be *famous.*

▶ PRACTICE PATTERNS

A. Select the infinitives in the following sentences. Tell whether each is used as subject, object, or complement.

1. Aurīga ambulāre nōn potest.
2. Bonōs laudāre semper dēbēmus.
3. Labōrāre bene est bonum.
4. Puerōs stāre jūssit.
5. Lūdōs spectāre est grātum.
6. Virī clāmāre nōn dubitant.

B. Translate into Latin. Tell the use of the infinitive in each sentence:

1. Caesar ordered the men to destroy the towns.
2. It is good to work with great diligence.
3. We ought to love our enemies.
4. The farmers were not able to plow the field.

## WORDS TO MASTER

**appropin′quō** (1), approach, *with* **ad + acc.,** *or with dat.* (*propinquity*)

**dē′leō, –ēre, –ēvī, –ētus** (2), destroy, wipe out (*delete*)

**du′bitō** (1), hesitate, doubt (*indubitable*)

**ini′tium, –ī,** *n.,* beginning, going in (*initial*)

**injū′ria, –ae,** *f.,* wrong, injustice, harm (*injury*)

**ju′beō, –ēre, jūssī, jūssus** (2), order, bid, command (*jussive*)

**le′vō** (1), raise (*elevate*)

**mo′ra, –ae,** *f.,* delay (*moratorium*)

**pūg′na, –ae,** *f.,* fight, battle (*pugnacious*)

**ro′ta, –ae,** *f.,* wheel (*rotary*)

**spa′tium, –ī,** *n.,* space, lap of a race-course, distance (*spatial*)

**temp′tō** (1,) try, test (*tempt*)

## BUILDiNG WORD POWER

Underlying many words in our English language is an interesting life story. It seems that on one of the hills of Rome there was a temple dedicated to the goddess **Jūnō Monētā,** Juno the Warner (**monēre,** *to warn*). According to one story, the temple got its name when, during an earthquake, Juno's voice was heard warning the Romans to appease the gods by sacrifice. The name also may have arisen from the other meaning of **monēre,** *to advise*, because Juno often gave advice, especially to women and girls.

Eventually the temple became a place where the Romans coined their money; the **Monēta** became a *mint*. By a roundabout way, through Old French, **monēta** became *money*. The word *monetary, pertaining to money,* came directly into English from the Latin.

Speaking of money, our word *salary,* from **sālārius,** *pertaining to salt*, originally meant the money the Roman soldiers received to buy salt. It was called their **sālārium,** from the Latin word **sāl,** which means *salt.*

## SENTENCE PATTERNS

A. Translate into English:

1. Caesar cōpiās agrōs vāstāre jūssit.
2. Temptāvēruntne virī ad mūrōs appropinquāre?
3. Vir nōtus miserīs auxilium dare dubitāvit.
4. Facta mala virōrum memoriā tenēre nōn dēbēmus.
5. Quōrum injūriās puerīs narrāre temptās?
6. Pecūniam dēbēre est multās cūrās habēre.
7. Quae sīgna dominus servōs levāre jūssit?
8. Eratne longa mora inter initium et terminum pūgnae?
9. Quibuscum puerī per lūdum sedēbant?
10. Quōs equōs spectāre puerī dēsīderāvērunt?

B. Translate into Latin the italicized words and phrases:

1. The boys *with many words tried to urge on* the charioteers.
2. *After a long delay* they gave the signal *by means of a trumpet.*
3. *The master* of the games *raised* the white flag, and the horses *rushed into the arena.*
4. He *commanded* his *slave to destroy the wheel.*
5. *The wheel* of the chariot broke, but *the injuries* to the rider were not *great;* he *ought to try again tomorrow.*

## The Chariot Race

**R**oman public games and spectacles, the establishment of which was attributed to Romulus, were originally religious festivals. For centuries they were held at the Circus Maximus, situated in a valley between the Aventine and Palatine Hills. This circus was an elliptical outdoor racecourse, about six hundred yards long and two hundred yards wide.

The most popular and the most frequent form of entertainment in the Circus Maximus was the chariot race. Modern interest in horse and auto racing pales in comparison with the frenzied enthusiasm of the spectators at these contests in ancient times.

Roman chariots were two-wheeled vehicles with three sides in which the charioteer stood to drive his four-horse team. The charioteers, *aurigae*, were either slaves or freedmen, who belonged to leagues and racing syndicates called the *factiones*. They wore liveries the color of their particular faction: red, white, blue, or green. Thus, in the races the chariots could be easily recognized by admirers or by those who had bet large sums of money on the most promising aurigae. So keen was the rivalry among the factions and so reckless the betting that it was necessary to protect horses and drivers from being drugged or poisoned.

Before the race began, the teams were driven into small vaulted chambers known as *carceres*, and the doors were closed. When the starting signal was given by the presiding magistrate, who waved a white flag for that purpose, the doors flew open and every driver made a dash for the low stone wall, the *spina*, in the center of the arena, each striving to gain the inside position. To complete the race the chariot circled the course seven times. The judges stood on the spina near the *metae*, or goals.

All means, fair or foul, were encouraged to obstruct rival chariots. The more dangerous the tricks, the more thrilled were the spectators. It was not unusual for one driver to upset a rival's chariot deliberately. He might even drive out of a straight course in order to prevent a swifter chariot from passing his. The crucial spot was at the metae, where each driver tried to save space and time by keeping the inner course.

The winner of a chariot race was treated as a great hero. Crowned with a laurel wreath, he was permitted to leave the Circus by the Porta Triumphalis, an honor indeed for one who in most cases had been a poor slave. Winners received extravagant sums of money and even their freedom. Statues of favorite aurigae adorned the spina, and these were often carried in the opening parade.

After a charioteer was named a winner, homing pigeons, which had been brought from nearby towns and dyed with the color of the winner, were released — a quick and easy way to notify the gamblers and facilitate the paying of the winning bets.

## A Day at the Races (continued)

Prope terminum pompae erant aurīgae, competitōrēs in certāmine (*contest*). In quadrīgīs stābant. Prīmus aurīga tunicam albam et equōs nigrōs, secundus tunicam rubram (*red*) et equōs albōs habēbat.

Circum arēnam procēdēbat (*advanced*) pompa splendida. Cūnctī spectātōrēs stābant ac clāmābant. Per hōram initium certāminis exspectāverant. Mox jūdicēs super spīnam sedēbant. Vinicius post longam moram stetit. Dominus lūdōrum mappam albam levāvit. Quadrīgae in arēnam et ad mētās volāvērunt. Cūnctī aurīgae prīmī esse temptābant. Spectātōrēs clāmābant et aurīgās atque equōs incitābant: "Iō Āfer! Iō Syre! Iō Lyde! Iō Pūblī!"

Per septem spatia equī et quadrīgae atque aurīgae iterum iterumque circum spīnam volāvērunt. Māgnum erat perīculum aurīgārum ad mētās. Nunc Āfer et Pūblius sunt prīmī! "Iō Āfer! Incitā equōs! Incitā equōs!" clāmābant puerī.

Mox Āfer prīmum locum obtinēre temptābat. Intervallum inter quadrīgās erat nōn māgnum. Pūblius equōs māgnā cum arte (*skill*) agēbat (*was driving*). Subitō rota quadrīgārum frēgit (*broke*). Āfer in terram cecidit (*fell*); Pūblius prīmus calcem (*chalk line*) trānsiit (*crossed*). Fīnis certāminis erat.

Dominus lūdōrum Pūbliō praemia dedit. Servī Āfrum ex arēnā portāvērunt, sed vulnera nōn māgna erant. Hodiē mala erat Fortūna; victōriam Āfer nōn habēbat, sed crās iterum temptābit et victor fortasse *(perhaps)* erit. Sextus et Fabius victōriam Pūblī nōn probāvērunt quod amīcī Āfrō erant. Crās in lūdō *(school)* puerī esse dēbent.

"... the Sibyl of Cumae ... prophesied that I should 'give Rome water and winter bread.' The winter bread was a reference to Ostia, but the water meant the two great aqueducts I built."

—Claudius in *Claudius the God*
Robert Graves, 1895–

# *Unit* XX

## CONVERSATION

MAGISTER: Cōnsīdite, puerī et puellae. In librīs vestrīs est pictūra. Quās ruīnās in pictūrā vidēs, Anna?

ANNA: Ruīnās Colossēī videō, magister. Quid est Colossēum?

MAGISTER: Colossēum, nōtum aedificium Rōmae, amphitheātrum erat, ubi populum Rōmānum spectācula et lūdī dēlectābant.

CORNĒLIA: Nōnne virī gladiīs cum virīs in Colossēō pūgnābant?

MAGISTER: Virī etiam sine armīs contrā bestiās interdum pūgnāvērunt. Dominus inīquus servum miserum Androclum sine armīs cum leōne pūgnāre jūssit.

ANNA: Quis erat Androclus? Narrā nōbīs *(to us)* fābulam.

MAGISTER: Crās vōbīs *(to you)* fābulam longam narrābō.

PAULUS: Num populus Rōmānus lūdōs crūdēlēs *(cruel)* jam probat?

MAGISTER: Minimē. Nunc benīgnī esse dēsīderant; sed semper dīcunt *(they say)*: " Quam diū *(As long as)* stat Colossēum, stat et *(also)* Rōma; quandō cadet *(will fall)* Colossēum, cadet et Rōmā! Cadet et mundus *(world)*!"

## SECTION 1 Parsing

▶ DISCUSSION

Parsing means clearly identifying the form of a Latin word and giving the syntax of the word, i.e., its function in the sentence.

1. Identifying the form means giving the following information:

*Noun, pronoun, adjective:* part of speech, declension, person (except for adj.), gender, number, case

*Verb:* part of speech, kind (transitive or intransitive), conjugation, principal parts, voice, mood, tense, person, number

*Adverb, preposition, conjunction, interjection:* part of speech

2. Giving the syntax of a word means stating its function, i.e., its relationship to the other words in the sentence. Answers to the following questions will tell us the syntax:

*Noun:* What is the reason for the case?
*Pronoun:* What is the reason for the case? With what antecedent does it agree?
*Adjective:* What noun or pronoun does it modify and agree with?
*Verb:* With what does it agree? What is the reason for the mood? If an infinitive, how is it used?
*Adverb:* What verb, adjective, or other adverb does it modify?
*Preposition:* What noun or pronoun does it govern?
*Conjunction:* What words, phrases, or clauses does it connect, or what clause does it introduce?
*Interjection:* (Independent)

▶ PRACTICE PATTERNS

A. Parse the italicized Latin words:

Ōlim Androclus, *servus miser*, dominum malum *habebat*. Dominus *servō* erat *inīquus*, et servus ex *agrīs* ad *silvās properāvit ubi* in *cavernā* diū mānsit. Tum leō (lion) cavernam intrāvit (entered). Androclus cum *cūrā* spīnam (thorn) ex pede (foot) leōnis *benīgnē* extrāxit et mox leō iterum *ambulāre poterat*.

B. Give the syntax of the italicized Latin words:

*Servō grātus* (grateful) erat leō quod vir eum (him) *cūrāverat* et *auxiliō vītam* leōnis servāverat. *Diū* vir cum leōne *in* cavernā mānsit. Tum subitō servī *dominī malī* Androclum *vīdērunt* et ad dominum servum miserum portāvērunt. Dominus crūdēlis (cruel) Androclum in *arēnā* cum bestiīs pūgnāre *jūssit*. Necesse erat *servum* sine *armīs pūgnāre*.

C. Translate the italicized words into Latin.

A few days later, *many prisoners were fighting* with wild animals in the Colosseum. Soon the animals *had killed* all the victims. Then one man *without weapons* slowly walked *into the arena*. A large lion *from* the cave *under* the seats *flew* into the arena. When he reached the man, he *suddenly* stood still and crouched before him. The amazed spectators *shouted:* "The lion *likes* the man. They are *friends.*" After the slave told his *story*, the people *ordered the master to free* both *the man* and the lion. Afterward they walked together *in the streets*.

## SECTION 2 Expressions of Place

▶ DISCUSSION

You have already used prepositions with the accusative or ablative case in expressions that denote place. These uses follow rules that are stated here for contrast with the special rule for the names of towns or cities, small islands, and a few other place words that will be studied later.

1. Place where: *in* + ablative

    **In oppidō** habitat. He lives *in the town.*

2. Place to which: *in* or *ad* + accusative

    **In oppidum** properat. He is hastening *into the town.*

3. Place from which: *ab, dē,* or *ex* + ablative

    **Ex oppidō** properat. He is hastening *out of the town.*

*Special rule* for the names of towns or cities, small islands, and a few other places: no prepositions are used.

1. Place where: locative case

    **Rōmae (Athēnīs)** habitat. He lives *at Rome (Athens).*

The *locative case* has the form of the genitive in the singular of the first and the second declensions; but in the plural of the first and second declensions and throughout the third declension (to be taught later), the locative has the form of the ablative.

2. Place to which: accusative without a preposition.

    **Rōmam (Athēnās)** properat. He is hastening *to Rome (Athens).*

3. Place from which: ablative without a preposition.

    **Rōmā (Athēnīs)** properat. He is hastening *out of Rome (Athens).*

# SECTION 3 Review of Prepositions

▶ DISCUSSION

It is well to note the exact meaning of each of these prepositions used *to denote place:*

1. **ā** (**ab**) with the ablative = *away* from the *outside* of a place
2. **ē** (**ex**) with the ablative = *out* from the *inside* of a place
3. **dē** with the ablative = *down* from a *higher* to a *lower* place
4. **in** with the ablative = *in, at, on* a place
5. **sub** with the ablative = *under, at the foot of, near* a place
6. **ad** with the accusative = *to, toward, near* a place
7. **in** with the accusative = *into, onto* a place
8. **sub** with the accusative = *under, close to* (with verbs of motion to)

▶ STUDY HELPS

1. The forms *ab* and *ex* are used before words beginning with a vowel or silent *h;* *ā* or *ab,* *ē* or *ex* may be used before words beginning with a consonant.

2. **Prō, sine,** and **sub** with the ablative are used after verbs not expressing motion to or toward.

3. The prepositions **ante, apud, circum, contrā, inter, per, post, prope** govern the accusative case.

▶ PRACTICE PATTERNS

A. Translate into English:

| | | | | |
|---|---|---|---|---|
| dē caelō | ā patriā | Rōmae | ab aquā | circum oppidum |
| in terrā | Rōmā | in Galliā | ante mūrum | contrā inimīcōs |
| ē casā | ex Ītaliā | sub portā | post bella | sine morā |
| in silvam | Rōmam | sub aquam | apud amīcōs | prope impedīmenta |
| ad rīpam | ad Siciliam | prō patriā | inter vīcōs | per agrum |
| cum puerīs | cum laetitiā | sine cūrā | prope aquam | in Ītaliam |

B. Translate into Latin:

| | | |
|---|---|---|
| away from danger | through the town | among the people |
| out of the building | under the power | between places |
| down from the horse | for the children | after the battle |
| in the temple | without money | against the plans |
| into the village | close to the wall | near the end |
| to the place | before the shop | around the spaces |

## WORDS TO MASTER

**accū′sō** (1), blame (*accuse*)

**benīg′nus, –a, –um,** *adj.,* kind (*benign*); **benīg′nē,** *adv.,* kindly

**cōnsi′lium, –ī,** *n.,* plan, advice (*counsel*)

**inter′dum,** *adv.,* sometimes

**ī′ra, –ae,** *f.,* anger (*irate*)

**jam,** *adv.,* now, already; **nōn jam,** no longer

**li′gō** (1), tie, bind (*ligament*)

**me′dius, –a, –um,** *adj.,* middle, the middle of (*median*)

**neces′se,** *indecl. adj.,* necessary; **necesse est,** it is necessary, must

**oc′cupō** (1), seize, capture (*occupy*)

**si′ne,** *prep. with abl.,* without (*sinecure*)

**tan′dem,** *adv.,* finally, at last (*tandem*)

## BUILDING WORD POWER

The word *cardinal* has an interesting history. **Cardō, cardinis** means *hinge.* In the early Christian Church certain bishops were designated *cardinals.* They exercised important functions, and much depended, or *hinged,* upon them. The color of their red vestments has given the cardinal bird its name.

Now take **cappa,** *a hooded cloak or cape.* From this we have *cap,* *cape, cope,* and *chaplet,* all meaning *a covering for the head or the body. A little cape* was a **capella**, from which came the word *chapel.* The custodians of the chapel were called **capellani,** that is, *chaplains.*

There may be a wide gap today between the meanings of *chaplain* and *chaperon,* but in reality they spring from the same original **capa.** In former times the chaperon, who accompanied young people, could be recognized by the large hat she wore.

There was a time when *escape* and *escapade* meant slipping out of one's cloak, **ex capā.**

## SENTENCE PATTERNS

A. Translate into English the two paragraphs in Practice Patterns A and B, page 108.

B. Translate into Latin:
1. Was not the master sometimes kind to the slaves?
2. It was necessary for the men to fight without weapons.
3. Finally, because he feared the great anger of the people, he blamed the captives.
4. No longer did they fear the power of men.
5. It was necessary for the inhabitants to seize the neighboring town.

### Rome's Ancient Port

Ōlim Rōmānī oppidum parvum prope ōstium (*mouth*) Tiberis (*of the Tiber*) aedificāvērunt. Oppidum Ōstiam appellāvērunt (*called*). Multī incolae Hispāniae, Galliae, Āsiae, Āfricae, Aegyptī, īnsulārum propinquārum ad oppidum Ōstiam nāvigābant. Incolae Ōstiae multum commercium (*trade*) et māgnam pecūniam habēbant.

Nautae validī et servī miserī māgnam cōpiam frūmentī ē Prōvinciīs ad oppidum Ōstiam portābant. Posteā, incolae et servī Ōstiae ad oppidum propinquum Rōmam frūmentum portābant, et Rōmānī multum cibum habēbant. Vīcī oppidaque Ītaliae etiam cibum habēbant. Ubi cōpiae Rōmānae ad Galliam, Hispāniam, Āfricam, Āsiam properābant et cum incolīs inimīcīs pūgnābant, necesse erat Ōstiam hīs (*these*) cōpiīs et incolīs locōrum frūmentum dare.

Incolae Ōstiae villās pulchrās, casās parvās, tabernās (*shops*) albās, multa templa, theātra māgna in oppidō aedificāvērunt. Lūdī et spectācula incolīs Ōstiae erant grāta, et ad lūdōs et spectācula saepe properābant. Ex agrīs agricolae laetī quoque properābant. Interdum lēgātus, interdum tribūnus aderat.

Post longa bella multī captīvī et servī, virī et fēminae, Ōstiae habitābant. Dominī inīquī captīvōs et servōs raptāvērunt (*seized*) et in mediā arēnā pūgnāre saepe jussērunt, quod spectāre lūdōs incolīs Ōstiae grātum fuit. Interdum virī cum virīs gladiīs in arēnā pūgnābant; interdum virī cum bestiīs pūgnābant; interdum etiam necesse erat virōs sine tēlīs contrā leōnēs pūgnāre, sed bestiae virōs miserōs semper necāvērunt.

Tandem post multōs annōs barbarī (*barbarians*) ex Germāniā, Galliā, atque aliīs (*other*) terrīs Eurōpae incolās Ōstiae oppūgnāvērunt (*attacked*) et mox superāvērunt. Barbarī māgnā cum īrā templa, theātra, villās, casās vāstāvērunt. Nōn jam virī, fēminae, līberī Ōstiae habitābant. Nōn jam nautae frūmentum ad oppidum propinquum Rōmam et vīcōs Ītaliae portābant. Nōn jam incolae ad templa, theātra, spectācula, lūdōs properābant. Nōn jam virī cum bestiīs in arēnā pūgnābant. Ōstia dēserta erat.

Nunc Amēricānī ubi Ītaliam vīsitant māgnō cum studiō ruīnās Ōstiae spectant et laudant. Barbarōs ex terrīs antīquīs Eurōpae accūsant quod oppidum et aedificia Ōstiae vāstāvērunt.

# Comprehensive Review: Units XVI–XX

A. Write in Latin the nominative, genitive, and base of:

| | | | | | | |
|---|---|---|---|---|---|---|
| year | gate | arms | limit | delay | injury | weapons |
| deed | bank | space | anger | spirit | courage | beginning |
| plan | duty | fight | place | battle | memory | injustice |
| end | act | wall | wrong | wheel | letter | service |

B. Write in Latin the feminine and the neuter forms, nominative plural, of these adjectives. Give the English meanings.

aequus    medius    idōneus    nōtus    grātus    inīquus    benīgnus

C. Write the adverbs formed from the following adjectives. Give the English meanings of the adjectives and the adverbs.

aequus    benīgnus    inīquus    grātus

D. Write in Latin:

sometimes    finally    whence    already    for a long time    no longer

E. Write the English meanings of these prepositions, and tell the case each one governs:

contrā    apud    inter    sine    sub    circum    prō    ante    post

F. Write in Latin the principal parts of:

| | | | | | | |
|---|---|---|---|---|---|---|
| try | bind | wait | order | announce | approve | approach |
| fly | hold | blame | raise | obtain | delight | hesitate |
| kill | save | seize | incite | summon | destroy | lay waste |

G. Write the following synopses in Latin and translate each form:

1. second person, plural number, indicative mood, active voice:
possum, jubeō, occupō
2. third person, singular number, indicative mood, active voice:
dubitō, obtineō, occupō

H. Write in Latin the specified forms:

1. accusative singular: terminus, īra, factum, rīpa
2. genitive plural: spatium, annus, pūgna, porta
3. ablative singular: mora, animus, proelium, locus
4. nominative plural: officium, injūria, cōnsilium, memoria
5. ablative plural: arma, rota, initium, mūrus

I. Parse the italicized words in these sentences:

1. *Quibus* dominus malus *mandāta* dedit?
2. *Lūdōs* spectāre *puerīs* erat *grātum*.
3. *Quōcum* servus *pūgnāvit* et *quem* necāvit?
4. *Quae* puella *līberīs fābulam* narrābit?
5. *Cūjus* librum dēlēvit?
6. Virī *cum* virīs pūgnābant.
7. *Diū in* agrō mānsit.
8. *In* silvam ambulāvit.

J. Decline in the singular and plural and translate: what bank?

K. Translate into Latin the italicized words or phrases in these sentences:

1. *He could not walk* to school.
2. *To be kind* is *to be good.*
3. He ordered *the men to shout.*
4. It is necessary for *the boy to work.*

L. Conjugate in Latin and translate the pluperfect tense of: possum.

M. Write the following imperatives in Latin, singular, plural, positive and negative, and translate:

order      announce      destroy      bind

## SENTENCE PATTERNS

A. Translate into English:

1. Ad lūdōs properāre nōn dubitō.
2. Nōn saepe fīnitimī inimīcī cōpiās Rōmānās superāre poterant.
3. Locum altum obtinēre dēsīderāvī ubi propinquus amīcīs meīs esse potuī.
4. Necesse erat servōs stāre ante locum ubi Imperātor inīquus sedēbat.
5. Nōnne dominī servōs cum servīs pūgnāre jūssērunt?
6. Equōs spectāre cūnctīs līberīs est grātum.
7. Vir bonus aequusque miserīs benīgnus semper fuerat.
8. Cūr Spartacus sociōs incitāre temptāvit?
9. Quis servōs casās, domicilia, aedificia Rōmāna dēlēre jūssit?
10. Numquam posteā virī virōs gladiīs in arēnā necāvērunt.

B. Write in Latin:

1. The Romans could not be hostile to the allies of Rome.
2. We desired to have a place near the end of the field.

3. To wait for the parade was not pleasing to the boys.
4. Did not the leader order unjust men to blame the slaves?
5. To whom did the master of the games give the rewards?


## SIGHT TRANSLATION: PYGMALION

Pygmaliōn multam pecūniam et multōs servōs et domicilium pulchrum habēbat, sed fēminās nōn amābat.  Cotīdiē māgnā cum dīligentiā labōrābat et statuās pulchrās sculpēbat (*chiseled*).  Saepe Pygmaliōn virōs ac fēminās convocābat.  "Spectāte pulchrās meās statuās!"  Cūnctī māgnō cum studiō clāmābant: "Ō Pygmaliōn, statuae tuae pulchrae sunt!"

Tandem Pygmaliōn statuam marmoream (*marble*) puellae pulchrae creāvit.  Statuam amābat sed tristis (*sad*) erat quod statua nōn vīva (*alive*) erat.  Statuae vītam dare nōn potuit.  Ad templum properāvit et deōs deāsque ōrāvit.  Tum ad domicilium revertit (*returned*).  Ante portam stābat pulchra puella.  "Nōn jam statua," inquit (*she said*), "sed puella vīva sum."  Et posteā Pygmaliōn laetus cum statuā vīvā habitābat.

The Shrine of Juturna in Rome.

The Colosseum in Rome. This amphitheater seated 45,000.
The cellars contained dozens of rooms to house gladiators
and wild animals.

*A-2*

The Emperor Claudius, A.D. 41–54.

The Emperor Caligula, A.D. 37–41.

The Appian Way. The first large road in Italy. This is a prime example of the Romans as master road builders. Called "the queen of roads," it was built by Appius Claudius, circa 300 B.C.

The Trojan Horse. This modern reconstruction now stands in Turkey at the site of ancient Troy.

Sarcophagus. The bas-relief on this coffin depicts a battle between Romans and Germans, second century A.D.

A Roman bath (eighteenth-century restoration). Bath, England.

Inscription from a temple in the Forum.

Horses. This bas-relief comes from Herculaneum, a city buried during the eruption of Mount Vesuvius in A.D. 79.

Mosaic. This detail is from the Piazza Armerina.

Mosaic. This mosaic from Palestrina shows animals from the Nile River.

A faun, playing pipes, Panisca, and a frightened woman. This fresco comes from the Villa of Mysteries in Pompeii, a city buried during the eruption of Mount Vesuvius in A.D. 79.

Hadrian's villa at Tivoli, near Rome. Hadrian reigned from A.D. 117 to A.D. 138.

Hence loathèd Melancholy,
Of Cerberus and blackest Midnight born,
In Stygian caves forlorn,
'Mongst horrid shapes, and shrieks, and
  sights unholy.
　　　　　—John Milton, 1608–1674

## CONVERSATION

THETIS: Quōs, mī amor (*love*), ad nūptiās (*wedding*) invitāre dē-sīderās?

PĒLEUS: Homō sum, et hominēs clārōs Graecōrum vocābō.

THETIS: Dea sum. Deōs deāsque vocābō sed Erim nōn invitābō.

PĒLEUS: Cūr ad nūptiās Erim nōn vocābis? Quālis dea est Eris?

THETIS: Eris ad nūptiās cūncta mala portābit, quod dea discordiae est. Discordiam adesse nūptiīs nōn dēsīderāmus.

ERIS (*māgnā cum īrā*): Nūptiīs clam (*secretly*) aderō. Inter deās pōmum aureum (*golden apple*) jactābō (*I will throw*). Verbum "Pulcherrimae" (*For the most beautiful*) in pōmō erit.

JŪNŌ, VENUS, MINERVA: Ego sum pulcherrima! Mihi pōmum dā!

PĒLEUS: Patrī deōrum pōmum dā! Juppiter erit jūdex (*judge*)!

JUPPITER: Jūdex esse nōn possum. Jūnō uxor mea est; Venus et Minerva fīliae meae sunt; mēcum (*with me*) in Olympō habitant. Bellum nōn dēsīderō!

MERCURIUS (*patrī deōrum*): Paris Trōjānus jūdex bonus erit!

JUPPITER: Ad Paridem properāte! Pulcherrimae pōmum aureum dabit!

ERIS (*māgnā cum laetitiā*): Sed propter Paridis jūdicium bellum erit!

## Nouns of the Third Declension

▶ DISCUSSION

1. Nouns of the first declension are usually feminine; of the second usually masculine or neuter. Nouns of all three genders occur in the third declension.

2. We recognize nouns of the first declension by the genitive case indicator *–ae;* nouns of the second declension by *–ī;* nouns of the third declension by *–is.*

3. Just as we find the *base* of a noun by dropping the case indicator of the genitive singular, so we can find the *stem* of a noun by dropping the *–rum* or the *–um* of the genitive plural.

4. We refer to the first declension as the *a*-declension because its stem ends in –*ā;* the second declension as the *o*-declension because its stem ends in –*o;* but we refer to the third declension as the *consonant* declension or *i*-declension because the stems of some of its nouns end in a consonant and others end in –*i.*

| Declension | Genitive Singular | Base | Genitive Plural | Stem |
|---|---|---|---|---|
| First | **portae** | **port/** | **portārum** | **porta/** |
| Second | **servī** | **serv/** | **servōrum** | **servo/** |
| Third (consonant) | **hominis** | **homin/** | **hominum** | **homin/** |
| | **honōris** | **honōr/** | **honōrum** | **honōr/** |
| Third (–i) | **cīvis** | **cīv/** | **cīvium** | **cīvi/** |

Notice that in third declension *consonant-stem* nouns the base and the stem are identical.

5. Third declension nouns with consonant stems are divided into two general classes: (1) nouns whose nominative is the base only or the base slightly changed in spelling for the sake of pronunciation; (2) nouns that add –*s* to the base to form the nominative singular. In this unit we shall study the first type of consonant stems.

Many third declension nouns are declined as in these paradigms.

| | **honor, –ōris** | **pater, –tris** | **homō, –inis** | **regiō, –ōnis** | |
|---|---|---|---|---|---|
| | *m.* honor | *m.* father | *m.* man | *f.* region | |
| BASE: | **honōr/** | **patr/** | **homin/** | **regiōn/** | |
| | | SINGULAR | | | C.I. |
| Nom. | honor | pater | homō | regiō | — |
| Gen. | honōris | patris | hominis | regiōnis | –is |
| Dat. | honōrī | patrī | hominī | regiōnī | –ī |
| Acc. | honōrem | patrem | hominem | regiōnem | –em |
| Abl. | honōre | patre | homine | regiōne | –e |
| | | PLURAL | | | |
| Nom. | honōrēs | patrēs | hominēs | regiōnēs | –ēs |
| Gen. | honōrum | patrum | hominum | regiōnum | –um |
| Dat. | honōribus | patribus | hominibus | regiōnibus | –ibus |
| Acc. | honōrēs | patrēs | hominēs | regiōnēs | –ēs |
| Abl. | honōribus | patribus | hominibus | regiōnibus | –ibus |

▶ STUDY HELPS

1. Third declension nouns that refer to persons have natural gender.

2. Consonant stems ending in –*or* are usually masculine, and the –*ō* in the base is long: ***honor, –ōris,*** honor. ***Arbor, –oris,*** *tree,* is an exception.

3. Consonant stems ending in –*iō, –tūdō, –dō, –gō* are feminine. ***Ōrdō,*** *order,* and ***sermō,*** *speech,* are exceptions.

4. Masculine and feminine nouns of the third declension have the same case indicators; the nominative and accusative plural are alike; the dative and ablative plural are alike.

5. The short *-is* of the genitive singular of the third declension must not be confused with the long *-īs* of the dative and ablative plural of the first and second declensions.

6. The vocative in the third declension is like the nominative.

▶ PRACTICE PATTERNS

A. Write the declension of the following:

     pater bonus     homō līber     cōnsul nōtus     regiō pulchra

B. Write the genitive and accusative singular and plural of: dea, deus, ōrdō. Compare the case indicators.

C. Write in Latin the dative plural of: queen, wind; and the genitive singular of: maiden, row. Compare the case indicators.

D. Decline in Latin and translate each form: wife, maiden.


## WORDS TO MASTER

**cōn′sul, –is,** *m.,* consul (*consular*)
**dolus, –ī,** *m.,* device, trickery
**ho′mō, –inis,** *m.,* man (*homicide*)
**jūdi′cium, –ī,** *n.,* judgment (*judicial*)
**ōr′dō, –inis,** *m.,* row, rank, order (*ordinary*)
**pa′ter, –tris,** *m.,* father (*paternal*)

**prop′ter,** *prep. with acc.,* on account of
**re′giō, –ōnis,** *f.,* region (*regional*)
**trāns,** *prep. with acc.,* across, over (*transient*)
**ux′or, –ōris,** *f.,* wife (*uxorious*)
**ven′tus, –ī,** *m.,* wind (*ventilate*)
**vir′gō, –inis,** *f.,* maiden (*virgin*)


## BUILDING WORD POWER

The easiest way to learn the gender, the form, and the meaning of third declension nouns is to study the English derivatives from these nouns. In many instances the meaning has remained the same or almost the same as the original Latin.

A large group of masculine nouns of the third declension retain their Latin form in English. Formed from the perfect passive participle, they always terminate in *-tor* or *-sor* and denote the agent or the doer of the action. *Narrāre* means to *narrate*. A *narrator* is *one who narrates* or *tells a story*. If *spectāre* means *to look at*, who is a *spectator* at a football game?

Form agent nouns on the following verbs: *nāvigāre, līberāre, ōrāre, cūrāre, creāre, dēmōnstrāre.* Some agent nouns do not denote

*117*

persons, such as ***mōtor, accelerātor, generātor.*** You may define
them with *that which*. ***Accelerāre*** means *to speed up;* ***generāre,*** *to
produce.* Do *numerator* and *denominator* mean the same as their Latin
originals? The Romans did not use fractions, you know.

## SENTENCE PATTERNS

A. Complete and translate into English:

1. Propter jūdici____ homin____ erit bell____.
2. Facta bona fīliōrum era____ patr____ grāta.
3. Nōnne prīmus cōnsul Rōmae era____ Jūnius Brūtus?
4. Jūdicia homin____ timēre nōn dēbēmus.
5. Ad regiōn____ Trōjānās cum rēgis uxōr____ nāvigāvit.
6. Post bella multī homin____ erant servī.
7. Paris honōr____, fāmam, imperi____, pecūni____ nōn dēsīderābat.
8. Virgin____ Vestālibus et honōr____ et glōriam dabant.
9. Cōnsul Rōmānus māgnō cum studi____ ōrdin____ cōpiārum spectābat.
10. Factum inīqu____ fīlī rēgīnae benīgn____ erat initium bellī.

B. Translate into Latin the italicized words or phrases:

Juno, *queen of the gods and goddesses*, promised *money and power* to Paris;
Minerva, *goddess* of wisdom, *honor* and *fame;* Venus, goddess of love and beauty,
*a beautiful wife.* Paris, *son* of the king of Troy, *gave* the golden apple to Venus.
*The judgment* of Paris *was the cause* of the Trojan *War.* Priam, king of Troy
and *father* of Paris, *did not approve the wicked deed* of his *son.* The Greeks *loved*
Helen, *the wife* of Menelaus, king of Sparta. When *she sailed to the country* of
the Trojans with Paris, the Greeks immediately *built* ships. *It was necessary*
then for *the men* of those *regions to prepare war* against the hostile Trojans. *For
a long time* the Greeks *fought* with the Trojans. They *conquered* the Trojans
not *by means of arms* but *by trickery.*

Pluto, the god of the Underworld,
and Cerberus, the three-headed
dog who guarded the entrance.

## The Realms of the Dead

Jupiter, after the overthrow of Cronus, became the father of
the gods. He then divided his kingdom in such manner that his
brother Pluto became the ruler of the Underworld, a vast, mys-

terious region to which the souls of men passed at death. This realm of darkness was bounded by awful rivers, the Styx and the Acheron. Charon, a grim boatman, received the dead at the Acheron and ferried them across, provided they had been properly buried in the world above and had the coin for their passage in their mouths.

At the gate that opened into the abode of Pluto was Cerberus, a dog generally depicted as having three heads and a serpent's tail. He never molested the dead who entered but was ferocious indeed to those who tried to depart.

Hades, sometimes called Erebus, had several divisions. The spirits of the dead appeared for trial before the judges of the Lower Regions. Here their deeds in the world above were examined and sentence passed upon them. The souls of the innocent passed to the Elysian Fields, where each was permitted to enjoy a happy life in a land of eternal spring and song. Near these fields flowed the Lethe, the river of forgetfulness. Those who drank from its waters forgot everything that had happened to them in life.

Mortals who had sinned greatly were condemned to regions where all manner of torture awaited them at the hands of the Furies and the many-headed Hydra. The very wicked, especially those who had offended the gods themselves, were doomed to Tartarus, a place of untold misery for its unfortunate inhabitants. Among those whom the gods punished most severely were Tantalus, Ixion, Sisyphus, and the Danaïdes.

Tantalus, son of Jupiter and father of Niobe, had been a monarch favored by the gods, but imprudently he had divulged certain of their secret plans. After death he was condemned to eternal woe. He found himself standing in a pool in which the water barely reached his chin. Overhead hung branches of various fruit trees laden with ripe and tempting fruit. Every time the wretched Tantalus bent to quench his torturing thirst, the water receded from his parched lips. Every time he grasped for the fruit, the branches sprang up, leaving the fruit just out of reach.

Ixion, king of Thessaly, had shown deep disrespect for the gods. In Tartarus he was chained to a wheel that rolled forever down an endless road. Sisyphus, king of Corinth, was a man of avarice and deceit. After he died, he was condemned to roll a huge rock uphill. When it reached the top, it immediately rolled back to the bottom of the hill so that Sisyphus had to begin all over again.

The Danaïdes were fifty daughters of King Danaus of Argos,

all of whom had murdered their husbands on their wedding night. When the women died, they were punished in Tartarus by having continually to pour water into sieves.

## For the Most Beautiful

"Dā mihi (*to me*) pōmum aureum, et imperium et pecūniam habēbis, Paris," Jūnō, rēgīna deārum et hominum, prōmīsit.

"Honōrēs et glōriam et fāmam tibi (*to you*) dabō," inquit (*said*) Minerva, dea sapientiae (*of wisdom*), "si mihi pōmum dabis."

"Nōnne fēminam pulchram esse uxōrem dēsīderās?" rogāvit Venus, dea amōris (*of love*) et pulchritūdinis (*of beauty*).

Paris, pastor (*shepherd*) et fīlius Priāmī, nōn dubitāvit. Sine morā et māgnō cum studiō Venerī pōmum aureum dedit, sed jūdicium fatāle Paridis erat initium bellī Trōjānī.

Helena, soror (*sister*) Castoris et Pollūcis (*of Pollux*), erat uxor Menelāī. Graecī Helenam pulchram amāvērunt et Menelāō māgnum honōrem dedērunt. Menelāus, rēx (*king*) Spartae, apud Graecōs multum imperium habēbat. Auxiliō Veneris, Paris ad terram Spartānōrum nāvigāre parāvit. Mox cum multīs sociīs in domiciliō Menelāī erat. Rēx nōbilis Paridī inimīcus nōn fuit. Diū Paris cum rēge et rēgīnā Spartae mānsit. Tum pastor perfidus (*treacherous*) auxiliō sociōrum Helenam raptāvit (*carried off*) et trāns aquam ad ōrās (*shores*) Trōjae nāvigāvit. Perfidia Paridis et infidēlitās Helenae erant causae longī bellī inter Graecōs et Trōjānōs.

Menelāus māgnā cum īrā multitūdinem amīcōrum et sociōrum statim (*immediately*) convocāvit. Ex oppidīs et vīcīs, ex agrīs et silvīs, ex īnsulīs et montibus (*mountains*) sine morā properāvērunt. Cūnctī virī validī Menelāum adjuvāre dēsīderāvērunt, et ad Spartānōrum terram gladiōs, tēla, scūta, arma bellī portāvērunt.

Per duōs (*two*) annōs Graecī māgnās nāvēs (*ships*) parāverant. Agamemnōn inter Graecōs māgnum imperium habuit, et nāvēs ad Trōjae ōrās nāvigāre jūssit. Agamemnōn, autem (*however*), in silvīs ambulābat et cervum (*deer*) Diānae forte (*by chance*) necāvit. Dea īrāta ventōs esse tranquillōs jūssit. Calchās vātes (*prophet*) Agamemnonī nūntiāvit:

"Sī ventōs secundōs (*favorable*) dēsīderās, fīliam tuam Īphigenīam sacrificāre dēbēs. Est mandātum deae Diānae." Pater miser fīliam ante āram (*altar*) Diānae stāre jūssit, sed Diāna puellam pulchram ad templum portāvit. Posteā secundī erant ventī, et nāvēs ad ōrās Trōjae nāvigāre parāvērunt.

Was this the face that launch'd a thousand ships
And burnt the topless towers of Ilium?
Sweet Helen, make me immortal with a kiss.
—Christopher Marlowe, 1564–1593

# Unit XXII

## CONVERSATION

PRIĀMUS: Tū quis es? Cūr cum sociīs Graecīs tuīs nōn nāvigāvistī?

SINŌN: Ego, Ō rēx nōbilis, sum Sinōn, jam nōn Graecus quod Graecī mē necāre temptāvērunt. Mē Minervae immolāre dēsīderāvērunt.

PRIĀMUS: Nōlī timēre, mī amīce. Trōjānus nunc eris. Quae est causa equī līgneī?

SINŌN: Ō māgne rēx, Trōjānīs cūncta cōnsilia Graecōrum narrābo. Nihil (*Nothing*) Graecīs jam dēbeō.

PRIĀMUS: Cūr tam (*such*) māgnum equum Graecī aedificābant?

SINŌN: Equus Minervae dōnum est. Sī Trōjānī per Trōjae portās equum movēbunt, Graecōs superābunt.

PRIĀMUS: Equum, Ō Trōjānī, per Trōjae portās cum celeritāte movēte!

LĀOCOŌN: Nōlīte equum movēre! Nōnne dolum prīncipis Ulixis ac Graecōrum, Trōjānī, memoriā tenētis? Timeō Graecōs etiam dōna ferentēs (*bearing*)!

TRŌJĀNĪ: Spectāte! Serpentēs circum Lāocoontis ac fīliōrum corpora! Māgna est īra Minervae!

PRIĀMUS: Properāte, virī Trōjae! Equum māgna cum celeritāte movēte!

## SECTION 1 Third Declension Nouns with Nominative Ending in –s or –x

▶ DISCUSSION

Nouns of this class are masculine or feminine only. They are all formed by adding –s to the consonant stem. Observe:

1. A final –c or –g of the stem *unites* with –s to form –x.

**duc** + s = **ducs** = **dux**, *leader*     **reg** + s = **regs** = **rēx**, *king*

2. A final –t or –d of the stem *is dropped* before –s.

**ped** + s = **peḍs** = **pēs**, *foot*     **mīlit** + s = **mīliṭs** = **mīles**, *soldier*

**obsid** + s = **obsiḍs** = **obses**, *hostage*

Notice that the short –i in the stem is changed to –e.

**121**

**3.** Final *–p* or *–b remains unchanged* when *–s* is added.

princip + s = princips = princeps, *chief, leading man*

| | rēx, rēgis<br>*m.* king<br>BASE: rēg/ | pēs, pedis<br>*m.* foot<br>ped/ | prīnceps, –ipis<br>*m.* chief<br>prīncip/ | cīvitās, –tātis<br>*f.* state<br>cīvitāt/ | C.I. |
|------|------|------|------|------|------|
| | | | SINGULAR | | |
| Nom. | rēx | pēs | prīnceps | cīvitās | –s |
| Gen. | rēgis | pedis | prīncipis | cīvitātis | –is |
| Dat. | rēgī | pedī | prīncipī | cīvitātī | –ī |
| Acc. | rēgem | pedem | prīncipem | cīvitātem | –em |
| Abl. | rēge | pede | prīncipe | cīvitāte | –e |
| | | | PLURAL | | |
| Nom. | rēgēs | pedēs | prīncipēs | cīvitātēs | –ēs |
| Gen. | rēgum | pedum | prīncipum | cīvitātum | –um |
| Dat. | rēgibus | pedibus | prīncipibus | cīvitātibus | –ibus |
| Acc. | rēgēs | pedēs | prīncipēs | cīvitātēs | –ēs |
| Abl. | rēgibus | pedibus | prīncipibus | cīvitātibus | –ibus |

# SECTION 2 Neuter Nouns with Consonant Stems

▶ DISCUSSION

Some important *neuter* nouns are consonant stems that add no indicator to the base to form the nominative singular. Most of these nouns have: (1) stems in *–min–*, as *flūmen, flūminis, river;* (2) stems in *–or–* (the *–o–* is always short), as *corpus, corporis, body;* (3) stems in *–er–*, as *genus, generis, race.*

| | flūmen, –minis<br>*n.* river<br>BASE: flūmin/ | corpus, –oris<br>*n.* body<br>corpor/ | genus, –eris<br>*n.* birth<br>gener/ | iter, itineris<br>*n.* journey<br>itiner/ | C.I. |
|------|------|------|------|------|------|
| | | | SINGULAR | | |
| Nom. | flūmen | corpus | genus | iter | — |
| Gen. | flūminis | corporis | generis | itineris | –is |
| Dat. | flūminī | corporī | generī | itinerī | –ī |
| Acc. | flūmen | corpus | genus | iter | — |
| Abl. | flūmine | corpore | genere | itinere | –e |
| | | | PLURAL | | |
| Nom. | flūmina | corpora | genera | itinera | –a |
| Gen. | flūminum | corporum | generum | itinerum | –um |
| Dat. | flūminibus | corporibus | generibus | itineribus | –ibus |
| Acc. | flūmina | corpora | genera | itinera | –a |
| Abl. | flūminibus | corporibus | generibus | itineribus | –ibus |

A knowledge of the English derivatives is an aid in remembering the spelling of neuter nouns: *corporal, generous, nominate,* from **corpus, genus, nōmen,** respectively.

▶ PRACTICE PATTERNS

A. Decline the following; translate the dative and ablative cases.

flūmen lātum    māgna celeritās    corpus validum    dux clārus

B. Give the specified forms in Latin:

1. chief (direct object)
2. speed (ablative of manner)
3. journey (with ad)
4. leader (indirect object)
5. bodies (subject)
6. king (possessive)
7. chiefs (ablative of accompaniment)
8. rivers (with prope)
9. peace (direct object)
10. route (ablative of means)

C. These nouns have the same form in English and Latin. Write the gender and the genitive case of each:

| | | | | | |
|---|---|---|---|---|---|
| specimen | horror | conductor | terror | acūmen | genus |
| cōnsul | color | exterior | regimen | ōrātor | honor |
| tribūnal | tūtor | protector | animal | clāmor | stadium |

## WORDS TO MASTER

cele′ritās, –tātis, *f.,* speed, swiftness (*accelerator*)

cor′pus, –oris, *n.,* body (*corporal*)

dō′num, –ī, *n.,* gift (*donor*)

dux, du′cis, *m.,* leader, general (*duke*)

flū′men, –inis, *n.,* river (*flume*)

i′ter, iti′neris, *n.,* journey, route, march (*itinerary*); **māgnum iter,** forced march

līg′neus, –a, –um, *adj.,* wooden (*ligneous*)

o′culus, –ī, *m.,* eye (*ocular*)

pāx, pā′cis, *f.,* peace (*pacify*)

prīn′ceps, –cipis, *m.,* chief, leader, first (*principal*)

rēx, rē′gis, *m.,* king (*regal*)

sta′tim, *adv.,* immediately

## BUILDING WORD POWER

Keep in mind that nouns that are masculine or feminine in English by natural gender are the same gender in Latin. This lesson is about nouns that are neuter in English and feminine in Latin. They are abstract nouns denoting quality or condition, and have the suffixes –*ia,* –*tia,* –*ntia,* –*tās,* and –*tūdō.* The first three types have already been treated under first declension derivatives in preceding pages. The fourth type is formed in Latin by the addition of –*tās* to an adjective: **līber + tās = lībertās,** *liberty.*

The derivatives of these Latin nouns always end in *–ty* in English. What are the derivatives for these: **humilitās, antīquitās, gravitās, dīgnitās, necessitās, quālitās, quantitās, sēcūritās, vīcīnitās, ūtilitās, brevitās, sānitās, celeritās?**

Write the Latin for: *unity, paucity, loquacity, facility, civility, alacrity, asperity, anxiety, sobriety, piety, society.* The last four are derived from adjectives that end in *–ius:* **anxius, sobrius, pius, socius.**

## SENTENCE PATTERNS

A. Complete and translate the following sentences into English:
1. Graecī Minervae equum līgne____ cum celeritāt____ dedērunt.
2. Sī prīncip____ equum per portās in oppid____ mōverint, Trōjānī Graec____ superābunt.
3. Statim populus Trōjān____ māgnō cum studiō virōs valid____ equ____ līgneum in oppidum movēre jūss____.
4. Nōn armīs sed dol____ Graecī Trōjān____ superāvērunt.
5. Flūmin____ erant lāta et itinera erant long____.
6. Achillēs fīlium rēg____ Trōjae necāvit.
7. Nōnne posteā patr____ Priāmō corpus ded____?
8. Ante oculōs duc____ dea silvārum virgin____ pulchram ad templ____ portāvit.
9. Lāocoōn dōn____ equī līgneī timuit et Trōjānōs monu____.
10. Posteā Graecī Trōj____ dēlēvērunt et tum pāx in terr____ fuit.

B. Translate the italicized words into Latin:
1. The Greek captive *by trickery* remained *in Troy.*
2. *With great speed* Achilles dragged *the body* of Hector three times *around the walls* of Troy *before the eyes* of Hector's sad *father.*
3. Immediately the *king* ordered *the men* to move *the wooden horse into town.*
4. And on earth *peace to men!*
5. They feared *the long journeys and the deep rivers.*

### Not by Arms but by Treachery

Jūdicium pastōris et pulchritūdō fēminae erant causae bellī Trōjānī. Graecī cum multīs prīncipibus ad ōrās (*shores*) Trōjae multitūdine nāvium (*ships*) nāvigāvērunt. Inter Graecōs erant ducēs clārī, Ulixēs, Achillēs, Agamemnōn, Menelāus. Priāmus, rēx Trōjae, et fīlius Hector, et Aenēās, fīlius Anchīsae, erant ducēs clārī Trōjānī.

Per novem (*nine*) annōs Graecī inimīcī in agrīs propinquīs Trōjae cum Trōjānīs pūgnāvērunt, sed incolae Trōjae erant validī et patriam contrā Graecōs dēfendērunt. Jūnō et Minerva et Neptūnus Trōjānōs et Paridem nōn amāvērunt, et prō Graecīs pūgnāvērunt. Paris ac Trōjānī Venerī et Mārtī erant grātī, et prō Trōjānīs Venus et Mārs pūgnāvērunt.

Tum Achillēs Graecus hastā (*spear*) Hectōrem necāvit et ter (*thrice*) circum mūrōs Trōjae corpus Hectōris ante oculōs patris trāxit (*dragged*). Trōjānī autem (*however*) Trōjam etiam tenuērunt. Tandem Ulixēs, Graecōrum prīnceps, dolō malō Trōjānōs superāvit. Graecī māgnum equum līgneum, dōnum Minervae, extrā (*outside*) mūrōs oppidī aedificāvērunt. Altō in equō erant prīncipēs Graecōrum cum multitūdine hominum validōrum. Posteā ab ōrīs Trōjae nāvigāre simulāvērunt (*pretended*) sed nōn longē ā terrā mānsērunt.

Trōjānī laetī māgnā cum celeritāte extrā mūrōs oppidī properāvērunt. Sed Lāocoōn, sacerdōs (*priest*) Neptūnī, dē templō cucurrit (*ran*) et clāmāvit: "Nōnne dolum Ulixis et Graecōrum, Trōjānī, memoriā tenētis? Timeō Graecōs etiam dōna ferentēs."

Tum pastōrēs Trōjānī ad rēgem captīvum Graecum portāvērunt. "Sī respōnsa vēra dederis, vītam tuam servābimus." Sinōn captīvus cum terrōre respondit: "Equus est dōnum ā Graecīs Minervae. Sī Trōjānī equum in oppidum mōverint, Graecōs vērō superābunt."

Subitō māgnae serpentēs ex aquā māgnā cum celeritāte properāvērunt et Lāocoontem et fīliōs necāvērunt. Trōjānī mōnstrum virīs complētum (*filled*) per portās mōvērunt. Posteā laetī dormiērunt (*slept*). Pāx in terrā erat. Terminus bellī erat.

Noctū (*At night*) Graecī ab īnsulā ubi clam (*secretly*) mānserant ad ōrās Trōjae nāvigāvērunt. Sinōn sīgnum dedit et dē equō Ulixēs et prīncipēs Graecī dēscendērunt. Scūta, tēla, gladiōs, arma bellī portāvērunt. Per portās Trōjae properāvērunt Graecī. Nōn pūgna sed caedēs (*slaughter*) erat. Undique erat clāmor; undique erat terror; undique ambulāvit Mors (*Death*).

*Forsan et haec olim meminisse iuvabit.*
Perhaps someday it will be pleasant to
remember these things.
—Vergil, 70–19 B.C.
*Aeneid*

# Unit XXIII

## CONVERSATION

HENRĪCUS: Pauca, pater, dē pūgnā inter Aenēam et Turnum narrā!

ROBERTA: Cūr, mī pater, Turnus, prīnceps māgnus Rutulōrum, incolās regiōnum fīnitimōrum contrā Aenēam Trōjānum incitāvit?

PATER: Turnus Lāvīniam, fīliam pulchram Latīnī, rēgis Latī, in mātrimōnium dūcere dēsīderāvit, sed Latīnus negāvit.

FREDERĪCUS: Cūr Latīnus Turnō fīliam in mātrimōnium dare dubitāvit? Māgnum erat Turnī nōmen ac fāma.

PATER: Dum Trōjānus nāve parvā trāns mare ad Ītaliam nāvigat, deī Latīnum in somnō (*sleep*) monuerant: "Dux nōbilis ā terrā aliēnā ad Latium nunc properat. Dā ducī in mātrimōnium Lāvīniam. Latiō fāmam fortūnamque vir Trōjānus dabit."

HENRĪCUS: Eratne Latīnī jūdicium Turnō ac Rutulīs grātum, pater?

PATER: Dea Jūnō propter Paridis jūdicium Trōjānīs semper inimīca fuerat. Bellum inter Trōjānōs ac Rutulōs incitāvit. Diū Trōjānī cum Rutulīs pūgnāvērunt. Tandem Aenēās cum Turnō sōlō (*alone*) pūgnāvit. Aenēās victor cum Lāvīniā uxōre rēgnāvit, et cīvibus urbis lēgēs aequās dedit.

## Third Declension *i*–Stems

▶ DISCUSSION

*I*-stem nouns, so called because their stems end in *–i,* are an important class of third declension nouns. They differ in some respects from consonant stems. It is necessary to recognize these differences in order to use this class of nouns correctly. *I*-stem nouns include:

1. Nouns whose nominative ends in *–is* or *–ēs, not increasing in the genitive,* that is, having no more syllables in the genitive than in the nominative case singular: **cīvis, cīvis,** *m., citizen,* and **caedēs, caedis,** *f., slaughter* (gen. pl., **cīvium, caedium**).

2. Nouns whose nominative ends in *–ns* and *–rs:* **cliēns, clientis,**

*m., client,* (gen. pl., **clientium**), and **cohors, cohortis,** *f., cohort,* (gen. pl., **cohortium**).

3. Monosyllables ending in *–s* or *–x* whose base ends in two consonants: **urbs, urbis,** *f., city,* (gen. pl., **urbium**); **nox, noctis,** *f., night* (gen. pl., **noctium**).

4. Neuters in *–e, –al, –ar:* **mare, maris,** *n., sea,* (gen. pl., **marium**).

| | cīvis, cīvis<br>*m. & f.* citizen | caedēs, caedis<br>*f.* slaughter | urbs, urbis<br>*f.* city | mare, maris<br>*n.* sea | | |
|---|---|---|---|---|---|---|
| | | | | | CASE INDICATOR | |
| BASE: | **cīv/** | **caed/** | **urb/** | **mar/** | M. & F. | N. |
| | | | SINGULAR | | | |
| Nom. | cīvis | caedēs | urbs | mare | (–s) | –e, –al, –ar |
| Gen. | cīvis | caedis | urbis | maris | –is | –is |
| Dat. | cīvī | caedī | urbī | marī | –ī | –ī |
| Acc. | cīvem | caedem | urbem | mare | –em | –e, –al, –ar |
| Abl. | cīve | caede | urbe | marī | –e | –ī |
| | | | PLURAL | | | |
| Nom. | cīvēs | caedēs | urbēs | maria | –ēs | –ia |
| Gen. | cīvium | caedium | urbium | marium | –ium | –ium |
| Dat. | cīvibus | caedibus | urbibus | maribus | –ibus | –ibus |
| Acc. | cīvēs | caedēs | urbēs | maria | –ēs (–īs) | –ia |
| Abl. | cīvibus | caedibus | urbibus | maribus | –ibus | –ibus |

▶ STUDY HELPS

1. The genitive plural indicator *–ium* is characteristic of *all i*-stem nouns. Masculine and feminine *i*-stems differ from the consonant stems only in the genitive and the accusative plural.

2. Neuter *i*-stems *always* terminate in *–ī* in the ablative singular, and in *–ia* in the nominative and the accusative plural.

▶ PRACTICE PATTERNS

A. Write the genitive plural of these nouns and translate:

| | | | | | | | |
|---|---|---|---|---|---|---|---|
| mors | mare | cīvis | regiō | nōmen | cōnsul | iter | jūdicium |
| urbs | rēx | dōnum | nāvis | virgō | flūmen | ōrdō | prīnceps |
| vōx | lēx | mūrus | liber | pater | homō | corpus | ventus |

B. Decline in Latin in the singular and plural and translate:

    a long ship    a beautiful river    a faithful citizen

**BUILDING WORD POWER**

The fifth group of abstract quality nouns of feminine gender have the nominative and genitive in *–tūdō, –tūdinis.* These nouns always terminate in *–tude* in both English and French.

If the Latin word **multitūdō** became *multitude* in English, what is the Latin for *longitude, magnitude, altitude, fortitude, servitude, lassitude, solicitude, amplitude?* Notice that these nouns were formed by adding the suffixes to adjectives.

What do you understand by the *vicissitudes* of life? What do we mean by a condition of previous *servitude?* Would you like to be blessed with *pulchritude?* Have you ever experienced general *lassitude* after a strenuous game? On what day do we usually express our *gratitude* for all the good things of life? Have you ever longed for *solitude* on the crowded streets or *quietude* in the din of a noisy cafeteria?

*Solicitude* (from **sollus + citus**) etymologically means *all stirred up.* Notice that the English derivative has only one *l.*

## WORDS TO MASTER

**cī′vis, –is,** *m. & f.*, citizen (*civil*)
**dum,** *conj.*, while, *with present tense*
**lēx, lē′gis,** *f.*, law (*legal*)
**ma′re, –is,** *n.*, sea (*marine*)
**mors, mor′tis,** *f.*, death (*mortal*)
**nā′vis, –is,** *f.*, ship (*naval*); **nāvis longa,** war galley

**ne′gō** (1), say no, deny (*negative*)
**nō′men, –minis,** *n.*, name (*nominal*)
**pau′cī, –ae, –a,** *pl., adj.*, few, a few (*paucity*)
**rēg′nō** (1), reign, rule (*interregnum*)
**urbs, –is,** *f.*, city (*urban*)
**vōx, vō′cis,** *f.*, voice (*vocal*)

## SENTENCE PATTERNS

A. Translate into English:
1. Turnus, rēx Rutulōrum, cīvēs Latīnōs ad bellum incitāvit.
2. Nōnne Aenēās nautās ad terram nāvibus nāvigāre jūssit?
3. Post mortem Hectōris, Achillēs Priāmō corpus fīlī dedit.
4. Aenēās ex nōmine uxōris Lāvīniae oppidum Lāvīnium vocāvit.
5. Aedificāvitne Ascanius, fīlius Aenēae, urbem Albam Longam?
6. Hominēs in Āfricā manēre dēsīderāvērunt sed vōx deī negāvit.
7. Per paucōs annōs Aenēās rēgnābat et populō lēgēs aequās dedit.
8. Dum rēgīna cum fīliābus spectat, virī malī rēgem necāvērunt.
9. Quōrum nāvēs ē marī in flūmen nāvigāvērunt?
10. Diū terrā marīque ad terram novam properābunt.

B. Translate into Latin:
1. After the death of the king, they built the small city.
2. The voice of the people is often the voice of God.
3. The laws of the city were few while the foreign king was reigning.
4. He told the story about the journey to the queen.
5. The name of the new fatherland was Latium, where through long years Latinus had reigned.

The Trojan horse, the "gift" in which the Greeks gained entrance into Troy.

## From Troy to Carthage

Soon after leaving the smoldering Troy, Aeneas and his companions arrived at the island of Delos. There the famous oracle of Apollo decreed: "Seek thine ancient mother. There the race of Aeneas shall dwell and subdue all other nations."

The Trojans had a tradition that their ancestors originally came from the island of Crete. They sailed for the island, but ill luck was their constant companion. Soon sickness and poor harvests made them wanderers again. Then in a dream Aeneas was told to seek the land of Hesperia, the supposed birthplace of Dardanus, the true founder of the Trojans' race.

Again they set forth, this time for Hesperia, the land now called Italy. On the way they stopped at the island of the Harpies, hideous creatures with heads of women and bodies of birds. When the Trojans tried to eat, the Harpies descended upon the food and snatched it away with their long talons.

Forced to leave the island or die of hunger, the Trojans again embarked, accompanied by the curse of the Harpies. Avoiding the Cyclops, and Scylla and Charybdis, and surviving a storm raised by Juno, they reached Carthage without further mishap.

Aeneas arrived at Carthage when the beautiful Dido was ruler there. However, Carthage had not always been her kingdom. This unfortunate queen was the daughter of the king of Tyre and the wife of the wealthy Sichaeus. When her wicked and avaricious brother, Pygmalion, ascended the throne of Tyre, he killed Sichaeus for his wealth. Warned of coming danger, Dido gathered her friends together, loaded ships with her gold and jewels, and fled from Tyre to Africa.

In Africa she was permitted to buy only as much land as a bull's hide could cover. Craftily she ordered the Phoenicians to cut the hide into thin strips and stretched it in a continuous line until it enclosed enough land for the citadel that afterward became the famous and powerful Carthage, rival of Rome.

When Aeneas and his companions arrived at Carthage, Dido received them warmly, held games in their honor, and listened with absorbed interest to the tale of their adventures as related to her by Aeneas. Dido fell in love with the hero and offered herself and her kingdom to him.

But the gods were on the alert. Jupiter sent Mercury to remind Aeneas of his destiny in Italy. In spite of Dido's pleas and allurements, Aeneas sadly hoisted sail. In despair, Dido stabbed herself. Looking back, Aeneas saw with anguish the flames of the funeral pyre on which Dido's body was being consumed.

## The Trojan Hero

Aenēās, clārus Trōjae vir (*hero*), erat fīlius deae Veneris et Anchīsae. Māgnā cum celeritāte sociōs ad arma vocāvit, et in viīs Trōjae contrā Graecōs pūgnāvit. Sed Graecī mūrōs urbis tenuērunt et domicilia et aedificia inflammāverant. Ante oculōs patris, Pyrrhus Polītam, fīlium Priamī, et posteā rēgem Priamum necāvit, dum Hecuba, rēgīna Trōjae et uxor Priamī, cum fīliābus spectat.

Tum Aenēās per flammās patrem Anchīsam in humerīs (*shoulders*) cum celeritāte portāvit. Quod Trōjam servāre nōn potuit, ex urbe properāvit et cum patre Anchīsā et fīliō Ascaniō et paucīs sociīs ad terram novam nāvigāvit. Diū terrā marīque Aenēās errāvit (*wandered*). Post septem (*seven*) annōs, nāvēs Trōjānae in flūmen Tiberim nāvigāvērunt.

Incolae regiōnis erant Latīnī, rēxque erat Latīnus. Latium erat nōmen partis Ītaliae ubi nunc est clāra urbs Rōma. Latīnus rēx fīliam, nōmine Lāvīniam, habēbat. Turnus, prīnceps nōbilis Ītaliae, Lāvīniam pulchram in mātrimōnium dūcere (*to marry*) dēsīderābat. Sed pater Latīnus negāvit, quod vōcēs deōrum rēgem monuerant: "Externus (*Stranger*) Lāvīniam habēbit, et nōmen tuum propter facta externī clārum erit."

Latīnus rēx pācem cum Trōjānīs esse dēsīderābat, sed Amāta, uxor Latīnī, Aenēam Lāvīniam in mātrimōnium dūcere nōn dēsīderābat. Turnus, rēx Rutulōrum, fīliam rēgis amābat et māgnā cum īrā populum regiōnis incitāvit. Māgnās cōpiās habēbat. Aenēās cum paucīs hominibus auxilium ab Etrūscīs habēbat.

Inter Turnum et Aenēam multa erant proelia. Tum Turnus cum Aenēā sōlō (*alone*) pūgnāvit, sed Aenēae erat nōn pār *(equal).* Post mortem Turnī erat pāx inter Trōjānōs et Rutulōs. Latīnus Aenēae Trōjānō fīliam pulchram Lāvīniam in mātrimōnium dedit. Aenēās parvum oppidum in Latiō aedificāvit et ex nōmine uxōris Lāvīniae oppidum Lāvīnium appellāvit *(named).* Hīc *(Here)* per paucōs annōs rēgnāvit et rēgnum aequīs lēgibus administrāvit. Quod bonus vir et deōs et patrem ac fīlium amābat, poētae Rōmānī Aenēam semper laudābant.

Rome was not built in one day.
—John Heywood, 1497–1580

# *Unit* XXIV

## CONVERSATION

| | |
|---|---|
| PATER: | Dum Ascanius, Aenēae fīlius, puer est, Lāvīnia rēgnāvit. Tum propter incolārum Lāvīnī multitūdinem, mātrī *(mother)* urbem Ascanius dedit; urbem novam aedificāvit. |
| HENRĪCUS: | Ubi, pater, Aenēae fīlius urbem aedificāvit? |
| PATER: | Sub monte Albānō urbem novam, Albam Longam, aedificāvit. |
| ROBERTUS: | Nōnne multī rēgēs fortēs post Ascanium rēgnāvērunt? |
| PATER: | Multī rēgēs, fortēs audācēsque, Albae Longae imperium tenuērunt; multī autem Aenēae nōn similēs erant. |
| ROBERTA: | Num incolae Albae Longae erant Trōjānī? |
| ROBERTUS: | Aenēās regiōnis incolās Latīnōs appellāvit *(called)* quod locī nōmen fuit Latium, atque Latīnus rēx fuerat. |
| PATER: | Et clāra lingua incolārum Latī erat Latīna. |
| HENRĪCUS: | Aedificāvitne rēx Albānōrum Rōmam? |
| PATER: | Silvius Proca, Latīnōrum antīquōrum rēx, frātrum Romulī ac Remī avus *(grandfather)* erat. Puerī, fortēs et audācēs, omnēs hostēs superāvērunt et Rōmam aedificāvērunt. |

## SECTION 1 Third Declension Adjectives

▶ DISCUSSION

All Latin adjectives, except those declined like first and second declension nouns, belong to the third declension and have in the nominative singular either one, two, or three terminations.

These adjectives, with few exceptions, are declined like *i*-stem nouns of the third declension, the masculine and feminine like *cīvis*, and the neuter like *mare*. There is only one difference: in the ablative singular the adjective always ends in *-ī* (not *-e*).

## SECTION 2 Adjectives of Two Terminations

▶ DISCUSSION

Most third declension adjectives belong to the two-termination type. They have the same forms throughout the masculine and feminine genders in the singular and the plural. The neuter forms differ from the masculine and feminine only in the nominative and the accusative cases.

The following paradigm gives the declension of adjectives of two terminations. Drop the *-is* of the nominative feminine singular, and you have the base: *brev/is.*

**brevis, breve,** *short, brief* BASE: **brev/**

|  | SINGULAR | | PLURAL | |
| --- | --- | --- | --- | --- |
|  | M.&F. | N. | M.&F. | N. |
| Nom. | brevis | breve | brevēs | brevia |
| Gen. | brevis | | brevium | |
| Dat. | brevī | | brevibus | |
| Acc. | brevem | breve | brevēs (–īs) | brevia |
| Abl. | brevī | | brevibus | |

## SECTION 3 Adjectives of Three Terminations

▶ DISCUSSION

With the exception of the nominative masculine singular, these adjectives are declined like adjectives of two terminations. Only three of these adjectives are used in this book: *ācer, ācris, ācre, keen, fierce, sharp; alacer, alacris, alacre, eager, lively;* and **celer, celeris, celere,** *swift.*

**ācer, ācris, ācre,** *fierce, keen, sharp* BASE: **ācr/**

|  | SINGULAR | | | PLURAL | | |
| --- | --- | --- | --- | --- | --- | --- |
|  | M. | F. | N. | M. | F. | N. |
| Nom. | ācer | ācris | ācre | ācrēs | ācrēs | ācria |
| Gen. | | ācris | | | ācrium | |
| Dat. | | ācrī | | | ācribus | |
| Acc. | ācrem | ācrem | ācre | ācrēs (–īs) | ācrēs (–īs) | ācria |
| Abl. | | ācrī | | | ācribus | |

The base of third declension adjectives of three terminations always ends in *-r,* preceded by a consonant, except *celer, celeris, celere.* The English derivatives offer clues to the correct Latin form, as *acrid, alacrity,* and *accelerate.*

▶ PRACTICE PATTERNS

A. Decline in the singular: ācer hostis; brevis via; celere flūmen; in the plural: celer equus; fortis frāter; alacris fēmina. Translate the forms: celere flūmen, fortis frāter.

B. Write in Latin the specified forms, and give the Latin case of each:

1. swift horse (direct object)
2. fierce sailor (indirect object)
3. sharp swords (subject)
4. short journeys (with inter)
5. brave boy (with cum)
6. every mountain (with ad)

C. Decline in Latin: every street; a sharp tongue.

# SECTION 4 Adjectives of One Termination

▶ DISCUSSION

An important class of third declension adjectives has all three forms alike for the three genders in the nominative singular. These adjectives may end in the nominative in *-ns, -ar,* or *-x.* Otherwise they are declined like *brevis, breve.* The genitive singular of these adjectives is generally listed with the nominative in the vocabulary, so that it is easy to find the base.

The most numerous of these one-termination adjectives end in *-ns* with the base in *-nt,* as *potēns, potentis,* powerful.

potēns, potentis, *powerful*  BASE: **potent/**

| | SINGULAR | | PLURAL | |
|------|------------|------|----------|---|
| | M.&F. | N. | M.&F. | N. |
| Nom. | potēns | | potentēs | potentia |
| Gen. | potentis | | potentium | |
| Dat. | potentī | | potentibus | |
| Acc. | potentem | potēns | potentēs (-īs) | potentia |
| Abl. | potentī | | potentibus | |

Compare these adjectives of one, two, or three terminations:

| M. | ācer gladius | celer servus | brevis homō | potēns vir |
| F. | ācris lingua | celeris serva | brevis vīta | potēns rēgīna |
| N. | ācre proelium | celere flūmen | breve spatium | potēns verbum |

*133*

▶ STUDY HELPS

Third declension adjectives have in the positive degree *–is* in the genitive singular, *–ium* in the genitive plural, *–i* in the ablative singular. There are a few exceptions.

▶ PRACTICE PATTERNS

A. With as many of these nouns as possible, use the correct forms of audāx, omnis, celer:

      prīnceps    soror    hostis    serva    amīcus    nauta

B. Write in Latin the genitive plural of:

| | | |
|---|---|---|
| all the consuls | the swift rivers | the heavy baggage |
| the bold girls | the short streets | the powerful weapons |

## WORDS TO MASTER

---

**au′dāx, –ācis,** *adj.,* daring, bold; **au-dā′cia, –ae,** *f.,* daring, boldness (*audacity*)

**au′tem,** *postpositive conj.,* however, but, moreover

**dī′ligēns, –entis,** *adj.,* careful (*diligent*)

**for′tis, –e,** *adj.,* brave, strong (*fortitude*)

**frā′ter, –tris,** *m.,* brother (*fraternity*)

**gra′vis, –e,** *adj.,* heavy, serious, severe (*gravity*)

**hos′tis, –is,** *m.,* enemy, public enemy; *pl.,* the enemy (*hostile*)

**mōns, mon′tis,** *m.,* mountain (*montane*)

**nox, noc′tis,** *f.,* night (*nocturn*); **multā nocte,** late at night; **noctū,** at night; **prīmā nocte,** at nightfall

**om′nis, –e,** *adj.,* every, all (*omnipotent*)

**pār, pa′ris,** *adj.,* equal, same (*parity*)

**si′milis, –e,** *adj.,* like (*similar*)

## BUILDING WORD POWER

Many adjectives in Latin belong to the third declension. One large group has the suffix *–ālis* with the meaning *pertaining to*. Many of them are denominative, that is, they are formed on Latin nouns. The suffix is added to the base of the noun.

    **caput, capitis,** *head:* **capit/ + ālis = capitālis =** *capital*

Form adjectives with the suffix *–ālis* from the following nouns, and give the English derivatives: ***corpus, nātiō, nōmen, prīnceps, nāvis, fīnis, tempus, mūrus, annus, socius, lēx.***

The suffix *–īlis* has the same meaning as *–ālis.* Form Latin and English adjectives from: ***cīvis, hostis, puer, vir, servus.***

The Latin adjective ***gentīlis*** from ***gēns, gentis,*** *clan,* came into English under three different forms: *gentile,* belonging to a foreign clan, non-

**134**

Jewish; *gentle,* of good social standing because of belonging to one's clan; *genteel,* polite, worthy of a *gentle*man. *Genteel* is now used only in a humorous sense. Etymologically, what do we mean by a *gentle* horse or *gentle* breeze?

## SENTENCE PATTERNS

A. Complete and translate into English:

1. Ad Ītaliam nāvigāre, autem, fuit officium grav____ fort____ ducis.
2. Amūlius, fīlius audāx rēgis, rēgnum frātr____ occupāvit.
3. Nōnne celer____ nāvēs nautārum fort____ ad patriam properāvērunt?
4. Num omnia praemia erant par____?
5. Nōnne celer____ servī per montēs et inter flūmin____ viās aedificāvērunt?
6. Cūr hominēs potent____ et dīligent____ multā nocte ad urbem appropinquāvērunt?
7. Ācrēs host____ contrā dominōs Rōmān____ magnā cum īrā pūgnāvērunt.
8. Frātrēs audāc____ rēgem inīquum necāvērunt.
9. Rēgīna alacris Trōjānōs fort____ in Āfricā manēre dēsīderāverat.
10. Nōnne Virginēs Vestālēs inter Rōmānōs erant potent____?

B. Translate into Latin:

1. The boy was not equal to his brother. Was he like his father?
2. Every man cannot be swift and daring.
3. The powerful leader with his fierce troops seized the city at nightfall.
4. We love all the mountains, all the rivers, all the seas of America.
5. Did not the wicked king kill the son of his brother?

### The Rescue of the Twins

Post mortem Ascanī, fīlī Aenēae fortis, rēgēs et bonī et malī urbem Albam Longam administrāvērunt. Proca, rēx clārus Latīnōrum, diū magnā cum jūstitiā rēgnābat. Duōs fīliōs habēbat, Numitōrem, fortem ac benīgnum, et Amūlium, audācem atque inīquum. Post patris mortem Amūlius rēgnum occupāvit et frātrem Numitōrem expulit (*expelled*). Numitōris fīlium necāvit, et frātris fīliam, Rheam Silviam, Vestālem Virginem creāvit.

Contrā lēgēs Rhea Silvia geminōs (*twin*) fīliōs habēbat. Rōmulus et Remus mātrī (*mother*) erant cārī, sed Amūlius Rheam Silviam necāvit. Servōs geminōs in flūmen Tiberim jactāre (*throw*) jūssit. Servus benīgnus, autem, īnfantēs in alveō (*basket*) locāvit et in aquam prope rīpam alveum jactāvit. Forte (*by chance*) flūmen redundāvit (*overflowed*). Mox alveus in terrā erat. Fortūna geminōrum erat bona. Ācris lupa (*wolf*) puerōs cūrāvit et vītam īnfantium servāvit.

Faustulus, pastor rēgis, prope rīpam flūminis forte ambulābat. Subitō īnfantēs vīdit et in casam ad uxōrem portāvit. Acca Lārentia, uxor pastōris, erat laeta. Per vīgintī (*twenty*) annōs Rōmulus et Remus cum pastōribus manēbant. In agrīs labōrābant et in silvīs cum sociīs ambulābant.

Tum latrōnēs (*robbers*) ācrēs pecora (*cattle*) Faustulī raptābant (*were seizing*). Geminī fortēs et audācēs cum latrōnibus ācribus pūgnāvērunt, et Faustulō et pastōribus praedam latrōnum dedērunt. Latrōnēs māgnā cum īrā cum frātribus fortibus pūgnāvērunt. Virī potentēs Remum superāvērunt et captīvum ad rēgem portāvērunt. Rēx Amūlius latrōnēs Remum ad frātrem Numitōrem portāre jūssit.

Numitor, ubi captīvum fortem vīdit, Remum multum amāvit et rogāvit: "Esne fīlius Faustulī?" Remus Numitōrī benīgnō fābulam dē vītā geminōrum narrāvit. Numitor erat laetus. Frātrēs, audācēs fortēsque, erant nepōtēs (*grandsons*). Interim Rōmulus cum omnibus pastōribus ad rēgiam (*palace*) Amūlī properāvit. Remus cum servīs Numitōris frātrī audācī auxilium dedit, et frātrēs Amūlium potentem necāvērunt. Numitōrī rēgnum dedērunt.

Comes the blind Fury with th' abhorrèd shears
And slits the thin-spun life.
　　　　　—John Milton, 1608–1674

# Unit XXV

## CONVERSATION

REMUS: Bonus avus (grandfather) noster imperium Albae Longae bene administrat.

RŌMULUS: Urbem novam in flūminis rīpā aedificāre ubi Faustulus prīmus nōs (*us*) vīdit dēbēmus.

REMUS: Sīc honōrem ac glōriam gentī nostrae dabimus!

RŌMULUS: Urbis nostrae fāma perpetua erit!

REMUS: Alacriter ac dīligenter urbem novam aedificābimus!

RŌMULUS: Altīs mūrīs hostēs prohibēre poterimus!

REMUS: Adulēscentēs fortēs nōmine factīsque in urbe habitābunt!

RŌMULUS: Nihil timēbunt. Omnēs gentēs virtūte superābunt!

REMUS: Quid urbem nostram appellābimus?

RŌMULUS: Ego rēx esse et urbī nōmen meum dare dēsīderō!

REMUS.    Ego cum frātre meō pūgnāre nōn dēsīderō, sed rēx esse quoque dēbeō! Urbem ex nōmine meō appellābō!

RŌMULUS:  Deī nōs monēbunt! Vultūrēs spectābimus! Ego ad Palātium cum amīcīs properābō! Dīligenter augurium exspectābimus!

REMUS:    Et ego cum amīcīs meīs in Aventīnō alacriter spectābō!


# SECTION 1 Formation of Adverbs from Third Declension Adjectives

▶ DISCUSSION

You have already learned that adverbs are formed from adjectives of the first and second declension by adding –*ē* to the base of the positive degree of the adjective. Adverbs are regularly formed from adjectives of the third declension by adding –*iter* to the base of the positive degree of the adjective.

| *Adjective* | *Base* | + *Indicator* = *Adverb* |
|---|---|---|
| **fortis,** *brave* | **fort/** + | iter = **fortiter,** *bravely* |
| **ācer,** *sharp* | **ācr/** + | iter = **ācriter,** *sharply* |
| **celer,** *swift* | **celer/** + | iter = **celeriter,** *swiftly* |

If the adjectives of the third declension are of one termination with the base ending in –*nt,* –*er* is added to the base of the positive degree of the adjective: ***potent/er,*** *powerfully.*

▶ STUDY HELPS

The adverb of **audāx** is usually spelled **audācter,** *boldly;* ***facile,*** *easily,* is the accusative neuter of ***facilis,*** *easy.* The adverb ***prīmō,*** *at first,* refers to time; ***prīmum,*** *first,* refers to order.

▶ PRACTICE PATTERNS

A. Using the above formula, form adverbs from these third declension adjectives:

brevis, breve (short, brief)       similis, simile (like)
gravis, grave (heavy, serious)    dīligēns, dīligentis (careful)
alacer, –cris, –cre (eager)       ūtilis, ūtile (useful)

B. Memorize the meanings of the adjectives and adverbs on this page.

*137*

# SECTION 2 Ablative of Respect

▶ DISCUSSION

The ablative is used *without a preposition* to show *in what respect* the meaning of a noun, adjective, or verb applies. This use is called the *ablative of respect* or *of specification*. It answers the question: In what respect?

1. **Latīnus Aenēae amīcus nōmine et factīs erat.**  Latinus was a friend to Aeneas *in name and in deeds.*
2. **Cīvēs erant paucī numerō sed fortēs animō.**  The citizens were few *in number* but brave *in spirit.*

▶ PRACTICE PATTERNS

A. Translate into English:

| | | | |
|---|---|---|---|
| māgnus corpore | similis linguā | fortis bellō | Lāvīnia nōmine |
| benīgnus verbō | pārēs audāciā | clārī bellō | similis honōre |
| Brūtus nōmine | celeritāte pār | fortis pūgnā | aequus virtūte |

B. Translate into Latin:

| | | | |
|---|---|---|---|
| powerful in word | keen in mind | useful in battle | like in daring |
| strong in body | king in name | Cornelia by name | few in number |
| friend in deed | kind in deeds | bold in speech | great in war |

## WORDS TO MASTER

**admi′nistrō** (1), manage, direct, (*administer*)

**adulēs′cēns, –entis,** *m.*, young man (*adolescent*)

**al′tus, –a, –um,** *adj.*, high, deep (*alto*)

**appel′lō** (1), name, call (*appellation*)

**cas′tra, –ōrum,** *n., pl.*, camp

**gēns, gen′tis,** *f.*, tribe, nation (*gentile*)

**ho′nor, –ōris,** *m.*, distinction (*honor*)

**lo′cō** (1), place, put (*locate*)

**ni′hil,** *indecl. noun, n.*, nothing (*annihilate*)

**prohi′beō, –ēre, –uī, –itus** (2), restrain, keep away or out (*prohibit*)

**sīc,** *adv.*, so, in this manner

**vir′tūs, –tūtis,** *f.*, courage, manliness (*virtue*)

## BUILDING WORD POWER

Another group of masculine nouns of the third declension terminate in *–or,* but they are formed on the root of the verb. They denote act or condition, not agent, and have no *–t* or *–s* in their suffix. If *horrēre* means *to bristle with fear,* what is the true meaning of *horror?* Does one's hair really stand on end if one is seriously frightened?

*138*

Form the nouns ending in *-or* both in English and Latin that come from: *terrēre, tenēre, rigēre, liquēre, candēre, vigēre, valēre.*

The Latin verb *humēre* originally meant *to be moist;* therefore, *humor* meant *moisture.* The old Greeks thought that the human body had four moistures, or humors, which caused not only ailments but dispositions. In time *humor* began to be applied to a type of disposition that appreciated the amusing or comical side of things. When we speak of the *aqueous humor,* we are being consistent with the original meaning of the word. Considering the original meaning, how can we have *dry humor?*

## SENTENCE PATTERNS

A. Translate into English:

1. Apud Trōjānōs prīnceps fortis erat, nōmine Aenēās.
2. Rēx omnia dīligenter atque industriē administrābat.
3. Superāvēruntne Rōmānī Sabīnōs honōre et virtūte?
4. Num hostēs altīs in montibus castra locāvērunt?
5. Sīc prīnceps hostēs potentēs ab urbe fortiter prohibuit.
6. Adulēscentēs nihil timuērunt quod nōmine et factō erant fortēs.
7. Adulēscēns audāx urbem novam Rōmam appellāvit.
8. Erantne gentēs fīnitimae Rōmānīs amīcae?
9. In mediīs lūdīs dum Sabīnī laetī nihil timent, Romulus sīgnum celeriter dedit.
10. Sine armīs Sabīnī Rōmānīs potentibus erant nōn parēs.

B. Translate into Latin:

1. Did Romulus name the city Rome because he surpassed his brother in courage?
2. The kings, wicked in name and in deed, did not manage the kingdom well.
3. Fiercely and bravely the young men fought for their country.
4. Thus they were able to place the city near the river.
5. All the tribes were not hostile to the leaders, were they?

The Fates, Clotho, Lachesis, and Atropos.

## Realms of the Dead (continued)

**P**luto was not very happy about being assigned by Jupiter to the Lower Regions, even though he controlled the souls of the dead and had for his own all the precious stones and metals buried in the earth. He wanted a wife to share his destiny. Jupiter had promised him the beautiful Proserpina, the goddess of spring, but he had not dared keep this promise because he feared the anger of Ceres, the girl's mother, who was the goddess of the harvest. Then Pluto decided to take the matter into his own hands.

One day while Proserpina was playing with her companions and gathering flowers in the sunny fields, a dark, forbidding man suddenly appeared, seized the beautiful girl, and carried her off. Ceres was frantic with grief when she realized her daughter had disappeared. No one could tell her who the kidnaper was because Pluto possessed a magic cap of darkness that made him invisible when he visited the earth.

In her great grief Ceres neglected her duties. All over the land there was drought and famine, flood and plague. Jupiter tried to persuade the goddess of the harvest to resume her duties. She refused to do so until her daughter had been returned to her.

A compromise was effected. It was decided that Proserpina, goddess of spring, was to stay six months with her mother and six with the lord of Hades. Thus, even to this day when summertime is over, Ceres, sorrowing for her daughter, neglects the earth; winter comes and reigns until the following spring when Proserpina returns.

Close to the throne of Pluto in the Underworld sat three important and powerful personalities, the *Fates*. They were sometimes called the *Parcae*, meaning "sparers," although this was a misnomer since no mortal escaped their designs.

*Clotho*, the youngest, spun the thread of life; *Lachesis* twisted the thread into the pattern that determined each mortal's destiny; and *Atropos* controlled the fatal shears that cut the thread. With each snip of her scissors, a human life ended.

The gods, as well as all mankind, were subject to the Fates. Not even Jupiter could change the pattern or delay the close of a human destiny once the Fates had set forth a decree.

Another female trio who lived in Hades were the *Furies*, three creatures that attended Proserpina. They were imagined as horror-inspiring winged maidens, with serpents in their hair and blood dripping from their eyes. It was their particular task to punish with remorse those who had escaped punishment for their crimes.

*Hecate* was a mysterious divinity, the goddess of sorcery and witchcraft, who haunted crossroads and graveyards at night and terrorized the superstitious with her phantoms, demons, and dogs.

## The Eternal City Is Built

Rōmulus et Remus cum Numitōre Albae Longae per paucōs annōs mānsērunt. Numitor urbem bene administrāvit. Cīvēs rēgem cārum habēbant quod imperium et lēgēs erant jūstae. Sed adulēscentēs māgnam urbem propinquam locō ubi cum Faustulō et Accā Larentiā habitāverant aedificāre dēsīderāvērunt.

Statim contrōversia ācris dē locō et dē nōmine urbis novae fuit. Rōmulus in monte Palātiō et Remus in monte Aventīnō urbem aedificāre dēsīderāvērunt. "Rēx erō," clāmāvit Rōmulus, "et nōmen meum urbī dabō!" "Urbem nōmine meō appellābō, et in urbe rēgnābō!" ācriter respondit Remus.

Amīcī frātrum augurium nūntiāvērunt. "Vultūrēs servābimus (*wait for*). Vultūrēs sīgna bona semper dant." Ad Palātium Rōmulus cum amīcīs celeriter properāvit, et per longam noctem caelum dīligenter spectābat. Remus in Aventīnō quoque augurium alacriter exspectābat. Prīmā lūce (*At daybreak*) Rōmulus duodecim (*twelve*), Remus sex vultūrēs vīdit. Rōmulus fuit victor et in Palātiō urbem novam locāvit.

Mūrī urbis nōn erant altī, et Remus ubi mūrōs vīdit dērīsit (*mocked*): "Mūrī tuī hostēs nōn prohibēbunt. Nihil prohibēbunt." Statim Rōmulus māgnā cum īrā frātrem necāvit. Sīc Rōmulus imperium obtinuit et urbī novae nōmen Rōmam dedit. Posteā Rōmulus erat prīmus rēx Rōmanōrum.

# *Comprehensive Review: Units* XXI–XXV

A. Write in Latin the nominative, genitive, gender, and base of:

| | | | | | | | |
|---|---|---|---|---|---|---|---|
| eye | ship | king | youth | enemy | death | father | judgment |
| law | gift | city | chief | consul | night | device | mountain |
| man | name | camp | tribe | honor | peace | courage | trickery |
| row | wind | wife | voice | daring | region | journey | swiftness |
| sea | body | river | speed | virgin | leader | brother | citizen |

B. Write in Latin the feminine and neuter forms in the nominative plural for the following adjectives. Give the English meanings.

potēns audāx brevis altus similis ācer pār dīligēns
alacer celer fortis omnis līgneus gravis paucī ūtilis

C. Write in Latin the adverbs formed on the following adjectives. Give the English meanings of the adverbs formed.

ācer altus audāx brevis fortis longus similis
pār clārus celer gravis potēns alacer dīligēns

D. Write the English meanings of:

nihil    sīc    propter    statim    trāns    dum    autem

E. Translate into Latin:

| | | |
|---|---|---|
| through the night | against the enemy | on account of the law |
| across the sea | under water | in behalf of the brother |
| in the river | near death | among the citizens |
| into the ship | around the mountain | without the young men |
| about the leader | away from the camp | down from the mountain |
| after peace | out of the cities | with the leading man |

F. Write these synopses in the active voice, indicative mood, and translate each form:

1. administrō (third person singular)    4. appellō (third person plural)
2. prohibeō (second person plural)    5. sedeō (second person singular)
3. negō (first person plural)    6. locō (first person singular)

G. Write in Latin the present imperative plural of the following words, then change to the negative form.

restrain    reign    deny    place    manage    name

H. Decline and translate:

adulēscēns audāx    virgō potēns    jūdicium simile    iter breve

I. Write in Latin the specified forms and translate:

1. genitive plural: prīnceps, hostis, flūmen, urbs, rēx, dux
2. dative singular: cīvis, uxor, cōnsul, gēns, pater, virgō
3. nominative plural: corpus, regiō, nōmen, vōx, ōrdō, mare
4. ablative plural: nāvis, castra, adulēscēns, dolus, homō, rēx
5. accusative plural: virtūs, flūmen, frāter, mōns, lēx, iter
6. genitive singular: celeritās, mare, nox, jūdicium, dōnum, oculus


## SENTENCE PATTERNS

A. Translate into English:

1. Nōnne dux Trōjānus rēgem virtūte superābat?
2. Nūntiī ex urbe novā ad regiōnēs fīnitimās celeriter properāvērunt.
3. Cūnctī Sabīnī, patrēs et frātrēs virginum, Rōmānōs ācriter accūsāvērunt.
4. Prīncipēs ācrēs Sabīnōrum bellum contrā hostēs potentēs audācter parābant.
5. Sabīnī erant fortēs nōmine factīsque ac Rōmānīs audācibus virtūte erant parēs.
6. In locō castrīs idōneō māgnās cōpiās locāvērunt.
7. Paucī hominēs māgnīs in perīculīs semper fortēs sunt.
8. Rōmulus urbem dīligenter aedificāverat, sed Rōma paucōs incolās habēbat.
9. Cūr adulēscentēs Rōmānī dolō virginēs occupāvērunt?
10. Convocāvitne Rōmulus ad lūdōs incolās regiōnum fīnitimārum?

## B. Translate into Latin:

1. On account of serious wrongs the Sabines were hostile to the citizens of Rome.
2. Sometimes the Romans were not equal in number to their enemies.
3. Rome was in great danger because the daring enemy were near the city
4. We ought always be kind in word and in deed.
5. The powerful troops fought bravely and fiercely.


### SIGHT TRANSLATION: AENEAS

Apud Trōjānōs prīnceps fortis erat nōmine Aenēās. Virtūte et cōnsiliō sociōs superābat. Quod Graecī Trōjam occupāverant et dēlēverant, cum sociīs ex patriā properāre parāvit. Sīc Venus fīlium monuit: "Nōn jam Trōjae manē. In Ītaliam properā. Ibi cōnsiliō deōrum nova patria fīlium meum exspectat." Cum patre et fīliō parvō et paucīs sociīs fīdīs trāns mare nāvigāvit. Per septem (*seven*) annōs terrā marīque errāvit (*wandered*).

Saepe Aenēās rogāvit: "Quandō patriam novam vidēbimus?" Sed tamen deī eī (*to him*) nūntiāvērunt: "In Ītaliā cum sociīs habitābis, et in Ītaliā līberī Trōjae māgnam fāmam habēbunt." Trōjānīs fortibus multa erant perīcula. Propter pōmum aureum Jūnō et Minerva Trōjānōs novum oppidum habēre nōn dēsīderābant. "Trōjānī," inquit (*said*) Jūnō, "māgnō in perīculō saepe erunt." Tandem multa post perīcula, Aenēās parvā cum parte sociōrum et nāvium ad Ītaliam pervēnit (*arrived*).

## CONVERSATION

MAGISTER: Hodiē, puerī puellaeque, ego vōbīs fābulam longam narrābō.

ANNA: Num fābula dē multitūdine mīlitum est? Ego bellum nōn amō.

MĀRCUS: Nōnne tū mīlitēs amās? Ego mīlitēs et pūgnās vidēre semper dēsīderō. Mīlitēs sunt validī et multam potestātem habent.

STELLA: Māter mea mihi grātiam interdum dat et fābulās dē sōle et lūnā et stellīs narrat.

MAGISTER: Persōnae (*Characters*) fābulae meae sunt Echō, nympha pulchra, et Narcissus, adulēscēns pulcher. Echō erat nympha Diānae, deae lūnae. Nympha laeta cum Diānā per silvās semper properābat.

MĀRCUS: Quis erat Narcissus?

MAGISTER: Narcissus erat adulēscēns pulcher, sed quod nymphās timēbat, eās (*them*) nōn amābat. Sē amābat. Praetereā, cum sociīs cervōs in silvīs oppūgnābat.

DISCIPULĪ: Quid est fīnis fābulae? Sī tibi placet, magister, nunc nōbīs fābulam narrā!

## SECTION 1 Personal Pronouns

▶ DISCUSSION

The person indicators of the verb, *–ō, –s, –t, –mus, –tis, –nt,* tell us the person and number of the subject. *Personal pronouns,* however, are necessary for cases other than the nominative, as well as for the nominative when it is necessary to express emphasis or contrast. The personal pronouns of the first and second persons are declined as in these paradigms.

| | FIRST PERSON | | | SECOND PERSON | |
|------|------|------|------|------|------|
| | | SINGULAR | | | |
| Nom. | **ego** | *I* | | **tū** | *you* |
| Gen. | **meī** | *of me* | | **tuī** | *of you* |
| Dat. | **mihi** | *to, for me* | | **tibi** | *to, for you* |
| Acc. | **mē** | *me* | | **tē** | *you* |
| Abl. | **mē** | *from, by, with me* | | **tē** | *from, by, with you* |

**144**

| Nom. | **nōs** | *we* | **vōs** | *you* |
|------|---------|------|---------|-------|
| Gen. | **nostrum** <br> **nostrī** | } *of us* | **vestrum** <br> **vestrī** | } *of you* |
| Dat. | **nōbīs** | *to, for us* | **vōbīs** | *to, for you* |
| Acc. | **nōs** | *us* | **vōs** | *you* |
| Abl. | **nōbīs** | *from, by, with us* | **vōbīs** | *from, by, with you* |

Observe the use of the personal pronouns in these sentences:

1. *Ego tē* **laudō;** *tū mē* **laudās.**     *I* praise *you; you* praise *me.*
2. *Tū mihi* **librum dēmōnstrāvistī.**     *You* showed *me* a book.
3. **Vītam prō** *nōbīs* **dedit.**     He gave his life for *us.*

▶ STUDY HELPS

1. The possessive adjectives **meus, tuus, noster, vester** are used instead of the genitives of **ego** and **tū** when possession is expressed.

2. When the ablative forms of **ego** and **tū** are used with the preposition **cum,** the preposition follows the pronoun and is attached to it: **mēcum,** *with me;* **tēcum,** *with you;* **nōbīscum,** *with us;* **vōbīscum,** *with you.*

▶ PRACTICE PATTERNS

A. Translate into English:

| | | | | | |
|---|---|---|---|---|---|
| mihi | mēcum | ad mē | ante nōs | vōbīscum | propter tē |
| tuī | ā mē | tēcum | vestrum | dē nōbīs | circum vōs |
| meī | in mē | post tē | sine mē | inter nōs | contrā mē |

B. Translate into Latin:

| | | | | |
|---|---|---|---|---|
| of me | for you (pl.) | near me | against us | of us |
| of you (sing.) | for us | by us | from me | among you |
| for me | without us | by you (pl.) | toward me | concerning you (pl.) |

# SECTION 2 Reflexive Pronouns

▶ DISCUSSION

1. Pronouns that refer to the subject of the sentence are called *reflexive pronouns*, because through them the action expressed by the verb is reflected back upon the doer of the action, the subject.

*I* praise *myself. You* are true *to yourself. They* bought a book *for themselves.*

The person, gender, and number of the reflexive will always be the same as the subject to which it refers.

**145**

2. In English the endings *–self, –selves* are joined to personal pronouns and possessive adjectives to form the reflexive pronouns.

3. In Latin the first and second persons do not have special forms for the reflexive pronouns. The forms of the personal pronouns of the first and second persons, singular and plural, in all cases but the nominative are used for that purpose. The nominative case cannot be reflexive.

4. The *reflexive of the third person* is the same in form for all three genders, both singular and plural.

### REFLEXIVE PRONOUN, THIRD PERSON

| | | |
|---|---|---|
| Nom. | — | |
| Gen. | **suī** | *of himself, herself, itself, themselves* |
| Dat. | **sibi** | *to, for himself, herself, itself, themselves* |
| Acc. | **sē** or **sēsē** | *himself, herself, itself, themselves* |
| Abl. | **sē** or **sēsē** | *from, by, with himself, herself, itself, themselves* |

| | SINGULAR | | PLURAL | |
|---|---|---|---|---|
| First | **mē accūsō** | *I blame myself* | **nōs accūsāmus** | *we blame ourselves* |
| Second | **tē accūsās** | *you blame yourself* | **vōs accūsātis** | *you blame yourselves* |
| Third | **sē accūsat** | *he blames himself* | **sē accūsant** | *they blame themselves* |

▶ STUDY HELPS

**cum + sē = sēcum** = *with himself, herself, itself, themselves*

▶ PRACTICE PATTERNS

A. Translate into English:

| | | |
|---|---|---|
| sibi (m.) | propter sē | sē nōn laudat |
| sēcum (f.) | tū tē laudās | vōs accūsātis |
| suī (n.) | ego mē servāvī | sē nōn servāvit |
| inter sē | vir sibi grātus est | praeter vōs |

B. Translate into Latin:

| | | |
|---|---|---|
| of myself | for ourselves | among themselves |
| to yourself | of yourselves | I blamed myself. |
| from himself | of themselves | The girl is pleasing to herself. |
| ourselves (acc.) | with themselves | Did you save yourself? |

### BUILDING WORD POWER

There are a few common words in English that terminate in *–men* and that are identified with Latin neuter nouns of the third declension. The suffix *–men* is added to the present stem of a verb and denotes the means or the result of an action.

*Acūmen, acūminis*, from *acuere*, *to sharpen*, means *that which is sharpened*, but in English it has come to mean *mental sharpness*.

**146**

A *specimen*, from **specere**, *to look at with attention*, means *that by which a thing is distinguished, an example*. A *stamen* from **stāre**, *to stand*, is *that which bears the pollen of the flower*. The English plural is *stamens;* the Latin plural became the English word *stamina*, meaning *power to stand up under mental or physical hardship*.

**Volūmen**, *that which can be rolled*, originally referred to what the Romans meant by a book, which was a roll of parchment. *Volume*, the English derivative, still means *book*, but it has added meanings, especially *amount of space* or *loudness of sound*.

## WORDS TO MASTER

**fī'nis, –is,** *m.*, end, limit (*finite*); **fī'nēs, –ium,** *pl.*, boundaries, territory

**grā'tia, –ae,** *f.*, favor, grace (*gracious*)

**lū'na, –ae,** *f.*, moon (*lunatic*)

**mā'ter, mā'tris,** *f.*, mother (*maternal*)

**mī'les, –itis,** *m.*, soldier (*militia*)

**multitū'dō, –inis,** *f.*, great number (*multitude*)

**oppūg'nō** (1), attack, assault

**potes'tās, –tātis,** *f.*, power

**prae'ter,** *adv., and prep. with acc.*, besides, except (*preternatural*); **praete'reā,** *adv.*, besides

**sōl, sō'lis,** *m.*, sun (*solar*)

**stel'la, –ae,** *f.*, star (*stellar*)

**tem'pus, –oris,** *n.*, time (*temporal*)

## SENTENCE PATTERNS

A. Complete and translate into English:

1. Post breve temp____ rēx inīqu____ māgnam potestātem habuit.
2. Nōnne mātr____ līberīs bonum cōnsilium dabant?
3. Mīlit____ sibi arma parāvērunt et urb____ hostium oppūgnāvērunt.
4. Quis nōb____ sōlem, lūn____, stellās dedit?
5. Ego tēcum pūgnāre nōn dēsīder____, sed ego potestāt____ habēre dēsīderō.
6. Nōnne Rōmānī cum gentibus propinqu____ fīn____ Rōmae diū fortiter pūgnāvērunt?
7. Manēte nōbīscum, mīlitēs, quod hostēs ācr____ patriae timēmus.
8. Et ego et tū in perīcul____ esse fortēs debēmus.
9. Praetereā multitūdō mīlit____ urbem nostr____ oppūgnāba____.
10. Praeter grāti____ rēgis necesse est vōs arma habēre.

B. Translate into Latin:

1. The pretty girl is pleasing to herself but not to us.
2. Many ancient tribes adored the sun and the moon and the stars.
3. We cannot attack Rome's enemies because we do not have the power.
4. They praise the brave soldier, but he does not praise himself.
5. Did not a multitude of brave soldiers give their lives for you and for me and for all the inhabitants of our fatherland?

**147**

**A Handsome Boy and an Echo**

Ōlim Echō, nympha laeta Diānae pulchrae, in silvīs cum multitūdine nymphārum habitābat. Sōlem et stellās amābat, sed
lūnam māgnopere (*very much*) amābat, quod Diāna erat lūnae dea.
Echō autem fuit loquāx (*loquacious*), et praetereā verbum ūltimum habēre semper dēsīderābat. Jūnō, deārum māter et rēgīna,
erat invida (*jealous*) et nympham loquācem nōn amābat. Māgnā
cum potestāte nympham numquam iterum prīmum verbum sed
semper verbum ūltimum habēre jūssit.

Misera Echō ad altōs montēs properāvit et in silvīs et cavernīs
habitābat. Cotīdiē corpus nymphae ēvanēscēbat (*disappeared*) et
post breve tempus vōx sōla (*only*) manēbat. Tum adulēscentem
pulchrum vīdit et statim amāvit. Adulēscēns erat Narcissus. Sē
amābat, et omnēs incolās silvārum praeter nymphās quoque
amābat. Ōlim Narcissus cum amīcīs in silvīs erat, et subitō
amīcōs vidēre nōn poterat.

"Ubi estis, amīcī meī?" Narcissus clāmābat. "Ego adsum."

"Adsum," Echō respondit.

"Ad mē properāte! Tē dēsīderō," adulēscēns clāmābat.

"Tē dēsīderō," nympha laeta respondit. Echō prīmum clāmāre
nōn poterat sed Narcissum oculīs amāre poterat.

"Ego amīcōs meōs dēsīderō," ācriter nūntiāvit Narcissus. "Nōn
tē amō."

"Tē amō," respondit misera Echō et ad Narcissum properāvit.
Sed māgnā cum īrā clāmābat: "Nōlī ad mē appropinquāre!"

"Ad mē appropinquā," respondit Echō, sed Narcissus ā nymphā celeriter properāvit.

Posteā nympha nōn jam fuit; sed etiam hodiē ūltimum verbum
habet.

---

Far from the fiery noon and eve's one star,    *Unit* XXVII
Sat gray-hair'd Saturn, quiet as a stone.
       —John Keats, 1795–1821

## CONVERSATION

MAGISTER:    Ōlim nympha aquae Narcissō placēre (*to please*) temptāvit,
sed adulēscēns superbus (*proud*) timōrem simulāvit et ā
nymphā miserā properāvit. Narcissus nymphās nōn amābat
sed amābat sē.

STELLA: Quae erat causa? Cūr Narcissus sē amābat?

MAGISTER: Fābula est brevis. Ōlim imāginem (*reflection*) suam in stāgnō (*pond*) clārō vīdit, et statim pictūram suam amāvit. Properāvit hūc et eō, sed semper ad pictūram suī revēnit (*returned*). Cotīdiē imāginem suam obtinēre temptāvit, sed ubi aquam mōvit, nōn jam pictūram suī vidēre poterat.

ANNA: Nōnne nymphae adulēscentī auxilium dedērunt?

MAGISTER: Cotīdiē nymphae vigilābant et adulēscentem pulchrum servāre temptāvērunt; imāgō pulchra Narcissum spectābat, sed respondēre nōn poterat. Tandem mente perturbātus (*disturbed*) quod imāginem suam obtinēre nōn poterat, mortem sibi dēsīderābat. Etiam vīvus "Ēheu (*Alas*)! Ēheu!" saepe clāmābat. Et Echō semper "Ēheu! Ēheu!" triste (*sadly*) respondēbat.

## SECTION 1 Possessive Adjectives

▶ DISCUSSION

The personal pronouns **ego** and **tū** and the third person reflexive pronoun **suī** each has a corresponding adjective, called a possessive adjective. Here is the complete list:

| ego | meus, –a, –um | *my, my own, mine* |
| nōs | noster, –tra, –trum | *our, our own, ours* |
| tū | tuus, –a, –um | *your, your own, yours* |
| vōs | vester, –tra, –trum | *your, your own, yours* |
| suī | suus, –a, –um | *his, her, its, their (own), hers, theirs* |

The possessive adjectives are declined like adjectives of the first and second declensions and agree in gender, number, and case with the nouns they modify. They usually follow the nouns they modify, except when emphatic. They may be, and frequently are, omitted when easily understood from the person and number of the subject, unless emphasis or contrast is intended.

EMPHATIC: **Vir fīliōs *suōs* accūsāvit.**  The man blamed *his own* sons.

UNEMPHATIC: **Vir fīliōs amābat.**  The man loved his sons.

▶ STUDY HELPS

1. ***Tuus, –a, –um*** is used with reference to one person only; ***vester, –tra, –trum*** refers to more than one.

   **librī tuī** = *your* (sing.) *books*
   **librī vestrī** = *your* (pl.) *books*

2. ***Suus, –a, –um*** is always reflexive.

*149*

A. Translate into English:

| | | | |
|---|---|---|---|
| liber meus | liber tuus | librum suum | mātris meae |
| liber noster | liber vester | librōs suōs | mātrī tuae |
| librī meī | librī tuī | māter mea | patribus suīs |
| librī nostrī | librī vestrī | māter nostra | patrum suōrum |

B. Translate into Latin, using possessive adjectives:

| | | | |
|---|---|---|---|
| with my son | of his daughter | of your (pl.) daughters | in your camp |
| with her son | for their daughter | of my leader | for my wife |
| with his son | to their daughters | with their king | for our queen |
| with their son | her daughter (acc.) | of your (sing.) sons | of our flock |

# SECTION 2 Intensive Pronoun: *ipse, ipsa, ipsum*

▶ DISCUSSION

The *intensive pronoun* in Latin is ***ipse, ipsa, ipsum,*** *self.* It is de-clined like adjectives of the first and second declension, except for the genitive and dative cases singular. Its meaning changes according to person, number, and gender. Before translating into Latin an English word with the suffix –*self*, it is very important to know whether the word is a reflexive pronoun or an intensive pronoun, for in English both these pronouns are expressed by the suffix –*self*.

| | SINGULAR | | | PLURAL | | |
|---|---|---|---|---|---|---|
| | **M.** | **F.** | **N.** | **M.** | **F.** | **N.** |
| Nom. | **ipse** | **ipsa** | **ipsum** | **ipsī** | **ipsae** | **ipsa** |
| Gen. | **ipsīus** | **ipsīus** | **ipsīus** | **ipsōrum** | **ipsārum** | **ipsōrum** |
| Dat. | **ipsī** | **ipsī** | **ipsī** | **ipsīs** | **ipsīs** | **ipsīs** |
| Acc. | **ipsum** | **ipsam** | **ipsum** | **ipsōs** | **ipsās** | **ipsa** |
| Abl. | **ipsō** | **ipsā** | **ipsō** | **ipsīs** | **ipsīs** | **ipsīs** |

COMPARISON OF INTENSIVE AND REFLEXIVE PRONOUNS

| | |
|---|---|
| **Agricola *ipse* agrum arāvit.** | The farmer *himself* plowed the field. |
| **Agricola *sibi* agrum arāvit.** | The farmer plowed the field *for himself.* |
| ***Ipse* dux fīlium *sēcum* habuit.** | The leader *himself* had his son *with him.* |

▶ STUDY HELPS

1. *Ipse* may be used of all persons in all genders, numbers, and cases. The reflexive pronoun *suī* may never be used in the nominative case, and refers only to the third person.

2. *Ipse* merely gives additional emphasis to some noun or pronoun and may be omitted; *suī* may never be omitted without changing the thought of the sentence.

3. *Ipse* is regularly used as a pronoun or as an adjective; the reflexive pronoun *suī* is always used as a substantive pronoun.

4. *Ipse* is sometimes translated *very* or *actual*.

▶ PRACTICE PATTERNS

A. Decline: māter ipsa; pater ipse; vulnus ipsum.

B. Translate into English:

| | | |
|---|---|---|
| gregēs ipsōs | mentis ipsīus | simulācrō ipsī |
| mundō ipsī | lēgātōrum ipsōrum | dīligentiā ipsā |

C. Write in Latin the specified form, and give the case and the number used. Translate into English:

1. corpus ipsum (subject)
2. pecūnia ipsa (means)
3. homō ipse (accompaniment)
4. dīligentia ipsa (manner)
5. montēs ipsī (with prope)
6. lēgēs ipsae (direct object)

D. Translate into Latin:

we ourselves · the very man · about life itself · The queens praise themselves.
the very night · the actual fact · the building itself · The queens themselves work.

## WORDS TO MASTER

**grex, gre′gis,** *m.,* herd, flock (*gregarious*)

**lēgā′tus, –ī,** *m.,* envoy, ambassador (*legate*)

**mēns, men′tis,** *f.,* mind (*mental*)

**mun′dus, –ī,** *m.,* universe, world (*mundane*)

**mū′tō** (1), move, change (*mutation*)

**sa′lūs, –ūtis,** *f.,* safety, salvation (*salutary*)

**si′mulō** (1), pretend (*simulate*); **simulā′crum, –i,** *n.,* figure, image

**ti′mor, –ōris,** *m.,* fear, cowardice (*timorous*)

**ubī′que,** *adv.,* everywhere (*ubiquitous*)

**vi′gilō** (1), be awake, be on guard, watch (*vigilant*)

**vī′vus, –a, –um,** *adj.,* alive, living (*vivid*)

**vul′nus, –eris,** *n.,* wound (*vulnerable*)

## BUILDING WORD POWER

It is an almost invariable rule that nouns in English ending in *–tion* or *–sion* are derived from Latin nouns of the third declension, the suffix of which is *–iō* and the gender feminine. These Latin nouns have been formed on the stem of the perfect passive participle. Therefore, if you

**151**

know the meaning of the noun in English, you can usually figure out the Latin infinitive and its meaning.

*creation*: **creātiō, –ōnis,** from **creātus** (**creāre** = *to create*)

Using this method of procedure, figure out the Latin form of the nominative case and the infinitive of the first conjugation verbs from which the following English words are derived: *navigation, liberation, habitation, invocation, narration.*

*Vision, motion, mansion, session* are formed from participles of second conjugation verbs. Write the present active infinitives of these verbs.

A few derivatives in *–ion* are action nouns based on the root of the verb and do not have an *–s* or *–t*. What is the nominative case in Latin for: *legion, region, rebellion, suspicion, opinion?*

The word **legiō,** besides meaning *a gathering* or *choosing,* meant *a chosen body, a legion.* The legion was a division of the Roman army consisting of ten cohorts and comprising between 4200 and 6000 men. As a general rule, the legion was composed of Roman citizens. The standard was a silver eagle. It was considered a terrible disgrace to lose a standard in battle. The legions were usually designated by numerals, although sometimes special names were used, as **Victrix,** *the Victorious.* It was by means of her legions that Rome won and guarded her great empire.

**SENTENCE PATTERNS**

A. Translate into English:
1. Ego ipse tē propter virtūtem tuam laudō.
2. Lēgātus ipse amīcōs suōs servāvit, sed sē nōn servāvit.
3. Nōnne tū mentem tuam mūtāre potes?
4. Per longam noctem mīlitēs sine timōre vigilābant.
5. Vōs ipsī longē aberātis ā proeliīs et vulneribus.
6. Fēminae ipsae māgnum timōrem prō salūte līberōrum habēbant.
7. Deī erant ubīque, sed nōs deōs ipsōs vidēre nōn poterāmus.
8. Agricola bonus ipse gregēs suōs dīligenter cūrāvit.
9. Num simulācra deōrum erant vīva? Nōnne Rōmānī timōrem simulābant?
10. Servābantne māgnō cum studiō deī ipsī salūtem mundī?

B. Translate into Latin:
1. They themselves did not adore images of the gods, did they?
2. The master himself will give a great reward to us, will he not?
3. Did the Roman poets themselves tell stories about living gods?
4. Whose images could they see in the houses and in the temples?
5. Who watched carefully the words and the deeds of the children?

*152*

Janus, the two-faced god.

## Roman Divinities

Just as some deities are found only in the Greek religion, so others are strictly Roman inventions. Two-faced Janus was one such god. He occupied an important place in the Roman religion. He was the god of all beginnings, and his name was invoked first in all undertakings. January, named for him because he opened the year, was his special month and New Year's day his principal festival. His chief temple in Rome faced east and west for the beginning and the ending of the day. Between the doors stood his statue with two faces, one young and one old. These doors were closed only when there was peace. They were closed three times in the first seven hundred years of the city's life: in the reign of the good king Numa; after the First Punic War when Carthage was defeated in 241 B.C.; and "when the whole world was at peace" during the reign of Augustus. The latter closed the doors of the temple with his own hands.

The Saturnalia, a festival in honor of Saturn, the god of seed and sowing, was held every winter and was the merriest of all festivals. The Quirinalia was a festival in honor of Quirinus, a god of war. Romulus was exalted to a place among the immortals, and was thought to have been carried up to heaven on February 17, the date of the Quirinalia. Consequently, Quirinus and Romulus became identified with one another.

The god of landmarks or boundaries was Terminus. His statue was a stone placed in the ground marking boundaries of fields. His worship is supposed to have been instituted by Numa, who ordered a festival kept every year in his honor. The Terminalia was celebrated on February 21. Neighbors gathered around and crowned with garlands the landmarks between adjoining properties. This god could be worshiped only in the open air.

A festival called the Floralia was held at the end of April in honor of Flora, goddess of flowers. The Vertumnalia, in honor of Vertumnus, was celebrated in August to mark the transition from fall to winter. There were many other festivals in honor of deities (originally numina) who were closely associated with the simple acts of everyday life: Silvanus, god of the fields and forests; Faunus, god of the shepherds and agriculture; Pales, of pasture and cattle; Pomona, of fruit trees.

According to early Roman belief, each man had a Genius and each woman a Juno. These were spirits who had given them being and were their protectors through life.

Important heroes were deified and placed in the heavens as stars and constellations. The Romans even erected temples for their worship.

## Religion of the Early Romans

JŪLIA: Herī, Anna, tū mihi multa dē nymphā pulchrā et adulēscente pulchrō narrāvistī. Hodiē mihi fābulās dē deīs Rōmānīs antīquīs narrā, sī placet tibi.

ANNA: Poētae et Rōmānī et Graecī multās fābulās dē multitūdine deōrum et deārum narrābant. Magistrī Rōmānī līberōs fābulās in lūdō docēbant.

JŪLIA: Vidēbantne hominēs deōs ipsōs?

ANNA: In fābulīs hominēs deōs deāsque saepe vidēbant et interdum deī corpora hominum vīvōrum simulābant et cum hominibus mortālibus ambulābant.

JŪLIA: Quī, Anna, erant prīmī deī Rōmānī?

ANNA: Prīmō Rōmānī antīquī animās (*spirits*) Nātūrae adōrābant. Ubīque erant animae Rōmānae et ubīque vigilābant. Tōtum (*whole*) mundum clārē vidēbant. Salūtem līberōrum dīligenter servābant.

JŪLIA: Habēbantne Rōmānī aliōs (*other*) deōs?

ANNA: Posteā Rōmānī deōs Sabīnōs et Etrūscōs amābant et adōrābant. Sāturnus erat deus agricultūrae, Silvānus deus silvārum, Palēs deus pastōrum et gregum, Terminus deus terminōrum. Sāturnus populō Rōmānō grātus erat.

JŪLIA: Quī erant Larēs et Penātēs?

ANNA: Larēs erant animae mājōrum (*ancestors*). Omnia perīcula et mala ā domiciliīs prohibēbant. Penātēs erant deī domiciliōrum. Penātēs bona et pecūniam et gregēs familiae cūrābant.

JŪLIA: Habentne Rōmānī statuās deōrum ipsōrum?

ANNA: In domiciliīs et templīs erant simulācra deōrum.

JŪLIA: Ego simulācra antīqua deōrum et deārum vīdī. Suntne simulācra deōrum Rōmānōrum?

ANNA: Fortasse (*Perhaps*) erant simulācra deōrum Graecōrum. Crās tibi fābulās dē deīs deābusque Graecīs narrābō.

*154*

Death's boatman takes no bribe, nor brings
Ev'n skilled Prometheus back from Hades' shore.
—Horace, 65–8 B.C.

*Unit*

XXVIII

## CONVERSATION

ANNA: Mercurius erat celer nūntius deōrum.   Is aquilae similis ad terram volābat et ad hominēs mortālēs mandāta Jovis portābat.
Interdum fulmina ējus etiam portābat.

JŪLIA: Nōnne Jūnō etiam nūntium habēbat?

ANNA: Praeter culpās suās Jūnō, uxor et soror Jovis, nūntiam habēbat.

JŪLIA: Quod erat nōmen ējus?

ANNA: Nūntia Jūnōnis erat virgō pulchra, nōmine Īris.   Per noctem
ea cum deīs et deābus in Olympō habitābat;   sed prīmā lūce
Īris ad fīnēs mundī ventō similis properāvit.

JŪLIA: Ubi hominēs eam spectābant, quid vidēbant?

ANNA: Post tempestātem (*storm*) ubi Īris trāns caelum volābat, hominēs
virginem pulchram cum alīs (*wings*) multōrum colōrum vidēbant.

JŪLIA: Nōnne hominēs eam amābant?

ANNA: Omnēs eam deam amābant, sed agricolae eam māgnopere adōrābant quod caelō aquam dabat.   Ubi aqua dēscendit, agrōs jūvit.

JŪLIA: Laudem dare nūntiae Jūnōnis est grātum et facile.   Nōnne ea
Jūnōnī sacrificia et dōna fēminārum Rōmānārum dabat?

ANNA: Ita, dedit.   Crās ego tibi fābulās dē deīs Graecīs narrābō.

## SECTION 1 Demonstratives

▶ DISCUSSION

In English we have words that are frequently accompanied by a
pointing gesture.   We call these words *demonstratives* (*dē* + *mōnstrāre*
= *point out*).   They stand for or point out definitely a person or object
previously mentioned.   *This* and *that* are the demonstratives in English;
*is, īdem, hic, ille, iste* are the demonstratives in Latin.

These demonstratives may be either pronouns or adjectives and may
be used in all genders and all cases.   As *pronouns* they take the place
of nouns and must agree with their antecedents in gender and number,
but not in case.   As *adjectives* they must follow the rules in Latin and
agree with the nouns they modify in gender, number, and case.

**155**

Observe that the following paradigm is very similar to that of adjectives of the first and second declensions, except for the genitive and dative singular, which are alike for all genders. The same is true of the intensive pronoun *ipse* and the other demonstratives.

DECLENSION OF **Is, Ea, Id**

|  | M. |  | F. |  | N. |  |
|---|---|---|---|---|---|---|
|  |  |  | SINGULAR |  |  |  |
| Nom. | **is** | *he* | **ea** | *she* | **id** | *it* |
| Gen. | **ējus** | *his, of him* | **ējus** | *her, of her* | **ējus** | *its, of it* |
| Dat. | **eī** | *to, for him* | **eī** | *to, for her* | **eī** | *to, for it* |
| Acc. | **eum** | *him* | **eam** | *her* | **id** | *it* |
| Abl. | **eō** | *from, by, with him* | **eā** | *from, by, with her* | **eō** | *from, by, with it* |
|  |  |  | PLURAL |  |  |  |
| Nom. | **eī** | *they* | **eae** |  | **ea** |  |
| Gen. | **eōrum** | *their, of them* | **eārum** |  | **eōrum** |  |
| Dat. | **eīs** | *to, for them* | **eīs** |  | **eīs** |  |
| Acc. | **eōs** | *them* | **eās** |  | **ea** |  |
| Abl. | **eīs** | *from, by, with them* | **eīs** |  | **eīs** |  |

▶ STUDY HELPS

1. There are no special words for the pronouns of the third person in Latin. **Hic, ille, iste, is** may be used, but the forms of **is** are the most common in this use.

2. The nominative forms **is, ea, id** and their plurals are expressed as subjects for emphasis only.

3. **Is, ea, id** is the most frequently used demonstrative pronoun and adjective, but it is less forceful and less definite than the other demonstratives. The forms of **is, ea, id** may be translated as *this* or *that*.

## SECTION 2 Distinction Between ē*jus* and *suus*

▶ DISCUSSION

If the possessive adjectives *his, her, its* refer to the subject, the reflexive adjective **suus, –a, –um** must be used. If they do not refer to the subject, the genitive of the personal pronoun, **ējus** in the singular, **eōrum, eārum, eōrum** in the plural, *must* be used.

1. **Pater līberōs suōs amat.** The father loves *his* children (*his own*).
2. **Pater līberōs ējus amat.** The father loves *his* children (*someone else's*)

1. *Suus, -a, -um* is possessive in all cases; the demonstrative pronouns show possession only in the genitive case.

2. Demonstrative adjectives precede their nouns; possessive and reflexive adjectives usually follow the nouns they modify.

▶ PRACTICE PATTERNS

A. Translate into English; tell the gender, number, and case of each form. Use *his own*, etc., for the reflexive adjectives.

| | | | | |
|---|---|---|---|---|
| id | ab eō | librī eōrum | domicilia sua | prō eīs deābus |
| eī | prō eīs | librī suī | animus ējus | prō eīs deīs |
| eōs | propter ea | librōrum suōrum | eae noctēs | in eā lūce |
| eae | fulmen ējus | dīligentiā ējus | ea sacrificia | sacrificium ējus |
| ea | fulmina sua | domicilium eōrum | prope eam partem | sacrificia sua |

B. Tell the gender, number, and case of each possessive adjective and of each demonstrative pronoun or adjective; then write the correct form in Latin:

| | | | |
|---|---|---|---|
| to him | with them | their own faults | her praise |
| for her | of them | with their light | her own praise |
| for it | of that eagle | with their own light | her sister |
| of it | for them | to (ad) those parts | their faults |

## WORDS TO MASTER

**a'quila, -ae,** *f.*, eagle (*aquiline*)
**cul'pa, -ae,** *f.*, fault (*culpable*)
**fa'cilis, -e,** *adj.*, easy (*facile*)
**ful'men, -inis,** *n.*, thunderbolt (*fulminate*)
**laus, lau'dis,** *f.*, praise (*laudable*)
**lūx, lū'cis,** *f.*, light (*lucent*); **prīmā lūce,** at daybreak
**māgno'pere,** *adv.*, greatly, very much

**pars, par'tis,** *f.*, part, party; faction, usually *pl.* (*partner*)
**quot,** *indecl. interrog. adj.*, how many? (*quotient*)
**sa'cer, -cra, -crum,** *adj.*, holy (*sacred*)
**sacrifi'cium, -ī,** *n.*, sacrifice (*sacrificial*)
**so'ror, -ōris,** *f.*, sister (*sorority*)

## BUILDING WORD POWER

We have already considered the suffix *-ālis,* which has the general meaning of *pertaining to* when attached to nouns. If an *l* occurs in the last or second-to-last syllable of the noun to which the suffix *-ālis* is to be attached, the *l* in the suffix is changed to *r* and becomes *-āris.* Instead of being *populālis,* the word becomes *populāris,* from which we have the English adjective, *popular,* pertaining to the people.

What are the English words for: *oculāris, īnsulāris, lūnāris, familiāris?* What are the Latin adjectives for: *consular, solar?* A few of the English derivatives end in *-ary* instead of *-ar*, as *military* (**mīlitāris**) and *salutary* (**salutāris**).

Adjectives that end in *-āris* belong to the third declension. There is another group of adjectives that end in *-ārius* in Latin. These are declined like first and second declension adjectives. In English they end in *-ary, -arious,* or *-arian.* Note that the Latin for *military* is **mīlitāris;** for *temporary,* **temporārius.**

## SENTENCE PATTERNS

A. Translate into English:

1. Nōnne aquila patrī ipsī deōrum sacra erat?
2. Quot hominēs erant sine culpā?
3. Propter ea nōs ipsae Jūnōnī dōna et sacrificia dedimus.
4. Māgna laus nōbīs nōn est bona, sed nōs eam māgnopere amāmus.
5. Ubi Sabīnī Rōmānōs fīliās sorōrēsque sibi dare jūssērunt, Rōmānī respondērunt: "Eae nōbīscum laetae erunt."
6. Sōl lūx mundī est, sed multī hominēs eam lūcem vidēre nōn possunt.
7. Narrā, Ō magister, nōbīs fābulam dē patre deōrum et fulmine ējus.
8. Sorōrī ējus laudem dare est facile quod ipsa nōbīs māgnopere cāra est.
9. Quibus eās partēs dedērunt?
10. Amāvēruntne Rōmānī tandem fīliās sorōrēsque fīnitimōrum?

B. Translate into Latin:

1. This part is small; I do not like it.
2. His sister praises herself, but her friends do not praise her.
3. Did they greatly fear his thunderbolts and the eagle sacred to him?
4. How many sisters did the king of the gods have?
5. The man easily saved his children; he did not save himself.

## The Graeco-Roman Celestial Court

ANNA: Hodiē ego tibi fābulās dē deīs Graecīs narrābō. Post multa proelia Rōmānī Graecōs superāvērunt. Rōmānī fābulās et simulācra deōrum Graecōrum amābant; mox deōs ipsōs adōrābant.

JŪLIA: Quot erant deī Graecī?

ANNA: Duodecim (*Twelve*) erant māgnī deī et deae. Juppiter (Jovis Pater) erat pater et deōrum et deārum et rēx hominum.

JŪLIA: Ubi habitābat Juppiter?

ANNA: Is in Olympō altīs in montibus rēgnābat et māgnam potestātem habēbat. Juppiter sibi caelum, terram, rēgnum omnium deōrum tenēbat. Fulmen erat tēlum ējus et aquila eī erat sacra. Ea avis (*bird*) erat sīgnum potestātis ējus et posteā etiam legiōnum Rōmānōrum. Frātribus suīs ac sorōribus partēs rēgnī suī dedit. Jūnō, uxor ējus, erat rēgīna deōrum et deārum. Sed Jūnō erat invida (*envious*) et multās culpās habēbat.

JŪLIA: Num Rōmānī eam amābant?

ANNA: Eam timēbant, sed omnēs fēminae et virginēs eam ōrābant. Erant multa templa Jūnōnis in Ītaliā et in prōvinciīs.

JŪLIA: Trōjānīs benīgna nōn erat, et ego eam nōn amō.

ANNA: Tē eam amāre necesse nōn est. Plūtōnem et Neptūnum, frātrēs Jovis, amābis. Plūtō erat rēx Tartarī. Dextrā (*right hand*) clavem (*key*) tenēbat; sinistrā (*left hand*) sceptrum habēbat. Plūtō semper erat tristis (*sad*); lūcem nōn amābat.

JŪLIA: Cūr Plūtō erat tristis?

ANNA: Erat rēx mortuōrum (*dead*) et rēgnum ējus sub terrā erat. Prōserpina, fīlia pulchra Cereris, erat uxor ējus, sed per sex mēnsēs annī cum mātre habitābat. Propter multās causās erat tristis.

JŪLIA: Eratne Neptūnus frāter ējus quoque tristis?

ANNA: Crās ego tibi fābulam dē Neptūnō narrābō.

Like Niobe, all tears.
—William Shakespeare, 1564–1616
*Hamlet*

# Unit XXIX

## CONVERSATION

JŪLIA: Quis erat superba (*proud*) Niobē? Eratne dea, magistra?

MAGISTRA: Dea nōn erat. Ālās in pedibus suīs nōn habēbat. Īgnem focī nōn cūrābat. Undās maris nōn temperābat (*did not regulate*). Rēgīna superba Thēbārum (*of Thebes*) antīquārum erat.

JŪLIA: Cūr superba erat? Eratne pulchra fēmina?

MAGISTRA: Niobē erat superba quod septem fīliōs ac septem fīliās habēbat, sed ea rēgīna pulchra semper tristis (*sad*) erat.

CORNĒLIA: Quae erat causa? Nōnne līberōs suōs amābat?

MAGISTRA: Māgna īra eam mōvit quod cīvēs urbis ējus Lātōnae sacrificia dabant. "Cūr," rogāvit, "mihi ea sacrificia nōn datis? Lātōna ūnum fīlium, ūnam fīliam habet; ego septem fīliōs ac septem fīliās habeō."

CORNĒLIA: Nōnne ea verba rēgīnae superbae īram deae movēbant?

MAGISTRA: Ad līberōs sine morā Lātōna properāvit atque eōs auxilium rogāvit. Apollō prīmum, secundum, tertium, omnēs septem fīliōs necāvit; Diāna omnēs septem fīliās necāvit. Itaque Niobē tristis sōla (*alone*) mānsit.

# Numerals

▶ DISCUSSION

In both English and Latin we have *cardinal* and *ordinal* numbers. The cardinals tell us how many, as *one, two,* etc. The word *cardinal* is derived from the Latin **cardō, cardinis,** which means *hinge* or *pivot.* These numbers are called *cardinal* because they are considered the most important and because other kinds of numbers depend upon, or pivot around, them. In Latin one, two, and three are declined; from four to one hundred are indeclinable.

The word *ordinal* is derived from the Latin word **ōrdō, ōrdinis,** which means *order.* With few exceptions, the ordinals are adjectives derived from the cardinals.

| ARABIC | ROMAN | CARDINAL | ORDINAL |
|---|---|---|---|
| 1 | I | **ū′nus, –a, –um,** *one* | **prī′mus, –a, –um,** *first* |
| 2 | II | **du′o, du′ae, du′o,** *two* | **secun′dus, –a, –um,** *second* |
| 3 | III | **trēs, tri′a,** *three* | **ter′tius, –a, –um,** *third* |
| 4 | IV | **quat′tuor,** *four* | **quār′tus, –a, –um,** *fourth* |
| 5 | V | **quīn′que,** *five* | **quīn′tus, –a, –um,** *fifth* |
| 6 | VI | **sex,** *six* | **sex′tus, –a, –um,** *sixth* |
| 7 | VII | **sep′tem,** *seven* | **sep′timus, –a, –um,** *seventh* |
| 8 | VIII | **oc′tō,** *eight* | **octā′vus, –a, –um,** *eighth* |
| 9 | IX | **no′vem,** *nine* | **nō′nus, –a, –um,** *ninth* |
| 10 | X | **de′cem,** *ten* | **de′cimus, –a, –um,** *tenth* |
| 20 | XX | **vīgin′tī,** *twenty* | |
| 100 | C | **cen′tum,** *one hundred* | |
| 1000 | M | **mīl′le,** *one thousand* | |

DECLENSION OF NUMERALS

**Ūnus,** *one*　　　　　　　　　　　　　**Duo,** *two*

| | M. | F. | N. | M. | F. | N. |
|---|---|---|---|---|---|---|
| Nom. | ūnus | ūna | ūnum | duo | duae | duo |
| Gen. | ūnīus | ūnīus | ūnīus | duōrum | duārum | duōrum |
| Dat. | ūnī | ūnī | ūnī | duōbus | duābus | duōbus |
| Acc. | ūnum | ūnam | ūnum | duōs (duo) | duās | duo |
| Abl. | ūnō | ūnā | ūnō | duōbus | duābus | duōbus |

*160*

|  | Trēs, *three* | | Mille, *thousand* | |
| --- | --- | --- | --- | --- |
|  | M. & F. | N. | SINGULAR | PLURAL |
| Nom. | trēs | tria | mīlle | mīlia |
| Gen. | trium | trium | mīlle | mīlium |
| Dat. | tribus | tribus | mīlle | mīlibus |
| Acc. | trēs | tria | mīlle | mīlia |
| Abl. | tribus | tribus | mīlle | mīlibus |

▶ STUDY HELPS

1. The cardinal numbers are usually followed by *ex* with the ablative. In English we say *one of;* in Latin *one from* (*ūnus ex librīs*).

2. *Centum* (100) in the singular is indeclinable.

3. *Mīlle* (1000) in the singular is an indeclinable adjective; in the plural, *mīlia,* a noun, is declined like a neuter *i*-stem. Notice the spelling; there are two *l's* in the singular, one *l* in the plural form. The *plural* forms of *mīlia* are always followed by the genitive.

▶ PRACTICE PATTERNS

A. Translate into English:

| | | |
| --- | --- | --- |
| ūnī virō | tria flūmina | tribus agricolīs |
| centum librī | ūnīus nōminis | cum mīlle mīlitibus |
| centum līberī | duābus deābus | cum quīnque mīlibus mīlitum |

B. Count to ten in Latin by cardinal numbers; by ordinal numbers.

C. Decline in the singular:

septimus agricola    tertia hōra    ūna fīlia mea    secunda āla

D. Translate into Latin:

| | | | | |
| --- | --- | --- | --- | --- |
| first altar | third wave | fifth fireplace | seventh sister | ninth part |
| second foot | fourth fire | sixth head | eighth eagle | tenth messenger |

E. Decline in Latin:

| | | | | |
| --- | --- | --- | --- | --- |
| one head | two wings | three fires | four sailors | these five brothers |

## WORDS TO MASTER

ā'la, –ae, *f.,* wing (*alate*)

ā'ra, –ae, *f.,* altar

ca'put, –itis, *n.,* head (*capital*)

fo'cus, –ī, *m.,* hearth, fireplace (*focus*)

īg'nis, –is, *m.,* fire (*ignite*)

i'taque, *conj.,* and so, therefore

ō'ra, –ae, *f.,* shore; **ōra mari'tima,** seacoast

pēs, pe'dis, *m.,* foot (*pedal*)

pe'des, –itis, *m.,* foot soldier, *pl.,* infantry

sānc'tus, –a, –um, *adj.,* holy, sacred (*sanctity*)

ta'men, *conj.,* however, nevertheless, yet

un'da, –ae, *f.,* wave (*undulate*)

**161**

## BUILDING WORD POWER

All our cardinal numbers, except dozen and million, came into our language from the Anglo-Saxon and are therefore of Teutonic origin. All but one of our ordinal numbers are likewise of Teutonic origin; but the Latin cardinals and ordinals have given a large number of derivatives to our English language.

From what Latin cardinals are these words derived: *union, duet, quadrilateral, quintessence, sextant, trident?* Perhaps you can find your own derivatives from these ordinals: ***prīmus, secundus, octāvus, decimus, quārtus.***

Sometimes in your reading you come across words like *twofold.* The suffix *–fold* is Teutonic. The Latin for *fold* is ***plicāre.*** What are we really saying when we use the word *duplicate?*

The suffix from ***plicāre*** became in English *–ple, –ble, –ply, –plex,* as in *triple, treble, multiply, duplex. Duplicity* really means double folding. What does *simplicity* mean? It is derived from ***semel,*** *once,* and ***–plex,*** *fold.*

## SENTENCE PATTERNS

A. Translate the English word into Latin, and then translate the entire sentence into English:

1. Herī ego (myself) tibi quīnque librōs dedī. Ubi sunt eī librī?
2. Quot (heads) sunt tria et quattuor? Ūnum et octō?
3. Vulcānus, frāter Martis, erat deus (fire) et Vesta erat dea focī.
4. Nōnne Diāna ipsa fīliās (seven) rēgīnae necāvit?
5. Dux ūnum ex prīncipibus et duōs ex (infantry) accūsāvit.
6. Ubi Diāna et Apollō omnēs līberōs rēgīnae necābant, Niobē vītam (one) fīliae servāre temptāvit.
7. Undae prope ōram maritimam erant altae et āram (destroyed).
8. (However), sex Vestālēs Virginēs īgnem sacrum cūrābant.
9. Nāvis ab ōrā (twenty) pedēs aberat.
10. Dea frūmentī et dea focī erant duae (sisters) Jovis.

B. Translate into Latin:

1. Who killed the seven sons and the seven daughters of the daring queen?
2. One and one are two; two and two are four; three and three are six; four and four are eight; five and five are ten.
3. Why did thousands of foot soldiers rush to the shore?
4. The teacher gave rewards to the third, fifth, and ninth boys.
5. The leader ordered a hundred soldiers to attack the town.

*162*

The seahorse, a trident, and a dolphin — symbols of Neptune, god of the sea.

## Major Greek and Roman Gods

In ancient times it was the aim of an educated Roman to become familiar with Greek literature and with the stories of the gods as told by the Greeks. For many centuries after the downfall of Rome, Greek was practically unknown, whereas Latin was the second language of every educated person. For this reason the Latin names rather than the Greek ones came into Western literature. It is well, since many writers go back to the Greek forms, to be able to identify the gods in both Latin and Greek.

| GREEK | LATIN | SPHERE OF ACTIVITY | SYMBOLS |
|---|---|---|---|
| Zeus | Jupiter (Jove) | Ruler of the gods and mankind | Eagle, thunderbolts, oak |
| Hera | Juno | Queen of the gods; wife of Jove; patroness of married women | Pomegranate, peacock, cuckoo |
| Hades | Pluto (Dis) | God of the Underworld | Chariot, Cerberus, scepter, key to the Underworld |
| Poseidon | Neptune | God of sea, horses, and earthquakes | Trident, dolphin, horses |
| Apollo | Apollo | God of sun, poetry, music, medicine | Lyre,* arrows, sun chariot |
| Artemis | Diana | Goddess of moon, hunting; patroness of maidens | Crescent, stag, arrows |
| Hermes | Mercury | God of commerce, theft; messenger of the gods | Winged cap, winged sandals, caduceus † |
| Ares | Mars | God of war | Sword, shield, dogs, vultures |
| Hephaestus | Vulcan | God of fire, metalworkers | Anvil, forge |
| Demeter | Ceres | Goddess of agriculture | Sheaf of wheat, poppies, cornucopia |
| Pallas Athena | Minerva | Goddess of wisdom, war, weaving | Aegis,‡ owl, olive tree, shield |
| Aphrodite | Venus | Goddess of love and beauty | Doves, sparrows |
| Hestia | Vesta | Goddess of hearth, home | Hearth fire |

* A lyre was a musical instrument played like a harp.

† A caduceus was a winged staff with two serpents twined around it.

‡ An aegis was a shield or breastplate. The head of the Medusa was fixed on the aegis of Minerva.

## More About the Graeco-Roman Celestial Court

JŪLIA: Ubi rēgnāvit Neptūnus? Mihi fābulam narrā, sī placet tibi.

ANNA: Neptūnus sub aquā habitābat, sed frātrī suō Plūtōnī dissimilis (*unlike*) laetus erat. Is undās maris temperābat (*regulated*) et aquās omnēs cūrābat.

JŪLIA: Quae erant sīgna potestātis ējus?

ANNA: Is deus sinistrā (*in his left hand*) sceptrum tenēbat. Sceptrum erat tridēns. Delphīnī (*Dolphins*) post eum semper nātābant (*swam*). Currum (*chariot*) cum quattuor equīs habēbat. Interdum Nymphae marīnae cum eō erant. Nōn erat tristis (*sad*) quod delphīnōs, equōs, Nymphās amābat, et agitāre currum (*to drive a chariot*) deō maris semper grātum erat.

JŪLIA: Quot fīliōs habēbat Juppiter?

ANNA: Mārs, Vulcānus, Mercurius erant trēs fīliī Jovis. Prīmus erat deus bellī et arma ac proelia semper dēsīderābat. Mīlitēs deum bellī māgnopere amābant, quod semper Rōmānōs adjuvābat, et saepe mīlitibus eōrum victōriam dabat.

Secundus fīlius īgnem in potestāte suā tenēbat. Is sub Monte Aetnā habitābat, et ibi fulmina Jovis, et tēla et scūta et galeās (*helmets*) deōrum parābat. Vertex montis īgnem saepe ēmittēbat.

Tertius fīlius ālās celerēs in pedibus suīs habēbat, quod deōrum nūntius erat, et trāns caelum, mare, terram nūntiōs et mandāta deōrum ad hominēs portābat. Dextrā parvum saccum (*sack*) et sinistrā cadūceum (*herald's staff*) tenēbat, quod cadūceus nūntiōrum sīgnum erat. Officia Mercurī multa et varia erant. Domicilia servābat; mercātōrēs (*merchants*), viātōrēs (*travelers*), furēs (*thieves*) cūrābat.

JŪLIA: Fīliī Jovis certē gravia negōtia administrābant. Nōnne Juppiter sorōrēs habēbat?

ANNA: Vesta ac Cerēs sorōrēs Jovis erant. Prīma soror, Vesta, erat dea domicilī et focī. In omnī domiciliō Rōmānō erat āra Vestae atque in Forō Rōmānō templum deae. In eō templō sex Vestālēs Virginēs flammam sacram semper servābant.

JŪLIA: Quālis dea erat Cerēs? Habēbatne negōtia gravia?

ANNA: Secunda soror, Cerēs, dea frūmentī atque agrōrum, agricolās cūrābat. Prōserpina, fīlia ējus, Plūtōnis uxor erat.

JŪLIA: Num Minerva soror Jovis erat? Nōnne erat dea sapientiae (*wisdom*)?

ANNA: Ex capite Jovis Minerva nāta est (*was born*). Tamen bella ac proelia amābat, et serpentēs eī erant sacrae.

For mortal daring is too high.
In our blind folly we storm heaven itself.
—Horace, 65–8 B.C.

## CONVERSATION

APOLLŌ: Cūr, mī fīlī, hūc properāvistī? Quae hūjus itineris est causa? Via erat difficilis. Quid dēsīderās?

PHAETHŌN: Dā, mī pater, Ō lūx terrārum, omnibus hominibus sīgnum et tē patrem meum probā! Nōnne ego fīlius tuus sum?

APOLLŌ: Dōnum rogā, mī fīlī, et tibi id dabō. Fīlius meus es tū.

PHAETHŌN: Quadrīgās tuās quās (*which*) cotīdiē agitās mihi dā, atque ego equōs tuōs agitābō. Hoc est dēsiderium (*wish*) meum.

APOLLŌ: Contrā nātūrae lēgēs est dēsiderium istum. Puer es, sed deōrum labōrem cum studiō rogās.

PHAETHŌN: Equōs sōlis agitāre possum. Māgnā cum laetitiā in quadrīgīs stābō. Nōlī timēre! Cotīdiē illōs agitās!

APOLLŌ: Tristis pater sum ego. Māgnō cum perīculō equōs alacrēs agitābis. Īgnem ac flammās exspīrant (*They breathe forth*).

PHAETHŌN: In hunc diem (*day*) quadrīgās atque equōs postulō. In capite meō radiōs (*rays*) sōlis locā, mī pater!

APOLLŌ: Nōlī equōrum celeritātem augēre! Nunc valē! Propter superbiam istam, nōn honor sed dolor tuus erit!

## Demonstratives: *hic, ille, iste*

▶ DISCUSSION

In addition to the demonstratives *is, ea, id* are *hic, ille,* and *iste*.

1. *Hic, haec, hoc* usually means *this* (the nearer). It refers to what is close at hand.

*hic* vir = *this* man (here)

2. *Ille, illa, illud* usually means *that* (the farther). It points to what is farther away.

*ille* vir = *that* man (over there)

3. *Iste, ista, istud* means *this* or *that* (*of yours*). It points out persons or objects near the person spoken to.

*ista* causa = *that* reason (*of yours*)

**4.** *Hic* and *ille,* used in the same sentence, show contrast.

**Hic ager est lātus, *ille* est angustus.**   *This* field is wide, *that* one is narrow.

**5.** *Hic* and *ille,* used in the same sentence, may be translated the *latter,* the *former.* **Hic** refers to the *nearer* person or thing; **ille** to the *remoter* person or thing.

| | |
|---|---|
| **Spartacus et Tēlemachus servōs līberāre temptāvērunt; *hic* in arēnā, *ille* in bellō necātus est.** | Spartacus and Telemachus tried to free the slaves; the *latter* was killed in the arena, the *former* in war. |

|        | SINGULAR *this* | | | | SINGULAR *that* | | |
|--------|------|------|------|--|------|------|------|
|        | M.   | F.   | N.   |  | M.   | F.   | N.   |
| Nom.   | hic  | haec | hoc  |  | ille | illa | illud |
| Gen.   | hūjus | hūjus | hūjus |  | illīus | illīus | illīus |
| Dat.   | huic | huic | huic |  | illī | illī | illī |
| Acc.   | hunc | hanc | hoc  |  | illum | illam | illud |
| Abl.   | hōc  | hāc  | hōc  |  | illō | illā | illō |

|        | PLURAL *these* | | | | PLURAL *those* | | |
|--------|------|------|------|--|------|------|------|
| Nom.   | hī   | hae  | haec |  | illī | illae | illa |
| Gen.   | hōrum | hārum | hōrum |  | illōrum | illārum | illōrum |
| Dat.   | hīs  | hīs  | hīs  |  | illīs | illīs | illīs |
| Acc.   | hōs  | hās  | haec |  | illōs | illās | illa |
| Abl.   | hīs  | hīs  | hīs  |  | illīs | illīs | illīs |

▶ **STUDY HELPS**

**1.** *Iste, ista, istud* has the same forms as *ille, illa, illud.*

**2.** *Hic, iste, ille* are occasionally used for the personal pronouns of the third person: *he, she, it, they.*

**3.** *Hic, iste, ille* are more definite and emphatic than *is.*

**4.** *Ille* often means *that famous, that well-known.* In this use, *ille* regularly follows the noun:

> **dux *ille*** = *that famous* leader

**5.** Ordinarily, the demonstrative adjectives precede the nouns they modify:

> **hic dux** = *this leader*     **illa fēmina** = *that woman*

**6.** The demonstratives are frequently used without nouns:

> **haec** = *these things*     **eī** = *these men*     **illa** = *those things*

▶ **PRACTICE PATTERNS**

A. Translate into English:

| | | |
|---|---|---|
| hoc cor | illīus lēgis | per illud spatium |
| huic labōrī | hūjus noctis | sub illīs montibus |
| illārum sorōrum | ad hoc aedificium | prope istud domicilium |
| ex hōc mūrō | in hāc casā | propter hanc causam |

**166**

B. Write in Latin the specified forms:

1. these wrongs (genitive)
2. those evil deeds (nominative)
3. this keen sorrow (ablative)
4. those citizens (genitive)
5. that labor of yours (accusative)
6. this difficult work (dative)

C. Translate into Latin:

by this law
of those nights
for this citizen

through these gates
near that dwelling
these three hearts

behind these buildings
to (ad) those walls
with this brother

D. Decline in Latin and translate:

ille dolor    illud cor    illa causa    haec culpa    ista fīlia

## WORDS TO MASTER

a'gitō (1), drive, stir up (*agitate*)

au'geō, –ēre, auxī, auctus (2), increase (*augment*)

cau'sa, –ae, *f.*, cause, reason; causā, *with gen.*, for the sake of (*causal*)

cor, cor'dis, *n.*, heart (*cordial*)

diffi'cilis, –e, *adj.*, difficult (*difficulty*)

do'lor, –ōris, *m.*, grief, pain (*dolorous*)

hīc, *adv.*, here, in this place

hūc, *adv.*, hither, to this place

la'bor, –ōris, *m.*, labor, work, toil (*laborious*)

pos'tulō (1), demand (*postulate*)

super'bus, –a, –um, *adj.*, proud (*superb*); super'bia, –ae, *f.*, pride; super'bē, *adv.*, proudly

tris'tis, –e, *adj.*, sad, sorrowful

## BUILDING WORD POWER

You will easily distinguish between two apparently similar groups of English adjectives if you know their Latin background. In Latin the suffixes –*āx* and –*ōx* added to verb stems form adjectives meaning *having a tendency to* or *inclined to*. **Pūgnāre** means *to fight;* **pūgnāx,** *inclined to fighting,* from which we derive the English word *pugnacious.* From what Latin adjectives do we derive *tenacious, audacious, rapacious, loquacious, sagacious, vivacious, ferocious, atrocious, precocious?*

Now consider the English words that end in –*aceous,* usually scientific terms. They derive from Latin words ending in –**aceus,** meaning *belonging to* or *like.* If **crēta** in Latin means *chalk,* what does *cretaceous* mean? If the Latin **arbor** and **crusta** mean *tree* and *shell,* what do *arboraceous* and *crustaceous* mean? These adjectives are used in biology.

With regard to spelling, unless the adjective refers directly to something scientific, use the ending –*acious.* You will be correct. Besides, in Latin, –*āx* is affixed to *verb* stems, –*aceus* to *noun* stems.

## SENTENCE PATTERNS

### A. Translate into English:

1. Aenēās ille cum sociīs suīs ab Āsiā ad Ītaliam nāvigāvit.
2. Propter haec māgnus dolor corda eōrum occupāvit.
3. Crās nōs sōlem iterum vidēbimus quod fīlius audāx deī sōlis equōs patris suī nōn agitābit.
4. Quadrātus et Tarcisius erant amīcī; hic erat parvus puer, ille mīles validus.
5. Iste amīcus tibi nōn erit fīdus, quod is sibi nōn est fīdus.
6. Hīc Rōmae omnēs cīvēs erant tristēs quod perīculum augēbat.
7. Hūc hostēs superbī properābant.
8. Nōnne māgna superbia puerī erat causa mortis ējus?
9. Omnēs Americānī "Washington" et "Lincoln" laudant et amant; hic servōs līberāvit et patriam nostram in perīculīs bellī servāvit; ille erat prīmus in bellō, prīmus in pāce, prīmus in cordibus cīvium Āmēricānōrum.
10. Difficilem labōrem deōrum superbē postulābat.

### B. Translate into Latin:

1. What was the cause of this difficult journey?
2. You have hastened hither to my kingdom because you are proud.
3. Again and again the boy proudly demanded the horses.
4. Here in this house of yours, you will see that famous woman.
5. This work is easy; that is difficult.

### Space Trip Ends in Tragedy

Apollo erat ūnus ex multīs deīs Rōmānīs, et Phaethōn, fīlius ējus, in terrā habitābat. Cotīdiē deus sōlis equōs suōs cum quadrī-gīs aureīs (*golden chariot*) per caelum agitābat, et Phaethōn cum amīcīs suīs equōs et quadrīgās patris suī spectābat. Ūnus ex sociīs ējus erat invidus (*envious*) et eī clāmāvit: "Fābula ista est falsa! Apollō pater tuus nōn est!" Phaethōn māgnā cum īrā ācriter respondit: "Verba mea sunt vēra! Apollō, deus sōlis, est pater meus. Tibi illud probābō!"

Sine morā, fīlius Apollinis ad rēgnum patris suī properāvit. Iter erat difficile ac longum, sed celeriter ambulāvit et mox ad rēgiam (*palace*) sōlis erat. Numquam anteā (*before*) rēgiam patris suī vīsitāverat, sed equōs et quadrīgās saepe vīderat. Apollō puerum longē vīdit, quod omnēs terrās et maria oculīs ācribus suīs vidit.

"Quae itineris causa est?" rogāvit Apollō. "Cūr hūc ad rēgiam meam ambulāvistī, fīlī mī?" Statim Phaethōn tristis respondit: "Pater mī, socius meus mihi clāmāvit: 'Fīlius deī sōlis tū nōn es! Apollō pater tuus nōn est!'"

"Fīlius meus es tū. Vēra sunt verba tua!" graviter respondit. "Tum, pater bone, māgnum sīgnum omnibus hominibus dā! Hōc sīgnō mē fīlium tuum probābis."

"Omnibus hominibus hoc sīgnum dabō. Quid dēsīderās, fīlī mī?"

"Dā mihi equōs tuōs ac quadrīgās et hōs agitābō."

Apollō erat tristis. "Hoc est contrā lēgēs Nātūrae. Hic est labor deōrum, nōn puerōrum. Equī meī sunt ācrēs ac celerēs. Fortasse (*Perhaps*) hoc factum erit causa mortis tuae."

Tamen Phaethōn audāx et superbus iterum quadrīgās postulāvit. Illā ipsā nocte Apollō fīliō suō quadrīgās cum equīs ācribus dedit, et in capite ējus radiōs (*rays*) suōs locāvit. Prīmā lūce Phaethōn alacer in quadrīgīs patris suī superbē stābat. Equīs inquiētīs (*restless*) sīgnum dedit, et per portās Aurōrae eōs agitāvit.

Mox puer audāx circum caelum volābat. Equī jam prope terram, jam inter stellās properābant. Omnī hōrā celeritātem augēbant. Phaethōn, puer miser, māgnopere timēbat. Nōmina equōrum memoriā nōn tenēbat. Mox omnibus in partibus volābat. Prīmum inter spatia, inter lūnam et terram atque inter stellās et planētās homō volābat, sed ubīque in terrā erant īgnēs, in silvīs, in agrīs, in montibus. Flammae frūmentum dēlēvērunt. In flūminibus et in marī nūlla aqua erat.

Cerēs, dea terrae, māgnō cum dolōre patrem potentem deōrum auxilium rogāvit. "Ō rēx deōrum! Tū caelī terraeque imperium tenēs. Cūnctīs hominibus auxilium dā! Agrī, oppida, mare, caelum ardent (*burn*). Auxilium tuum exspectāmus. Nōs, Ō Juppiter, servā!"

Sed pater deōrum perīculum vīderat. Īrātus fulmen contrā quadrīgās jēcit (*hurled*). Corpus puerī superbī in flūmen cecidit (*fell*). Juppiter fīlium Apollōnis propter superbiam ējus necāverat.

# Comprehensive Review: Units XXVI–XXX

A. Write in Latin the dative singular and translate. Give the gender and base:

| | | | | | | | |
|---|---|---|---|---|---|---|---|
| pēs | ōra | laus | mīles | dolor | culpa | grātia | potestās |
| sōl | lūx | lūna | labor | soror | caput | stella | multitūdō |
| āra | cor | grex | fīnis | causa | focus | mundus | simulācrum |
| āla | pars | mēns | timor | pedes | aquila | tempus | sacrificium |
| | unda | īgnis | māter | fulmen | vulnus | lēgātus | |

B. Write in Latin the feminine and neuter forms, genitive singular:

living    sacred    proud    easy    holy    sad    difficult

C. Write the English meanings:

praeter   ubīque   māgnopere   quot   itaque   hīc   hūc   praestereā

D. Write in Latin the principal parts of these verbs:

attack   change   pretend   drive   increase   demand   watch

E. Write these synopses in the active voice, indicative mood:

1. third person plural: augeō
2. third person singular: postulō

F. Decline in the singular and translate:

hic timor   haec causa   hoc tempus   ille dolor   illa lūx   illud caput

G. Decline in the plural and translate:

is mīles   vir ipse   id fulmen   pater noster   māter tua   vulnus suum

H. Identify the case and the number of these forms:

| | | | | | | | | |
|---|---|---|---|---|---|---|---|---|
| tū | vōs | meī | sibi | duās | vōbīs | hūjus | ipsam | tribus |
| sē | ego | ūnī | illī | trēs | trium | nōbīs | prīmī | decimō |
| mē | eae | nōs | hunc | mihi | mīlia | ūnīus | tertiā | ipsīus |
| tē | duo | eōs | iste | hanc | eōrum | illud | quārtō | duōrum |

I. Write in Latin the specified forms, and translate:

1. nominative plural: haec unda, hic īgnis, is lēgātus
2. genitive singular: hoc vulnus, illud tempus, homō ipse
3. ablative singular: illa soror, is focus, illud flūmen
4. accusative plural: māter ipsa, ea lūx, is pēs
5. dative singular and plural: sacrificium suum, potestās mea

J. In each of the following groups, all the adjectives agree with the noun except one. Write the correct form of the incorrect adjective.

1. sorōrem: hāc, eam, ipsam, illam    5. fulmen: illud, hoc, ea, ipsum
2. caput: eam, hōc, ipsum, illud    6. dolōris: ipsīus, hūjus, illud, ējus
3. causās: eās, illa, hās, ipsās    7. fīnium: ipsōrum, eōrum, illōrum, hōrum
4. mentī: ipsa, illī, huic, eī    8. culpīs: is, illīs, ipsīs, hīs

K. Match the words in the first line with those in the second:

1. mīlitem   lēgātīs   sorōrēs   itineris   capita   stellārum   annō
2. quīntō   trium   tribus   prīmae   tria   ūnum   sextī

## SENTENCE PATTERNS

A. Select the word in parentheses that makes the sentence grammatically correct; then translate the sentence.

1. Mīlitēs duōs fīliōs cōnsulis (ipsīus, ipse) necāvērunt.
2. Nōnne lēgātus ad (illud, illōs) mūrōs appropinquāvit?

3. Sī pācem dēsīderātis, inimīcī (noster, nōbīs) esse nōn dēbētis.
4. Eī nōn sunt librī meī; mihi (eōs, ea) nōlī dare.
5. Posteā illī (nōbīscum, sēcum) ad id bellum properābunt.
6. Māter ipsa (nōs, sē) multa dē māgnīs bellīs Rōmānōrum docuit.
7. Nōlī oppūgnāre (illud, istum) oppidum. Mūtā (istam, illud) mentem.
8. Juppiter duās sorōrēs, Vestam et Cererem, habēbat; (illa, haec) erat dea frūmentī; (illa, haec) erat dea focī.
9. Dā, Ō lūx mundī, pater (mī, meum), sīgnum. Probā mē esse fīlium tuum.
10. Tū puer es, sed labōrem deōrum (ipsōs, ipsōrum) rogās.

B. Translate into Latin:

1. The leader is pleasing to himself but not to us.
2. You, O Romans, attack us and give us many difficult orders.
3. The girl increased her sacrifices for the safety of her sister.
4. Shall we be able to change these plans?
5. The soldiers were demanding many favors for themselves.


**SIGHT TRANSLATION:** FAMOUS TWINS

Castor et Pollūx erant frātrēs fortēs et benīgnī et pulchrī. In multīs bellīs māgnā virtūte pūgnābant et multōs hostēs superāvērunt. Ōlim māgna tempestās (*storm*) ad nāvem appropinquābat, sed auxiliō deōrum discessit (*scattered*). Tum nautae in capitibus Castoris et Pollūcis duās stellās vīdērunt. "Deī ipsī in capitibus frātrum hās stellās locāvērunt," clāmāvērunt omnēs. "Frātrēs bonī sunt causae salūtis nostrae!"

Posteā ācer hostis Castorem necāvit et ad īnferōs (*Lower Regions*) hic properāvit. Māgnus dolor Pollūcem occupāvit. Is erat immortālis quod fīlius deī erat. Sine frātre suō Pollūx erat miser et tristis. Multīs verbīs et māgnō dolōre auxilium patrem ipsum deōrum ōrāvit. "Ego laetus vītam meam," inquit (*he said*), "prō frātre meō dabō."

Juppiter autem statuit ūnum diem (*day*) vītae Castorī, ūnum diem mortis Pollūcī dare. Itaque domicilium frātrum cotīdiē mūtāvit. Juppiter duās stellās in caelō locāvit. Hominēs eās Geminōs (*Twins*) appellābant et frātrēs ut (*as*) deōs adōrābant.

*Tanta stultitia mortalium est.*
—Seneca, 8 B.C.–A.D. 65

# Unit XXXI

Lord, what fools these mortals be!
—William Shakespeare, 1564–1616
*A Midsummer Night's Dream*

## CONVERSATION

MAGISTER: Ōlim inter populōs Athēnārum ac Crētae, īnsulae propinquae Graeciae, bellum fuit.

CORNĒLIUS: Quis illō tempore rēx Crētae fuit?

MAGISTER: Mīnōs tyrannus multōs annōs in īnsulā Crētā rēgnāvit.

CORNĒLIA: Cūr incolae Crētae Graecīs amīcī nōn erant?

MAGISTER: Incolae Athēnārum Androgeum, fīlium ējusdem rēgis, necāvērunt quod in lūdīs Graecīs erat victor.

JŪLIUS: Brevī tempore post fīlī suī mortem, Mīnōs cum Graecīs pūgnāvit. Māgnae cōpiae tyrannī Athēniēnsēs (*Athenians*) superāvērunt.

MAGISTER: Mīnōs inīquus post victōriam septem ē puerīs, septem ē puellīs Graecīs quotannīs (*yearly*) postulāvit.

CORNĒLIUS: Cūr rēx Crētae līberōs Graecōs postulāvit?

MAGISTER: Ille Mīnōtaurō, mōnstrō horribilī, līberōs Graecōs dedit.

JŪLIUS: Mīnōtaurus corpus hominis et caput taurī habēbat.

MAGISTER: Mōnstrum intrā labyrinthum habitābat. Dum līberī per multās labyrinthī viās ambulant, illōs Mīnōtaurus necāvit.

## SECTION 1 The Demonstrative *īdem*

▶ DISCUSSION

The demonstrative *īdem, eadem, idem,* the *same,* may be used, like other demonstratives, both as a pronoun and as an adjective. Compounded of *is + dem,* it differs little from *is* in declension. Throughout the declension the suffix *–dem* remains unchanged. Like the other demonstratives it precedes its noun when used as a modifying adjective: *īdem puer = the same boy.*

|  | SINGULAR | | | PLURAL | | |
|---|---|---|---|---|---|---|
|  | M. | F. | N. | M. | F. | N. |
| Nom. | īdem | eadem | idem | eīdem | eaedem | eadem |
| Gen. | ējusdem | ējusdem | ējusdem | eōrundem | eārundem | eōrundem |
| Dat. | eīdem | eīdem | eīdem | eīsdem | eīsdem | eīsdem |
| Acc. | eundem | eandem | idem | eōsdem | eāsdem | eadem |
| Abl. | eōdem | eādem | eōdem | eīsdem | eīsdem | eīsdem |

*172*

1. *Is + dem = īdem;* the *–s* is dropped before *–dem.* *Id + dem = idem;* the *–d* is dropped before *–dem.* The masculine *īdem* is distinguished from the neuter *idem* by the long *–ī* in the masculine.

2. The letter *–m* becomes *–n* before *–dem.*

3. *Īdem* is sometimes translated *also* or *at the same time.* *Ego īdem vīdī = I also saw.*

4. *Ibidem* (*ibid.*) = *in the same place;* *idem* (*id.*) = *the same as above, the same.*

▶ PRACTICE PATTERNS

A. Translate into English:

| | | |
|---|---|---|
| idem tempus | propter eundem dolōrem | cum eōdem imperātōre |
| eādem vigiliā | eōrundem cīvium | ab eīsdem victōriīs |
| īdem taurus | ējusdem cordis | eadem aestās |

B. Write in Latin the specified forms:

1. accusative singular: the same night watch
2. ablative singular: the same night
3. dative singular: the same victory
4. accusative plural: the same contest
5. ablative plural: the same bull
6. nominative plural: the same flight

C. Write in Latin:

| | | |
|---|---|---|
| we also | of the same flight | near the same walls |
| the same summer | in the same place | the same time |
| of the same brothers | the same as above | of the same wings |
| of the same sisters | with the same girl | the same winter |

# SECTION 2 Expressions of Time

▶ DISCUSSION

1. In English we express the time at which or within which an act takes place by a preposition and its object: *at night, in summer, within three hours.* In Latin we express the time at which something happens, or within which it happens, by the *ablative case without a preposition:*

**prīmā lūce,** *at daybreak* **aestāte,** *in summer* **quīnque hōrīs,** *within five hours*

*The ablative of time* always answers the question *when?* or *within what time?*

*173*

2. If we wish to express how long a time the action took, we use the *accusative case without a preposition:*

***multōs annōs*** = *for many years*

The *accusative of duration of time* always answers the question *how long?* In English it is often called the adverbial objective to distinguish it from the direct object.

▶ STUDY HELPS

1. *In, on, at, within which,* when used with words *expressing time,* take the ablative case without a preposition.

2. Not all expressions that answer the question *when?* come under the heading *ablative of time.* **In bellō,** *in war,* or **in pāce,** *in peace,* or **in perīculō,** *in danger,* are usually accompanied by the preposition **in,** since the words *war, peace,* and *danger* do not in themselves denote time; *summer, winter, day,* etc., do. If *war* or *peace* is modified by adjectives, the preposition may be omitted, as: **bellō cīvīlī,** *in the civil war.*

3. The prepositions **ante, post, per** with the accusative case may be used to indicate *time before, after,* and *during which* an event takes place.

▶ PRACTICE PATTERNS

A. Translate into English:

| | | |
|---|---|---|
| aestāte | eōdem tempore | hieme |
| tertiā hōrā | paucīs annīs | post duās hōrās |
| multās hōrās | longum tempus | per hiemem |
| illō tempore | omnī hōrā | in bellō |
| sex hōrīs | eō tempore | prīmā lūce |
| tertiā vigiliā | breve tempus | ante prīmam lūcem |
| octō hōrās | in pāce | in perīculō |

B. Translate into Latin:

| | | |
|---|---|---|
| for seven years | every night | at daybreak |
| within three hours | that very night | within a year |
| in winter and summer | at the same time | at the second watch |
| for a few years | after five hours | through many years |

BUILDING WORD POWER

Hundreds of English words terminate with the suffix *–ble.* The corresponding Latin suffix is **–bilis.** Combined chiefly with verb stems, it forms adjectives meaning *capable of being, able to,* or *inclined to.*

If **portāre** means *to carry, portable* must mean *able to be carried.* Notice the passive idea in the word. What do these adjectives mean: *adorable, curable, donable, habitable, laudable?*

174

Not all words in English ending in *–ble* are Latin derivatives. Sometimes *–ble* is attached to purely English words, both verbs and nouns, but it usually retains its original significance. *Believable* means the same as *credible*, though *believe* is a non-Latin word.

Sometimes this suffix is joined to the stem of the perfect passive participle, as *visible, divisible, persuasible.*

Write the Latin for: *horrible, terrible, arable, possible, stable, separable, superable, memorable, flexible, honorable.*

## WORDS TO MASTER

**aes′tās, –tātis,** *f.,* summer

**cu′pidus, –a, –um,** *adj.,* desirous of (*cupidity*)

**frūs′trā,** *adv.,* in vain (*frustrate*)

**fu′ga, –ae,** *f.,* flight (*fugitive*)

**fūr′tim,** *adv.,* by stealth, secretly (*furtive*)

**hi′ēms, hi′emis,** *f.,* winter

**imperā′tor, –ōris,** *m.,* commander, general (*emperor*)

**pu′tō** (1), think, suppose (*impute*)

**scien′tia, –ae,** *f.,* knowledge (*science*)

**tau′rus, –ī,** *m.,* bull (*toreador*)

**victō′ria, –ae,** *f.,* victory (*victorious*)

**vigi′lia, –ae,** *f.,* a watch, night watch (*vigil*)

## SENTENCE PATTERNS

A. Translate the phrases in parentheses into Latin, and then translate the sentences into English:

1. (Within a few hours) Daedalus cum fīliō suō ad eandem īnsulam nāvigāvit.
2. (In summer and in winter) multōs annōs vir miser patriam suam dēsīderābat, sed frūstrā auxilium exspectābat.
3. (At that time) ad sē parvōs līberōs vocāvit.
4. In ipsā īnsulā (the same) taurus omnēs incolās terruit.
5. Prīmīs annīs (the same) vir rēgī ipsī erat grātus.
6. (In a few hours) īgnis sōlis ālās dēlēvit.
7. Num vir, fugae cupidus, imperātōrem (at the same hour) necāvit?
8. (At the second watch) puer taurum līberāre fūrtim temptāvit.
9. Victōria erit nostra sī (for a short time) fortēs fuerimus.
10. Dux māgnam scientiam bellī habēbat, sed (in danger) fortis et audāx nōn erat.

B. Translate the italicized words into Latin:

*At the same time the king* of Athens *had a son,* Theseus. *This same youth* was famous for *his deeds.* He announced *his plan to the king.* "*I shall hasten* to go to Crete. *If I kill* the Minotaur, you and the fatherland *will be free,* and *I likewise shall have great glory.*" Theseus *with the help* of Ariadne, daughter of the king of Crete, *did kill* the monster.

**Roman Writing**

When Roman children first learned to write, they used wax tablets called *tabella*. A tabellum was made of wood covered with wax and resembled the small toy chalkboards that children use today. Sometimes the tabella were even made of ivory. A raised boxlike edge kept the wax in place and protected the writing so two tablets of equal size could be placed face to face without danger of being erased. When fastened along one edge, they opened like a book.

The writing on the wax was done with a sharp, pointed instrument of bone or ivory, called a *stylus*. Since one end of the stylus was flat, the impression of writing could be smoothed out when necessary, and the tabella used over and over again. The wax was usually black, and the writing appeared in the color of the underlying wood or ivory.

When these tabella were used for writing letters, from two to five leaves could be used. A string was passed through holes on the edges of the tabella, the ends tied together, and the knot made fast by sealing wax into which the writer impressed the seal of his ring. This seal was the guarantee that the letter was genuine. When a letter was opened, the thread was cut in such manner as to leave the seal undisturbed.

Boys in the Roman grammar school learned how to make their own textbooks. The teacher dictated, and they wrote in good ink with a reed on *papyrus*, paper obtained from reeds that grew plentifully in Egypt. The ends of the papyrus sheets were fastened to wooden rods. As one end was being unrolled for reading, the other was rolled. These also could be fastened with string and sealed with wax when used for letters or important documents.

The writing on these scrolls was done crosswise in equal columns about three inches wide. A label bearing the title was attached to the upper edge so that when the scrolls were placed in a box, they could be easily identified. These rolls of writing were called *volumina* from the verb *volvere*, to roll. What does volume mean today?

## The First Astronauts

Ōlim vir, nōmine Daedalus, Athēnīs habitābat. Īdem māgnam scientiam habēbat, sed inimīcum necāverat, et cīvēs Athēnārum eum ad mortem condemnāverant. Ille fūrtim trāns mare ad māgnam īnsulam Crētam fūgit (*fled*) et ibi multōs annōs mānsit. Eōdem tempore erat in Crētā mōnstrum horribile, Mīnōtaurus. Corpus hominis et caput taurī habēbat, et multōs incolās jam necāverat. Omnēs incolae illum māgnopere timēbant. Quis illōs hōc perīculō līberāre poterat?

Mīnōs, rēx Crētae, Daedalum rogāvit: "Nōnne locum parābis unde hoc mōnstrum fugere (*to flee*) nōn poterit?" Respondit Daedalus: "Labyrinthum ubi mīlle itinera erunt aedificābō. Mīnōtaurus mox in labyrinthō erit captīvus unde fugere numquam poterit."

Rēx ipse et incolae īnsulae erant laetī, et breve tempus Daedalō erant amīcī. Sed posteā is rēgī erat nōn grātus et in īnsulā captīvus erat. Saepe vir miser patriam suam vidēre dēsīderābat, et iterum iterumque dē fugā frūstrā putābat.

"Ego trāns aquās lātās altāsque nāvigāre nōn possum, quod nāvem nōn habeō. Ab hāc terrā ad patriam meam ambulāre nōn possum. Iter novum brevī tempore parābō. Ego erō similis avī (*bird*). Ālas formābō et per caelum volābō. Paucīs hōrīs patriam vidēbō."

Quattuor ālās pennīs (*feathers*) et cērā (*wax*) dīligenter parāvit. Tum Daedalus fīlium suum, nōmine Icarum, vocāvit et puerum volāre fūrtim docuit. Corporī Icarī ālās accommodāvit (*fitted*), et illum hīs verbīs monuit: "Prope terram volā, fīlī mī; sī prope sōlem volābis, cēra hārum ālārum īgne sōlis dissolvet (*will melt*) et māgnō in perīculō eris. Verba mea memoriā tenē, et ad patriam nostram itinere novō volābimus."

Tandem ille omnia parāverat. Et pater et fīlius alacrēs altum in caelum volāvērunt. Icarus, per caelum lātum ālīs novīs volandī (*of flying*) cupidus, verba patris suī memoriā nōn tenuit. Altius (*Higher*) et altius volāvit. "Icare! Icare!" clāmāvit pater illīus, "altius (*too high*) volās! Nōlī volāre altius!"

Iterum iterumque pater anxius vocāvit. "Icare!" clāmāvit, "Icare, ubi es?" Tum brevī tempore pennās in undīs vīdit. Prope sōlem volāverat audāx puer, et cēra dissolverat. Ālae ex humerīs (*shoulders*) ējus et Icarus ipse dē spatiō altum in mare ceciderant (*had fallen*). Numquam posteā ille per caelum volāvit. Daedalus ipse autem ad Graeciam patriam tūtō (*safely*) volāvit.

# Unit XXXII

## CONVERSATION

MĪLES SABĪNUS: Spectāte! Puella Rōmāna aquam ex flūmine intrā mūrōs arcis (*citadel*) portat! Est inopia aquae in urbe!

TITUS TATIUS (*rēx Sabīnōrum*): Apprehendite (*Seize*) puellam!

TARPĒJA (*fīlia prīncipis Rōmānī*): Quae est voluntās tua?

RĒX SABĪNŌRUM: Dēmōnstrā nōbīs iter in arcem! Dā nōbīs auxilium!

TARPĒJA: Sī mihi ornāmenta bracchiōrum (*arms*) sinistrōrum dabitis, iter vōbīs ā mē dēmōnstrābitur!

RĒX SABĪNŌRUM: Tibi ea certē dabimus! Post tē intrā mūrōs arcis statim properābimus! [*Mox Sabīnī intrā mūrōs validōs stābant.*]

TARPĒJA (*cupidē*): Nōnne armillae (*bracelets*) ē bracchiīs sinistrīs mihi ā vōbīs nunc dabuntur?

TITUS TATIUS: Promissum nostrum tibi, puella perfida, servābitur. Scūta, nōn armillae, ē bracchiīs sinistrīs nostrīs erunt praemium tuum. [*Sine morā sīgnum ā rēge datum est* (was given), *et scūta contrā puellam miseram ā mīlitibus jacta sunt* (were thrown). *Puella perfida sine vītā dē Capitōlīnō praecipitāta est* (was hurled).]

## SECTION 1 Passive Voice

▶ DISCUSSION

1. A verb in the *active voice* presents its subject as *doing* something. A verb in the *passive voice* presents its subject as *receiving* the action. Usually only transitive verbs, that is, verbs that take an object, may be used in the passive voice.

    ACTIVE VOICE    The slave *was carrying* grain.
    PASSIVE VOICE   Grain *was being carried* by the slave.

In the first sentence the subject, *slave*, is the *doer* of the action, *was carrying*. The verb, therefore, is in the *active voice*. In the second sentence the subject, *grain*, is the receiver of the action, *was being carried*. The verb, therefore, is in the passive voice.

**178**

Pompeiian patio. This patio is outside the house of the Vettii
family. Filled with myriad statues, sculptures, and mosaics,
it was excavated seventeen centuries after its burial in A.D. 79.

Vesta (a relief from the Villa Albani, Rome). Goddess of hearth and home, she is identified with the Greek goddess Hestia. Vestal virgins tended her sacred fire in the temple dedicated to her in Rome.

Aesculapius. Son of Apollo, he was
the Roman god of medicine and healing,
identified with the Greek god Asclepius.

Diana. Goddess of the moon
and of hunting, she
is identified with the
Greek goddess Artemis.

*B-3*

Bronze animals, circa 25 B.C.–A.D. 200.

Relief of a cobbler and spinner at work, circa A.D. 150.

Woman storing linens. This terra-cotta plaque was made around 450 B.C.

Ceres, Neptune, Juno. Ceres was goddess of agriculture, identified with the Greek goddess Demeter. Neptune, god of the sea, was often depicted holding a trident. He is identified with Poseidon. Juno, the sister and wife of Jupiter, was goddess of marriage and queen of the gods, and is identified with the Greek Hera.

Medusa. In Greek mythology Medusa was one of the Gorgons, three sisters with snakes for hair. Any person who looked at them was turned to stone. Perseus, son of Zeus (Jupiter) and Danae, slew Medusa.

Etruscan fresco. The Etruscans comprised an early civilization predating the Roman Empire and located in Etruria, an area north of Rome.

A Roman lady, end of
the first century A.D.

Etruscan jewelry. Made of gold and semiprecious stones, these fibulae
(clasps) and other ornaments were fashioned about 500 B.C.

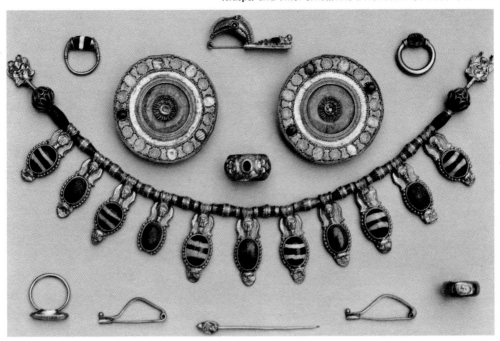

2. In English the passive voice is formed by using some tense of the verb *to be* as an auxiliary along with the past participle of the verb: *was carried*. In Latin the passive voice of the present, imperfect, and future tenses of all conjugations is formed by dropping the active person indicators and adding the passive person indicators.

### PRESENT INDICATIVE PASSIVE, FIRST CONJUGATION

*Pres. Stem + Pass. P.I. =    Form*

SINGULAR

| | | | | | |
|---|---|---|---|---|---|
| First | vocā(o) | + | r | = vocor | *I am called* |
| Second | vocā | + | ris | = vocāris | *you are called* |
| Third | vocā | + | tur | = vocātur | *he, she, it is called* |

PLURAL

| | | | | | |
|---|---|---|---|---|---|
| First | vocā | + | mur | = vocāmur | *we are called* |
| Second | vocā | + | minī | = vocāminī | *you are called* |
| Third | vocā | + | ntur | = vocantur | *they are called* |

### IMPERFECT INDICATIVE PASSIVE, FIRST CONJUGATION

*Pres. Stem + T.I. + Pass. P.I. =    Form*

SINGULAR

| | | | | | | |
|---|---|---|---|---|---|---|
| First | vocā | + bā + | r | = vocābar | *I was (being) called* |
| Second | vocā | + bā + | ris | = vocābāris | *you were (being) called* |
| Third | vocā | + bā + | tur | = vocābātur | *he, she, it was (being) called* |

PLURAL

| | | | | | | |
|---|---|---|---|---|---|---|
| First | vocā | + bā + | mur | = vocābāmur | *we were (being) called* |
| Second | vocā | + bā + | minī | = vocābāminī | *you were (being) called* |
| Third | vocā | + bā + | ntur | = vocābantur | *they were (being) called* |

### FUTURE INDICATIVE PASSIVE, FIRST CONJUGATION

*Pres. Stem + T.I. + Pass. P.I. =    Form*

SINGULAR

| | | | | | | |
|---|---|---|---|---|---|---|
| First | vocā | | bi(o) | | r | = vocābor | *I shall be called* |
| Second | vocā | + bi(e) + | ris | = vocāberis | *you will be called* |
| Third | vocā | + bi + | tur | = vocābitur | *he, she, it will be called* |

PLURAL

| | | | | | | |
|---|---|---|---|---|---|---|
| First | vocā | + bi + | mur | = vocābimur | *we shall be called* |
| Second | vocā | + bi + | minī | = vocābiminī | *you will be called* |
| Third | vocā | + bi(u) + | ntur | = vocābuntur | *they will be called* |

The present, imperfect, and future tenses passive of the *second conjugation* are formed like those of the *first*.

| | | | |
|---|---|---|---|
| Present Passive | monē(o) + | — + r = moneor | *I am warned* |
| Imperfect Passive | monē | + bā + r = monēbar | *I was warned* |
| Future Passive | monē | + bi(o) + r = monēbor | *I shall be warned* |

1. The letter *–r,* which appears in all but one (***vocāminī***) of the passive endings, may be called the *passive indicator.*

2. The short *–i* always becomes short *–e* before *–ris.*

3. The present and imperfect tenses in the passive may be translated progressively:

**vocātur** = *he is called, is being called*
**vocābātur** = *he was called, was being called*

Do not confuse the active *I was calling* with the passive *I was being called.*

4. The passive of the verb ***videō,*** *see,* may be translated *seem.*

**videor** = *I am seen,* or *I seem*
**vidētur** = *it is seen,* or *it seems*

▶ **PRACTICE PATTERNS**

A. Write the specified forms in the passive voice and translate into English:

| | | |
|---|---|---|
| moneō (imperfect) | terreō (future) | dēmōnstrō (present) |
| nōminō (present) | augeō (imperfect) | incitō (imperfect) |
| augeō (future) | vulnerō (present) | vītō (future) |
| dō (future) | deleō (imperfect) | videō (imperfect) |

B. Write in Latin:

| | | |
|---|---|---|
| It was changed. | He was wounded. | It was pointed out. |
| We are moved. | I was saved. | I was being held. |
| He was watched. | You were held. | You will be avoided. |
| It is destroyed. | They will be seized. | I was frightened. |
| We shall be seen. | He is being avoided. | They were shunned. |

# SECTION 2 Ablative of Agent

▶ **DISCUSSION**

In English we cannot ask a question containing the phrase *by whom* without using the passive voice.

*By whom* was the grain carried? The grain was being carried *by the slave.*

In Latin, the answer to *by whom* is in the ablative case. It is called the ablative of personal agent because it names the personal agent by whom a thing is done. The ablative of agent is always a *person,* used with a passive verb, and the *preposition* ***ā*** or ***ab,*** meaning *by.*

*Formula:*    *Person + Passive + Preposition = Ablative of Agent*
**Frūmentum ā servō portābātur.**

## WORDS TO MASTER

amīci'tia, –ae, *f.*, friendship (*amity*)

cer'tus, –a, –um, *adj.*, sure, certain; cer'tē, *adv.*, certainly

dēmōn'strō (1), show, point out (*demonstrate*)

dex'ter, –tra, –trum, *adj.*, right (*dexterous*); dex'tra, –ae, *f.*, right hand

ino'pia, –ae, *f.*, lack, need

in'trā, *adv. and prep. with acc.*, within (*intramural*)

lī'bertās, –tātis, *f.*, freedom (*liberty*)

per'fidus, –a, –um, *adj.*, faithless; perfi'dia, –ae, *f.*, treachery (*perfidy*)

sinis'ter, –tra, –trum, *adj.*, left (*sinister*); sinis'tra, –ae, *f.*, left hand

vī'tō (1), avoid, shun (*inevitable*)

volun'tās, –tātis, *f.*, wish, good will (*voluntary*)

vul'nerō (1), wound (*vulnerable*)

## BUILDING WORD POWER

We are frequently confused about the spelling of words that end in –*able* or –*ible* in English. Which shall we use? There is no inflexible rule, but a few suggestions may be helpful.

1. If the word is derived from a first conjugation verb, the chances are that the word will end in –*able*. Usually there is an English noun ending in –*ation* derived from the same stem. For example, *navigation* and *navigable* are derived from **nāvigāre,** a first conjugation verb.

2. The suffix –*able* is used if the ending can be dropped and still leave a complete word: *agreeable, respectable, favorable, honorable. Agree, respect, favor, honor* are complete words.

3. If the word ends in mute –*e*, the –*e* is dropped and –*able* added: *excusable, curable, endurable. Excuse, cure, endure* end in mute –*e*. If the ending is –*ce* or –*ge*, the mute –*e* is retained to keep the soft sound: *effaceable, chargeable.* There are exceptions to all these rules. Can you think of any?

## SENTENCE PATTERNS

A. Translate into English:

1. Dextrā mīles gladium habuit; sinistrā scūtum portāvit.
2. Propter inopiam cibī aquaeque vīrī fēminaeque terrēbantur.
3. Omnēs rēgēs bonam voluntātem populī nōn habēbant.
4. Post multa bella erant pāx et amīcitia inter hās gentēs.
5. Nōnne Rōmulus ipse ab hostibus graviter vulnerābitur?
6. Num haec praemia puellae perfidae dabuntur?
7. Sabīnī ā Rōmānīs ipsīs virtūte nōn superābantur.

8. Ego ipse tibi viam intrā mūrōs certē dēmōnstrābō.
9. Rōmānī ipsī lībertātem amābant, sed fīnitimīs eam nōn dabant.
10. Propter puellae perfidiam cīvēs fortēs ab hostibus occupābantur.

B. Translate into Latin:

1. Liberty was desired by the Romans.
2. On the right were seen the treacherous enemy, on the left the faithful allies.
3. The way was sure, but they did not avoid all the dangers.
4. For many years there were peace and friendship between the men.
5. The short way was shown to the enemy by the girl.


## The Women Have the Last Word

Prīmus prīnceps urbis Rōmae atque imperī fuit Rōmulus ille,
deī Martis et Rheae Silviae fīlius. Rōmulus urbem aedificāvit
et urbem novam ex nōmine suō appellāvit. Ad Rōmulī urbem
multitūdō hominum properāvit. Fugitīvīs ex fīnitimīs populīs
asȳlum dedit. Concilium (*Council*) populī ā Rōmulō habēbātur.
Omnibus incolīs lībertās atque aequa jūra (*rights*) dabantur.
Etiam creāvit centum senātōrēs quī (*who*) patrēs quoque appellābantur.

Jam fīrma erat urbs nova et fīnitimīs gentibus bellō pār.
Rōma incolārum plēna (*full*) erat, sed cūnctus populus virōrum
erat. Rōmulus ipse sibi uxōrem dēsīderābat. Virī Rōmānī sibi
uxōrēs māgnō cum studiō dēsīderābant. Tum Rōmulus lēgātōs
ad fīnitimōs vīcōs properāre jūssit. Lēgātī cūnctīs populīs nūntiāvērunt: "Rōmulus rēx lūdōs māgnōs et spectācula habēbit.
Virōs ac fēminās ad eōs lūdōs ac spectācula vocat."

Multae gentēs fīnitimae cum līberīs atque uxōribus ad urbem
Rōmam cum laetitiā properāvērunt. Dum hominēs alacrēs lūdōs
spectant, et perīculum nōn timent, sīgnum ā Rōmulō dabātur.
Statim Rōmānī omnēs, virī puerīque, sibi Sabīnōrum fīliās com-
prehendērunt (*seized*) et cum eīs in casās suās properāvērunt.
Virī Sabīnī fīliās servāre nōn potuērunt quod arma nōn habuērunt.
Sīc Rōmānī sibi uxōrēs obtinuērunt.

Frūstrā puellae clāmāvērunt; frūstrā matrēs eārum implōrāvērunt; frūstrā patrēs frātrēsque Rōmānōs fīliās sorōrēsque
suās sibi dare jūssērunt. Rōmānī Sabīnīs respondērunt: "Fīliae
vestrae et sorōrēs nōbīscum laetae erunt. Eīs omnia jūra
Rōmānōrum dabuntur."

Sabīnī autem māgnā cum īrā arma parāvērunt. Post longum tempus ad urbem Rōmam properāvērunt et cum Rōmānīs ācriter pūgnāvērunt. Multī Sabīnī et multī Rōmānī vulnerābantur. Multōs annōs Sabīnī extrā mūrōs urbis Rōmae et exspectābant et pūgnābant. Tandem propter Tarpējae perfidiam māgnō in perīculō erat Rōma. Arx ā Sabīnīs tenēbātur; urbs Rōma facile oppūgnābātur. In eō locō ubi nunc Forum Rōmānum est, longa et ācris erat pūgna. Subitō Sabīnae fīliae atque uxōrēs Rōmānae inter Sabīnōs et Rōmānōs volāvērunt, et pācem atque amīcitiam ā patribus ac virīs (*husbands*) implōrāvērunt. Dūces eō factō movēbantur et posteā ē multīs ūnum rēgnum fēcērunt (*made*).

The first who was king was a fortunate soldier: Who serves his country well has no need of ancestors.

—Voltaire, 1694–1778

# Unit

# XXXIII

## CONVERSATION

MAGISTER: Quī rēx in cordibus omnium cīvium Rōmānōrum prīmus semper fuit?

PAULUS: Rōmulus māgnus rēx ā Rōmānīs semper habēbātur.

PAULA: Posteā Rōmānī Rōmulum prō deō adōrāvērunt et eī nōmen Quirīnum dedērunt.

MAGISTER: Quibuscum rēx Rōmae bellum multōs annōs gerēbat?

JŪLIUS: Bellum longum contrā fīnitimōs inimīcōs ā Rōmulō gerēbātur, dum urbem Rōmam rēgit.

MAGISTER: Ā quibus Sabīnī in bellō superābantur?

JŪLIA: Sabīnī cum Rōmānīs illō tempore contendēbant, sed illī ā Rōmānīs post prīncipis mortem regēbantur.

MAGISTER: Quī rēx clārus ac bonus post Rōmulum Rōmānōs regēbat?

CORNĒLIUS: Incolae Rōmae ā Numā Pompiliō, rēge Sabīnō, regēbantur. Pācem amīcitiamque cum gentibus fīnitimīs cōnfīrmāvit.

PAULUS: Quis fuit tertius rēx Rōmānōrum? Rōmānusne fuit?

MAGISTER: Tullus Hostīlius Rōmānus ā senātōribus populōque tertius rēx dēligēbātur. Neque pācem neque amīcitiam cum fīnitimīs cōnfīrmāre temptāvit. Vir cupidus bellī erat.

# Third Conjugation

▶ DISCUSSION

1. All verbs whose present stem ends in short *–e* belong to the third conjugation. The principal parts of *regere, to rule,* are:

| *Pres. Indic.* | *Pres. Infin.* | *Perf. Indic.* | *Perf. Pass. Part.* |
|---|---|---|---|
| **regō** | **regere** | **rēxī** | **rēctus** |
| *I rule* | *to rule* | *I have ruled, I ruled* | *having been ruled, ruled* |
| | *Pres. Stem* | *Perf. Stem* | *Participial Stem* |
| | **rege/** | **rēx/** | **rēct/** |

### PRESENT INDICATIVE ACTIVE, THIRD CONJUGATION

*Pres. Stem + P.I.   = Form*

SINGULAR

| First | **regé** | **+ ō** | **= regō** | *I rule, am ruling, do rule* |
|---|---|---|---|---|
| Second | **regé(i)** | **+ s** | **= regis** | *you rule, are ruling, do rule* |
| Third | **regé(i)** | **+ t** | **= regit** | *he, she, it rules, is ruling, does rule* |

PLURAL

| First | **regé(i)** | **+ mus** | **= regimus** | *we rule, are ruling, do rule* |
|---|---|---|---|---|
| Second | **regé(i)** | **+ tis** | **= regitis** | *you rule, are ruling, do rule* |
| Third | **regé(u)** | **+ nt** | **= regunt** | *they rule, are ruling, do rule* |

The short *–e* of the third conjugation changes to short *–i* in forming the *present tense*, except in the third person plural where it becomes *–u,* and in the first person singular where it is absorbed by the *–ō.*

2. The *imperfect tense* of the third conjugation has the same formation as that of the first and second conjugations:

*Formula: Present Stem + Tense Indicator + Person Indicator = Form*
**regēbam, regēbas, regēbat, regēbāmus, regēbātis, regēbant,** *was (were) ruling, ruled*

3. The *future tense* of the *third conjugation* is formed by dropping the short *–e* of the present stem and adding the tense indicator (*–a* in the first person singular and long *–ē* in the others) and the person indicators.

### FUTURE INDICATIVE ACTIVE, THIRD CONJUGATION

*Pres. Stem + T.I. + P.I. =  Form*

SINGULAR

| First | **regé** | **+ a** | **+ m** | **= regam** | *I shall rule* |
|---|---|---|---|---|---|
| Second | **regé** | **+ ē** | **+ s** | **= regēs** | *you will rule* |
| Third | **regé** | **+ ē** | **+ t** | **= reget** | *he, she, it will rule* |

| First | regę́ | + ē | + mus | = regēmus | *we shall rule* |
| Second | regę́ | + ē | + tis | = regētis | *you will rule* |
| Third | regę́ | + ē | + nt | = regent | *they will rule* |

4. In Latin the passive voice of the present, imperfect, and future tenses of the third conjugation is formed by substituting the passive person indicators for the active. Observe the following:

### Present Active

| regō | regis | regit | regimus | regitis | regunt |
|------|-------|-------|---------|---------|--------|

### Present Passive

| regor | regeris | regitur | regimur | regiminī | reguntur |
|-------|---------|---------|---------|----------|----------|

### Imperfect Active

| regēbam | regēbās | regēbat | regēbāmus | regēbātis | regēbant |
|---------|---------|---------|-----------|-----------|----------|

### Imperfect Passive

| regēbar | regēbāris | regēbātur | regēbāmur | regēbāminī | regēbantur |
|---------|-----------|-----------|-----------|------------|------------|

### Future Active

| regam | regēs | reget | regēmus | regētis | regent |
|-------|-------|-------|---------|---------|--------|

### Future Passive

| regar | regēris | regētur | regēmur | regēminī | regentur |
|-------|---------|---------|---------|----------|----------|

▶ STUDY HELPS

The second person singular forms of the present and future passive are identical in spelling but not in pronunciation: **re'geris, regē'ris.** The macron makes the difference.

▶ PRACTICE PATTERNS

A. Conjugate and translate:

1. gerō (present, imperfect, future active)
2. vertō (present, imperfect, future passive)

B. Give the voice, tense, person, and number, and translate:

| gerent | dēligēminī | timent | contendunt | pellar | terrēmur |
| dīvidēmur | scrībentur | dēligēmur | regēbāminī | scrībunt | gerēris |
| postulant | cōnfīrmābam | videntur | nōminābunt | movētur | statuent |

C. Write in Latin:

| it seemed | they will write | you (sing.) were demanding |
| he is chosen | it was being divided | he is being avoided |

**185**

## WORDS TO MASTER

cōnfīr'mō (1), make firm, strengthen, establish (*confirm*)

conten'dō, –ere, –tendī, — (3), struggle, hasten, fight (*contend*)

dē'ligō, –ere, –lēgī, –lēctus (3), choose, select

dī'vidō, –ere, –vīsī, –vīsus (3), divide (*division*)

ge'rō, –ere, gessī, gestus (3), bear, carry, wear (*digest*); **bellum gerere,** wage war

mēn'sis, –is, *m.*, month

ne'que (nec) *conj.,* and . . . not, nor, neither

neque . . . neque, neither . . . nor

nō'minō (1), name, call (*nominate*)

pel'lō, –ere, pepulī, pulsus (3), strike, drive out (*pulse*)

re'gō, –ere, rē'xī, rēctus (3), guide, rule (*regulate*)

scrī'bō, –ere, scrīp'sī, scrīp'tus (3), write (*scribe*)

sta'tuō, –ere, –uī, statūtus (3), place, establish, determine (*statute*)

## BUILDING WORD POWER

In English we frequently put two words together to make one compound word, as *seaside, sunshine.* In Latin, too, we find many compound words, as **agricultūra,** meaning *cultivation of the field.*

The Romans had several ways of making compounds, and one of these was to use prepositions as prefixes (**prae,** *before* + **fixus,** *fixed*) at the beginning of a root or a stem, thus changing the meaning of the word. Originally prepositions were adverbs.

Usually these prefixes appear in English with the same meanings as in Latin. The preposition **ab,** *away, from,* became the prefix **ab–.** Notice that before the consonants **–m, –p, –v,** the **–b** drops out, as in **āmovēre,** *to move away;* before **–c** or **–t, ab–** becomes **abs–,** as in **abstinēre,** *to hold away from, abstain.*

Our word *absent* is derived from **absum,** *I am away from.* What is the difference in meaning between *vocation* and *avocation?* Would stamp collecting ordinarily be a vocation or an avocation? What is your most absorbing avocation?

## SENTENCE PATTERNS

A. Translate into English:

1. Rōma multōs annōs ā Rōmulō regēbātur.
2. Fābulās scrībere est negōtium illīus.
3. Pāx et amīcitia inter gentēs inimīcās cōnfīrmābuntur.
4. Dux mīlitēs suōs servāre et nōn necāre statuit.
5. Nōnne cōpiae Rōmānae ad terram Albānōrum contendēbant?

*186*

6. Sī Rōmānī Albānōs superābunt, Alba Longa ā Rōmānīs regētur.
7. Eō tempore hostēs ex Ītaliā ā cīvibus fortibus pellēbantur.
8. Neque Sabīnī neque Albānī Rōmānōs tandem superāvērunt.
9. Senātōrēs populusque Rōmānus rēgem novum nōmināvērunt.
10. Annus in mēnsēs ā rēge bonō dīvidēbātur.

## B. Write in Latin:

1. Many stories about the gods will be written by the poets.
2. Were not the leaders chosen by the king?
3. The bold general tried to strengthen neither peace nor friendship.
4. That nation waged war for many years with neighboring peoples.
5. The wicked kings did not determine to write the new laws, did they?

### Kings Rule Rome

Post Rōmulī mortem, prīmī rēgis Rōmae, per breve interrēgnum ūnīus annī Rōma ā senātōribus potentibus regēbātur. Tum omnēs incolae urbis rēgem novum postulāvērunt. Numa Pompilius, Sabīnus, rēx prūdēns et homō pācis, dēligēbātur. Virōs bonōs scrībere multās lēgēs aequās jūssit; senātōrēs hās populum docuērunt. Rēx jūstus populōs fīnitimōs amābat et cum hīs contendere nōn dēsīderābat. Ubi hī auxilium rōgābant, Numa Pompilius hīs auxilium dedit. Templa aedificāvit et ea cūrāre multōs virōs nōmināvit. Virginēs Vestālēs dēligēbat, templum Jānī aedificāvit, annum ad cursum (*course*) lūnae in duodecim mēnsēs dīvīsit. Numa annōs trēs et quadrāgintā (*forty*) prūdenter rēgnābat.

Iterum interrēgnum breve fuit, et posteā Tullus Hostīlius Rōmam regēbat. Numa Pompilius, prūdēns vir, pācis cupidus fuerat, sed Tullus Hostīlius, audāx et ācer, bellī cupidus fuit. Populus autem pācem hōc tempore amābat, et virī puerīque agricolae esse dēsīderābant. Cum gentibus fīnitimīs contendere nōn dēsīderābant.

Sed propter rēgem bellicōsum Rōmānī cum Albānīs saepe ācriter contendēbant. Iterum iterumque Rōmānī in agrīs Albānōrum bellum gerēbant, et Albānī eōs ex agrīs semper pellēbant. Rōmānī et Albānī virtūte et numerō virōrum paene parēs erant. Neque Rōmānī neque Albānī erant semper victōrēs.

Illō tempore dux Albānus prūdēns mortem multōrum virōrum fortium vītāre voluit (*wished*). Rēgī Rōmānō cōnsilium breviter explānāvit.

The Roman standard.
S.P.Q.R. is the abbreviation for *Senatus Populusque Romanus.*

## The Story of Early Rome, 753–31 B.C.

In this book there are many Latin reading lessons through which the history of Rome is gradually unfolded from its legendary beginnings to the establishment of the Empire. The following chart will serve as a guide for important dates and events.

IMPORTANT PERIODS AND EVENTS

| | | |
|---|---|---|
| | | Descendants of Aeneas rule Alba Longa until 753 B.C. |
| 700 B.C.— | **Period of Kings** | Romulus: founds city of Rome, 753 B.C.<br>Numa Pompilius: establishes state religion. |
| | | Tullus Hostilius: warrior king.<br>Ancus Marcius: extends Roman power.<br>Tarquinius Priscus: great builder. |
| 600 B.C.— | | Servius Tullius: reorganizes the people.<br>Tarquinius Superbus: tyrant; expelled, 510 B.C. |
| 500 B.C.—<br>to<br>300 B.C.— | **Period of the Republic** | Beginning of long series of wars, 510–275 B.C. |
| 200 B.C.— | | Defeat of Pyrrhus: Rome, mistress of Italy, 275 B.C.<br>First Punic (Carthaginian) War, 264–241 B.C.<br>Second Punic (Carthaginian) War, 218–202 B.C. |
| 100 B.C.— | | Third Punic (Carthaginian) War, 149–146 B.C.<br>Rome, mistress of Mediterranean World, 133 B.C.<br>One hundred years of revolution and civil wars: the Gracchi; Sulla and Marius . . . |
| | | . . . Caesar and Pompey; Octavius and Antony.<br>Octavius: master of Roman World, 31 B.C.; founds Empire and receives name Augustus. |
| | | The Empire, from 31 B.C. |

To endure is greater than to dare; to tire out hostile fortune; ... who can say this is not greatness?
—William Makepeace Thackeray, 1811–1863

## CONVERSATION

MAGISTER: Numa ā Rōmānīs laudābātur quod vir cupidus pācis erat.

PAULA: Ā quō Rōmānī post Numam regēbantur?

MAGISTER: Tullus Hostīlius tertius rēx ā senātōribus populōque Rōmānō dēligēbātur. Bellum gerere eī grātum erat.

JŌSĒPHUS: Quā cum gente Hostīlius prīmō bellum gessit?

MAGISTER: Māgnae cōpiae ab Hostīliō contrā Albānōs ducēbantur.

ANNA: Probāvēruntne Albānī bellum? Timēbantne Rōmānōs?

MAGISTER: Mettius Fūfetius, Albānōrum dux, bellum nōn probāvit. Prō patriā autem Albānī pūgnāvērunt. Ab hostibus nōn cucurrērunt.

ROBERTUS: Quod cōnsilium Mettius Fūfetius cēpit?

MAGISTER: Servāre et nōn necāre virōs suōs in animō habuit. Ducī Rōmānō cōnsilium nūntiāvit. "Paucī ex Rōmānīs cum paucīs ex Albānīs armīs contendent. Victōrēs Rōmānōs et Albānōs regent."

ROBERTA: Quid Hostīlius fēcit? Dēlēgitne virōs parēs aetāte?

MAGISTER: Cum laetitiā cōnsilium probāvit. Forte trēs frātrēs Rōmānī ac trēs frātrēs Albānī virtūte atque aetāte erant parēs. Hīs certāminis cūra data est.

PAULA: Ubi frātrēs Rōmānī cum frātribus Albānīs contendērunt?

MAGISTER: In medium agrum longum lātumque properāvērunt. Rōmānī prō suīs castrīs, Albānī prō suīs pūgnam spectābant et victōriam exspectābant.

## SECTION 1 Third Conjugation Verbs Ending in –iō

▶ DISCUSSION

1. Many verbs in the third conjugation end in –iō in the first person singular of the present indicative. They are called –iō verbs. They are like all other verbs in the third conjugation in having a short –e in the present infinitive. The present stem ends in –e.

**189**

The principal parts are like those in the following model:

| Pres. Indic. | Pres. Infin. | Perf. Indic. | Perf. Pass. Part. |
|---|---|---|---|
| **capiō** | **capere** | **cēpī** | **captus** |
| *I take* | *to take* | *I have taken, I took* | *having been taken, taken* |
| | Pres. Stem | Perf. Stem | Participial Stem |
| | **cape/** | **cēp/** | **capt/** |

2. In the present tense the conjugation of **capiō** differs from that of **regō** in the first person singular and the third person plural, where the vowel –*i* appears before the usual ending.

PRESENT TENSE

| Active | **capiō** | **capis** | **capit** | **capimus** | **capitis** | **capiunt** |
|---|---|---|---|---|---|---|
| | **regō** | **regis** | **regit** | **regimus** | **regitis** | **regunt** |
| Passive | **capior** | **caperis** | **capitur** | **capimur** | **capiminī** | **capiuntur** |
| | **regor** | **regeris** | **regitur** | **regimur** | **regiminī** | **reguntur** |

3. In the imperfect tense, active and passive, **capiō** differs from **regō** in the vowel –*i,* which appears in all forms before the long –*ē.*

IMPERFECT TENSE

| Active | **cap–iēbam** | **–iēbās** | **–iēbat** | **–iēbāmus** | **–iēbātis** | **–iēbant** |
|---|---|---|---|---|---|---|
| | **reg–ēbam** | **–ēbās** | **–ēbat** | **–ēbāmus** | **–ēbātis** | **–ēbant** |
| Passive | **cap–iēbar** | **–iēbāris** | **–iēbātur** | **–iēbāmur** | **–iēbāminī** | **–iēbantur** |
| | **reg–ēbar** | **–ēbāris** | **–ēbātur** | **–ēbāmur** | **–ēbāminī** | **–ēbantur** |

4. In the future tense, active and passive, **capiō** differs from **regō** in the vowel –*i,* which appears in all forms before the tense indicator.

FUTURE TENSE

| Active | **capiam** | **capiēs** | **capiet** | **capiēmus** | **capiētis** | **capient** |
|---|---|---|---|---|---|---|
| | **regam** | **regēs** | **reget** | **regēmus** | **regētis** | **regent** |
| Passive | **capiar** | **capiēris** | **capiētur** | **capiēmur** | **capiēminī** | **capientur** |
| | **regar** | **regēris** | **regētur** | **regēmur** | **regēminī** | **regentur** |

▶ PRACTICE PATTERNS

A. Conjugate and compare, as above. Give English meanings.

1. present tense, active and passive voice: rapiō, dūcō
2. imperfect tense, active and passive voice: capiō, regō
3. future tense, active and passive voice: jaciō, jungō

B. Translate into Latin:

| | | |
|---|---|---|
| he was seized | it will be joined | you (sing.) did hurl |
| we were making | I am being taken | they will be ruled |
| they were turned | they were running | we are being moved |
| she was leading | you (pl.) were being led | you (pl.) will turn |
| you (sing.) were led | they will be led | she is being taken |

*190*

# SECTION 2 The Perfect System Indicative Active of the Third Conjugation

▶ **DISCUSSION**

The formation of the tenses based upon the perfect system is the same for all verbs. Notice the following synopses in the active for both types of third conjugation verbs.

SYNOPSES: THIRD PERSON PLURAL INDICATIVE ACTIVE

| | **regō, regere, rēxī, rēctus** | | **capiō, capere, cēpī, captus** | |
|---|---|---|---|---|
| Present | **regunt** | *they rule* | **capiunt** | *they take* |
| Imperfect | **regēbant** | *they were ruling* | **capiēbant** | *they were taking* |
| Future | **regent** | *they will rule* | **capient** | *they will take* |
| Perfect | **rēxērunt** | *they ruled* | **cēpērunt** | *they took* |
| Pluperfect | **rēxerant** | *they had ruled* | **cēperant** | *they had taken* |
| Fut. Perfect | **rēxerint** | *they will have ruled* | **cēperint** | *they will have taken* |

▶ **PRACTICE PATTERNS**

A. Conjugate in the specified forms of the active voice:

1. capiō, regō (perfect tense)
2. faciō, dūcō (pluperfect tense)
3. jaciō, scrībō (future perfect tense)
4. capiō, jungō (imperfect tense)

B. Give synopses as follows:

1. third person plural, indicative mood, active voice: vertō
2. second person singular, indicative mood, active voice: capiō

C. Give the tense, person, and number of each of the following:

| | | | | |
|---|---|---|---|---|
| jēcit | gessit | cēpimus | fēcērunt | currēbam |
| jūnxī | regunt | capitis | cucurrit | jēcērunt |
| facit | capiam | fēcimus | manēbant | vertitis |
| gerit | amābit | jacient | faciēmus | sedēbunt |
| movet | gerent | scrībēs | dūxērunt | currimus |
| dūxit | faciet | dūxeram | jēceris | gesserant |

D. Translate into Latin. Give the voice, tense, person, and number of each of the following:

| | | |
|---|---|---|
| they ran | it was joined | it was written |
| we threw | we were throwing | it was being changed |
| he hurled | we were thrown | we shall be led |
| it is turning | she had ruled | it will be written |
| he was taken | they have made | he will have joined |

# SECTION 3 Ablative of Place from Which

▶ DISCUSSION

The ablative of *place from which* has been familiar in practice since the introduction of the prepositions **ā, ab, dē, ē, ex.** (The preposition is omitted with the names of towns, small islands, and a few other words denoting place.) This ablative denotes motion from one point to another and is regularly accompanied by one of the prepositions **ā, ab, dē, ē,** or **ex.**

| | |
|---|---|
| **Nūntius ab urbe ad castra properāvit.** | *The messenger hastened from the city to the camp.* |

# SECTION 4 Ablative of Separation

▶ DISCUSSION

The ablative of separation emphasizes the state of being apart. Sometimes the separation is figurative, with such verbs as those meaning *to set free, deprive, sustain,* and the preposition is omitted. If the word in the ablative refers to a person, a preposition is regularly used.

| | |
|---|---|
| **Patriam *perīculō* līberāvit.** | He freed his country *from danger.* |
| **Patriam *ab hostibus* līberāvit.** | He freed his country *from the enemy.* |

▶ STUDY HELPS

The preposition **ab** with the *ablative of agent* always means *by;* with the *ablative of separation* it means *from, away from.*

## WORDS TO MASTER

ae'tās, –tātis, *f.*, age (*eternal*)

ca'piō, –ere, cē'pī, captus (3), take, seize (*capture*)

certā'men, –inis, *n.*, contest

cur'rō, –ere, cucur'rī, cursūrus (3), run (*current*)

dū'cō, –ere, dū'xī, ductus (3), lead (*duct*)

fa'ciō, –ere, fē'cī, factus (3), make, do (*fact*)

for'te, *adv.*, by chance (*fortuitous*)

gau'dium, –ī, *n.*, joy, gladness (*gaudy*)

in'teger, –gra, –grum, *adj.*, whole, untouched, unimpaired, unwearied, fresh (*integer*)

ja'ciō, –ere, jē'cī, jactus (3), throw, hurl (*reject*)

jun'gō, –ere, jūn'xī, jūnctus (3), join (*junction*)

ver'tō, –ere, ver'tī, versus (3), turn (*vertigo*)

## BUILDING WORD POWER

Sometimes the final consonant of a prefix, instead of dropping out, is changed so that it will harmonize with the initial consonant of the word to which the prefix is attached. This change makes pronunciation easier. It is called *assimilation* (*ad*, *to*, + *similis*, *like*). The prefixes most frequently assimilated are: *ad–*, *com–*, *ex–*, *in–*, *ob–*, *sub–*.

In English and Latin, *ad–* has the meaning *to*, *at*, *toward*, *near*. In the following words, the *–d* has become the same as the initial consonant of the word to which it is affixed: *abbreviate*, *accelerate*, *affirm*, *aggravate*, *allocate*, *annunciation*, *approbation*, *arrogate*, *assimilate*, *attempt*. The knowledge of this rule should be a guide to correct spelling.

Notice the retention of the *–d* in these compounds: *adapt*, *adept*, *adhere*, *adjacent*, *admit*, *adore*, *adsorb*, *adulterate*, *advocate*.

Usually the *–d* before *–s* becomes *–s*, or is dropped, as in *ascribe* (*ad* + *scrībō*) and *ascend* (*ad* + *scandō*).

## SENTENCE PATTERNS

A. Translate into English:
1. Nōnne Horātiī erant parēs aetāte Cūriātiīs?
2. Trēs virī arma cēpērunt et inter duās gentēs cucurrērunt.
3. Forte ille integer fuit, sed ūnus vir tribus pār nōn fuit.
4. Propter mortem duōrum Rōmānōrum Albānī cum gaudiō clāmāvērunt.
5. Ille sē vertit; ūnus Cūriātius nōn longē ab illō aberat.
6. Rēx potēns Albānōs cum Rōmānīs jūnxit et lēgēs novās fēcit.
7. Mīlitēs perīculō līberābantur sed ab hostibus nōn erant līberī.
8. Brevī tempore illī sex virī in agrō stābant.
9. In ūnō certāmine hostēs ā servīs capiēbantur.
10. Tēla valida contrā mūrōs urbis jaciēbantur.

B. Translate into Latin:
1. He led one man away from his brothers and then killed him.
2. The contest was brief, but the Horatii did not surpass the Curiatii in bravery.
3. Did the wall around Rome keep the enemy from the city?
4. Whom did the six brave men free from danger?
5. In what contest did the enemy shout with joy?

### A Six-Man Battle

"Dēlige trēs virōs ex cōpiīs tuīs, et ego trēs ex meīs dēligam. Hī sex virī prō mīlitibus fortibus Rōmae et Albae Longae contendent. Sī Rōmānī erunt victōrēs, Albānōs regent; sī Albānī

Rōmānōs superābunt, hī ab Albānīs regentur. Probāsne cōnsilium meum?" "Cōnsilium tuum nōn est difficile et Rōmānīs grātum est," Hostīlius celeriter respondit.

Forte apud Rōmānōs erant trēs frātrēs, nōmine Horātiī, et apud Albānōs etiam erant trēs frātrēs, nōmine Cūriātiī. Horātiī et Cūriātiī amīcī semper fuerant, sed illī dēfēnsōrēs (champions) ā ducibus suīs dēligēbantur et prō gente suā in certāmine contendere dēsīderābant. Sex adulēscentēs fortēs sē armāvērunt et sine timōre in medium agrum cucurrērunt. Mīlitēs Rōmānī prō castrīs suīs, mīlitēs Albānī prō suīs sedēbant.

Intereā (Meanwhile) omnēs Rōmānī et Albānī praeter fēminās ad locum certāminis aderant. Amīcī et sociī adulēscentium fortium pūgnam spectāre parāvērunt et verbīs laudis illōs stimulāre. Inter duās gentēs Horātiī et Cūriātiī sine timōre stābant.

"Prō patriā Rōmā pūgnābimus!" clāmāvērunt Horātiī. "Prō lībertāte Albānōrum!" celeriter respondērunt Cūriātiī.

Prīncipēs duōrum populōrum tubā sīgnum dedērunt. Certāmen ācre fuit. Paene statim Cūriātiī duōs Horātiōs gladiīs necāvērunt sed Rōmānī trēs Albānōs vulnerāverant. Manēbat ūnus Horātius, sed ille erat integer. Horror ācer animōs Rōmānōrum cēpit. Albānī māgnō cum gaudiō clāmābant: "Victōria est nostra! Victōria est nostra!" Fīnis certāminis cum tranquillitāte exspectābātur.

Trēs Cūriātiī vulnerātī (wounded) circum ūnum Horātium stābant. Albānī celerem victōriam exspectābant. Sed ūnus Horātius erat alacer animō et celer pede. Subitō ā Cūriātiīs celeriter properāvit et fugam simulāvit. Rōmānī māgnō cum dolōre movēbantur, quod illī causam fugae nōn vidēbant. Eratne Horātius Rōmānus timidus?

Horātius neque perīculum neque mortem timēbat. Per agrum cucurrit et fugā suā ab sē Cūriātiōs vulnerātōs sēparāvit. Post Horātium trēs Cūriātiī cum difficultāte quoque cucurrērunt. Inter Cūriātiōs erant māgna intervalla. Subitō sē vertit et prīmum Cūriātium necāvit; deinde (then) secundum. Tertius manēbat. Horātius illum defessum (wearied) et vulnerātum facile superāvit et necāvit.

"Nostra est victōria!" clāmāvērunt Rōmānī laetī. "Alba Longa posthāc (hereafter) ā nōbīs regētur!" Posteā Tullus Hostīlius cum mīlitibus ācribus Albam Longam dēlēvit et Albānōs ad urbem Rōmam dūxit. Tum rēx ācer populōs duōrum oppidōrum jūnxit et prō Albānīs et prō Rōmānīs lēgēs gravēs scrīpsit. Multōs annōs Rōma ā rēge bellicōsō regēbātur.

The mathematician has reached the highest rung on the ladder of human thought.
—Havelock Ellis, 1859–1939

*Unit* XXXV

## CONVERSATION

ROBERTA: Quis fuit Tarquinius, quīntus rēx Rōmānōrum? Unde vēnit?

MAGISTER: Vir ipse erat ex genere Graecōrum, sed uxor ējus Tanaquil Etrūsca erat. Ex Etrūriae oppidō vēnērunt.

PETRUS: Quālis fēmina erat Tanaquil?

MAGISTER: Fēmina nōbilis ac superba multa sacra deōrum sciēbat.

ROBERTUS: Cūr Rōmam contendēbant? Num Etrūriam amābant?

MAGISTER: Fortūna illōrum in Etrūriā nōn erat bona; Rōma illīs temporibus erat nova. Praetereā sibi imperium cupiēbant.

ROSA: Ambulābantne ex Etrūriā ad urbem Rōmam?

MAGISTER: Carpentō (*wagon*) cum equīs vēnērunt. Post longum iter ad Jāniculum pervēnērunt. Tarquinius pilleum (*cap*) in capite gerēbat. Apud nōbilēs Rōmānōs pilleum gerere mōs nōn erat. Subitō ē caelō volāvit aquila atque ā Tarquiniō pilleum rapuit. Tum altum in caelum volāvit. Post breve tempus iterum vēnit et pilleum in capite ējus posuit. "Hoc est ōmen futūrae potestātis. Rēx eris!" exclāmāvit Tanaquil.

## SECTION 1 Fourth Conjugation

▶ DISCUSSION

1. All verbs whose present stem ends in long –*ī* belong to the fourth conjugation. The principal parts are like those in the following model:

| Pres. Indic. | Pres. Infin. | Perf. Indic. | Perf. Pass. Part. |
|---|---|---|---|
| **audiō** | **audīre** | **audīvī** | **audītus** |
| *I hear* | *to hear* | *I have heard, I heard* | *having been heard, heard* |

| | Pres. Stem | Perf. Stem | Participial Stem |
|---|---|---|---|
| | **audī/** | **audīv/** | **audīt/** |

2. The conjugation of **audiō** in the *present tense* differs from that of **capiō** in the quantity of the vowel –*i* in some forms, and in the spelling of the second person singular in the *passive voice*.

*195*

Compare the present tense, active and passive, of **audiō** and **capiō**.

| Active | audiō | audīs | audit | audīmus | audītis | audiunt |
|---|---|---|---|---|---|---|
| | capiō | capis | capit | capimus | capitis | capiunt |

| Passive | audior | audīris | audītur | audīmur | audīminī | audiuntur |
|---|---|---|---|---|---|---|
| | capior | caperis | capitur | capimur | capiminī | capiuntur |

3. The conjugation of the *imperfect* and *future tenses* of **audiō** is identical with that of the same tenses of **capiō**.

▶ PRACTICE PATTERNS

A. Conjugate and compare the following. Give the English translation of each form.

1. present tense, passive: rapiō, pōnō
2. imperfect tense, active: cupiō, sciō
3. future tense, active and passive: sentiō, jungō

B. Translate into Latin:

| | | |
|---|---|---|
| he came | I was coming | they were being heard |
| he feels | it was heard | he will have perceived |
| we arrived | they had come | they will be coming |
| you (pl.) know | they were hearing | she has arrived |

# SECTION 2 The Perfect System Indicative Active of the Fourth Conjugation

▶ DISCUSSION

The formation of the tenses based upon the perfect system is the same for all verbs.

| CONJUGATION: | FIRST | SECOND | THIRD | THIRD –io | FOURTH | T.I. |
|---|---|---|---|---|---|---|
| Perfect | vocāvit | monuit | rēxit | cēpit | audīvit | — |
| Pluperfect | vocāverat | monuerat | rēxerat | cēperat | audīverat | erā |
| Fut. Perfect | vocāverit | monuerit | rēxerit | cēperit | audīverit | eri |

▶ PRACTICE PATTERNS

A. Conjugate in the perfect, pluperfect, and future perfect tenses, active voice: sentiō, cupiō. Translate each form.

B. Write synopses in the active voice, third person plural. Translate each form.

vītō    augeō    pōnō    cupiō    sciō

C. Give the tense, person, and number of each of the following:

| | | | | | | |
|---|---|---|---|---|---|---|
| sēnsī | audīveris | vīcerātis | vēnērunt | interfēcistī | sciēbat | vincam |
| posuit | rapiunt | sēnserant | cupiēs | pervēnerō | vēnistis | rapueram |

D. Translate into Latin. Tell voice, tense, person, and number of each:

| | | |
|---|---|---|
| we know | they will be killed | you (sing.) perceived |
| I had come | they pitched camp | it will be perceived |
| he heard | it had arrived | he was being placed |
| they knew | she will desire | she will have desired |
| she was coming | he was conquered | they were being seized |

## WORDS TO MASTER

au'diō, –īre, –īvī, –ītus (4), hear, hear of, listen to (*audit*)

cu'piō, –ere, –īvī, –ītus (3), desire (*cupidity*)

ge'nus, –eris, *n.*, race, kind (*generate*)

interfi'ciō, –ere, –fēcī, –fectus (3), kill

perve'niō, –īre, –vēnī, –ventūrus (4), arrive, *with* ad

pō'nō, –ere, po'suī, po'situs (3), place, put (*position*); **castra pōnere,** pitch camp

pōns, pon'tis, *m.*, bridge (*pontoon*)

ra'piō, –ere, ra'puī, raptus (3), seize and carry off, snatch, seize (*rapt*)

sci'ō, –īre, –īvī, –ītus (4), know, know how (*science*)

sen'tiō, –īre, sēn'sī, sēnsus (4), feel, perceive (*sense*)

ve'niō, –īre, ve'nī, ventūrus, come (*venture*)

vin'cō, –ere, vī'cī, vic'tus (3), conquer (*victor*)

## BUILDING WORD POWER

Sometimes a short –*a* or a short –*e* in the base of a noun or the root of a verb is changed to a short –*i*. For example, *in*– (*not*) + *amīcus* (*friendly*) = *inimīcus* (*unfriendly*).

*Faciō, capiō,* and *jaciō* form many compounds with prefixes in Latin. Since the –*a* in the root of each of these verbs is short, it is changed to short –*i* in the infinitive: *af/ficere; ac/cipere; ad/jicere.* Because –*ē* in the third principal part of the original verbs is long, it remains long in the compounds *affēcī, accēpī, adjēcī.* Short –*a* in the fourth principal part changes to short –*e* in the compounds *affectus, acceptus, adjectus.*

Diphthongs are always long. When the word containing the diphthong is compounded, the diphthong changes to a long vowel. *Caedere* means *to cut down, to kill.* Notice the long –*ī* in *accīdere.* Do not confuse this

**197**

word with **accidere** (**ad** + **cadere**, *fall*). They are two different words. The long –*ī* in the first makes the difference. *Accident* and *occident* are from **cadere**; *homicide* and *suicide* from **caedere.**

A. Translate into English:
1. Lūcius Tarquinius ipse sibi rēgnum occupāre cupīvit.
2. Fīlia rēgis ā patre suō rēgnum occupāre temptāvit.
3. Ubi rēx ipse ad Cūriam pervēnit, Lūcius Tarquinius amīcīs suīs tēla dedit.
4. Nōnne Tarquinius Prīscus ex genere Graecōrum erat et ex Etrūriā vēnerat?
5. Servius ubi omnia haec audīvit ad Cūriam contendit.
6. Tum Tarquinius rēgem rapuit et illum ē Cūriā jēcit.
7. Posteā amīcī Lūcī Tarquinī rēgem miserum interfēcērunt.
8. Rēx bonus Sabīnōs vīcerat, lēgēs aequās scrīpserat, templum Diānae fēcerat.
9. Prope pontem hostēs māgnā cum celeritāte castra posuerant.
10. Num puerī fābulam dē aquilae fugā sciēbant?

B. Translate into Latin the italicized words or phrases:
1. *The king himself arrived* at the Curia and *desired to know the reason* for the assembly. *The friends* of Tarquin *seized the king* in the street and *killed him with their swords.* When *the people heard* the story about *the death* of the good king, *they did not approve the wicked deeds of his daughter.*
2. *The enemy had perceived* the weakness of the Romans and *had pitched camp near the bridge.*

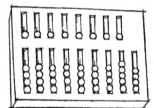

An abacus, a counting device used by the Romans.

## Roman Arithmetic

**A**rithmetica Romana held an important place in Roman schools. Mental calculation was stressed. A rather elaborate system of finger counting was developed. The pupils knew the digits from one to ten because they could count that far on their *digiti*, fingers or toes. In modern arithmetic, figures from one to nine are digits.

The fingers were held up to denote the numbers. One finger was represented by I, three fingers by III. The angle between the forefinger and the thumb resembled a V, and this was used to represent five. It is thought that two V's placed together with vertices coinciding formed X, which represented ten.

Probably the fingers on the left hand were used to count units and tens; on the right hand hundreds and thousands. The figure I added to X formed XI or eleven; placed before X it formed IX or nine. XX was twenty; L, fifty; C, one hundred; D, five hundred; M, a thousand.

There were no plus or minus signs. These came later, in the Middle Ages, when the owners of the warehouses needed signs to indicate overweight and underweight. Our word *plus* is a short form of *surplus* (*super + plus*); the Latin word *minus* means *less*.

The first mechanical calculator on record was the *abacus*, a counting frame with a long and somewhat hazy history. Originally numbers were represented by matchstick figures; then by notches on a stick (*talea*), from which we see a survival in the words *tally* and *tailor*. Then pebbles (*calculi*) were used to count (*calculate*). The next development seems to have been the use of bead-shaped pebbles on a stick. From this developed the abacus.

It is thought that the Romans borrowed the abacus from the Etruscans. We know that the use of the abacus for counting was common in China hundreds of years before it was introduced into Rome. It is still used with great skill in China and Japan and in many of the Chinese shops here in America. Perhaps you used a toy one before you went to school, or a large one for counting in the first grade. Nobody knows who brought the abacus to America, but the Spanish explorers found the Peruvians and Mexicans skilled in its use when they arrived.

Even the abacus did not make arithmetic easy for the Romans because in written calculations they were forced to use Roman numerals. There were no Arabic figures such as we use and no character to represent zero. At most, a Roman could figure out problems involving addition and subtraction of whole numbers. Fractions, multiplication, and division were unknown processes in those days.

Strange as it may seem to us with our electronic robots and mechanical calculators, the Romans went on using the abacus and their Roman numerals until the late Middle Ages; then the new arithmetic with its Arabic numbers was adopted from the Moorish universities in Spain. It was really the discovery of the zero by the Hindus that freed Western civilization from finger counting.

We, however, still find Roman numerals useful, although some

**199**

people find them difficult to learn.  If you have forgotten how difficult they can be, try writing *fourteen ninety-two* in Roman numerals.

### Kings Rule Rome (continued)

Ancus Mārcius, nepōs (*grandson*) Numae Pompilī, Rōmae erat quārtus rēx.  Ille rēx bonus prūdēnsque fuit, et similis Numae cum fīnitimīs pūgnāre nōn cupīvit.  Sed Rōma ā Latīnīs saepe oppūgnābātur.  Rēx nōn timidus bellum contrā Latīnōs statim gessit.  Urbem hostium dēlēvit et cīvēs ad urbem Rōmam dūxit. Cīvibus novīs Montem Aventīnum dedit.

Pontem sublicium (*wooden*) trāns Tiberim rēx fēcit, et Jāni-culum cum urbe hōc ponte jūnxit.  Carcer (*Prison*) prope Forum et sub monte Capitōlīnō aedificābātur, et Ostia, portus (*port*) Rōmae, in ōre (*mouth*) Tiberis condēbātur (*was founded*).  Agrum fīnēsque Rōmae ad mare extendit et populī Rōmānī imperium auxit.

Post Ancum Mārcium rēgnum obtinuērunt prīncipēs Etrūscī. Tarquinius Prīscus cum uxōre suā ex Etrūriae oppidō ad urbem Rōmam migrāverat.  Māgnam laudem et rēgis et populī Rōmānī celeriter sibi obtinuit, et tandem tūtor duōrum fīliōrum rēgis fuit.

Fīdus et bonus tūtor fuit, sed post mortem Ancī Mārcī ipse rēx esse cupīvit et imperium facile obtinuit.  Multa bella gessit et multōs agrōs hostium audācter occupāvit.  Circum Māximum aedificāvit et lūdōs Rōmānōs statuit.  Et in bellō et in pāce Rōmam bene rēxit Tarquinius.

Interim duo fīliī Ancī Mārcī Tarquinium interficere et rēgnum occupāre statuērunt.  Illī duōs pastōrēs rēgem interficere jus-sērunt.  Sed hī pastōrēs rēgem vulnerāvērunt; illum nōn statim interfēcērunt.  Tanaquil rēgīna mortem rēgis nōn nūntiāvit donec (*until*) propter auctōritātem ējus (*her*) Servius Tullius grātiam populī obtinuerat et rēx ā populō creātus est.

Tarquinius Prīscus Servium Tullium prō fīliō ēdūcāverat quod Tanaquil puerum amāvit.  Tum post Tarquinī Prīscī mortem Servius Tullius sibi rēgnum facile obtinuit.  Prūdenter imperium administrāvit.  Prīmus ille cēnsum populī Rōmānī habērī (*to be held*) jūssit.

Sed Lūcius Tarquinius, fīlius Tarquinī Prīscī, Rōmam regere māgnopere cupīvit.  Cum malā uxōre, fīliā Servī Tullī, rēgem interfēcit et imperium occupāvit.

# Comprehensive Review: Units XXXI–XXXV

A. Write the ablative singular, gender, base, and meaning:

| | | | | | |
|---|---|---|---|---|---|
| fuga | imperātor | scientia | taurus | gaudium | mēnsis |
| hiēms | victōria | amīcitia | inopia | vigilia | aetās |
| genus | lībertās | voluntās | certāmen | aestās | pōns |

B. Give the English meanings:

| | | | | |
|---|---|---|---|---|
| cupidus | dexter | integer | fūrtim | neque |
| certus | sinister | frūstrā | intrā | forte |

C. Write in Latin the principal parts of these verbs. After the first principal part, write the number indicating to which conjugation each belongs.

| | | | | | | |
|---|---|---|---|---|---|---|
| regō | dēligō | vulnerō | interficiō | putō | audiō | nōminō |
| sciō | scrībō | cōnfirmō | dēmōnstrō | dūcō | pellō | statuō |
| gerō | dīvidō | contendō | perveniō | vincō | capiō | vertō |

D. Decline in Latin and translate:
1. the same summer (singular)
2. the same joy (plural)

E. Write these synopses, active voice, indicative mood, and translate each form:

1. jaciō (second person singular)
2. currō (third person plural)
3. faciō (second person plural)
4. veniō (third person singular)
5. cupiō (third person plural)
6. pōnō (second person plural)

F. Conjugate in the present and future tenses, active and passive voices:

vītō    augeō    jungō    rapiō    sentiō

G. Write in Latin the specified forms, and translate:
1. dative singular: mēnsis, hiēms, fuga
2. dative plural: pōns, imperātor, vigilia
3. genitive singular: scientia, aetās, aestās
4. genitive plural: gaudium, victōria, genus
5. ablative singular: voluntās, inopia, lībertās
6. accusative plural: taurus, certāmen, amīcitia

H. With each of the following nouns, use the correct form of īdem, eadem, idem:

| | | | | | | |
|---|---|---|---|---|---|---|
| hiēms | fugam | gaudiō | aestāte | voluntās | mēnsibus | certāmine |
| pontī | taurī | tempus | generis | amīcitia | victōriae | imperātōrēs |

I. Complete the following sentences by translating into Latin the words in parentheses. Name the rule governing each phrase.

1. (With weapons) pūgnāvērunt.
2. (With his mother) pervēnit.
3. (By the soldier) servābātur.
4. (For many years) habitābunt.
5. (From danger) līberābātur.
6. (From the town) properāvērunt.

7. (Within a short time) aderit.
8. (For three hours) spectābant.
9. (At the same time) vēnērunt.
10. (In word and deed) erat benīgnus.

## SENTENCE PATTERNS

A. Translate into English:

1. Antīquīs tempōribus multa bella ā Rōmānīs gerēbantur.
2. Aestāte et hieme pontēs ā servīs aedificābuntur.
3. Cīvēs Rōmānī contrā multitūdinem hostium tēla jaciēbant.
4. Pāx et amīcitia cum sociīs cōnfīrmantur.
5. Saepe deī ab hominibus vidēbantur, ita poētae scrībunt.
6. Ex oppidō suō ab eīsdem mīlitibus pellentur.
7. Eōdem tempore imperātor Rōmānōs māgnō timōre līberāvit.
8. Subitō ab hostibus celeriter cucurrit et fugam simulāvit.
9. Forte sex frātrēs erant parēs aetāte et virtūte.
10. Ā quibus gentibus Rōmānī in bellō superābuntur?

B. Translate into Latin:

1. Who were free from danger because the bridge was being destroyed?
2. At the third hour the city will be freed from the enemy by the brave general and his soldiers.
3. Danger never is conquered without danger.
4. Did the people hear about the death of the good king?
5. The soldiers are being led away from the city to the camp.

## SIGHT TRANSLATION: THE SWORD OF DAMOCLES

Fuit ōlim in Siciliā rēx potēns nōmine Dionȳsius. In domiciliō māgnō ac pulchrō habitābat, sed propter cōnsilia inimīcōrum perīculum mortis cotīdiē timēbat. Ūnō diē eum cīvis quīdam (*certain*) nōmine Damoclēs vīsitāvit. Ubi domicilium pulchrum spectāvit, māgnitūdinem cubicu-lōrum (*of the rooms*) atque hortōrum (*of the gardens*) māgnō cum studiō laudāvit. "Ō Dionȳsī, tū es homō fortūnātus! Propter mūnificentiam (*generosity*) tuam ab amīcīs laudāberis; propter potestātem ab inimīcīs timēberis. Numquam hominem tam fortūnātum cōgnōvī (*knew*)!"

Tum respondit: "Ō Damoclēs, falsa est opīniō tua. Hāc nocte ad cēnam (*banquet*) meam venī. Vēra dē meā fortūnā sciēs."

Circā (*About*) decimam hōram ad cēnam pervēnit Damoclēs. Māgna servōrum multitūdō aderat. Illī manūs (*hands*) Damoclis aquā pūrā lāvērunt (*washed*). In capite corōnam (*crown*) rosārum posuērunt. Ac-cubuit (*reclined*) Damoclēs, et cum eō Dionȳsius ipse et multī cīvēs nō-bilēs quoque accubuērunt.

In mediā cēnā rēx Damoclem rogāvit: "Dēlectatne tē haec cēna?"

Respondit Damoclēs: "Sī centum annōs vīvam (*shall live*), nihil melius (*better*) ā mē vidēbitur." "Tolle (*Lift up*) oculōs tuōs," jūssit rēx. Statim Damoclēs timōre superābātur. Super (*Above*) caput ūnō fīlō (*thread*) suspendēbātur gladius nūdus. Tum māgnō cum terrōre, "Cūr hunc perīculum mihi parāvistī?" rogāvit.

Dionȳsius respondit: "Hoc est exemplum vītae meae. Dum multīs gaudiīs dēlector, multīs quoque perīculīs terreor. Māgna est rēgis potestās, sed māgnae etiam sunt cūrae ējus."

This fellow's wise enough to play the fool, **Unit** XXXVI
And to do that well craves a kind of wit.
—William Shakespeare, 1564–1616
*Twelfth Night*

## CONVERSATION

MAGISTER: Lūcius Tarquinius, rēx Rōmānus, Superbus appellātus est quod prīmus rēgum bellum gerī, pācem cōnfīrmārī cum multīs gentibus per sē sine auctōritāte senātūs jūssit.

ROBERTUS: Nōnne portentum terribile illō tempore vīsum est?

MAGISTER: Māgnus serpēns in rēgis domiciliō inventus est.

HENRĪCUS: Quid rēx propter portentum agī dēsīderābat?

MAGISTER: Ille duōs fīliōs ad Delphicum ōrāculum in Graeciam mīsit et eōs deum Apollinem causam portentī rogāre jūssit. Fīliī rēgis sēcum in itinere Jūnium Brūtum dūxērunt.

ROBERTA: Respônditne adulēscentibus Apollō?

MAGISTER: Puerī patris mandāta fēcērunt et tum ōrāculum rogāvērunt: "Ō māgne Apollō, ad quem nostrum veniet imperium Rōmānum?" Quid, Cornēlia, erat deī respōnsum?

CORNĒLIA: "Imperium Rōmae habēbit quī prīmus ōsculum (*kiss*) mātrī dederit." Statim Brūtus terrae, mātrī omnium hominum, ōsculum dedit.

ROBERTUS: Eratne Brūtus umquam (*ever*) rēx? Habēbatne Rōmae imperium?

MAGISTER: Multitūdō Rōmānōrum ē rēgnō Tarquinium Superbum pellere māgnopere dēsīderābat, sed ducem nōn habēbant. Posteā Brūtum auxilium rogāvērunt quod propter multās injūriās regis multum labōrāverat. Brūtus cōnsul creātus est et rēgem mālum et superbum expulit.

## SECTION 1 Perfect System, Passive Voice

▶ DISCUSSION

In English the passive forms of the perfect system, third person singular, indicative are: perfect, *he has been called;* pluperfect, *he had been called;* future perfect, *he will have been called.* In Latin these same tenses are formed by combining the perfect passive participle with the present, imperfect, and future tenses of *sum.*

The following graphic formulas will serve as guides for the formation of these tenses for verbs that have a perfect passive participle.

*204*

| | PERFECT | PLUPERFECT | FUTURE PERFECT |
|---|---|---|---|
| Formulas | Perf. pass. part. + pres. tense of **sum** | Perf. pass. part. + imperf. tense of **sum** | Perf. pass. part. + fut. tense of **sum** |
| Singular | | | |
| First | **vocātus, –a, –um sum** | **vocātus, –a, –um eram** | **vocātus, –a, –um erō** |
| Second | **es** | **erās** | **eris** |
| Third | **est** | **erat** | **erit** |
| Plural | | | |
| First | **vocātī, –ae, –a sumus** | **vocātī, –ae, –a erāmus** | **vocātī, –ae, –a erimus** |
| Second | **estis** | **erātis** | **eritis** |
| Third | **sunt** | **erant** | **erunt** |
| Translation | *I have been called* *I was called (once)* | *I had been called* | *I shall have been called* |

▶ STUDY HELPS

1. The perfect passive participle is an adjective, declined like an adjective of the first or second declension. It must agree with the subject of the compound passive verb in gender, number, and case.

> **Puellae vocātae sunt.** The girls were called.
> **Puer vocātus erat.** The boy had been called.
> **Oppida oppūgnāta erunt.** The towns will have been attacked.

2. The verb *faciō* uses forms of the verb *fīō* for the passive of the present, imperfect, and future tenses. *Fīō* will be taught in a later lesson. The other tenses form the passive voice regularly. The passive of *faciō* may be translated by *become, be made,* or *be done.*

▶ PRACTICE PATTERNS

A. Conjugate as indicated and also write English translations:
1. perfect passive: dō, moneō, mittō, inveniō, creō
2. pluperfect passive: jaciō, audiō, cūstōdiō, videō, putō
3. future perfect passive: vocō, dūcō, moneō, jaciō

B. Write synopses, active and passive, third person plural, and translate:

> rogō    videō    mittō    rapiō    sentiō

C. Write in Latin:

| | | |
|---|---|---|
| she was ruled | they were expelled | they have been elected |
| he was called | he had been sent | it will have been guarded |
| it was saved | it has been found | he will have been led |
| they were driven | she had been killed | we shall have been ruled |
| they were fleeing | they shall have been | you (sing.) had fled |

# SECTION 2 Present Passive Infinitive

▶ DISCUSSION

In English *to be* is the indicator of the present passive infinitive, just as *to* indicates the active infinitive. Active: *to call*; passive: *to be called*. In Latin the present passive infinitive is formed in all conjugations except the third by changing the final *–e* of the present active infinitive to *–ī*:

**vocāre** = *to call*     **vocārī** = *to be called*

In the third conjugation the short *–e* of the stem is changed to long *–ī.*

| Conjugation | Act. Infin. | Pass. Infin. |
|---|---|---|
| First | **vocāre,** *to call* | **vocārī,** *to be called* |
| Second | **monēre,** *to warn* | **monērī,** *to be warned* |
| Third | **regere,** *to rule* | **regī,** *to be ruled* |
| Third –io | **capere,** *to seize* | **capī,** *to be seized* |
| Fourth | **audīre,** *to hear* | **audīrī,** *to be heard* |

▶ PRACTICE PATTERNS

A. Write the active and passive infinitives of these verbs and translate:

| | | | | | |
|---|---|---|---|---|---|
| sciō | vertō | cupiō | habeō | spectō | cōnfīrmō |
| negō | dēbeō | dēleō | mittō | dēligō | appellō |
| rapiō | vincō | vāstō | jungō | vocō | respondeō |
| servō | jaciō | videō | scrībō | sentiō | inveniō |

B. Translate into Latin:

| | | | |
|---|---|---|---|
| to run | to be able | to be moved | to be guarded |
| to sail | to be avoided | to be elected | to be entrusted |
| to drive | to be taken | to be prepared | to be expelled |
| to kill | to delight | to overcome | to determine |

# SECTION 3 The Present Imperative

▶ DISCUSSION

In accordance with the rule already learned, the present imperative singular of verbs is formed by dropping the *–re* of the present infinitive when the subject understood is singular:

**vocā** = *call*     **monē** = *warn*     **rege** = *rule*
**cape** = *take*     **audī** = *hear*

If the subject understood is plural, *–te* is added to this imperative form; but in verbs of the third conjugation, the short stem vowel *–e* changes to short *–i* before *–te:*

**vocāte** = *call* (pl.)   **monēte** = *warn* (pl.)   **regite** = *rule* (pl.)
**capite** = *take* (pl.)   **audīte** = *hear* (pl.)

▶ STUDY HELPS

There are four verbs whose present imperative is irregular: *dīc, speak; dūc, lead; fac, make;* and *fer, carry.* The plural forms are: *dīcite, dūcite, facite, ferte.* The irregular verb *ferō* will be taught in a later lesson.

▶ PRACTICE PATTERNS

A. Translate:

scrībīte    pelle    gerite    cūstōdī    venīte    mitte    mittite    invenī

B. Write in Latin the present imperative, singular and plural, of these verbs:

run    throw    join    flee    commit    drive    conquer    feel    arrive    kill

## WORDS TO MASTER

**a′gō, –ere, ē′gī, āctus** (3), drive, lead, do (*agent, act*); **grātiās agere,** give thanks; **vītam agere,** lead a life

**auctō′ritās, –tātis,** *f.,* influence, authority (*authority*)

**commit′tō, –ere, –mīsī, –missus** (3), commit, entrust (*commission*); **proelium committere,** begin battle

**cre′ō** (1), create, make, produce, elect (officials) (*creation*)

**cūstō′diō, –īre, –īvī, –ītus** (4), watch, guard (*custody*)

**expel′lō, –ere, –pulī, –pulsus** (3), drive out, expel (*expulsion*)

**fu′giō, –ere, fū′gī, —** (3), flee, escape (*fugitive*)

**inve′niō, –īre, –vēnī, –ventus** (4), come upon, find, find out, discover (*invention*)

**malefi′cium, –ī,** *n.,* evil deed, crime

**mit′tō, –ere, mī′sī, missus** (3), send (*mission*)

**mōs, mō′ris,** *m.,* custom, habit (*moral*); *pl.,* manners, character

**occī′dō, –ere, –cīdī, –cīsus** (3), strike down, beat to the ground, cut down, kill, slay

## BUILDING WORD POWER

There are two prefixes spelled *in–*. One is from the preposition *in,* which may mean *in, into, within, on, toward, very.* It follows the rules for assimilation and becomes *il–* before words beginning with *l–; ir–* before *r–;* and *im–* before *m–, p–,* and *b–.* Note: *illusion, irrigation, immigrant,* and *imbibe.*

The other is the *inseparable* prefix *in–*, which is not an independent preposition and is not able to be separated from the root or base to which it is affixed. It corresponds to the English prefix *un–*, as in *unnecessary*, and always has a negative meaning, as *without, no, not.* Before *–gn–*, the negative prefix *in–* forms the combination *ign–*, as in *ignoble, ignominy*, and *ignorance.*

Which *in–* is used in the following italicized words? What did the doctor really do when he gave you an *injection* of Salk vaccine? What does *inoculate* have to do with eyes? The children were *inseparable.* If *fārī* means *to speak*, what is the true meaning of *infant?* Why were boys who attended knights called *infantry?*

## SENTENCE PATTERNS

A. Translate into English.

1. Brūtus populum incitāvit, et rēgīna inīqua ex urbe expulsa est.
2. Semper rēx malus ā mīlitibus suīs cūstōdiēbātur.
3. Multa maleficia ā familiā rēgis commissa erant.
4. Num erat mōs rēgum perfidōrum lēgēs bonās statuere?
5. Multī Rōmānī occīsī sunt quod amīcī Servī Tullī fuerant.
6. Paucīs hōrīs maleficium fīlī rēgis inventum est.
7. Cōnsulēs ā populō creātī sunt et multōs annōs māgnam auctōritātem habēbant.
8. Nōnne servus cōnsilia fīliōrum cōnsulis audīvit et ad Brūtum nūntium mīsit?
9. Quī Tarquinius ex Etrūriā vēnit, et quī Tarquinius ad Etrūriam fūgit?
10. Necesse erat rēgem inīquum ex urbe expellī.

B. Write this story in Latin:

Once upon a time Rome was ruled by kings. Lucius Tarquinius Superbus was a bad king. He desired all the power and authority for himself. He ordered all the friends of Servius Tullius to be put to death or expelled from the city. Sextus, son of the bad king, was also wicked. The Tarquinii, father and son, had few friends and many enemies. Finally these bad men were driven from the city and two consuls were elected by the people. Never again was Rome ruled by kings.

### Brutus, the First Roman Consul

Rōma ā rēge inīquō multōs annōs regēbātur. Hic rēx appellātus est L. Tarquinius Superbus. Vī (*By force*) rēgnum occupāverat et vī rēgnum administrāvit. Multī cīvēs Rōmānī ab illō aut ex urbe expulsī sunt aut interfectī sunt. Omnēs fīliī sorōris

Tarquiniae occīsī sunt quod eōs timuit. Ūnus puer, nōmine Jūnius, stultitiam (*foolishness*) simulāvit ac se ā morte servāvit. Propter hoc Brūtus appellātus est.

Malus rēx nōn erat laetus. Amīcōs fīdōs nōn habēbat et perīculum semper timēbat. Eum omnī tempore cūstōdīrī ā mīlitibus suīs necesse erat. Māgnus numerus cīvium eum expellī ā rēgnō cupīvit, sed dux bonus invenīrī nōn potuit. Tandem virum quī (*who*) cōpiās rēgis in fugam dare (*put to flight*) poterat invēnērunt. Dux erat Jūnius Brūtus quī multōs annōs stultitiam simulāverat.

Lūcius Tarquinius erat malus, sed fīlius ējus, nōmine Sextus, erat pējor quam (*worse than*) rēx ipse. Is maleficia horribilia semper committēbat. Propter eum Lūcrētia, domina Rōmāna, sē occīdit. Brūtus aderat et patrī et conjugī (*husband*) ējus jūrāvit (*swore*): "Audīte me! Lūcium Tarquinium cum uxōre et omnibus līberīs ex urbe Rōmā agam. Numquam Tarquinius Rōmae iterum rēgnābit!"

Brūtus dux ā populō Rōmānō dēlectus est. Rēgīnam, similem nātūrā rēgī, ex urbe expulsit. Cum illā erant fīliae ējus et amīcī rēgis. Tum rēx mūrōs Ardeae oppūgnābat, et ubi nūntium dē perīculō suō accēpit, cōpiās ex Ardeā ad urbem Rōmam dūxit. Mīlitēs dē mūrīs Rōmānīs exspectābant, et ubi rēx et fīliī ējus vīsī sunt, portae urbis clausae sunt (*were closed*). Tum rēx malus in Etrūriam fūgit et Sextus ab inimīcīs interfectus est.

Sīc rēgēs Rōmā expulsī sunt. Duo cōnsulēs creātī sunt, Lūcius Jūnius Brūtus et Tarquinius Collātīnus. Tamen pars populī novum rēgnum neque amābat neque laudābat. Paucī Tarquinium iterum rēgem esse cupīvērunt. Inter eōs ipsī fīliī Brūtī cōnsulis erant. Contrā cōnsulēs conjūrāvērunt (*conspired*) et rēgem in urbem nocte dūcere statuērunt. Servus cōnsilia eōrum audīvit et Brūtō cōnsulī omnia haec narrāvit. Ille omnēs cīvēs quī hoc cōnsilium cēperant gladiō statim interficī jūssit.

Prīmō Brūtus suōs fīliōs inter conjūrātōs (*conspirators*) nōn sēnsit, sed tandem eōs vīdit. Ubi puerī patrem auxilium rogāvērunt, eīs veniam (*pardon*) negāvit. "Mihi fīliī meī cārī sunt," inquit (*he said*), "sed lībertās patriae meae cārior (*dearer*) est." Rōmānī patrem propter lībertātis et patriae amōrem (*love*) laudāvērunt.

*Unit* XXXVII

## CONVERSATION

MAGISTER: Ad arma! Cīvēs Rōmānī ad arma! Nōlīte pontem relinquere!

PAULUS: Quid est, magister? Cūr clāmās: "Ad arma!"

MAGISTER: Lārs Porsena, cūjus mīlitēs māgnam partem montis Jāniculī celeriter cēpērunt, ad pontem prōcēdit. Facile hostēs pontem ā quō est breve iter in urbem occupābunt. Quid facere possumus? Necesse est pontem mūnīrī.

PATRICIUS: Dēlēte, cīvēs, pontem! Ego in itinere angustō stābō et hostēs prohibēbō. Quī mēcum pontem dēfendent?

MAGISTER: Quis es tū? Cūr salūtem fugā nōn petis?

PATRICIUS: Horātius Coclēs sum ego. Illō nōmine appellātus sum quod in proeliō cum hostibus ācribus oculum āmīsī.

ROBERTUS: Ego, nōmine Spurius Lārcius, quī sum clārus genere factīsque, dextrā tuā stābō et tēcum hostēs prohibēbō.

HENRĪCUS: Titus Herminius appellātus sum. Sinistrā tuā erō ego.

PATRICIUS: Nōs, cīvēs, caput pontis dēfendēmus. Vōs, quibus deī auxilium dabunt, īgne gladiōque post (*behind*) nōs pontem dēlēte!

## Relative Pronouns

▶ DISCUSSION

The English relative pronouns, *who, which, what,* and *that,* introduce a subordinate clause and connect the clause with some preceding noun or pronoun called its *antecedent* (**ante** + **cēdere,** *go*).

*Who* always refers to *persons,* and *which* to *things.* *That* may refer to *either* persons or things. *Which* and *that* do not change form to indicate case, but *who* does: nominative, *who;* possessive, *whose;* objective, *whom.* These same forms are used for both singular and plural.

In Latin there are masculine, feminine, and neuter forms for both singular and plural. The relative pronoun in both English and Latin agrees with its antecedent in person and number but not in case.

|        | M.      | F.                                          | N.                              |
|--------|---------|---------------------------------------------|---------------------------------|
|        |         | **SINGULAR**                                |                                 |
| Nom.   | **quī** | **quae,** *who, which, that*                | **quod,** *which, that*         |
| Gen.   | **cūjus** | **cūjus,** *whose, of whom, of which*     | **cūjus,** *of which*           |
| Dat.   | **cui** | **cui,** *to, for whom, which*              | **cui,** *to, for which*        |
| Acc.   | **quem** | **quam,** *whom, which, that*              | **quod,** *which, that*         |
| Abl.   | **quō** | **quā,** *from, by, with whom, which*       | **quō,** *from, by, with which* |
|        |         | **PLURAL**                                  |                                 |
| Nom.   | **quī** | **quae,** *who, which, that*                | **quae,** *which, that*         |
| Gen.   | **quōrum** | **quārum,** *whose, of whom, of which*   | **quōrum,** *of which*          |
| Dat.   | **quibus** | **quibus,** *to, for whom, which*        | **quibus,** *to, for which*     |
| Acc.   | **quōs** | **quās,** *whom, which, that*             | **quae,** *which, that*         |
| Abl.   | **quibus** | **quibus,** *from, by, with whom, which* | **quibus,** *from, by, with which* |

▶ STUDY HELPS

1. The interrogative adjective and the relative pronoun are identical in form; the interrogative pronoun and the relative pronoun are identical in the plural only.

2. Clauses introduced by relative pronouns are usually adjective clauses and are always subordinate clauses.

3. A verb having a relative pronoun as its subject has the same person and number as the antecedent of the relative pronoun.

> **Sum ego *quī* virum vīdī.** It is I *who* saw the man.

*Vīdī* is first person singular because the antecedent of **quī,** subject of *vīdī,* is **ego.**

4. When the relative pronoun is used with the preposition *cum, cum* is usually attached to the relative pronoun, forming one word: **quōcum, quācum, quibuscum.**

▶ PRACTICE PATTERNS

A. Translate into English:

| | |
|---|---|
| librī cūjus | domina quae ambulat |
| librī quōrum | mūrī quōs vīdistī |
| is quī clāmat | puellae quibus librōs dedit |
| flūmen quod fluit | oppidum in quod contendērunt |
| Ego sum quī sum | mīles cui pecūniam dedērunt |

B. Translate into Latin the italicized words or phrases:

I *who* saw Rome      the town *which* is near the river
the man *whose* name      the gates *which* they stormed
the girl *whose* mother      the men *with whom* we worked
the men *whose* deeds      the lady *with whom* you walked
the boy *to whom* you spoke      the plot *which* we discovered

## WORDS TO MASTER

**acci′piō, –ere, –cēpī, –ceptus** (3), receive (*accept*)

**āmit′tō, –ere, –mīsī, –missus** (3), send away, lose

**ca′dō, –ere, cecidī, cāsūrus** (3), fall (*cadence*)

**dēfen′dō, –ere, –fendī, –fēnsus** (3), defend, protect (*defense*)

**flu′ō, –ere, flū′xī, flūxūrus** (3), flow (*fluent*)

**īnsi′diae, –ārum,** *f. pl.*, treachery, plot (*insidious*)

**mū′niō, –īre, –īvī, –ītus** (4), fortify (*munitions*)

**perter′reō, –ēre, –uī, –itus** (2), terrify, alarm

**pe′tō, –ere, –īvī, –ītus** (3), seek, beg (*petition*)

**post′quam,** *conj.*, after

**prōcē′dō, –ere, –cessī, –cessūrus** (3), go forward, advance (*proceed*)

**relin′quō, –ere, –līquī, –lictus** (3), leave, leave behind, abandon, give up (*relinquish*)

## BUILDING WORD POWER

A very frequently used prefix is **ē–** (**ex–**) with the meaning *out, from, beyond, without*. **Ex–** is used before vowels and **h–, c–, p–, q–, s–, t–,** as in **exclāmō, explōrō, exquīrō, exspectō, extendō**. Assimilation takes place before **–f**, as **ex– + faciō = efficiō**. In English derivatives as *expect, exert, expatiate*, the *–s–* is dropped.

As you know, **pēs, pedis** means *foot*, so if you are *expeditious* (*quick*) about anything, it is because there is nothing for you to trip over. An *expedient* (*resource*) is something advantageous to free your feet. When you *expedite* (*hurry*) some business, you see there is nothing in the way of your feet. When you go on an *expedition*, your feet must be free. On the contrary, to *impede* someone is to entangle his feet. In what way is an *impediment* a hindrance? Why is baggage called *impedimenta?*

The prefix **extra–** is a close relative of **ex–**, and it means *outside, beyond*. *Extraordinary* means *beyond the ordinary*. What is the true meaning of *extravagant* (**vagō** = *wander*)?

## SENTENCE PATTERNS

A. Translate into English:

1. Nōnne castra flūmine quod per urbem fluēbat mūnīta sunt?
2. Pōns quem Horātius dēfendēbat in flūmen cecidit.
3. Multitūdō mīlitum Etrūscōrum ā quibus Jāniculum captum erat ad pontem celeriter cucurrit.
4. In flūmine fuit pōns quō hostēs iter facile ad urbem habēbant.
5. Rōmānī quī māgnopere perterritī sunt ad pontem prōcessērunt.
6. Nōlīte salūtem fugā petere! Nōlīte pontem relinquere!
7. Rōmānī propter īnsidiās puellae victōriam paene āmīsērunt.
8. Cīvēs virum cūjus pūgnam fortem spectāverant māgnō cum gaudiō accēpērunt.
9. Horātius postquam pōns dēlētus est in flūmen sē jēcit.
10. Ā quō Tarquinius post mortem Brūtī auxilium petīvit?

B. Translate into Latin. Tell the number, gender, and case of the relative pronouns.

1. The river by which Rome was fortified flowed through the city.
2. Did not the citizens whom Porsena had terrified seek safety in flight?
3. The brave man by whom Rome was saved received a large reward, didn't he?
4. On the river was a bridge by which the enemy could easily come into the city.
5. He was called by that name because he had lost an eye in battle.

### The Roman Toga

For more than a thousand years the characteristic garment of the Roman citizen was the *toga*. It was the outer garment for formal wear in public. Semicircular in shape, about eighteen feet by seven feet, and made of undyed white wool, it enveloped the whole figure, to which it added grace and dignity. No one but a Roman citizen could wear it, and he had to wear it for all formal occasions. If a citizen was banished, he was not permitted to take his toga, because it was widely known as a sign of Roman citizenship.

The Roman boy wore the same kind of garments as his father; these consisted primarily of the tunic and the toga. The *tunic* was an undergarment extending from the neck to the calf of the leg. This was usually white and made of wool. It was worn in the house and for work. Until he reached the age of manhood, a boy's toga had a border of Roman purple. This was called the *toga praetexta* and was worn also by magistrates, censors, dictators, and important officials of free towns and colonies.

The *toga virilis* of an ordinary citizen was plain white. Those running for public office used chalk to give their toga a shiny or glossy effect. It was called a *toga candida*, and those who wore it were called *candidati*, from which we get our word *candidate*. The *toga picta* was crimson, embroidered in gold, and was worn by victorious generals in triumphal processions and also by the emperors.

## A One-eyed Hero Saves Rome

Tarquinius, secundō annō postquam ex urbe expulsus est, contrā Rōmānōs bellum gessit. Eī auxilium ā Porsenā, rēge Etrūscō datum est. Illō tempore Etrūscī erant hostēs Rōmānōrum, et Porsena cum multīs cōpiīs Rōmam prōcēdēbāt. Rōmānī, quī māgnopere perterritī sunt quod mōns Jāniculum ā Porsenā facile occupātus erat, ex agrīs in urbem fugiēbant. Līberī et fēminae et servī intrā mūrōs ductī sunt.

Inter montem Jāniculum et urbem Rōmam fluēbat Tiberis. Urbs multīs mūrīs et flūmine celerī mūnīta est. In hōc flūmine erat pōns sublicius (*wooden*) quī hostibus iter paene dedit. Pōns autem erat angustus et paucī eōdem tempore trāns eum ambulāre poterant.

Hostēs postquam Jāniculum cēpērunt, celeriter ad flūmen contendērunt. Vir fortis, Horātius Coclēs, quī illō nōmine appellātus est quod in proeliō oculum āmīserat, prīmus māgnum perīculum sēnsit. Coclēs, quī prope caput pontis forte positus erat, māgnā vōce ad sociōs suōs clāmāvit: "Cūr fugitis, virī Rōmānī? Nōlīte relinquere pontem. Nōnne perīculum sentītis? Sī pontem relinquētis, hostēs in urbem mox venient. Eum īgne et gladiō dēlēte! Contrā Etrūscōs pūgnābō! Ego corpore meō pontem dēfendam!"

Prōcessit in prīmam partem pontis ipsāque audāciā hostēs turbāvit (*confused*). Duo Rōmānī, Spurius Lārcius et Titus Herminius, clārī genere factīsque, cum eō stetērunt et trēs virī breve tempus hostēs ā ponte prohibuērunt. Tum Horātius duōs sociōs salūtem fugā petere jūssit. "Pōns mox cadet. Ad rīpam statim properāte!"

Sed Horātius Coclēs pontem nōn relīquit. Etruscī māgnō clāmōre undique in ūnum hostem tēla jēcērunt. Subitō pōns in flūmen cecidit. "Tiberīne Pater," inquit (he said), "tē, sāncte, ōrō! Haec arma et hunc mīlitem propitiō (favorable) flūmine accipe!"

Circum virum fortem multa tēla cadēbant ubi sē in Tiberim jēcit. Sed ad rīpam sine vulneribus pervēnit. Alacriter cīvēs eum accēpērunt cūjus factum forte laudem certē meruit (deserved). Horātiō populus Rōmānus māgnam partem terrae pūblicae dedit, et in Forō statua ējus posita est. Praemia idōnea duōbus mīlitibus Rōmānīs quī cum illō pontem dēfenderant quoque data sunt. Fortitūdō ūnīus virī cūnctam urbem servāvit.

<table>
<tr><td>If all the world were just,<br>There would be no need of valor.<br>—Plutarch, A.D. 46–120<br>Lives</td><td>Unit XXXVIII</td></tr>
</table>

## CONVERSATION

CŌNSUL: Quis es, adulēscēns? Unde vēnistī? Cūr hīc es?

MŪCIUS: Gājus Mūcius, clārus propter genus atque audāciam meam sum ego.

CŌNSUL: Quid cupis, Mūcī? Senātōribus ac patribus dīc!

MŪCIUS: Multōs diēs jam prope urbem rēx Etruscōrum cum māgnīs cōpiīs mānsit. Frūmentum in urbem portārī nōn potest. Nūllum cibum nunc habēmus. Ego bonum cōnsilium cēpī.

CŌNSUL: Nōbīs cōnsilium tuum celeriter narrā, fortis adulēscēns!

MŪCIUS: Sōlus sed armātus ad castra hostium trāns flūmen prōcēdere cupiō. Porsenam occīdere in animō habeō! Ita cīvēs Rōmānī morte ūnīus hominis tōtō perīculō līberābuntur!

CŌNSUL: Quid aliud facere possumus? Nēmō ex urbe excēdere potest. Populus neque aquam neque cibum habēre potest.

MŪCIUS: Neque perīculum neque dolōrem neque mortem timeō. Sī cōnsul mihi potestātem fēcerit, aut tūtus rēgem Etruscōrum necābō aut nōn jam vīvam! Valēte, meī amīcī!

# Adjectives of Special Declension

▶ DISCUSSION

There are ten adjectives in Latin that are called irregular, but they are declined like adjectives of the first and second declensions with the exception of only two cases: (1) the genitive singular, which ends in –*ius* in all genders; (2) the dative singular, which ends in –*ī* in all genders. Only the singular of the following adjectives is given here since their plural declension is regular.

<table>
<tr><td></td><td colspan="3">SINGULAR</td><td colspan="3">SINGULAR</td></tr>
<tr><td></td><td colspan="3">**nūllus, nūlla, nūllum**</td><td colspan="3">**neuter, neutra, neutrum**</td></tr>
<tr><td></td><td colspan="3">*none, no*</td><td colspan="3">*neither (of two)*</td></tr>
<tr><td></td><td>M.</td><td>F.</td><td>N.</td><td>M.</td><td>F.</td><td>N.</td></tr>
<tr><td>Nom.</td><td>nūllus</td><td>nūlla</td><td>nūllum</td><td>neuter</td><td>neutra</td><td>neutrum</td></tr>
<tr><td>Gen.</td><td>nūllīus</td><td>nūllīus</td><td>nūllīus</td><td>neutrīus</td><td>neutrīus</td><td>neutrīus</td></tr>
<tr><td>Dat.</td><td>nūllī</td><td>nūllī</td><td>nūllī</td><td>neutrī</td><td>neutrī</td><td>neutrī</td></tr>
<tr><td>Acc.</td><td>nūllum</td><td>nūllam</td><td>nūllum</td><td>neutrum</td><td>neutram</td><td>neutrum</td></tr>
<tr><td>Abl.</td><td>nūllō</td><td>nūllā</td><td>nūllō</td><td>neutrō</td><td>neutrā</td><td>neutrō</td></tr>
<tr><td></td><td colspan="3">**alter, altera, alterum**</td><td colspan="3">**alius, alia, aliud**</td></tr>
<tr><td></td><td colspan="3">*the other (of two)*</td><td colspan="3">*other, another*</td></tr>
<tr><td>Nom.</td><td>alter</td><td>altera</td><td>alterum</td><td>alius</td><td>alia</td><td>aliud</td></tr>
<tr><td>Gen.</td><td>alterius</td><td>alterius</td><td>alterius</td><td>alīus</td><td>alīus</td><td>alīus</td></tr>
<tr><td>Dat.</td><td>alterī</td><td>alterī</td><td>alterī</td><td>aliī</td><td>aliī</td><td>aliī</td></tr>
<tr><td>Acc.</td><td>alterum</td><td>alteram</td><td>alterum</td><td>alium</td><td>aliam</td><td>aliud</td></tr>
<tr><td>Abl.</td><td>alterō</td><td>alterā</td><td>alterō</td><td>aliō</td><td>aliā</td><td>aliō</td></tr>
</table>

Five of these adjectives, **nūllus, sōlus, tōtus, ūllus, ūnus,** with the *exception* of the genitive and dative singular, are declined like *fīdus, –a, –um*; three, **neuter, uter, uterque,** are declined like *pulcher, –chra, –chrum*; **alter** is declined like *līber, lībera, līberum*; **alius,** like *industrius, –a, –um*.

These adjectives and their meanings are easily remembered if they are studied in related groups as follows:

<table>
<tr><td>✴ **alius, alia, aliud**</td><td>*another, other (of several), else*</td></tr>
<tr><td>**alter, altera, alterum**</td><td>*the other, the one (of two)*</td></tr>
<tr><td></td><td></td></tr>
<tr><td>**uter, utra, utrum**</td><td>*which (of two)*</td></tr>
<tr><td>**uterque, utraque, utrumque**</td><td>*each (of two), both*</td></tr>
<tr><td>**neuter, neutra, neutrum**</td><td>*neither (of two)*</td></tr>
</table>

| | |
|---|---|
| ūnus, ūna, ūnum | *one, alone; only* (pl.) |
| ūllus, ūlla, ūllum | *any* |
| nūllus, nūlla, nūllum | *none, no* |
| sōlus, sōla, sōlum | *alone, sole, only, single* |
| tōtus, tōta, tōtum | *the whole, entire, all* |

▶ STUDY HELPS

1. These adjectives are emphatic and always precede the nouns they modify. They have no vocative case.

2. *Alterius* is commonly used for the genitive of *alīus.*

3. *Nūllus = nē + ūllus (not any)*; *neuter = nē + uter (neither of two).*

4. *Tōtus = whole, not capable of being divided; omnēs* (pl.) *= all, the whole, complete collection of units and parts; omnis* (sing.) *= each, every, the whole; cūnctus = all, all collectively, the whole.*

5. *Nūllus = not any, no;* it is always an adjective. *Nihil = not a thing, nothing;* it is always an indeclinable noun. *Nēmō = no man, no one;* it is always a noun.

6. *Alius* and *alter* are frequently used in pairs with the following meanings:

(a) *alius ... alius = one ... another:* **Alius mūrus lātus est, alius angustus.** *One* wall is wide, *another* is narrow.

(b) *aliī ... aliī = some ... others:* **Aliī puerī aquam, aliī terram amant.** *Some* boys like the water, *others* like the land.

(c) *alter ... alter = the one ... the other:* **Magister alterum puerum laudāvit; alterum accūsāvit.** The teacher praised *the one* boy; *the other* he blamed.

▶ PRACTICE PATTERNS

A. Decline in Latin and translate:

| | | |
|---|---|---|
| Singular: tōta urbs | altera causa | utrum cōnsilium |
| Plural: dux sōlus | neutrum nōmen | aliud maleficium |

B. Translate into English:

| | | |
|---|---|---|
| alterius cōnsulis | utrique rēgēs | tōtī multitūdinī |
| aliud oppidum | nūllum auxilium | alter ego |
| nōminis sōlīus | ūnī ducī | ūllī cōpiae |

C. Write in Latin the specified form, and give the case of each:

1. which king (subject)
2. one contest (direct object)
3. any soldier (possession)
4. the whole kingdom (with ab)
5. no plan (with propter)
6. neither brother (possession)
7. another consul (indirect object)
8. the same camp (direct object)
9. the other rivers (subject)
10. the man alone (with cum)

**armā′tus, –a, –um,** *adj.,* armed (*armature*)

**aut,** *conj.,* or; **aut . . . aut,** either . . . or

**circum′dō, –are, –dedī, –datus** (1), *irreg.,* place around, surround

**conjū′rō** (1), swear (an oath) together, take an oath, conspire, form a league (*conjure*)

**discē′dō, –ere, –cessī, –cessūrus** (3), go away, depart

**excē′dō, –ere, –cessī, –cessūrus** (3), go away, depart (*exceed*)

**īrā′tus, –a, –um,** *adj.,* angered (*irate*)

**i′ta,** *adv.,* so, thus

**nē′mō, —,** *dat.,* **nēminī,** *acc.,* **nēminem,** *m. & f.,* no one, nobody

**perfi′ciō, –ere, –fēcī, –fectus** (3), accomplish, finish (*perfect*)

**tū′tus, –a, –um,** *adj.,* safe (*tutor*)

**vī′vō, –ere, vī′xī, victūrus** (3), live, be alive (*vivid*)

## BUILDING WORD POWER

The little word **nē**, an adverb and a conjunction in Latin, has the meaning of *not* in compounds, some of which became important English derivatives. *Negative* is from **negāre**, which means *to assert that a thing is not*. When you *negotiate* a business deal, you give up your leisure. **Negōtium**, meaning *business*, is formed from **nē + ōtium**, *leisure, ease*. The –g between two vowels is for euphony.

That which is without legal force is *null* from **nūllus**, *none, not one, nobody, no*. **Nūllus = nē + ūllus**. **Ūllus**, *any*, is the diminutive of **ūnus**, *one*. **Uter** can mean *either of two* or, interrogatively, *which (of two)*; **neuter = nē + uter**, *neither of two*. If you are *neutral* at a game, you are rooting for neither side. Do you know who told Polyphemus, the giant, that his name was **Nēmō (nē + homō)**? It was Ulysses. In this way he saved himself and his companions from certain death. To *annihilate* something literally means *to reduce it to a thread;* **nihil**, the Latin word for *nothing*, is ultimately from **nē + fīlum**, *thread*.

## SENTENCE PATTERNS

A. Translate into English:

1. Aliī in bellō interfectī erant; aliī ab hostibus captī erant.
2. Inter hōs mīlitēs fuērunt duo virī; alter eīs pecūniam dabat; alter prope eum stābat. Uter fuit rēx Etrūscōrum?
3. Vir sōlus ad castra hostium prōcēdere cupīvit.
4. Neuter eōrum virōrum alterum timēbat; uterque nēminem timēbat.
5. Nihil in tōtā urbe āctum est quod utrīque nōn grātum erat.
6. Ita nūllō tempore incolae Rōmae tūtī ex urbe excēdere poterant.

7. Mox ā mīlitibus armātīs circumdatus est neque discēdere potuit.
8. Porsena ipse virtūtem Mūcī laudāvit, sed hic erat tristis quod maleficium nōn perfectum erat.
9. Sī hīc manēbis, tūtus nōn eris neque diū vīvēs.
10. Aut ex urbe discēde aut tē occīdēmus. Multī adulēscentēs īrātī contrā tē conjūrāvērunt.

B. Translate into Latin:
1. Armed with one weapon, Mucius departed from the city.
2. There was no route by which he could escape alive.
3. The angered soldiers surrounded the daring young man.
4. Without any battle Rome was freed by one man from great danger
5. Mucius told his whole plan to the consul alone.


### Another One-Man Victory

Lārs Porsena postquam ita ab Horātiō expulsus est, nōn statim in patriam suam discesserat, sed cum māgnīs cōpiīs suīs in castrīs trāns flūmen manēbat. Quod agrōs Rōmānōrum occupāverat māgna inopia cibī in urbe erat. Aliī sociī Rōmae frūmentum in urbem portāre nōn poterant. Nāvēs etiam ex Ostiā quae erat prope mare dēlētae sunt quod frūmentum ad Rōmānōs portābant. Nēmō ex urbe excēdere poterat; nēmō in urbem prōcēdere poterat.

Incolae miserī Rōmae jam famem (*starvation*) sentiēbant et mortem exspectābant, ubi Gājus Mūcius, adulēscēns nōbilis, ad senātōrēs fortiter vēnit et audācter nūntiāvit: "In media castra hostium prōcēdam et rēgem Porsenam gladiō occīdam. Ego sōlus prōcēdere cupiō, et sōlus hōc perīculō cīvēs Rōmānōs līberābō!"

Senātōrēs cōnsilium illīus probābant quī statim trāns flūmen ad castra hostium discessit. Tum Mūcius gladiō armātus castra Etrūscōrum fūrtim intrāvit (*entered*) et rēgis scrībam (*secretary*), nōn rēgem ipsum, occīdit. Adulēscēns audāx currere temptāvit sed ā mīlitibus captus est et ad rēgem tractus est (*was dragged*).

"Cūr sine ūllā causā scrībam meum occīdistī?" māgnā cum īra rogāvit Porsena. "Rēgem, nōn scrībam, occīdere cupīvī. Id autem perficere eō tempore nōn potuī. Sed tē moneō, Ō rēx. Multīs perīculīs et īnsidiīs semper circumdaberis. Nec ego sōlus tē occīdere cupiō. Multī Rōmānī contrā tē conjūrāvērunt. Ūnus nostrum tē occīdet. Sī hīc manēbis, nōn diū vīvēs."

Porsena īrātus sed perterritus (*terrified*) respondit: "Nisi (*Unless*) mihi cōnsilia Rōmānōrum narrāveris, igne cōnsūmēris."

"Cīvis Rōmānus neque dolōrem neque mortem timet," superbē nūntiāvit adulēscēns audāx, et posuit dextram in īgne quī prope in ārā erat. Ibi eam fortiter tenuit dum īgne cōnsūmitur.

"Tū es fortis!" clāmāvit rēx quī et animō et audāciā Mūcī mōtus est. "Tūtus ex castrīs meīs propter fortitūdinem tuam statim excēdere potes." Mox cum Rōmānīs pācem cōnfīrmāvit et omnibus cum cōpiīs suīs ex agrīs Rōmānīs excessit. In nūllō proeliō cum adulēscentibus Rōmānīs similibus Mūciō pūgnāre cupīvit.

Propter māgnum Mūcī animum Rōmānī eī agrōs lātōs ac praemia māgna dedērunt. "Scaevola" (*Lefty*) appellātus est quod dextra īgne cōnsūmpta erat. Bis (*Twice*) Rōma virtūte ūnīus virī servāta est. Alter ūnum oculum, alter ūnam manum (*hand*) habēbat. Utrīque praemium datum est, sed nūllum praemium virtūtī eōrum pār erat.

She moves a goddess, and she looks a queen.
—Homer, *circa* 850 B.C.
*Iliad*

# Unit
# XXXIX

## CONVERSATION

MAGISTER: Apud Rōmānōs antīquōs erant duo māgna genera, plēbs ac patriciī. Quī erant patriciī, Paule?

PAULUS: Aliī nōbilēs patriciōs, aliī patrēs appellāvērunt. Tōta potestās, agrī, pecūnia ā patriciīs habēbantur.

ROBERTUS: Quae plēbs possēdit (*possess*), magister?

MAGISTER: Postquam Tarquinius Superbus Rōmā expulsus est, condiciō plēbis erat mala. Plēbs erat pauper; nūlla jūra habēbat; patriciōs in mātrimōnium dūcere nōn poterat.

ROBERTA: Cūr plēbs nūlla jūra habēbat? Nōnne erant lēgēs?

MAGISTER: Patriciī omnēs lēgēs dedērunt, sed nūllae lēgēs prō plēbe scrīptae sunt. Plēbs ā patriciīs pressa est.

PAULA: Num plēbī auxilium datum est ubi patriciōs rogāvit?

MAGISTER: Praetereā plēbs ubi agrōs relīquit et prō patriā pūgnāvit nūllam pecūniam accēpit. Uxōrēs et līberī sine ūllō cibō erant. Post bella paene tōta plēbe aere aliēnō (*debt*) premēbātur. Etiam in servitūtem dūcēbātur.

PAULUS: Plēbs īrāta contrā patriciōs incitāta est.

# SECTION 1 Verbs with Two Accusatives

▶ DISCUSSION

In Latin, as well as in English, some transitive verbs take a second accusative in addition to their direct object. This second accusative is either a *predicate accusative* or a *secondary object*.

1. Verbs of naming, choosing, appointing, making, showing, considering, and the like in the active voice may take two accusatives denoting the same person or thing. The second accusative may be an adjective. This use is known as the *predicate accusative*.

> **Cicerōnem cōnsulem creāvērunt.** They elected Cicero *consul.*
> **Cicerōnem clārum habent.** They consider Cicero *famous.*

In changing from the active to the passive voice, the *predicate accusative* becomes *predicate nominative*.

> **Cicerō cōnsul creātus est.** Cicero was elected *consul.*
> **Cicerō clārus habētur.** Cicero is considered *famous.*

2. Some verbs of asking and teaching may take two accusatives, one of the *person* (direct object) and the other of the *thing* (secondary object).

> **Rēgem auxilium rogāvit.** He asked *the king for help.*
> **Rēgem multa docuit.** He taught *the king many things.*

3. Verbs compounded with **circum** and **trāns** may take two accusatives, one depending on the verb, the other on the preposition.

> **Flūmen impedīmenta trānsportā-** They carried *the baggage across the river.*
> **vērunt.**

▶ PRACTICE PATTERNS

Translate the sentences, and identify the accusatives:

1. Nōs multa docet.
2. Mīlitēs mare trānsportāvit.
3. Urbem Rōmam appellābant.
4. Omnēs hunc hominem malum putant.
5. Virum pecūniam rogāvērunt.
6. Populus Brūtum ducem dēlēgit.

# SECTION 2 Idioms

▶ DISCUSSION

An idiom is an expression peculiar to a language. Every language has its own idioms. *Good-by*, which is a contraction of *God be with you*, is one of many idioms in English. There are many important idioms in Latin that it is well to memorize. Remember that it is not always desirable to reproduce in English the exact translation of the idiom. The translation should represent the thought of the original rather than the grammatical construction.

Following is a list of the more common verbal idioms.

| | |
|---|---|
| **bellum gerere** | *to wage war* |
| **castra movēre** | *to break camp* |
| **castra pōnere** | *to pitch camp* |
| **cōnsilium capere** | *to adopt a plan* |
| **grātiās agere** | *to thank* |
| **grātiam habēre** | *to feel grateful* |
| **in fugam dare** | *to put to flight* |
| **in fugam sē dare** | *to flee* |
| **in mātrimōnium dūcere** | *to marry* |
| **inter sē dare** | *to exchange* |
| **iter dare** | *to give right of way* |
| **iter facere** | *to march* |
| **memoriā tenēre** | *to remember* |
| **ōrātiōnem habēre** | *to make a speech* |
| **poenam dare** | *to suffer punishment* |
| **proelium committere** | *to begin battle* |
| **verba facere** | *to make a speech* |
| **viam mūnīre** | *to build a road* |

▶ PRACTICE PATTERNS

Translate into idiomatic English:

1. Poenam dabis.
2. Cōnsilium cēpit.
3. Ōrātiōnem habuerat.
4. Castra pōnere temptāvit.
5. Memoriā proelium tenēmus.
6. Servō grātiās egērunt.
7. Dux castra movēbit.
8. In fugam sē dedērunt.
9. Iter mīlitibus dedit.
10. Hostēs in fugam dedimus.
11. Servī viam mūnīvērunt.
12. Per montēs iter fēcērunt.
13. Vir verba faciēbat.
14. Captīvōs inter sē dabant.

## WORDS TO MASTER

**cae′dēs, –is,** *f.,* slaughter

**jūs, jū′ris,** *n.,* right, justice (*jury*)

**ni′si,** *conj.,* if not, unless, except

**patri′ciī, –ōrum,** *m. pl.,* the nobles, the patricians (*patrician*)

**pau′per, –eris,** *adj.,* poor, lowly; *noun, m.,* poor man (*pauper*)

**plēbs, plē′bis,** *f.,* common people (*plebeian*)

**poe′na, –ae,** *f.,* punishment (*penal*)

**praesi′dium, –ī,** *n.,* protection, garrison (*presidium*)

**pre′mō, –ere, pressī, pressus** (3), press, press hard (*pressure*)

**re′liquus, –a, –um,** *adj.,* remaining, rest of (*relic*)

**ser′vitūs, –tūtis,** *f.,* slavery (*servitude*)

**susti′neō, –ēre, –uī, –tentus** (2), hold out, withstand (*sustain*)

222

## BUILDING WORD POWER

In this unit we shall treat of some words that are compounded with
**dē-**, which as a prefix means *down from, away from, off, utterly*. It also
has a negative force or an unfavorable meaning.

We have frequently used the word *derivative*. The word *derive* is
itself a Latin derivative from **dē-**, *down*, + **rīvus**, *stream*. A **rīvus**
was a little stream by which water was drawn from a larger body of
water. We make the meaning of one word flow from another.

Strangely enough, *river* and *arrive* are not derived from **rīvus** but
from **rīpa,** *bank of a river*. **Rīpārius,** *belonging to a river bank*, eventually
became *river*. **Arrīpāre,** *to reach the bank*, became our very useful word
*arrive*.

**Dēspicere** (**dē + specere**), *look down upon*, became *despise*. It also
became *despite* (*in spite of*) and *spite* (*malice*). *Despise, despite*, and *spite*
are triplets.

*Debit* and *debt* are doublets from **dēbēre** (**dē + habēre**), *to have a*
*thing from someone*, therefore, *owe*.


## SENTENCE PATTERNS

A. Translate the sentences into English, and explain the syntax of
the italicized words:

1. Plēbs *patriciōs auxilium* rogāvit, sed *illī* nōn datum est.
2. Num plēbs ūlla *jūra* Rōmae habuit?
3. Cūr cōnsulēs *inīquōs* putās?
4. Reliquī in *urbe* manēbant, sed neque cibum neque *pecūniam* habēbant.
5. Plēbs pauper, quae *ā cōnsulibus* pressa est, *injūriās* sustinēre nōn potuit et
   *ex urbe* discessit.
6. Rōmānī māgnā cum *caede* in fugam ab hostibus datī sunt.
7. Nōnne Coriolānus ad hostēs *quōs* ipse vīcerat sē in fugam dedit?
8. Oppūgnāvēruntne urbem quae sine *praesidiō* relicta erat?
9. Plēbs Rōmam nōn dēfendet nisi lēgēs et jūra *ā patriciīs* scrībentur.
10. Mīlitēs quī nūllam *pecūniam* habēbant in *servitūtem* ductī sunt.

B. Translate into Latin:

At that time the common people were not able to marry men or women of the
other class. The patricians had all the rights; the common people had none.
When the common people left their fields and fought with the enemy, neither
money nor booty was given to them for their services. Unless the farmers
could labor in the fields, their wives and children could have no food. Then
the common people adopted a plan. They determined to fight for Rome no
longer.

## Women's Fashions

The wearing apparel of Roman women was very similar to that of men. It consisted of an under tunic and an outer tunic. This outer tunic was the *stola*, the distinctive dress of Roman women. Generally sleeveless, it was gathered at the waist with a belt and fastened at the shoulders with brooches or buttons. The *palla* was a large oblong shawl made of woolen goods for outdoor wear.

In the earliest days Roman ladies wore only woolen garments. Later linen was used, and cotton and silk were imported. Silk from China was rare and expensive. White was the prevailing color for clothing, but during the Empire a few other colors were produced. The first artificial color used in Rome was purple.

The ladies' sandals were like the men's but were made of softer and finer leather. Their winter shoes often had cork soles. Sometimes the soles were quite thick so as to make a lady appear to be taller. Stockings were not worn, but when necessary, people wrapped their legs with strips of woolen cloth.

Many of the secrets of the modern hairdresser were known and used. Every imaginable hair style is seen in statues that have been preserved. Sometimes hair was dyed golden red. Black dye came from India. The female hairdresser, usually a slave, was skilled with the curling iron that shaped the ringlets and the crude scissors that cut the bangs. She was familiar with oils and tonics to make the hair soft and lustrous and to increase its growth.

Face powder was a mixture of powdered chalk and white lead. Rouge for cheeks and lips was ocher or the lees of wine. Eyebrows and lashes were blackened with ashes or powdered antimony, and teeth glistened with enamel. Once made up, the lady chose her jewels, a diadem of precious stones for her hair, earrings, at least one necklace, rings for her fingers, bracelets for wrists, and circlets for her ankles.

When she appeared on the street in her multicolored robes and shawls and sparkling adornments, she must have made a dazzling appearance indeed. If it was hot, an attendant carried a parasol, usually covered in bright green, which she held over her mistress' head. With a gorgeous fan another attendant kept her cool, or brushed away the flies.

## The First Sit-Down Strike

Prīmīs temporibus urbis Rōmae līberae māgna fuit discordia. Incolae Rōmae antīquae in duo genera dīvīsī sunt. Nōbilēs patrēs aut patriciī appellābantur; reliquī plēbs nōminābantur. Patriciī potestātem, agrōs, pecūniam habēbant; plēbs erat pauper nec ūlla jūra habēbat. Plēbs multās ā patriciīs injūriās accēpit. Patriciī lēgēs fēcērunt et administrāvērunt, sed lēgēs nōn scrīptae sunt. Plēbs patriciōs in mātrimōnium dūcere nōn poterat. Plēbs neque pecūniam neque agrōs possēdit (possessed).

Postquam ūltimus (last) rēx Rōmā expulsus est erat dissensiō inter patrēs et plēbem propter aes aliēnum (debt). Dēbitōrēs ā crēditōribus servī factī sunt. Paene tōta plēbs post bella aere aliēnō premēbātur quod plēbī, quae agrōs suōs relīquerat et cum hostibus pūgnāverat, pecūnia et praeda nōn datae sunt. Praetereā uxōrēs et līberī per tempus bellī sine cibō et cōpiīs erant.

Ubi plēbs cōnsulēs auxilium rogāvit, nūllum auxilium illī datum est. Subitō bellum cum Volscīs nūntiātum est. Plēbs māgnō gaudiō clāmāvit: "Nōn pūgnābimus. Ex agrīs nostrīs ad bellum nōn prōcēdēmus. Uxōrēs et līberōs et casās nōn relinquēmus."

Volscī erant hostēs ācrēs et jam prope urbem erant. Cōnsulēs et patriciī quī perterritī sunt plēbī nūntiāvērunt: "Sī prō Rōmā et patriā pūgnāveritis, praeda et pecūnia mīlitibus dabuntur et lēgēs scrībentur." Tum plēbs uxōrēs, līberōs, agros, casas relīquit et iterum cum hostibus pūgnāvit. Volscī victī sunt; tamen post bellum praemia plēbī nōn data sunt, mīlitēs sine stipendiō (pay) erant, dēbitōrēs in servitūtem ductī sunt, lēgēs nōn scrībēbantur.

Injūstitia et violentia cōnsulum ad īram plēbem incitāvērunt. Prīmō dē caede cōnsulum et senātōrum dēlīberāvērunt. Tum inter sē statuērunt: "Rōmam relinquēmus et novum oppidum aedificābimus." Māgna pars plēbis ex urbe ad Sacrum Montem sēcessit. Ibi diū manēbat.

Intereā (Meanwhile) Rōmae cōnsilium plēbis cōnsulibus et patribus nūntiātum est. Māgnus terror hōs occupāvit. Cibum et frūmentum nōn habēbant; nūllī agricolae in agrīs labōrābant. Perterritī sunt quod hostēs erant ācrēs et Rōmae paucī erant mīlitēs. Ad plēbem missus est Menēnius Agrippa, ipse plēbēius (*of the people*) et plēbī cārus.

Jupiter has loaded us with a couple of wallets: the one, filled with our own vices, he has placed at our backs; the other, heavy with those of others, he has hung before.
—Phaedrus, *circa* A.D. 8

# *Unit* XL

## CONVERSATION

ROBERTUS: Plēbs omnia perīcula et dolōrēs bellī, patrēs sōlī omnia praemia victōriārum habēbant.

PAULUS: Id neque jūstum neque aequum erat.

ROBERTA: Mīlitēs, quī in bellō prō lībertāte atque imperiō pūgnāvērunt, domī ā cōnsulibus ac patriciīs oppressī sunt.

PAULA: Illō tempore exercitus Volscōrum ad fīnēs Rōmānōs appropinquāvit atque agrōs vāstābat. Senātus, quī adventum illōrum timuit, plēbem auxilium rogāvit.

ROBERTUS: Volscī aliīque populī fīnitimī victī sunt, sed plēbs etiam nūlla jūra habēbat. Statim populus in Sacrum Montem, Rōmā breve spatium, sēcessit et ibi castra posuit.

PAULUS: Nūllī agricolae quī in agrīs labōrābant Rōmae relinquebantur; nūllī mīlitēs erant quī urbem dēfendere poterant. Metus impetūs animōs ducum occupāverat.

ROBERTA: "Sī reveniēs," patriciī plēbī nūntiāvērunt, "magistrātūs legere poteris quōrum officium erit jūra tua dēfendere."

## SECTION 1 Fourth Declension

▶ DISCUSSION

Nouns of the fourth declension end in *–us* or *–ū* in the nominative case. Those that end in *–us* are usually masculine. A very few are feminine, as **domus,** *house,* and **manus,** *hand* or *band.* Likewise, a very few are neuter. **Cornū,** *horn* or *wing of an army,* is the only common

*226*

neuter noun of this declension. The genitive ending of all nouns of the fourth declension is long –**ūs.**

| | impetus, –ūs *m.* attack | | | cornū, –ūs *n.* horn, wing of an army | |
|---|---|---|---|---|---|
| BASE: | **impet/** | | | **corn/** | |
| | | C.I. | SINGULAR | | C.I. |
| Nom. | impet**us** | –**us** | | corn**ū** | –**ū** |
| Gen. | impet**ūs** | –**ūs** | | corn**ūs** | –**ūs** |
| Dat. | impet**uī** | –**uī** | | corn**ū** | –**ū** |
| Acc. | impet**um** | –**um** | | corn**ū** | –**ū** |
| Abl. | impet**ū** | –**ū** | | corn**ū** | –**ū** |
| | | | PLURAL | | |
| Nom. | impet**ūs** | –**ūs** | | corn**ua** | –**ua** |
| Gen. | impet**uum** | –**uum** | | corn**uum** | –**uum** |
| Dat. | impet**ibus** | –**ibus** | | corn**ibus** | –**ibus** |
| Acc. | impet**ūs** | –**ūs** | | corn**ua** | –**ua** |
| Abl. | impet**ibus** | –**ibus** | | corn**ibus** | –**ibus** |

▶ STUDY HELPS

1. The characteristic vowel –*u* appears in all cases except the dative and ablative plural.

2. The nominative and accusative cases singular of the *second* and *fourth* declension nouns are the same. *Second* declension nouns usually mean *persons* or *concrete* objects; *fourth* declension nouns seldom mean *persons* and usually have an *abstract* or *collective* meaning.

3. Many nouns of the fourth declension are the same in form as the fourth principal part of the verb: **adventus,** *approach, arrival,* from **advenīre, adventus,** *come forward* or *come to.*

4. **Domus,** *house,* is partly of the fourth and partly of the second declension. In both declensions it is feminine. The forms most used are: **domus,** *house,* **domī,** *at home* (locative); **domum,** *homeward;* **domō,** *from home.*

▶ PRACTICE PATTERNS

A. Decline: exercitus fortis, utraque manus, cornū sinistrum. Translate the forms: utraque manus.

B. Translate into Latin:

| | |
|---|---|
| at my home | on account of fear |
| of the band | on the right hand |
| of the army | at the coming of the army |
| after the attack | for the senate and the Roman people |
| on the left wing | with good armies |

# SECTION 2 Accusative of Extent of Space

You have already learned that words in Latin that answer the question *how long?* (*extent* or *length of time*) are in the accusative case without a preposition. Words that answer the question *how far?* (*extent of space, distance*) are also in the accusative case without a preposition.

EXTENT OF TIME: **Octō annōs Caesar in Galliā bellum gerēbat.**
*How long?*    For *eight years* Caesar waged war in Gaul.
EXTENT OF SPACE: **Castra *decem pedēs* ā mūrō posuērunt.**
*How far?*    They pitched camp *ten feet* from the wall.

▶ **PRACTICE PATTERNS**

A. Translate into English:

| | | |
|---|---|---|
| centum pedēs latum | octō pedēs altum | paucōs mēnsēs |
| multōs pedēs altum | quattuor diēs | decem pedēs |
| multōs annōs posteā | sex pedēs longum | sex mēnsēs |
| ūnum pedem longum | quīnque hōrās | decem annōs |

B. Translate into Latin:

1. The sea is many feet deep.
2. The soldiers walked for three hours.
3. He could not plow ten feet.
4. The wall is eight feet high.
5. They worked for two hours.
6. He reigned for nine years.
7. They remained a few months.
8. The water is seven feet deep.

## WORDS TO MASTER

**adven'tus, –ūs,** *m.,* arrival, coming (*advent*)

**cōgnōs'cō, –ere, –nōvī, –nitus** (3), learn; *perf.,* know (*recognize*)

**cōnspec'tus, –ūs,** *m.,* sight, view (*conspectus*)

**cor'nū, –ūs,** *n.,* horn, wing of an army (*cornet*)

**exer'citus, –ūs,** *m.,* army (*exercise*)

**im'petus, –ūs,** *m.,* attack (*impetus*)

**le'gō, –ere, lēgī, lēctus** (3), read, choose (*lecture*)

**magistrā'tus, –ūs,** *m.,* officer, magistrate, magistracy

**ma'nus, –ūs,** *f.,* hand, band of men (*manual*)

**me'tus, –ūs,** *m.,* fear, dread, terror (*meticulous*)

**ōs, ō'ris,** *n.,* mouth, face (*oral*)

**senā'tus, –ūs,** *m.,* senate (*senator*)

## BUILDING WORD POWER

Many nouns of the fourth declension have the same spelling as the perfect passive participle; consequently they terminate in *–tus* or *–sus.* Some of these fourth declension nouns retain their Latin form in English, as *apparatus, prospectus, status.*

The following are all derived from the fourth principal parts of verbs: *advent, cult, cant, habit, debit, event, exit, convent, congress, egress.* Add *–us* and you have a fourth declension noun. They are usually abstract nouns and denote action or the result of an action.

What English words are derived from these nouns of the fourth declension: *ūsus, gradus, lacus, senātus, spīritus, concursus?* Do not confuse *cōnsēnsus* and *cēnsus.* The former is derived from *con + sentīre, to think,* and the latter from *cēnsēre, to enroll.* Both *sentīre* and *cēnsēre* have several meanings, one of which is *to think.* Perhaps that is the reason the spelling of these two words is sometimes confused.

## SENTENCE PATTERNS

A. Translate into English:

1. Senātus populusque Rōmānus adventū hostium perterritus est.
2. Nōnne patria nostra multōs annōs tūta sine māgnīs exercitibus erat?
3. In cōnspectū Deī omnēs hominēs sunt līberī parēsque.
4. Nōnne Rōmānī impetum ācrem in hostēs fēcērunt?
5. Hodiē puer domī suae est sed crās domum frātris perveniet.
6. Cīvēs Rōmānī lēgēs novās legere et cōgnōscere ā magistrātibus jūssī sunt.
7. Ōs cibum accipere necesse est aut vīta ē corpore discēdet.
8. Manus mīlitum longum spatium per montēs iter fēcit.
9. Propter māgnum metum magistrātūs pater exercitum auxilium rogāvit.
10. Vir Scaevola appellātus est quod manum dextram āmīserat.

B. Translate into Latin:

1. Because of his great fear the leader of the right wing of the army did not attack the enemy quickly.
2. Two magistrates were chosen from the people.
3. It was the duty of the ten men to write the laws and of the citizens to read and to learn them.
4. If the mouth does not receive the food, the body will not be strong.
5. For many years they walked every day for many miles.

### The First Sit-Down Strike (continued)

Ubi Menēnius Agrippa ad castra pervēnit, adventus ējus plēbī grātus erat quae eum bene accēpit. Populō (ita fāma erat) hanc fābulam narrāvit lēgātus. "Corpus hūmānum multa membra habet, inter quae sunt manūs, ōs, dentēs, venter (*stomach*). Ōlim reliquae partēs corporis īrātae erant, quod venter omnia accēpit sed nihil sibi ēgit. Tum inter sē hoc cōnsilium cēpērunt.

"Dentēs nūllum cibum mandere (*chew*), ōs nūllum cibum accipere, manūs nūllum cibum ad ōs ferre (*carry*) statuērunt. Itaque venter alī (*to be nourished*) nōn poterat, et tōtum corpus ē vītā discessit. Nōlīte, Ō cīvēs, propter discordiam vestram patriam eōdem modō (*manner*) dēlēre."

Necesse erat corpus humānum omnēs partēs habēre; ita necesse erat patriam et patrēs et plēbem habēre. Plēbs fābulam lēgātī intellēxit (*understood*) et condiciōnēs pācis accēpit. Novī magistrātūs creātī sunt quōrum erat officium contrā violentiam cōnsulum plēbī auxilium semper dare. Duo tribūnī ex genere plēbis dēlēctī sunt quī multōs annōs jūra cīvium Rōmānōrum dēfendēbant.

Post haec breve tempus inter patrēs plēbemque erat pāx. Cōnsulēs autem tōtam potestātem sibi tenēre cupīvērunt. Tribūnī auctōritātem jūraque plēbis augēre quoque cupīvērunt. Tandem trēs lēgātī dēlēctī sunt et Athēnās missī sunt. Officium erat lēgātōrum lēgēs Solōnis et mōrēs Graecōrum cōgnōscere.

Ubi lēgātī ē Graeciā revertērunt (*returned*), decemvirī prō duōbus cōnsulibus creātī sunt. Tōta potestās hīs decemvirīs ūnum annum data est. Officium decemvirōrum erat lēgēs scrībere. Erat inter decemvirōs Appius Claudius, prīnceps tōtīus magistrātūs, quī prīmō senātuī et cīvibus grātus erat. Ille puellam, nōmine Verginiam, fīliam centuriōnis, amābat. Socius decemvirī puellam capere jūssus est. "Verginia erat," inquit (*he said*), "fīlia ūnīus ex servīs ējus." Puella serva nōn erat, sed hoc maleficium commissum est. Ad tribūnal Appī jūdicis (*judge*) ducta est.

Eō tempore exercitus erat in castrīs nōn longē ab urbe. Nūntius ad patrem puellae missus est quī Rōmam celeriter vēnit. Ubi patrem miserum nēmō juvāre cupīvit, quod omnēs decemvirum inīquum timēbant, fīliam suam occīdit et ad exercitum fūgit. Mīlitēs quibus omnia nūntiāvit cum ferē omnī plēbe ad Montem Sacrum prōcessērunt. Decemvirī ē magistrātū expulsī sunt, et cōnsulēs tribūnīque plēbis iterum creātī sunt.

# *Comprehensive Review: Units* XXXVI–XL

A. Write the dative singular, gender, base, and meaning:

| | | | | | |
|---|---|---|---|---|---|
| ōs | plēbs | cornū | praesidium | servitūs | exercitus |
| mōs | poena | manus | cōnspectus | adventus | maleficium |
| jūs | metus | caedēs | auctōritās | impetus | magistrātus |

B. Write in Latin the feminine and neuter forms in the nominative singular and give meanings:

armātus    īrātus    tūtus    pauper    reliquus

C. Write the English meanings:

postquam    aut    nēmō    ita    nisi    īnsidiae    patriciī

D. Decline in Latin and translate: powerful army; sharp attack.

E. Write the principal parts and the meaning of the second principal part of these verbs. Place a figure after the first principal part to indicate the conjugation to which each belongs.

| | | | | | | |
|---|---|---|---|---|---|---|
| agō | vīvō | fugiō | prōcēdō | conjūrō | cūstōdiō | cōgnōscō |
| legō | cadō | mūniō | occīdō | accipiō | expellō | committō |
| fluō | creō | mittō | āmittō | inveniō | relinquō | circumdō |
| petō | premō | excēdō | dēfendō | discēdō | perficiō | perterreō |

F. Write these synopses, and give English meanings:

1. creō (third person singular, passive)
2. sustineō (third person plural, passive)
3. vīvō (third person plural, active)
4. accipiō (first person plural, active)
5. mūniō (second person singular, active and passive)

G. Translate these forms:

| | | | | | |
|---|---|---|---|---|---|
| cui | ā quō | dē quā | quārum | ā quibus | quibuscum |
| quī | in quā | quōrum | in quod | per quem | trāns quae |
| quae | ex quō | quōcum | ad quem | dē quibus | prope quās |

H. Translate into Latin the italicized forms:

the boy *with whom*  
the river *across which*  
she *who* is  
the soldier *whom*

the children *to whom*  
the river *to which*  
the messengers *whom*  
the name *about which*

I. Write in Latin the specified forms and translate:

1. genitive singular: poena, maleficium, caedēs, manus
2. dative singular: metus, plēbs, mēnsis, fuga
3. accusative singular: servitūs, praesidium, mōs, vigilia
4. ablative singular: jūs, inopia, adventus, auctōritās
5. accusative plural: exercitus, pōns, victōria, praesidium
6. ablative plural: īnsidiae, cornū, impetus, genus

J. Write in Latin the specified forms:

1. ablative feminine singular: nūllus, uter, sōlus, quī, is
2. dative neuter singular: alter, ille, quī, alius, tōtus
3. genitive masculine singular: ūllus, neuter, ipse, hic, quis
4. genitive masculine plural: quī, is, ille, hic, ipse, īdem
5. dative feminine plural: quis, quī, īdem, nūllus, uter, sōlus

**K.** Write the idioms in Latin:

| | | |
|---|---|---|
| to flee | to wage war | to adopt a plan |
| to thank | to live a life | to put to flight |
| to march | to pitch camp | to begin battle |

**L.** Observe carefully the person indicators and tense indicators before translating these verbs:

| | | | | |
|---|---|---|---|---|
| ēgit | fugient | āmissī erunt | prōcēdent | cōgnitī sunt |
| creās | vīxerit | perterrēbant | sustinētis | conjūrāverit |
| lēgit | occīdit | expulsus est | excēdēbant | relicta erunt |
| mūnit | premētur | discessērunt | missī sunt | committuntur |
| flūxit | petuntur | committentur | invēnērunt | dēfendēbātur |
| cadunt | flūxerat | cūstōdīverat | perficient | discessistis |

**M.** Write in Latin:

| | | |
|---|---|---|
| in war | for five hours | in the province |
| a mile | for five miles | in the first month |
| by swords | ten feet high | away from the city |
| with joy | by our soldiers | brave in deed |
| from Rome | with weapons | three miles long |

## SENTENCE PATTERNS

**A.** Translate into English:

1. Post multōs annōs omnibus cīvium jūra data sunt.
2. Pāx amīcitiaque cum fīnitimīs ā Rōmānīs cōnfīrmātae erunt.
3. Mīlitēs quī in Galliam iter fēcerant adventum imperātōris exspectābant.
4. Num dux sine vulnere parvā nāve trāns flūmen sē in fugam dabat?
5. Parvum oppidum quod ā nōmine Lāvīniā Lāvīnium appellātum est ā Trōjānīs aedificātum est.
6. Rōma, ita narrātur, septem rēgēs habuit quōrum aliī erant aequī, aliī inīquī.
7. Hostēs ipsī nūllōs agrōs illīus tōtīus regiōnis vāstāre statuērunt.
8. Utrum praesidium ab exercitū hostium in cōnspectū prīncipis dēlētum est?
9. Aenēās et sociī ējus, quī in Āfricā multōs mēnsēs mānserant, ab urbe quae ā Dīdōne regēbātur fugere nōn cupīvērunt.
10. Quī puerōs multa docērī jussērunt?

**B.** Translate into Latin:

1. The magistrate defended some citizens; others he drove out.
2. Which of the two armies will depart from the city?
3. The brave man who had saved the city was elected consul.
4. Did not the king order many men to be driven from the towns?
5. The consuls with the soldiers, whom the enemy had conquered by treachery, arrived at the city of Rome.

Ōlim duo virī ā locō ad locum multās hōrās ambulābant et cīvēs cibum rogābant. Nēmō illīs cibum dedit. Tandem ad casam parvam ac pauperem ubi vir bonus, Philēmōn, et Baucis, uxor ējus, habitābant pervēnērunt. "Salvēte, amīcī," inquit ūnus ex virīs, "cibum aquamque petimus." "Multa nōn habēmus, sed vōbīs id quod habēmus dabimus," alacriter respondit Philēmōn. Cibus ā Baucide bonā celeriter parātus est. Post cibum alter ex virīs nūntiāvit: "Ego sum Mercurius, nūntius deōrum. Ante vōs stat Juppiter, rēx et pater deōrum, quī imperium caelī et terrae tenet ac deīs hominibusque lēgēs aequās dat. Nōlīte timēre. Vīcus et incolae malī dēlēbuntur. Vōs sōlī servābiminī. Nōbīscum ad montem venīte, et tūtī eritis."

Ubi ad summum montem pervēnērunt, post sē spectāvērunt. Omnia praeter casam eōrum sub aquā erant. Eōrum casa in templum pulchrum versa est. Posteā multōs annōs Philēmōn et Baucis dīligenter templum cūrābant.

"One more such victory against the Romans,"
said Pyrrhus, "and I am lost."
—Plutarch, A.D. 46–120
*Morals*

*Unit* XLI

## CONVERSATION

MAGISTER: Cūr Pyrrhus, Epīrī rēx, contrā Rōmānōs bellum diū gessit?

PAULUS: Rōmānī propter injūriās quās graviōrēs putābant Tarentum oppūgnābant. Rōmānī erant potentiōrēs quam Tarentīnī, quī Pyrrhum auxilium rogāvērunt.

MAGISTER: Quis Rōmānōs contrā Epīrī rēgem dūxit?

ROBERTUS: Valerius cōnsul contrā Pyrrhum ā Rōmānīs missus est.

MAGISTER: Eratne Pyrrhus fortior aut fīrmior Valeriō?

HENRĪCUS: Et Pyrrhus et Valerius erant fortēs ac firmī, sed prīmō
fortūna Rōmānōs fēliciōrēs adjūvit et exercitus Pyrrhī
superātus est. Rōmānī erant laetiōrēs.

MAGISTER: Quōmodo Pyrrhus posteā Rōmānōs vīcit?

CORNĒLIUS: Rēx Epīrī elephantōs in Rōmānōs agī jūssit.

MAGISTER: Cūr Rōmānī commōtī sunt ubi elephantōs vīdērunt?

PAULUS: Rōmānī, quī numquam anteā contrā elephantōs pūgnāverant, fūgērunt quod perterritī sunt.

MAGISTER: Num mīlitēs Pyrrhī erant audāciōrēs quam Rōmānī?

ROBERTUS: Paucī mīlitēs fortiōrēs Rōmānīs umquam (*ever*) erant.

## SECTION 1 Comparison of Adjectives

▶ DISCUSSION

1. Most adjectives describe the quality of an object, as: *pretty* girl,
*brave* boy. But one girl may be prettier than another, and a boy may
be braver than his companion. We can also say: the *prettiest* girl, the
*bravest* boy. There is a difference in amount between *pretty*, *prettier*,
*prettiest*. This difference we call *degree*. The first degree, *pretty*, is called
the *positive;* the second degree, *prettier*, is called the *comparative* and is
used only when comparing *two* objects; the third degree, *prettiest*, is
called the *superlative* and is used when comparing more than two
objects.

2. To give the three degrees of an adjective is to *compare* it. Some
adjectives, such as *all, each, first,* cannot be compared.

# SECTION 2 Comparative Degree of Adjectives

▶ DISCUSSION

1. In English the comparative degree is regularly formed by adding
*-er* to the positve: *large, larger*. Sometimes the adverb *more* is used
with the positive: *frequent, more frequent*.

2. In Latin the nominative singular of the comparative of adjectives
of the first, second, and third declensions is regularly formed by adding
*-ior*, masculine and feminine, and *-ius*, neuter, to the base of the positive.

| *Positive* | *Base* | + | *Indicators* | = *Comparative of Adjective* | |
|---|---|---|---|---|---|
| | | | M.&F. | N. | |
| **clārus** | **clār/** | + ior | **ius** = **clārior, clārius** | | *clearer* |
| **fortis** | **fort/** | + ior | **ius** = **fortior, fortius** | | *braver* |
| **audāx** | **audāc/** | + ior | **ius** = **audācior, audācius** | | *bolder* |
| **potēns** | **potent/** | + ior | **ius** = **potentior, potentius** | | *more powerful* |

Adjectives in the comparative degree are declined as follows:

| | SINGULAR | | PLURAL | |
|---|---|---|---|---|
| | M.&F. | N. | M.&F. | N. |
| Nom. | **fortior** | **fortius** | **fortiōrēs** | **fortiōra** |
| Gen. | **fortiōris** | | **fortiōrum** | |
| Dat. | **fortiōrī** | | **fortiōribus** | |
| Acc. | **fortiōrem** | **fortius** | **fortiōrēs** | **fortiōra** |
| Abl. | **fortiōre** | | **fortiōribus** | |

▶ STUDY HELPS

1. Comparatives do not have *-ium* in the genitive plural, *-ia* in the
nominative and accusative plural neuter, and usually do not have *-ī*
in the ablative singular.

2. Sometimes a comparison is implied but not expressed. It can then
be translated by *too* or *rather:* This lesson is *too* short (shorter than it
ought to be). This lesson is *rather* short (shorter than others). The
comparative **brevior, brevius** may be translated: *shorter, too* short,
*rather* short.

▶ PRACTICE PATTERNS

A. Write the comparative in Latin and translate:

| cārus | gravis | fēlīx | dīligēns | facilis | alacer | sacer |
|---|---|---|---|---|---|---|
| ācer | potēns | altus | cupidus | certus | fīrmus | brevis |

B. Decline throughout in the comparative degree: facilis labor.

C. Write in Latin:

| the braver man | too high a wall | rather high | firmer walls |
|---|---|---|---|
| a deeper ditch | a shorter way | more certain | happier girls |

## SECTION 3 Comparison with *quam*

▶ DISCUSSION

In English we use the adverb *than* in comparisons; and the two persons, places, or things being compared are in the same case. The same rule is true in Latin with the adverb *quam* (*than*).

**Honor** mihi cārior est *quam* vīta.    *Honor* is dearer to me *than life.*
  **Vallum** altius *quam mūrum*    We saw a *rampart* higher *than a wall.*
  vīdimus.

## SECTION 4 Ablative of Comparison

▶ DISCUSSION

In Latin *quam* is sometimes omitted. The word being compared, which follows *than* in English, is placed in the ablative case in Latin. This use is called the *ablative of comparison*. This ablative may be used only when the persons, places, or things being compared would be in the *nominative* or *accusative* case if *quam* were used.

**Omnia cōnsilia tua sunt clāriōra**
  **nōbīs *quam lūx*.**              All your *plans* are clearer to us *than*
**Omnia cōnsilia tua sunt clāriōra**    *light.*
  **nōbīs *lūce*.**

▶ PRACTICE PATTERNS

Translate into Latin in two ways, if possible:
1. The Roman troops were more powerful than the army of the enemy.
2. I have never seen mountains higher than those.
3. Fame was dearer to the Romans than money.
4. Were they braver in battle than their enemies?
5. No one was more famous than he.

**BUILDING WORD POWER**

When the preposition *cum* is used as a prefix in Latin, it always changes its spelling. *Cum,* meaning *with, together with,* was spelled *quom* before the time of Augustus. Therefore, it is not surprising that when *cum* is joined to another word, the *u* becomes an *o*. It is usually *con–,* but it follows the laws of assimilation as in the following words: *collocō, corrigō, combūrō, committō, comparō.* Notice the *co–* before vowels and before *–h* and *–gn,* as in *coaequālis, cohibeō, cōgnōscō.*

*236*

Sometimes this prefix has the idea of *very much*. For example, *movēre* means *to move*, **commovēre**, *to move very much*, therefore, *to disturb* or *alarm*. What is a *commotion?*

Do you know that companions (**cum + panis,** *bread*) are those who eat their bread together? When people *concur* in a plan, they run together (**cum + currere,** *run*); but when they *concoct* a plan, they cook it together (**cum + coquere,** *cook*). *Consider,* meaning *to ponder,* originally meant *to observe the stars* (**cum + sīdus,** *star*). What is the true meaning of *concord* (**cum + cor,** *heart*)?

## WORDS TO MASTER

**an'teā,** *adv.,* before

**au'rum, –ī,** *n.,* gold (*auriferous*)

**commo'veō, –ēre, –mōvī, –mōtus** (2), alarm, startle (*commotion*)

**dī'cō, –ere, dīxī, dictus** (3), say, tell (*diction*)

**do'mus, –ūs,** *f.,* house, home (*domestic*); *locative,* **domī,** at home

**fē'līx, –īcis,** *adj.,* happy, successful (*felicitous*)

**fīr'mus, –a, –um,** *adj.,* firm, strong, solid

**for'tūna, –ae,** *f.,* fortune, luck, chance

**fos'sa, –ae,** *f.,* ditch, trench (*fossil*)

**mo'dus, –ī,** *m.,* manner, way, kind (*mode*); **quōmodo,** how

**mū'nus, –eris,** *n.,* duty, task, gift (*munificent*)

**vāl'lum, –ī,** *n.,* rampart (*wall*)

## SENTENCE PATTERNS

A. Translate into English:

1. Haec fossa est lātior quam illa; hoc flūmen est altius illō.
2. Nōnne Rōmānī erant potentiōrēs fīnitimīs?
3. Rōmānī nōn erant similiōrēs Craecīs quam aliīs hostibus.
4. Eratne haec domus pulchrior illā?
5. Num aurum et alterum mūnus graviōra erant?
6. Pyrrhus amīcitiam fīrmiōrem cum Rōmānīs cupīvit.
7. Eratne Fabricius fortior et fēlīcior quam Pyrrhus?
8. Nūllō modō rēx Fabricium aurō movēre potuerat; posteā hunc timōre commovēre temptāvit.
9. Vālla circum castra exercitūs Rōmānī sunt altiōra quam mūrī circum Rōmam.
10. Numquam anteā dīligentiōrēs servōs aut vīderant aut audīverant.

B. Translate into Latin in two ways if possible:

1. Gold and gifts were not dearer to the man than his honor.
2. The rampart was rather high and the ditch too wide.
3. Were not the Romans more daring than the Trojans?

4. Then the king said: "Take this gold and these gifts."
5. Were these soldiers more successful in battle than the Greeks?

Orpheus playing his lyre.

## Orpheus and Eurydice

Orpheus was the son of Apollo, the god of music. His mother was the Muse Calliope. It is not surprising, therefore, that he was a great musician. There was no limit to his power when he played and sang. He moved the stones in the field and turned the courses of the streams. Even the wild animals forgot their savage nature to gather around him when he played his lyre.

Where he first met and how he wooed the one he loved, Eurydice, we do not know. They were married, but their joy was short-lived. Directly after the wedding, while Eurydice was walking with her bridesmaids in a meadow, she was bitten by a viper and died in the arms of her husband.

Orpheus decided to follow Eurydice to the realms of Hades and beg for the return of her life. There he played his celestial lyre so sweetly and sadly that the vast multitude of the underworld were charmed to stillness. Even Tantalus forgot his thirst, Ixion stood at his wheel entranced, and Sisyphus ceased his labor.

At the throne of Pluto and Proserpina, he pleaded his cause to the music of the lyre so eloquently that Pluto relented and granted the prayer of the lover on one condition, that he would not cast a glance at Eurydice as she followed him until they had reached the upper world. At the last moment, longing overcame him, and he gave a swift backward glance. Instantly she was gone. Orpheus heard but one faint word, "Farewell!" Disconsolate, Orpheus thereafter wandered in deep gloom from country to country until death finally united him with his beloved.

## A Man of Integrity

Antīquīs temporibus Rōmānī contrā populōs fīnitimōs multa et ācria bella gessērunt. Etrūscī, Samnītēs, Latīnī ā Rōmānīs victī sunt quod Rōmānī erant armīs potentiōrēs quam fīnitimī. Propter haec bella illī sibi māgnam potestātem obtinēre potuērunt.

Ōlim Tarentīnī contrā Rōmānōs, quibuscum bellum gerēbant, Pyrrhum, rēgem Epīrī, auxilium rogāvērunt. Hic cum exercitū et vīgintī elephantīs ad Ītaliam statim nāvigāvit. Tum prīmum Rōmānī cum trānsmarīnīs (*from across the sea*) hostibus contendērunt. Contrā Pyrrhum et exercitum ējus Valerius cōnsul ā senātū missus est.

Cōnsul proelium cum hostibus commīsit. Prīmō mīlites Pyrrhī, quī impetum Rōmānōrum sustinēre nōn potuērunt, sē in fugam dedērunt. Statim Pyrrhus elephantōs in Rōmānōs agī jūssit. Jam fortūna proelī celeriter mūtāta est. Rōmānī, quī numquam anteā elephantōs aut vīderant aut audīverant, māgnopere commōtī sunt et ā Pyrrhō facile victī sunt. Nox fīnem huic proeliō fēcit.

Tamen mīlitēs cōnsulis fortiter pūgnāverant, et dux Rōmānus, quī partem exercitūs ā morte servāverat, mīlitēs suōs integrōs sēcum in castra dūxit. Pyrrhus erat victor sed mīlia mīlitum suōrum āmīserat. Tum vērō rēx māgnō cum dolōre manūs ad caelum levāvit et māgnā vōce clāmāvit: "Sī iterum eōdem modō illōs Rōmānōs superāverō, sōlus ego sine ūnō mīlite domum ad Epīrum discēdam."

Quod multī mīlitēs Rōmānī in manū Pyrrhī tenēbantur, senātus ad illum dē captīvīs lēgātōs mīsit. Ūnus ex lēgātīs erat Fabricius, cīvis bonus, quem Rōmānī propter integritātem māgnopere amābant. Per tōtam vītam pauper fuerat et in domō parvā habitāverat. Eī Pyrrhus mūnera et aurum dare cupīvit, sed frūstrā. Honor Fabriciō erat cārior quam vīta, et dōna nōn accēpit.

Posteā rēx Pyrrhus Fabricium terrēre temptāvit. Ūnus ex elephantīs jūssū (*order*) rēgis post aulaeum (*curtain*) prope Rōmānum stābat. Subitō aulaeum removēbātur, et elephantus strīdōrem (*noise*) horribilem ēmittēbat (*let out*). Rēgī Fabricius ita dīxit: "Herī aurum et mūnera tua mē nōn temptāvērunt. Hodiē elephantus tuus mē nōn perterret."

I am tired and sick of war. Its glory is
all moonshine. . . . War is hell.
—General William Tecumseh Sherman, 1820–1891

*Unit* XLII

## CONVERSATION

MAGISTER: Quibuscum Rōmānī tria bella longissima gessērunt, Jūlia?

JŪLIA: Ā Rōmānīs tria bella gravissima ac crūdēlissima cum Poenīs (*Carthaginians*) gesta sunt. Post tertium bellum Poenī Rōmānīs sē trādidērunt. Carthāgō dēlēta est.

MAGISTER: Eratne Carthāgō multa mīlia passuum ab Ītaliā?

ANNA: Carthāgō in Āfricā contrā Siciliam locāta est.

MAGISTER: Quōmodo multa mīlia Rōmānōrum mare trāductī sunt, Cornēlia? Num nāvēs longās (*war galleys*) habēbant?

CORNĒLIA: Rōmānī māgnam classem nāvium longārum aedificāvērunt et prīmum prope Siciliam cum Poenīs contendērunt.

MAGISTER: Cūr Rōmānōs māgnam classem aedificāre necesse erat?

MĀRCELLA: Rōmānī exercitum potentissimum sed nūllās nāvēs habēbant; Poenī multās nāvēs sed nūllum exercitum potentem habēbant. Sīc Rōmānī ac Poenī erant dissimilēs.

MAGISTER: Poterantne Rōmānī nāvēs longās eō tempore bene administrāre?

JŪLIA: Prīmō nāvēs administrāre Rōmānōs difficillimum erat.

## SECTION 1 Superlative Degree of Adjectives

▶ DISCUSSION

When we consider only two objects or persons for comparison, we use the *comparative degree;* but when more than two are being considered, we use the *superlative degree:* the *braver* of *two,* the *bravest* of *three;* the *more powerful* of *two,* the *most powerful* of *three.*

All adjectives of the first, second, and third declensions that are *regularly* compared add *–issimus, –a, –um* to the base of the positive.

*Positive* *Base* + *Indicators* = *Superlative of Adjective*
　　　　　　　　　 M.　 F.　 N.

**clārus** **clār/** + issimus, –a, –um = clārissimus, –a, –um　*clearest*
**fortis** **fort/** + issimus, –a, –um = fortissimus, –a, –um　*bravest*
**audāx** **audāc/** + issimus, –a, –um = audācissimus, –a, –um　*boldest*
**potēns** **potent/** + issimus, –a, --um = potentissimus, –a, –um　*most powerful*

240

Comparison of Adjectives
Ending in *–er* and *–lis*

▶ DISCUSSION

1. Some adjectives have an unusual comparison. All adjectives whose masculine singular in the positive degree ends in *–er* form the *superlative* by adding *–rimus* to this positive. The *comparative* of these adjectives is formed regularly.

| Positive | Comparative | Superlative |
|---|---|---|
| **līber, –era, –erum** | **līberior, līberius** | **līberrimus, –a, –um** |
| **ācer, ācris, ācre** | **ācrior, ācrius** | **ācerrimus, –a, –um** |

2. Six adjectives whose masculine singular in the positive ends in *–lis* form the *superlative* by adding *–limus* to the base of the positive. The *comparative* is formed regularly.

| Positive | Comparative | Superlative |
|---|---|---|
| **similis, simile** | **similior, similius** | **simillimus, –a, –um** |

The six adjectives thus compared are: **similis,** *like;* **dissimilis,** *unlike;* **facilis,** *easy;* **difficilis,** *difficult;* **humilis,** *low;* **gracilis,** *slender.*

▶ STUDY HELPS

Sometimes the superlative degree is used to show that a noun has a quality in a very high degree, but not necessarily the highest. This usually is translated *very.*

**fortissimus** vir      a *very brave* man

Great care should be taken to use the translation that makes the best sense in a particular context.

▶ PRACTICE PATTERNS

A. Compare and give English translation:

firmus   crūdēlis   dissimilis   pulcher   pauper   celer   ācer
gravis   nōbilis   dīligēns   alacer   cārus   miser   fēlīx

B. Decline in all genders, singular and plural: gravissimus, pulcherrimus, humillimus.

C. Translate into Latin in all genders, singular and plural:

| | | | |
|---|---|---|---|
| freer | quickest | too heavy | quite difficult |
| longer | difficult | very unjust | the very poor |
| easiest | boldest | most unlike | more unfortunate |
| eternal | very easy | rather poor | most beautiful |

# SECTION 3 Partitive Genitive

▶ DISCUSSION

1. The *partitive genitive*, sometimes called the *genitive of the whole*, designates the *whole* of which a *part* is taken. It is used with nouns, pronouns (interrogative or indefinite), adjectives, adverbs (of quantity, degree, or place), comparatives, superlatives, and ordinal numbers. In these expressions, the genitive denotes the *whole*, modifying a word denoting a *part*.

2. *Ex* or *dē* with the *ablative case* is generally used instead of the genitive with numerals, especially cardinal numbers (except *mīlia*), and with *quīdam, a certain one.* Ordinals generally take the genitive.

1. **pars montis,** part *of the mountain*
2. **ūnus ex līberīs,** one *of the children*
3. **duo mīlia mīlitum,** two thousand *soldiers*
4. **prīmus omnium,** first *of all*
5. **quīdam ex lēgātīs,** certain *of the legates*
6. **quis nostrum?** who *of us?*
7. **pulchrior puellārum,** the prettier *of (two) girls*
8. **hōrum fortissimī,** the bravest *of these*

▶ STUDY HELPS

1. Words like **cūnctus, omnis,** and **tōtus,** which mean the *whole*, cannot be followed by the genitive, but agree with the nouns they modify.

2. There is no exact translation for the English word *mile*. **Mīlle passūs** means *a thousand paces*, a Roman mile. To express the plural, *miles*, **mīlia passuum,** *thousands of paces*, must be used. A Roman mile was about 450 feet less than an English mile. By **passūs** the Romans meant the distance between two successive positions of the same foot. It is therefore longer than the English pace.

▶ PRACTICE PATTERNS

A. Translate into English:

| | | |
|---|---|---|
| nōs omnēs | pars pecūniae | gravissimus hominum |
| tōtus mundus | quis vestrum? | duo mīlia passuum |
| cūnctī virī | trēs ex librīs | fortissimī mīlitum |
| quīdam ex virīs | fēlīcior puellārum | hōrum celerrimī |

B. Translate into Latin:

| | |
|---|---|
| a mile | part of the city |
| first of all | the most cruel of the soldiers |
| who of them? | the most unjust of the kings |

A lady from Sicily. This detail is from a terra-cotta vase
from Centuripe, Sicily, made about 250 B.C.

Marcus Aurelius on the Capitoline hill. The Capitoline hill,
one of the seven hills of Rome, was the site of the Temple of Jupiter.

Pantheon, Rome. This temple, dedicated to all the gods, was built by Agrippa in 27 B.C., then rebuilt by Hadrian in the second century A.D. After 609, it was used as a Christian church.

Pont-du-Gard Aqueduct, near Nîmes in southern France.

Silenus. This bronze handle attachment from a situla (libation jar) is a fine example of
Roman metalwork from the first century A.D. Silenus was leader of the satyrs
and the foster father of Bacchus, earlier called Dionysus by the Greeks.

C-4

Medusa. This huge head, made during the second century A.D., comes from a temple of Apollo located in modern-day Turkey.

Silver bowl handle, circa A.D. 150.

The Daphne wine-jug. In Greek mythology, the nymph Daphne escaped from Apollo by becoming a laurel tree. This glass wine-jug dates from around the third century A.D. and possibly comes from Antioch, Syria, which was part of the Roman Empire.

Wall painting from a villa at Boscoreale, near Pompeii, first century B.C.

Zeus. This statue is now in a Vatican City museum. Zeus,
the king of the gods, is identified with the Roman god Jupiter.

| | |
|---|---|
| four miles | the wider of the rivers |
| the tallest of the buildings | many thousands of soldiers |
| the quickest of them | the swiftest of the ships |

## WORDS TO MASTER

**aeter'nus, –a, –um,** *adj.*, perpetual, lasting (*eternal*)

**clas'sis, –is,** *f.*, division, fleet (*class*)

**crūdē'lis, –e,** *adj.*, cruel

**dissi'milis, –e,** *adj.*, unlike, dissimilar

**dīvi'tiae, –ārum,** *f. pl.*, riches

**i'gitur,** *adv.*, therefore, then, so, accordingly

**jū'dex, –icis,** *m.*, judge (*judicial*)

**ob'ses, –idis,** *m. & f.*, hostage

**osten'dō, –ere, –tendī, –tentus** (3), show, point out (*ostentation*)

**pas'sus, –ūs,** *m.*, step, stride (*pace*); **mīlle passūs,** a thousand paces, a mile

**trā'dō, –ere, –didī, –ditus** (3), hand over, give up, deliver (*tradition*)

**trādū'cō, –ere, –dūxī, –ductus** (3) lead across, bring over, transport (*traduce*)

## BUILDING WORD POWER

*Trāns*, the preposition meaning *across*, is frequently found as *trāns*- or *trā*– in Latin and English words. It may express the idea of *beyond*, *above*, or *through*. What is the true meaning of: *transport, transmit, transmarine, translucent, transcribe?*

*Tradition* (*trāns* + *dare*, *give*) originally meant *betrayal*, and we find that interpretation in the word *treason*, a doublet for *tradition*. The word *betray* is a *hybrid* (a word made up of two or more elements from different languages). *Be–* is from medieval English; *–tray* from *trādere*, *to hand over*. *Tradition* now means unwritten teachings or customs handed down by word of mouth from generation to generation.

*Trajectory* is the curved path of something hurtling through space, especially that of a *projectile*. Are satellites projectiles? *To transpire* really means *to breathe across, to leak out, to become known*. Sometimes it is carelessly used to mean *happen*. What does your dictionary have for the meaning of this word?

## SENTENCE PATTERNS

A. Translate into English:

1. Exercitus Rōmānus in Āfricam ā Regulō trāductus est.
2. Hostēs tōtam Siciliam et māgnās dīvitiās Rōmānīs trādidērunt.
3. Aliī in proeliō ācerrimō interfectī sunt; aliī captī sunt.
4. Obses sibi laudem aeternam obtinuit quod fīdum sē ostendit.

5. Statim duo mīlia mīlitum salūtem fugā petīvērunt.
6. Rēgulus igitur ab hostibus crūdēlissimīs interfectus est quod Rōmānī cum Poenīs pācem nōn fēcērunt.
7. Nōnne jūdex inīquissimus injūriās graviōrēs commīsit?
8. Illō tempore Rōmānī prīmam classem nāvium aedificāvērunt.
9. Nautae celerrimī quīnque mīlia passuum prope terram nāvigāvērunt.
10. Hōrum audācissimus sibi glōriam aeternam cupīvit.

B. Translate into Latin:

1. The Romans were very unlike the inhabitants of Africa.
2. Was not the city many miles away from Rome?
3. Many thousands of captives, therefore, were transported to Italy.
4. Regulus, who delivered himself into the hands of the very cruel enemy, saved his fatherland.
5. Honor was dearer to him than riches or his own safety.


## Rome's First Naval Battle

Postquam rēx Epīrī ex Ītaliā discessit, Rōma domina tōtīus Ītaliae erat. Rōmānī jam aliud et gravius bellum cum Carthāginiēnsibus (*Carthaginians*) gessērunt. Urbs Carthāgō in Āfricā contrā Siciliam locāta est. Incolae Poenī quoque appellābantur quod ē Phoeniciā vēnerant.

Initiō trium bellōrum gravissimōrum, quae bella Pūnica appellāta sunt, et Rōma et Carthāgō erant urbēs potentēs. Rōmānī exercitum potentissimum sed nūllās nāvēs habēbant; Poenī māgnās dīvitiās et māgnam scientiam rērum (*affairs*) nāvālium (*naval*) sed nūllās validās cōpiās habēbant.

Illō tempore necesse erat Rōmānōs multa mīlia mīlitum nāvibus trādūcere ex Ītaliā ad Siciliam. Rōmānī igitur multās nāvēs longās celeriter aedificāvērunt simillimās nāvī longae quae in aquīs prope Ītaliam inventa erat. Mox prīmam classem Rōmānam nāvium longārum habēbant.

Quīntō annō bellī Pūnicī prīmī Gājus Duillius, cōnsul Rōmānus, Ōstiā nāvigāvit. Ille Poenōs in marī invēnit ubi jam diū imperium habēbant. Corvī (*Gangways*) in nāvibus Rōmānīs aedificātī erant. Poenī, quī proelium cum Rōmānīs commīsērunt, facillimam victōriam exspectāvērunt. Ubi nāvēs Poenōrum ad nāvēs Rōmānās appropinquābant, Duillius corvōs dēmittī (*to be let down*) jūssit. Rōmānī, quī rēs nāvālēs īgnōrābant (*did not know*) neque nāvēs bene regere poterant, trāns corvōs in nāvēs hostium cucurrērunt et gladiīs atque aliīs tēlīs māgnum numerum hostium occīdērunt.

Quīnquāgintā (*Fifty*) ex nāvibus Poenōrum dēlētae sunt, et rōstra (*beaks*) nāvium quae captae erant Rōmam missa sunt ubi in Forō posita sunt et ubi diū manēbant. Haec vērō erat prīma victōria Rōmāna nāvālis; nūlla victōria Rōmānīs grātior erat. Illī sē validiōrēs in proeliō nāvālī quam hostēs ostenderant.

Nōnō annō bellī, Regulus, cōnsul Rōmānus, prīmus exercitum in Āfricam trādūxit. Poenī auxilium ā Graecīs petīvērunt, quī Xanthippum ducem ācerrimum mīsērunt. Ab illō Rōmānī māgnā caede victī sunt, et Regulus ipse captus est.

Posteā īdem Regulus obses ā Poenīs Rōmam missus est. Hī Regulum pācem et permūtātiōnem (*exchange*) captīvōrum cum Rōmānīs facere jūssērunt. Ubi Rōmam pervēnit, senātum monuit: "Nōlīte facere pācem aut permūtātiōnem captīvōrum cum Poenīs." Statim vir fortis captīvus Rōmā discessit et post adventum suum in Āfricam ā Poenīs occīsus est. Fidem (*promise*) cum hostibus servāverat et sibi laudem aeternam obtinuit.

*Semper eadem.*
Ever the same.
—Motto of Queen Elizabeth I, 1533–1603

# *Unit* XLIII

## CONVERSATION

ROBERTUS: Post prīmum bellum Punicum tōta Sicilia prōvincia Rōmāna erat; post secundum, Hispānia in duās prōvinciās dīvīsa est; post tertium, Poenī Rōmānīs Āfricam, quae prōvincia Rōmāna facta est, cessērunt.

ANNA: Nōnne Hannibal in paucīs proeliīs Rōmānōs vīcit?

ROBERTUS: Hannibal postquam in Ītaliam vēnit Pūblium Scipiōnem cōnsulem apud flūmen Trebiam vīcit.

HENRĪCUS: Tum Gājus Flāminius cōnsul cum exercitū inter montēs et Lacum Trasumēnum ab Hannibale undique oppūgnātus est.

ROBERTUS: Flāminius suōs stāre ac pūgnāre jūssit; sed tum quandō angustiās (*difficulties*) comprehendit, clāmāvit: "Per mediōs hostēs gladiīs viam facite et vōbīs salūtem fortitūdine petite."

ROBERTA: Subitō eques Gallus impetum ācerrimum per turbam fēcit ac cōnsulem pīlō occīdit. Nūllum iter fugae erat, etsī per

angustiās (*the pass*) et per lacum Rōmānī fugere temptābant.

MAGISTER: Haec est ad Trasumēnum pūgna quae inter paucās calami
tātēs populī Rōmānī memoriā tenētur.

## Subordinate Clauses

▶ DISCUSSION

In Latin as in English a clause is a group of words having a subject
and a predicate. A clause that expresses a complete thought is called
an *independent*, or *principal*, *clause;* a clause that by itself does not have
a complete meaning is called a *dependent*, or *subordinate*, *clause.*

In previous lessons you have frequently translated subordinate clauses.
The following summary will help you to remember the important facts
about these clauses, which have had their verbs in the indicative mood.

1. *Adjective clauses*, also called *relative* clauses, modify nouns or pronouns, are introduced by *relative pronouns*, and may take any tense of
the verb.

The Romans, *who fought with the Car-*    **Rōmānī, quī cum Poenīs pūgnā-**
*thaginians*, were very daring.    **vērunt, audācissimī erant.**

2. *Adverbial clauses* modify verbs and are introduced by subordinate
conjunctions, as follows:

(a) *Causal clauses* are introduced by **quod,** *because,* and tell *why* the
action of the verb in the principal clause took place.

**Illō tempore dictātor dēlēctus est**    At that time a dictator was elected *be-*
**quod cīvēs perīculum timēbant.**    *cause* the citizens feared the danger.

(b) *Temporal clauses* are introduced by **dum,** *while,* **ubi,** *when,* and
**postquam,** *after.*

     (1) **Dum,** *while,* is regularly followed by the *present* tense in Latin
which must be translated by the English *imperfect.*

**Dum haec geruntur, Rōmānī**    *While* these things *were going on*, the
**māgnopere perterritī sunt.**    Romans were greatly terrified.

     (2) **Ubi,** *when,* and **postquam,** *after,* are followed by the *perfect*
tense in Latin, if past time is expressed; this may be trans-
lated by the English *perfect* or *pluperfect.*

**Poenī, ubi proelium cum Rōmānīs**    *When* the Carthaginians *began* battle
**commīsērunt, facillimam vic-**    with the Romans, they expected a
**tōriam exspectābant.**    very easy victory.

| | |
|---|---|
| **Poenī,** *postquam* **proelium cum Rōmānīs** *commīsērunt,* **nōn jam facilem victōriam exspectābant.** | *After* the Carthaginians *had begun* battle with the Romans, they no longer expected an easy victory. |

If both the principal and subordinate clauses in the same sentence have the same subject, the subject is placed *before* the dependent clause, as in the two preceding sentences.

(c) *Conditional clauses* are introduced by **sī,** *if,* and **nisi,** *if not, unless.* Any tense in the indicative may be used in the conditional clause. In English we frequently use the *present* tense after *if* when in Latin the *future* or the *future perfect* are used.

| | |
|---|---|
| **Sī Sicilia** *vincētur,* **quid agēs?** | *If* Sicily *is conquered,* what will you do? |

(d) *Concessive clauses* are introduced by **etsī,** *although, even if.* These clauses, like conditions, may take any tense of the indicative.

| | |
|---|---|
| **Rōmānī,** *etsī* **multa proelia āmīsērunt, Poenōs vīcērunt.** | *Although* the Romans lost many battles, they conquered the Carthaginians. |

▶ PRACTICE PATTERNS

Translate into English; classify the subordinate clauses.

1. Cōnsul cui hoc cōnsilium nōn grātum erat\proelium commīsit.
2. Postquam Scīpiō ad Āfricam nāvigāvit, Hannibal revocātus est.
3. Quod pāx neutrī urbī grāta erat, bellum iterum gestum est.
4. Nisi pūgnābitis, hostēs nōn vincētis.
5. Rōmānī, dum Ītaliam vincunt, multōs agrōs vāstābant.
6. Scīpio, ubi Hispāniam vīcit, exercitum in Āfricam trādūxit.
7. Etsī mīles fuerat fortis, dux eum interficī jūssit.

## WORDS TO MASTER

**cē′dō, –ere, cessī, cessūrus** (3), yield, go away (*cede*)

**cī′vitās, –tātis,** *f.,* state, citizenship, body of citizens (*city*)

**com′parō** (1), prepare, make ready, get together

**comprehen′dō, –ere, –hendī, –hēnsus** (3), seize, catch, understand (*comprehend*)

**cōnsti′tuō, –ere, –uī, –ūtus** (3), decide, determine (*constitute*)

**conve′niō, –īre, –vēnī, –ventūrus** (4), come together, assemble (*convene*)

**e′ques, –itis,** *m.,* horseman, knight; *pl.,* cavalry

**et′sī,** *conj.,* even if, although

**fī′niō, –īre, –īvī, –ītus** (4), end, finish (*finite*)

**fortitū′dō, –inis,** *f.,* bravery, courage (*fortitude*)

**pī′lum, –i,** *n.,* javelin, spear (*pile driver*)

**re′vocō** (1), call back (*revoke*)

## BUILDING WORD POWER

All the world today is *interested* (*inter* + *esse*) in *international affairs* (*inter* + *nātiō*). An *intelligent* (*inter* + *legere*) person has the ability to recognize relations and differences, and therefore is quick to learn. The prefix *inter–* has the general idea of *between, at intervals*.

Keeping this in mind, analyze the italicized words: 1. The policeman *intercepted* the secret letter. 2. A man from the rear of the hall *interjected* a question. 3. The *interurban* bus is always on time. 4. During *intermission* we went out to the lobby. 5. The young soldier was suffering from *intermittent* fever. 6. During the *interregnum* there was great unrest.

*Intra–* and *intro–* mean *within*. *Intra–* is used only in modern coined words, as *intramural, intravenous*. *Intro–* is found in very few words, as *introduce, introspection, introversion*.

Which words in the above paragraph describe the following: *self-examination, injection, athletics, to make acquainted?*

## SENTENCE PATTERNS

A. Translate into English:

1. Eō tempore multa mīlia Rōmānōrum interfecta sunt quod duo cōnsulēs bonum cōnsilium Fabī nōn comprehendērunt.
2. Postquam exercitus victus est, nōn necesse erat equitēs dēlērī.
3. Dum Scipiō bellum in Āfricā gerit, Hannibal revocātus est.
4. Māgna fuit caedēs quam cīvitās Rōmāna ad Lacum accēpit.
5. Num mīles, etsī pīlō vulnerātus est, hostī cessit?
6. Postquam bellum in Āfricā fīnītum est, Carthāgō dēlēta est.
7. Etsī senātus nōn probāvit, populus bellum dēbēre gerī cōnstituit.
8. Hannibal, quī exercitum trāns altissimōs montēs trādūxit, omnia comparāverat.
9. Num incolae Carthāginis Rōmānōs fortitūdine et virtūte superāvērunt?
10. Zamae duo exercitūs convēnērunt, sed Fortūna Rōmānīs victōriam dedit.

B. Translate into Latin:

1. Because Hannibal did not yield to the Roman leader, the very beautiful city of Carthage was destroyed.
2. Never did the Roman state have a braver citizen and leader.
3. After they had marched for many miles, the cavalry and infantry arrived at the very deep river.
4. Scipio was called by the poet "the thunderbolt of war."
5. While Hannibal was leading his army across the Alps, he lost many thousands of his foot soldiers and cavalry.

A Roman boy wearing a *bulla*, an elaborate locket containing charms against evil.

## Naming the Roman Baby

As soon as a child was born, it was carried to the father and laid at his feet. If he lifted the child into his arms, he thereby acknowledged his parentage and gave assurance that the baby would be cared for and reared with all the rights and privileges of his family. If an infant had some physical defect or if for some reason the father did not want it, he had the right, according to Roman custom, to dispose of it as he saw fit.

Normally, however, a new baby was received with joy. A wreath was hung at the street door to announce the fact to passers-by. The mother was usually overwhelmed with congratulations and gifts from friends. Then came the grand celebration, the *dies lustricus*, the name day for the baby.

The name given to the boy was simply a first name, a *praenomen*, because his *nomen*, or second name, and his *cognomen*, or third name, were already his from his father. The nomen was the gentile name, that is, the name of the clan (*gens*). The cognomen indicated the particular family of the clan to which his father belonged. Thus, Publius Cornelius Scipio was Publius of the Cornelian clan of the family of the Scipios.

A girl was usually given her father's praenomen in feminine form, as Lucia from Lucius, or she might be given the feminine form of her father's gentile name, as the daughter of Marcus Tullius Cicero was Tullia, and of Gaius Julius Caesar, Julia.

Occasionally girls were given more individual names, as Rutila (red-head) from the color of her hair, or Prima because she was the first, Tertia because she was the third daughter. The girls seemed to have the advantage in choice of names because there were only eighteen Roman praenomina for men, and famous families used the same two or three over and over again. It was good that there were no telephone directories in those days.

After the father had solemnly announced to the assembled relatives and friends: "Let the boy be named Lucius!" all came forward and presented the baby with tiny metal trinkets which, strung together and hung around his neck, amused him with their jingling or rattling. They were called the *crepundia* (rattles).

But far more important was the *bulla*, an elaborate locket, made
of gold if the parents were wealthy, or of leather if the parents
were poor. The bulla contained charms against the power of the
evil *numina*, vague, brooding spirits acting on the life of the child.
The father himself hung this charm about the neck of the child.
It was never removed permanently until the day the boy as-
sumed the *toga virilis*, which proclaimed his Roman citizenship,
or until the girl laid it aside on her wedding eve. The bulla,
however, was carefully protected and kept throughout life.

## ROMAN NAMES

| Given Name | | Clan Name | Family Branch |
|---|---|---|---|
| PRAENŌMEN | | NŌMEN | COGNŌMEN |
| Name | Abbrev. | (Gens = Clan) | (Originally a nickname) |
| Mārcus | M. | Tullius | Cicerō: "with the wart" |
| Gājus | C. | Jūlius | Caesar: "sharp" |
| Gnaeus | Cn. | Aemilius | Albus: "white" |
| Lūcius | L. | Claudius | Barbātus: "with the beard" |
| Pūblius | P. | Cornēlius | Longus: "tall" |
| Quīntus | Q. | Horātius | Nāsō: "with the nose" |

About the first century B.C. only eighteen praenomina were
in common use. The eldest son of each generation duplicated
his father's name. Father and son were distinguished by adding
*pater* or *filius* to the praenomen: Lucius pater or Lucius filius.
A second son might be called Secundus.

## The Mighty African Warrior

Post prīmum bellum Pūnicum ubi pāx cōnfīrmāta est, Poenī
Rōmānīs tōtam Siciliam et māgnās dīvitiās cessērunt. Sicilia
igitur erat prīma prōvincia Rōmāna. Hamilcar, quī in hoc bellō
imperātor fuerat, imperium et dīvitiās in Hispāniā augēre cupīvit.
Trāns mare exercitum trādūxit, et sēcum Hannibālem, parvum
fīlium suum, quī tum novem annōs habēbat.

Post mortem Hamilcaris, Hasdrubal Poenicī exercitūs dux dēlēctus est. Octō annōs hic exercitum Poenōrum rēxerat, et ubi ab
inimicō occīsus est, Hannibal imperātor creātus est. Illō tempore Hannibal vīgintī annōs habuit. Rōmānōs vincere cōnstituit,
et trēs exercitūs potentissimōs comparāvit, ē quibus ūnum in Āfricam mīsit, alterum cum frātrē Hasdrubāle in Hispāniā relīquit,
tertium in Ītaliam sēcum dūcere statuit.

Erant duo itinera quibus imperātor Poenōrum exercitum in Ītaliam dūcere potuit, alterum terrā, alterum marī. Hannibal, quod victoriās Rōmānōrum in aliīs proeliīs nāvālibus memoriā tenēbat, terrā ad Ītaliam prōcēdere cōnstituit.

Postquam omnēs gentēs hostilēs Hispāniae et Galliae victae sunt, Hannibal trāns altissimōs Alpēs montēs māgnum numerum peditum, equitum, elephantōrum, equōrum trādūcere temptāvit. Tandem, etsī māgnam partem et exercitūs et equōrum et elephantōrum āmīsit, in Ītaliam pervēnit et complūribus (*very many*) proeliīs Rōmānōs vīcit.

Populus Romanus, ubi haec dē Hannibāle cōgnōvit, perterritus est. Ūnā vōce cīvēs dictātōrem postulāvērunt, et dictātor, Quīntus Fabius, ā senātū creātus est. Mīlitibus Rōmānīs ille dīxit: "Nōlīte pūgnāre cum Hannibālis exercitū! Morā sōlā Hannibal vincētur!"

Cōnsilium erat bonum sed cōnsulī nōn grātum. Hic posteā proelium cum Poenīs commīsit, sed multa mīlia corporum mīlitum Rōmānōrum in agrīs relicta sunt et multa mīlia mīlitum Rōmānōrum Poenīs sē trādidērunt aut captīvī factī sunt. Nūllam calamitātem māiōrem (*greater*) quam hanc Cannīs Rōmāni accēpērunt.

Etsī Hannibal multās urbēs occupāvit, et multās partēs Ītaliae dēlēvit, Rōmānī pācem numquam petīvērunt. Postquam senātus Publium Cornēlium Scīpiōnem bellum gererc in Āfricā contrā Poenōs jūssit, Hannibal ad urbem Carthāginem revocātus est, et ā Scīpiōne in proeliō victus est. Secundum bellum Pūnicum fīnītum erat.

[Mercy is] mightiest in the mightiest.
—William Shakespeare, 1564–1616
*The Merchant of Venice*

## *Unit* XLIV

## CONVERSATION

TIBERIUS: Ō miserrimī cīvēs, fēlīciōrēs quam vōs sunt bestiae Ītaliae; illī domicilia habent. Vōs, autem, quī prō Ītaliā pūgnāvistis ac vulnerātī estis, nūlla domicilia ubi habitāre potestis habētis!

GĀJUS: Undique per Ītaliam agrī ā paucīs tenentur, nec jam ā cīvibus līberīs sed ā servīs coluntur.

| | |
|---|---|
| TIBERIUS: | Cīvitās Rōmāna cotīdiē fit (*becomes*) mājor ac potentior; condiciō plēbis fit pējor et miserior. |
| GĀJUS: | Etsī dominī orbis terrārum (*of the world*) appellāminī, nūllam terram prō vōbīs tenētis. |
| TIBERIUS: | Causam populī pauperrimī suscipere cōnstituō. Lēgem novam rogābō (*propose*). Fortūnās omnium aequārī cupiō. |
| GĀJUS: | Senātōrēs, quī nunc māximās dīvitiās habent, ob lēgēs novās māgnopere commovēbuntur. |
| TIBERIUS: | Tribūnus plēbis creātus sum. Agrī pūblicī ā nōbilibus ementur ac cīvibus pauperrimīs dabuntur. |

## SECTION 1 Irregular Comparison of Adjectives

▶ DISCUSSION

1. In Latin as in English, very many common adjectives are *irregular in comparison*, that is, they do not form their comparative and superlative degrees on the base of the positive. The most important are given here.

| Positive | Comparative | Superlative |
|---|---|---|
| bonus, –a, –um *good* | melior, melius *better* | optimus, –a, –um *best* |
| malus, –a, –um *bad* | pējor, pējus *worse* | pessimus, –a, –um *worst* |
| māgnus, –a, –um *great* | mājor, mājus *greater* | māximus, –a, –um *greatest* |
| parvus, –a, –um *small* | minor, minus *smaller* | minimus, –a, –um *smallest* |
| multus, –a, –um *much* | ——, plūs *more* | plūrimus, –a, –um *most* |
| multī, –ae, –a *many* | plūrēs, plūra *more* | plūrimī, –ae, –a *most* |

2. The following adjectives are also used rather frequently although the positive forms seldom occur. Notice that the irregularity in the comparison occurs in the superlative degree.

| Positive | Comparative | Superlative |
|---|---|---|
| exterus, –a, –um *outside* | exterior, –ius *outer* | extrēmus, –a, –um *outermost* |
| īnferus, –a, –um *low* | īnferior, –ius *lower* | īnfimus, –a, –um<br>īmus, –a, –um }<br>*lowest, the base of* |

| posterus, –a, –um | posterior, –ius | postrēmus, –a, –um |
|---|---|---|
| *following* | *latter* | *last* |
| superus, –a, –um | superior, –ius | suprēmus, –a, –um ⎫ |
| *high* | *higher* | summus, –a, –um ⎰ |
| | | *highest, the top of* |

▶ STUDY HELPS

1. There is no masculine or feminine form for the comparative of *multus*. *Plūs* is followed by the partitive genitive. The genitive of *plūs* is *plūris*.

2. The adjectives *summus, extrēmus, īnfimus, reliquus, medius,* and a few others are not followed by the genitive case, but agree in gender, number, and case with the nouns they modify, as *summus mōns, the top of the mountain.*

▶ PRACTICE PATTERNS

A. Translate into English:

| | | |
|---|---|---|
| vir melior | pessimum malum | proximum iter |
| mājor mīles | reliquī mīlitēs | ad īnfimum montem |
| summum bonum | plūrima pecūnia | dē māximā et optimā virtūte |
| plūs cōnsilī | inferior Gallia | in extrēmō ponte |
| īnfimus mōns | minimus metus | ad exterius vallum |

B. Compare in Latin, giving all the genders for each degree:

| | | | | | | |
|---|---|---|---|---|---|---|
| high | good | great | free | small | bad | brief |
| true | bold | clear | many | noble | low | safe |
| much | keen | brave | dear | swift | poor | wide |

C. Write the specified forms in Latin:

1. better army (nominative)
2. smaller house (accusative)
3. worse fears (genitive)
4. supreme good (dative)
5. larger part (genitive)
6. worst wounds (ablative)
7. deeper water (ablative)
8. smallest fires (genitive)
9. largest walls (dative)
10. end of the road (ablative)
11. rather good weapons (nominative)
12. the rest of the men (accusative)
13. middle of the journey (ablative)
14. the top of the mountain (genitive)

# SECTION 2 The Ablative of Cause

▶ DISCUSSION

The ablative without a preposition may be used to express the cause or reason of an action, state, or feeling. It is generally used with ad-

**253**

jectives or verbs of emotion. **Propter** and **ob** with the accusative may be used instead of the ablative of cause.

**Fīliī Cornēliae** *virtūte* **laudātī sunt.**
**Filiī Cornēliae** *propter virtūtem*
   **laudātī sunt.**

The sons of Cornelia were praised *because of their bravery.*

▶ PRACTICE PATTERNS

A. Write two Latin sentences, using the ablative of cause, and two with propter or ob.

B. Write the Latin of the italicized words:
1. *Because of fear* the soldiers fled.
2. The people suffered *from lack of food.*
3. The man was proud *on account of his work.*
4. Terrified *because of the danger,* she ran.
5. The men fought bravely *on account of their leader's praise.*

# SECTION 3 Adverbs of Place

▶ DISCUSSION

There are nine adverbs of place that should be distinguished and learned because they are frequently met in stories.

| Place Where | | Place from Which | | Place to Which | |
|---|---|---|---|---|---|
| **ibi** | *there* | **inde** | *thence* | **eō** | *to that place, there* |
| **hīc** | *here* | **hinc** | *hence* | **hūc** | *to this place, hither* |
| **ubi** | *where* | **unde** | *whence* | **quō** | *to what place, where* |

*(handwritten annotations: "from that place", "from this place", "from what place")*

▶ STUDY HELPS

1. **Ubi**, *where*, **unde**, *whence*, and **quō**, *where*, can be used as relative or interrogative adverbs. **Ubi** has two meanings, *where* and *when.* **Eō**, *there*, **hūc**, *to this place*, and **quō**, *where*, are used with verbs expressing motion to or toward a place or thing.

2. **Hīc** with a long –*ī* is the adverb *here*; **hic** with a short –*i* is the demonstrative pronoun *this.*

▶ PRACTICE PATTERNS

Translate into Latin:

1. Where are you?
2. Where are you running?
3. Come here.
4. Remain here.
5. Remain there.
6. Whence is he?
7. Thence he is.
8. He ran to that place.
9. When will he come?

**254**

ae′quō (1), make equal, equalize (*equation*)

co′lō, −ere, −uī, cultus (3), cultivate, worship (*cult*)

colō′nia, −ae, *f.*, farm, colony (*colonist*)

condi′ciō, −ōnis, *f.*, terms (*condition*)

e′mō, −ere, ē′mī, ēmptus (3), buy (*redemption*)

nō′bilis, −e, *adj.*, famous, wellborn, noble; nōbilēs, −ium, *m. pl.*, nobles

ob, *prep. with acc.*, on account of; quam ob rem, for what reason?

o′pus, −eris, *n.*, work, task (*opera*)

pū′blicus, −a, −um, *adj.*, of the people, public (*publicity*)

susci′piō, −ere, −cēpī, −ceptus (3), undertake (*susceptible*)

to′ga, −ae, *f.*, toga, robe worn in time of peace by Roman citizens

ūl′timus, −a, −um, *adj.*, last, farthest (*ultimate*)

## BUILDING WORD POWER

In the comparative forms of the adjectives, you will recognize a number of words with which you are familiar: *īnferior, exterior, superior, posterior, minor, minus, mājor, prior, interior.* We have two English words from *mājor: mayor* and *major*.

From what Latin forms were the following derived: *optimist, pessimist, maximum, minimize, extreme, supreme, summit, ameliorate, prime, pejorative, plurality, posthumous?*

*Praeter,* an adverb and preposition meaning *except, beyond, outside the bounds of,* is used in a few words. For a bird to sing is *natural,* but for a bird to answer a question would be *preternatural,* beyond his natural powers, because a bird cannot think or speak. Parrots can be trained to laugh, cry, and enunciate words, but they do so without understanding. These acts are not *preternatural.*

## SENTENCE PATTERNS

A. Translate into English:

1. Tiberius agrōs pūblicōs dīvidī et sīc fortūnās omnium aequāre cupīvit.
2. Ob māximam potestātem nōbilium plūrimī agrī ā paucīs tenēbantur.
3. Officium gravissimum erat tribūnī causam plēbis suscipere.
4. Condiciō populī erat miserrima quod agricolae nūllam terram quam colere poterant habēbant.
5. Utrum nōbīs dabitis, cibum aut agrum?
6. Gajus Gracchus, quī frātrī simillimus fuit, plēbis causam suscēpit.
7. Cūr ille colōniās ad prōvinciās ūltimās mīsit?

8. Plūrimum frūmentum pecūniā pūblicā ēmit et plēbī dedit.
9. Optimum cōnsilium cēpit, sed opus erat difficilius.
10. Nōnne cīvēs pessimī ducēs optimōs occīdērunt?

B. Translate into Latin:

1. Where did the soldiers come from, and where are they hastening?
2. In time of peace, a Roman citizen wore a toga.
3. The condition of many citizens was unfortunate because they had no land.
4. Come here. There is less danger here.
5. All the best leaders feared the very great works of the brothers.

## Might Is Right at Rome

Ōlim Rōmae habitābant duo frātrēs, clārissimī et integerrimī. Tiberius Gracchus et frāter ējus Gājus fīliī erant Semprōnī Gracchī et Cornēliae, Scīpiōnis Āfricānī fīliae. Post mortem patris duo puerī ā mātre doctī sunt. Ipsa puerōs esse fortēs, jūstōs, fīdōs docuit, et saepe fābulās dē factīs Rōmānōrum fortissimōrum et optimōrum, quī vītam prō patriā dederant, narrābat.

Illō tempore condiciō plēbis miserrima erat. Dum cōnsulēs ducēsque Rōmānī bella gerunt, plūrimī rēgēs, urbēs, gentēs victī sunt. Cīvitās Rōmāna major et potentior facta erat, sed in secundō bellō Pūnicō agrī agricolārum pauperum dēlētī sunt. Undique per Ītaliam agrī ā paucīs nōbilibus tenēbantur. Nūllī cīvēs līberī sed plūrimī servī agrōs colēbant.

Multī cīvēs in urbēs fūgērunt ubi neque cibum neque casās habēbant. Necesse erat pecūniam pūblicam illīs darī, sed fēlīcēs nōn erant. Agrōs et alia jūra māximē cupīvērunt.

Tiberius et Gājus Gracchus, postquam togam virīlem accēpērunt et cīvēs Rōmānī factī sunt, erant benīgnissimī agricolīs et pauperibus. Tiberius tribūnus plēbis creātus est, et suscipere causam pauperum cōnstituit. Ille lēgēs jūstās scrīpsit quibus agrōs pūblicās dīvīsit et agricolīs pauperibus dedit. Sīc fortūnās omnium aequāre poterat.

Sed agrōs dīvidī et pauperibus darī senātōribus erat nōn grātum. Eō tempore lēx Rōmāna virum esse tribūnum ūnum annum jūssit. Contrā illam lēgem Tiberius iterum tribūnus creātus est. Dum cīvēs inter sē in viīs contendunt, Scīpiō Nāsīca senātōribus clāmābat: "Vōs quī lēgēs servārī cupīvistis mēcum venīte!" Armātī Tiberium quī erat sine tēlīs invēnērunt, et illum cum plūrimīs amīcīs interfēcērunt. Corpora in flūmen Tiberim jacta sunt. Tum nōbilēs pessima cōnsilia cēpērunt et agrōs quī inter plēbem dīvīsī erant occupāvērunt.

Decimō annō post Tiberī mortem Gājus Gracchus tribūnus plēbis creātus est, et similis frātrī causam plēbis suscēpit. Multās lēgēs optimās prō plēbe scrīpsit. Mīlitibus et pauperibus agrōs et pecūniam dedit. Colōniās ad loca idōnea mīsit, viās mūnīvit, horrea (*barns*) pūblica aedificāvit. Hoc opus difficillimum erat, sed nihil eī erat difficilius. Nōbilēs autem īrātissimī erant et Gājum interficere cōnstituērunt. Fūgit, sed posteā servum suum eum interficere jūssit; quod fēcit.

<table>
<tr><td>... one Senator seldom proclaims his own inferiority to another, and still more seldom likes to be told of it.<br>—Henry Brooks Adams, 1838–1918</td><td>Unit XLV</td></tr>
</table>

## CONVERSATION

JŌSĒPHUS: Cūr certāmen pessimum inter Marium ac Sullam erat?

MAGISTER: Prīmō certāmen inter plēbem ac nōbilēs Rōmae erat. Utraque factiō sibi multō plūs auctōritātis cupīvit.

PHILIPPUS: Nōnne utraque factiō illō tempore multō plūs ōtī et dīvitiārum quam Rōmānī superiōribus temporibus habuit?

MAGISTER: Paucī nōbilēs magistrātūs gessērunt; ducēs plēbis potestātis amōre (*love*) commōtī sunt. Multae aliae causae discordiae cīvīlis erant.

ROBERTUS: Quōmodo Marius māximus dux factus est?

MAGISTER: Marius, humillimus homō dē plēbe, adulēscēns cum exercitū Scīpiōnis in Hispāniam prōcessit. Scīpiōnī erat cārus.

JŌSĒPHUS: Nōnne Marius cīvitātem Rōmānam ex summō perīculō saepe servāvit? Eī Rōmānī plūrimōs honōrēs dedērunt.

MAGISTER: Tribūnus, legātus, cōnsul creātus est. Quam prīmum bellum cum Jugurthā cōnfēcit; in Galliā Teutōnēs vīcit; Cimbrōs quī in Ītaliā cōnsīdere postulāvērunt expulit.

PHILIPPUS: Posteā Sullae, ducī nōbilium, quam inimīcissimus erat.

## SECTION 1 Comparison of Regular Adverbs

▶ DISCUSSION

Most ordinary adverbs are derived from adjectives and therefore depend upon them for comparison. Observe the following:

*257*

|  | Positive | Comparative | Superlative |
|---|---|---|---|
| Adjective | cārus, *dear* | cārior, cārius, *dearer* | cārissimus, *dearest* |
| Adverb | cārē, *dearly* | cārius, *more dearly* | cārissimē, *most dearly* |
| Adjective | ācer, *keen* | ācrior, ācrius, *keener* | ācerrimus, *keenest* |
| Adverb | ācriter, *keenly* | ācrius, *more keenly* | ācerrimē, *most keenly* |

The following are models for the comparison of regular adverbs.

| Positive | Comparative | Superlative |
|---|---|---|
| clārē, *clearly* | clārius, *more clearly* | clārissimē, *most clearly* |
| līberē, *freely* | līberius, *more freely* | līberrimē, *most freely* |
| fortiter, *bravely* | fortius, *more bravely* | fortissimē, *most bravely* |
| celeriter, *quickly* | celerius, *more quickly* | celerrimē, *most quickly* |
| similiter, *similarly* | similius, *more similarly* | simillimē, *most similarly* |

▶ STUDY HELPS

1. The comparative degree of the adverb may be translated with *more, too,* and *rather: more clearly, too clearly, rather clearly.*

2. The superlative degree of the adverb may be translated with *most* or *very: most clearly, very clearly.*

3. **Quam** with the superlative of an adverb or adjective is translated *as ... as possible:* **quam celerrimē,** *as quickly as possible;* **quam plūrimae nāvēs,** *as many ships as possible.*

# SECTION 2 Comparison of Irregular Adverbs

▶ DISCUSSION

Some adverbs, like the adjectives from which they are derived, show peculiarities in comparison.

| Positive | Comparative | Superlative |
|---|---|---|
| bene, *well* | melius, *better* | optimē, *best* |
| male, *badly* | pējus, *worse* | pessimē, *worst* |
| māgnopere, *greatly* | magis, *more* | māximē, *most* |
| multum, *much* | plūs, *more* | plūrimum, *most* |
| parum, *little* | minus, *less* | minimē, *least* |

▶ PRACTICE PATTERNS

A. Compare and give the English translation:

longē  lātē  līberē  graviter  benīgnē  laetē  fēlīciter  difficile  pulchrē

B. Translate into English:

| | | | | | |
|---|---|---|---|---|---|
| malē | melius | ācriter | miserrimē | plūs | ācerrimē |
| magis | minus | gravius | pulchrius | optimē | nōbilissimē |

C. Translate into Latin:

| | | | | |
|---|---|---|---|---|
| freely | narrowly | rather joyfully | worse | very clearly |
| sharply | very badly | most bravely | least | most boldly |
| briefly | very nobly | most quickly | most | too clearly |
| bravely | very justly | too strongly | best | most humbly |

# SECTION 3 Ablative of Degree of Difference

▶ **DISCUSSION**

When two things are compared, the amount of difference between them is often specified. This amount of difference is expressed by the ablative, called the *ablative of degree of difference*. This ablative is usually expressed by **paulō, multō,** or some phrase containing a *number*.

Study these sentences:

1. The journey was a little less difficult (less *by a little* = **minus paulō**).
2. This journey was much harder (harder *by much* = **difficilius multō**).
3. The river rose three feet higher (higher *by three feet* = **altius tribus pedibus**).
4. We rose a little before daybreak (before *by a little* = **ante paulō**).
5. We rose a little after daybreak (after *by a little* = **post paulō**).

▶ **PRACTICE PATTERNS**

A. Translate into English:

| | | |
|---|---|---|
| decem pedibus altior | tribus hōrīs ante | plūs tribus hōrīs |
| longior paulō | post duōbus annīs | multīs pedibus altius |
| multō fortior | minus decem annīs | septem post noctīs |

B. Translate into Latin:

| | | |
|---|---|---|
| two miles longer | little less water | two years more |
| three feet higher | much easier | after three months |
| much more grace | a little after daybreak | five hours before |

## BUILDING WORD POWER

If I *preside* (**prae + sedēre**) at a meeting, I *sit before* its members. The *president* is, of course, the one presiding. If your father gave you, the eldest of five boys, an expensive car for a graduation present, he would be establishing a *precedent*. (Notice that this word used as a noun is accented on the first syllable.) A *precedent* (**prae + cēdere**) is an act that serves as an example, reason, or justification for a future similar act. What do you think your four brothers will expect when they graduate?

*259*

If you have a *prejudice* (***prae*** + ***jūdicium***) against someone or something, you have formed your judgment before knowing the facts. A *preposterous* (***prae***, *before* + ***post***, *after*) statement is absurd or ridiculous because the true meaning of ***praeposterus*** is *having the last first*, something contrary to reason.

Give the true meaning of: *prescription, premonition, preserve, presentiment, prevent, prevision, previous.*

## WORDS TO MASTER

**cīvī'lis, –e,** *adj.,* of a citizen, civil (*civil*)

**cō'gō, –ere, –ēgī, –āctus** (3), collect; *with infin.,* force, compel (*cogent*)

**cōnfi'ciō, –ere, –fēcī, –fectus** (3), accomplish, perform, complete, end (*confection*)

**cōnsī'dō, –ere, –sēdī, –sessūrus** (3), sit down, settle

**cōnsulā'tus, –ūs,** *m.,* consulship (*consulate*)

**dē'nique,** *adv.,* finally, at last

**hu'milis, –e,** *adj.,* low, humble, wretched (*humility*)

**mīlitā'ris, –e,** *adj.,* of a soldier, military (*military*)

**ō'tium, –ī,** *n.,* leisure, ease (*otiose*)

**prōdū'cō, –ere, –dūxī, –ductus** (3), lead out (*produce*)

**reve'niō, –īre, –vēnī, –ventūrus** (4), come back, return (*revenue*)

**tribū'nus, –ī,** *m.,* tribune, military tribune (*tribunal*)

## SENTENCE PATTERNS

A. Translate into English:

1. Gājus Marius, etsī homō humillimī generis, tribūnus plebis, cōnsul, imperātor creātus est.
2. Dēnique māximā virtūte et scientiā bellī ad summum imperium pervēnerat.
3. Marius quam prīmum domum revēnit et brevī tempore cōnsul factus est et bellum cōnficere jūssus est.
4. Voluntāte et potestāte nōbilium paucōrum negōtium cīvīle et mīlitāre gerēbātur.
5. Annō ūltimō Marius bellum quam celerrimē cōnficere cōnstituit.
6. Nōnne plēbs et nōbilēs multō plūs ōtī habēbant quam Rōmānī antīquōrum temporum?
7. Populus Rōmānus māximē perterrēbātur ubi Cimbrī in Ītaliā cōnsīdere cōnstituērunt.
8. Hīc exercitum prōdūxit et quam prīmum proelium cum eīs fēcit.
9. Marius erat multō cārior Scīpiōnī quam aliī mīlitēs.
10. Īdem postquam septimum cōnsulātum accēpit Rōmā fugere coāctus est.

B. Translate into Latin:

1. At that very time the general was finishing the war as quickly as possible.

2. As soon as possible the leader attacked the enemy and forced them to flee.
3. The enemy fought bravely, but the men of those tribes fought much more fiercely.
4. Because of his very great knowledge of war, the same man was chosen general of the Roman army.
5. This route is two miles longer than that.

The Roman senate chamber.

## Roman Politics

**A** Roman aspiring to political distinction in the Roman Republic sought election to the following offices in this order: *quaestor, aedile, praetor, consul.* If he was a plebeian, he might hold the office of tribune of the people before becoming aedile. An ambitious politician tried to hold each of these offices at the earliest possible date: quaestor at thirty-one, tribune at thirty-seven, praetor at forty, and consul at forty-three.

Quaestors were primarily financial officers. Some served in Rome and some in Italy. One quaestor accompanied each general or provincial governor as treasurer or paymaster. Aediles supervised commerce in the market place, food supplies, streets, public buildings, games, and festivities. Tribunes were the representatives of the plebeians. Praetors acted as judges in legal disputes, as provinicial governors, and as managers of public spectacles. Consuls, two in number, headed the government. Like all magistrates, except the *censors*, they held office one year. All magistrates served without pay.

At intervals of five years, two magistrates were appointed, who were called censors. They drew up the census of the people, showed the amount of property owned by each, and supervised the morals and conduct of the citizens. They made contracts for the collection of taxes and for the erection and repair of public buildings, roads, and other public works.

The Roman senate under the kings was an advisory council of elders (*senatores*), and it continued to be an advisory council

*261*

to the magistrates of the Republic. In Cicero's day the senate was composed exclusively of ex-magistrates, many of them with long records of public service. They held office for life.

## A Struggle for Supremacy

Post Gracchōrum mortem condiciōnēs Rōmae pējōrēs factae sunt. Certāmen pessimum inter plēbem et nōbilēs erat. Uterque sibi omnia cupīvit. Paucī nōbilēs negōtium cīvīle ac mīlitāre administrāvērunt; paucī nōbilēs omnēs agrōs et dīvitiās habēbant; paucī nōbilēs cūnctōs magistrātūs, praedam prōvinciārum, laudem, glōriam obtinuērunt. Et nōbilēs et plēbs multō plūs ōtī et bonōrum quam Rōmānī antīquī habuerant.

Gājus Marius, vir humilis generis, mīles erat in exercitū Scīpiōnis cui grātissimus fuit. Postquam tribūnus plēbis creātus est, causam populī contrā nōbilēs suscēpit; hinc grātus erat neque nōbilibus neque senātōribus.

Paulō post Rōmānī cum Jugurthā, rēge Numidiae, in Āfricā bellum gerēbant. Marius lēgātus ad Āfricam nāvigāvit, sed ille imperātor esse māximē cupīvit. Rōmam revēnit ubi cōnsul creātus est et bellum fīnīre jūssus est. Ūnō annō bellum cōnfēcit et rēgem Jugurtham captīvum Rōmam dūxit.

Dum haec in Āfricā geruntur, duae potentissimae gentēs Germānicae novōs agrōs et domūs petēbant, quārum altera, Teutōnēs, ad Galliam pervēnerant, altera, Cimbrī, in Ītaliā cōnsīdere cupīvērunt. Rōmānī summō perīculō perterrēbantur et quam prīmum contrā hostēs ācerrimōs exercitum mīsērunt. Quīnque exercitūs Rōmānī dēlētī sunt.

Virtūte et arte mīlitārī Marius Rōmae clārissimus erat. Populus ā lēgibus discessit et hunc cōnsulem iterum creāvit. Cum exercitū ad Teutōnēs quam celerrimē contendit. Teutōnēs fortissimē et ācerrimē pūgnāvērunt sed ā Rōmānīs victī sunt. Multī captīvī factī sunt apud quōs rēx ipse erat. Marius, postquam quīntum cōnsulātum accēpit, in Ītaliam revēnit. Cimbrī in Ītaliā cōnsēderant et ad Marium lēgātiōnem superbam mīsērunt.

"Nōbīs et amīcīs nostrīs terram et urbēs dā. In Ītaliā cōnsīdere cupimus." Hic erat nūntius Cimbrōrum audācissimōrum.

"Quī sunt amīcī vestrī?" postulāvit Marius.

"Teutōnēs sunt amīcī et sociī nostrī," superbē respōnsum est.

"Illī *erant* amīcī et sociī vestrī," Marius dīxit et rīsit (*smiled*).

"Plūrimī eōrum terram quam ā nōbīs accēpērunt nunc tenent et eam semper tenēbunt." Tum reliquī ducēs Teutōnum in catēnīs (*chains*) prōductī sunt. Dēnique Marius caedem Cimbrōrum māximam fēcit et apud plēbem Rōmānam plūrimīs victōriīs māximō in honōre fuit.

# *Comprehensive Review: Units* XLI–XLV

A. Write the dative singular, gender, and meaning of these words:

| | | | | | | |
|---|---|---|---|---|---|---|
| opus | eques | domus | ōtium | colōnia | classis | tribūnus |
| toga | modus | fossa | vallum | fortūna | jūdex | fortitūdō |
| mūnus | obses | aurum | passus | cīvitās | condiciō | cōnsulātus |

B. Write the nominative singular of the feminine and neuter forms and give meanings:

| | | | | | | |
|---|---|---|---|---|---|---|
| fēlīx | fīrmus | gravis | cīvīlis | humilis | nōbilis | ūltimus |
| dīligēns | aeternus | pūblicus | crūdēlis | mīlitāris | dissimilis | alacer |

C. Write the meanings of the following:

| | | | | | | |
|---|---|---|---|---|---|---|
| etsī | ubi | hīc | anteā | dēnique | quō | unde |
| ibi | ob | hinc | igitur | inde | hūc | eō |

D. Write the present passive infinitive of these verbs. Translate.

| | | | | | | |
|---|---|---|---|---|---|---|
| suscipiō | emō | colō | revocō | ostendō | comparō | cōnficiō |
| comprehendō | dīcō | trādō | fīniō | trādūcō | prōdūcō | commoveō |

E. Write the perfect passive participle of each of the verbs listed above under D. Translate.

F. Write the third principal part of these verbs. Translate.

cōnstituō    aequō    cōgō    conveniō    cōnsīdō    cēdō    reveniō

G. Write the comparative in the nominative singular. Translate.

| | | | | | | | |
|---|---|---|---|---|---|---|---|
| fēlīx | malus | bonus | fīrmus | gravis | multus | crūdēlis | ācer |
| miser | līber | audāx | māgnus | parvus | similis | dīligēns | lātus |

H. Write the superlative in the nominative plural. Translate.

| | | | | | | |
|---|---|---|---|---|---|---|
| pauper | aequus | longus | celer | multus | bonus | superbus |
| parvus | doctus | māgnus | malus | brevis | pulcher | difficilis |

I. Form adverbs from these adjectives and compare them:

| | | | | | |
|---|---|---|---|---|---|
| ācer | potēns | certus | similis | superbus | līber |
| cārus | gravis | fortis | cupidus | integer | grātus |

J. Compare these adverbs and translate each form:

bene    male    māgnopere    parum    multum

K. Decline in Latin:

| | |
|---|---|
| the better farmer | the best condition |
| the deepest river | the most just tribune |

L. Write the English meaning of:

alterum mūnus    illud tōtum iter    hic eques ipse    eadem cīvitās    sōla nāvis
aliud opus       uterque obses     ūnīus flūminis    hūjus modī     ūllus vir

M. Express in Latin:

1. This ditch is deeper than that river. (two ways)
2. This ditch is three feet deeper than that river.
3. The infantry fled because of fear. (two ways)
4. The rampart was five miles long.
5. The best of these were our men.

## SENTENCE PATTERNS

A. Translate into English:

1. Rēx potentissimus, quī Rōmānīs inimīcior quam omnibus aliīs gentibus erat, in Rōmānōs impetūs ācerrimōs fēcerat.
2. Apud senātum ōrātiōnem brevissimam habuit.
3. Facillimum erat hoc iter sed propter metum hostium equitī difficillimum vīsum est.
4. Sine morā longiōre ad oppidum postrēmum quam celerrimē contendit.
5. Tribūnus quod rēgem numquam vīderat nūllō modō hunc cōgnōvit.
6. Rōmānī templa pulchriōra quam aedificia pulcherrima nostra aedificābant.
7. Salūs cīvitātis erat multō cārior Rōmānō vītā ipsā.
8. Incolae illārum regiōnum quam prīmum auxilium petere coāctī sunt.
9. Etsī mīlitēs fortissimē pūgnābant, ab hostibus vincēbantur.
10. Nisi properāveris, domum hodiē nōn perveniēs.

B. Translate into Latin:

1. The river near which the Romans had pitched camp was many feet wider than the Tiber.
2. After peace was established, Sicily was a Roman province.
3. The inhabitants defended their state as bravely as possible.
4. Because of lack of food, they were forced to surrender.
5. Although conditions in Rome were bad, outside the city they were worse.

## SIGHT TRANSLATION: DESTROYED BY A FLOOD

Multīs annīs ante quod hominēs pessimī erant, Juppiter ipse māximā īrā commovēbātur et illōs dēlēre cōnstituit. Deucaliōnem autem et Pyrrham uxōrem ējus servāre māgnopere cupiēbat quod optimī erant. Pater deōrum Neptūnum terram plūrimā aquā circumdare et tergere (*and cover*) jūssit. Hic, potentissimus deus maris, id fēcit, etsī Deucaliōn et uxōr benīgnissima monitī erant et sē servāre potuērunt. Ille māximam nāvem aedificāverat et in eā cum uxōre cārissimā multōs mēnsēs mānsit. Posteā etsī omnia aquīs dēlēta sunt, cōnsiliō deōrum plūrimī virī et fēminae in terrā iterum vīvēbant.

I had rather be the first in this town
than the second in Rome.
—Plutarch, A.D. 46–120
*Lives,* Caesar

*Unit* XLVI

## CONVERSATION

PAULA: Annō sextī cōnsulātūs Marī erat initium illīus bellī quod bellum sociāle appellātum est.

MAGISTER: Quae sociī ā Rōmānīs hōc tempore petīvērunt, Anna?

ANNA: Sociī, quī prō rē pūblicā saepe pūgnāverant et reī pūblicae pecūniam atque auxilium dederant, esse pars cīvitātis Rōmānae et jūra cīvium Rōmānōrum habēre cupīvērunt.

MAGISTER: Rōmānīne sociīs haec jūra statim dedērunt, Jūlia?

JŪLIA: Exercitum centum mīlia mīlitum comparāvērunt et cum sociīs duōs annōs contendērunt. Etsī sociī in aciē victī sunt, et nūllam fidem nec ūllam spem habēbant, tamen eīs multa jūra cīvium posteā data sunt.

MAGISTER: Quī imperātor clārus apud populum Rōmānum post bellum sociāle māximō in honōre erat, Cornēlia?

CORNĒLIA: Sulla, vir nōbilis generis, doctus et potēns sed cupidior glōriae, ā populō laudātus est. Mariō nōn grātum erat tantam laudem Sullae darī.

## SECTION 1 Fifth Declension

▶ DISCUSSION

The fifth declension includes all nouns with nominative in *–ēs* and genitive in *ēī–* (*–eī* after a consonant). The stem ends in *–e,* and the vowel *–e* appears in all cases. Nouns of the fifth declension are *feminine* with the exception of *diēs,* which is always masculine in the plural and generally so in the singular, except when it refers to some specified time, as *tertiā diē.* Only *diēs* and *rēs* have all the plural forms.

|  | **diēs, –ēī** | | | **rēs, –eī** | | |
|  | *m.* day | | | *f.* thing | | |
| BASE: | **di/** | | | **r/** | | |
|  | SINGULAR | | C.I. | PLURAL | | C.I. |
| Nom. | diēs | rēs | –ēs | diēs | rēs | –ēs |
| Gen. | diēī | reī | –ēī, –eī | diērum | rērum | –ērum |
| Dat. | diēī | reī | –ēī, –eī | diēbus | rēbus | –ēbus |
| Acc. | diem | rem | –em | diēs | rēs | –ēs |
| Abl. | diē | rē | –ē | diēbus | rēbus | –ēbus |

**265**

1. The noun **rēs** has sometimes been called a blank check because the translator fills in the word most suitable to the meaning of the context. Literally **rēs** means *thing;* but avoid this translation when possible by using *affair, matter, event, fact,* and the like.

2. The noun **rēs** with descriptive adjectives forms many idiomatic expressions: **rēs pūblica** *(public affair), the commonwealth, the state:* **rēs mīlitāris,** *military affairs, warfare;* **rēs frūmentāria,** *grain supply;* **rēs novae,** *revolution.* Both words in these idioms are declined.

▶ PRACTICE PATTERNS

A. Decline in the singular: rēs pūblica; brevis diēs; omnis spēs; prīma aciēs; in the plural: rēs mīlitāris; trēs diēs.

B. Write in Latin the specified forms:

1. our commonwealth (accusative)
2. this day (ablative)
3. very many things (genitive)
4. the same hope (dative)
5. each thing (nominative)
6. both things (dative)
7. which (of two) things (accusative)
8. three days (accusative)

# SECTION 2 Horizontal Comparison of Case Indicators

1. The nominative singular is often irregular and must be learned from the vocabulary. The nominative singular of *masculine* and *feminine* nouns originally ended in **-s,** but the **-s** has disappeared from the first declension, from second declension nouns like **ager** and **vir,** and from some third declension consonant-stem nouns like **cōnsul.**
2. The accusative singular of masculine and feminine nouns ends in **-m** in all declensions, with the preceding vowel short.
3. The accusative plural of masculine and feminine nouns ends in **-s** in all declensions, with the preceding vowel long.
4. In neuters the nominative and accusative singular are alike, and the nominative and accusative plural are alike and always end in short **-a.**
5. The ablative singular ending is the stem vowel, except in consonant stems and most masculine and feminine **i-**stems, which end in **-e.**
6. In each declension the dative plural is like the ablative plural. The ending is **-īs** in the first and second declensions, **-bus** in the others.
7. In all declensions the genitive plural ends in **-um,** which is preceded by **-r** in the first, second, and fifth declensions.
8. The vocative is like the nominative except in the singular of second declension nouns in **-us** (vocative **-e**) and **-ius** (vocative **-ī**).

| Declension | | First | Second | | Third Cons. Stems | | Third i-Stems | | Fourth | | Fifth |
|---|---|---|---|---|---|---|---|---|---|---|---|
| Stem Vowel | | -a | -o | | | | | | -u | | -e |
| Gender | | F. | M. | N. | M.&F. | N. | M.&F. | N. | M. | N. | F. |
| **SINGULAR** | | | | | | | | | | | |
| Subject | Nom. | -a | -us | -um | (as in vocabulary) | | (as in vocabulary) | | -us | -ū | -ēs |
| Possession (*of*) | Gen. | -ae | -ī | -ī | -is | | -is | | -ūs | -ūs | -ēi, -ei |
| *To, for* | Dat. | -ae | -ō | -ō | -ī | | -ī | | -uī | -ū | -ēi, -ei |
| Object; **in**, *into;* **ad**, *to, toward* | Acc. | -am | -um | -um | -em | (nom.) | -em | (nom.) | -um | -ū | -em |
| *From, with, by, in, on, at;* **ā, ab;** *from, by;* **ē, ex,** *out of, from;* **cum,** *with;* **in,** *in, on* | Abl. | -ā | -ō | -ō | -e | | -e, -ī | -ī | -ū | -ū | -ē |
| **PLURAL** | | | | | | | | | | | |
| | Nom. | -ae | -ī | -a | -ēs | -a | -ēs | -ia | -ūs | -ua | -ēs |
| | Gen. | -ārum | -ōrum | -ōrum | -um | -um | -ium | -ium | -uum | -uum | -ērum |
| | Dat. | -īs | -īs | -īs | -ibus | | -ibus | | -ibus | | -ēbus |
| | Acc. | -ās | -ōs | -a | -ēs | -a | -ēs, -īs | -ia | -ūs | -ua | -ēs |
| | Abl. | -īs | -īs | -īs | -ibus | | -ibus | | -ibus | | -ēbus |

9. With names of cities, towns, and small islands, *place where* is expressed by the locative case. The locative has the same form as the genitive in the singular nouns of the first and second declensions. In the singular of nouns of the third declension and in all plural nouns, it has the same form as the ablative.

▶ PRACTICE PATTERNS

Identify the case and number of these forms:

| | | | | | |
|---|---|---|---|---|---|
| aciē | pedēs | virōrum | tempora | cornuum | mīlitibus |
| dōna | impetū | nōmina | vulnera | tabulārum | cīvitātēs |
| rēbus | passuum | librum | hominis | imperātōrī | prōvinciā |
| fideī | itinere | oppidō | salūtis | hostibus | diēbus |

## WORDS TO MASTER

**a′ciēs, –eī,** *f.*, edge, line, line of battle, army

**dēpō′nō, –ere, –posuī, –positus** (3), lay aside, put down (*deposit*)

**di′ēs, –eī,** *m.*, day (*diary*); **multō diē,** late in the day

**doc′tus, –a, –um,** *adj.*, learned, skilled (*doctor*)

**fi′des, –eī,** *f.*, faith, pledge, confidence, trust (*fidelity*)

**incen′dō, –ere, –cendī, –cēnsus** (3), set on fire, kindle (*incense*)

**in′trō** (1), enter, go in (*entrance*)

**redū′cō, –ere, –dūxī, –ductus** (3), lead back (*reduce*)

**rēs, re′ī,** *f.*, thing (*real*)

**spēs, spe′ī,** *f.*, hope

**ta′bula, –ae,** *f.*, record, list (*table*)

**tan′tus, –a, –um,** *adj.*, so great, so much (*tantamount*)

## BUILDING WORD POWER

Two fifth declension nouns came into English with spelling unchanged, **speciēs** from **specere,** *to look at,* and **seriēs,** from **serere,** *to join.* A *species* is a kind, class, or group, distinguished by its appearance or other characteristic. A distinct kind of plant or animal is a species. A red maple is a species of maple. The ablative of this word is **speciē.** In English the word *specie* now means minted metal coin as contrasted with paper money. Silver dollars are *specie.*

*Series* is a number of things arranged in a row or in succession. What do we mean by a series of concerts? a serial story? the World Series? From **rēs** meaning *thing,* we have *real, reality,* and *rebus.* A *dismal* day was originally a **diēs malī,** *a day of evil,* an unlucky day. **Diārium,** *an allowance for a day,* became *diary;* **diurnālem,** *daily,* is our *journal;* **diurnus,** *daily,* is *journey;* **subdiurnāre,** *to stay day after day,* shortened to *sojourn;* **meridiēs** from **medī diē** (*at the middle of the day*) changed to *meridian.*

## SENTENCE PATTERNS

A. Translate into English:
1. Nōnne Sulla cōnsul exercitum Rōmam paucīs diēbus redūxit?
2. Tabulae nōminum plūrimōrum in Forō locātae sunt.
3. Post trēs annōs summum imperium subitō dēposuit.
4. Domus imperātōris incēnsa est atque uxor fugere coācta est.
5. Nēmō ex eīs quī amīcī Marī putābantur ūllam spem fugae habēbat.
6. Victōriīs et scientiā reī mīlitāris Sulla anteā laudābātur.
7. Posteā facta pessima ējus semper memoriā tenēbantur.
8. Cūr imperium tantī bellī Sullae trāditum est?
9. Sine fidē et spē certāmen intrāre nōn dēbēmus.
10. Num Marius, etsī ācerrimus in aciē erat, doctus habēbātur?

B. Translate into Latin:
1. There were very many brave soldiers in that battle line, weren't there?
2. The first leader was bad, the second was worse, but the third was worst of all.
3. With faith and hope we can accomplish very great things.
4. He was a very learned man, but he loved himself more than the commonwealth.
5. After a few days he led the army back to Italy and a little later entered Rome.

## A Struggle for Supremacy (continued)

Annō ultimō bellī cum Jugurthā Gājus Marius erat cōnsul et imperātor; Lūcius Cornēlius Sulla quaestor ējus erat. Hic gentis patriciae potentissimus mīles et doctissimus vir erat sed inimīcissimus Mariō; ille humilis generis fortissimus et audācissimus imperātor erat. Hic senātuī et nōbilibus semper fuerat amīcus; ille causam plebis pauperis suscēperat.

Marius postquam rem pūblicam ā Teutōnibus et Cimbrīs līberāvit apud populum Rōmānum māximō in honōre erat et cōnsul iterum creātus est. Hōc annō sextī cōnsulātūs erat initium bellī sociālis. Sociī, quod cīvēs Rōmānī esse cupivērunt, cum Rōmānīs bellum gerere cōnstituērunt. Inter imperātōrēs clārōs reī pūblicae quī eō tempore cum sociīs pūgnābant erat Sulla. Virtūte et scientiā reī mīlitāris ille ā Rōmānīs laudātus est et cōnsul creātus est. Tandem sociī ā Sullā superātī sunt, sed posteā Rōmānī eīs jūra quae petīverant dedērunt.

Paucīs post annīs Rōmānī cum Mithridāte, Ponticō rēge, quī multa mīlia cīvium Rōmānōrum in Āsiā occīderat, bellum gerēbant. Ubi perīculum gravissimum factum est, Sulla cōnsul ā senātū dēlēctus est et in Āsiam cum exercitū quam celerrimē prōcēdere jūssus est. Mariō autem nōn grātum erat imperium tantī bellī Sullae trādī. Itaque postquam Sulla ad exercitum prōcessit, Pūblius Sulpicius, tribūnus plēbis, lēgem scrīpsit quā Gājus Marius dux hūjus bellī creātus est. Sulla, quī Rōmā sed nōn ab Ītaliā discesserat, exercitum Rōmam redūxit, urbem paucīs diēbus occupāvit, Marium cum fīliō multīsque amīcīs fugere coēgit.

Dum Sulla in Graeciā et in Āsiā contrā Mithridātem contendit, Marius Rōmam ab ūnō ē cōnsulibus revocātus est. Ille omnēs amīcōs Sullae quīnque diēs noctēsque in templīs, in domibus eōrum, in viīs petīvit et eōs crūdēlissimē occīdit. Domus Sullae incēnsa est atque uxor līberīque fugere coāctī sunt. Alter cōnsulum et plūrimī nōbilēs interfectī sunt, et corpora in viās jacta sunt. Subitō Marius ipse ē vītā excessit postquam septimum cōnsulātum suscēpit.

Ubi haec Sullae narrāta sunt, ex Asiā excessit et in Ītaliam ad bellum cīvīle properāvit. Mithridātem etsī hic pācem cōnfīrmāre coāctus est nōn vīcit. Cōnsulēs superāvit et victor Rōmam intrāvit. Amīcīs Marī erat nūlla spēs. Sulla mīlia cīvium occīdī jūssit. Dictātor ā senātū creātus est et lēgēs reī pūblicae statim mūtāvit. Tribus post annīs summum imperium dēposuit et in villā propinquā marī reliquam vītam ēgit.

If you aspire to the highest place, it is no disgrace to stop at the second, or even the third.
—Marcus Tullius Cicero, 106–43 B.C.

# Unit XLVII

## CONVERSATION

ROBERTUS: Cūr Pompējus, Rōmānōrum legiōnum imperātor, ā populō Māgnus appellātus est, magister?

MAGISTER: Pompējus ab omnibus Māgnus appellārī poterat quod māgnās rēs optimē gessisse dīcitur. Ut (As) Cicerō, ōrātōrum Rōmānōrum clārissimus, dīxit: "Pompējus quattuor hās rēs habēbat: scientiam reī mīlitāris, virtūtem, auctōritātem, fēlīcitātem (good luck)."

PHILIPPUS: Quandō Cicerō prō Pompējō ōrātiōnem clāram habuit?

MAGISTER: Cicerō praetor prō Pompējō prīmam ōrātiōnem habuit.

PAULUS: Quae Cicerō illō tempore dīxit?

MAGISTER: Haec dīxit: "Prīmum, nūllus erat mājor scientiā bellī quam Pompējus; secundum, plūra bella gessit quam cēterī lēgērunt; tertium, labor in negōtiīs, virtūs in perīculīs, celeritās, cōnsilium, fidēs erant mājōra in hōc ūnō imperātōre quam in omnibus reliquīs imperātōribus quōs aut vīdimus aut audīvimus."

# SECTION 1 Perfect Active Infinitive

▶ DISCUSSION

In English *to have* is the indicator of the perfect active infinitive, which is formed by combining *to have* with the perfect participle: *to have + called = to have called.* In Latin the perfect active infinitive is formed by adding the indicator *–isse* to the *perfect stem:*

$$\textbf{vocāv/} + \textbf{isse} = \textbf{vocāvisse} = \textit{to have called}$$

PERFECT ACTIVE INFINITIVE

| CONJUGATION | *Perf. Stem* | + | *Indicator* | = | *Form* | |
|---|---|---|---|---|---|---|
| First | **vocāv** | + | **isse** | = | **vocāvisse** | *to have called* |
| Second | **monu** | + | **isse** | = | **monuisse** | *to have warned* |
| Third | **rēx** | + | **isse** | = | **rēxisse** | *to have ruled* |
| Third –io | **cēp** | + | **isse** | = | **cēpisse** | *to have taken* |
| Fourth | **audīv** | + | **isse** | = | **audīvisse** | *to have heard* |

▶ PRACTICE PATTERNS

Write the present and perfect active infinitives of these verbs. Place a number after each, indicating the conjugation to which it belongs. Translate each form into English.

| | | | | | |
|---|---|---|---|---|---|
| cōgō | sciō | dēpōnō | accidō | reducō | cōnsīdō |
| colō | lūdō | terreō | incendō | cōnficiō | cōnstituō |
| fīniō | dēdō | intrō | nūntiō | accipiō | existimō |
| mittō | stō | videō | maneō | locō | transportō |

# SECTION 2 Perfect Passive Infinitive

▶ DISCUSSION

In English *to have been* is the indicator of the perfect passive infinitive, which is formed by combining *to have been* with the perfect participle:

*to have been + called = to have been called.* In Latin the perfect passive infinitive is formed by combining the *perfect passive participle* with **esse:**

**vocātus** + **esse** = **vocātus esse** = *to have been called*

PERFECT PASSIVE INFINITIVE

| CONJUGATION | *Perf. Pass. Part.* | *+ esse =* | *Form* |
|---|---|---|---|
| First | **vocātus, –a, –um** | + esse = | **vocātus, –a, –um esse** *to have been called* |
| Second | **monitus, –a, –um** | + esse = | **monitus, –a, –um esse** *to have been warned* |
| Third | **rēctus, –a, –um** | + esse = | **rēctus, –a, –um esse** *to have been ruled* |
| Third –io | **captus, –a, –um** | + esse = | **captus, –a, –um esse** *to have been taken* |
| Fourth | **audītus, –a, –um** | + esse = | **audītus, –a, –um esse** *to have been heard* |

▶ PRACTICE PATTERNS

A. Write the present and perfect passive infinitives of these verbs. Place a number after each, indicating the conjugation to which it belongs. Translate each form into English:

| | | | | | |
|---|---|---|---|---|---|
| dō | augeō | vertō | mittō | statuō | perficiō |
| colō | vāstō | teneō | nūntiō | recipiō | trānsportō |
| petō | jubeō | premō | sentiō | prōdūcō | incipiō |

B. Translate into Latin and indicate the conjugation to which each Latin infinitive belongs:

| | | |
|---|---|---|
| to order | to have demanded | to have been given |
| to be held | to accomplish | to be carried over |
| to be sent | to have entered | to have been divided |
| to have taken | to have defended | to have finished |
| to be recalled | to have departed | to have been laid aside |
| to have come | to have been done | to have ordered |

C. Write the present and perfect infinitives in Latin of: sum, possum, adsum, absum. Translate into English.

## BUILDING WORD POWER

The prefix **sub–** generally has the meaning of *under, beneath, inferior to.* **Sus–** is often used before words beginning with *c, p,* or *t.* **Sur–** is found in *surreptitious (done by stealth), surrogate (substitute),* and in the compound *resurrect.* What law is evident in: *success, sufficient, suggest, summon, support?*

**Subter,** a Latin adverb meaning *below, secretly,* is used in very few English words, as *subterfuge* (**subter** + *fugere*), which means literally *a plan to flee secretly.* What is the prefix in *subterranean?* Is it *subter–?*

**Super,** an adverb, preposition, and prefix, has the general meaning of *above, over, excessive,* and appears in many English words as *sur–* from ear-Latin. **Supra–** as a prefix is equivalent to *super–.* *Supercilium* (**super** + **cilium,** *eyelid*) means *eyebrow.* By raising his **supercilia,** a haughty person expresses disdain or contempt, hence our English word *supercilious.* Why is an actor having an insignificant part in a play called a *supernumerary?*

## WORDS TO MASTER

**ac'cidō, –ere, –cidī, —** (3), befall, happen (*accident*)

**cē'terī, –ae, –a,** *adj.,* the rest, the others (*et cetera*)

**co'hors, –hortis,** *f.,* a division of a legion, cohort (*cohort*)

**inci'piō, –ere, –cēpī, –ceptus** (3), begin (*incipient*)

**le'giō, –ōnis,** *f.,* a division of the army, legion (*legionary*)

**nam,** *conj.,* for

**ōrā'tiō, –ōnis,** *f.,* speech, plea, language (*oration*); **ōrātiōnem habēre,** deliver a speech

**ōrā'tor, –ōris,** *m.,* speaker (*orator*)

**quam,** *interrog. adv.,* how?; *adv. and conj.,* than; *with superlatives,* as . . . as possible; **quam diū,** how long? **quam longē,** how far?

**quan'tus, –a, –um,** *interrog. adj.,* how great? how large? how much? (*quantity*)

**reci'piō, –ere, –cēpī, –ceptus** (3), take back, receive (*recipient*); **sē recipere,** withdraw, return

**trānspor'tō** (1), bring over, carry, carry over (*transport*)

## SENTENCE PATTERNS

A. Translate into English. Identify the infinitives.

1. Pompējus plūra proelia commīsit quam cēterī aut vīdērunt aut audīvērunt.
2. Eī ducēs dē imperiō reī pūblicae inter sē contendere incēpērunt.
3. Nam uterque potentior alterō esse māgnopere dēsīderābat.
4. Necesse fuit imperātōrem trāns mare legiōnēs trādūcere.
5. Quanta erat potestās Crassī in rē pūblicā?
6. Hoc nūllī ducī cohortis anteā acciderat.
7. Caesar magistrātum alium post alium habuisse dīcitur.
8. Nōnne Cicerō, ōrātor clārissimus, prō Pompējō ōrātiōnem habuit?
9. Impedīmenta trāns flūmen trānsportāta esse debent.
10. Num legiōnēs Caesaris in castra sē recipere cupīvērunt?

B. Translate into Latin:

1. How great a gift did the others receive?
2. Now nothing in the entire state could be done that was not pleasing to the others.
3. Caesar began to prepare as large an army as possible.
4. For it is a very great honor to have fought for our country.
5. The senate did not desire Caesar to be remembered at Rome.

### Perseus and the Medusa

The lovely Danae had been imprisoned in a tower because an oracle had told her father, King Acrisius, that his daughter's son would one day be the cause of his death. According to the legend, Jupiter himself visited the unhappy girl in her prison. In time Danae bore Jupiter's son whom they named Perseus.

Acrisius became furiously angry and enclosed the mother and child in a large wooden chest, closed the top, and set the chest adrift on the sea. In the course of time, the strange vessel came to rest on an island. A kind fisherman forced open the lid and brought the two unfortunate castaways to Polydectes, king of that country. He immediately fell in love with Danae, but she refused to marry him because she wanted to devote all her time and love to her son.

At last, when Perseus was grown up, Polydectes determined to get rid of him, hoping that when he was out of the way, Danae would change her mind and marry him. He ordered the young man to bring him the head of the Gorgon Medusa, who at that time was laying waste the country. The Medusa, it seems, had once been a maiden whose crowning glory was her hair; but she dared to vie in beauty with Minerva, who, enraged, turned her rival's hair into hissing serpents with wings and claws and enormous teeth.

The Gorgon Medusa was a monster so frightful in appearance that one glance turned the beholder to stone. Perseus, helped by Minerva and Mercury, approached the cave of the Three Gray

Sisters, who alone could help him in his task. The Three Sisters, who had been gray from birth, possessed only one eye, which they passed from one to the other. As the eye was being passed, all three were blind.

Perseus, standing silent nearby, watched for his opportunity and snatched the eye. He would not return it until they told him the hiding place of the Gorgons, as well as the place where he could obtain three things: the helmet of Pluto, which would render him invisible; the winged shoes with which he could fly with the speed of the wind; and the pouch used to carry the Medusa's head after he had severed it from her body. Reluctantly they granted all his demands.

Then Minerva gave Perseus her highly polished shield so that he could see the Medusa as in a mirror; for if he looked at the monster directly, he would turn to stone. Mercury lent his finely sharpened sickle with which Perseus could cut off the Medusa's head. Quickly the deed was done, and Perseus was on his homeward journey with the Medusa's head in his pouch.

## The Great Pompey

Per annōs bellī cīvīlis senātus Rōmānus paene omnem auctōritātem potestātemque dēposuit. Ducēs, quī exercitūs potentissimōs et māximam scientiam reī mīlitāris habēbant, summum imperium Rōmae habēbant. Inter eōs fuit Gnaeus Pompējus, quī in Sullae exercitū lēgātus fuerat.

Mox post Sullae mortem, ubi pīrātae plūrimī omnia maria īnfēstābant et urbēs Ītaliae dēlēbantur, contrā eōs Pompējus missus est. Pīrātās statim superārī necesse erat quod nāvigātiō nōn erat tūta et frūmentum ē prōvinciīs Rōmam trānsportārī nōn poterat. Brevissimō tempore Pompējus omnia maria illā peste līberāvit. Nihil hāc victōriā erat celerius, nam ante quadrāgēsimam (*fortieth*) diem tōtō marī expulsī sunt pīrātae.

Dum Pompējus contrā pīrātās bellum gerit, Mithridātēs, quī ā Sullā annīs ante paucīs paene victus erat, iterum contrā Rōmānōs bellum in Āsiā gerēbat. Pompējus Mithridātem vīcit, quī in Pontum fūgit et ibi ā mīlite interfectus est. Tum ille Tigrānem, rēgem Armēniae, vīcit. Posteā ad Jūdaeam prōcessit et prīmus Jūdaeōs superāvit. Hierosolymam (*Jerusalem*), caput gentis, cēpit, et templum jūre victōriae intrāvit.

Ubi rēs Āsiae cōnfectae sunt, Rōmam revēnit, nōn cum exercitū suō, ut (*as*) plūrimī timuerant, sed sine legiōnibus. Rōmae per spatium duōrum diērum māgnus imperātor triumphāvit, id quod nēminī anteā acciderat. Cohortēs Sertōrī in Hispaniā, pīrātās Ciliciae, Mithridātem, rēgem Pontī, Tigrānem, rēgem Armēniae, Jūdaeōs Palaestīnae Pompējus māgnus vīcerat.

Posteā Pompējus, etsī tantum imperium jam habēbat, multō mājōrem auctōritātem et honōrēs dēsīderāvit. Senātuī erat grātissimus, sed erat ūnus dux potēns quem māximē timuit. Ille homō erat Gājus Jūlius Caesar, quī ipse esse prīmus Rōmae māgnopere cupīvit.

Itaque hī duo ducēs, Pompējus et Caesar, cum Mārcō Crassō, quī māximās dīvitiās habēbat, societātem (alliance) inter sē jungere statuērunt. Hōc modō rēs cīvitātis administrāvērunt. Eōdem annō Pompējus et Caesar erant cōnsulēs. Posteā hic Galliam, ille Hispāniam obtinēbat. Caesar māximō cum gaudiō cum legiōnibus ad Galliam contendit; Pompējus autem Rōmae mānsit quod illī esse prope senātum et nōbilēs erat grātum. Ubi Caesar Rōmā discēdere statuit, senātus laetus erat quod nōbilēs eum memoriā tenērī nōn cupīvērunt.

... the die was now cast; I had passed the Rubicon: Swim or sink, live or die, survive or perish. ...
—John Adams, 1735–1826

# Unit XLVIII

## CONVERSATION

MAGISTER: Exīstimāsne Jūlium Caesarem māgnum imperātōrem fuisse?

JŌSĒPHUS: Complūrēs dīcunt Caesarem māximum imperātōrem omnium saeculōrum esse. Hoc nōndum exīstimō.

MAGISTER: Quibuscum dīcunt illum societātem (alliance) fēcisse?

HENRĪCUS: Ille societātem cum Pompējō ac Crassō fēcit.

MAGISTER: Quam ob rem societātem fēcit?

ROBERTUS: Caesar ferē omnēs nōbilēs sibi inimīcissimōs esse et futūrōs esse scīvit. Pompējum auctōritāte, Crassum pecūniā eum adjuvāre posse intellēxit. Sē dīvitiīs Crassī et imperiō Pompējī rem pūblicam bene administrātūrum esse spērāvit. Sē vocāvērunt triumvirōs.

MAGISTER: Nihil agī potuit dē rēbus cīvitātis nisi trēs virī probāvērunt. Quam prōvinciam Caesar post cōnsulātum cēpit?

CORNĒLIUS: Caesar sē Galliam prōvinciam acceptūrum esse dīxit.
MAGISTER: Quī Rōmānus prīmus Germānōs superāvit?
PETRUS: Caesar ipse scrībit sē prīmum Germānōs vīcisse.

## SECTION 1 Future Active Infinitive

▶ DISCUSSION

In English there is no special form for the future active infinitive. In Latin the future active infinitive is a combination of the *future active participle* + **esse.** The future active participle is made up of the participial stem + **ūr** + **us, -a, -um:**

> **vocāt/ + ūr + us, -a, -um = vocātūrus, -a, -um** = *about to call*

The indicator for the future participle is **-ūr-.**

> **vocātūrus + esse = vocātūrus esse** = *to be about to call*

FUTURE ACTIVE INFINITIVE

| CONJUGATION | *Fut. Act. Part.* | + esse = | *Form* |
|---|---|---|---|
| First | **vocātūrus, -a, -um** | + esse = | **vocātūrus esse** *to be about to call* |
| Second | **monitūrus, -a, -um** | + esse = | **monitūrus esse** *to be about to warn* |
| Third | **rēctūrus, -a, -um** | + esse = | **rēctūrus esse** *to be about to rule* |
| Third -io | **captūrus, -a, -um** | + esse = | **captūrus esse** *to be about to take* |
| Fourth | **audītūrus, -a, -um** | + esse = | **audītūrus esse** *to be about to hear* |

▶ PRACTICE PATTERNS

Write the future active infinitives of these verbs. Indicate the conjugation to which each belongs. Translate into English:

| | | | | | |
|---|---|---|---|---|---|
| dō | lūdō | dēpōnō | incipiō | inveniō | respondeō |
| dēdō | sciō | veniō | incendō | postulō | interficiō |
| stō | putō | occīdō | sentiō | existimō | intellegō |

## SECTION 2 Indirect Statement

▶ DISCUSSION

1. Suppose, on the way from school, your friend John says: "My father is building a new house." At home you announce to your father:

"John *says that* his father is building a new house." The original statement was made *directly* to you, but your father hears it only *indirectly* through you. When you repeated John's words, you changed them to an objective clause introduced by *that*, and you used the word *says*.

2. In Latin when a simple statement is indirectly quoted, the verb is changed from the indicative mood in the direct statement to the *infinitive* in the indirect statement, and the subject is changed from the *nominative* to the *accusative* case.

Direct statement: **Vir ambulat.**      *The man is walking.*
Indirect statement: **Dīcit virum ambulāre.**    He says *that the man is walking.*

| ENGLISH | LATIN |
|---|---|
| The verb is finite. | The verb is in the infinitive. |
| The introductory word *that* is used. | There is no introductory word. |
| The subject is in the nominative case. | The subject is in accusative case. |

3. Indirect statements usually follow verbs of *mental action*, such as *say, know, think, hear, perceive,* and the like. These verbs should be memorized:

     **dīcō** (3), *say, tell*      **sciō** (4), *know*      **nūntiō** (1), *announce*
     **putō** (1), *think*      **audiō** (4), *hear*      **sentiō** (4), *feel, perceive*
     **negō** (1), *say not, deny*      **videō** (2), *see*      **exīstimō** (1), *think*

4. The present infinitive denotes the *same* time as the main verb; the perfect denotes time *before* that of the main verb; the future denotes time *after* that of the main verb.

Present: **Dīcit virum *ambulāre.***   He says that the man *is walking, walks.*
         **Dīxit virum *ambulāre.***   He said that the man *was walking, walked.*
Perfect: **Dīcit virum *ambulāvisse.***   He says that the man *was walking, walked.*
         **Dīxit virum *ambulāvisse.***   He said that the man *had walked.*
Future: **Dīcit virum *ambulātūrum esse.***   He says that the man *will walk.*
         **Dīxit virum *ambulātūrum esse.***   He said that the man *would walk.*

▶ STUDY HELPS

1. The participle of the compound infinitive in indirect discourse is always in the accusative case and agrees with its subject in gender and number.

**Caesar *sē* nāvēs *dēlētūrum esse* cōgnōvit.**    Caesar knew that *he would destroy* the ships.

2. A predicate noun or adjective used with an infinitive in indirect discourse is always in the accusative case and agrees with its subject in gender and number.

**Mīles *impedīmenta* esse *gravia* putāvit.**    The soldier thought that the *baggage* was *heavy.*

*278*

3. When the speaker makes a statement about himself in indirect discourse, the reflexive pronoun is used.

**Caesar *sē* exercitum trāductūrum esse dīxit.**   Caesar said that *he* would lead his army across.

4. The verb of saying, thinking, etc., is regularly placed at the end of the complete sentence.

▶ PRACTICE PATTERNS

Write in Latin the active and passive infinitives, and translate:

| | | | | | | | |
|---|---|---|---|---|---|---|---|
| legō | petō | dūcō | cupiō | vertō | jungō | vincō | expellō |
| creō | pōnō | mittō | capiō | augeō | premō | sentiō | cūstōdiō |

## WORDS TO MASTER

**complū'rēs, –a,** *pl.*, *adj.*, very many, several

**dē'dō, –ere, –didī, –ditus** (3), give up, surrender

**exīs'timō** (1), think, suppose

**fe'rē,** *adv.*, almost

**intel'legō, –ere, –lēxī, –lēctus** (3), understand (*intelligent*)

**inte'reā,** *adv.*, in the meantime; **in'-terim,** *adv.*, meanwhile (*interim*)

**jūven'tūs, –tūtis,** *f.*, youth, young men

**lū'dō, –ere, lūsī, lūsus** (3), play, mock (*delude*)

**nōn'dum,** *adv.*, not yet

**rūr'sus,** *adv.*, again, in turn

**sae'culum, –ī,** *n.*, age, century, generation (*secular*)

**ve'nia, –ae,** *f.*, indulgence, pardon (*venial*)

## BUILDING WORD POWER

***Contrā,*** an adverb in Latin meaning *against* or *opposite*, came into English in three forms: *contra–*, *contro–*, and from ear-Latin *counter–*. Analyze the following words, and give their true meaning: *contradict, contraposition, contravene, countersign, controvert.*

*Control* came from *counter-roll,* a rolled-up piece of parchment on which debts were listed. *Country* (***contrāta terra***) probably meant the land outside the city.

You have frequently used the preposition ***prō*** with the meaning *for, in behalf of, in front of.* Used as a prefix, it has the added meanings of *forward, in place of, favoring.* In the word *prodigal* (***prō–*** + ***agere***), *–d–* is inserted for euphony. ***Prō*** became *por–* in a few words, such as *portend,* from ***prōtendere,*** *to stretch forth to the future, to foretell.* What do you mean by a *portent? proslavery? pronoun? the pro's and con's of an argument?*

Give the English words derived from: ***prōducere, prōmissum, prō-clāmāre, prōpellere, prōspectus, prōjectus, prōpositus.***

## SENTENCE PATTERNS

A. Translate into English. Explain the syntax of the Latin infinitives.

1. Nōnne hostēs summam scientiam reī mīlitāris habuisse exīstimant?
2. Interim Caesar sē exercitum suum flūmen trādūctūrum esse dīxit.
3. Quālem virum Mārcum Crassum fuisse dīcunt?
4. Intellēxēruntne Caesarem eōs nōn lūdere?
5. Intereā senātus oppida Caesarī sine pūgnā sē dedisse audīvit.
6. Quandō mīlitēs sē Rōmam ventūrōs esse nūntiāvērunt?
7. Prīmō saeculō ante Chrīstum hominēs clārōs vīxisse cōgnōvimus.
8. Caesar complūrēs cohortēs rūrsus laudāvit quod hās quam fortissimē semper pūgnāre intellēxit.
9. Quam ob rem eum hostibus veniam datūrum esse negāvērunt?
10. Interim ferē omnēs senātōrēs ex urbe fūgērunt ubi Caesarem legiōnēs trāns flūmen trādūxisse audīvērunt.

B. Translate into Latin. Explain the syntax of the Latin infinitives used.

1. Do you know that Caesar was killed in the first century before Christ?
2. Many thought that Caesar would not lead his army across the river.
3. In the meantime the general said that the senate had acted against the laws.
4. When did he find out that the senators had left Rome?
5. They did not know that several towns were being destroyed.

## The Man Who Came, Who Saw, and Who Conquered

Prīmō saeculō ante Chrīstum erant Rōmae multī prīncipēs māximī, inter quōs erat Gājus Jūlius Caesar, vir nōbilissimī generis. Ubi adulēscēns fuit, bellum cīvīle inter Marium et Sullam gerēbātur. Sulla, ubi ex puerīs (*boyhood*) Caesar excessit, cōnsul creātus est et eī inimīcissimus erat quod Caesar fīliam Cinnae, quī fuerat amīcus Mariō, in mātrimōnium dūxit.

Sulla dīxit sē Caesarem pūnitūrum esse. Posteā autem adulēscentī, quod Caesaris amīcī id postulābant, veniam dare cōgēbātur. Ille autem hōs amīcōs dē Caesare monuit. Exīstimāvit Caesarem futūrum esse inimīcum nōbilibus et nūntiāvit multōs Mariōs esse in Caesare. Post Sullae mortem Caesar ad īnsulam Rhodum nāvigāre cōnstituit, nam in hāc īnsulā eō tempore clārissimum dīcendī (*of oratory*) magistrum esse audīverat. Hūc dum nāvigat, ā pīrātīs captus est mānsitque apud eōs prope quadrāgintā (*forty*) diēs. Interim sociī pecūniam compārāvērunt quam pīrātīs dēdidērunt.

Caesar pīrātīs dīxerat sē eōs captūrum atque interfectūrum esse. Pīrātae eum lūdere exīstimābant; sed Caesar ubi ex manibus pīrātārum evāsit (*escaped*), aliās nāvēs invēnit et pīrātās quoque quōs crucifīxit. Inde ad īnsulam Rhodum prōcessit. Postquam studium dīcendī cōnfectum est, Caesar Rōmam sē recēpit et tribūnus mīlitāris dēlectus est et posteā quaestor Hispāniae. Omnem magistrātum, alium post alium, sibi obtinuit; aedīlis, pontifex māximus, praetor, cōnsul creātus est.

Caesar scīvit nōbilēs sibi inimīcissimōs esse. Illō tempore Pompējus māximam potestātem, Crassus māximās dīvitiās habēbat. Caesar, Pompējus, Crassus amīcī factī sunt et sē triumvirōs appellāvērunt. Ob auxilium hōrum virōrum, Caesar cōnsul creātus est. Nihil in tōtā cīvitāte factum est quod ūllī ex tribus nōn grātum erat.

Caesar post cōnsulātum prōvinciam Galliam accēpit. In Galliā ferē decem annōs manēbat et hīs annīs omnem Galliam vīcit. Pompējus in urbe Rōmā mānserat ubi victōriās Caesaris māximās audīvit. Illō tempore Crassus ā Parthīs interfectus erat; et Jūlia, uxor Pompējī et fīlia Caesaris, ex hāc vītā excesserat. Tum Pompējus sōlus cōnsul ā senātū creātus est, quī Caesarem exercitum dīmittere et Rōmam statim venīre jūssit. Hic exercitum suum Rubicōnem trādūxit et contrā Pompējum et nōbilēs bellum gessit.

Beauty is that Medusa's head
Which men go armed to seek and sever.
—Archibald MacLeish, 1892–

# Unit XLIX

## CONVERSATION

MAGISTER: Quandō Caesar dictātor in perpetuum creātus est?

ANNA: Caesarem dictātōrem in perpetuum creātum esse post bellum cīvīle putō. Deinde superbē rēgnāre incipiēbat.

MAGISTER: Cūr populus Rōmānus lībertātem āmittēbat?

CORNĒLIUS: Omnem potestātem auctōritātemque ā senātū rapuit, cupiēns superior cēterīs in rē pūblicā esse. Senātōrēs ad sē venientēs sedēns excēpit.

MAGISTER: Quis corōnam (*crown*) in Caesaris capite in sellā aureā (*golden chair*) prō Rōstrīs sedentis posuit?

CORNĒLIA: Antōnius, Caesaris in omnibus bellīs et tum cōnsulātūs socius, prope (*nearby*) stāns corōnam in Caesaris capite posuit.  Caesar corōnam ex Antōnī manibus nōn accēpit, sed nūllō modō īram ostendit.

MAGISTER:  Quīdam Rōmānī dīxērunt Caesarem spērāre populum eum rēgem creātūrum esse.  Cūr nōmen rēgis nōn accēpit?

JŪLIUS:  Id nōmen, ut suprā dēmōnstrāvimus, Rōmānīs nōn grātum erat.

# SECTION 1 Participles; Present Active Participle

▶ DISCUSSION

1. A participle is a *verbal adjective*.  As a *verb* it has tense and voice, may be modified by an adverb, and may govern an object.  As an *adjective* it is declined to agree in gender, number, and case with the noun or pronoun it modifies.

2. In English there are *four* participles: present, active and passive; and perfect, active and passive.  In Latin there are *three* participles: present active, future active, and perfect passive.  In this unit we shall study only the present participle.

3. In English present participles are found in both the active and passive voice, as *calling, being called*.  In Latin the present participle is found only in the active voice, as **vocāns,** *calling*.  *Being called* cannot be expressed in Latin in the same manner as in English.  In English the form of the present participle may be used with forms of the verb *to be* as the progressive form of the finite verb.  In Latin the present participle is used only as a participle.  Compare these two sentences:

The soldiers *attacking* the town heard the signal.  (Present participle)
The soldiers *were attacking* the town.  (Main verb, progressive form)

4. The present active participle in Latin is formed by adding –*ns* to the *present stem* of the verb, except in the fourth conjugation and the –*io* verbs of the third conjugation, where a long –*ē* is inserted between the stem and the ending.

PRESENT ACTIVE PARTICIPLE

| CONJUGATION | Pres. Stem | + Indicator | = | Form | |
|---|---|---|---|---|---|
| First | **vocā** | +. **ns** | | = **vocāns** | *calling* |
| Second | **monē** | + **ns** | | = **monēns** | *warning* |
| Third | **rege** | + **ns** | | = **regēns** | *ruling* |
| Third –io | **cape** + *iē* + | **ns** | | = **capiēns** | *taking* |
| Fourth | **audī** + *ē* + | **ns** | | = **audiēns** | *hearing* |

The present active participle is declined in the *third* declension as a *one-termination* adjective.

282

**vocāns, vocant/is,** *calling*     BASE: **vocant/**

|  | SINGULAR | | PLURAL | |
| --- | --- | --- | --- | --- |
|  | M.&F. | N. | M.&F. | N. |
| Nom. | vocāns | | vocant**ēs** | vocant**ia** |
| Gen. | vocant**is** | | vocant**ium** | |
| Dat. | vocant**ī** | | vocant**ibus** | |
| Acc. | vocant**em** | vocāns | vocant**ēs** | vocant**ia** |
| Abl. | vocant**e** (**–ī**) | | vocant**ibus** | |

▶ STUDY HELPS

1. The vowel before **–ns** in the nominative singular is always long; before **–nt** in the base it is always short.

2. The present active participle in English always ends in *–ing.*

3. The ablative ends in **–ī** when it is used as an adjective; as a pure participle, it ends in **–e.**

| | |
| --- | --- |
| **Vir ā mīlite** *fugientī* **necātus est.** | The man was killed by the *fleeing* soldier. (Adjective) |
| **Vir ā mīlite ab hostibus** *fugiente* **necātus est.** | The man was killed by the soldier *fleeing* from the enemy. (Participle) |

# SECTION 2 Use of the Present Active Participle

▶ DISCUSSION

Participles are frequently used in Latin to express in brief and concise form ideas that are usually expressed in English by clauses introduced by *while, as, when,* or by a relative pronoun. Observe these translations:

**Multī** *fugientēs* **captī sunt.**
1. Many *fleeing (while fleeing)* were captured.
2. Many were captured *while they were fleeing.*
3. Many were captured *as they were fleeing.*
4. Many were captured *when they were fleeing.*
5. Many *who were fleeing* were captured.

The present participle *always* denotes the same time as that of the main verb. Therefore, a present participle connected with a main verb of present time is translated by a clause indicating present time. The same is true of all the tenses.

▶ PRACTICE PATTERNS

A. Write the present participles of these verbs in the case, number, and gender indicated.

1. accusative plural neuter: moveō, dēpōnō, perficiō
2. dative singular feminine: vīvō, sustineō, stō

3. genitive plural masculine: dīmittō, excipiō, suspiciō
4. nominative plural feminine: postulō, premō, fīniō
5. ablative plural neuter: vertō, fluō, teneō

B. Write in Latin:
1. I saw the soldiers fleeing.
2. They are giving land to the people dwelling in the provinces.
3. They will find the man laboring.
4. They killed him while he was standing.

## WORDS TO MASTER

**conjūrā'tiō, –ōnis,** *f.*, conspiracy, plot (*conjure*)
**dein'de,** *adv.*, thence, from there, next
**dīmit'tō, –ere, –mīsī, –missus** (3), send away (*dismiss*)
**exci'piō, –ere, –cēpī, –ceptus** (3), receive, welcome (*except*)
**Ī'dūs, –uum,** *f. pl.*, the Ides (the 15th of March, May, July, October, and the 13th of the other months)
**invi'dia, –ae,** *f.*, envy (*invidious*)

**perpe'tuus, –a, –um,** *adj.*, unbroken, lasting (*perpetual*); **in perpetuum,** forever
**quī'dam, quae'dam, quod'dam** or **quid'dam,** *indef. adj. and pron.*, certain, a certain one
**spē'rō** (1), hope, hope for (*desperation*)
**su'prā,** *adv., and prep. with acc.*, above
**suspi'ciō, –ere, –spēxī, –spectus** (3), distrust (*suspect*)
**um'quam,** *adv.*, ever, at any time

## BUILDING WORD POWER

A large number of present participles came into English as adjectives, sometimes also as nouns. If derived from first conjugation verbs, they regularly end in *–ant;* from the other conjugations they end in *–ent.* The present participle in French, however, ends in *–ant*, regardless of the Latin conjugation. As a result, we sometimes are confused about the spelling of some words.

For example, we have the adjective *confident* directly from the Latin present participle **cōnfidēns, cōnfidentis** and the noun *confidant* from the same Latin participle but coming into English from French. Distinguish between *dependent* and *dependant*.

What English words are derived from: ***accidēns, incidēns, antecēdēns, agēns, sentiēns, currēns, continēns, cōnstāns, prōvidēns, efficiēns, recipiēns, conveniēns, patiēns, regēns?***

All Latin nouns derived from present participles end in *–ntia*, the English derivatives in *–nce* or *–ncy*. What is the English for: ***patientia, efficientia, cōnstantia, prōvidentia?***

## SENTENCE PATTERNS

### A. Translate into English:

1. Pompējus, Caesaris facta jam suspiciēns, nūntium ad eum mittit.
2. Vir magistrātum habēns in jūdicium vocārī nōn poterat.
3. Ūnus ē multīs prīncipibus prope Caesarem stantibus eum vulnerāvit.
4. Nōnne eum exercitum dīmittere et Rōmam revenīre jūssit?
5. Imperātōrem invidiā contrā Caesarem commōtum esse sēnsērunt.
6. Quīdam vir Caesarī dīxit eum Īdibus Mārtiīs māximō in perīculō futūrum esse.
7. Pompējus, spērāns sē coāctūrum esse Caesarem sine exercitū Rōmam revenīre, mīlitēs ējus dīmittī jūssit.
8. Deinde putāns sē in illā terrā amīcōs habēre in Āfricam nāvigāvit.
9. Num Caesar sedēns senātōrēs ad sē venientēs excipere dēbet?
10. Ducēs conjurātiōnis, ut suprā dēmōnstrāvimus, in perpetuum memoriā tenēbuntur.

### B. Translate into Latin:

1. Caesar thought that fear of death was worse than death itself.
2. Because of envy Pompey, knowing the facts, said he would destroy Caesar.
3. Suspecting nothing, the greatest of Rome's leaders came into the senate on the Ides of March.
4. Did Caesar ever know that a conspiracy had been formed?
5. Did we not show above that Pompey was defeated in a war?

### Perseus and Andromeda

On his return journey Perseus flew over a country in Ethiopia ruled by King Cepheus. From afar he saw a beautiful young woman chained to a rock. Wishing to know the reason, he landed from the sky at her feet. At first she was frightened, but finally she revealed her sad story. Her mother, Cassiopeia, the queen of Cepheus, had boasted that she was more beautiful than the nymphs. They became very angry and begged Neptune to punish the proud queen. This he did by sending a horrible sea monster that ravaged the coast and devoured both people and cattle.

The king, in anguish and despair, consulted an oracle, who declared that the only way to appease the offended nymphs was to sacrifice his daughter Andromeda to the monster. Now, chained to the rock, she awaited her doom.

While they were yet speaking, a terrifying sound was heard as the monster lashed his way to the rock. Quick as a flash Perseus mounted the back of the monster, who fought in vain against his winged and unseen foe. After watching the combat from the shore, the Ethiopians joyously released Andromeda as soon as the monster was dead.

Joyfully Perseus and Andromeda, with her parents, made their way to the palace of Cepheus. There a banquet was prepared to celebrate Perseus' bravery, Andromeda's rescue, and their marriage to each other. Into the midst of the festivities rushed Phineus, who had once been betrothed to the bride but who had made no attempt to save her in her deadly peril.

A fierce struggle ensued. Perseus, fearing he would lose Andromeda, produced the Gorgon's head, and his enemies were instantly turned to stone. Cepheus provided the young people with a handsome ship, in which they sailed to the island where Danae lived. They arrived just in time to rescue her from Polydectes and turn that wicked tyrant to stone.

The charmed helmet, the winged shoes, and the pouch were returned to their owners, but Perseus presented the head of Medusa to Minerva, who thereafter wore its image on her breastplate or on her shield.

### Beware the Ides of March

Caesar, ut suprā dēmōnstrātum est, cum Pompējō et Crassō prīmum triumvirātum fēcit. In librīs dē bellō Gallicō Caesar ipse sē esse in Galliā ferē decem annōs et hīs annīs omnem Galliam vīcisse scrīpsit. Ille etiam exercitum flūmen Rhēnum in Germāniam trādūxit, et posteā in Britanniam nāvigāvit. Neque omnem Germāniam neque omnem Britanniam vīcit quod Germānī et Britannī fuērunt virī fortissimī.

Legimus Pompējum in urbe Rōmā mānsisse. Ubi dē multīs victōriīs clārissimīs Caesaris intellēxit, invidiā contrā Caesarem commōtus est. Quod illum dēlēre cupīvit, cōgere eum sine exercitū et sine magistrātū revenīre Rōmam cōnstituit.

Caesar Pompējum et senātum contrā lēgēs Rōmānās agere scīvit, et ipse contrā lēgēs exercitum Rubicōnem trādūxit. Ubi

Pompējus et senātus Caesarem cum exercitū sine proeliō per Ītaliam iter facere audīvērunt, Rōmā fūgērunt. Pompējus cum exercitū suō Brundisium pervēnit atque inde nāvibus ad Graeciam nāvigāvit.

Tandem duo māximī imperātōrēs Rōmānī inter sē in Thessaliā ad Pharsālum contendērunt. Pompējus exercitum mājōrem, Caesar mīlitēs fortiōrēs habēbat. Legiōnēs Pompējī ā minōribus cōpiīs Caesaris victae sunt et Pompējus, rēgem Aegyptī eī auxilium datūrum esse putāns, eō fūgit; sed mandātīs rēgis ipsīus interfectus est et caput ējus ad Caesarem missum est.

Post fīnem bellī Caesar in Āsiam Minōrem iter fēcit et Phārnacem, fīlium Mithridātis, quī Pompējō auxilium dederat, vīcit. Id dīcitur fuisse bellum Caesaris brevissimum, quī ad senātum hunc nūntium mīsit: "Vēnī, vīdī, vīcī." Posteā pauca proelia et in Āfricā et in Hispāniā gessit et tandem domum revēnit ubi victōriārum quattuor triumphōs ēgit. Quārtum cōnsulātum ēripuit (*seized*) et dictātor creātus est.

Caesar multa prō bonō pūblicō cōnfēcisse dīcitur; sed quod omnem potestātem auctōritātemque ā senātōribus et nōbilibus ēripuerat, populus Rōmānus nōn jam lībertātem habēbat.

Complūrēs senātōrēs et nōbilēs conjūrātiōnem contrā Caesarem fēcērunt quod ipsī eum esse rēgem cupere exīstimāvērunt. Caesar Īdibus Mārtiīs, dē quō diē monitus erat, sine timōre in senātum vēnit. Ūnus ē nōbilibus prope eum stantibus sīgnum dedit. Prīmō Caesar sē dēfendit, sed amīcum Brūtum apud reliquōs vidēns, "Et tū quoque, Brūte," clāmāvit neque jam contendit.

*Civis Romanus sum.*
I am a Roman citizen!
—Marcus Tullius Cicero, 106–43 B.C.

# *Unit* L

## CONVERSATION

MAGISTER: Quot ōrātiōnēs omnīnō in Catilīnam Cicerō habuit?

HENRĪCUS: Cicerō quattuor ōrātiōnēs immortālēs in Catilīnam habuit.

MAGISTER: Recitā prīmae ōrātiōnis partem, Mārce.

MĀRCUS: "Ō tempora! Ō mōrēs! Senātus haec intellegit, cōnsul videt; hic tamen vīvit. Vīvit? Etiam in senātum venit. Dēsīgnat (*Points out*) oculīs ad caedem quemque nostrum."

MAGISTER: Optimē, Mārce. Quam partem memoriā tenēs, Cornēlia?

CORNĒLIA: "Habēmus senātūs cōnsultum in tē, Catilīna. Mūtā jam istam mentem. Tenēris undique. Lūce sunt clāriōra nōbīs

tua cōnsilia omnia.  Ubi putāvistī tē nocturnō impetū
Praeneste occupātūrum esse, sēnsistīne illam colōniam meīs
praesidiīs, custōdiīs, vigiliīs esse mūnītam?"

ROBERTUS:   Ego etiam partem prīmae ōrātiōnis recitāre possum.  "Dīcō
tē priōre nocte vēnisse Mārcī Laecae domum, et convēnisse
ad eundem locum complūrēs ējusdem generis sociōs.  Num
negāre audēs (dare)?"

# SECTION 1 Perfect Passive Participle

▶ DISCUSSION

1. In English the perfect participles are used in the active and passive
voice: *having called, having been called*.  In Latin the perfect participle
is found only in the passive voice.  As you have already learned, it is
the fourth principal part of the verb, always ends in *–tus* or *–sus*,
and grammatically is a verbal adjective of the first and second declensions.  It is used with **sum, eram, erō** to form the tenses of the perfect
passive system.

2. This participle is often used in Latin, but its literal translation may
be unsuitable in the English sentence.  Frequently a better way to express
exact meaning is by a clause.  The subordinate clause may be introduced by *after, since, because, although, if,* or a relative pronoun.  When
translating, keep in mind that the perfect passive participle denotes time
*previous* to that of the main verb.

**Mīlitēs *vulnerātī* captī sunt.**

The soldiers {
1. As participle:   a. *wounded*
                    b. *having been wounded*
2. As subordinate clause:
   (temporal)       c. *when they had
                       been wounded*
   (causal)         d. *since they had
                       been wounded*
                    e. *because they had
                       been wounded*
   (concessive)     f. *although they had
                       been wounded*
   (conditional)    g. *if they had
                       been wounded*
   (relative)       h. *who had been wounded*
3. As a main clause:
                    i. *had been wounded and*
} were seized.

The best way to get a good idiomatic translation of a participial phrase is to translate the Latin participle literally by an English participle with the noun or pronoun it modifies. From this rough translation the thought will be clear. This thought can then be rendered by a clause that best suits the sense of the passage. Translations 1 (a) and (b) above are literal translations of *vulnerātī.*

▶ PRACTICE PATTERNS

A. Translate into English in three ways:

| | |
|---|---|
| cōnsul ab hostibus victus | cum exercitū āmissō |
| cīvēs ē perīculō ēreptī | ad castra incēnsa |
| plēbī ā patriciīs oppressae | hostēs ā Rōmānīs inventī |

B. Write in Latin the perfect passive participles, in the nominative singular masculine, of the following verbs. Translate each participle into English in three ways:

| | | | | | |
|---|---|---|---|---|---|
| send | blame | snatch | increase | undertake | give |
| turn | make | crush | fortify | lead forth | advise |
| lose | find | compel | conquer | lead across | have |

# SECTION 2 Use of the Future Active Participle

▶ DISCUSSION

You have already learned the formation of the future participle and one of its users. It is rarely used in simple agreement with a noun. Generally it is found in combination with forms of *sum.* Grammatically it is a verbal adjective, declined like first and second declension adjectives; if used in the predicate, it agrees in gender, number, and case with the subject. It denotes time after that of the main verb.

Since there is no future participle in English, the Latin is best translated by the expressions *about to, going to, intend to, on the point of.*

| | |
|---|---|
| **Quid dē salūte reī pūblicae factūrī sunt?** | What are they *about to* (*going to, intending to*) do about the welfare of the state? |

▶ PRACTICE PATTERNS

A. Write in Latin the future active participles of the verbs listed in Practice Patterns in Section 1B of this unit. Translate each participle.

B. The table on page 290 gives the participles of vocō. Using this as a model, write the participles of: moneō, regō, capiō, audiō.

| | ACTIVE | PASSIVE |
|---|---|---|
| Present | vocāns, vocantis, *calling* | |
| Perfect | | vocātus, –a, –um, *having been called* |
| Future | vocātūrus, –a, –um, *about to call* | |

▶ STUDY HELPS

The verb **sum** has one participle: *futūrus, –a, –um, about to be;* **possum** has one participle, **potēns,** used as an adjective.

## WORDS TO MASTER

**ars, ar'tis,** *f.,* skill, art, branch of learning

**con'jūnx, –jugis,** *m. & f.,* husband, wife (*conjugal*)

**cōnsul'tum, –ī,** *n.,* decree, order (*consultation*)

**cūstō'dia, –ae,** *f.,* watch, guard (*custody*)

**ēri'piō, –ere, –uī, –reptus** (3), snatch, rescue

**immortā'lis, –e,** *adj.,* immortal, eternal

**omnī'nō,** *adv.,* in all, altogether

**op'primō, –ere, –pressī, –pressus** (3), overwhelm, crush (*oppress*)

**pos'terus, –a, –um,** *adj.,* next, following (*posterity*); **postrīdiē,** on the following day

**pri'or, pri'us,** *comp. adj.,* former, first (*priority*); *superl.,* **prīmus, –a, –um,** first, foremost (*prime*)

**quī'que, quae'que, quod'que,** *indef. adj.,* each; **quis'que, quid'que,** *indef. pron.,* each one

**ū'nā,** *adv.,* together; **ūnā cum,** together with, along with

## BUILDING WORD POWER

The prefix **per–** ordinarily means *through* or *thoroughly.* Originally *through* and *thorough* were the same word: *through and through = thoroughly.* **Permanēre** means *to stay through;* **perterrēre,** *to frighten through and through, thoroughly.* **Per–** can also mean *very,* as **perpaucī** means *very few.*

If **colāre** means *to strain,* what is the purpose of a coffee *percolator?* If a young lady gets a *permanent,* what is she hoping about that curl? If your father plants *perennials,* what does he expect will happen every year? If a person says you have *perspective,* does he mean you can see through glass or that you see events and people in their right relations? If your work is *perfect,* you do it thoroughly, through and through.

Do you know that the prefix **per-** is disguised in *pilgrim?* Originally a *pilgrim* was a **peregrīnus,** a foreigner who journeyed through the land (**per + agrum**), foreign land, outside Rome.

## SENTENCE PATTERNS

A. Translate into English:

1. Cicerō cōnsul factus Catilīnae conjūrātiōnem praesidiīs, vigiliīs, cūstōdiīs oppressūrus erat.
2. Ōrātor dīxit Catilīnam quemque nostrum ad caedem dēmōnstrāvisse.
3. Sēnsistīne urbem praesidiīs mūnītam futūram esse tūtam?
4. Ō deī immortālēs! In quā urbe vīvimus? Quam rem pūblicam habēmus?
5. Nōnne Cicerō Catilīnam priōre nocte domum socī intrāvisse scīvit?
6. Habēmus senātūs cōnsultum in Catilīnam ācre et grave.
7. Ōrātiōnēs bene habēre erat ars quam Cicerō ex puerō habēbat.
8. Catilīna bellum gerere in animō habēns ūnā cum virīs pessimīs in patriam prōcessit.
9. Sociī ējus comprehēnsī paucīs post diēbus sine jūdiciō interfectī sunt.
10. Cicerō rem pūblicam, bōna, fortūnās, conjugēs līberōsque, urbem pulcherrimam omnīnō ex īgne atque gladiō ēripuit.

B. Translate into Latin. Use participles where possible.

1. About to wage war against Rome, he went on the following day to the army which had been prepared.
2. His allies, after they had been overwhelmed, were killed in the city.
3. Did you think you would destroy the city fortified by my guards?
4. The senate and the Roman people, who had been rescued from fire and sword, called Cicero the father of his country.
5. Catiline, while he was fighting bravely, fell in battle.

### Rome's Greatest Orator

Dum Caesar et Pompējus inter sē dē summō imperiō contendunt, Rōmae vivēbat clārissimus ōrātor nōmine Mārcus Tullius Cicerō. Ille erat vir humilis generis quī per sē ad summōs magistrātūs ascenderat. Rōmam ā patre missus, studiīs et jūrī tōtō sē animō dedit. Ab optimīs magistrīs doctus est inter quōs erant Mūcius Scaevola et Archiās.

Paucīs post annīs in īnsulam Rhodum nāvigāvit ubi multa dē arte rhētoricā ā Molōne, Graecō magistrō nōtissimō, didicit (*learned*). Apud ōrātōrēs clārissimōs erat optimus. Postquam Rōmam revēnit, ōrātiōnēs clārās habēre coepit. Sextum Roscium dēfendit et Sullam dictātōrem offendit. Melius igitur erat Cicerōnem Rōmā discedere.

Post Sullae mortem Cicerō magistrātūs petere incipiēbat. Omnēs magistrātūs, alium post alium, sibi obtinuit. Quaestor, aedīlis, praetor, cōnsul creātus est. Paulō ante cōnsul creātus rem pūblicam ē māximō perīculō ēripuit. Lūcius Sergius Catilīna, vir pessimus ōrdinis senātōriī, cōnsul creārī cupīvit, sed nōn potuit. Postquam Cicerō et Antōnius cōnsulēs factī sunt, Catilīna ūnā cum cēterīs sibi similibus, conjūrātiōnem fēcit et senātum occīdere, cōnsulēs interficere, urbem incendere, dīvitiās rapere cōnstituit. Cicerō, dē perīculīs ab amīcīs monitus, omnīnō quattuor ōrātiōnēs in Catilīnam habuit.

Catilīna, ubi post ōrātiōnem prīmam Cicerōnis in senātū intellēxit omnia cōnsilia sua cōgnita esse, Rōmā ad exercitum quem parāverat fūgit. Aliī sociī ējus quī in urbe mānserant captī sunt et paucīs post diēbus sine jūdiciō interfectī sunt. Catilīna ipse fortissimē pūgnāns in proeliō occīsus est.

Post mortem Catilīnae Cicerō multōs honōrēs accēpit. Posteā inimīcī ējus sub duce Clōdiō, pessimō virō, ex urbe eum expulērunt quod cīvēs Rōmānōs sine jūdiciō interficī jūsserat. Per labōrēs autem multōrum amīcōrum Cicerō Rōmam revocātus est.

Cicerō nōn jam negōtiīs pūblicīs sē dedit, sed trēs annōs multōs librōs dē rēbus philosophīcīs et rhētoricīs scrīpsit. Post mortem Caesaris multās ōrātiōnēs ācerrimās contrā Mārcum Antōnium scrīpsit. Posteā ubi Antōnius, Octāvius, Lepidus secundum triumvirātum fēcērunt, Antōnius Cicerōnem prōscrīpsit (*listed for death*). Hic fugiēns ab Antōnī mīlitibus captus et occīsus est. Caput et manūs māximī ōrātōris et scrīptōris Rōmānī in Rōstrīs, ubi Cicerō ōrātiōnēs clārissimās habuerat, positae sunt.

# *Comprehensive Review: Units* XLVI–L

A. Write the ablative singular, the gender, and meanings of these nouns. Indicate the declension to which each belongs.

| | | | | | |
|---|---|---|---|---|---|
| rēs | fidēs | ōrātor | conjūnx | juventūs | cōnsultum |
| ars | diēs | aciēs | tabula | invidia | cūstōdia |
| spēs | legiō | cohors | ōrātiō | saeculum | conjūrātiō |

B. Write the Latin:

| | | | | | | |
|---|---|---|---|---|---|---|
| when | above | former | several | following | in all | certain one |
| ever | again | learned | immortal | so great | the others | on account of |
| how | thence | almost | perpetual | each one | how great | of what kind |

C. Decline in Latin and give meanings:

  SINGULAR: a more learned orator; a stronger faith; greater hope
  PLURAL: greatest thing; longest day; bravest legion

D. Compare in Latin and translate:

  doctus    parum    multum    gravis

E. Decline in Latin and translate:

cūstōdia    tribūnus    cōnsultum    cohors    impetus    aciēs (sing.)

F. Write in Latin and translate all the infinitives, active and passive, of these verbs:

  trānsportō    sustineō    incendō    dēdō    incipiō    mūniō

G. Write in Latin and translate the present and future active and the perfect passive participles of these verbs:

  exīstimō    respondeō    ēripiō    dēpōnō    sciō

H. Write in Latin and translate the present imperative, singular and plural, positive and negative, of these verbs:

  intrō    excipiō    spērō    mūniō    augeō    lūdō    occīdō

I. Write in Latin and translate these synopses, active and passive, in the indicative mood: third person singular: opprimō, exīstimō; second person plural: intellegō, sentiō.

J. Write in Latin the specified forms and translate:
1. dative plural: ea legiō
2. ablative singular: ōrātor ipse
3. accusative plural: cōnsultum grave
4. passive participle: suspiciō, redūcō
5. present and future participles: dīmittō
6. perfect infinitives, active and passive: cūstōdiō
7. comparative and superlative: bonus, male

## SENTENCE PATTERNS

A. Translate into English. Identify the participles and infinitives:
1. Dīcunt neque Caesarem neque Pompēium parem habēre cupīvisse.
2. Mārius ab equitibus Sullae fugiēns captus est.
3. Caesar intellegēbat prōvinciās gladiō occupātās gladiō administrārī dēbēre.
4. Tandem Rōmānī complūribus gentibus in prōvinciīs habitantibus plūrima jūra cīvium Rōmānōrum cessērunt.
5. Nōnne multī eum monuerant mortem ad eum Īdibus Mārtiīs ventūram esse?
6. Sulla intellēxit imperium tōtīus bellī Māriō datum esse.
7. Multōs cīvēs captōs ad oppidum dūcī audīvimus.
8. Ducēs exercitūs deōs Rōmānīs auxilium datūrōs esse spērāvērunt.
9. Hunc rēgem ab imperātōre vincī posse putābant.
10. Num exercitum Rōmānum hostēs in fugam dedisse audīvērunt?

*293*

B. Translate into Latin.

1. I saw the army of Caesar entering the city.
2. He hoped that the consuls would give him other orders.
3. Did he know that the senate was hostile to him?
4. They always thought that their city could not be taken.
5. They said that they saw the soldiers who had been wounded.

## SIGHT TRANSLATION: PANDORA

Antīquīs temporibus (ita ā poētis narrātur) genus gigantum (*giants*) in terrā vīvēbat. Apud gigantēs erant duo frātrēs, Promētheus et Epimētheus. Aliī dīcunt Promētheum īgnem ex caelō rapuisse et hominibus miserīs dedisse. Juppiter maleficiō Promētheī īrātus erat et eum gravissimē pūnīre cōnstituit. Dīcitur deus igitur Vulcānum, deum īgnis, prīmam fēminam creāre prō Promētheō jūssisse.

Māximā cum cūrā ex argillā (*clay*) facta est et Pandōra appellāta est, quod omnia dōna, pulchritūdō, sapientia, mūsica, et cētera, eī ā deīs ac deābus data sunt. Mercurius puellam pulchram ad Promētheum dūxit, quī dīxit sē illam habēre nōn cupere.

Frāter ējus autem eam vīdit et māgnō cum studiō Pandōram petītam uxōrem obtinuit. Arcam (*box*) eī ā Jove datam habuit. Arca multās rēs et sēcrētās tenuit, sed pater deōrum eam arcam aperīre (*open*) vetuit (*forbade*). Pandōra conjugī suō arcam dedit, sed dum conjūnx abest, cūriōsitāte eam aperuit. Statim morbī (*diseases*) et multa mala ex arcā volāvērunt et haec super tōtam terram extendisse dīcunt.

Pandōra perterrita arcam vacuam Epimētheō dēmōnstrāvit. Spēs autem ex arcā nōn fūgerat. Epimētheus īrātus sē conjugem pūnītūrum esse prōmīsit, sed spēs posteā dolōrēs et mala vītae levāvit.

"This was the noblest Roman of them all!"
—Marc Antony (spoken about Brutus)
William Shakespeare, 1564–1616
*Julius Caesar*

# *Unit* LI

## CONVERSATION

MAGISTER: Quis, Caesare interfectō, Rōmae imperium obtinuit?

PETRUS: Mārcus Antōnius, optimus Caesaris amīcus, omnem potestātem cēpit, sed rēs pessimē administrāvit.

MAGISTER: Cūr prīncipēs conjūrātiōnis, Brūtō et Cassiō ducentibus, summum imperium nōn sūmpsērunt?

JŪLIA: Ob Antōnī ōrātiōnem populus Rōmānus, brevī tempore intermissō, Brūtī ac Cassī ac cēterōrum mortem postulāvit. Hī quam celerrimē ex urbe fūgērunt et sēcum māgnās cōpiās ēdūxērunt.

MAGISTER: Quem Caesar ante mortem adoptāverat?

HENRĪCUS: Octāvius, sorōris Caesaris nepōs (*grandson*), ā Caesare adoptātus erat. Morte Caesaris cōgnitā, Rōmam quam prīmum prōcessit et exercitum cōnscrīpsit.

MAGISTER: Cum Antōniō diū contendit. Uterque alterum vincere temptābat, sed nihil effectum est. Tandem pāx inter eōs cōnfīrmāta est, et Lepidus eīs sē jūnxit. Triumvirī, inimīcīs prōscrīptīs atque interfectīs, bona rapuērunt.

# Ablative Absolute

▶ DISCUSSION

1. In English we sometimes say: *Such being the case, we shall not go on.* *Such being the case* is grammatically independent of the rest of the sentence. This construction is called the *nominative absolute* because the noun or its substitute is in the nominative case and, with the participle, is *independent* of all other parts of the sentence. In Latin this construction is frequently used, but the words are in the *ablative* instead of the nominative case. Hence, the phrase is called *ablative absolute*.

2. An ablative absolute may consist of:

A noun or pronoun and a participle.

**Obsidibus datīs,**    *Hostages having been given,*
**Caesar pācem faciet.**    Caesar will make peace.

A noun or pronoun and an adjective.

| | |
|---|---|
| *Mīlitibus fortibus,* | *The soldiers (being) brave,* |
| **urbs servāta est.** | the city was saved. |

Two nouns.

| | |
|---|---|
| *Caesare duce,* | *Caesar (being) leader,* |
| **mīlitēs fortiter pūgnāvērunt.** | the soldiers fought bravely. |

3. The meaning of the ablative absolute is usually best expressed in English by an adverbial clause. Always choose the translation that seems to express the thought most accurately in English. Observe carefully each translation of the following Latin sentence:

### *Obsidibus datīs,* **Caesar pācem fēcit.**

Literal translation:      a. *The hostages having been given,*

As subordinate clause:

(temporal)      b. *When the hostages were (had been) given,*

     c. *After the hostages were (had been) given,*

     d. *As soon as the hostages were (had been) given,*

(causal)      e. *Since the hostages were (had been) given,*

     f. *Because the hostages were (had been) given,*

     g. *As the hostages were (had been) given,*

(concessive)      h. *Although the hostages were (had been) given,*

(conditional)      i. *If the hostages were (had been) given,*

As a main clause:      j. *The hostages were (had been) given, and*

Caesar made peace.

▶ STUDY HELPS

1. Since the perfect passive participle denotes time before that of the main verb, it may be translated by the pluperfect tense, as in the translations above.

2. *Caesare duce* (composed of two nouns) may be translated: *with Caesar as leader,* or *under Caesar's leadership.*

3. *Caesare vīvō* (composed of a noun and an adjective) may be translated: *while Caesar was alive.*

4. *Hostibus venientibus* (composed of a noun and present participle)

is generally translated into English by a clause with *when* or *while:*
*when* or *while the enemy were coming.*

5. The noun or pronoun in the ablative absolute *never* denotes the same person or things as the subject or the object of the main verb; therefore, do not confuse the *participle used as a clause* and the *ablative absolute.*

**Mīles *vulnerātus* captus est.**   The soldier *who was wounded* was seized.

***Vulnerātus*** is a *participle* agreeing with the subject **mīles.**

**Mīlite *vulnerātō*, amīcus ējus**   *The soldier having been wounded,* his
**fūgit.**                            friend fled.

***Mīlite vulnerātō*** is an *ablative absolute* and has no grammatical connection with the rest of the sentence.

▶ PRACTICE PATTERNS

A. Translate into English as many ways as possible:

| | | |
|---|---|---|
| aciē īnstrūctā | imperiō sumptō | mīlitibus cōnscrīptīs |
| Augustō duce | portīs clausīs | Cicerōne prīvātō |
| pāce effectā | cōnsultō gravī | brevī tempore intermissō |
| inimīcīs prōscrīptīs | exercitū ēductō | virīs inter sē pūgnantibus |

B. Translate into Latin:

the fields having been laid waste     the baggage being light
the men being private citizens     with me as your general
while the soldiers were fortifying     the gates having been closed

## WORDS TO MASTER

**clau′dō, −ere, clausī, clausus** (3), close, shut in (*clause*)

**cōnscrī′bō, −ere, −scrīpsī, −scrīptus** (3), enroll, enlist (*conscription*)

**ēdū′cō, −ere, −dūxī, −ductus** (3), lead out (*educate*)

**effi′ciō, −ere, −fēcī, −fectus** (3), bring about, complete (*effect*)

**īgnō′tus, −a, −um,** *adj.,* unknown, strange

**īn′struō, −ere, −strūxī, −strūctus,** arrange, build (*instruct*); **aciem īnstruere,** draw up a line of battle

**intermit′tō, −ere, −mīsī, −missus** (3), interrupt, cease; *pass.,* elapse (*intermission*)

**le′vis, −e,** *adj.,* light, fickle (*levity*)

**prīvā′tus, −a, −um,** *adj.,* private; **prīvā′tus, −ī,** *m.,* private citizen (*private*)

**prōscrī′bō, −ere, −scrīpsī, −scrīptus** (3), outlaw, list publicly for death (*proscribe*)

**sū′mō, −ere, sūmpsī, sūmptus** (3), take up (*sumptuous*)

**ves′per, −erī,** *m.,* evening (*Vespers*)

## BUILDING WORD POWER

*Ante* as a preposition and as a prefix means *before, prior to, in front of.* Do you know that if someone tells you your hat is *antediluvian,* he means that it was in style before the Flood?

*Antīquus (antīcus)* is one of the few words in Latin composed only of a prefix and a suffix (*ante + -icus*). Most words that end in *-ic* in English end in *-ique* in French, as *antic* and *antique* from the original Latin *antīquus.* The word *antic* was first used in connection with designs and figures unearthed in Rome because they were *ancient.* What is old or ancient often seems strange or ludicrous to a more modern generation. Now the word *antic* means a *fantastic trick* or *caper,* although originally it meant *ancient.*

*Circum* means *around,* from the Latinized Greek word *circus,* meaning *ring.* The Circus Maximus was a circular place for exhibitions. Is our modern *circus* a circular place?

Who first *circumnavigated* the globe? When you *circumscribe* a triangle, which is on the outside, the triangle or the circle? If a person is *circumspect* or cautious, he looks all around the matter before he acts. *Circumlocution* means talking around; it is the use of many words to say something that could be said in a few words. What does *circumvent* mean?

## SENTENCE PATTERNS

A. Translate into English:

1. Paucīs diēbus intermissīs, imperātor omnia ad bellum pertinentia parāvit.
2. Numā rēge, portae templi Jānī clausae sunt.
3. Potestāte ab Antōniō sūmptā, Octāvius cum eō diū contendit.
4. Mīlibus mīlitum cōnscrīptīs, cōnsul ad prōvinciam properāvit.
5. Lepidus captus Rōmam missus est ubi prīvātus vīxit.
6. Factīs Brūtī īgnōtīs, Caesar illum esse optimum amīcum putābat.
7. Cōpiīs ēductīs et īnstructīs, imperātor mandāta nūntiāvit.
8. Pāce effectā, Octāvius sōlus summum imperium tenēbat.
9. Inimīcīs proscrīptīs, Antōnius bona eōrum ēripere poterat.
10. Cīvēs pācem post plūrima bella habentēs studiīs litterārum sē dant.

B. Using the ablative absolute where possible, translate into Latin:

1. After the soldiers were led out, battle was begun without delay.
2. Although several months had elapsed, he still did not manage the affairs well.
3. All the wars having been finished, there was peace.
4. They say he began to prepare all things pertaining to war.
5. While Caesar was alive, Brutus seemed to be his best friend.

## On with the Show

In the ancient Roman world there were no commercial theaters. Plays were presented at the times of the games on temporary wooden stages. The first permanent theater was erected in 55 B.C. under the direction of Pompey in the Campus Martius at Rome. It was built of stone and had a seating capacity of about 27,000.

Although it was patterned after the Greek theater, it differed in several ways. Greek theaters were excavated out of the side of a hill. A circular space in front of the stage, where choruses and actors performed, was called the *orchestra*. Roman theaters were built on level ground; as Roman plays seldom had a chorus, what might have been the orchestra became a semicircle in front of the stage.

The Romans never liked tragedies and therefore never wrote original tragedies. The comedies written by Plautus and Terence were really translations from Greek plays, dealt with Greek life, and were given in Greek costumes. Large portions of these comedies were recited to music or were sung while the actors danced.

Since there was no artificial lighting in the theaters, plays had to be presented in the daytime. They seem to have lasted about two hours. Sometimes the audience did not think this was long enough and refused to go home. Then understudies of the famous actors would come out and imitate them in what was similar to amateur vaudeville shows.

The actors in the plays were all slaves. Men played the parts of women. The stock characters were rich man, king, soldier, slave, young man, and young woman. Sometimes an actor played two or more parts in the same play; the only important change needed was of a mask or wig. The masks and wigs used in tragedies differed from those used in comedies.

The masks, a necessity for all actors, had cheek supports and resonance chambers that acted as amplifiers. Gray wigs were used for old men, black for young men, red for slaves. Young men wore brightly colored clothing; old men wore white. Thus the characters could be easily identified.

For a comedy the stage scenery usually represented a street, with an entrance at each end, one toward the town, the other toward the sea. The fronts of two or three houses, with doors that opened, provided backstage scenery. Entrances and exits were through the doors or at either end of the street. Later, stage scenery in the form of prisms was used. These could be turned to represent a palace, prison, or whatever was needed.

If a murder was essential to the plot, a platform was rolled out suddenly onto the stage. The murderer stood with his dripping dagger. The victim was at his feet. Nothing was said. After the audience had duly gasped, the platform was rolled back, the indications of murder were washed away, and the supposed corpse would reappear in another part.

Admission to these plays was free to every citizen. Women were not admitted to comedies, but they could be present at tragedies. In later times no such restrictions were made. The chariot races and gladiatorial combats were always more popular than plays, which gradually degenerated info the lowest and the coarsest pantomimes and mimes. Finally, under the influence of Christianity, these disappeared entirely.

### Augustus: Imperātor et Prīnceps

Mārcus Brūtus, quod hominem interficere prō bonō pūblicō jūstum esse exīstimābat, conjūrātiōnem contrā Caesarem, amīcum suum, facere nōn dubitāvit. Populō Rōmānō māgnopere incitātō ab Antōniō contrā hominēs quī Caesarem interfēcerant, Brūtus et sociī ex urbe fūgērunt. Antōnius, dux Caesaris partis (*party*) creātus, bellum cīvīle effēcit. Caesar, quī nūllum fīlium habēbat, Gājum Octāvium fīlium fīliae sorōris adoptāverat.

Caesare interfectō, Octāvius in Ītaliam quam celerrimē vēnit et cum Antōniō bellum gessit. Magistrātum Caesaris sibi capere cupīvit, sed ante adventum ējus Antōnius, parte Caesaris adjuvante, in manūs omnem potestātem cēperat.

Brevī tempore intermissō, multīs cōpiīs novīs cōnscrīptīs, Octāvius cum duābus legiōnibus Caesaris quae eī sē trādiderant, cum Antōniō diū contendit. Antōniō victō, Octāvius cum Antōniō et Lepidō secundum triumvirātum fēcit. Illī plūrimōs inimīcōs prōscrīpsērunt, inter quōs, ut suprā dēmōnstrāvimus, erat Cicerō, quī ōrātiōnēs multās et ācrēs contrā Antōnium habuerat. Inimīcīs interfectīs, bona et dīvitiās rapere poterant.

Jūnctīs triumvirōrum exercitibus, Octāvius et Antōnius in Graeciam nāvigāvērunt et in māgnō proeliō Philippīs Brūtum et Cassium vīcērunt. Brūtus statim sē interfēcit. Bellō cōnfectō, Lepidus in Āfricam, Āntōnius in Āsiam prōcessit. Octāvius sōlus Rōmam properāvit.

Quīnque annīs intermissīs, Octāvius in Siciliam nāvigāvit et ibi Sextum, fīlium Pompējī, facillimē vīcit. Octāvius, quī Lepidum auxilium Sextō dedisse exīstimāvit, hunc captum Rōmam mīsit, ubi Lepidus prīvātus per reliquam vītam suam ēgit. Antōnius in Aegyptō, quod sē Cleopātram rēgīnam amāre putābat, uxōrem suam Octāviam, sorōrem Octāvī, dīmīsit.

Octāvius īrātus omnēs rēs ad bellum pertinentēs parāvit, et ad Aegyptum nāvigāvit. Apud Actium, oppidum Graecum, pūgnātum est. Uterque classem in aciē īnstrūxit. Aliae nāvēs Antōnī sē in fugam dēdērunt; aliae Octāviō sē trādidērunt. Antōnius, postquam exercitus ējus etiam Octāviō sē trādidit, in Aegyptum fūgit.

Proximō annō Octāvius in Aegyptum nāvigāvit, sed Antōnius et Cleopātra, quī eum venīre audīvērunt, sē interfēcērunt. Omnibus inimīcīs victīs, Octāvius sōlus Rōmae summum imperium tenēbat. Augustus, Imperātor, Prīnceps ā senātū appellātus est.

The only good histories are those written by the persons themselves who commanded in the affairs whereof they write.
—Michel de Montaigne, 1533–1592

# Unit LII

## CONVERSATION

MAGISTER: Caesar scrībit Helvētiōs reliquōs incolās Galliae virtūte superāvisse. Crēdisne Caesarī?

ROBERTUS: Scīmus antīquīs temporibus Helvētiōs ferē cotīdiānīs (*daily*) proeliīs Germānīs restitisse et nocuisse.

MAGISTER: Quam ob rem Helvētiī cum Germānīs contendēbant?

MĀRCELLA: Interdum suīs fīnibus Germānōs prohibēbant; interdum ipsī in eōrum fīnibus bellum gerēbant.

MAGISTER: In quō locō habitābant Helvētiī?

HENRĪCUS: Gēns Helvētiōrum eam partem Galliae habitābat quae nunc "Switzerland" appellātur. Proximī erant Germānīs quī trāns Rhēnum vīvēbant. Genāva, māgnum oppidum quod erat in prōvinciā Rōmānā et in rīpīs Rhodanī (*Rhône*), proxima Helvētiōrum fīnibus erat.

MAGISTER: Imperāvitne Caesar obsidēs hostibus?

STEPHĀNUS: Hostibus victīs, Caesar obsidēs illīs saepe imperāvit, et illīs quī eī restitērunt nōn pepercit.

## SECTION 1 Dative with Special Verbs

▶ DISCUSSION

Certain verbs that are transitive in English have an indirect object in Latin instead of a direct object; but the dative is translated as if it were the accusative. Such verbs are: *favor, help, injure, please, trust, distrust, command, obey, serve, resist, threaten, envy, pardon, spare,* and *persuade.*

Notice in these sentences that the transitive English verbs really contain the idea of giving or showing that we find in verbs taking an indirect object.

| | |
|---|---|
| 1. *Suīs amīcīs* **favet.** | He favors (shows favors to) *his friends.* |
| 2. *Mihi* **imperat.** | He orders (gives orders to) *me.* |
| 3. *Hostibus* **restitērunt.** | They resisted (gave resistance to) *the enemy.* |
| 4. *Helvētiīs* **persuāsit.** | He persuaded (offered persuasion to) *the Helvetians.* |
| 5. **Patrēs** *plēbī* **nocuērunt.** | The patricians wronged (gave injury or harm to) *the people.* |
| 6. **Sociī** *pācī* **studēbant.** | The allies desired (were eager for) *peace.* |
| 7. *Cicerōnī* **cōnfīdēbant.** | They trusted (gave confidence to) *Cicero.* |

▶ STUDY HELPS

There are some exceptions to this rule, as *juvō,* help; *jubeō,* order; and *dēlectō,* please. These govern the accusative case.

▶ PRACTICE PATTERNS

A. Translate into English:

| | | | |
|---|---|---|---|
| parce mihi | vōbīs imperō | mihi persuāsit | vōbīs credent |
| tibi crēdō | hostī nocēbit | virīs imperat | amīcīs favēmus |
| nōbīs parce | pācī student | ducī persuāsit | hostibus resistam |

B. Translate into Latin:

| | | |
|---|---|---|
| Trust him. | He commanded the army. | Who trusts an enemy? |
| Believe me. | Spare your people. | I shall persuade you. |
| Resist them. | I was eager for help. | Did Caesar harm Rome? |
| Don't harm me. | He was eager for peace. | Who helped the leader? |

## SECTION 2 Dative with Compound Verbs

▶ DISCUSSION

Many verbs compounded with prepositions govern the dative of indirect object. They may be divided into two classes:

1. Intransitive verbs which cannot take a direct object.

    **Pompējus exercituī** *praefuit.*   Pompey *was in command of* the army.

2. Transitive verbs which can take a direct object and a dative of the indirect object, the indirect object depending on the preposition compounded with the verb.

    **Senātus Octāvium exercituī**   The senate *placed* Octavius *in com-*
        **praefēcit.**                *mand of* the army.

▶ STUDY HELPS

1. The following are among the prefixes used in these verbs: *ad, ante, con* (*cum*), *de, in, inter, ob, post, prae, pro, sub,* and *super.*

2. If the prefix is only adverbial, the accusative of the direct object only is used.

    **Cōpiās** *praemīsit.*   He *sent* the troops *ahead.*


## SECTION 3 Irregular Verb eō

▶ DISCUSSION

Certain verbs are called irregular because their inflection is different from that of the regular verbs. Learn the conjugation of the irregular verb **eō,** *go,* because it is very frequently used.

PRINCIPAL PARTS: **eō, īre, iī (īvī), itūrus**

INDICATIVE ACTIVE

| | Present Tense | | | Imperf. | **ībam** |
|---|---|---|---|---|---|
| | SING. | PL. | | Fut. | **ībō** |
| First | **eō** | **īmus** | | Perf. | **iī (īvī)** |
| Second | **īs** | **ītis** | | Pluperf. | **ieram (īveram)** |
| Third | **it** | **eunt** | | Fut. Perf. | **ierō (īverō)** |

▶ STUDY HELPS

1. The present stem *ī–* becomes *e–* before *a, o,* or *u.*
2. The future follows the model of the first conjugation.

3. The imperfect, perfect, pluperfect, and future perfect tenses are regular; the imperative is regular; the infinitives are regular, but the perfect infinitive may be **īsse** or **īvisse**.

4. The passive forms of **eō** are rare since it is intransitive. The compounds **adeō**, *I approach;* **ineō**, *I enter;* and **trānseō**, *I go across*, are transitive.

▶ **PRACTICE PATTERNS**

A. Write a synopsis of eō in the third person singular. Translate.

B. Prefix the following prepositions to īre and translate into English:

ab    ad    circum    ex    per    in    sub    trāns

C. Translate into Latin:

| | | | |
|---|---|---|---|
| He sent me ahead. | He went. | She had gone. | We shall go. |
| He was in command of the army. | I was going. | She has gone. | We are going. |
| | She will go. | She did go. | You (pl.) went. |
| He influences them. | We had gone. | I shall go. | Are you going? |

## WORDS TO MASTER

**addū′cō, –ere, –dūxī, –ductus (3)**, lead to, influence (*adduce*)

**conti′neō, –ēre, –uī, –tentus (2)**, hold together, hem in (*contain*)

**crē′dō, –ere, –didī, –ditus (3)**, trust, believe (*credible*)

**e′ō, īre, iī (īvī), itūrus, *irreg.*,** go, pass, march (*exit*)

**im′perō (1)**, order, command, rule, levy (*imperative*)

**indū′cō, –ere, –dūxī, –ductus (3)**, lead on, influence (*induce*)

**no′ceō, –ēre, –uī, — (2)**, injure, harm (*nocuous*)

**par′cō, –ere, pepercī, parsūrus (3)**, spare (*parsimony*)

**permo′veō, –ēre, –mōvī, –mōtus (2)**, influence, disturb, alarm

**persuā′deō, –ēre, –suāsī, –suāsūrus (2)**, persuade (*persuasion*)

**propte′reā, *adv.*,** on this account; **propte′reā quod, *conj.*,** because

**resis′tō, –ere, –stitī, — (3)**, withstand, resist (*resistance*)

## BUILDING WORD POWER

The usual meaning for the preposition **ob** is *on account of*. With verbs of motion it means *toward* or *to*. The prefix **ob–** has other meanings such as *against, before, upon*. Assimilation occurs before words beginning with **–c, –f,** or **–p**. The **–b** is dropped before **–m**. *Omission* (**omittere**) has only one **–m**, not two. What is the prefix in: **occurrere, officere, oppōnere?**

Did you ever toss a coin for heads or tails? How do you know which side is which? The face of a coin that has the principal figure or inscription, such as the head of Washington on a twenty-five-cent piece, is called the *obverse* side because it is turned toward you. This side is called *heads;* the reverse side, *tails.* The *obverse* side of anything is the side that is *facing* you; the *reverse* side is the opposite.

That which is *obvious* (**ob** + **via**) is facing you so that you cannot fail to see it. If we *obviate* something, we go toward it, meet it, and take it out of the way.

## SENTENCE PATTERNS

A. Translate into English:

1. Prīmā lūce proelium commīsērunt et hostibus diū restitērunt.
2. Helvētiī omnium rērum inopiā adductī lēgātōs ad Caesarem mīsērunt.
3. Itaque hāc ōrātiōne inductī et auctōritāte Orgetorīgis permōtī cōnstituērunt dē fīnibus suīs cum omnibus cōpiīs exīre.
4. Helvētiī undique flūminibus, montibus, lacū continēbantur.
5. Hōc modō facillimē sociīs persuāsit.
6. Prōvinciae quam māximum potest mīlitum numerum imperat.
7. Proptereā quod sē fīnēs habēre angustiōrēs crēdēbant, patriam relinquere statuērunt.
8. Ubi ea rēs Helvētiīs nūntiāta est, ducī conjūrātiōnis nōn pepercērunt.
9. Diē cōnstitūtā omnis familia Orgetorīgis ad jūdicium iit.
10. Nōnne dux, bellī et glōriae cupidus, patriae nocuit?

B. Translate into Latin:

1. Casticus, induced by the influence of Orgetorix, determined to seize the power in his own state.
2. The Helvetians believed that their country was too small.
3. The leaders were disturbed by the reasons of Orgetorix.
4. He, led on by the speech of the chief, made a conspiracy.
5. They prepared as large a number of men and as great a supply of grain as possible.

### The Fighting Helvetians

Saepe audīvimus Galliam in partēs trēs dīvīsam esse. Helvētiī eam partem Galliae quae nunc "Switzerland" appellātur habitābant. Illī erant proximī Germānīs, quī trāns flūmen Rhēnum (*Rhine*) habitābant. Reliquōs Gallōs virtūte superābant quod ferē cotīdiānīs (*daily*) proeliīs cum Germānīs contendēbant.

ORGETORIX ASSUMES LEADERSHIP

Apud Helvētiōs longē nōbilissimus fuit Orgetorīx. Ille summum imperium māgnopere cupīvit et conjūrātiōnem nōbilitātis fēcit. Helvētiōs dēbēre cum omnibus cōpiīs terrās novās ā Germānīs remōtās petere dīxit.

Facilius eīs persuāsit quod Helvētiī undique locī nātūrā continēbantur; ūnā ex parte flūmine Rhēnō, lātissimō et altissimō, quī agrum Helvēticum ā Germānīs dīvīsit; altera ex parte monte Jūrā altissimō; tertiā Lacū Lemannō (*Geneva*) et flūmine Rhodanō, quī prōvinciam Rōmānam ab Helvētiīs dīvīsit.

Prō (*in proportion to*) multitūdine autem hominum et prō glōriā bellī atque fortitūdinis sē angustiōrēs fīnēs habēre exīstimābant. Proptereā hominēs bellī cupidī fīnēs suōs relinquere cupiēbant.

### THE HELVETIANS PLAN THEIR GREAT MIGRATION

Hīs rēbus adductī et auctōritāte Orgetorīgis permōtī, Helvētiī carrōrum quam māximum numerum, frūmentī quam māximam cōpiam parābant. Cum proximīs cīvitātibus pācem et amīcitiam cōnfirmāre cōnstituērunt.

### CONSPIRACY OF ORGETORIX

Orgetorix dux creātus sibi lēgātiōnem ad cīvitātēs fīnitimās suscēpit. In hōc itinere Casticus Sēquanus, auctōritāte Orgetorīgis inductus, rēgnum in cīvitāte suā occupāre statuit, quod pater ante habuerat. Itaque Dumnorīgī Haeduō, frātrī Dīviciācī, quī eō tempore prīncipātum in cīvitāte obtinēbat, idem persuāsit, eīque fīliam suam in mātrimōnium sē datūrum esse prōmīsit. "Ipse meae cīvitātis imperium obtentūrus sum. Facillimē rēgnum occupāre atque tōtīus Galliae imperium obtinēre possumus. Omnibus meīs cōpiīs vōs adjūvābō." Orgetorīx hīs verbīs trēs fīrmissimōs populōs conjūnxit.

### BETRAYAL AND TRIAL OF ORGETORIX

Ea rēs Helvētiīs nūntiāta est. Omnis familia Orgetorīgis ad jūdicium vēnit, sed Orgetorīx causam suam numquam dīxit (*pleaded his case*). Ipse sē interfēcit.

Temple of Antoninus and Faustina. Inside this temple in the Roman Forum a baroque Catholic church was built in the seventeenth century. The statue in the foreground shows a vestal virgin.

The Arch of Titus. Titus, a general, ruled Rome from A.D. 79 to A.D. 81.

D-2

Roman milestones.

The Judaean triumph of Titus. Detail from the Arch of Titus.

A street in Pompeii.

A Roman "taxicab."

Double-arched aqueduct in Segovia, Spain. The Romans
built this conduit for carrying water about A.D. 100.

The Temple of Cybele. Cybele was a nature goddess of ancient Asia Minor and is identified with Ops, the Roman goddess of the harvest and wife of Saturn. Located near the Forum, this first-century B.C. structure is also wrongly known as the Temple of Vesta.

D-6

The theatre at Aspendos. Built in the second century A.D.,
this is the best-preserved Roman amphitheatre in Asia Minor.

Detail from the Column of Marcus Aurelius Antoninus. Marcus Aurelius ruled as emperor from A.D. 161 to A.D. 180. He is remembered as a Stoic philosopher.

# *Unit* LIII

## CONVERSATION

MAGISTER: Vultisne plūrēs fābulās dē Caesare audīre?

PAULUS: Puerī fābulās dē bellīs saepe audīre volunt.

PAULĪNA: Paucae puellae dē proeliīs fābulās audīre volunt, etsī patrēs ac frātrēs eārum in bellō prō patriā pūgnāvērunt.

JŪLIA: Ego dē bellō numquam audīre volō, sed Caesarem admīror.

PAULUS: Quid Caesar fēcit ubi eī nūntiātum est Helvētiōs ex agrīs exīsse et per prōvinciam Rōmānam iter facere cōnārī? Num eōs prōvinciam Rōmānam inīre passus est?

MAGISTER: Caesar, quī prōvinciae Galliae praefuit, Rōmā profectus quam māximīs potest itineribus in Galliam contendit et ad Genāvam pervēnit. Quid deinde, Paule, Caesarem facere voluisse arbitrāris?

PAULUS: Cōpiae eī dēfuērunt, et prōvinciae quam plūrimōs poterat mīlitēs imperāvit. Etiam pontem quī erat ad Genāvam dēlērī voluit. Ad Genāvam erat lacus.

PAULĪNA: Helvētiī ad fīnēs suōs redīre nōn potuērunt. Lēgātōs igitur ad Caesarem mīsērunt, nōbilissimōs cīvitātis.

## SECTION 1 Deponent Verbs

▶ DISCUSSION

1. A deponent verb is *passive* in *form* and *active* in *meaning.* Such a verb is called *deponent* (from **dēpōnere,** *lay aside*) because it has *laid aside* or lost its active forms and passive meanings.

2. Deponent verbs are found in all the four regular conjugations. They are conjugated throughout the indicative and the subjunctive like regular verbs of the four conjugations in the *passive.* The principal parts of model deponent verbs given here should be carefully memorized.

| CONJUGATION | PRES. INDIC. | PRES. INF. | PERF. INDIC. |
|---|---|---|---|
| First | **cōnor** = *I attempt* | **cōnārī** | **cōnātus sum** |
| Second | **vereor** = *I fear* | **verērī** | **veritus sum** |
| Third | **sequor** = *I follow* | **sequī** | **secūtus sum** |
| Third–**io** | **patior** = *I suffer* | **patī** | **passus sum** |
| Fourth | **largior** = *I bestow* | **largīrī** | **largītus sum** |

**307**

A. Write synopses of these verbs in the third person singular. Translate

  cōnor   vereor   sequor   patior   largior

B. Write in Latin:

| | | | |
|---|---|---|---|
| Shall I try? | He will follow. | I endured. | Are you trying? |
| Have I tried? | We will set out. | She bestowed. | Does he fear? |

# SECTION 2 Participles of Deponent Verbs

▶ DISCUSSION

Deponent verbs have all the *participles* of regular verbs. There is one difference in translation. The perfect participle of the deponent verb is the exact equivalent of the English active participle: **cōnātus** = *having tried*. It must *not* be translated *having been tried*.

▶ PRACTICE PATTERNS

A. Translate:

  veritus   secūtus   passus   largītus   profectus

B. Write and translate all the participles of:

  cōnor   vereor   sequor   patior   largior   proficīscor

C. Write in Latin the masculine singular:

| | | | |
|---|---|---|---|
| setting out | fearing | about to set out | having followed |
| having feared | following | having bestowed | about to bestow |
| having tried | suffering | about to suffer | about to try |

# SECTION 3 Infinitives of Deponent Verbs

▶ DISCUSSION

Deponent verbs have three *infinitives*, all active in meaning. The present and the perfect are passive in form, active in meaning: **cōnārī** = *to try;* **cōnātus esse** = *to have tried.* The future is active in form and in meaning: **cōnātūrus esse** = *to be about to try.*

▶ PRACTICE PATTERNS

A. Write all the infinitives of the following verbs and translate:

  cōnor   vereor   sequor   patior   largior

B. Write a synopsis in the third person plural, and write all the participles and the infinitives of: proficīscor. Translate.

# SECTION 4 Irregular Verb *volō*

▶ **DISCUSSION**

The present indicative of **volō**, *be willing, wish*, is irregular. The other tenses are regularly formed. There is no passive and no imperative. **Volēns,** *willing*, is the only participle.

PRINCIPAL PARTS: **volō, velle, voluī, —**

INDICATIVE ACTIVE

| | Present Tense | | | |
|---|---|---|---|---|
| | SING. | PL. | Imperf. | **volēbam** |
| | | | Fut. | **volam** |
| First | **volō** | **volumus** | Perf. | **voluī** |
| Second | **vīs** | **vultis** | Pluperf. | **volueram** |
| Third | **vult** | **volunt** | Fut. Perf. | **voluerō** |

▶ **PRACTICE PATTERNS**

A. Write a synopsis in the third person plural of: volō. Translate.

B. Translate into English:

| duce volente | quid vīs? | volō scrībere |
|---|---|---|
| vidēre volēbant | nēmō vult | volō eum scrībere |

C. Translate into Latin:

| to wish | he, wishing to set forth | they wish to be in command of |
|---|---|---|
| to have wished | he wishes to go out | the man being willing |

## WORDS TO MASTER

**cō'nor** (1), *dep.,* strive, try, attempt (*conative*)

**dē'sum, –esse, –fuī, –futūrus,** *irreg.,* be wanting, fail

**ex'eō, –īre, –iī, –itūrus,** *irreg.,* go forth, go out (*exit*)

**in'eō, –īre, –iī, –itus,** *irreg.,* go into, enter on (*initiate*)

**la'cus, –ūs,** *m.,* lake

**pa'tior, patī, passus sum** (3), *dep.,* suffer, endure, undergo, allow, permit (*patient*)

**praefi'ciō, –ere, –fēcī, –fectus** (3), place in command of (*perfect*)

**prae'sum, –esse, –fuī, –futūrus,** *irreg.,* be in command of (*present*)

**proficīs'cor, –ī, –fectus sum** (3), *dep.,* set out, start out

**re'deō, –īre, –iī, –itūrus,** *irreg.,* go back, return

**se'quor, –ī, secūtus sum** (3), *dep.,* follow (*sequence*)

**vo'lō, vel'le, vo'luī, —,** *irreg.,* wish, be willing (*volition*)

## BUILDING WORD POWER

Not all words that begin with *post–* are from the Latin preposition **post,** which means *behind* or *after*. *Post* meaning *mail* and *post* meaning *a military position* are both derived from **positus,** the perfect passive participle of **pōnere,** *to place.* The *post* of *doorpost* is from **postis,** which is the Latin word for *doorpost.*

Many think that the word *posthumous, following after death,* is from **post + humus** *(ground),* but it is really from the Latin word **postumus,** meaning *last,* the superlative degree of **posterus,** which in turn is derived from **post,** *after.*

Did you ever write a *postscript* to a letter or *postpone* an engagement or take a *postprandial* nap? What are the youth of today doing to pass on the torch of liberty to the *posterity* of America?

**SENTENCE PATTERNS**

A. Translate into English:

1. Voluēruntne Helvētiī per prōvinciam nostram iter facere?
2. Nōnne fīnitimī, oppidīs incēnsīs, Helvētiōs sequī cōnātī sunt?
3. Caesar ab urbe profectus est et ad Genāvam pervēnit.
4. Voluntne hostēs sine ūllō maleficiō ē fīnibus suīs exīre?
5. Num intellegistis illōs prōvinciam nostram inīre voluisse?
6. Quī Caesarem hunc lēgātum cōpiīs praeficere velle dīxit?
7. Fortūnā volente, nōbīs cibus auxiliumque numquam dēerunt.
8. Nōlīte hostēs patī iter facere per prōvinciam.
9. Quam ob rem lēgātus prīmae legiōnī praefuit?
10. Oppida vīcōsque incendērunt quod sē nōn reditūrōs esse spērāvērunt.

B. Translate into Latin:

1. Did Caesar wish the Helvetians to return to their own territory?
2. Caesar, who was in command of the province, placed Labienus in charge of the tenth legion.
3. They said they would do no harm, didn't they?
4. We are about to set out at once.
5. Caesar tried to levy as many soldiers as possible.

Bellerophon about to attack the chimera.

**Bellerophon and Pegasus**

**W**hen Bellerophon, a son of the king of Corinth, came to visit Iobates, King of Lycia, he learned that a chimera was destroying the fields of Lycia and killing many of its citizens. A chimera was a horrible monster whose body was a compound of a lion and a goat, its hind legs those of a dragon, and its breath of fire. The king of Lycia had sought in vain throughout Greece for a hero capable of destroying the monster.

In a letter that Bellerophon brought from Proteus, son-in-law of Iobates, were instructions to kill the bearer, who, of course, knew nothing of the contents of the letter. Iobates, thinking Bellerophon could not possibly return from such a mission, sent the hero to fight the chimera.

Before going into combat, he consulted an oracle of the gods and was counseled to seek the winged horse Pegasus, which had sprung from the blood of the Gorgon Medusa. This horse had been caught by Minerva and had been presented by her to the Muses. These nine daughters of Jupiter and Mnemosyne were patronesses of various phases of literature, art, and science.

Bellerophon passed the night in the temple of Minerva. While he slept, the goddess brought him a golden bridle. With the help of this bridle, he captured and mastered Pegasus. Riding the winged horse, Bellerophon sped through the air, found the chimera, and, avoiding its deadly breath, sent his arrows into the monster from every side.

Afterward Bellerophon died in a rash attempt to reach Olympus, and Pegasus returned to the service of the Muses.

## A Deserted Homeland

Post Orgetorīgis mortem Helvētiī id quod cōnstituērunt facere cōnātī sunt, id est, ē fīnibus suīs exīre. Ubi sē ad eam rem parātōs esse putāvērunt, oppida sua omnia plūrimōsque vīcōs incendērunt. Frūmentum omne, praeter quod sēcum portātūrī erant, eōdem tempore incendērunt, quod exīstimābant sē, spē reditūs āmissā, facilius omnia perīcula sustentūrōs esse. Haec eadem fīnitimīs suīs persuāsērunt. Suīs oppidīs vīcīsque incēnsīs, quattuor gentēs Gallicae cum Helvētiīs proficīscī parāvērunt.

### A CHOICE OF ROUTES

Erant itinera duo quibus domō exīre possent (*they could*); ūnum per Sēquanōs, angustum et difficile, inter montem Jūram et flūmen Rhodanum; alterum, multō facilius, per prōvinciam nostram. Prīncipēs Helvētiōrum suīs nūntiāvērunt: "Per prōvinciam Rōmanam iter faciēmus." Omnibus rebus comparātīs, diē cōnstitūtā ad rīpam Rhodanī omnēs convēnērunt.

### THE FIRST BLITZKRIEG

Caesarī, quī prōvinciae Galliae praefuit, nūntiātum est Helvētiōs per prōvinciam nostram iter facere cōnārī. Ab urbe profectus est et quam māximīs poterat itineribus in Galliam contendit et ad (in the vicinity of) Genāvam pervēnit. Prōvinciae tōtī quam māximum poterat mīlitum numerum imperāvit, et pontem quī erat ad Genāvam dēlērī jūssit. Ubi dē ējus adventū Helvētiī cōgnōvērunt, lēgātōs ad eum mīsērunt, nōbilissimōs cīvitātis. Dīxērunt sē sine ūllō maleficiō iter per prōvinciam factūrōs esse et sē aliud iter nūllum habēre.

### CAESAR'S REPLY

Caesar, quod memoriā tenēbat Lūcium Cassium cōnsulem occīsum (esse) exercitumque ējus ab Helvētiīs pulsum (esse) et sub jugum missum (esse), eīs hoc concēdere nōlēbat (was unwilling). Tamen quod mīlitēs quōs imperāverat nōndum convēnerant, respondit sē tempus ad dēlīberandum (to deliberate) sūmptūrum (esse); atque eōs ad Īdūs Aprīlēs revenīre jūssit.

O Julius Caesar! thou art mighty yet!
Thy spirit walks abroad, and turns our swords
In our own proper entrails.
  —William Shakespeare, 1564–1616
   *Julius Caesar*

# *Unit* LIV

## CONVERSATION

MAGISTER: Caesar erat vir māgnā virtūte quī summus dux factus est. Cōnsiliīs Helvētiōrum cōgnitīs, quid fecit?

CORNĒLIUS: Ubi Caesarī nūntiātum est Helvētiōs cōnsilium cēpisse per agrum Sēquanōrum et Haeduōrum trānsīre in eōs fīnēs prope prōvinciam Rōmānam, commōtus cōnsilia sua cēpit.

MAGISTER: Quam ob rem cōnsilium Helvētiōrum Caesarī nōn grātum erat?

CORNĒLIA: Hoc māximō cum perīculō prōvinciae futūrum esse scīvit.

MAGISTER: Quae Caesar illō tempore fierī volēbat?

JŪLIUS: Caesar Helvētiōs vī ac virtūte repellere studēbat. Rīpās flūminis mūniēbat et item eī mūnītiōnī quam fēcerat Titum Labiēnum lēgātum, mīlitem māgnā fortitūdine, praefēcit.

MAGISTER:    Cūr Caesar ipse in Ītaliam māgnīs itineribus contendit?
CORNĒLIUS:   In Ītaliā duās legiōnēs cōnscrīpsit et trēs legiōnēs veterānās
             ēdūxit. Vir māximae celeritātis per Alpēs cum hīs quīnque
             legiōnibus impedīmenta ferentibus contendit.

# SECTION 1 Irregular Verb *ferō*

▶ DISCUSSION

*Ferō,* *bear, carry,* may be considered a verb of the third conjugation
with a few irregular forms in the present tense of the indicative, the imperative, and the infinitive.

PRINCIPAL PARTS: **ferō, ferre, tulī, lātus**

INDICATIVE ACTIVE

|        | Present Tense |          |           |            |
|--------|--------|----------|-----------|------------|
|        | SING.  | PL.      |           |            |
|        |        |          | Imperf.   | **ferēbam** |
|        |        |          | Fut.      | **feram**   |
| First  | **ferō** | **ferimus** | Perf.   | **tulī**    |
| Second | **fers** | **fertis**  | Pluperf.| **tuleram** |
| Third  | **fert** | **ferunt**  | Fut. Perf. | **tulerō** |

▶ STUDY HELPS

1. The –*i* is lost in the second and third persons singular and in the
second person plural of the active voice, as above.
2. The formation of the passive of **ferō** is regular except that –*i* is
lost in the third person singular, *feri̸tur = fertur,* and –*e* is lost in the
second person singular, *feri̸ris = ferris.*
3. The present imperative, singular and plural, is *fer, ferte.*
4. The present infinitive active is *ferre, to carry;* passive, *ferrī, to
be carried.*

▶ PRACTICE PATTERNS

A. Write a synopsis, third person singular, active and passive of the
verb: ferō. Translate each form.
B. Write the participles and infinitives, active and passive, of ferō
and translate each form.
C. Write in Latin:

| | | |
|---|---|---|
| they were carried | I was being carried | it is carried |
| carrying (m. pl.) | having been carried (n. pl.) | we shall carry |
| I was carrying | about to carry (m. sing) | you (sing.) had carried |

**313**

# SECTION 2 Ablative and Genitive of Description

▶ DISCUSSION

1. The ablative modified by an adjective may be used to describe a person or thing:

**homō *māgnā virtūte***    a man *of great courage*
                     a man *with great courage*

2. The genitive modified by an adjective may also be used to describe a person or thing:

**mūrus *trium pedum***      a wall *of three feet*

3. The ablative is regularly used to express temporary qualities, but is sometimes also used for permanent ones. The genitive for the most part is used to express measure, number, and permanent (never temporary) qualities.

4. External qualities are usually expressed by the ablative; internal, by the genitive.

▶ STUDY HELPS

In this descriptive use of the genitive and the ablative, the describing noun is always modified by an adjective. If the describing noun is not modified by an adjective, it is translated in Latin by an adjective:

a man *of courage* = **vir *fortis***

▶ PRACTICE PATTERNS

A. Translate:

| | | |
|---|---|---|
| fossa decem pedum | puer māgnae virtūtis | dux fortī animō |
| mūrus hūjus modī | vir māgnā virtūte | rēx multī beneficī |
| dux inimīcī animī | mīles fortis animī | rīpa quīnque pedum |

B. Write in Latin:

| | | |
|---|---|---|
| man of high courage | wall of five feet | distance of one mile |
| boy with large hands | man of twenty years | life of seven years |
| march of three days | two days' march | girl with pretty a mouth |

# SECTION 3 Irregular Verb *fīō*

▶ DISCUSSION

The passive forms of the present, imperfect, and future tenses of the verb *faciō* are lacking. The missing forms are replaced by the irregular

*314*

verb *fīō, become, be made.* The regularly formed perfect system tenses in the passive of both verbs are identical and have the same meaning.

PRINCIPAL PARTS: **fīō, fierī, factus sum**

INDICATIVE PASSIVE

| | Present Tense | | Imperf. | **fīēbam** |
|---|---|---|---|---|
| | SING. | PL. | Fut. | **fīam** |
| First | **fīō** | — | Perf. | **factus sum** |
| Second | — | — | Pluperf. | **factus eram** |
| Third | **fit** | **fīunt** | Fut. Perf. | **factus erō** |

▶ STUDY HELPS

1. The stem vowel *-ī* is long throughout, except before *-er* and final *-t.*
2. Compounds of *faciō* form their passive regularly.
3. *Fīō* may be used with a predicate noun or adjective.

> **Dux** *clārus* **fīēbat.** The leader was becoming *famous.*

▶ PRACTICE PATTERNS

A. Write in Latin a synopsis of each of the following verbs in the third person singular, active and passive: faciō and cōnficiō. Translate each form.

B. Write the infinitives, active and passive, of faciō. Translate.

C. Write in Latin:

| | | | |
|---|---|---|---|
| it happened | it was done | it was made | I become |
| it will happen | it has been done | no one becomes | can it be done? |

---

## WORDS TO MASTER

**angus′tiae, –ārum,** *f. pl.,* narrow pass; difficulties

**benefi′cium, –ī,** *n.,* kindness, service (*beneficial*)

**cupi′ditās, –tātis,** *f.,* desire, eagerness, greed (*cupidity*)

**dēji′ciō, –ere, –jēcī, –jectus** (3), throw down, destroy, disappoint (*dejected*)

**fe′rō, ferre, tulī, lātus,** *irreg.,* bear, carry, endure (*circumference*)

**fī′ō, fi′erī, factus sum,** *irreg.,* become, be made, happen (*fiat*)

**invī′tus, –a, –um,** *adj.,* unwilling, reluctant

**i′tem,** *adv.,* likewise (*item*)

**repel′lō, –ere, reppulī, repulsus** (3), drive back (*repel*)

**stu′deō, –ēre, –uī, —** (2), be eager for (*study*); **novīs rēbus studēre,** desire a change in government

**trāns′eō, –īre, –iī (īvī), –itus,** *irreg.,* cross over, go across (*transit*)

**vīs, —, —, vim, vī;** *pl.,* **vīrēs, vīrium,** *f.,* force, violence (*vim*); **vim facere,** use force

## BUILDING WORD POWER

*Ambi–*, *sē–*, and *dis–* are strictly prefixes and are never prepositions. *Ambi–* means *around* or *both*. *Ambition* (*ambi + īre*) originally meant going around to win favor or votes. An *ambiguous* (*ambi + agere*) statement can have two or more possible meanings. An *ambidextrous* (*ambi + dexter*) person is able to use both hands with equal ease.

*Sē* (*sed–* before vowels) has the meaning of *apart*. What did the people do when they seceded (*sē + cēdere*) from Rome? *Sedition* (*sēd + īre*) is a going apart for the purpose of revolt. *Segregation* (*sē + grēx*) is a going apart from a group.

*Dis–* (*di–*, *dif–*) also has the general meaning of *apart, asunder, aside*, as well as a *negative* meaning. What do *dismiss, dissimilar, differ, divert* mean? Occasionally a Latin word in *dis–* came into English through ear-Latin as *de–: defy*, from *diffidāre, to distrust*.


## SENTENCE PATTERNS

A. Translate into English:
1. Helvētiī eā spē dējectī sunt et flūmen trānsīre cōnātī sunt.
2. Prīnceps Haeduōrum diū novīs rēbus studēbat.
3. Helvētiī per fīnēs fīnitimōrum arma ferre cōnātī sunt.
4. Nōnne amīcī Sēquanīs fierī volēbant?
5. Sēquanīs invītīs, necesse erat Helvētiōs vim facere.
6. Hī flūmen trānsīre temptābant sed ā Rōmānīs repulsī sunt.
7. Dux quam plūrimās cīvitātēs suō beneficiō amīcās sibi habēre volēbat.
8. Propter angustiās per Sēquanōs īre nōn poterant.
9. Persuāsitne prīnceps hūjus gentis Sēquanīs?
10. Item obsidēs inter sēsē dedērunt.

B. Translate into Latin:
1. Did not Cicero, a man of great learning, become a consul?
2. The Helvetians said they would not use force.
3. Dumnorix became a leader with great influence.
4. Caesar being unwilling, they did not pass through our territory.
5. A wall of ten feet is not too high.


### They Shall Not Pass!

Ubi ea diēs quam cōnstituerat cum lēgātīs vēnit et lēgātī ad eum revēnērunt, negāvit sē posse iter ūllī per prōvinciam dare; et sē eōs cōnantēs prohibitūrum esse ostendit. Helvētiī eā spē dējectī Rhodanum trānsīre cōnātī sunt, sed operis mūnitiōne (*fortification*) et mīlitum tēlīs repulsī hoc facere nōn potuērunt.

Ūna via per Sēquanōs relinquēbātur sed erat difficilis et angusta. Sēquanīs invītīs, trānsīre nōn poterant. Helvētiī igitur dē hōc itinere lēgātōs ad Sēquanōs mīsērunt. Dumnorīx, quī erat prīnceps Haeduōrum, Helvētiīs erat amīcus quod ex eā cīvitāte Orgetorīgis fīliam in mātrimōnium dūxerat. Apud Sēquanōs plūrimum poterat (*was very powerful*). Ille propter haec lēgātiōnī praeerat. Eō tempore Dumnorīx, cupiditāte rēgnī adductus, novīs rēbus studēbat et quam plūrimās cīvitātēs suō beneficiō habēre sibi obstrictās (*under obligations*) volēbat. Itaque hanc rem suscēpit et Sēquanī, eō petente, per fīnēs suōs Helvētiōs trānsīre passī sunt.

<h3 style="text-align:center">CAESAR REINFORCES HIS ARMY</h3>

Caesarī nūntiātum est Helvētiōs in animō habēre per agrum Sēquanōrum et Haeduōrum iter in eōs fīnēs facere quī nōn longē ā Tolōsātium fīnibus aberant, quae cīvitās erat in prōvinciā. Hoc māgnō cum perīculō prōvinciae futūrum esse intellegēbat. Ob eās causās eī mūnitiōnī quam fēcerat Titum Labiēnum praefēcit.

Ipse in Ītaliam māgnīs itineribus contendit duāsque ibi legiōnēs cōnscrīpsit, et trēs ex hībernīs ēdūxit; et in ulteriōrem Galliam per Alpēs cum hīs quīnque legiōnibus īre contendit. Ibi quaedam gentēs itinere exercitum prohibēre cōnātae sunt, sed pulsae sunt.

<h3 style="text-align:center">APPEALS FOR HELP</h3>

Helvētiī jam per angustiās et fīnēs Sēquanōrum suās cōpiās trādūxerant et in Haeduōrum fīnēs pervēnerant; eōrumque agrōs vāstābant. Haeduī lēgātōs ad Caesarem dē auxiliō mīsērunt. Eōdem tempore aliae gentēs Caesarī nūntiāvērunt sē, vāstātis jam agrīs, nōn facile ab oppidīs vim hostium prohibēre posse. Item Allobrogēs, quī trāns Rhodanum vīcōs habēbant, fugā sē ad Caesarem recēpērunt et auxilium petīvērunt.

There are many who recite their writings. . .
while bathing. The closeness of the place
gives melody to the voice.
                        —Horace, 65–8 B.C.

# *Unit* LV

## CONVERSATION

MAGISTER:  Quā dē causā (*Why*) Helvētiī per fīnēs Sequānōrum suās
           cōpiās trādūcunt?
JŪLIUS:    In Haeduōrum fīnēs properant ut eōrum agrōs vāstent.
MAGISTER:  Possuntne Haeduī sē ab eīs dēfendere?
JŪLIA:     Lēgātōs ad Caesarem mittunt quī hunc certiōrem faciant
           Helvētiōs in Haeduōrum fīnēs jam pervēnisse.  Auxilium
           rogant.
MAGISTER:  Nōnne aliae gentēs ā Caesare auxilium petunt?
ROBERTUS:  Eōdem tempore aliae gentēs Caesarem certiōrem faciunt sē,
           vāstātis jam agrīs, nōn facile ab oppidīs vim hostium pro-
           hibēre posse.  Intereā Helvētiī flūmen Ararim trānseunt.
MAGISTER:  Trēs partēs cōpiārum id flūmen jam trādūxērunt.  Quid
           facit Caesar nē Helvētiī quārtam partem trādūcant?
ROBERTA:   Ē castrīs proficīscitur ut in eōs impedītōs impetum faciat.
           Māgnam partem occīdit.  Reliquī aegrē fugiunt.
MAGISTER:  Cōnsēquiturne exercitus Rōmānus eōs fugientēs?
JŪLIUS:    Helvētiī in proximās silvās sē abdunt nē capiantur.

## SECTION 1 Subjunctive Mood

▶ DISCUSSION

1. In both English and Latin there are three finite moods: the *indicative*, the *imperative*, and the *subjunctive*.  The *indicative* in both languages
is commonly used to state a fact or to ask a direct question.  The *imperative* in both languages expresses a command.

2. In English the *subjunctive* mood is not so commonly used as formerly, but it is still often heard in such sentences as: *If this be true*, . . .,
*If I were he*, . . ., *Long live the King!*  In Latin, however, forms of the
verb in the subjunctive appear on almost every page of normal text.

3. The subjunctive may be used in principal (independent) and subordinate (dependent) clauses.  It can express the ideas of command,
purpose, result, indirect question, and the like, and the English translation must contain these ideas.

4. Sometimes the Latin subjunctive may be translated by the English

**318**

indicative, and sometimes with the aid of auxiliary verbs such as *may, might, can, could, would,* and *should.*

5. The subjunctive mood in Latin has four tenses. It has no future or future perfect.

6. The person indicators, active and passive, are the same as in the indicative, except that *–m,* never *–ō,* is always used in the first person active. The indicators of the perfect indicative active differ from those of the other tenses, as has been noted before.

# SECTION 2 Formation of the Present Subjunctive

▶ DISCUSSION

1. The *base,* or *root,* of a verb is the same as the present stem minus the inflection vowel: *vocā–, monē–, rege–, cape–, audī–* are *present stems; voc/, mon/, reg/, cap/, aud/* are bases, or roots.

2. Each tense of the subjunctive has its own indicator by which the particular form can be easily identified. In the first conjugation the tense indicator for the present tense is long *–ē,* and for the second, third, and fourth conjugations it is long *–ā.*

PRESENT SUBJUNCTIVE ACTIVE, FIRST CONJUGATION

| | Base + | T.I. + | P.I. = | Form | Possible Translation |
|---|---|---|---|---|---|
| | | | SINGULAR | | |
| First | voc/ + | ē + | m | = vocem | *I may call* |
| Second | voc/ + | ē + | s | = vocēs | *you may call* |
| Third | voc/ + | ē + | t | = vocet | *he, she, it may call* |
| | | | PLURAL | | |
| First | voc/ + | ē + | mus | = vocēmus | *we may call* |
| Second | voc/ + | ē + | tis | = vocētis | *you may call* |
| Third | voc/ + | ē + | nt | = vocent | *they may call* |

The Latin present subjunctive is translated into English not only by *may,* but by *let, should, would,* or by the indicative present or future, according to the nature of the clause in which the subjunctive stands.

PRESENT SUBJUNCTIVE ACTIVE

| CONJUGATION: | SECOND | THIRD | THIRD –io | FOURTH |
|---|---|---|---|---|
| | *Base + eā* | *Base + ā* | *Base + iā* | *Base + iā* |
| | | SINGULAR | | |
| First | **moneam** | **regam** | **capiam** | **audiam** |
| Second | **moneās** | **regās** | **capiās** | **audiās** |
| Third | **moneat** | **regat** | **capiat** | **audiat** |

| First | moneāmus | regāmus | capiāmus | audiāmus |
| Second | moneātis | regātis | capiātis | audiātis |
| Third | moneant | regant | capiant | audiant |

▶ STUDY HELPS

1. The vowel before the personal ending remains the same throughout.
2. The quantity of vowels changes as in the indicative mood.
3. The passive voice is formed regularly by substituting the passive indicators for the active ones.

## PRESENT SUBJUNCTIVE, DEPONENT VERBS

| CONJUGATION: | FIRST | SECOND | THIRD | THIRD –io | FOURTH |
| | Base + ē | Base + eā | Base + ā | Base + iā | Base + iā |

SINGULAR

| First | cōner | verear | sequar | patiar | largiar |
| Second | cōnēris | vereāris | sequāris | patiāris | largiāris |
| Third | cōnētur | vereātur | sequātur | patiātur | largiātur |

PLURAL

| First | cōnēmur | vereāmur | sequāmur | patiāmur | largiāmur |
| Second | cōnēminī | vereāmini | sequāminī | patiāminī | largiāminī |
| Third | cōnentur | vereantur | sequantur | patiantur | largiantur |

## PRESENT SUBJUNCTIVE, IRREGULAR VERBS

| Sum | Possum | Volō | Eō | Ferō | Fīō |
|-----|--------|------|-----|------|-----|
| sim | possim | velim | eam | feram | fīam |
| sīs | possīs | velīs | eās | ferās | fīās |
| sit | possit | velit | eat | ferat | fīat |
| sīmus | possīmus | velīmus | eāmus | ferāmus | fīāmus |
| sītis | possītis | velītis | eātis | ferātis | fīātis |
| sint | possint | velint | eant | ferant | fīant |

▶ STUDY HELPS

*Volō, nōlō, mālō, sum* and its compounds are the only Latin verbs which have an –*i* in the present subjunctive.

▶ PRACTICE PATTERNS

A. Write the third person singular of the present subjunctive, active and passive, of the following verbs. Translate by using *may*.

postulō     teneō     abdō     jaciō     impediō

B. Translate into Latin:

| he may be present | we may follow | you (pl.) may run |
| she may be absent | you (sing.) may set out | she may hide |
| it may be lacking | they may bring in | they may pursue |

# SECTION 3 Clauses Expressing Purpose

▶ DISCUSSION

1. In English when we say: He comes to school *to study*, the infinitive expresses the purpose of his coming. Instead of an infinitive in a simple sentence, we may use a clause in a complex sentence: He comes to school *in order that he may study*.

2. In Latin prose we do not use an infinitive to express purpose. We must use a subordinate clause introduced by **ut** if the clause is positive; by **nē**, if negative. After verbs meaning *choose, send,* or *leave,* purpose may be expressed by a relative clause. The antecedent of the relative pronoun is usually the object of the main verb.

| | |
|---|---|
| **Pūgnant *ut vincant*.** | They fight *to conquer (in order that they may conquer)*. |
| **Pūgnant *nē vincantur*.** | They fight *in order not to be conquered (in order that they may not be conquered; lest they be conquered)*. |
| **Nūntiōs *quī haec dīcant* mittimus.** | We are sending messengers *to say these things (who shall say these things)*. |

▶ STUDY HELPS

1. Purpose clauses answer the question *why?* and are adverbial clauses.

2. The present tense of the subjunctive is used in a purpose clause after a main verb whose tense expresses present or future time.

3. The conjunction **ut** with the subjunctive may mean either *that, so that,* or *in order that;* with the *indicative* it may mean *as* or *when*.

4. The conjunction **nē** with the subjunctive may mean *that . . . not; in order that . . . not; lest;* or *in order not to . . . .*

## WORDS TO MASTER

**ab′dō, –ere, –didī, –ditus** (3), put away, hide

**ae′grē,** *adv.,* with difficulty

**cā′sus, –ūs,** *m.,* fall, accident, chance (*casualty*)

**certiō′rem faciō,** inform; **certior fierī,** *pass.,* be informed

**cōn′sequor, –ī, –secūtus sum** (3), *dep.,* pursue, overtake, attain (*consequence*)

**explōrā′tor, –ōris,** *m.,* scout (*exploratory*)

**impe′diō, –īre, –īvī, –ītus** (4), hinder, entangle (*impede*)

**īn′ferō, –ferre, –tulī, illātus,** *irreg.,* bring in, inflict (*infer*); **bellum īnferre,** make war

**īnsīg′nis, –e,** *adj.,* marked, distinguished (*insignia*)

**ju′gum, –ī,** *n.,* yoke, ridge (*subjugate*)

**lo′quor, –ī, locūtus sum** (3), *dep.,* speak (*loquacious*)

**red′dō, –ere, –didī, –ditus** (3), give back, pay (*rendition*)

## BUILDING WORD POWER

There are many words in English derived from Latin that have the inseparable prefix *re-* or *re-d-*. This prefix may mean *back* or *again*. If you use an insect *repellent*, you drive *back* annoying or destructive pests. When you *recreate* by playing games or listening to good music, you really *create* your body or mind *again*. A person's *reputation* (*re-*, *again* + *putare*, *to think*) is what is thought about him. *Reputable* means having a good reputation. When we respect (*re-*, *back* + *specere*, *to look*) someone, we *look back* with attention, and then we esteem.

**Unda** means *wave;* **undāre**, *to flow in waves;* **redundāre**, *to flow back in waves, to overflow*. A *redundant* syllable or word is one that is not needed. In the sentence: "Have you got a pencil?" *got* is *redundant*. The adverb **iterum** means *again*. **Iterāre** means *to iterate, to say* or *do again*. In the word *reiterate*, the prefix *re-* is *redundant* because it is not needed for the sense of the word.

Analyze the following words, and decide whether the prefix means *back* or *again:* remit, repetition, reject, reduce, remain, redemption, recede, recur, remove. Use these words in English sentences. Write the Latin from which they are derived.

## SENTENCE PATTERNS

A. Translate into English. Pick out the purpose clauses.

1. Caesar pontem facit ut cōpiās Helvētiōrum cōnsequī possit.
2. Superatne cōnsulem ut ējus exercitum sub jugum mittat?
3. Imperātor ē castrīs proficīscitur ut eōs impedītōs capiat.
4. Lēgātōs īnsīgnēs mittunt quī cum Caesare loquantur.
5. Caesar ab explōrātōribus certior factus est trēs partēs cōpiārum hostium id flūmen trānsīsse.
6. Nōnne reliquī fugiunt ut in proximās silvās sē abdant?
7. Pontem dēlent nē hostēs exercitum trādūcant.
8. Cāsū pars cīvitātis Helvetiae quae injūriās populō Rōmānō intulerat prīma poenās dedit.
9. Pontem aegerrimē faciunt ut trānseant.
10. Explōrātōrēs ducem certiōrem fēcērunt gentēs frūmentum reddere.

B. Translate into Latin. Pick out the purpose clauses.

1. Distinguished men are being sent to Caesar to speak about peace.
2. Was not the consul killed and his army sent under the yoke?
3. Caesar hastens lest the army of the enemy escape.
4. Are scouts being sent to learn the nature of the place?
5. They are hastening in order that they may inform Caesar about their wrongs.

The Baths of Caracalla.

## Roman Country Clubs

Socially the baths, *thermae*, were to the Romans of the Empire what country clubs are today to many Americans. Attending the baths was part of the daily routine. They were the places where men, women, and children of all classes of Roman society met and spent a large part of their leisure time.

There were baths throughout the Roman world, but in Rome itself there were hundreds of them. The most prominent were large and elaborate. The best-preserved of the larger bathing establishments are those of Diocletian, covering an area of thirty-two acres, and those of Caracalla, twenty-seven acres. The ruins of the Thermae of Diocletian today include the magnificent Roman church called St. Mary of the Angels; another church, the Oratory of St. Bernard; the National Roman Museum; and several other smaller buildings.

In the center of the thermae were the buildings for bathing purposes. The dressing rooms adjoined the *tepidarium*, a large vaulted hall slightly warmed. This was between the *frigidarium*, a very large cold water swimming pool about two hundred by one hundred feet, and the *calidarium*, heated by vapor circulating beneath the pavement. This last was for hot-water baths and contained small rooms for private bathing. South of the calidarium there were very hot rooms for steam baths.

Besides providing every type of bath that human ingenuity could devise, the baths became little worlds for the enjoyment of all the luxuries of the times. Around the main building were porticos filled with shops, where food, ointments, clothing, and other commodities could be purchased. There were enclosed gardens and covered promenades, gymnasiums and rooms for massage, libraries and museums. Everywhere there were splashing fountains and magnificent marble statues, masterpieces donated by the emperor or wealthy benefactors.

Although all senators and wealthy knights had sumptuous private baths with walls and swimming pools of marble and with

*323*

ceilings covered with all varieties, of paintings, they frequently attended the public thermae. There they could enjoy perhaps better than anywhere else the good fellowship that resulted from the free and relaxed atmosphere of the baths, where social barriers were partly forgotten and informality prevailed. Even the emperors were known to swim with the poorest of their subjects.

## Divide and Conquer

Flūmen est Arar, quod per fīnēs Haeduōrum et Sēquanōrum in Rhodanum flūit. Per explōrātōrēs Caesar certior factus est trēs jam partēs cōpiārum Helvētiōs hoc flūmen trādūxisse; quartum partem citrā (*on this side*) flūmen Ararim relinquam esse.

Itaque Caesar dē tertiā vigiliā cum legiōnibus tribus ē castrīs profectus est, et quam celerrimē vēnit ad eam partem cōpiārum quae nōndum flūmen trānsierat. In eōs ex itinere impedītōs impetum fēcit māgnamque partem eōrum occīdit. Reliquī sē in fugam dedērunt atque in proximās silvās sē abdidērunt.

### PAST WRONGS AVENGED

Is pāgus (*district*) appellābātur Tigurīnus; nam omnis cīvitās Helvētia in quattuor partēs aut quattuor pāgōs dīvīsa est. Hic pāgus patrum nostrōrum memoriā Lūcium Pīsōnem, cōnsulem Rōmānum, interfēcerat et ējus exercitum sub jugum mīserat.

Ita aut casū aut cōnsiliō deōrum immortālium, pars cīvitātis Helvētiae, quae īnsīgnem calamitātem populō Rōmānō intulerat, ea prīma poenam dedit. In hāc rē Caesar nōn sōlum publicās sed etiam prīvātās injūriās ultus est (*avenged*).

### CAESAR AND THE HELVETIAN EMBASSY

Hōc proeliō factō, Caesar, quī reliquās cōpiās Helvētiōrum cōnsequī vult, ūnō diē pontem in Ararī facit ut ita exercitum trādūcat. Tum Helvētiī id quod ipsī diēbus xx aegerrimē cōnfēcerant illum ūnō diē fēcisse intellegunt. Hāc de causā, māgnopere adventū ējus commōtī, lēgātōs ad eum quī pācem petant mittunt; cūjus lēgātiōnis Dīvicō est prīnceps.

### DIVICO SPEAKS

Is ita loquitur: "Sī pācem populus Rōmānus cum Helvētiīs faciet, in eam partem ibunt atque ibi erunt Helvētiī, ubi eōs tū cōnstituēs atque esse volēs. Sin (*but if*) bellum īnferre persevērābis (*persist*), memoriā tenē veterem (*ancient*) calamitātem populī Rōmānī et prīstīnam (*former*) virtūtem Helvētiōrum."

Hīs Caesar respondet sē omnia haec memoriā tenēre, sed sē quoque cōgnōscere eōs iter facere per prōvinciam per vim cōnātōs esse et sociīs Rōmānīs injūriās tulisse. "Sī, autem, obsidēs ā vōbīs mihi dabuntur, et sī Haeduīs et Allobrogibus dē injūriīs quās ipsīs sociīsque eōrum intulistis satisfaciētis (*make amends*), vōbīscum pācem faciam."

# Comprehensive Review: Units LI–LV

A. Write in Latin the nominative, genitive, and gender of these nouns. Give English translation of each.

vīs   lacus   cāsus   jugum   beneficium   cupiditās   explōrātor   angustiae

B. Write the English meanings of:

| | | | |
|---|---|---|---|
| item | aegrē | invītus | prīvātus |
| levis | īgnōtus | īnsīgnis | proptereā |

C. Write in Latin the specified forms:

1. what lake (accusative)
2. this scout (ablative)
3. many things (genitive)
4. the same kindness (dative)
5. no force (accusative)
6. that desire (genitive)
7. which (of two) lakes (nominative)
8. greater accident (ablative)
9. any day (genitive)
10. a very heavy yoke (accusative)

D. Write the principal parts and meanings of these verbs. Indicate the conjugation to which each belongs, or mark it *irregular*.

| | | | | | |
|---|---|---|---|---|---|
| eō | redeō | ēdūcō | trānseō | sequor | prōscrībō |
| ferō | reddō | addūcō | loquor | dējiciō | cōnsequor |
| sūmō | parcō | claudō | resistō | praesum | persuadeō |
| exeō | crēdō | patior | contineō | repellō | intermittō |
| ineō | dēsum | indūcō | permoveō | īnstruō | volō (irreg.) |
| abdō | noceō | īnferō | pertineō | efficiō | proficīscor |
| cōnor | studeō | imperō | impediō | cōnscrībō | praeficiō |

E. Write the following synopses; translate each form.

1. active and passive indicative, third person plural: permoveō, impediō
2. active indicative: ferō, second person plural
   volō, *wish*, third person singular
   volō, *fly*, first person plural
   eō, third person plural
3. indicative: cōnor, first person plural
   sequor, third person singular
   loquor, third person plural

F. Write in Latin the infinitives, active and passive, and translate each form: sūmō, contineō.

G. Write in Latin the participles, active and passive, and translate each form:

<blockquote>impediō    efficiō    cōnscrībō    permoveō    imperō</blockquote>

H. Conjugate in the present subjunctive active:

<blockquote>possum    studeō    resistō    praeficiō</blockquote>

I. Translate into Latin:

| | |
|---|---|
| a ten-foot wall | Believe me. |
| to command the army | Spare the people. |
| a soldier of great courage | Do not harm the boy. |
| to be in charge of the troops | He persuaded the leader. |
| to place in charge of the army | No one ought to resist a friend. |

## SENTENCE PATTERNS

A. Translate into English:

1. Equitātum quī impetum hostium sustineat mittit.
2. Orgetorīx erat vir māgnā virtūte.
3. Nōnne castra mūnit ut eōs prohibēre possit?
4. Caesar animadvertit Sēquānōs nihil eārum rērum efficere.
5. Amīcum in perīculō vidēns, mīles fortis eum ēripere cōnātur.
6. Imperātōre dūcente, nēmō pūgnāre dubitat.
7. Sīgnō datō, proelium commīsērunt.
8. Mīlitēs ad montēs properant nē ab hostibus videantur.
9. Sunt in exercitū ducēs quī hostibus parcent.
10. Eō duce, oppidum oppūgnābimus.

B. Translate into Latin:

1. Caesar placed a man of great bravery in command of the rampart three feet high.
2. The Helvetians, influenced (led on) by the words of Orgetorix, decided to leave home.
3. Under the leadership of a very brave general we destroyed the largest town.
4. He is sending scouts in all directions to learn the plans of the enemy.
5. These tribes are resisting the Romans in order that they may not be made captives.

## SIGHT TRANSLATION: JULIUS CAESAR

Octō annōs Caesar in Galliā proelia plūrima et ācerrima gessit. Ā mīlitibus amātus est quod eum fortissimum aequumque esse cōgnōvērunt. Hostēs quibuscum pūgnāvit eum timuērunt sed admīrātiōne māgnae virtūtis in bellō et clēmentiae admīrābilis in pāce permovēbantur. Prīmō annō bellī Gallicī quaedam gēns, appellāta Helvētia, domō cum omnibus cōpiīs exīre statuit. Sē fīnēs habēre angustiōrēs exīstimāvērunt prō multitūdine hominum et prō glōriā bellī, et lātiōrēs terrās māximē cupiēbant.

Illō tempore Caesar erat prōcōnsul in Galliā. Ubi certior factus est dē consiliīs hūjus gentis, quam celerrimē ad Galliam profectus est. Impetū in Helvētiōs factō, tōtam gentem vīcit. In fīnēs suōs unde erant profectī Helvētiōs redīre jūssit. Omnī cibō Helvētiōrum dēlētō, Caesar fīnitimam gentem eīs frūmentum dare, et ipsōs oppida vīcōsque quōs incenderant iterum aedificāre quoque jūssit.

An army marches on its stomach.
—Napoleon Bonaparte, 1769–1821

## CONVERSATION

CAESAR: Diem ex diē nōs dūcunt (*put off*) Haeduī. Frūmentum cōn-
ferrī, portārī, adesse dīcunt; tamen nūllum frūmentum habēmus. Convocā prīncipēs Haeduōrum ut cum eīs loquar.

PRĪNCIPĒS: Properāvimus, imperātor, nē tardī (*late*) essēmus.

CAESAR: Nōs precibus vestrīs adductī bellum suscēpimus ut agrōs
vestrōs dēfenderēmus. Nunc nūllum frūmentum habēmus.
Neque id emere neque sūmere ex agrīs possumus. Cūr
nōbīs id nōn datis? Cibum habēre volumus nē superēmur.

LISCUS: Quīdam ex Haeduīs māgnam potestātem apud nōs habent,
etsi prīvātī nōn magistrātūs sunt. Seditiōsā ōrātiōne hōrum
multitūdō frūmentum nōn cōnfert quod dēbet.

CAESAR: Quae ducēs conjūrātiōnis multitūdinī dīcunt, Lisce?

LISCUS: Melius est, sī jam imperium Galliae obtinēre nōn possumus,
Gallōrum quam Rōmānōrum imperia perferre (*endure*). Ab
eīsdem cōnsilia tua atque ea quae in castrīs geruntur hostibus
nūntiantur. Hī ā mē continērī nōn possunt.

## SECTION 1 Formation of the Imperfect Subjunctive

▶ DISCUSSION

The imperfect subjunctive, active and passive, for all Latin verbs is
formed by adding the regular person indicators, active and passive, to
the present active infinitive.

IMPERFECT SUBJUNCTIVE ACTIVE, FIRST CONJUGATION

| *Pres. Act. Inf.* + *P.I.* = *Form* | | | | *Possible Translation* |
|---|---|---|---|---|
| SINGULAR | | | | |
| First | **vocāre** | + **m** | = **vocārem** | *I might call* |
| Second | **vocāre** | + **s** | = **vocārēs** | *you might call* |
| Third | **vocāre** | + **t** | = **vocāret** | *he, she, it might call* |
| PLURAL | | | | |
| First | **vocāre** | + **mus** | = **vocārēmus** | *we might call* |
| Second | **vocāre** | + **tis** | = **vocārētis** | *you might call* |
| Third | **vocāre** | + **nt** | = **vocārent** | *they might call* |

The Latin imperfect subjunctive is translated into English not only by *might* but also by *would* and the past tenses of the indicative, according to the nature of the clause in which the subjunctive stands.

▶ STUDY HELPS

1. The passive voice of the imperfect subjunctive is formed regularly by substituting the passive indicators for the active ones.

2. The syllable *–re* may be considered the tense indicator of the imperfect subjunctive.

IMPERFECT SUBJUNCTIVE ACTIVE

*Pres. Act. Inf. + P.I. = Form*

| CONJUGATION: | SECOND | THIRD | THIRD **–io** | FOURTH |
|---|---|---|---|---|
| | | SINGULAR | | |
| First | **monērem** | **regerem** | **caperem** | **audīrem** |
| Second | **monērēs** | **regerēs** | **caperēs** | **audīrēs** |
| Third | **monēret** | **regeret** | **caperet** | **audīret** |
| | | PLURAL | | |
| First | **monērēmus** | **regerēmus** | **caperēmus** | **audīrēmus** |
| Second | **monērētis** | **regerētis** | **caperētis** | **audīrētis** |
| Third | **monērent** | **regerent** | **caperent** | **audīrent** |

IMPERFECT SUBJUNCTIVE, DEPONENT VERBS

The imperfect subjunctive of the deponent verbs is formed regularly as in the passive voice of regular verbs.

| **cōnārer** | **verērer** | **sequerer** | **paterer** | **largīrer** |
|---|---|---|---|---|

IMPERFECT SUBJUNCTIVE, IRREGULAR VERBS

The imperfect subjunctive of the irregular verbs is formed regularly.

| **essem** | **possem** | **vellem** | **īrem** | **ferrem** | **fierem** |
|---|---|---|---|---|---|

When the main verb is in a *secondary* or *past* tense, the imperfect subjunctive is ordinarily used in *purpose* clauses:

| **Vēnērunt *ut vidērent*.** | They came *in order that they might see (to see)*. |
|---|---|
| **Vēnērunt *nē vidērentur*.** | They came *in order that they might not be seen (lest they be seen)*. |
| **Virōs mīsit *quī vidērent*.** | He sent men *that they might see (to see; who should see)*. |

▶ PRACTICE PATTERNS

A. Write the third person plural, imperfect subjunctive active of the following verbs. Translate by using the auxiliary verbs *might* or *would:*
abstineō    convertō    superō    incipiō    mūniō    sum    eō    ferō    volō

B. Conjugate in the imperfect subjunctive: cōnor, sequor, fīō.

**329**

C. Translate into Latin:

| | | |
|---|---|---|
| I might be present | they might see | you (pl.) might suffer |
| they might be absent | they might be frightened | we might be driven out |
| she might be able | you (sing.) might ask | he might persuade |
| they might bestow | she might become | he might try |

## SECTION 2 Review of the Accusative Case

As a review of the accusative case, place in the parentheses the letter of the rule that explains the use of the accusative case. Translate.

a. Direct object of a transitive verb
b. Direct object of a preposition
c. Place to which
d. Place to which without a preposition
e. Duration or extent of time
f. Extent of space
g. With objective infinitive
h. Indirect statement
i. After verbs of naming, etc.
j. Verbs compounded with prepositions
k. After verbs of asking, etc.
l. With subjective infinitive

1. Augustus multōs annōs rēgnāvit. (___)
2. Sciō mīlitēs venīre. (___)
3. Caesar mīlitēs pūgnāre jūssit. (___)
4. Illum cōnsulem creāvērunt. (___)
5. Mīlitēs castra mūnīvērunt. (___)
6. In urbem vēnit. (___)
7. Multa mīlia passuum ambulāvērunt. (___)
8. Rōmam vēnit. (___)
9. Mē īre necesse erat. (___)
10. Rēgem multa docuit. (___)
11. Flūmen exercitum trādūxit. (___)
12. Ipse ad eōs contendit. (___)
13. Ante bellum erant līberī. (___)
14. Virum esse mīlitem putābant. (___)

Explain the syntax of the italicized accusatives. Translate.

1. Eīs *cōnsilium* suum ostendit.
2. Ille *iter* esse *facile* dīxit.
3. *Hostēs praedam* facere prohibēbat.
4. Trēs *diēs exercitum* Helvētiōrum sequēbātur.
5. Virī quī *multa mīlia* passuum ambulāvērunt tandem *Rōmam* pervēnērunt.
6. *Equitātum* ante sē mīsit.
7. *Virum* perītum *ducem* creāvērunt.
8. Lēgātus *equitēs* jūssit *hostēs agrōs* vāstāre prohibēre.
9. Caesar *cōpiās* in proximum *collem* dūxit.
10. Ipse contrā *eōs* pūgnāvit.
11. Necesse erit *mīlitēs mūrōs* cūstōdīre multōs *mēnsēs*.

**BUILDING WORD POWER**

Sometimes compound words were formed in Latin by uniting a noun or verb with an adjective or an adverbial modifier. Originally **bonus,**

*330*

good, was **benus,** from which we have the adverb **bene,** *well, rightly.*
From **bene** and *facere, do* or *make,* we have some interesting descriptive
Latin words that came into English, such as *benefactor, benefice, benefit.*
What do *benevolence, benignity, benign,* and *benediction* mean?

From **malus,** *bad, evil,* we have **male,** *badly, ill.* Notice that **male**
is an *antonym* (word opposite in meaning) for **bene** in *malevolence, malign,
malediction, malefactor.* *Malady* (**male + habitus**) originally meant
*badly kept.* *Malaria* (**male + aria**) was named from the bad air around
the marshes, instead of the mosquitos that carry the disease.

Which one of the following words would be used by a dentist? a med-
ical doctor? a psychiatrist? *Malocclusion, malnutrition, maladjustment.*

## WORDS TO MASTER

**absti′neō, –ēre, –uī, –tentus** (2),
restrain, refrain (*abstinence*)

**ag′men, –minis,** *n.,* marching column, line of march, army on the
march

**animadver′tō, –ere, –vertī, –versus**
(3), notice, observe, perceive (*ani-
madvert*)

**ascen′dō, –cre, –scendī, –scēnsus**
(3), climb, mount (*ascend*)

**ci′trā,** *prep. with acc.,* on this side of

**col′lis, –is,** *m.,* hill

**cōn′ferō, –ferre, –tulī, collātus,**
*irreg.,* gather, compare (*confer,
collate*); **sē cōnferre,** go, flee

**conver′tō, –ere, –vertī, –versus** (3),
turn about, change (*convert*)

**equitā′tus, –ūs,** *m.,* cavalry

**perī′tus, –a, –um,** *adj. with gen.,*
skilled

**praemit′tō, –ere, –mīsī, –missus**
(3), send ahead

**prex, precis,** *f.,* prayer, entreaty;
*regularly in plural* (*precarious*)

## SENTENCE PATTERNS

A. Translate into English. Pick out the purpose clauses.

1. Mīlitēs fortiter pūgnābant ut castra dēfenderent.
2. Nūntium praemīsit quī Caesarem dē proeliō certiōrem faceret.
3. Proeliō abstinēbat nē nostrī ab hostibus superārentur.
4. Explōrātōrēs quī nātūram montis cōgnōscerent praemīsit.
5. Pūblius Cōnsidius reī mīlitāris perītissimus habēbātur.
6. Equitātus cupidius agmen hostium sequēbātur.
7. Postquam id animadvertit iter convertit.
8. Caesar dēnique duās legiōnēs quī collem ascenderent mīsīt.
9. Necesse erit mīlitēs citrā flūmen multās hōrās pūgnāre.
10. Helvētiī Rōmānōs discēdere ā castrīs exīstimābant.

B. Translate into Latin:

1. Did he not send skilled men ahead to prepare the camp?

2. When the mountain had been seized, Labienus, refraining from battle, awaited our men.
3. Did Caesar build a bridge in order to lead his army across the river?
4. Considius, who was very skilled in military affairs, was sent ahead with the scouts.
5. He refrained from battle lest his men be killed.

### A Surprise Attack

Posterō diē Helvētiī castra ex eō locō mōvērunt. Item Caesar fēcit, et omnem equitātum praemīsit quī iter hostium cōgnōsceret. Hī cupidius agmen secūtī aliēnō locō cum equitātū Helvētiōrum proelium commīsit. Paucī dē nostrīs cecidērunt. Caesar autem suōs ā proeliō continēbat ac hostēs praedam facere prohibēbat.

Quīndecim (*Fifteen*) diēs Caesar exercitum Helvētiōrum sequēbātur. Tum ab explōrātōribus certior factus est hostēs sub monte castra posuisse ab ipsīus castrīs octō mīlia passuum. Explōrātōrēs quī nātūram et ascēnsum montis cōgnōscerent mīsit. Illī ascēnsum esse facilem nūntiāvērunt.

Itaque dē tertiā vigiliā Titum Labiēnum lēgātum cum duābus legiōnibus et eīs ducibus quī iter cōgnōverant summum jugum montis ascendere jūssit. Eīs cōnsilium suum ostendit. Ipse dē quārtā vigiliā eōdem itinere quō hostēs ierant ad eōs contendit et omnem equitātum ante sē mīsit. Pūblium Cōnsidium, quī reī mīlitāris perītissimus habēbātur, cum explōrātōribus praemīsit.

### AN OFFICER'S BLUNDER

Prīmā lūce, dum summus mōns ā Labiēnō tenētur, ipse ab hostium castrīs nōn longē aberat, neque aut ipsīus adventus aut Labiēnī cōgnitus est, Cōnsidius ad eum, equō incitātō, accessit. Dīxit montem nōn ā Labiēnō sed ab hostibus tenērī; id sē ā Gallicīs armīs atque īnsīgnibus cōgnōvisse. Caesar igitur cōpiās suās in proximum collem dūxit et aciem īnstrūxit.

Intereā Labiēnus, monte occupātō, nostrōs exspectābat et proeliō abstinēbat quod Caesar eum adventum suum exspectāre jūsserat ut undique ūnō tempore in hostēs impetus fieret. Multō dēnique diē per explōrātōrēs Caesar cōgnōvit et montem ā suīs tenērī et Helvētiōs castra mōvisse. Cōnsidius enim, timōre perterritus, id quod nōn vīderat prō vīsō (*as seen*) Caesarī nūntiāverat. Hostēs autem castra sua mōverant. Itaque eō diē cum eīs proelium committere nōn poterat.

Helvētiī Rōmānōs timōre perterritōs discēdere exīstimābant. Posterō diē illī, mūtātō cōnsiliō, iter convertērunt et in nostrōs impetūs facere incipiēbant. Postquam id animadvertit, cōpiās suās Caesar in proximum collem dūxit et equitātum praemīsit. Ipse in colle mediō aciem īnstrūxit legiōnum quattuor veterānārum. In summō jugō duās legiōnēs, quās in Galliā proximē cōnscrīpserat, et omnia auxilia locārī jūssit.

Oh, this age! how tasteless and ill-bred it is.
—Catullus, 87–54 B.C.

# *Unit* LVII

## CONVERSATION

CAESAR: Haec esse vēra cōgnōvī. Ipse est Dumnorīx, summā audāciā, apud plēbem māgnā grātiā, rērum novārum cupidus.

VALERIUS: Ille tantum numerum equitum circum sē semper habet ut capī nōn possit.

CLAUDIUS: Neque Caesarem neque Rōmānōs amat, quod eōrum adventū auctōritās ējus minor facta est, et quod Dīviciācus, frāter ējus, in antīquō locō grātiae et honōris locātus est. Tam īrātus erat Dumnorīx ut frātrī suō nocēre cōnārētur.

CAESAR: Dīviciācus amīcus meus est. Cōgnōvī eum summum ad populum Rōmānum studium et ad mē habēre. Voluntātem, fidem, jūstitiam, temperantiam habet. Ego Dīviciācō nocēre nōn cupiō. Vocā eum ad mē ut cum eō loquar.

DĪVICIĀCUS: Adsum, nōbilis Caesar. Quid vīs?

CAESAR: Tālia, Dīviciāce, sunt maleficia frātris tuī ut ego eī parcere nōn dēbeam. Cōgnōvistīne haec?

DĪVICIĀCUS: Haec sciō, sed tam adulēscēns est Dumnorīx ut nihil cum eō agere possim. Parce eī nē populus mē perfidiae accūset.

## SECTION 1 Result Clauses

▶ DISCUSSION

1. In English the verb in a *clause of result* is expressed by the indicative mood because a result is something that has actually happened. A

**333**

fact is stated. In Latin the verb is in the subjunctive mood, and the clause, whether affirmative or negative, is introduced by **ut.** In a negative clause the negative adverb **nōn** is placed before the verb. In the English translation the auxiliary verbs *may, might, should, would* are *never* used.

2. In Latin as in English, some word in the main clause serves as a warning indicator that a result clause is coming. *Ita* and *sīc,* both of which mean *so,* are usually used with verbs. *Tam,* also meaning *so,* is used with adjectives and adverbs. *Tantus, so great,* and *tālis, such,* are adjectives.

| | |
|---|---|
| **Rōmānī** *tam* **fortiter pūgnāvērunt** *ut* **hostēs superārent.** | The Romans fought *so* bravely *that* they overcame the enemy. |
| **Numerus hostium erat** *tantus ut* **Rōmānī eōs** *nōn* **superārent.** | The number of the enemy was *so great that* the Romans did *not* overcome them. |

▶ PRACTICE PATTERNS

A. Translate these main clauses into English:

1. Ita hostēs territī sunt . . .
2. Tālēs erant condiciōnēs pācis . . .
3. Tanta est altitūdō flūminis . . .
4. Mīlitēs tantā virtūte pūgnāvērunt . . .
5. Mōns tam longē aberat . . .
6. Quis est tam fortis . . .

B. Match these subordinate clauses with the above clauses:

1. ut fugerent.
2. ut nihil timeat.
3. ut hostēs eās nōn acciperent.
4. ut hostēs suōs paene semper superārent.
5. ut necesse esset virōs multōs diēs ambulāre.
6. ut exercitum trādūcere nōn possit.

PURPOSE AND RESULT CLAUSES: COMPARISON

| PURPOSE | RESULT |
|---|---|
| 1. **ut,** positive; **nē,** negative | 1. **ut,** positive; **ut . . . nōn,** negative |
| 2. *that, in order that; that . . . not; lest;* with an infinitive | 2. *that, so that; that . . . not;* never with an infinitive |
| 3. *may* or *might* | 3. never *may* or *might* |
| 4. incomplete action: possibility | 4. complete action: fact |
| 5. for what purpose? why? | 5. with what result? |

PURPOSE

**Rōmānī fortiter pūgnāvērunt** *ut* **hostēs superārent.** The Romans fought bravely *that* they *might* overcome the enemy.

RESULT

**Rōmānī** *tam* **fortiter pūgnāvērunt** *ut* **hostēs superārent.** The Romans fought *so* bravely *that* they *did* overcome the enemy.

# SECTION 2 Review of the Genitive Case

Identify the nouns in the genitive case in these sentences as: (a) genitive of possession; (b) genitive of description; (c) genitive of the whole (partitive genitive). Translate each sentence.

1. Mīlia passuum tria ab eōrum castrīs castra posuit.
2. Ūnus ex lēgātīs captīs erat vir māgnī studī.
3. Ad vallum vīgintī pedum pervēnērunt.
4. Mājor pars exercitūs Rōmam iter fēcit.
5. Exercitus Caesaris omnem Galliam superāvit.

## WORDS TO MASTER

**conji'ciō, –ere, –jēcī, –jectus** (3), throw, hurl (*conjecture*)

**dēdi'tiō, –ōnis,** *f.,* surrender

**dēfes'sus, –a, –um,** *adj.,* tired out, exhausted

**ēgre'dior, –ī, –gressus sum** (3), *dep.,* go out, leave (*egress*)

**expūg'nō** (1), take by storm, storm, capture

**hiber'na, –ōrum,** *n. pl.,* winter quarters (*hibernate*)

**obji'ciō, –ere, –jēcī, –jectus** (3), throw against, pile up against (*object*)

**prōgre'dior, –ī, –gressus sum** (3), *dep.,* go forth, advance (*progress*)

**prōji'ciō, –ere, –jēcī, –jectus** (3), throw forth, cast, betray (*project*)

**reti'neō, –ēre, –uī, –tentus** (2), hold back, detain (*retention*)

**tā'lis, –e,** *adj.,* such, of such kind

**tam,** *adv.,* so, to such a degree

## BUILDING WORD POWER

We have two prefixes spelled *mis–*, one of which is from Anglo-Saxon, the other from the Latin *minus*, the comparative neuter of *parvus*, meaning *little*. In words compounded with the Latin prefix, the *mis–* is negative or depreciatory. *Mischief* (*minus + caput*) is the bad head to which things come. A *miscreant* (*minus + crēdō*), now a *wretch*, was originally an *unbeliever*, a term applied to the Saracens and then to evildoers in general. *Misnomer* (*minus + nōmen*) is a wrong name. The word *student* would be a misnomer if applied to a pupil who does not study.

*Bi–* is a prefix from the adverb *bis* meaning *twice*. A *biannual* event occurs twice a year; *biennial* every two years. What is the difference between *bisect* and *dissect* (*secāre, cut*)? How many *bicuspid* (*cuspis, point*) teeth do you have? What is the name of the large muscle in your upper arm (*bi + caput*)? Do you know that *biscuit* (*bis + coquere, cook*) can be a cracker, a color, or a piece of pottery before glazing?

A. Translate into English. Distinguish between purpose and result clauses.

1. Imperātor equitātum quī castra hostium expūgnāret praemīsit.
2. Ab septimā hōrā ad vesperum pūgnātum est tam ācriter ut mīlia mīlitum ex utrīsque exercitibus interficerentur.
3. Vulneribus tam dēfessī erant ut eō sē recipere inciperent.
4. Prō vallō carrōs objēcerant ut ē locō superiōre in nostrōs venientēs tēla conjicerent.
5. Helvētiī tantum numerum virōrum āmīserant ut lēgātōs dē dēditiōne ad Caesarem mitterent.
6. Multī virī nocte ēgressī sunt nē captīvī Rōmānōrum essent.
7. Ē castrīs prōgressī sunt ut ad pedēs Caesaris sē prōjicerent.
8. Imperia imperātōris erant tālia ut captīvī in Germāniam fugere nōn possent.
9. Cum omnibus carrīs secūtī impedīmenta in ūnum locum contulērunt.
10. Bellum ita gesserat ut Helvētiī vincerentur.

B. Translate into Latin:

1. The soldiers were so exhausted that they could not fight.
2. To that place they hastened in order to surrender.
3. Both armies fought so fiercely that thousands lost their lives.
4. The enemy lost so many men that they were not able to win.
5. They guarded the river carefully lest the captives escape.

Monuments of the dead along the Appian Way.

## Fashions in Funerals

All Romans, except perhaps the extremely poor, anticipated their own funerals with interest. This event was their one moment of posthumous glory. If poor, they scrimped and saved enough money in order to join one of the many co-operative burial societies that would ensure a memorable funeral. If rich, they left nothing undone to plan a grandiose ceremony.

In the early days funerals were held at night, but at the time of the Empire they took place in daylight. After the torchbearers at the head of the procession, marched the musicians, playing mournful music on their flutes, lyres, and dulcimers.

Professional clowns and buffoons came next, singing and shouting to amuse the spectators. Behind them walked an actor, dressed as the deceased and imitating his speech, mannerisms, gait, and perhaps even mocking the dead man's foibles.

The most important attraction of the display was composed of actors, carrying wax images of all the outstanding ancestors of the man's family, and dressed as consuls, generals, or other officials, according to the position each held in life. When Marcellus, nephew of Augustus, died, six hundred such actors walked in the procession, each bearing a mask of an important ancestor.

Slaves carried placards on which were written accounts of the deeds of the dead man. Then came the deceased, ornately gowned and carried on an elaborately decorated couch by eight pallbearers. The family, friends, freedmen, and ex-slaves followed. The women, their hair disheveled as an indication of grief, wore white, and the friends were dressed in dark-colored togas.

The funeral advanced first to the Forum, where the mourners and actors were provided with seats. An important kinsman mounted the Rostra and delivered a suitable eulogy. Then the procession reassembled and marched outside the city gates, where the body was cremated; the ashes were collected by a son of the deceased and deposited in a funeral urn. This was placed inside the tomb in a chamber called the *columbarium*, because each of the many niches resembled a dovecot.

The remains of magnificent tombs on all roads leading out of Rome illustrate the types of architecture used by wealthy Romans to impress passers-by with the importance of their families.

### Preparation for Battle

Interim Helvētiī omnia impedīmenta sua in ūnum locum contulērunt. Ipsī, rejectō (*hurled back*) nostrō equitātū, phalange (*phalanx*) factā, ad prīmam nostram aciem prōcessērunt. Caesar, postquam cōpiās īnstrūxit, sīgnum dedit et proelium cum Helvētiīs commīsit.

VICTORY FOR THE ROMANS

Nostrī, pīlīs ē locō superiōre missīs, facile hostium phalangem perfrēgērunt (*broke through*), et in eōs gladiīs impetum fēcērunt. Ita diū et ācriter pūgnātum est. Helvētiī prīmum impetum nostrōrum sustinēre nōn poterant; atque aliī in montem, aliī ad impedīmenta et carrōs suōs sē contulērunt.

Hī tamen ab hōrā septimā ad vesperum ex castrīs cōpiās ēducēbant. Ad multam noctem (*late at night*) etiam prope impedīmenta pūgnātum est, proptereā quod Helvētiī prō vallō carrōs objēcerant et ē locō superiōre in nostrōs venientēs tēla conjiciēbant, eu inter carrōs pīla longa subjiciēbant (*kept thrusting*) nostrōsque vulnerābant. Tandem illī, vulneribus dēfessī, sē nōn diūtius (*longer*) dēfendere poterant. Impedīmentīs castrīsque eōrum expūgnātīs, Helvētiī sē recipere incēpērunt. Ibi Orgetorīgis fīlia atque ūnus ē fīliīs captus est. Ex eō proeliō circiter (*about*) CXXX mīlia hominum superfuērunt (*survived*), eāque tōtā nocte continenter iērunt. Posteā Caesar cum omnibus cōpiīs eōs sequī incēpit.

### THE HELVETIANS SURRENDER

Helvētiī omnium rērum inopiā adductī dē dēditiōne lēgātōs ad Caesarem mīsērunt. Sē ad pedēs prōjēcērunt. Caesar Helvētiōs in eō locō manēre et adventum suum exspectāre jūssit. Eō postquam pervēnit, obsidēs, arma, servōs quī ad eōs fūgerant postulāvit. Dum ea geruntur, circiter hominum mīlia sex prīmā nocte ē castrīs Helvētiōrum ēgressī ad Rhēnum fīnēsque Germānōrum contendērunt. Quod ubi Caesar cōgnōvit, hōs quōrum per fīnēs ierant eōs redūcere jūssit. Eōs reductōs in numerō hostium habuit.

### TERMS OF PEACE

Reliquōs omnēs, obsidibus, armīs, servīs trāditīs, Caesar in dēditiōnem accēpit. Helvētiōs et alterās gentēs in fīnēs suōs unde erant prōfectī, redīre jūssit, et oppida quae incenderant iterum aedificāre jūssit. Sīc māximus imperātor, Gājus Jūlius Caesar, bellum tam bene gesserat ut paucīs mēnsibus tōtum bellum Helvēticum cōnficeret.

Oh, it is excellent to have a giant's strength,
But it is tyrannous to use it like a giant.
—William Shakespeare, 1564–1616
*Measure for Measure*

# *Unit* LVIII

## CONVERSATION

GALLUS: Quis vestrum tam fortis est ut mēcum sōlus pūgnet?

MĀNLIUS: Quid! Nūllus Rōmānus cum hōc hoste audācī contendet!

CĪVIS RŌMĀNUS (*magnō cum dolōre*): Nēmō!

MĀNLIUS: Cūr nēmō ex exercitū audet contrā illum prōcēdere?

CĪVIS RŌMĀNUS: Ille quidem (*indeed*) cēterōs Gallōs et vīribus et māgnitūdine et adulēscentiā atque virtūte superābat.

MĀNLIUS: Ego ipse prōcēdam neque patiar virtūtem Rōmānam ā Gallō spoliārī (*to be despoiled*).

CĪVIS RŌMĀNUS: Vidēsne quam ingēns sit? Scūtum longum habet et gladiōs duōs; quoque torquem (*necklace*) aureum circum collum (*neck*) suum gerit. Intellegō cūr omnēs eum vereantur.

MĀNLIUS: Scūtum ējus meō scūtō percutiam, et dē locō eum dējiciam. Posteā hunc Gallum audācem occīdam, torquem dētraham et in collō meō impōnam. Pro patriā meā!

## SECTION 1 Formation of the Perfect Subjunctive Active

▶ DISCUSSION

The perfect subjunctive active for all Latin verbs is formed by adding the tense indicator *-eri* plus the person indicators to the perfect stem.

PERFECT SUBJUNCTIVE ACTIVE, FIRST CONJUGATION

| | *Perf. Stem.* + *T.I.* + *P.I.* = | | | | *Form* | *Possible Translation* |
|---|---|---|---|---|---|---|
| | | | **SINGULAR** | | | |
| First | vocāv | + eri | + | m | = vocāverim | *I may have called* |
| Second | vocāv | + eri | + | s | = vocāverīs | *you may have called* |
| Third | vocāv | + eri | + | t | = vocāverit | *he, she, it may have called* |
| | | | **PLURAL** | | | |
| First | vocāv | + eri | + | mus | = vocāverīmus | *we may have called* |
| Second | vocāv | + eri | + | tis | = vocāverītis | *you may have called* |
| Third | vocāv | + eri | + | nt | = vocāverint | *they may have called* |

*339*

| CONJUGATION: | SECOND | THIRD | THIRD –io | FOURTH |
|---|---|---|---|---|
| | | SINGULAR | | |
| First | monuerim | rēxerim | cēperim | audīverim |
| Second | monuerīs | rēxerīs | cēperīs | audīverīs |
| Third | monuerit | rēxerit | cēperit | audīverit |
| | | PLURAL | | |
| First | monuerīmus | rēxerīmus | cēperīmus | audīverīmus |
| Second | monuerītis | rēxerītis | cēperītis | audīverītis |
| Third | monuerint | rēxerint | cēperint | audīverint |

▶ **STUDY HELPS**

1. The perfect subjunctive active is like the future perfect indicative active except for the long –ī in the first person plural and the second person singular and plural, and for the use of –m instead of –ō in the first person singular for the person indicator.

2. The Latin perfect subjunctive is translated into English not only by *may have* but by other forms, according to the nature of the clause in which the subjunctive is found.

3. The perfect subjunctive of the irregular verbs is formed regularly: *fuerim, potuerim, voluerim, ierim (īverim), tulerim.*

4. The *passive* forms of the perfect subjunctive can be found in the *Appendix.*

▶ **PRACTICE PATTERNS**

A. Conjugate the following verbs in the perfect subjunctive active. Translate into English, using the auxiliary verbs *may have.*

   dētrahō  percutiō  cōnferō  volō  adsum  possum

B. Write in Latin:

    he may have come      we may have thrown
    they may have gone     you (pl.) may have heard
    you (sing.) may have been  I may have borne
    he may have been present   she may have been absent

# SECTION 2 The Sequence of Tenses

▶ **DISCUSSION**

The tense of the subjunctive in a subordinate clause depends on the tense of the main verb. This tense relationship between the verbs in the principal clauses and in the subordinate clauses is called *sequence of tenses.*

| SEQUENCE | IF THE MAIN VERB IS: | THE SUBORDINATE CLAUSE USES: |
|---|---|---|
| Primary | present<br>future<br>present perfect<br>   (*has, have*)<br>future perfect<br>imperative<br>present subjunctive | 1. the *present subjunctive* (to express same time as, *or* time future to that of the main verb)<br>2. the *perfect subjunctive* (to express time before that of the main verb) |
| Secondary | imperfect<br>perfect (simple)<br>pluperfect | 1. the *imperfect subjunctive* (to express same time as, *or* time future to that of the main verb)<br>2. the *pluperfect subjunctive* (to express time before that of the main verb) |

▶ STUDY HELPS

1. Primary tenses follow primary tenses; secondary follow secondary.

2. The *present perfect* in English always uses *has* or *have;* it is a *primary* tense. The *simple perfect* expresses past time without auxiliary verbs; it is a secondary tense: primary = *I have called;* secondary = *I called.*

# SECTION 3 Indirect Questions

▶ DISCUSSION

1. In English and in Latin there are two kinds of questions:

| | | |
|---|---|---|
| *Direct* | *What are you doing?* | **Quid facis?** |
| *Indirect* | *I ask what you are doing.* | **Rogō quid faciās.** |

A *direct* question becomes *indirect* when it is used as the direct object of verbs meaning *ask, know, perceive, show,* etc. It is always introduced by an interrogative word. In English the verb of an indirect question is in the indicative mood; in Latin it is in the subjunctive mood, although the English translation is like the indicative.

2. Indirect questions must not be confused with indirect statements.

| INDIRECT STATEMENT | INDIRECT QUESTION |
|---|---|
| **Sciō eum vēnisse.**<br>I know *that* he came. | **Sciō cūr vēnerit.**<br>I know *why* he came. |
| 1. Introduced by *that* in English, but has no introductory word in Latin<br>2. Verb in the infinitive<br>3. Subject in the accusative | 1. Introduced in both English and Latin by a *question* word or phrase<br>2. Verb in the subjunctive<br>3. Subject in the nominative |

*341*

Change the following direct questions to indirect questions in English, using verbs of asking, knowing, perceiving, showing, etc. Translate into Latin:

1. Who led the army to the mountain?
2. Why did the cavalry of the Helvetians follow our army?
3. At what time will they come?
4. Where have the enemy pitched camp?
5. Whence did they come?
6. To whom did the Helvetians surrender?

## WORDS TO MASTER

adulēscen'tia, –ae, f., youth (adolescence)

dētra'hō, –ere, –trāxī, –trāctus (3), draw off, remove (detract)

ēve'niō, –īre, –vēnī, –ventūrus (4), come out, result

ēven'tus, –ūs, m., outcome (event)

fā'tum, –ī, n., destiny (fate)

impō'nō, –ere, –posuī, –positus (3), place upon (impose)

in'gēns, –gentis, adj., huge

la'tus, –eris, n., side, flank, wing of an army (lateral)

mā'ne, adv., in the morning

o'vis, –is, f., sheep (ovine)

percu'tiō, –ere, –cussī, –cussus (3), strike through, pierce (percussion)

val'lēs, –is, f., valley

vix, adv., barely, scarcely

## BUILDING WORD POWER

Many verbs in Latin were derived from nouns or adjectives. They are called *denominatives* (*dē* + *nōmen*), which means *from nouns*, although they are also derived from adjectives. Trace the original nouns or adjectives in these Latin verbs: *līberāre, locāre, mīlitāre, nōmināre, domināre, validāre, aequāre, associāre.* Write the English verb which ends in –ate that is derived from each of the foregoing Latin verbs.

A few denominatives are found in the other conjugations, as *pūnīre,* punish, from *poena; fīnīre,* finish, from *fīnis; lūdere,* play, from *lūdus; flōrēre,* flower, from *flōs* (*flōris*).

Very often if you know the meaning of a noun or adjective in Latin, you can form and tell the meaning of a first conjugation verb formed on that noun or adjective. Form first conjugation verbs on these nouns and adjectives; tell the English meaning: *aliēnus; anima; antīquus; genus* (*generis*); *terminus.* From what Latin nouns or adjectives were these Latin verbs derived: *accelerāre, renovāre, ēlabōrāre, accommodāre, ēlevāre?* Name English derivatives from these Latin verbs.


## SENTENCE PATTERNS

A. Translate into English:

1. Cōgnōvēruntne Rōmānī cūr Gallī in Ītaliam pervenīrent?
2. Nōnne Rōmānī dīxērunt ēventum reī hostibus nōn grātum esse?
3. Num Gallus māgnitūdine corporis ingēns rem contrā sē ēventūram esse putat?
4. Hostis audāx superbē rogāvit quālēs mīlitēs Rōmānī essent.
5. Ex alterō latere vallis exercitus Gallōrum, et ex alterō latere exercitus Rōmānōrum certāmen spectābat.
6. Hostem occīdere erat fātum adulēscentis fortis.
7. Mīlitēs vix vidēre potuērunt quō modō Mānlius gladium suum dētraheret.
8. Nunc sciunt quam ob rem scūtum scūtō percusserit.
9. Scūtō in corpus impositō, Gallus impetum Mānlī exspectat ut eum occīdat.
10. Quis Rōmānōrum erat tam īrātus ut hostem ingentem māne oppūgnāret?

B. Translate into Latin:

1. Does he know with what weapon the Roman struck the enemy?
2. He believed that the outcome of the affair would be pleasing to him.
3. Does Manlius understand that the Gaul from his youth was a soldier?
4. The man of huge body is asking why the fate of both armies cannot be decided by one battle.
5. Morning and evening the soldiers wait on both sides of the bridge to kill the boy's sheep.


### Manlius, the Giant-Killer

Rōmānī cum Gallīs, quī in Ītaliam dēscenderant, bellum gerēbant (381 B.C.). Jam ad pontem, ā quō nōn longē Gallī erant, pervēnerant. Et Gallī et Rōmānī castra prope flūmen Aniēnem (*Anio*) ita posuērunt ut pōns inter duōs exercitūs esset. Deinde māne quīdam Gallus, māgnitūdine corporis ingēns, scūtum gerēns et gladiōs duōs manibus tenēns, atque torque (*necklace*) aureō dēcorātus, in prīmam aciem prōcessit. Ille cēterōs Gallōs et vīribus et māgnitūdine et adulēscentiā atque virtūte superābat.

Commissō proeliō, atque utrīsque summō studiō pūgnantibus, Gallus et Gallīs et Rōmānīs manū sīgnificāre (*to make a sign*) incipiēbat. Pūgnae pausa facta est. Statim silentiō factō, cum vōce māximā ūnum ex Rōmānīs ad certāmen singulāre prōvocāvit. "Quis Rōmānōrum," rīsit, "tam fortis est ut mēcum sōlus pūgnet?"

Id Titō Mānliō, nōbilī adulēscentī Rōmānō, māgnō dolōrī erat. Is māximē īrātus quod ē tantō exercitū nēmō audēbat propter ējus māgnitūdinem ingentem et ācrem vultum (*expression*) cum Gallō pūgnāre. Hīs ā Gallō dictīs, Mānlius fortis prōcessit, neque passus est virtūtem Rōmānum ab hoste rīdērī. Scūtō pedestrī (*infantry*) et gladiō brevī cinctus (*girded*) contra Gallum cōnstitit. Timōre māgnō ea congressiō (*meeting*) in ipsō pontī, exercitibus utrōque latere pontis spectantibus, facta est.

Gallus suō mōre scūtum suum prōjēcit et impetum Mānlī exspectāvit. Mānlius, animō magis quam arte cōnfīsus (*trusting*), scūtō scūtum percussit. Dum Gallus locum suum recuperāre (*recover*) cōnātur, Mānlius iterum scūtum percussit et hominem ingentem dē locō iterum dējēcit. Hoc modō sub gladium Gallicum successit et gladiō suō hostem occīdit, torquem dētrāxit, et in collō (*neck*) suō imposuit.

## CONVERSATION

PYTHIAS: Salvē, Dāmōn, amīce optimē! Dīc mihi cūr Syrācūsam vēnerīs?

DĀMŌN: Nōnne cōnspicis tōtam urbem mīlitibus Agrigentō complētam (*filled*) esse? Nōnne nōvistī quā dē causā Dionȳsius sociīque Agrigentō arcem occupāverint et arma frūmentumque rapuerint? Tyrannus creārī rēx in animō nunc habet.

PYTHIAS: Rēx! Rēx! Dionȳsius auctōritātem obtinēre rēgis cōgitat! Haec crēdere nōn possum!

DĀMŌN: Vērum est. Probābuntne senātōrēs haec? Num trādentur urbem huic tyrannō?

PYTHIAS: Ego quidem (*indeed*) nōn probābō. In conciliō (*meeting*) senātōrum contrā tyrannum ōrātiōnem habēbō.

\*   \*   \*

PYTHIAS (*post ōrātiōnem*): Senātus caecus est! Nunc nūllam auctōritātem ostendit sed ā lēge discedēns tyrannum rēgem creat! Et ego ad mortem dūcor! Ah! Dāmōnem cārum amīcum meum cōnspiciō! Calamitāte meā audītā, ad mē celeriter contendit!

## SECTION 1 Formation of the Pluperfect Subjunctive Active

▶ DISCUSSION

The pluperfect subjunctive active for all Latin verbs is formed by adding the tense indicator *–isse* plus the regular person indicators to the perfect stem.

PLUPERFECT SUBJUNCTIVE ACTIVE, FIRST CONJUGATION

| *Perf. Stem* + *T.I.* + *P.I.* = | *Form* | *Possible Translation* |
|---|---|---|
| SINGULAR | | |
| First **vocāv** + isse + **m** | = **vocāvissem** | *I might have called* |
| Second **vocāv** + isse + **s** | = **vocāvissēs** | *you might have called* |
| Third **vocāv** + isse + **t** | = **vocāvisset** | *he, she, it might have called* |

**345**

| First | vocāv + isse + mus = vocāvissēmus | *we might have called* |
|---|---|---|
| Second | vocāv + isse + tis = vocāvissētis | *you might have called* |
| Third | vocāv + isse + nt = vocāvissent | *they might have called* |

## PLUPERFECT SUBJUNCTIVE ACTIVE

| CONJUGATION: | SECOND | THIRD | THIRD –io | FOURTH |
|---|---|---|---|---|
| | | SINGULAR | | |
| First | monuissem | rēxissem | cēpissem | audīvissem |
| Second | monuissēs | rēxissēs | cēpissēs | audīvissēs |
| Third | monuisset | rēxisset | cēpisset | audīvisset |
| | | PLURAL | | |
| First | monuissēmus | rēxissēmus | cēpissēmus | audīvissēmus |
| Second | monuissētis | rēxissētis | cēpissētis | audīvissētis |
| Third | monuissent | rēxissent | cēpissent | audīvissent |

▶ STUDY HELPS

1. The pluperfect subjunctive active may also be formed by adding the regular person indicators to the perfect active infinitive: **vocāvisse + m,** etc.

2. The Latin pluperfect subjunctive may be translated into English by *might have, would have,* and by other forms, according to the nature of the clause in which the subjunctive is found.

3. The pluperfect subjunctive of the irregular verbs is formed regularly: **fuissem, potuissem, voluissem, īssem (īvissem), tulissem.**

4. The *passive* forms of the pluperfect subjunctive can be found in the *Appendix.*

▶ PRACTICE PATTERNS

A. Write the third person plural pluperfect subjunctive active of the following verbs. Translate into English, using *might have.*

cōgitō   cōnspiciō   nōscō   teneō   sciō   eō   ferō   volō   adsum   possum

B. Write synopses in the subjunctive active only:

1. cōgitō (first person singular)
2. cōnspiciō (second person singular)
3. sciō (second person plural)
4. sum (third person singular)
5. nōscō (third person singular)
6. vetō (first person plural)
7. augeō (third person plural)
8. eō (third person plural)

C. Write in Latin:

1. They might have been absent.
2. You (pl.) might have pondered.
3. I might have known.
4. You (sing.) might have seen.
5. He might have been able.
6. We might have perceived.

# SECTION 2 Review of the Dative Case

The datives below are used: (a) with special adjectives; (b) with special verbs; (c) with compound verbs; (d) as indirect object. Translate these sentences, and explain the syntax of the datives.

1. Nihil nōbīs nocēre potest.
2. Fortis imperātor exercituī praeerat.
3. Ea amīcitia erat grāta mātrī.
4. Pater fīliō praemium dedit.
5. Lēgātum fortem exercituī praefēcērunt.
6. In eō itinere Casticō persuāsit.
7. Ea rēs Helvētiīs nūntiāta est.
8. Propinquī sunt Germānīs.
9. Populō Rōmānō bellum intulērunt.
10. Castrīs idōneum locum dēlēgit.
11. Caesar captīvīs lībertātem dedit.
12. Lībertās eīs ā Caesare data est.

## WORDS TO MASTER

**ar'bitror** (1), *dep.*, consider, think, judge (*arbitrate*)

**beā'tus, –a, –um,** *adj.*, happy, blessed (*beatify*)

**cae'cus, –a, –um,** *adj.*, blind

**cala'mitās, –tātis,** *f.*, disaster (*calamity*)

**clam,** *adv.*, secretly

**cō'gitō** (1), ponder, think about, consider (*cogitate*)

**cōnspi'ciō, –ere, –spēxī, –spectus** (3), catch sight of, perceive (*conspicuous*)

**mor'tuus, –a, –um,** *adj.*, dead (*mortuary*)

**nōs'cō, –ere, nōvī, nōtus** (3), learn, come to know; *perf.*, know (*noted*)

**peccā'tum, –ī,** *n.*, sin, crime (*peccable*)

**sce'lus, –eris,** *n.*, crime, wicked deed

**ve'tō, –āre, –uī, –itus** (1), *irreg.*, forbid (*veto*)

## BUILDING WORD POWER

When the Romans wanted to denote repeated or intensified action, they made the stem of the perfect passive participle the stem of a first conjugation verb. Thus, **dīcere, dictus,** *say*, developed into **dictāre,** *to say repeatedly, to dictate.* Such verbs are called *frequentatives.*

From **pellere, pulsus,** *strike*, we have **pulsāre,** *keep on striking, beat.* What frequentative was developed from **habēre?** Sometimes **–itō** was added to the present stem of a verb, as **agitāre,** *to put in constant motion*, from **agō,** *drive.*

Besides verbs in *–ate* we have many verbs in English derived from participles of Latin verbs. What are the derivatives from: **objectus, respectus, āctus, īnfectus, inductus, afflictus?**

Write as many English verbs as you can think of that end in the following syllables: *–cept, –dict, –duct, –fect, –ject, –press, –rect, –rupt, –sect, –spect, –vent.* Give the Latin present infinitive for as many of these verbs as you can, as for example: *conduct* from **condūcere.**

## SENTENCE PATTERNS

A. Translate into English. Explain the reasons for the subjunctive mood in some of the sentences.

1. Imperātōribus mortuīs, incolae urbis convēnērunt ut ducēs novōs creārent.
2. Intellēxērunt rēgem malum scelera contrā lēgēs commīsisse.
3. Tālia scelera ducis rēgī nūntiāta sunt ut ducem occīdī dēbēre arbitrārētur.
4. In hīs calamitātibus Dāmōn dīxit sē amīcō auxilium datūrum esse.
5. Diē quōdam Pythias rogāvit cūr Dionȳsius rēgem creārī vellet.
6. Senātor nōverat quis peccāta rēgis cōnspēxisset.
7. Nōnne adulēscēns sēnsit quam ob rem amīcus caecus esset?
8. Clam autem dux inīquus cōgitābat quō modō potestātem obtinēre posset.
9. Dionȳsius incolās Syrācūsae lēge temptārī vetuit.
10. Cīvēs urbis sē brevī tempore futūrōs esse beātōs arbitrātī sunt.

B. Translate into Latin:

1. Have you not heard that the young man saved the life of his friend?
2. No one understood why the leader had killed the generals.
3. Secretly he thought about the crimes of the soldier (who was) trying to be elected king.
4. Did the people perceive who was in command of the troops?
5. Damon knows where his friend has gone and when he will return.

## Pyramus and Thisbe

**A**ccording to the Roman poet Ovid, the purple fruit of the mulberry tree was once the color of snow. The tree changed its color after the death of Pyramus and Thisbe, whose story appears here.

Once upon a time there lived in Babylon a handsome youth named Pyramus and a lovely maiden called Thisbe. Because their houses adjoined, they played together as children; but when their childhood friendship deepened into love, their parents would not allow their marriage. Since they were forbidden to speak to each other, they could converse only by signs and glances.

Then one day they discovered a crack in the wall that separated their houses. Through this crack they could whisper expressions of their devotion; but that was not enough. With great fear and trepidation they arranged to meet each other at twilight near a white mulberry tree outside the city walls. As Thisbe at the appointed hour approached the meeting place, she saw a fierce-looking lioness. Terrified, she fled, dropping her veil as she ran. The beast picked up the veil in her bloody mouth, but soon dropped it and ambled off to the woods.

Just then Pyramus appeared. Filled with anguish when he recognized the blood-stained veil, he plunged his sword into his side just as Thisbe, wishing to warn him of the danger, came forth from her hiding place. Filled with anguish, she too killed herself; and the mingled blood of the unfortunate lovers stained the roots of the mulberry tree, whose fruit ever since has been a deep purple.

### Damon and Pythias

Ōlim habitābat Syrācūsīs in īnsulā Siciliā cīvis quīdam nōmine Dionȳsius quī urbem pulchram regere māgnopere volēbat. Illō tempore incolae Syrācūsae bellum cum Carthāginiēnsibus gerē-bant. Post bellum Carthāgō victor ex pūgnā discessit. Incolae Syrācūsae arbitrātī sunt Dionȳsium, mīlitem prīvātum, māgnam virtūtem ostendisse, et ob hanc causam multī eum laudāvērunt.

Posteā conciliō (*meeting*) convocātō, populus victus dē condi-ciōnibus bellī agēbat. Nēmō illō tempore intellēxit cūr Dionȳsius contrā lēgem ōrātiōnem habēret in quā nūntiāvit imperātōrēs exercitūs Syrācūsae contrā rem pūblicam ēgisse et mortem hōrum imperātōrum postulāvit. Clam autem alia cōnsilia cōgitābat.

Populus ab hāc ōrātiōne incitātus, imperātōribus mortuīs, ducēs novōs apud quōs Dionȳsius erat creāvit. Brevī tempore, populus eum prīncipem ducum creāre coāctus est. Hōc factō, cīvēs sē esse beātōs arbitrātī sunt, sed mox sēnsērunt cūr Dionȳsius sum-mam potestātem māgnopere cupīvisset. Nōn jam cīvēs erant caecī. Dionȳsius quidem dictātor Syrācūsae factus erat, et etiam dominus operum mīlitārium urbis erat. Paulō post, quod dīxit hostēs lībertātis ipsum oppūgnāvisse et vulnerāvisse, sescentōs (*six hundred*) hominēs dēlēctōs cohortem praetōriam (*bodyguard*) obtinuit. Senātus et concilia (*assemblies*) convēnērunt, sed nūllam auctōritātem nec potestātem habuērunt. Scelus post scelus contrā patriam fēcit. Nēmō lēge temptātus est. Lēgēs novās vetuit. Dionȳsius jam vērō tyrannus erat.

Quīdam senātor nōmine Pythias, ubi nōvit arcem et omnēs rēs mīlitārēs ā Dionȳsiō obtentās esse, commōtus est; nam dē lībertāte cīvitātis māximē timēbat. Cum prīmum cōgnōvit Dionȳsium rēgem creārī in animō habēre, in senātum contendit. Audācter loquēns senātum rogāvit cūr ā lēge discessissent et tyrannum rēgem creārent. Senātō statim dīmissō, Pythias ab mīlitibus Dionȳsī captus est et interficī jūssus est. Dum Pythias ad mortem trahitur, amīcum Dāmōnem cōnspēxit, quī, calamitāte amīcī audītā, ad eum celeriter contendēbat.

Elysium is as far to
The very nearest room,
If in that room a friend await
Felicity or doom.
　—Emily Dickinson, 1830–1886

# *Unit* LX

## CONVERSATION

DIONȲSIUS: Quis es tū? Unde vēnistī?

DĀMŌN: Tūne, Dionȳsī, quaeris ā mē quis sim et unde vēnerim? Dāmōn, mīles Agrigentō, ego sum. Ex puerīs ego et Pythias amīcī fidēlēs fuimus. Uterque alterum tōtō animō amat.

DIONȲSIUS: Pythias hodiē sē mihi inimīcum ostendit et jam eum interficī jūssī. Abī!

DĀMŌN: Pythias fīlium et uxōrem rūrsus vidēre māximē cupit. Ego mē vadem (*pledge*) dabō prō Pythiā ut amīcus meus moram mortis habeat et ad domicilium redeat.

DIONȲSIUS: Ego nōn crēdō ūllum amīcum prō alterō ē vītā excēdere velle, sed vidēbimus. Nōvistīne ubi uxor et fīlius ējus habitent?

DĀMŌN: Prope ōram maritimam quae vīgintī mīlia passuum abest.

DIONȲSIUS: Sex hōrās moram mortis dabō. Nōlī pūtāre amīcum tuum, ā perīculō līberātum, reventūrum esse. Tū autem reditum ējus in carcere (*prison*) exspectābis. Fīne sex hōrārum, illō nōn reveniente, tū, Dāmōn, interficiēris.

DĀMŌN: Crēde mihi. Neuter nostrum fidem alterī āmittet.

## SECTION 1 Review of the Ablative Case

In each of these sentences, a noun or pronoun is used in the ablative case. A list is given of the ablatives used in this book. Match Column I with Column II. Translate the sentences.

| COLUMN I | COLUMN II |
|---|---|
| a. Means | 1. Trēs legiōnēs ex hībernīs ēdūxit. (_____) |
| b. Manner | 2. Cum lēgātīs ad urbem iit. (_____) |
| c. Agent | 3. Cōpiae ā ducibus īnstruentur. (_____) |
| d. Accompaniment | 4. Urbem perīculō līberāvit. (_____) |
| e. Description | 5. Gladiō pūgnābat. (_____) |
| f. Time when | 6. Sine timōre ante rēgem stābat. (_____) |
| g. Time within which | 7. Dux erat benīgnus verbīs et factīs. (_____) |
| h. Cause | 8. Mōns altior est colle. (_____) |
| i. Place where | 9. Sīgnō datō proelium commīsērunt. (_____) |
| j. Place from which | 10. In Ītaliā diū habitābant. (_____) |
| k. Separation | 11. Rōmānī timōre commovēbantur. (_____) |
| l. Ablative absolute | 12. Paucīs hōrīs oppidum dēlētum est. (_____) |
| m. Specification (respect) | 13. Virum māgnā scientiā dēlēgērunt. (_____) |
| n. Comparison | 14. Mōns multō altior est colle. (_____) |
| o. Degree of difference | 15. Illō tempore aberat. (_____) |
| p. With prepositions | 16. Ad certāmen māgnō cum gaudiō properāvit. |
| | (_____) |

## SECTION 2 Review of the Nominative, Vocative, and Locative Cases

Match Column I with Column II. Translate the sentences.

| COLUMN I | COLUMN II |
|---|---|
| a. Subject of finite verb | 1. Rōmae remānsit. (_____) |
| b. Predicate nominative | 2. Estis benīgnī, Cornēlī et Mārce. (_____) |
| c. Predicate adjective | 3. Puerī domī labōrāvērunt. (_____) |
| d. Locative | 4. Fīlius meus es tū. (_____) |
| e. Vocative | 5. Ego sum quī sum. (_____) |
| | 6. Illī aderant. (_____) |

# SECTION 3 General Review of Cases

Account for the cases of the italicized words. Translate the sentences.

1. *Classī* praeerat.
2. *Urbs* ā *mīlitibus* oppūgnāta est.
3. *Rōmam* vēnērunt.
4. Rēx benīgnus *virō* erat.
5. *Puer* māgnā *virtūte* erat.
6. Equus *virī* capiētur.
7. *Mīles* pūgnat.
8. *Servō* cibum dedit.
9. *Mūrum* sex *pedum* fēcērunt.
10. *Multō* fortius pūgnābat.
11. Ab *urbe* fūgit.
12. Multa *mīlia* passuum ambulāvit.
13. Puer *patrī* crēdidit.
14. Multōs *annōs* passus est.
15. *Tēlō* vulnerātus est.
16. Māgnā cum *cūrā* scrīpsit.
17. Sciō *puellās* īsse.
18. *Urbe* captā incolae fūgērunt.
19. *Scientiā* frātrem superāvit.
20. *Rōmae* habitat.
21. *Domum* cucurrit.
22. Cicerō *cōnsul* creātus est.
23. Īte in *casam, Jūlī* et *Paule.*
24. Per *agrōs* contendērunt.
25. In *ponte* stābat.
26. *Victōriā* laetus erat.
27. Fortissima *puellārum* erat.
28. Cum *dolōre* urbem relinquēbant.
29. Cum *amīcō* ībō.
30. Vīsus est *beātus.*
31. Oportet *virum* īre.
32. *Nocte* apprehensī sunt.
33. Decem *diēbus* urbs capta est.
34. Fortiōrēs *Rōmānīs* erant.
35. Sine *cūrā* lūdēbant.
36. Dux erat multae *scientiae.*

## WORDS TO MASTER

**am′bō, −ae, −ō** (declined like **duo**), both (*ambidextrous*)

**apprehen′dō, −ere, −ī, −hēnsus** (3), seize, lay hold of (*apprehend*)

**aspec′tus, −ūs,** *m.*, appearance, sight (*aspect*)

**ingre′dior, −ī, −gressus sum** (3), *dep.*, enter (*ingress*)

**ju′venis, −e,** *adj.*, young, youthful (*juvenile*); **ju′venis, −is,** *m.*, young man, a youth

**lū′men, −inis,** *n.*, light (*luminous*)

**nūp′tiae, −ārum,** *f. pl.*, marriage, nuptials (*nuptial*)

**opor′tet, −ēre, oportuit** (2), *impers.*, it is fitting, it is proper, ought

**quae′rō, −ere, quaesīvī, quaesītus** (3), inquire, seek, ask (*inquisitive*)

**rema′neō −ēre, −mānsī, −mansūrus** (2), stay behind, remain (*remain*)

**salū′tō** (1), greet (*salute*)

**tra′hō, −ere, trāxī, trāctus** (3), drag, draw (*tractor*)

## BUILDING WORD POWER

Many Latin verbs of the third conjugation were formed from other verbs by adding −sc− to the present stem. They are sometimes called familarly −scō verbs, but the more technical term is *inceptive* or *inchoative*, both of which words express the idea of beginning. For example,

*352*

*flōs* means *flower;* *flōrēre,* *to flower;* *flōrēscere,* *to begin to flower.*
The trees are *florescent* when they begin to flower. Do not confuse
*florescent* with *fluorescent,* a coined word for the type of light we may use
over our desks in school and perhaps at home.

When you remove the cap from a soft drink bottle, the liquid *effervesces.* It has the appearance of boiling. *Fervēre* means *to boil.* What
do *fervēscere* and *effervēscere* mean? Watch the development of
this word: *alere* = *feed;* *alēscere* = *increase, grow up;* *adolēscere*
= *come to maturity.* An adolescent is one who is developing from childhood to maturity. *All* Latin *–scō* verbs and their English derivatives
have *–esce–,* a good rule for spelling.

## SENTENCE PATTERNS

A. Translate into English:
1. Nōnne imperātor ā mīlitibus quaesīvit ad quem locum captīvus fūgisset?
2. Apprehende illum ut cōgnōscāmus ubi arma abdiderit?
3. Rēx rogāvit ambōs juvenēs cūr in urbe remānsissent.
4. Dīxēruntne oportēre nōs ex castrīs ēgredī?
5. Haec locūtus in domicilium amīcī ingressus est.
6. Nōvistīne ā quibus amīcī lūmina Siciliae appellārentur?
7. Ēgressus Pythias juvenem audācem aspectū in viā stantem invēnit et illum salūtāvit.
8. Calamitāte amīcī audītā, Dāmōn ad rēgem contendit ut causam Pythiae ageret.
9. Num intellēxit quam ob rem hostis adulēscentem ad illud locum trāxisset?
10. Juvenis tam celeriter cucurrit ut nūptiīs amīcī adesse posset.

B. Translate into Latin:
1. The man entering the house said he knew which young man had been seized.
2. Didn't the king understand why both men had been faithful to each other?
3. It is not fitting that either Damon or Pythias be put to death.
4. Did the inhabitants of the city inquire what kind of leader he was?
5. He thought that Pythias, freed from all danger, would remain at home.

## Damon and Pythias (continued)

Dāmōn Agrigentō vēnerat et Syrācūsīs paucōs diēs manēbat,
nam Calanthem in mātrimōnium dūcere dēsīderābat. Temporibus
prīstinīs (*former*) Dāmōn et Pythias fuerant amīcī nōtī. Eō
tempore ex puerīs excesserant, sed etiam amīcī fidēlēs erant,
ūnus mīles fortis, alter senātor honestus (*honored*). Ambō juvenēs

*353*

erant nōbilēs aspectū et factō, et uterque alterum cārum habēbat.

Dāmōn māgnō cum dolōre amīcum salūtāvit. Bene intellēxit quam ob rem Pythias ad mortem traherētur, et ab hōc quaesivit quae māgnopere vellet. Pythias respondit sē ante mortem puerum parvum et uxōrem fīdam rūrsus vidēre tōtō animō cupere, sed Dionȳsius id vetuerat. Statim Dāmōn ad tyrannum Dionȳsium properāvit ut causam Pythiae expōneret. Tyrannus rogāvit ubi uxor Pythiae habitāret. Dāmōn eī dīxit Pythiae domicilium ferē vīgintī mīlia passuum abesse, sed hunc sex hōrīs revenīre posse. Dāmōn Pythiam reventūrum esse prōmīsit, et dīxit sē ipsum vadem (*pledge*) prō amīco datūrum esse.

Dionȳsius nōn arbitrātus est ūllum amīcum prō alterō vītam dare velle, sed rēge volente Pythias ad domicilium propinquum ōrae maritimae māximā cum celeritāte contendit, dum Dāmōn apprehenditur et in carcerem (*prison*) trahitur.

Interim Dionȳsius et omnēs amīcī Pythiae et Dāmōnis reī ēventum exspectābant, et quaerēbant inter sē uter eōrum in fīde remanēret. Fīne sex hōrārum accedente nec illō reveniente, Dāmōn ad mortem ducī jūssus est, nam aut Dāmōnem aut Pythiam interficī oportet. Ambō juvenēs vītam cupiēbant, sed neuter eōrum fidem alterī āmīsit. Uterque alterō crēdidit.

Ipsā igitur hōrā ā tyrannō statūtā, subitō ille cui vas (*pledge*) datus erat carcerem māgnā cum celeritāte ingressus est. Dionȳsius, aspectū Pythiae permōtus, amīcōs fidēlēs salūtāvit et in admīrātiōne poenam remīsit (*remitted*). Deinde hīs amīcīs fidēlibus sē socium tertium hūjus amīcitiae jungere volēbat. Multī incolae Syrācūsae ad nūptiās Dāmōnis et Calanthis properāvērunt. Dāmōn et Pythias lūmina tōtīus Siciliae in perpetuum tenēbantur.

# Comprehensive Review:  Units LVI–LX

A. Write the genitive, the gender, and the meaning of these nouns:

| | | | | | |
|---|---|---|---|---|---|
| ovis | lūmen | collis | ēventus | aspectus | calamitās |
| fātum | latus | vallēs | nūptiae | hīberna | equitātus |
| agmen | scelus | juvenis | peccātum | dēditiō | adulēscentia |

B. Write the meanings of:

| | | | | | | | |
|---|---|---|---|---|---|---|---|
| eō | clam | beātus | tālis | perītus | ambō | dēfessus | ingēns |
| vix | māne | caecus | citrā | mortuus | tam | proximus | deinde |

C. Identify these forms and translate:

| | | | | | |
|---|---|---|---|---|---|
| peccāta | mortuōs | lūminī | proximīs | caecus | beātissimō |
| collium | vesperī | perītior | aspectūs | equitātū | adulēscēns |
| ingentī | latera | hībernīs | ducum | vallibus | nūptiārum |

D. Write in Latin the specified forms:

1. any fate (genitive)
2. what hill (dative)
3. this side (accusative)
4. that crime (ablative)
5. both sides (nominative)
6. the whole valley (dative)
7. the greatest sins (ablative)
8. no surrender (genitive)
9. very happy nuptials (nominative)
10. very beautiful evenings (genitive)
11. which (of two) sheep (accusative)
12. no calamity (nominative)
13. rather pleasing appearance (genitive)
14. the longer line of march (dative)
15. which light (accusative)
16. a very deep valley (ablative)

E. Write the voice, mood, tense, person, and number of these forms:

| | | | | |
|---|---|---|---|---|
| ēveniat | cōnspēxit | prōjēcerit | convertētur | ēgressus es |
| oportet | cōgitēmus | abstinēbat | ascendisset | arbitrātus est |
| vetētur | cōnferret | dētrāximus | expūgnāverint | ingrediēbantur |
| traheret | nōverāmus | objiciātur | conjēcissēmus | percussum erat |
| possētis | apprehendō | quaererētur | animadvertunt | impositī erant |
| nōverimus | nocuerīmus | remanēbāmus | abstinērentur | prōgressī sunt |

F. Write a synopsis, active and passive, indicative and subjunctive, third person singular, of nōscō.

G. Write the infinitives and participles and give meanings:

| | | | | |
|---|---|---|---|---|
| impōnō | expūgnō | abstineō | conjiciō | cūstōdiō |

H. Translate into Latin:

| | | |
|---|---|---|
| in Rome | from the town | the enemy seeking peace |
| in Italy | at that time | a leader in name and deed |
| at home | by the soldier | the best of the soldiers |
| from Rome | into the city | because of his good deeds |
| a mile | two feet higher | an attack having been made |
| three miles | with great sorrow | on account of many reasons |
| the soldiers | five thousand soldiers | a gift pleasing to the boy |
| with the king | five of his companions | to give a gift to the boy |

## SENTENCE PATTERNS

### A. Translate into English:

1. Lēgātī vēnērunt ut pācem peterent.
2. Legiōnem tertiam ibi relīquit nē hostēs flūmen trānsīrent.
3. Nōlī spem tuam in dīvitiīs aut potestāte pōnere.
4. Duce juvante patriam nostram adjuvāre et servāre possumus.
5. Nōnne Caesar negāvit sē ūllī iter per prōvinciam datūrum esse?
6. Num Rōmānī Gallīs equitātū superiōrēs erant?
7. Mūrus tam altus factus erat ut oppidum bene dēfenderētur.
8. Magister rogāvit quid fēcissem.
9. Mīlitēs tantā virtūte pūgnāvērunt ut oppidum occupāre possēmus.
10. Ita vīxī ut nōn frūstrā mē vīxisse exīstimem.

### B. Translate into Latin:

1. So skilled was the leader, so brave were the soldiers that the Romans overcame the enemy within a short time.
2. Marius asked them who their brothers were.
3. Do you know who I am and from what city I have come?
4. The soldiers fought bravely that they might not be conquered.
5. No one understood why they had surrendered to the enemy.

## SIGHT TRANSLATION: SAVED BY THE GEESE

Ōlim Gallī ex fīnibus excesserant ut oppida vīcōsque Etrūscōrum raperent. Etrūscī perterritī auxilium ā Rōmānīs petīvērunt. Itaque cōnsul Rōmānus exercitum contrā Gallōs dūxit, sed mīlitēs Rōmānī ferōcissimō aspectū barbarōrum perterritī sunt et fūgērunt. Gallī corpora ingentis magnitūdinis habēbant et cornua pecorom (*cattle*) in capitibus suīs gerēbant.

Victōria Gallōrum erat tam facilis ut Rōmam ipsam expūgnāre cōnstituerent. Urbem intrāvērunt. Cīvēs Rōmānī cum uxōribus līberīsque in arcem ascendērunt ut sē ibi omnī modō dēfenderent. Arx erat in summō colle. Multīs domibus raptīs et incēnsīs, hostēs post paucōs diēs impetum in arcem ipsam facere cōnstituērunt.

Silentiō noctis, Gallī, aliī aliōs trahentēs, in arcem ascendere clam cōnātī sunt. Complūrēs ad summum collem tantō silentiō pervēnērunt ut cūstōdēs nihil sentīrent. Sed subitō anserēs (*geese*) Jūnōnis sacrī Gallōs audīvērunt et clāmōre suō Mānlium, ducem praesidī, excitāvērunt. Mānlius aliōs cūstōdēs vocāns statim in prīmum Gallum impetum ācerrimum fēcit et eum dē saxō (*rock*) dējēcit. Gallus cāsū aliōs quoque perturbāvit, et hostēs facillimē repulsī sunt. Sīc arx Rōmāna ab ānseribus sacrīs servāta est.

# *Appendix*

## Pronunciation of Latin

The pronunciation of Latin will not be difficult. Nearly every sound in Latin has an equivalent English sound. At first you will learn the correct pronunciation of Latin by imitating your teacher. The rules outlined here are as close to the original Roman pronunciation as it is possible to infer from reliable sources.

### Vowels

The same vowels are used in both languages. Vowels may be either long or short. All long vowels have one sustained sound; therefore it takes more time to pronounce a vowel when it is long than when it is short. In the Roman method of pronunciation, the vowels are sounded as follows:

| Long | English | Latin | Short | English | Latin |
|------|---------|-------|-------|---------|-------|
| ā | as in *par* | **pāx** | a | as in *idea* | **pater** |
| ē | as in *pay* | **pēs** | e | as in *pet* | **pedes** |
| ī | as in *peal* | **pīlum** | i | as in *pit* | **piger** |
| ō | as in *pole* | **pōnō** | o | as in *pot* | **populus** |
| ū | as in *pool* | **pūniō** | u | as in *put* | **putō** |

### Quantity of Vowels

We learn the quantity of a vowel, that is, whether it is long or short, chiefly by observation, but the following rules serve as good guides:

1. A vowel is *long* if it is marked with a *macron* above it, as **ā** in **pāx.**

2. A vowel is long before –**nf**, –**ns**, –**nx**, –**nct**, –**gn**, –**scō**, as: **īnferus, amāns, lānx, cūnctus, māgnus, crēscō.**

3. A vowel resulting from a contraction is *long;* as **cōgō** (**co** + **agō**); **dēbeō** (**dē** + **habeō**); **nīl** (**nihil**).

4. A vowel is usually *short* before another vowel or –**h**, as **sua, vehere.**

5. A vowel is *short* before –**nd**, –**nt**, –**ss**; and final –**m**, –**r**, –**t**: as: **amandum, vident, missus; eram, amor, audit.**

### Diphthongs

Sometimes two adjacent vowels are pronounced together to give one sound. Thus linked, they are called *diphthongs.* Diphthongs are always long, but they do not have a macron over them.

| Diphthong* | English | Latin |
|:---:|:---:|:---:|
| ae | as in *pine* | pae'ne |
| oe | as in *poise* | poe'na |
| au | as in *pout* | pau'sa |
| eu | as in *feud* | Eurō'pa |
| ei | as in *weight* | hei |
| ui | as in *squeak* | huic |

Note that the diphthong **ui** is used almost exclusively in **cui** (pronounced *kwee*) and in **huic** (pronounced *wheek*).

## Semivowels

The letters **i** and **u** are both vowels and consonants. As a consonant **i** is pronounced like the *y* in English; **u** as a consonant is pronounced like the *w* in English. In this book, the **i**-consonant will be written as **j**: **injūria**, *injury* (pronounced in Latin in-yu'ri-a); and the **u**-consonant as **v**: **vīnum**, *wine* (pronounced in Latin wee'num). Notice that the word **vīnum** has also the letter **u** as a vowel.

The letters **i** and **u** are used as consonants if they begin a syllable and are followed by a vowel, or if they occur between vowels, as **jūbeō, ējus, ventus, ēventus.**

## Consonants

Most of the Latin consonants are pronounced as in English. The following exceptions must be noted.

| English Letter | | Latin |
|:---:|:---|---:|
| *b* | before **s** or **t** has the sound of *p*. | **urbs, obtineō** |
| *c* | always has the sound of *k*. | **cadō, Cicerō** |
| *g* | always has the sound of *g* in *gum*. | **Germānia, īgnis** |
| *j* | has the sound of *y* in *yes*. | **jam, injūria** |
| *n* | before **c, g, x** has the sound of *–ng* in *hang*. | **jungō, vincō** |
| *r* | is rolled at the tip of the tongue. | **rēs, ēripiō** |
| *s* | always has a hissing sound as in *sin*. | **salve, īnsīgnis** |
| *t* | always has the sound of *t* in *tin*. | **teneō, initium** |
| *ι* | always has the sound of *w* as in *wine*. | **vīnum, invidia** |
| *x* | always has the sound of *ks*. | **lēx, dīxī** |
| *z* | always has the sound of *dz* as in *adz*. | **zōna** |
| *qu* | before a vowel has the sound of *qu* as in *quit*. | **quis, relinquō** |
| *gu* | before a vowel has the sound of *gu* as in *language*. | **lingua** |
| *ch* | always has the sound of *k* as in *chorus*. | **pulcher** |

* These vowels do not always form diphthongs, as **po-ē'-ta, de-in'-de**, etc.

## Syllabication

1. A syllable is the smallest pronounceable unit. It consists of a vowel or a diphthong with or without one or more consonants. Hence a Latin word has as many syllables as it has vowels or diphthongs or both. There are no silent letters in Latin: **sa/lū/tā/ris, pae/ne.**

2. Whenever possible a Latin syllable begins with a consonant. A single consonant between two vowels goes with the second: **rē/gī/na.** A prefix generally remains as a whole: **ad/est (ad + est).**

3. If two or more consonants occur between vowels, the first consonant is joined with the preceding vowel: **hos/tis, obs/cū/ra.**

4. Double consonants, as **tt** or **ss,** are always separated: **mit/tō, mis/sus.**

5. The letter **x** is treated as a double consonant, but is pronounced with the preceding vowel: **dūx/ī, rēx/it.**

6. Whenever a mute, **p, b, t, d, c, g,** is followed by a liquid, **l** or **r,** both the mute and the liquid are pronounced in the following syllable: **sa/crum, cas/tra, pū/blicus.**

## Quantity of Syllables

1. A syllable is *long by nature* if it contains a long vowel or a diphthong: **mā/ter, a/māns, cau/sa.**

2. A syllable is *long by position* if it contains a short vowel followed in the same word by two or more consonants, or by the double consonant **x (x = c + s,** or **g + s).** The vowel retains its short sound: **noc/tis, mit/tō; nox.**

3. A syllable is short if it contains a short vowel, followed by a vowel or a single consonant: **vi/a, pe/des.**

## Accent or Stress

1. Accent is the emphasis given to a syllable by stress, pitch, or both.

2. In Latin the last syllable of a word, the ultima, is almost never stressed.

3. The first syllable of a word of two syllables is always stressed, whether the vowel is long or short: **vi'/a, vī'/ta.**

4. In a word of more than two syllables the second-to-last syllable, the penult (**paene,** *almost* + **ūltima,** *last*), if long, is stressed: **nā/tū'/ra, in/jūs' tus;** if the penult is short, the third-last syllable, the antepenult, is stressed: **īn'su/la, pe'/di/tēs. Ante** means *before.*

## Question Words

| | | | | | |
|---|---|---|---|---|---|
| **Quis? Qui?** | *Who?* | | **Cūjus? Quōrum?** | | *Whose?* |
| **Quem? Quōs?** | *Whom?* | | **Quōcum? Quibuscum?** | | *With whom?* |
| **Quid? Quae?** | *What?* | | **Ā quō? Ā quibus?** | | *By whom?* |

| Cui?   Quibus?     | *To (For) whom?*          | Quandō?           | *When?*       |
|--------------------|---------------------------|-------------------|---------------|
| Quī, Quae, Quod?   | *Which? What?*            | Quotiēns?         | *How often?*  |
| Uter?              | *Which (of two)?*         | Quā?              | *By what*     |
| Quot?              | *How many?*               |                   | *way?*        |
| Quantus?           | *How large?*              | Quam?             | *How?*        |
| Quālis?            | *What kind of?*           | Quōmodo?          | *How?*        |
| Quō in tempore?    | *When?*                   | Quamdiū?          | *How long?*   |
| Quō in locō?       | *Where?*                  | Cūr?              | *Why?*        |
| Ubi?               | *Where?*                  | Quā dē causā?     | *Why?*        |
| Quō?               | *Whither? Where (to)?*    | Quam ob rem?      | *Why?*        |
|                    |                           | Quā rē?           | *Why?*        |
| Unde?              | *Whence?*                 | Quō cōnsiliō?     | *Why?*        |

## Classroom Conversation

The following terms may be used in routine questions and answers in Latin.

| *question* | interrogātiō | *case* | cāsus |
|------------|--------------|--------|-------|
| *answer* | respōnsum | *nominative* | nōminātīvus |
| *declension* | dēclīnātiō | *genitive* | genitīvus |
| *conjugation* | conjugātiō | *dative* | datīvus |
| *noun* | nōmen | *accusative* | accūsātivus |
| *pronoun* | prōnōmen | *ablative* | ablātīvus |
| *adjective* | adjectīvus | *vocative* | vocātīvus |
| *adverb* | adverbium | *locative* | locātīvus |
| *preposition* | praepositiō | *verb* | verbum |
| *conjunction* | conjūnctiō | *transitive* | trānsitīvum |
| *interjection* | interjectiō | *intransitive* | intrānsitīvum |
| *pronoun* | prōnōmen | *voice* | vōx |
| *personal* | persōnāle | *active* | āctīva |
| *possessive* | possessīvum | *passive* | passīva |
| *demonstrative* | dēmōnstrātīvum | *mood* | modus |
| *intensive* | intentīvum | *indicative* | indicātīvus |
| *person* | persōna | *imperative* | imperātīvus |
| *first* | prīma | *infinitive* | īnfīnitīvus |
| *second* | secunda | *subjunctive* | subjūnctīvus |
| *third* | tertia | *tense* | tempus |
| *number* | numerus | *present* | praesēns |
| *singular* | singulāris | *imperfect* | imperfectum |
| *plural* | plūrālis | *future* | futūrum |
| *gender* | genus | *perfect* | perfectum |
| *masculine* | masculīnum | *pluperfect* | praeterītum perfectum |
| *feminine* | fēminīnum | | |
| *neuter* | neutrum | *fut. perfect* | futūrum perfectum |

| voice | vōx | tense | tempus |
|---|---|---|---|
| active | āctīva | present | praesēns |
| passive | passīva | imperfect | imperfectum |
| mood | modus | future | futūrum |
| indicative | indicātīvus | perfect | perfectum |
| imperative | imperātīvus | pluperfect | praeteritum |
| infinitive | īnfīnitīvus | | perfectum |
| subjunctive | subjūnctīvus | fut. perfect | futūrum |
| | | | perfectum |

The following directions and questions are often used in the classroom.

**Omnēs surgite (cōnsīdite).** *All rise (be seated).*
**Aperīte librōs vestrōs.** *Open your books.*
**Claudite librōs vestrōs.** *Close your books.*
**Respondē (Respondēte) Latīne.** *Answer in Latin.*
**Redde (Reddite) Latīne.** *Translate into Latin.*
**Lege (Legite) Latīne.** *Read in Latin.*
**Dīligenter auscultā (auscultāte).** *Listen carefully.*
**Intellegisne (Intellegitisne) hoc?** *Do you understand this?*
**Distribue (Distribuite) chartās.** *Pass the papers.*
**Incipe (Incipite) legere.** *Begin to read.*
**Ad tabulam aspice (aspicite).** *Look at the board.*
**Scrībe (Scrībite) in tabulā.** *Write on the board.*
**Quid est subjectum?** *What is the subject?*
**Quae dēclīnātiō?** *What declension?*
**Cūjus generis est nōmen?** *Of what gender is the noun?*
**In quō cāsū est nōmen?** *In what case is the noun?*
**Estne in nōminātīvō?** *Is it in the nominative?*
**Quid est praedicātum?** *What is the predicate?*
**Quae conjugātiō?** *What conjugation?*
**In quā vōce est verbum?** *In what voice is the verb?*
**In quō modō est verbum?** *In what mood is the verb?*
**In quō tempore est verbum?** *In what tense is the verb?*
**Estne sententia plēna?** *Is it a complete sentence?*
**Sī placet. Grātiās tibi (vōbīs) agō.** *Please. I thank you.*

# Latin Forms

## Declension of Nouns

FIRST      SECOND
DECLENSION    DECLENSION

### SINGULAR

| Nom. | puella | servus | puer | ager | vir | fīlius | oppidum |
|------|--------|--------|------|------|-----|--------|---------|
| Gen. | puellae | servī | puerī | agrī | virī | fīlī | oppidī |
| Dat. | puellae | servō | puerō | agrō | virō | fīliō | oppidō |
| Acc. | puellam | servum | puerum | agrum | virum | fīlium | oppidum |
| Abl. | puellā | servō | puerō | agrō | virō | fīliō | oppidō |

### PLURAL

| Nom. | puellae | servī | puerī | agrī | virī | fīliī | oppida |
|------|---------|-------|-------|------|------|-------|--------|
| Gen. | puellārum | servōrum | puerōrum | agrōrum | virōrum | fīliōrum | oppidōrum |
| Dat. | puellīs | servīs | puerīs | agrīs | virīs | fīliīs | oppidīs |
| Acc. | puellās | servōs | puerōs | agrōs | virōs | fīliōs | oppida |
| Abl. | puellīs | servīs | puerīs | agrīs | virīs | fīliīs | oppidīs |

In form the vocative case is always the same as the nominative case; but the vocative singular of nouns in –us is –e; **fīlius** and proper names in –ius have –ī: **serve, fīlī, Cornēlī.**

## THIRD DECLENSION

*Masculine and Feminine Consonant Stems*

### SINGULAR

| Nom. | honor | pater | regiō | rēx | prīnceps | cīvitās | pēs |
|------|-------|-------|-------|-----|----------|---------|-----|
| Gen. | honōris | patris | regiōnis | rēgis | prīncipis | cīvitātis | pedis |
| Dat. | honōrī | patrī | regiōnī | rēgī | prīncipī | cīvitātī | pedī |
| Acc. | honōrem | patrem | regiōnem | rēgem | prīncipem | cīvitātem | pedem |
| Abl. | honōre | patre | regiōne | rēge | prīncipe | cīvitāte | pede |

### PLURAL

| Nom. | honōrēs | patrēs | regiōnēs | rēgēs | prīncipēs | cīvitātēs | pedēs |
|------|---------|--------|----------|-------|-----------|-----------|-------|
| Gen. | honōrum | patrum | regiōnum | rēgum | prīncipum | cīvitātum | pedum |
| Dat. | honōribus | patribus | regiōnibus | rēgibus | prīncipibus | cīvitātibus | pedibus |
| Acc. | honōrēs | patrēs | regiōnēs | rēgēs | prīncipēs | cīvitātēs | pedēs |
| Abl. | honōribus | patribus | regiōnibus | rēgibus | prīncipibus | cīvitātibus | pedibus |

Some masculine and feminine nouns of the third declension end in –s in the nominative. If the stem of a noun ends in –c or –g, the nominative will end in –x, as **reg– + s = rēx; duc– + s = dux.** Nouns with stems ending in –tr have the nominative ending in –ter, as **pater** from **patr–.** A final –t or –d of the stem is dropped before –s, as **ped– + s = pēs.**  Short –i in the stem of more than one syllable changes to short –e in the nominative, as **prīncip– + s = prīnceps.** Nouns with stems ending in –**din** and –**gin** end in –**ō** in the nominative, as **virgō, virginis** and **multitūdō, multitūdinis.**

*Neuter Consonant Stems*

SINGULAR

|      |         |          |         |         |           |
|------|---------|----------|---------|---------|-----------|
| Nom. | flūmen  | corpus   | genus   | caput   | iter      |
| Gen. | flūminis | corporis | generis | capitis | itineris  |
| Dat. | flūminī | corporī  | generī  | capitī  | itinerī   |
| Acc. | flūmen  | corpus   | genus   | caput   | iter      |
| Abl. | flūmine | corpore  | genere  | capite  | itinere   |

PLURAL

|      |           |           |          |          |            |
|------|-----------|-----------|----------|----------|------------|
| Nom. | flūmina   | corpora   | genera   | capita   | itinera    |
| Gen. | flūminum  | corporum  | generum  | capitum  | itinerum   |
| Dat. | flūminibus | corporibus | generibus | capitibus | itineribus |
| Acc. | flūmina   | corpora   | genera   | capita   | itinera    |
| Abl. | flūminibus | corporibus | generibus | capitibus | itineribus |

**i-**Stems

SINGULAR

*Masculine and Feminine*                                      *Neuter*

|      |        |         |        |         |           |         |
|------|--------|---------|--------|---------|-----------|---------|
| Nom. | cīvis  | caedēs  | urbs   | nox     | cohors    | mare    |
| Gen. | cīvis  | caedis  | urbis  | noctis  | cohortis  | maris   |
| Dat. | cīvī   | caedī   | urbī   | noctī   | cohortī   | marī    |
| Acc. | cīvem  | caedem  | urbem  | noctem  | cohortem  | mare    |
| Abl. | cīve   | caede   | urbe   | nocte   | cohorte   | marī    |

PLURAL

|      |           |            |           |           |            |         |
|------|-----------|------------|-----------|-----------|------------|---------|
| Nom. | cīvēs     | caedēs     | urbēs     | noctēs    | cohortēs   | maria   |
| Gen. | cīvium    | caedium    | urbium    | noctium   | cohortium  | marium  |
| Dat. | cīvibus   | caedibus   | urbibus   | noctibus  | cohortibus | maribus |
| Acc. | cīvēs (–īs) | caedēs (–īs) | urbēs (–īs) | noctēs (–īs) | cohortēs (īs) | maria   |
| Abl. | cīvibus   | caedibus   | urbibus   | noctibus  | cohortibus | maribus |

Masculine and feminine **i**-stem nouns fall into three classes:
1. Nouns ending in –**is** or –**es** and having the same number of syllables in the genitive as the nominative.
2. Monosyllables in –**s** or –**x** whose base ends in a double consonant.
3. Nouns ending in –**ns** or –**rs.**

Neuter nouns ending in –**e, –al, –ar** are **i**-stems.

| | M.&F. | N. | M. | F. |
|---|---|---|---|---|
| | | SINGULAR | | |
| Nom. | impet**us** | corn**ū** | di**ēs** | r**ēs** |
| Gen. | impet**ūs** | corn**ūs** | di**ēī** | r**eī** |
| Dat. | impet**uī** | corn**ū** | di**ēī** | r**eī** |
| Acc. | impet**um** | corn**ū** | di**em** | r**em** |
| Abl. | impet**ū** | corn**ū** | di**ē** | r**ē** |
| | | PLURAL | | |
| Nom. | impet**ūs** | corn**ua** | di**ēs** | r**ēs** |
| Gen. | impet**uum** | corn**uum** | di**ērum** | r**ērum** |
| Dat. | impet**ibus** | corn**ibus** | di**ēbus** | r**ēbus** |
| Acc. | impet**ūs** | corn**ua** | di**ēs** | r**ēs** |
| Abl. | impet**ibus** | corn**ibus** | di**ēbus** | r**ēbus** |

## Declension of Adjectives

### FIRST AND SECOND DECLENSIONS

| | SINGULAR | | | PLURAL | | |
|---|---|---|---|---|---|---|
| | M. | F. | N. | M. | F. | N. |
| Nom. | bon**us** | bon**a** | bon**um** | bon**ī** | bon**ae** | bon**a** |
| Gen. | bon**ī** | bon**ae** | bon**ī** | bon**ōrum** | bon**ārum** | bon**ōrum** |
| Dat. | bon**ō** | bon**ae** | bon**ō** | bon**īs** | bon**īs** | bon**īs** |
| Acc. | bon**um** | bon**am** | bon**um** | bon**ōs** | bon**ās** | bon**a** |
| Abl. | bon**ō** | bon**ā** | bon**ō** | bon**īs** | bon**īs** | bon**īs** |
| | | | | | | |
| Nom. | miser | miser**a** | miser**um** | miser**ī** | miser**ae** | miser**a** |
| Gen. | miser**ī** | miser**ae** | miser**ī** | miser**ōrum** | miser**ārum** | miser**ōrum** |
| Dat. | miser**ō** | miser**ae** | miser**ō** | miser**īs** | miser**īs** | miser**īs** |
| Acc. | miser**um** | miser**am** | miser**um** | miser**ōs** | miser**ās** | miser**a** |
| Abl. | miser**ō** | miser**ā** | miser**ō** | miser**īs** | miser**īs** | miser**īs** |
| | | | | | | |
| Nom. | pulcher | pulchr**a** | pulchr**um** | pulchr**ī** | pulchr**ae** | pulchr**a** |
| Gen. | pulchr**ī** | pulchr**ae** | pulchr**ī** | pulchr**ōrum** | pulchr**ārum** | pulchr**ōrum** |
| Dat. | pulchr**ō** | pulchr**ae** | pulchr**ō** | pulchr**īs** | pulchr**īs** | pulchr**īs** |
| Acc. | pulchr**um** | pulchr**am** | pulchr**um** | pulchr**ōs** | pulchr**ās** | pulchr**a** |
| Abl. | pulchr**ō** | pulchr**ā** | pulchr**ō** | pulchr**īs** | pulchr**īs** | pulchr**īs** |

### THIRD DECLENSION

| | *Two Terminations* | | *Three Terminations* | | | *One Termination* | |
|---|---|---|---|---|---|---|---|
| | SINGULAR | | | | | | |
| | M.&F. | N. | M. | F. | N. | M.&F. | N. |
| Nom. | brev**is** | brev**e** | ācer | ācr**is** | ācr**e** | potēns | |
| Gen. | brev**is** | | ācr**is** | | | potentis | |
| Dat. | brev**ī** | | ācr**ī** | | | potent**ī** | |
| Acc. | brev**em** | brev**e** | ācr**em** | ācr**em** | ācr**e** | potent**em** | potēns |
| Abl. | brev**ī** | | ācr**ī** | | | potent**ī** | |

|      | M.&F. | N. | M.&F. | N. | M.&F. | N. |
|------|-------|-----|-------|-----|-------|-----|
| Nom. | brevēs | brevia | ācrēs | ācria | potentēs | potentia |
| Gen. | brevium | | ācrium | | potentium | |
| Dat. | brevibus | | ācribus | | potentibus | |
| Acc. | brevēs (–īs) | brevia | ācrēs (–īs) | ācria | potentēs (–īs) | potentia |
| Abl. | brevibus | | ācribus | | potentibus | |

## PRESENT ACTIVE PARTICIPLE

|      | SINGULAR | | PLURAL | |
|------|----------|----|--------|----|
|      | M.&F. | N. | M.&F. | N. |
| Nom. | vocāns | | vocantēs | vocantia |
| Gen. | vocantis | | vocantium | |
| Dat. | vocantī | | vocantibus | |
| Acc. | vocantem | vocāns | vocantēs (–īs) | vocantia |
| Abl. | vocante (–ī) | | vocantibus | |

When the present participle is used as an adjective, the ablative indicator is **–ī.**

## ADJECTIVES OF SPECIAL DECLENSION

The following adjectives have a genitive singular termination in **–īus,** a dative singular termination in **–ī,** and their other forms like **fīdus, līber,** and **pulcher.**

**alius, alia, aliud,** *other, another*
**alter, altera, alterum,** *the other*
**uter, utra, utrum,** *which (of two)?*
**uterque, utraque, utrumque,** *each of two, both*
**neuter, neutra, neutrum,** *neither (of two)*

**ūnus, ūna, ūnum,** *one, alone*
**ūllus, ūlla, ūllum,** *any*
**nūllus, nūlla, nūllum,** *none*
**sōlus, sōla, sōlum,** *only, single, alone*
**tōtus, tōta, tōtum,** *the whole, entire, all*

For the declension of these adjectives *see* page 216.

## REGULAR COMPARISON OF ADJECTIVES

| *Positive* | *Comparative* | *Superlative* |
|-----------|--------------|--------------|
| **clārus, –a, –um** | **clārior, clārius** | **clārissimus, –a, –um** |
| **fortis, –e** | **fortior, fortius** | **fortissimus, –a, –um** |
| **audāx (audācis)** | **audācior, audācius** | **audācissimus, –a, –um** |
| **potēns (potentis)** | **potentior, potentius** | **potentissimus, –a, –um** |
| **līber, –era, –erum** | **līberior, līberius** | **līberrimus, –a, –um** |
| **ācer, ācris, ācre** | **ācrior, ācrius** | **ācerrimus, –a, –um** |
| **similis, –e** | **similior, similius** | **simillimus, –a, –um** |

## IRREGULAR COMPARISON OF ADJECTIVES

| | | |
|---|---|---|
| **bonus, –a, –um** | **melior, melius** | **optimus, –a, –um** |
| **malus, –a, –um** | **pējor, pējus** | **pessimus, –a, –um** |
| **māgnus, –a, –um** | **mājor, mājus** | **māximus, –a, –um** |
| **parvus, –a, –um** | **minor, minus** | **minimus, –a, –um** |
| **multus, –a, –um** | **———, plūs** | **plūrimus, –a, –um** |
| **multī, –ae, –a** | **plūrēs, plūra** | **plūrimī, –ae, –a** |

# DECLENSION OF COMPARATIVE ADJECTIVES

## SINGULAR

|  | M.&F. | N. | M.&F. | N. |
|---|---|---|---|---|
| Nom. | clārior | clārius | — | plūs |
| Gen. | | clāriōris | — | plūris |
| Dat. | | clāriōrī | — | — |
| Acc. | clāriōrem | clārius | — | plūs |
| Abl. | | clāriōre | — | plūre |

## PLURAL

|  | M.&F. | N. | M.&F. | N. |
|---|---|---|---|---|
| Nom. | clāriōrēs | clāriōra | plūrēs | plūra |
| Gen. | | clāriōrum | | plūrium |
| Dat. | | clāriōribus | | plūribus |
| Acc. | clāriōrēs (–īs) | clāriōra | plūrēs (–īs) | plūra |
| Abl. | | clāriōribus | | plūribus |

In the singular **plūs** is used as a neuter noun and has no masculine or feminine forms.

# Adverbs

| REGULAR COMPARISON | | | IRREGULAR COMPARISON | | |
|---|---|---|---|---|---|
| *Positive* | *Comparative* | *Superlative* | *Positive* | *Comparative* | *Superlative* |
| clārē | clārius | clārissimē | bene | melius | optimē |
| līberē | līberius | līberrimē | male | pējus | pessimē |
| fortiter | fortius | fortissimē | māgnopere | magis | māximē |
| celeriter | celerius | celerrimē | multum | plūs | plūrimum |
| similiter | similius | simillimē | parum | minus | minimē |

# Numerals

## DECLENSION OF
### duo, trēs, mīlia

|  | M. | F. | N. | M.&F. | N. | N. |
|---|---|---|---|---|---|---|
| Nom. | duo | duae | duo | trēs | tria | mīlia |
| Gen. | duōrum | duārum | duōrum | trium | | mīlium |
| Dat. | duōbus | duābus | duōbus | tribus | | mīlibus |
| Acc. | duōs, duo | duās | duo | trēs | tria | mīlia |
| Abl. | duōbus | duābus | duōbus | tribus | | mīlibus |

In the singular **mīlle**, *thousand*, is an indeclinable adjective. In the plural **mīlia** is a neuter noun followed by the genitive of the noun denoting the persons or things that are numbered.

For the declension of **ūnus** *see* page 160.

# LIST OF NUMBERS

| Arabic | Roman Numerals | Cardinal | Ordinal |
|---|---|---|---|
| 1 | I | ūnus, –a, –um | prīmus, –a, –um |
| 2 | II | duo, duae, duo | secundus, alter |
| 3 | III | trēs, tria | tertius |
| 4 | IV | quattuor | quārtus |
| 5 | V | quīnque | quīntus |
| 6 | VI | sex | sextus |
| 7 | VII | septem | septimus |
| 8 | VIII | octō | octāvus |
| 9 | IX | novem | nōnus |
| 10 | X | decem | decimus |
| 11 | XI | ūndecim | ūndecimus |
| 12 | XII | duodecim | duodecimus |
| 13 | XIII | tredecim | tertius decimus |
| 14 | XIV | quattuordecim | quārtus decimus |
| 15 | XV | quīndecim | quīntus decimus |
| 16 | XVI | sēdecim | sextus decimus |
| 17 | XVII | septendecim | septimus decimus |
| 18 | XVIII | duodēvīgintī | duodēvīcēsimus |
| 19 | XIX | ūndēvīgintī | ūndēvīcēsimus |
| 20 | XX | vīgintī | vīcēsimus |
| 21 | XXI | ūnus et vīgintī, vīgintī ūnus | vīcēsimus prīmus |
| 28 | XXVIII | duodētrīgintā | duodētrīcēsimus |
| 29 | XXIX | ūndētrīgintā | ūndētrīcēsimus |
| 30 | XXX | trīgintā | trīcēsimus |
| 40 | XL | quadrāgintā | quadrāgēsimus |
| 50 | L | quīnquāgintā | quīnquāgēsimus |
| 60 | LX | sexāgintā | sexāgēsimus |
| 70 | LXX | septuāgintā | septuāgēsimus |
| 80 | LXXX | octōgintā | octōgēsimus |
| 90 | XC | nōnāgintā | nōnāgēsimus |
| 100 | C | centum | centēsimus |
| 101 | CI | centum (et) ūnus | centēsimus (et) prīmus |
| 200 | CC | ducentī, –ae, –a | ducentēsimus |
| 300 | CCC | trecentī, –ae, –a | trecentēsimus |
| 400 | CCCC | quadringentī | quadringentēsimus |
| 500 | D | quīngentī | quīngentēsimus |
| 600 | DC | sescentī | sescentēsimus |
| 700 | DCC | septingentī | septingentēsimus |
| 800 | DCCC | octingentī | octingentēsimus |
| 900 | DCCCC | nōngentī | nōngentēsimus |
| 1,000 | M | mīlle | mīllēsimus |
| 2,000 | MM | duo mīlia | bis mīllēsimus |

# Declension of Pronouns

## PERSONAL

| | *First Person* | | | *Second Person* | |
| | SINGULAR | PLURAL | | SINGULAR | PLURAL |
|---|---|---|---|---|---|
| Nom. | ego | nōs | | tū | vōs |
| Gen. | meī | nostrum, nostrī | | tuī | vestrum, vestrī |
| Dat. | mihi | nōbīs | | tibi | vōbīs |
| Acc. | mē | nōs | | tē | vōs |
| Abl. | mē | nōbīs | | tē | vōbīs |

There is no personal pronoun of the third person. Its place is taken either by a demonstrative pronoun (usually **is**, *he;* **ea**, *she;* **id**, *it*) or, if the antecedent is the subject of the sentence or clause, by a reflexive pronoun.

## REFLEXIVE

| | *First Person* | | *Second Person* | | *Third Person* | |
| | SINGULAR | PLURAL | SINGULAR | PLURAL | SINGULAR | PLURAL |
|---|---|---|---|---|---|---|
| Nom. | — | — | — | — | — | — |
| Gen. | meī | nostrī | tuī | vestrī | suī | suī |
| Dat. | mihi | nōbīs | tibi | vōbīs | sibi | sibi |
| Acc. | mē | nōs | tē | vōs | sē, sēsē | sē, sēsē |
| Abl. | mē | nōbīs | tē | vōbīs | sē, sēsē | sē, sēsē |

## POSSESSIVE

### Referring to Singular Antecedent

First Person    **meus, –a, –um,** *my, mine*
Second Person    **tuus, –a, –um,** *your, yours*
Third Person    **suus, –a, –um,** *his, her, hers, its* (reflexive)
                **ējus** (gen. sing. of **is**) *his, her, hers, its* (not reflexive)

### Referring to Plural Antecedent

First Person    **noster, –tra, –trum** *our, ours*
Second Person    **vester, –tra, –trum** *your, yours*
Third Person    **suus, –a, –um** *their, theirs* (reflexive)
                **eōrum, eārum, eōrum** (gen. pl. of **is**) *their, theirs* (not reflexive)

The vocative masculine singular of **meus** is **mī. Meus, tuus, suus, noster, vester** are used as adjectives, agreeing with the thing possessed.

## DEMONSTRATIVE PRONOUNS AND ADJECTIVES

| | SINGULAR | | | PLURAL | | |
| | M. | F. | N. | M. | F. | N. |
|---|---|---|---|---|---|---|
| Nom. | hic | haec | hoc | hī | hae | haec |
| Gen. | | hūjus | | hōrum | hārum | hōrum |
| Dat. | | huic | | | hīs | |
| Acc. | hunc | hanc | hoc | hōs | hās | haec |
| Abl. | hōc | hāc | hōc | | hīs | |

|        | SINGULAR |          |          | PLURAL   |          |          |
|--------|----------|----------|----------|----------|----------|----------|
|        | M.       | F.       | N.       | M.       | F.       | N.       |
| Nom.   | ille     | illa     | illud    | illī     | illae    | illa     |
| Gen.   |          | illīus   |          | illōrum  | illārum  | illōrum  |
| Dat.   |          | illī     |          |          | illīs    |          |
| Acc.   | illum    | illam    | illud    | illōs    | illās    | illa     |
| Abl.   | illō     | illā     | illō     |          | illīs    |          |

|        | M.       | F.       | N.       | M.       | F.       | N.       |
|--------|----------|----------|----------|----------|----------|----------|
| Nom.   | is       | ea       | id       | eī, iī   | eae      | ea       |
| Gen.   |          | ējus     |          | eōrum    | eārum    | eōrum    |
| Dat.   |          | eī       |          |          | eīs, iīs |          |
| Acc.   | eum      | eam      | id       | eōs      | eās      | ea       |
| Abl.   | eō       | eā       | eō       |          | eīs, iīs |          |

|        | M.       | F.       | N.       | M.       | F.       | N.       |
|--------|----------|----------|----------|----------|----------|----------|
| Nom.   | iste     | ista     | istud    | istī     | istae    | ista     |
| Gen.   |          | istīus   |          | istōrum  | istārum  | istōrum  |
| Dat.   |          | istī     |          |          | istīs    |          |
| Acc.   | istum    | istam    | istud    | istōs    | istās    | ista     |
| Abl.   | istō     | istā     | istō     |          | istīs    |          |

## DEMONSTRATIVE PRONOUN AND ADJECTIVE

|        | SINGULAR  |           |        | PLURAL        |              |          |
|--------|-----------|-----------|--------|---------------|--------------|----------|
|        | M.        | F.        | N.     | M.            | F.           | N.       |
| Nom.   | īdem      | eadem     | idem   | eīdem, īdem   | eaedem       | eadem    |
| Gen.   |           | ējusdem   |        | eōrundem      | eārundem     | eōrundem |
| Dat.   |           | eīdem     |        |               | eīsdem, iīsdem |        |
| Acc.   | eundem    | eandem    | idem   | eōsdem        | eāsdem       | eadem    |
| Abl.   | eōdem     | eādem     | eōdem  |               | eīsdem, iīsdem |        |

## INTENSIVE PRONOUN AND ADJECTIVE

|        | SINGULAR  |           |          | PLURAL    |          |          |
|--------|-----------|-----------|----------|-----------|----------|----------|
|        | M.        | F.        | N.       | M.        | F.       | N.       |
| Nom.   | ipse      | ipsa      | ipsum    | ipsī      | ipsae    | ipsa     |
| Gen.   |           | ipsīus    |          | ipsōrum   | ipsārum  | ipsōrum  |
| Dat.   |           | ipsī      |          |           | ipsīs    |          |
| Acc.   | ipsum     | ipsam     | ipsum    | ipsōs     | ipsās    | ipsa     |
| Abl.   | ipsō      | ipsā      | ipsō     |           | ipsīs    |          |

## RELATIVE PRONOUN

|        | SINGULAR  |           |          | PLURAL    |          |          |
|--------|-----------|-----------|----------|-----------|----------|----------|
|        | M.        | F.        | N.       | M.        | F.       | N.       |
| Nom.   | quī       | quae      | quod     | quī       | quae     | quae     |
| Gen.   |           | cūjus     |          | quōrum    | quārum   | quōrum   |
| Dat.   |           | cui       |          |           | quibus   |          |
| Acc.   | quem      | quam      | quod     | quōs      | quās     | quae     |
| Abl.   | quō       | quā       | quō      |           | quibus   |          |

# INTERROGATIVE PRONOUN AND ADJECTIVE

| | SINGULAR | | | | | PLURAL | | |
|---|---|---|---|---|---|---|---|---|
| | *Pronoun* | | *Adjective* | | | *Pronoun and Adjective* | | |
| | M.&F. | N. | M. | F. | N. | M. | F. | N. |
| Nom. | quis | quid | quī | quae | quod | quī | quae | quae |
| Gen. | cūjus | | cūjus | | | quōrum | quārum | quōrum |
| Dat. | cui | | cui | | | | quibus | |
| Acc. | quem | quid | quem | quam | quod | quōs | quās | quae |
| Abl. | quō | | quō | quā | quō | | quibus | |

The interrogative adjective in the singular is the same as the relative pronoun, except that the nominative masculine may be either **quis** or **quī**. The plural of the interrogative adjective and the interrogative pronoun is the same as that of the relative pronoun.

## Conjugation of Regular Verbs

### PRINCIPAL PARTS

| *First Conj.* | *Second Conj.* | *Third Conj.* | *Third Conj.* (–io) | *Fourth Conj.* |
|---|---|---|---|---|
| vocō | moneō | regō | capiō | audiō |
| vocāre | monēre | regere | capere | audīre |
| vocāvī | monuī | rēxī | cēpī | audīvī |
| vocātus | monitus | rēctus | captus | audītus |

### STEMS*

| | | | | |
|---|---|---|---|---|
| vocā/ | monē/ | rege/ | cape/ | audī/ |
| vocāv/ | monu/ | rēx/ | cēp/ | audīv/ |
| vocāt/ | monit/ | rēct/ | capt/ | audīt/ |

## INDICATIVE MOOD
### *Active Voice*
#### PRESENT

| *I call, am calling, do call* | *I warn, am warning, do warn* | *I rule, am ruling, do rule* | *I take, am taking, do take* | *I hear, am hearing, do hear* |
|---|---|---|---|---|
| vocō | moneō | regō | capiō | audiō |
| vocās | monēs | regis | capis | audīs |
| vocat | monet | regit | capit | audit |
| vocāmus | monēmus | regimus | capimus | audīmus |
| vocātis | monētis | regitis | capitis | audītis |
| vocant | monent | regunt | capiunt | audiunt |

*In the following paradigms the stem or the part of a stem that is used in a given form appears in light-face type. **The tense indicator and person indicator appear in bold-face type.** *Generally, letters that are neither a part of the stem nor a part of the indicators appear in italics.* **In certain forms where such type distinction is impractical, the entire form appears in bold-face type.**

| *I was calling, called, used to call* | *I was warning, warned, used to warn* | *I was ruling, ruled, used to rule* | *I was taking, took, used to take* | *I was hearing, heard, used to hear* |
|---|---|---|---|---|
| vocābam | monēbam | regēbam | capiēbam | audiēbam |
| vocābās | monēbās | regēbās | capiēbās | audiēbās |
| vocābat | monēbat | regēbat | capiēbat | audiēbat |
| vocābāmus | monēbāmus | regēbāmus | capiēbāmus | audiēbāmus |
| vocābātis | monēbātis | regēbātis | capiēbātis | audiēbātis |
| vocābant | monēbant | regēbant | capiēbant | audiēbant |

| *I shall call* | *I shall warn* | *I shall rule* | *I shall take* | *I shall hear* |
|---|---|---|---|---|
| vocābō | monēbō | regam | capiam | audiam |
| vocābis | monēbis | regēs | capiēs | audiēs |
| vocābit | monēbit | reget | capiet | audiet |
| vocābimus | monēbimus | regēmus | capiēmus | audiēmus |
| vocābitis | monēbitis | regētis | capiētis | audiētis |
| vocābunt | monēbunt | regent | capient | audient |

| *I called, have called* | *I warned, have warned* | *I ruled, have ruled* | *I took, have taken* | *I heard, have heard* |
|---|---|---|---|---|
| vocāvī | monuī | rēxī | cēpī | audīvī |
| vocāvistī | monuistī | rēxistī | cēpistī | audīvistī |
| vocāvit | monuit | rēxit | cēpit | audīvit |
| vocāvimus | monuimus | rēximus | cēpimus | audīvimus |
| vocāvistis | monuistis | rēxistis | cēpistis | audīvistis |
| vocāvērunt | monuērunt | rēxērunt | cēpērunt | audīvērunt |

| *I had called* | *I had warned* | *I had ruled* | *I had taken* | *I had heard* |
|---|---|---|---|---|
| vocāveram | monueram | rēxeram | cēperam | audīveram |
| vocāverās | monuerās | rēxerās | cēperās | audīverās |
| vocāverat | monuerat | rēxerat | cēperat | audīverat |
| vocāverāmus | monuerāmus | rēxerāmus | cēperāmus | audīverāmus |
| vocāverātis | monuerātis | rēxerātis | cēperātis | audīverātis |
| vocāverant | monuerant | rēxerant | cēperant | audīverant |

| *I shall have called* | *I shall have warned* | *I shall have ruled* | *I shall have taken* | *I shall have heard* |
|---|---|---|---|---|
| vocāverō | monuerō | rēxerō | cēperō | audīverō |
| vocāveris | monueris | rēxeris | cēperis | audīveris |
| vocāverit | monuerit | rēxerit | cēperit | audīverit |
| vocāverimus | monuerimus | rēxerimus | cēperimus | audīverimus |
| vocāveritis | monueritis | rēxeritis | cēperitis | audīveritis |
| vocāverint | monuerint | rēxerint | cēperint | audīverint |

## Passive Voice

### PRESENT

| *I am called* | *I am warned* | *I am ruled* | *I am taken* | *I am heard* |
|---|---|---|---|---|
| vocor | moneor | regor | capior | audior |
| vocāris | monēris | regeris | caperis | audīris |
| vocātur | monētur | regitur | capitur | audītur |
| vocāmur | monēmur | regimur | capimur | audīmur |
| vocāminī | monēminī | regiminī | capiminī | audīminī |
| vocantur | monentur | reguntur | capiuntur | audiuntur |

### IMPERFECT

| *I was called* | *I was warned* | *I was ruled* | *I was taken* | *I was heard* |
|---|---|---|---|---|
| vocābar | monēbar | regēbar | capiēbar | audiēbar |
| vocābāris | monēbāris | regēbāris | capiēbāris | audiēbāris |
| vocābātur | monēbātur | regēbātur | capiēbātur | audiēbātur |
| vocābāmur | monēbāmur | regēbāmur | capiēbāmur | audiēbāmur |
| vocābāminī | monēbāminī | regēbāminī | capiēbāminī | audiēbāminī |
| vocābantur | monēbantur | regēbantur | capiēbantur | audiēbantur |

### FUTURE

| *I shall be called* | *I shall be warned* | *I shall be ruled* | *I shall be taken* | *I shall be heard* |
|---|---|---|---|---|
| vocābor | monēbor | regar | capiar | audiar |
| vocāberis | monēberis | regēris | capiēris | audiēris |
| vocābitur | monēbitur | regētur | capiētur | audiētur |
| vocābimur | monēbimur | regēmur | capiēmur | audiēmur |
| vocābiminī | monēbiminī | regēminī | capiēminī | audiēminī |
| vocābuntur | monēbuntur | regentur | capientur | audientur |

### PERFECT

*I was called, have been called*

vocātus, -a, -um { sum / es / est }
vocātī, -ae, -a { sumus / estis / sunt }

*I was warned, have been warned*

monitus, -a, -um { sum, etc. }
monitī, -ae, -a

*I was ruled, have been ruled*

rēctus, -a, -um { sum, etc. }
rēctī, -ae, -a

*I was taken, have been taken*

captus, -a, -um { sum, etc. }
captī, -ae, -a

*I was heard, have been heard*

audītus, -a, -um { sum, etc. }
audītī, -ae, a

| *I had been called* | | *I had been warned* | | *I had been ruled* | |
|---|---|---|---|---|---|
| vocātus, −a, −um | eram<br>erās<br>erat | monitus, −a, −um | eram, *etc.* | rēctus, −a, −um | eram, *etc.* |
| vocātī, −ae, −a | erāmus<br>erātis<br>erant | monitī, −ae, −a | | rēctī, −ae, −a | |

| *I had been taken* | | *I had been heard* | |
|---|---|---|---|
| captus, −a, −um | eram, *etc.* | audītus, −a, −um | eram, *etc.* |
| captī, −ae, −a | | audītī, −ae, −a | |

## FUTURE PERFECT

| *I shall have been called* | | *I shall have been warned* | | *I shall have been ruled* | |
|---|---|---|---|---|---|
| vocātus, −a, −um | erō<br>eris<br>erit | monitus, −a, −um | erō, *etc.* | rēctus, −a, −um | erō, *etc.* |
| vocātī, −ae, −a | erimus<br>eritis<br>erunt | monitī, −ae, −a | | rēctī, −ae, −a | |

| *I shall have been taken* | | *I shall have been heard* | |
|---|---|---|---|
| captus, −a, −um | erō, *etc.* | audītus, −a, −um | erō, *etc.* |
| captī, −ae, −a | | audītī, −ae, −a | |

## SUBJUNCTIVE MOOD

### *Active Voice*

#### PRESENT

| | | | | |
|---|---|---|---|---|
| vocem | moneam | regam | capiam | audiam |
| vocēs | moneās | regās | capiās | audiās |
| vocet | moneat | regat | capiat | audiat |
| vocēmus | moneāmus | regāmus | capiāmus | audiāmus |
| vocētis | moneātis | regātis | capiātis | audiātis |
| vocent | moneant | regant | capiant | audiant |

#### IMPERFECT

| | | | | |
|---|---|---|---|---|
| vocārem | monērem | regerem | caperem | audīrem |
| vocārēs | monērēs | regerēs | caperēs | audīrēs |
| vocāret | monēret | regeret | caperet | audīret |

| | | | | |
|---|---|---|---|---|
| vocārēmus | monērēmus | regerēmus | caperēmus | audīrēmus |
| vocārētis | monērētis | regerētis | caperētis | audīrētis |
| vocārent | monērent | regerent | caperent | audīrent |

PERFECT

| | | | | |
|---|---|---|---|---|
| vocāverim | monuerim | rēxerim | cēperim | audīverim |
| vocāverīs | monuerīs | rēxerīs | cēperīs | audīverīs |
| vocāverit | monuerit | rēxerit | cēperit | audīverit |
| vocāverīmus | monuerīmus | rēxerīmus | cēperīmus | audīverīmus |
| vocāverītis | monuerītis | rēxerītis | cēperītis | audīverītis |
| vocāverint | monuerint | rēxerint | cēperint | audīverint |

PLUPERFECT

| | | | | |
|---|---|---|---|---|
| vocāvissem | monuissem | rēxissem | cēpissem | audīvissem |
| vocāvissēs | monuissēs | rēxissēs | cēpissēs | audīvissēs |
| vocāvisset | monuisset | rēxisset | cēpisset | audīvisset |
| vocāvissēmus | monuissēmus | rēxissēmus | cēpissēmus | audīvissēmus |
| vocāvissētis | monuissētis | rēxissētis | cēpissētis | audīvissētis |
| vocāvissent | monuissent | rēxissent | cēpissent | audīvissent |

*Passive Voice*

PRESENT

| | | | | |
|---|---|---|---|---|
| vocer | monear | regar | capiar | audiar |
| vocēris | moneāris | regāris | capiāris | audiāris |
| vocētur | moneātur | regātur | capiātur | audiātur |
| vocēmur | moneāmur | regāmur | capiāmur | audiāmur |
| vocēminī | moneāminī | regāminī | capiāminī | audiāminī |
| vocentur | moneantur | regantur | capiantur | audiantur |

IMPERFECT

| | | | | |
|---|---|---|---|---|
| vocārer | monērer | regerer | caperer | audīrer |
| vocārēris | monērēris | regerēris | caperēris | audīrēris |
| vocārētur | monērētur | regerētur | caperētur | audīrētur |
| vocārēmur | monērēmur | regerēmur | caperēmur | audīrēmur |
| vocārēminī | monērēminī | regerēminī | caperēminī | audīrēminī |
| vocārentur | monērentur | regerentur | caperentur | audīrentur |

PERFECT

| | | | | | | |
|---|---|---|---|---|---|---|
| vocātus, −a, −um | sim sīs sit | monitus, −a, −um | sim, *etc.* | rēctus, −a, −um | sim, *etc.* |
| vocātī, −ae, −a | sīmus sītis sint | monitī, −ae, −a | | rēctī, −ae, −a | |

**374**

| captus,<br>–a, –um | sim,<br>etc. | audītus,<br>–a, –um | sim,<br>etc. |
|---|---|---|---|
| captī,<br>–ae, –a | | audītī,<br>–ae, –a | |

## PLUPERFECT

| vocātus,<br>–a, –um | essem<br>essēs<br>esset | monitus,<br>–a, –um | essem,<br>etc. | rēctus,<br>–a, –um | essem,<br>etc. |
|---|---|---|---|---|---|
| vocātī,<br>–ae, –a | essēmus<br>essētis<br>essent | monitī,<br>–ae, –a | | rēctī,<br>–ae, –a | |

| captus,<br>–a, –um | essem,<br>etc. | audītus,<br>–a, –um | essem,<br>etc. |
|---|---|---|---|
| captī,<br>–ae, –a | | audītī,<br>–ae, –a | |

## IMPERATIVE MOOD

### *Active Voice*

#### PRESENT

| | | | | | | | | | |
|---|---|---|---|---|---|---|---|---|---|
| SING. | vocā, *call* | monē, *warn* | rege, *rule* | cape, *take* | audī, *hear* |
| PL. | vocāte, *call* | monēte, *warn* | regite, *rule* | capite, *take* | audīte, *hear* |

## INFINITIVES

| *Active Voice* | | | *Passive Voice* | | |
|---|---|---|---|---|---|
| PRES. | vocāre<br>monēre<br>regere<br>capere<br>audīre | *to* { *call*<br>*warn*<br>*rule*<br>*take*<br>*hear* | vocārī<br>monērī<br>regī<br>capī<br>audīrī | *to be* { *called*<br>*warned*<br>*ruled*<br>*taken*<br>*heard* |
| PERF. | vocāvisse<br>monuisse<br>rēxisse<br>cēpisse<br>audīvisse | *to<br>have* { *called*<br>*warned*<br>*ruled*<br>*taken*<br>*heard* | vocātus, –a, –um esse<br>monitus, –a, –um esse<br>rēctus, –a, –um esse<br>captus, –a, –um esse<br>audītus, –a, –um esse | *to<br>have<br>been* { *called*<br>*warned*<br>*ruled*<br>*taken*<br>*heard* |
| FUT. | vocātūrus, –a, –um esse<br>monitūrus, –a, –um esse<br>rēctūrus, –a, –um esse<br>captūrus, –a, –um esse<br>audītūrus, –a, –um esse | *to be<br>about to* { *call*<br>*warn*<br>*rule*<br>*take*<br>*hear* | | |

# PARTICIPLES

| | Active Voice | | Passive Voice | |
|---|---|---|---|---|
| PRES. | vocāns, –antis<br>monēns, –entis<br>regēns, –entis<br>capiēns, –entis<br>audiēns, –entis | *calling*<br>*warning*<br>*ruling*<br>*taking*<br>*hearing* | | |
| PERF. | | | vocātus, –a, –um<br>monitus, –a, –um<br>rēctus, –a, –um<br>captus, –a, –um<br>audītus, –a, –um   *having been* | *called*<br>*warned*<br>*ruled*<br>*taken*<br>*heard* |
| FUT. | vocātūrus, –a, –um<br>monitūrus, –a, –um<br>rēctūrus, –a, –um<br>captūrus, –a, –um<br>audītūrus, –a, –um   *about to* | *call*<br>*warn*<br>*rule*<br>*take*<br>*hear* | | |

Deponent verbs are conjugated like the passive voice of regular verbs. *See* pages 307, 308, 320, 329, 340, 346.

## Conjugation of Irregular Verbs

### Sum, *I am*

PRINCIPAL PARTS: **sum, esse, fuī, futūrus**

#### INDICATIVE MOOD

| PRESENT | IMPERFECT | FUTURE |
|---|---|---|
| *I am* | *I was* | *I shall be* |
| **sum** | **eram** | **erō** |
| **es** | **erās** | **eris** |
| **est** | **erat** | **erit** |
| **sumus** | **erāmus** | **erimus** |
| **estis** | **erātis** | **eritis** |
| **sunt** | **erant** | **erunt** |

| PERFECT | PLUPERFECT | FUTURE PERFECT |
|---|---|---|
| *I have been, was* | *I had been* | *I shall have been* |
| **fuī** | **fueram** | **fuerō** |
| **fuistī** | **fuerās** | **fueris** |
| **fuit** | **fuerat** | **fuerit** |
| **fuimus** | **fuerāmus** | **fuerimus** |
| **fuistis** | **fuerātis** | **fueritis** |
| **fuērunt** | **fuerant** | **fuerint** |

## SUBJUNCTIVE MOOD

| PRESENT | IMPERFECT | PERFECT | PLUPERFECT |
|---------|-----------|---------|------------|
| sim | essem | fuerim | fuissem |
| sīs | essēs | fuerīs | fuissēs |
| sit | esset | fuerit | fuisset |
| sīmus | essēmus | fuerīmus | fuissēmus |
| sītis | essētis | fuerītis | fuissētis |
| sint | essent | fuerint | fuissent |

## IMPERATIVE MOOD

SING. es, *be*
PL. este, *be*

## INFINITIVES

PRES. esse, *to be*
PERF. fuisse, *to have been*
FUT. futūrus, –a, –um esse,
*to be about to*
(*to be going to*) *be*

## PARTICIPLE

FUT. futūrus, –a, –um
*about to*
(*going to*) *be*

---

**Possum,** *I am able, I can*

PRINCIPAL PARTS: **possum, posse, potuī**

## INDICATIVE MOOD

| PRESENT | IMPERFECT | FUTURE |
|---------|-----------|--------|
| *I am able, I can* | *I was able, I could* | *I shall be able* |
| possum | poteram | poterō |
| potes | poterās | poteris |
| potest | poterat | poterit |
| possumus | poterāmus | poterimus |
| potestis | poterātis | poteritis |
| possunt | poterant | poterunt |

| PERFECT | PLUPERFECT | FUTURE PERFECT |
|---------|------------|----------------|
| *I have been able, I could* | *I had been able* | *I shall have been able* |
| potuī | potueram | potuerō |
| potuistī | potuerās | potueris |
| potuit | potuerat | potuerit |
| potuimus | potuerāmus | potuerimus |
| potuistis | potuerātis | potueritis |
| potuērunt | potuerant | potuerint |

## SUBJUNCTIVE MOOD

| PRESENT | IMPERFECT | PERFECT | PLUPERFECT |
|---------|-----------|---------|------------|
| possim | possem | potuerim | potuissem |
| possīs | possēs | potuerīs | potuissēs |
| possit | posset | potuerit | potuisset |
| possīmus | possēmus | potuerīmus | potuissēmus |
| possītis | possētis | potuerītis | potuissētis |
| possint | possent | potuerint | potuissent |

**377**

| INFINITIVES | PARTICIPLE |
|---|---|
| PRES. **posse,** *to be able* | PRES. potēns (adj.), *powerful* |
| PERF. potu**isse,** *to have been able* | |

**Ferō,** *I bear, I bring*

PRINCIPAL PARTS: **ferō, ferre, tulī, lātus**

*Active Voice*          *Passive Voice*

## INDICATIVE MOOD

| | | | | |
|---|---|---|---|---|
| PRES. | fero | fer*i*mus | fer*o*r | fer*i*mur |
| | fers | fertis | ferris | fer*i*minī |
| | fert | fer*u*nt | fertur | fer*u*ntur |

| | | |
|---|---|---|
| IMPERF. | ferēbam | ferēbar |
| FUT. | feram | ferar |
| PERF. | tulī | lātus, –a, –um sum |
| PLUPERF. | tuleram | lātus, –a, –um eram |
| FUT. PERF. | tulerō | lātus, –a, –um erō |

## SUBJUNCTIVE MOOD

| | | |
|---|---|---|
| PRES. | feram | ferar |
| IMPERF. | ferrem | ferrer |
| PERF. | tulerim | lātus, –a, –um sim |
| PLUPERF. | tulissem | lātus, –a, –um essem |

## IMPERATIVE MOOD

| | | |
|---|---|---|
| SING. | fer | — |
| PL. | ferte | — |

## INFINITIVES

| | | |
|---|---|---|
| PRES. | ferre | ferrī |
| PERF. | tulisse | lātus, –a, –um esse |
| FUT. | lātūrus, –a, –um esse | — |

## PARTICIPLES

| | | |
|---|---|---|
| PRES. | ferēns | — |
| PERF. | — | lātus, –a, –um |
| FUT. | lātūrus, –a, –um | — |

## Eō, *I go*

PRINCIPAL PARTS: **eō, īre, iī (īvī), itūrus**

### INDICATIVE MOOD

| PRES. | | IMPERF. | **ībam** |
|---|---|---|---|
| ēō | īmus | FUT. | **ībō** |
| īs | ītis | PERF. | **iī(īvī)** |
| it | e*u*nt | PLUPERF. | **ieram** |
| | | FUT. PERF. | **ierō** |

### SUBJUNCTIVE MOOD

| PRES. | **ĕam** |
|---|---|
| IMPERF. | **īrem** |
| PERF. | **ierim** |
| PLUPERF. | **īssem** |

### IMPERATIVE MOOD

| SING. | **ī** |
|---|---|
| PL. | **īte** |

### INFINITIVES

| PRES. | **īre** |
|---|---|
| PERF. | **īsse (iisse)** |
| FUT. | **itūrus, –a, –um esse** |

### PARTICIPLES

| PRES. | **iĕns,** *e*u**ntis** |
|---|---|
| FUT. | **itūrus, –a, –um** |

---

## Fīō, *I am made* (passive of **faciō**)

PRINCIPAL PARTS: **fīō, fierī, factus sum**

### INDICATIVE MOOD

| PRES. | | IMPERF. | **fīēbam** |
|---|---|---|---|
| fīō | — | FUT. | **fīam** |
| — | — | PERF. | **factus sum** |
| fit | fīunt | PLUPERF. | **factus eram** |
| | | FUT. PERF. | **factus erō** |

### SUBJUNCTIVE MOOD

| PRES. | **fīam** |
|---|---|
| IMPERF. | **fierem** |
| PERF. | **factus sim** |
| PLUPERF. | **factus essem** |

### IMPERATIVE MOOD

| SING. | **fī** |
|---|---|
| PL. | **fīte** |

### INFINITIVES

| PRES. | **fierī** |
|---|---|
| PERF. | **factus, –a, –um esse** |

### PARTICIPLE

| PERF. | **factus, –a, –um** |
|---|---|

---

## Volō, *I am willing, I wish*

PRINCIPAL PARTS: **volō, velle, voluī**

### INDICATIVE MOOD

| PRES. | | IMPERF. | vol*ē*bam |
|---|---|---|---|
| volō | vol*u*mus | FUT. | volam |
| **vīs** | vultis | PERF. | voluī |
| **vult** | vol*u*nt | PLUPERF. | volueram |
| | | FUT. PERF. | voluerō |

### SUBJUNCTIVE MOOD

| PRES. | **velim** |
|---|---|
| IMPERF. | **vellem** |
| PERF. | voluerim |
| PLUPERF. | voluissem |

### INFINITIVES

| PRES. | **velle** |
|---|---|
| PERF. | voluisse |

### PARTICIPLES

| PRES. | vol*ē*ns |
|---|---|

# Summary of Rules of Syntax

The word *syntax* is derived from a Greek word meaning to draw up an army in orderly array. In the terminology of grammar, it is the orderly arrangement of words as elements in a sentence to show their use and their relationships to other words. To explain the syntax of a given word is to state its form, the reason for the form, and the word on which it depends. It is important to identify the part of speech before giving the syntax.

## Agreement

1. A verb agrees with its subject in person and number.
2. Adjectives agree in gender, number, and case with the nouns to which they refer or which they modify.

> *Modify* (**modus** + **facere**) means to limit or restrict the meaning of one word by means of another: a *large* house. The word *large* restricts the meaning of *house*.

3. Adjectives are sometimes used as nouns:

> **nostrī,** *our men*    **multa,** *many things*

4. A predicate adjective after a *linking* verb agrees with the subject of the verb in gender, number, and case.

> The chief linking verbs in English are: *be, appear, seem, become, feel, look, taste, smell.* In Latin, forms of the verb **sum** and passive forms of **videō** and **faciō** are the most frequently used of the linking verbs.

5. A predicate adjective after a complementary infinitive is in the nominative case, agreeing with the subject of the main verb:

> **Amīcus *fīdus* esse dēbet.**    A friend ought to be *faithful*.

6. A predicate adjective after an objective infinitive is in the accusative case, agreeing with the subject of the infinitive:

> **Vir *amīcum fīdum* esse cupit.**    The man wishes his *friend* to be *faithful*.

7. An appositive agrees in case with the noun it explains:

**In Āmēricā, *patriā nostrā*, sunt urbēs pulchrae.**    In America, *our native land*, are beautiful cities.

8. A relative pronoun agrees with its antecedent in person, gender, and number, but its case depends upon its use in its own clause:

**Nōs *quī* sumus cīvēs cīvitātem servā- bimus.**    We *who* are citizens will save the state.

9. A participle agrees in gender, number, and case with a noun or pronoun expressed or understood:

> **Nōs *moritūrī* tē salūtāmus!**    We, *(who are) about to die,* salute you!

# Noun Syntax

1. *Nominative Case*
   a. The *subject* of a finite verb is in the nominative case.
   b. A *predicate noun* is in the nominative case. It is connected with the subject by a linking verb, or by a passive form of a verb meaning *to call, choose, name, elect.*

   > Sum *incola* **Americae.**  I am an *inhabitant* of America.
   > [**Brūtus** *cōnsul* **creātus est.**  Brutus was elected *consul.*

2. *Genitive Case*
   a. The genitive case is used to denote *possession* or *close connection:*

   > **liber** *puerī,* *the boy's* book  **tribūnus** *populī,* tribune *of the people*

   b. A genitive naming the whole may depend upon words that express a part of that whole. Instead of the *genitive of the whole* (partitive genitive), the ablative with **ex** or **dē** is regularly used with **quīdam** (*a certain one*) and with cardinal numerals except **mīlia:**

   > **pars** *mīlitum,* part *of the soldiers*
   > **quīdam** *ē mīlitibus,* certain *of the soldiers*
   > **decem** *ē mīlitibus,* ten *of the soldiers*

   c. The genitive modified by an adjective may be used to describe a person or thing and is called the *genitive of description:*

   > **hominēs** *māgnae virtūtis,* men *of great courage*

3. *Dative Case*
   a. The *indirect object* of a verb is in the dative case. Verbs meaning *to give, tell, show, offer* often have an indirect object and also a direct object:

   > **Servō** pecūniam dedit.  He gave money *to the slave.*

   b. Many *intransitive verbs* take a dative of indirect object. Among them are: **crēdō, imperō, noceō, parcō, persuādeō, resistō, studeō.**

   > **Cīvibus** persuāsit.  He persuaded *the citizens.*

   c. Many *compound verbs* with the prefixes **ad–, ante–, con–, dē–, in–, inter–, ob–, post–, prae–, prō–, sub–,** and **super–** take the dative.

   > **Brūtus** *nāvibus* **praeerat.**  Brutus was in command of *the ships.*

   d. The dative case is used after Latin adjectives meaning likeness, fitness, nearness, friendliness, usefulness, and their opposites.

   > **Arēna erat** *lūdīs* **idōnea.**  The arena was suitable *for games.*

4. *Accusative Case*
   a. The *direct object* of a transitive verb is in the accusative case:

   > **Patriam** laudāmus.  We praise our *native land.*

   b. The accusative is used without a preposition to express *extent of space* and *of time* (duration of time).

   > **Mīlitēs** *decem mīlia* **passuum iter fēcērunt.**  The soldiers marched *ten miles.* (Extent of space)

> **Rēx decem annōs rēgnāvit.** The king reigned (*for*) *ten years*.
> (Duration of time)

    c. The *place to which* or *limit of motion* is regularly expressed by the accusative with **ad** or **in.**

> **In urbem venit.** He comes *into the city*.

With the names of cities, towns, small islands, **domus,** and a few other place words, the preposition is omitted.

> **Rōmam venit.** He comes *to Rome*.

    d. Verbs of making, choosing, calling, and the like take a *predicate accusative*, referring to the same person or thing as the direct object.

> **Populus Rōmānus Brūtum *cōnsulem* creāvit.** The Roman people elected Brutus *consul*.

    e. Verbs of asking, demanding, teaching sometimes take *two accusatives*, one of the person and one of the thing.

> **Rōmānī multās *gentēs lēgēs* docuērunt.** The Romans taught many *nations laws*.

    f. **Circumdūcō, trādūcō, trānsportō** take *two accusatives*, one the object of the verb, the other of the preposition.

> **Mīlitēs *pontem* trādūxit.** He led *the soldiers* across *the bridge*.

    g. The *subject of an infinitive* is in the accusative case.

> **Puerum īre necesse est.** The boy must go. (It is necessary that *the boy* go.)
>
> **Scīmus *puerum* īre.** We know that *the boy* is going.

    h. Certain *prepositions* govern the accusative case. Among the most important are: **ad, ante, apud, circum, contra, inter, ob, per, post, praeter, prope, propter, trāns; in** and **sub** take the accusative when they show direction toward which a thing moves (place to which).

5. *Ablative Case*

    a. *Place in which* (place where) is expressed by the ablative with **in,** except with names of cities, towns, small islands, **domus,** and a few other place words which take the *locative* case.

> **Rōma est *in Ītaliā*.** Rome is *in Italy*.

    b. *Place from which* is expressed by the ablative with **ab, dē,** or **ex,** except with names of cities, towns, small islands, **domus,** *etc.*, when the ablative without a preposition is used.

> **Ex urbe fūgērunt.** They fled *from the city*.
>
> **Rōmā fūgērunt.** They fled *from Rome*.

    c. The person by whom an action is done is regularly expressed by the *ablative of personal agent*. This requires the *passive* voice, a *person*, and the *preposition* **ā** or **ab.**

> **Frūmentum *ā servīs* portābātur.** The grain was carried *by the slaves*.

    d. The ablative with **cum** is used to express *accompaniment* or *conflict*.

> **Puer *cum patre* ambulat.** The boy is walking *with his father*.
>
> **Graecī *cum Rōmānīs* pūgnāvērunt.** The Greeks fought *with the Romans*.

With personal, relative, and sometimes interrogative pronouns, **cum** becomes an enclitic:

**mēcum,** *with me* **vōbīscum,** *with you* **quōcum,** *with whom*

e. The ablative without a preposition is used to denote the *means* by which an act is performed.

**Gladiō pūgnābat.** He was fighting *with a sword.*

f. The *ablative of comparison*, without a preposition, may be used instead of **quam** and the nominative, or **quam** and the accusative.

**Mārcus erat fortior** *quam* **Sextus.**
**Mārcus erat fortior** *Sextō.* Marcus was braver *than Sextus.*

**Quam** must be expressed if the first of the two things compared is in the genitive, dative, or ablative.

**Erant cupidiōrēs** *bellī* **quam** *pācis.* They were more eager *for war* than *for peace.*

g. The ablative without a preposition is used with comparatives and words involving comparison (as **post, ante**) to denote the *degree of difference.*

*Pede* **altior quam frāter est.** He is *a foot* taller (taller *by one foot*) than his brother.

h. The *ablative of description*, without a preposition but always with an adjective modifier, is used to describe a noun. It is often translated by *of.*

**Erat vir** *summā audāciā.* He was a man *of the greatest boldness.*

i. The *ablative of specification*, without a preposition, is used to indicate in what respect the meaning of a verb, noun, or adjective applies. It answers the question: "In what respect?" and is often called the *ablative of respect.*

**Sociōs** *virtūte* **superābat.** He surpassed his companions *in courage.*

j. The ablative without a preposition is used to denote the *time when* or the *time within which* an action takes place.

*Illō tempore* **hostēs erant prope urbem.** *At that time* the enemy was near the city. (Time when)

*Decem annīs* **multa oppida vīdit.** *Within ten years* he saw many towns. (Time within which)

k. An *ablative absolute* is equivalent to an adverbial clause and is expressed by a noun and a participle, a noun and an adjective, or two nouns in the ablative case. It is grammatically independent of the rest of the sentence. It may represent clauses of time, cause, condition, etc.

**Rēge interfectō** ... *After he had killed the king* ... (Time)
**Superātīs Belgīs** ... *Since the Belgians were conquered* ... (Cause)
**Pāce factā** ... *If peace is made* ... (Condition)
**Caesare vīvō** ... *During Caesar's lifetime* ... (Noun and an adjective)
**Regulō duce** ... *With Regulus as leader* ... (Two nouns)

l. The ablative is used to express *separation* with or without the prepositions **ab, dē,** or **ex.** It emphasizes a state of being apart. With words denoting persons, a preposition is regularly used; with verbs meaning *to free, to lack,* and *to deprive,* the preposition is regularly omitted.

**Cīvēs** *perīculō* **līberāvit.**    He freed the citizens *from danger.*

**Hostēs** *ab urbe* **prohibuērunt.**    They kept the enemy *away from the city.*

**Patriam** *ab hostibus* **līberāvit.**    He freed the fatherland *from the enemy.*

m. The ablative of abstract nouns with **cum** is used to express the *manner* of an action, but **cum** may be omitted if the ablative phrase contains an adjective modifier.

**Puer** *cum studiō* **labōrat.**    The boy is working *with zeal (zealously).*

**Puer** *māgnō cum studiō* (*māgnō studiō*) **labōrat.**    The boy is working *with great zeal (very zealously).*

n. The ablative is used to express the *cause,* the reason, or the motive of the action of a verb. It is generally used without a preposition, sometimes with **dē** or **ex.**

*Timōre* **oppidum relīquērunt.**    *Because of fear* they left the town.

Cause is frequently expressed by **propter** or **ob** with the *accusative.*

**Propter** (*ob*) *perīculum grave* **oppidum relīquērunt.**    *On account of the serious danger,* they left the town.

o. The ablative is used with the *prepositions* **ab, cum, dē, ex, prae, prō, sine;** also with **in** and **sub** to express *place where:*

**in aquā,** *in the water*    **sub ponte,** *under the bridge*

### 6. *Vocative Case*

a. The person or thing addressed is in the vocative case. The vocative commonly stands after one or more words in the sentence.

**Nūllum aurum,** *rēgīna māgna,* **rogō!**    I ask for no gold, *great queen!*

b. The form of the vocative is regularly like the nominative, except in the second declension. Nouns and adjectives of this declension ending in −**us** have a vocative singular in −**e:**

**amīce cāre!**    *O dear friend!*

and proper nouns in −**ius** and **fīlius** have a vocative in −**ī** (not −**iī**):

**Lūcī, fīlī**

c. **Meus** has the vocative **mī;** the vocative plural of **meus** is **meī.**

### 7. *Locative Case*

a. Names of cities, towns, small islands, *etc.,* in the singular of the first and second declensions express *place where* by the *locative case.* The form of the locative is identical with the genitive:

**Rōmae,** *at Rome*    **domī,** *at home*

b. For names of cities, towns, small islands, *etc.,* found in the first and second declension plural, and for the third declension, the locative is formed like the dative or ablative:

**Athēnīs,** *at Athens*    **Carthāginī** or **Carthāgine,** *at Carthage*

# Verb Syntax

1. *Moods.* There are three moods in Latin: the indicative, subjunctive, and imperative.

    a. The *indicative* mood asserts a fact or asks a question. It is used in principal (independent) and subordinate (dependent) clauses.

    b. The *subjunctive* mood represents an act as willed, desired, conditioned, or prospective. It is often translated as the English indicative. It may be used in both principal and subordinate clauses.

    c. The *imperative* mood is used to express a command.

        **Nūntium ad urbem mitte!**   Send a messenger to the city.

        **Nōlī** (**nōlīte**) followed by the infinitive is the regular expression for a negative imperative.

| | |
|---|---|
| **Nōlī (nōlīte) nūntium ad urbem mittere!** | *Don't (Be unwilling to) send a messenger to the city.* |

2. *Tenses of the Indicative*

    a. The *present* tense indicates present time.

        **In viā ambulant.**   They *are walking* on the street.

    b. The *imperfect* tense represents an action or condition as continuing, customary, repeated, or attempted in the past.

        **Rōmānī in Forō stābant.**   The Romans *were standing* (*used to stand, kept on standing, stood*) in the Forum.

    c. The *future* tense indicates future time.

        **Rōmānī in Forō stābunt.**   The Romans *will stand* in the Forum.

    d. The *perfect* tense has two uses:

        (1) It may indicate an action completed at the present time, corresponding to the English present perfect with *has* and *have*.

            **Vir vēnit**   The man *has come.*

        (2) It may indicate an action completed at some indefinite past time.

            **Vir vēnit.**   The man *came.*

    e. The *pluperfect* (past perfect) tense represents an action as completed at or before a certain past time. It corresponds to the English past perfect tense.

        **Vir pervēnerat.**   The man *had arrived.*

    f. The *future perfect* tense represents an action as completed before some future time. It corresponds to the English future perfect tense, but is much commoner in Latin than in English.

        **Ante noctem id fecerit.**   Before night he *will have done* this.

3. *Indicative in Subordinate (Dependent) Clauses*

    a. *Adjective clause.* An *adjective*, or *relative*, clause which states a fact about a definite person or thing is in the indicative.

    **Vir quem laudās pater meus est.**   The man *whom you praise* is my father.

b. *Adverbial clauses*

(1) A *causal* clause gives the reason of the action. Causal clauses introduced by **quod** are used with the indicative when the reason is given on the authority of the *speaker* or the *writer*.

*Quod plēbs nūlla jūra habēbat*, **ex urbe** **discessit.**      *Because the common people had no rights, they departed from the city.*

(2) A *temporal* clause introduced by **postquam,** *after*, or **ubi,** *when*, regularly takes the perfect indicative to refer to a single past act, and is often translated by the pluperfect.

**Rēx** *postquam perīculum intellēxit*, **cum hostibus pācem fēcit.**      *After the king (had) understood the danger, he made peace with the enemy.*

(3) A *temporal* clause introduced by **dum** regularly takes the present indicative to denote continued action even in past time.

**Hoc** *dum narrat*, **forte audīvī.**      *By chance I heard this while he was telling it.*

(4) A *conditional* clause is introduced by **sī,** *if*, or **nisi,** *if not, unless.* These clauses are called conditional because they state the condition or circumstances in which the action expressed in the main clause is true. Simple conditions of fact take the indicative and are called past, present, or future according to their time.

Present: **Sī** *adest*, **bene est.** *If he is (now) here*, it is well.
Past (Imperfect or Perfect): **Sī** *aderat*, **bene erat.** *If he was here*, it was well.
Future: **Sī** *aderit*, **bene erit.** *If he is (shall be) here*, it will be well.
Future Perfect: **Sī** *adfuerit*, **bene erit.** *If he is (shall have been) here*, it will be well.

(5) A clause of *concession* introduced by **etsī** (*although*) is regularly expressed by the indicative.

**Mīles,** *etsī vulnerātus erat*, **fortiter** **pūgnābat.**      *The soldier was fighting bravely, although he had been wounded.*

4. *Subjunctive in Subordinate Clauses*

a. The subjunctive is used in a subordinate clause to express the *purpose* of an act stated in the main clause. The subordinate clause if affirmative is introduced by **ut** (*that, in order that*); if negative by **nē** (*that . . . not, in order that . . . not, lest*). English regularly uses an *infinitive*, but sometimes uses *may* or *might*. (See p. 321.)

    **Venimus** *ut videāmus*.      *We come to see (that we may see).*
    **Fugit** *nē capiātur*.      *He flees in order that he may not be captured.*

b. The subjunctive is used in a subordinate clause that expresses *result*. The subordinate clause is introduced by **ut** (*so that, that*); if negative, **ut . . . nōn** is used. The English translation is like the indicative. The result clause is often anticipated in the main clause by the indicators: **tam, sīc, ita, tantus, tālis.**

**Sīc labōrat** *ut omnēs eum laudent.*      *He so works that all praise him.*
**Ita bene erat oppidum mūnītum** *ut* **nōn capī posset.**      *So well had the town been fortified that it could not be taken.*

c. A question *indirectly* quoted (hence no longer a question) after such verbs as *ask, doubt, learn, know, tell, hear* has its verb in the subjunctive and is introduced by an interrogative pronoun, adjective or adverb. The English translation is like the indicative.

**Rogant *quis sit*.**   They ask *who he is*.

d. In a complex sentence the verb in the principal clause sets the time (past, present, future) for the whole sentence. Therefore the tense of the verb in the subordinate clause must follow the division of time indicated by the main verb. This is known as *sequence of tenses*.

The law of sequence of tenses requires that a primary tense in the principal clause be followed by a primary tense in the subordinate clause, and that a secondary tense in the main clause be followed by a secondary tense in the subordinate clause.

> Primary Tenses (referring to present or future time)
>     Indicative:   present, future, present perfect, future perfect
>     Subjunctive:  present, perfect
> Secondary Tenses (referring to the past)
>     Indicative:   imperfect, perfect, pluperfect
>     Subjunctive:  imperfect, pluperfect

### Primary Sequence

**Rogō (Rogābō, Rogāverō, Rogāvī) ubi habitet (habitāverit).**   *I ask (shall ask, shall have asked, have asked) where he lives (has lived (or) lived).*

### Secondary Sequence

**Rogāvī (Rogābam, Rogāveram) ubi habitāret (habitāvisset).**   *I asked (was asking, had asked) where he lived (had lived).*

5. *Infinitives.* An infinitive is an indeclinable verbal noun. Its form is not limited by person and number, though it is limited by tense and voice. It has several important uses.

a. The *complementary* infinitive is used to complete the meaning of certain verbs, such as **dēbeō, cupiō, possum, volō, parō, properō, contendō,** etc.

   (1) The complementary infinitive has no accusative subject because its subject is the same as the nominative subject of the verb on which it depends.

**Īre potest.**   He can *go* (is able *to go*).

   (2) A predicate noun or adjective after a complementary infinitive is in the nominative case.

**Hic vir *cōnsul* esse vult.**   This man wishes to be *consul*.

b. The *objective* infinitive, with an accusative subject, is used as the object of another verb.

**Eōs īre jūssit.**   He ordered *them to go*.

*387*

(1) The objective infinitive has an accusative subject, the complementary infinitive has not.

(2) The objective infinitive may be found after the following verbs: **jubeō, cōgō, cupiō, prohibeō, patior,** etc.

c. The *subjective* infinitive, with or without a subject accusative, may be the subject of a verb used impersonally. The predicate adjective referring to the subjective infinitive is neuter.

| | |
|---|---|
| *Legere* **est grātum.** | It is pleasant *to read* (*to read* is pleasant). |
| *Legere bonōs librōs* **est grātum.** | It is pleasant *to read good books.* |
| *Puerum* **bonōs librōs** *legere* **oportet.** | *The boy* ought *to read* good books. (It is necessary that *the boy read* good books.) |

d. The infinitive, with accusative subject, is used in *indirect statements* after verbs of saying, thinking, knowing, and perceiving. The tenses of the infinitive denote time relative to that of the main verb.

(1) The present infinitive is used to denote action going on at the same time as that of the main verb.

**Dīxit sē** *vincere.*   He said that he *was conquering.*

(2) The perfect infinitive refers to action previous to that of the main verb.

**Dīxit sē** *vīcisse.*   He said that he *had conquered.*

(3) The future infinitive refers to action that is to take place after the time of the main verb.

**Dīxit sē** *victūrum esse.*   He said that he *would conquer.*


6. *Participles.* Regular transitive verbs have three participles: the present and the future in the active voice, and the perfect in the passive. They are verbal adjectives and agree with some noun, expressed or understood, in gender, number, and case.

a. The present active participle indicates an act going on at the same time as the main verb.

**Pompam arēnam** *intrantem* **videō (vīdī, vidēbō).**   I see (I saw, I shall see) the procession *entering* the arena.

b. The perfect passive participle denotes an act completed before the time of the main verb.

**Urbēs ab hostibus** *captae* **incenduntur (incēnsae sunt, incendentur).**   The cities *captured* by the enemy are being burned (were burned, will be burned).

c. The future active participle denotes an act taking place after the time of the main verb.

*Moritūrī* **tē salūtāmus (salūtāvimus, salūtābimus).**   We, *who are going (about) to die,* salute you (saluted you, will salute you).

# Prefixes and Suffixes

## Latin-English Prefixes

| Prefix | General Meaning | Examples |
|---|---|---|
| ab–, a–, abs– | *away, from, down* | abduct, avert, abstain |
| ad–, ab–, ac–, af–, ag–, al–, an–, ap–, ar–, as–, at–, a– | *to, at, toward, near* | adduce, abbreviate, accept, affect, aggravate, allude, announce, approximate, arrogate, assimilate, attempt, ascribe |
| ante–, anti– | *before, prior to, in front of* | antecedent, antiquity, anticipate |
| circum– | *around, about, on both sides* | circumnavigate, circumspect |
| com– (cum), co–, col–, con–, cor– | *together with, joint, equally, very* | commission, composition, coequal, collect, conduce, correct, council |
| contra–, contro– | *against, opposite* | contradict, controversy, countersign |
| de– | *down, off, away from, entirely, undo* | deduce, depart, defect |
| dis–, di–, dif– | *separation, not, away, intensity, opposite* | dismiss, divert, differ, dishonest |
| ex–, e–, ef– | *out, out of, away from, former* | exact, erect, effect |
| extra–, extro– | *outside, beyond* | extraordinary, extrovert |
| in–, il–, im–, ir– | *in, into, within, on, toward, very* | induce, illusion, immanent, irrigate |
| in–, ig–, il–, im–, ir– | *not, without, opposing* | inactive, ignoble, illegal, immature, irregular |
| inter– | *between, among, reciprocal* | intercept, interact |
| intra– | *within, inside of* | intramural, intravenous |
| intro– | *into, within, inward* | introduce, introvert |
| ob–, o–, oc–, of–, op– | *over, against, toward, vary, before, upon* | obviate, omit, occasion, offer, opponent |
| per– | *through, very* | perfect, perform, pervious |
| post– | *after, following, later, behind* | postscript, postpone, post-mortem |
| pre– (prae–) | *before* (in time, place, or rank) | precede, prejudice, presentiment, preside |
| preter– (praeter) | *past, beyond* | pretermission, preternatural |
| pro– | *before, forward, for, in behalf of, in place of, favoring* | proclaim, produce, procure, prolong, pronoun, proslavery |
| re–, red– | *back, again* | recede, reiterate, redundant |
| retro– | *backward, back, behind* | retroactive, retrograde, retrospect |

| Prefix | General Meaning | Examples |
|---|---|---|
| **se–, sed–** | *away, aside, without, apart from* | secede, secure, sedition |
| **sub–, suc–, suf–, sug–, sum–, sup–, sur–, sus–, su–** | *under, beneath, below, inferior* | substance, success, suffer, suggest, summon, suppress, surreptitious, suspense, suspect |
| **subter–** | *below, under* | subterfuge |
| **super–, sur–** | *over, above, on top, excessive* | supersede, superscript, supersonic, survey |
| **trans–, tra–** | *across, beyond, over* | transact, transcribe, translucent, traduce, tradition |
| **ultra–** | *beyond, excessive, beyond the range of, extreme* | ultraviolet, ultramodern, ultramarine, ultrasonic |

## Latin-English Suffixes

| Suffix | General Meaning | Latin Words | English Derivatives |
|---|---|---|---|
| –āceus | *made of; like; belonging to* | crētāceus | cretaceous |
| –ācea (n. pl.) | | crustācea | crustacea |
| –ālis | *pertaining to; like* | lēgālis | legal |
| –ānus | *pertaining to; belonging to* | Rōmānus | Roman |
| | | hūmānus | human; humane |
| | | subterrāneānus | subterranean |
| –ārius | *pertaining to; belonging to* | ōrdinārius | ordinary |
| –ārium (n.) | *nouns denoting place* | aviārium | aviary |
| | | aquārium | aquarium |
| –āris | *pertaining to; belonging to* | populāris | popular |
| –āticus | *pertaining to; belonging to* | aquāticus | aquatic |
| –icus | | pūblicus | public |
| –āticum (n.) | | viāticum | viaticum |
| | | foliāticum | foliage |
| **–ātus** | | | |
| (verbs) | *(perfect passive participles changed to verbs in English)* | creātus | create |
| | | nāvigātus | navigate |
| (adj.) | *shaped like; concerned with* | dentātus | dentate |
| | | prīvātus | private |
| (nouns) | *one who* | lēgātus | legate |
| | *office* | senātus | senate |
| –āx (–ācis) | *tendency to; inclined to* | pūgnāx | pugnacious |
| + –tās | *abstract nouns of quality* | pūgnācitās | pugnacity |

| Suffix | General Meaning | Latin Words | English Derivatives |
|---|---|---|---|
| –bilis | able to be, capable of being; inclined to | laudābilis<br>vīsibilis | laudable<br>visible |
| –brum<br>–crum<br>–trum | means; place of action | vertebra (f.)<br>fulcrum<br>rōstrum | vertebra<br>fulcrum<br>rostrum |
| –bulum<br>–culum<br>–ulum | means; place of action | vestibulum<br>vehiculum<br>rīdiculum | vestibule<br>vehicle<br>ridicule |
| –ernus<br>–urnus<br>–erna (f.) | pertaining to | modernus<br>nocturnus<br>caverna<br>taberna | modern<br>nocturn<br>cavern<br>tavern |
| –ia<br>–tia<br>–ntia | abstract nouns of quality<br><br>(from base of pres. part.) | miseria<br>jūstitia<br>frequentia | misery<br>justice<br>frequence, –cy |
| –idus | possessing the quality of | timidus | timid |
| –ilis | pertaining to; capable of being, able to be | puerīlis<br>cīvīlis<br>facilis<br>ductilis | puerile<br>civil<br>facile<br>ductile |
| –īnus<br><br>–iēnus | pertaining to, like | marīnus<br>aquilīnus<br>aliēnus | marine<br>aquiline<br>alien |
| –īna (f.) | nouns | doctrīna | doctrine |
| –iō (n.) +<br>present stem<br>of verb | nouns of action; state; result of action | legiōn– | legion |
| –io (n.) +<br>stem of perfect<br>pass. part. | abstract nouns of action | āctiōn–<br>versiōn– | action<br>version |
| –ium<br>–cium<br>–tium | neuter nouns of place; result of action | studium<br>aedificium<br>hospitium<br>praemium<br>collēgium | study<br>edifice<br>hospice<br>premium<br>college |
| –ius | characterized by; belonging to | varius<br>anxius | various<br>anxious |
| –īvus | pertaining to; tendency; capable of | āctīvus<br>missīvus | active<br>missive |
| –lentus | full of; disposed to | corpulentus | corpulent |
| –culus<br>–ellus<br>–olus<br>–ulus | implying smallness; affection; contempt; diminutives | articulus<br>libellus<br>gladiolus<br>scrūpulus<br>fōrmula (f.)<br>corpusculum (n.) | article<br>libel<br>gladiola<br>scruple<br>formula<br>corpuscle |

| Suffix | General Meaning | Latin Words | English Derivatives |
|---|---|---|---|
| **-men** | means; action; result of action | **regimen** | regimen |
| | | **specimen** | specimen |
| **-mentum** | means; result of action | **regimentum** | regiment |
| **-mōnium** | abstract nouns of action; | **sānctimōnium** | sanctimony |
| **-mōnia** | result of action | **ācrimōnia** | acrimony |
| **-nt-** | (stem of present participle) relating to | **dīligent-** | diligent |
| | | **sentient-** | sentient |
| **-or** + present stem of verb | abstract and collective nouns denoting action or condition | **clāmor** | clamor |
| **-or** + stem of perfect pass. part. | denoting an agent | **narrātor** | narrator |
| **-ōrius** | pertaining to; belonging to | **audītōrius** | auditory |
| | | **nōtōrius** | notorious |
| **-ōrium** (n.) | nouns denoting place | **audītōrium** | auditorium |
| | | **factōrium** | factory |
| **-ōsus** | full of | **verbōsus** | verbose |
| **-ōx** | tendency to; inclined to; | **ferōx** | ferocious |
| + **-tās** | abstract nouns of quality | **ferōcitās** | ferocity |
| **-tās** | abstract and collective nouns denoting quality | **gravitās** | gravity |
| | | **lībertās** | liberty |
| **-tūdō** | abstract nouns denoting quality | **altitūdō** | altitude |
| **-tum** | (neuter ending of perf. pass. part.) result of action; completed act | **factum** | fact |
| | | **habitum** | habit |
| **-tūra** | result of action | **captūra** | capture |
| **-sūra** | | **fissūra** | fissure |
| **-ūra** | | **figūra** | figure |
| **-tus** | fourth declension nouns | **adventus** | advent |
| **-sus** | identical in form with the perf. pass. part. | **sēnsus** | sense |
| **-tūs** | abstract nouns denoting quality | **virtūs** | virtue |
| **-us** | second declension masculine adjective | **barbarus** | barbarous |
| | | **sevērus** | severe |
| **-uus** | belonging to | **continuus** | continuous |
| | | **assiduus** | assiduous |

# Glossary of Proper Names

Latin proper names in English translation should be pronounced as in English words.

## A

**Acca Lārentia, –ae, f.**, the wife of Faustulus and the nurse of Romulus and Remus.

**Achillēs, –is, m.**, a Greek hero in the Trojan War; son of Peleus and Thetis.

**Actium, –ī, n.**, promontory in west Greece, near which Octavianus (later Augustus) conquered Antony and Cleopatra.

**Aegyptus, –ī, m.**, Egypt, a country in northern Africa.

**Aemilius, –ī, m.**, name of a Roman gens; Aemilia Via, road leading from Ariminum to Placentia.

**Aenēās, –ae, m.**, son of Venus and Anchises; hero of Vergil's Aeneid; ancestor of the Romans.

**Aequī, –ōrum, m. pl.**, a people of central Italy with whom the Romans waged war.

**Aetna, –ae, f.**, a volcano in Sicily.

**Āfrica, –ae, f.**, the continent of Africa.

**Agamemnōn, –onis, m.**, leader of the Greek expedition to Troy.

**Agrippa, –ae, m.**, a Roman family name; Menenius Agrippa is said to have reconciled the patricians and the plebeians.

**Alba, –ae, f.**, white; **Alba Longa**, the oldest Latin town, built by Ascanius, destroyed by Tullus Hostilius; **Albānī, –ōrum, m. pl.**, the Albans.

**Allobrogēs, –um, m. pl.**, a Gallic people.

**Alpēs, –ium, f. pl.**, the Alps.

**Amāta, –ae, f.**, wife of King Latinus and the mother of Lavinia.

**Amērica, –ae, f.**, America; **Amēricānus, –ī, m.**, an American.

**Amūlius, –ī, m.**, king of Alba Longa, who drove his elder brother, Numitor, from throne, and left Numitor's grandsons, Romulus and Remus, to die in the Tiber.

**Anchīsēs, –ae, m.**, father of Aeneas.

**Ancus (Mārcius), –ī, m.**, fourth king of Rome.

**Androclus, –ī, m.**, a Roman slave.

**Androgeus, –ī, m.**, son of King Minos of Crete.

**Antōnius, Mārcus, –ī, m.**, Mark Antony, bitter enemy of Cicero, triumvir with Octavianus and Lepidus, defeated by Octavianus at the battle of Actium, 31 B.C.

**Apollō, –inis, m.**, son of Jupiter and Latona; brother of Diana; god of the sun.

**Appius, –ī, m.**, Roman praenomen. **Appius Claudius**, a Roman censor, who began the Appian Way, which led from Rome to Capua and was later extended to Brundisium; **Appia Aqua**, an aqueduct, was constructed by the same.

**Aprilis, –is, m.**, the month of April.

**Arar, –is, m.**, a river in Gaul.

**Archiās, –ae, m.**, a Greek poet of Antioch, a teacher of Cicero.

**Archimēdēs, –is, m.**, a celebrated Greek mathematician and inventor.

**Ardea, –ae, f.**, town of the Rutuli in Latium.

**Armenia, –ae, f.**, a country in Asia Minor.

**Ascanius, –ī, m.**, son of Aeneas and Creusa; founder of Alba Longa.

**Āsia, –ae, f.**, the continent of Asia.

**Assyria, –ae, f.**, a country in Asia.

**Athēnae, –ārum, f. pl.**, Athens; **Atheniēnsēs**, the Athenians.

**Augustus, –ī, m.**, a name granted to Octavianus and other Roman emperors.

**Aventīnum, –ī, n.**, the Aventine, one of the seven hills of Rome.

## B

**Baucis, –is, f.**, an aged Phrygian, wife of Philemon.

**Belgae, –ārum, m.**, the Belgians.

**Britannī, –ōrum, m.**, the Britains; **Britannia, –ae, f.**, Britain; **Britannicus, –a, –um**, British.

**Brundisium,** –ī, *n.,* now Brindisi, a town in Calabria, Italy.

**Brūtus,** –ī, *m.,* Roman cognomen; **L. Jūnius Brūtus,** who freed Rome from the kings; elected first Roman consul; **M. Jūnius Brūtus,** one of the murderers of Caesar.

## C

**C.,** *abbr. for* **Gājus,** a Roman praenomen.

**C. Jūlius Caesar,** –aris, *m.,* general, author, statesman; conquered Pompey; overthrew power of senate; became dictator with supreme power; was murdered by Brutus and Cassius.

**Calchās,** –antis, *m.,* soothsayer to the Greeks before Troy.

**Caligula,** –ae, *m.,* Roman emperor, son of Germanicus.

**Cannae,** –ārum, *f. pl.,* a small town in Apulia; scene of the defeat of the Romans by Hannibal, 216 B.C.

**Capitōlīnus,** –ī, *m.;* the Capitoline Hill.

**Capitōlium,** –ī, *n.,* the Capitol, a temple of Jupiter in Rome; one of the seven hills of Rome.

**Carthāgō,** –inis, *f.,* a city in northern Africa.

**Cassius,** –a, –um, name of a Roman gens; **C. Cassius Longīnus,** one of the murderers of Caesar.

**Casticus,** –ī, *m.,* a Sequanian noble.

**Castor,** –oris, *m.,* twin brother of Pollux and brother of Helen.

**Catilīna,** –ae, *m.,* Roman of noble birth who headed a conspiracy against the state, which Cicero exposed.

**Catō,** –ōnis, *m.,* Roman cognomen; **M. Porcius Catō,** the censor, author of books on agriculture.

**Cerēs, Cereris,** *f.,* goddess of agriculture; sister of Jupiter; mother of Proserpina.

**Chrīstus,** –ī, *m.,* Christ; **Chrīstiānus,** –ī, *m.,* a Christian.

**Cicerō,** –ōnis, *m.,* M. Tullius Cicero, great Roman writer and orator.

**Cilicia,** –ae, *f.,* a region in Asia Minor.

**Cimbrī,** –ōrum, *m.,* a German tribe that invaded Italy; defeated by Marius.

**Cincinnātus,** –ī, *m.,* L. Quinctius Cincinnatus, Roman farmer who was summoned from the farm to become dictator, 458 B.C.

**Cinna,** –ae, *m.,* partisan of Marius in the civil war against Sulla.

**Circus Māximus,** –ī, *m.,* the greatest circus in Rome.

**Claudius (Clodius),** –ī, *m.,* **Appius Claudius Crassus,** notorious decemvir, 451 B.C.; **Appius Claudius Caecus,** censor, 312 B.C., builder of public works; **Emperor Claudius** (10 B.C.–A.D. 54).

**Cleopātra,** –ae, *f.,* queen of Egypt.

**Colossēum,** –ī, *n.,* the Colosseum, a Roman amphitheater.

**Concordia,** –ae, *f.,* the goddess Concord; Temple of the goddess in the Forum.

**Comitium,** –ī, *n.,* place of assembly at the end of the Roman Forum.

**Cornēlia,** –ae, *f.,* wife of Ti. Sempronius Gracchus; mother of the Gracchi.

**Corsica,** –ae, *f.,* island of Corsica in the Mediterranean Sea.

**Crassus,** –ī, *m.,* wealthy Roman, member of the first triumvirate with Caesar and Pompey.

**Crēta,** –ae, *f.,* an island south of Greece.

**Cūria,** –ae, *f.,* meeting place of the Roman senate.

**Cūriātii,** –ōrum, *m. pl.,* name of an Alban gens, from which three champions fought with the Horatii.

**Cyclōpēs,** –um, *m. pl.,* one-eyed giants; descendants of Uranus and Gaea.

## D

**Daedalus,** –ī, *m.,* Greek craftsman, builder of the Cretan labyrinth; mythical aviator.

**Damoclēs,** –is, *m.,* courtier of Dionysius, the tyrant of Syracuse.

**Delos,** –ī, *f.,* small island in the Aegean Sea; supposed birthplace of Apollo and Diana.

**Delphī,** –ōrum, *m.,* a small town famous for the oracle of Apollo.

**Deucaliōn,** –ōnis, *m.,* survivor of the flood.

**Diāna,** –ae, *f.,* goddess of the moon, the hunt, and the forest; sister of Apollo.

**Dīdō, –ōnis,** *f.,* queen of Carthage.

**Dionysius, –ī,** *m.,* the tyrant of Syracuse.

**Dīviciācus, –ī,** *m.,* Haeduan chief.

**Divicō, –ōnis,** *m.,* Helvetian chieftain.

**Duīlius, –ī,** *m.,* Roman consul; gained great naval victory over the Carthaginians.

**Dumnorīx, –īgis,** *m.,* brother of Diviciacus.

## E

**Epimētheus, –ī,** *m.,* husband of Pandora; brother of Prometheus.

**Epīrus, –ī,** *m.,* a region in northwest Greece.

**Eris, –idis,** *f.,* Eris, the goddess of discord.

**Etrūria, –ae,** *f.,* a district in northwest Italy.

**Etrūscī, –ōrum,** *m. pl.,* people of Etruria.

**Eurōpa, –ae,** *f.,* the continent of Europe.

## F

**Fabius, –ī,** *m.,* Q. Fabius Maximus Cunctator, opponent of Hannibal in second Punic War.

**Fabricius, –ī,** *m.,* Roman general renowned for his integrity.

**Faustulus, –ī,** *m.,* shepherd who brought up Romulus and Remus.

**Flāminius, –ī,** *m.,* C. Flaminius Nepos, defeated by Hannibal at Lake Trasumene; **Flāminia Via,** road built by the above.

**Forum, –ī,** *n.,* a market place; **Forum Rōmānum,** at the foot of the Palatine and Capitoline hills.

## G

**Gaea, –ae,** *f.,* Mother Earth.

**Gallī, –ōrum,** *m. pl.,* the Gauls; **Gallus, –ī,** *m.,* a Gaul; **Gallia, –ae,** *f.,* Gaul, ancient France.

**Genāva, –ae,** *f.,* a town of the Allobroges, now Geneva.

**Germānī, –ōrum,** *m. pl.,* the Germans; **Germānia, –ae,** *f.,* Germany.

**Gracchus, –a, –um,** name of a Roman gens; **Tiberius** and **Gājus,** the **Gracchī,** Roman reformers, second century B.C.

**Graecī, –ōrum,** *m. pl.,* the Greeks; **Graecus, –a, –um,** Greek; **Graecia, –ae,** *f.,* Greece.

## H

**Haeduī (Aeduī), –ōrum,** *m. pl.,* a Gallic tribe living in modern Burgundy.

**Hamilcar, –aris,** *m.,* Carthaginian general in first Punic War; father of Hannibal.

**Hannibal, –alis,** *m.,* leader of the Carthaginians in the second Punic War.

**Hasdrubal, –alis,** *m.,* Carthaginian general; brother-in-law of Hannibal.

**Hector, –oris,** *m.,* son of Priam.

**Hecuba, –ae,** *f.,* wife of Priam.

**Helena, –ae,** *f.,* wife of Menelaus; carried off by Paris, who thus caused the Trojan War.

**Helvētiī, –ōrum,** *m. pl.,* inhabitants of what is now Switzerland.

**Hibernia, –ae,** *f.,* Ireland.

**Hispānia, –ae,** *f.,* Spain.

**Horātius, –a, –um,** name of a Roman gens; the three **Horātiī** who fought against the Curiatii; **Horātius Coclēs** who defended the bridge over the Tiber against Porsena; **Quīntus Horātius Flaccus,** the Roman poet.

**Hostīlius, –ī,** *m.,* Tullus Hostilius, the third king of Rome.

## I

**Icarus, –ī,** *m.,* the son of Daedalus; drowned in the Aegean Sea while flying from Crete with wings made by his father.

**Ītalī, –ōrum,** *m. pl.,* the Italians. **Ītalia, –ae,** *f.,* Italy; **Ītalicus, –a, –um,** Italian.

## J

**Jāniculum, –ī,** *n.,* one of the hills of Rome, on the left bank of the Tiber.

**Jānus, –ī,** *m.,* the god of the year, represented with two faces; the guardian of doorways and beginnings.

**Jūdea, –ae,** *f.,* Judea, or Palestine; **Jūdaeī, –ōrum,** *m. pl.,* the Jews.

**Jugurtha, –ae,** *m.,* king of Numidia; conquered by Marius.

**Jūlius, –a, –um,** name of Roman gens; *see* **Caesar; Jūlia, –ae,** *f.*, feminine of Julius.

**Jūnius, –a, –um,** name of a Roman gens; *see* **Brūtus.**

**Jūnō, –ōnis,** *f.*, sister and wife of Jupiter.

**Juppiter, Jovis,** *m.*, Jupiter, king of the gods.

**Jūra, –ae,** *f.*, chain of mountains between the Rhine and the Rhone.

## L

**L.,** *abbr. for* Lucius, a Roman praenomen.

**Labiēnus, –ī,** *m.*, a lieutenant of Julius Caesar.

**Lacus Lemannus, –ī,** *m.*, Lake Geneva.

**Laeca, –ae,** *m.*, one of Catiline's fellow conspirators against Cicero.

**Lāocoön, –ontis,** *m.*, a priest of Neptune in Troy, who warned the Trojans against the Greeks and, with his two sons, was killed by serpents.

**Larēs, –um,** *m. pl.*, Roman household gods.

**Latīnē,** *adv.*, in Latin.

**Latīnus, –ī,** *m.*, king of Latium.

**Latium, –ī,** *n.*, region of Italy in which Rome was situated.

**Latōna, –ae,** *f.*, mother of Apollo and Diana.

**Lāvīnia, –ae,** *f.*, Latin princess, bride of Aeneas.

**Lāvīnium, –ī,** *n.*, city of Latium, founded by Aeneas in honor of his wife.

**Lepidus, –ī,** *m.*, M. Aemilius, a triumvir with Antonius and Octavianus.

**Liscus, –ī,** *m.*, a chief magistrate of the Haeduans.

**Lūcrētia, –ae,** *f.*, Roman matron whose death led to the expulsion of the kings.

## M

**M.,** *abbr. for* Marcus, a Roman praenomen.

**Mānlius, –a, –um,** name of a Roman gens; **M. Mánlius Capitōlīnus,** who repulsed the Gauls.

**Mārcius, Ancus, –ī,** *m.*, fourth king of Rome.

**Marius, –a, –um,** name of a Roman gens; **C. Marius,** seven times consul; conqueror of Jugurtha and the Cimbri and Teutones; rival of Sulla; leader of the popular party at Rome.

**Mārs, Martis,** *m.*, god of war.

**Menelāus, –ī,** *m.*, brother of Agamemnon; husband of Helen.

**Mercurius, –ī,** *m.*, messenger of the gods; patron of travelers, thieves, and merchants.

**Minerva, –ae,** *f.*, goddess of wisdom.

**Mīnōs, Mīnōis,** *m.*, king of Crete.

**Mīnōtaurus, –ī,** *m.*, a monster, half man and half bull.

**Mīthridātēs, –is,** *m.*, king in Pontus, defeated by Pompejus (Pompey).

**Mōns Sacer, Montis Sacrī,** *m.*, the Sacred Mountain, a hill near Rome.

**Mūcius, –a, –um,** name of a Roman gens; **M. Mūcius Scaevola** (Left-handed), who made an attempt on the life of Porsena.

## N

**Neptūnus, –ī,** *m.*, the god of the sea.

**Nerō, –ōnis,** *m.*, the fifth Roman emperor, persecutor of the Christians.

**Niobē, –ēs,** *f.*, queen of Thebes, turned to stone by Latona.

**Numa, –ae,** *m.*, Numa Pompilius, second king of Rome.

**Numidia, –ae,** *f.*, a country of North Africa.

**Numitor, –ōris,** *m.*, king of Alba Longa; father of Rhea Silvia; grandfather of Romulus and Remus.

## O

**Octāvius, –a, –um,** name of a Roman gens. **Octāviānus, –ī,** *m.*, name of the Emperor Augustus, signifying that he was adopted from the family called Octavius; **Octāvia, –ae,** *f.*, sister of Augustus and wife of Mark Antony.

**Olympus, –ī,** *m.*, a famous mountain in Thessaly; home of the gods.

**Orgetorīx, –īgis,** *m.*, a Helvetian chieftain.

**Ōstia, –ae,** *f.*, an ancient seaport in Rome at the mouth of the Tiber.

## P

**P.,** *abbr. for* **Pūblius,** a Roman praenomen.

**Palātium, –ī,** *n.,* one of the seven hills of Rome; **Palātīnus, –a, –um,** relating to the Palatine Hill.

**Palēs, –is,** *m.,* goddess of herds and shepherds.

**Pandōra, –ae,** *f.,* wife of Epimetheus; endowed with all gifts by the gods.

**Paris, –idis,** *m.,* son of Priam; carried away Helen, wife of Menelaus, and thus caused the Trojan War.

**Parthia, –ae,** *f.,* an ancient country southeast of the Caspian Sea.

**Pēleus, –ī,** *m.,* king of Thessaly; husband of Thetis; father of Achilles.

**Penātēs, –ium,** *m.,* ancient Italian household gods.

**Phaethon, –thontis,** *m.,* son of Apollo; killed by a thunderbolt of Jupiter.

**Phārnacēs, –is,** *m.,* king in Pontus; son of Mithridates; conquered by Caesar.

**Pharsālus, –ī,** *f.,* a town in Thessaly near which Caesar defeated Pompey.

**Philēmōn, –onis,** *m.,* husband of Baucis.

**Philippī, –ōrum,** *m. pl.,* city in Macedonia, where Octavian and Antony defeated Brutus and Cassius.

**Phoenicia, –ae,** *f.,* a country of Syria.

**Plineus, –ī,** *m.,* the Elder, author of books on natural history; the Younger, author of letters.

**Plūtō, –ōnis,** *m.,* king of the Underworld; husband of Proserpina.

**Poenus, –ī,** *m.,* a Carthaginian; **Pūnicus, –a, –um,** Punic, Carthaginian.

**Polītēs, –ae,** *m.,* Polites, son of King Priam of Troy.

**Pollūx, –ūcis,** *m.,* the twin brother of Castor and brother of Helen.

**Pompējus, –a, –um,** name of Roman gens; **Cn. Pompējus,** Pompey the Great, triumvir with Caesar and Crassus.

**Pompilius, –ī,** *m.,* Numa Pompilius, second king of Rome.

**Pontus, –ī,** *m.,* country on the shores of the Black Sea; **Ponticus, –a, –um,** belonging to Pontus.

**Porsena, –ae,** *m.,* an Etruscan king.

**Praeneste, –is,** *n.,* a strongly fortified town of Latium.

**Proca, –ae,** *m.,* a king of Alba Longa.

**Promēthēus, –ī,** *m.,* the mythical hero who made man of clay and stole fire from Heaven.

**Pyrrhus, –ī,** *m.,* king of Epirus, in Greece; enemy of Rome.

**Pyrrha, –ae,** *f.,* wife of Deucalion.

## Q

**Quirīnus, –ī,** *m.,* the name given to the deified Romulus.

## R

**Rēgulus, –ī,** *m.,* **M. Atīlius Rēgulus,** Roman consul and general in first Punic War.

**Remus, –ī,** *m.,* twin brother of Romulus.

**Rhea Silvia, –ae,** *f.,* mother of Romulus and Remus.

**Rhēnus, –ī,** *m.,* the Rhine river between Gaul and Germany.

**Rhodanus, –ī,** *m.,* the Rhone, a river in Gaul.

**Rōma, –ae,** *f.,* Rome.

**Rōmānus, –a, –um,** Roman; **Rōmānus, –ī,** a Roman.

**Rōmulus, –ī,** *m.,* legendary founder of Rome.

**Rōstra, –ōrum,** *n. pl.,* the speaker's platform in the Forum.

**Rubicō, –ōnis,** *m.,* the Rubicon, river in northern Italy at the boundary of the Roman Republic and its provinces.

**Rutulī, –ōrum,** *m. pl.,* the Rutuli or Rutulians, a people of Latium, central Italy.

## S

**Sabīnus, –a, –um,** Sabine; **Sabīnī, –ōrum,** *m. pl.,* a tribe living near Rome.

**Sacra Via, –ae,** *f.,* a street in Rome; **Sacer Mōns,** a hill in the Sabine country.

**Samnitēs, –ium,** *m. pl.,* inhabitants of Samnium, a region of central Italy.

**Sardinia, –ae,** *f.,* an island in the Mediterranean Sea.

**Saturnus, -ī,** *m.,* god of agriculture.

**Scotia, -ae,** *f.,* Scotland.

**Scipiō, -ōnis,** *m.,* a family name of the gens Cornelia. Scipio Africanus defeated Hannibal at Zama and thus finished the second Punic War.

**Sertōrius, -ī,** *m.,* a general of Marius.

**Servius Tullius, Servī Tullī,** *m.,* sixth king of Rome.

**Sēquanī, -ōrum,** *m. pl.,* the Sequanians, a tribe of Celtic Gaul.

**Sibylla, -ae,** *f.,* a Sibyl, priestess and oracle of Apollo.

**Sicilia, -ae,** *f.,* the island of Sicily.

**Silvius Proca, Silvī Procae,** a king of Alba Longa.

**Sinōn, -ōnis,** *m.,* a Greek spy in the Trojan War.

**Sparta, -ae,** *f.,* the capital of Laconia.

**Spartacus, -ī,** *m.,* leader in a revolt of the gladiators.

**Sulla, -ae,** *m.,* dictator; leader of the nobility; enemy of Marius.

**Sulpicius, -a, -um,** name of a Roman gens; **P. Sulpicius Rūfus,** one of Caesar's lieutenants.

### T

**Tarentum, -ī,** *n.,* a town in Italy.

**Tarquinius, -ī,** *m.,* Tarquin, a king of Rome; **T. Superbus,** Tarquin the Proud, last king of Rome.

**Teutonēs, -um,** *m. pl.,* Teutons, a German people defeated by Marius.

**Thēbae, -ārum,** *f. pl.,* Thebes, a city of ancient Greece.

**Thessalia, -ae,** *f.,* Thessaly, a region of Greece.

**Tiberis, -is,** *m.,* the Tiber, the river on which Rome is situated.

**Tigurīnī, -ōrum,** *m. pl.,* a tribe of the Helvetians.

**Titanī, -ōrum,** *m.,* Titans, a race of handsome giants, descendants of Uranus and Gaea.

**Tolōsātēs, -ium,** *m. pl.,* people of Tolosa, a town in Gaul, now Toulouse.

**Trōja, -ae,** *f.,* Troy, city of Asia Minor.

**Trōjānus, -ī,** *m.,* Trojan.

**Tullus Hostīlius, Tullī Hostīlī,** *m.,* third king of Rome.

### U

**Uranus, -ī,** *m.,* god of heaven; husband of Gaea; father of the Titans, the Cyclopes, and the Furies.

### V

**Valerius, -ī,** *m.,* a Gallic interpreter and confidential friend of Caesar.

**Venus, -eris,** *f.,* goddess of love and beauty.

**Vergilius, -ī,** *m.,* Publius Vergilius Maro, Vergil, the great Latin poet.

**Vesta, -ae,** *f.,* the goddess of the hearth; Vestal virgin, a priestess of Vesta.

**Volscī, -ōrum,** *m. pl.,* a people of Latium.

**Vulcānus, -ī,** *m.,* Vulcan, the god of fire.

### X

**Xanthīppus, -ī,** *m.,* a Greek who took Regulus prisoner.

# Vocabulary

## Latin-English

The words in the vocabulary that have been listed under Words to Master are printed here without an asterisk. The words that are preceded by an asterisk are used only in the Latin reading lessons and Conversations. Many of these words can be recognized by their likeness to English words. If not, they have been translated in context wherever they appear in the readings and Conversations. Prefixes and suffixes are listed separately on pages 389–392.

The future active participle is usually given as the fourth principal part of verbs that are wholly, or generally, intransitive.

### A

**ā, ab,** *prep.* + *abl.*, from, away from, by.

**abdō, –ere, –didī, –ditus,** 3, hide, conceal.

**abstineō, –ēre, –uī, –tentus,** 2, restrain, refrain, abstain.

**absum, –esse, āfuī, āfutūrus,** *irreg.*, be away, be absent, be distant.

**ac,** *see* **atque.**

**accēdō, –ere, –cessī, –cessūrus,** 3, approach.

**accidō, –ere, –cidī, —,** 3, befall, happen.

**accipiō, –ere, –cēpī, –ceptus,** 3, receive, accept.

**accūsō, –āre, –āvī, –ātus,** 1, blame, accuse.

**ācer, ācris, ācre,** *m/f/n.,* 3, sharp, keen, active, fierce.

**aciēs, aciēī,** *f.,* 5, edge, line of battle, battle line.

***ācrimōnia, –ae,** *f.,* 1, sharpness, acrimony.

**ācriter,** *adv.,* sharply, fiercely.

***āctiō, –ōnis,** *f.,* 3, action.

**ad,** *prep.* + *acc.,* to, toward, near, about.

**addūcō, –ere, –dūxī, –ductus,** 3, lead to, influence.

**adjuvō, –āre, –jūvī, –jūtus,** 1, *irreg.*, aid, help.

**administrō, –āre, –āvī, –ātus,** 1, manage, direct, administer.

***admīrābilis, –e,** *mf/n.,* 3, admirable.

***admīror, –ārī, –ātus,** 1, *dep.*, wonder at, admire.

***adoptō, –āre, –āvī, –ātus,** 1, adopt.

***adōrnō, –āre, –āvī, –ātus,** 1, furnish, adorn.

**adōrō, –āre, –āvī, –ātus,** 1, worship, adore.

**adsum, –esse, –fuī, –futūrus,** *irreg.*, be present, be near, be at hand.

**adulēscēns, –entis,** *m.,* 3 (–ium), youth, young man.

**adulēscentia, –ae,** *f.,* 1, youth.

***adultus, –a, –um,** *m/f/n.,* 1, 2, grown up, adult.

***advena, –ae,** *mf.,* 1, stranger.

**adventus, –ūs,** *m.,* 4, coming, arrival, advent.

***adverbium, –ī,** *n.,* 2, adverb.

***adversus,** *adv./prep.* + *acc.,* opposed to, against.

**aedificium, –ī,** *n.,* 2, building, house.

**aedificō, –āre, –āvī, –ātus,** 1, build, construct.

***aedīlis, –is,** *m.,* 3 (–ium), aedile, a public officer at Rome.

***aeger, –gra, –grum,** *m/f/n.,* 1, 2, sick, ill.

**aegrē,** *adv.,* hardly, with difficulty.

***aequālis, –e,** *mf/n.,* 3, equal.

**aequō, –āre, –āvī, –ātus,** 1, make equal, equalize.

**aequus, –a, –um,** *m/f/n.,* 1, 2, equal, just, even, fair.

aestās, –tātis, *f.*, 3, summer.

aetās, –tātis, *f.*, 3, age.

aeternus, –a, –um, *m/f/n.*, 1, 2, perpetual, eternal; **in aeternum,** forever.

ager, agrī, *m.*, 2, field, territory, land.

agitō, –āre, –āvī, –ātus, 1, drive, stir up.

agmen, –inis, *n.*, 3, column of march, line of march.

agō, –ere, ēgī, āctus, 3, drive, lead, do, act; **grātiās agere,** give thanks; **vītam agere,** spend or lead a life; **negōtium agere,** transact business; **causam agere,** plead a cause.

agricola, –ae, *m.*, 1, farmer.

*agrīcultūra, –ae, *f.*, 1, agriculture.

āla, –ae, *f.*, 1, wing.

alacer, –cris, –cre, *m/f/n.*, 3, eager, lively, alert.

alacriter, *adv.*, eagerly.

albus, –a, –um, *m/f/n.*, 1, 2, white.

aliēnus, –a, –um, *m/f/n.*, 1, 2, another's, foreign.

alius, –a, –ud, *m/f/n.*, 1, 2, *gen.*, –īus, *dat.*, –ī, another, other; **aliī ... aliī,** some ... others; **alius (–a, –ud) post alium (–am, –ud),** one after the other.

*alligō, –āre, –āvī, –ātus, 1, tie to, bind to.

alter, –era, –erum, *m/f/n.*, 1, 2, *gen.*, –īus, *dat.*, –ī, the other (of two), the second; **alter ... alter,** the one ... the other.

*altitūdō, –inis, *f.*, 3, height, depth.

altus, –a, –um, *m/f/n.*, 1, 2, high, tall, deep.

*amantissimus, –a, –um, *m/f/n.*, 1, 2, most (very) loving.

ambō, –ae, –ō, *m/f/n.*, *declined like* **duo,** both.

ambulō, –āre, –āvī, –ātūrus, 1, walk, march.

amīcitia, –ae, *f.*, 1, friendship.

amīcus, –a, –um, *m/f/n.*, 1, 2, friendly; **amīcus, –ī,** *m.*, 2, friend; **amīca, –ae,** *f.*, 1, friend.

āmittō, –ere, –mīsī, –missus, 3, send away, let go, lose.

amō, –āre, –āvī, –ātus, 1, love, like.

*amor, –ōris, *m.*, 3, love.

*amphitheātrum, –ī, *n.*, 2, amphitheater.

*angelus, –ī, *m.*, 2, angel.

angustus, –a, –um, *m/f/n.*, 1, 2, narrow, difficult; **angustiae, –ārum,** *f. pl.*, 1, narrow pass, difficulties.

*anima, –ae, *f.*, 1, soul, breath of life.

animadvertō, –ere, –vertī, –versus, 3, notice, observe, perceive.

*animal, –ālis, *n.*, 3 (–ium), animal.

animus, –ī, *m.*, 2, spirit, mind, courage; **in animō habēre,** to have in mind, intend.

annus, –ī, *m.*, 2, year.

ante, *prep.* + *acc.*, before, in front of; *adv.*, before, formerly, ago.

anteā, *adv.*, before, formerly.

antīquus, –a, –um, *m/f/n.*, 1, 2, ancient, old.

*anxius, –a, –um, *m/f/n.*, 1, 2, anxious, troubled.

appellō, –āre, –āvī, –ātus, 1, name, call upon, address.

apprehendō, –ere, –prehendī, –prehēnsus, 3, seize, lay hold of.

appropinquō, –āre, –āvī, –ātus, 1, approach.

apud, *prep.* + *acc.*, near, at, among, at the house of.

aqua, –ae, *f.*, 1, water.

*aquaeductus, –ūs, *m.*, 4, aqueduct.

aquila, –ae, *f.*, 1, eagle.

āra, –ae, *f.*, 1, altar.

arbitror, –ārī, –ātus, 1, *dep.*, think, judge.

*arca, –ae, *f.*, 1, box.

*arēna, –ae, *f.*, 1, arena, sand.

arma, –ōrum, *n. pl.*, 2, arms, weapons.

armātus, –a, –um, *m/f/n.*, 1, 2, armed.

*armō, –āre, –āvī, –ātus, 1, arm.

arō, –āre, –āvī, –ātus, 1, plow.

ars, artis, *f.*, 3 (–ium), skill, art.

*arx, arcis, *f.*, 3 (–ium), citadel, fortress.

ascendō, –ere, –scendī, –scēnsus, 3, mount, climb, ascend.

*ascēnsus, –ūs, *m.*, 4, ascent.

aspectus, –ūs, *m.*, 4, appearance, sight, aspect.

*asȳlum, –ī, *n.*, 2, asylum.

atque (ac), *conj.*, and, and also.

*atrium, –ī, *n.*, 2, atrium, principal room of a Roman house.

auctōritās, –tātis, *f.*, 3, influence, authority.

**audācia, –ae,** *f.,* 1, daring, boldness.
**audācter,** *adv.,* boldly.
**audāx, –ācis,** *mfn.,* 3, daring, bold.
**audiō, –īre, –īvī, –ītus,** 4, hear, hear of.
**augeō, –ēre, auxī, auctus,** 2, increase.
*****augur, –uris,** *m.,* 3, augur, soothsayer.
*****augurium, –ī,** *n.,* 2, augury, soothsaying.
*****aureus, –a, –um,** *m/f/n.,* 1, 2, golden.
*****aurīga, –ae,** *m.,* 1, driver, charioteer.
**aurum, –ī,** *n.,* 2, gold.
*****auspicium, –ī,** *n.,* 2, divination by the flight of birds, auspices.
**aut,** *conj.,* or; **aut . . . aut,** either . . . or.
**autem,** *conj., always postpositive,* however, but, moreover.
**auxilium, –ī,** *n.,* 2, help, aid.
*****avis, –is,** *f.,* 3 (–ium), bird.

# B

*****barbarus, –a, –um,** *m/f/n.,* 1, 2, barbarous, uncivilized.
*****basilica, –ae,** *f.,* 1, building, meeting-place, basilica.
**beātus, –a, –um,** *m/f/n.,* 1, 2, happy, blessed.
*****bellicōsus, –a, –um,** *m/f/n.,* 1, 2, warlike, bellicose.
**bellum, –ī,** *n.,* 2, war; **bellum gerere,** wage war; **bellum cōnficere,** end a war successfully; **bellum īnferre,** make war upon.
**bene,** *adv.,* well; *comp.,* **melius;** *superl.,* **optimē.**
*****beneficentia, –ae,** *f.,* 1, kindness, beneficence.
**beneficium, –ī,** *n.,* 2, kindness, service.
**benīgnē,** *adv.,* kindly.
**benīgnus, –a, –um,** *m/f/n.,* 1, 2, kind, kindly, friendly.
*****bestia, –ae,** *f.,* 1, beast.
**bonus, –a, –um,** *m/f/n.,* 1, 2, good; *comp.,* **melior;** *superl.,* **optimus;** **bonum, –ī,** *n.,* 2, a good thing; **bona, –ōrum,** *n. pl.,* 2, goods, property.
**brevis, –e,** *mf/n.,* 3, short, brief.

# C

**cadō, –ere, cecidī, cāsūrus,** 3, fall.
*****cādūceus, –ī,** *m.,* herald's staff, Mercury's staff, caduceus.

**caecus, –a, –um,** *m/f/n.,* 1, 2, blind.
**caedēs, –is,** *f.,* 3 (–ium), slaughter, carnage.
**caelum, –ī,** *n.,* 2, heavens, sky.
**calamitās, –tātis,** *f.,* 3, disaster, calamity.
*****camera, –ae,** *f.,* 1, vaulted chamber, room.
**capiō, –ere, cēpī, captus,** 3 (–io), take, seize; **cōnsilium capere,** form a plan.
**captīvus, –a, –um,** *m/f/n.,* 1, 2, captive; **captīvus, –ī,** *m.,* 2, prisoner, captive.
**caput, capitis,** *n.,* 3, head.
**cārē,** *adv.,* dearly, at a high price.
**carrus, –ī,** *m.,* 2, cart, wagon.
**cārus, –a, –um,** *m/f/n.,* 1, 2, dear.
**casa, –ae,** *f.,* 1, cottage, hut, house.
**castra, –ōrum,** *n. pl.,* 2, camp.
**cāsus, –ūs,** *m.,* 4, chance, happening, fall.
**causa, –ae,** *f.,* 1, cause, reason.
*****cavea, –ae,** *f.,* 1, hollow place, cave.
*****caverna, –ae,** *f.,* 1, cavern.
**cēdō, –ere, cessī, cessūrus,** 3, yield, go away.
**celer, celeris, celere,** *m/f/n.,* 3, swift, quick.
**celeritās, –tātis,** *f.,* 3, speed, swiftness, celerity.
**celeriter,** *adv.,* quickly, speedily; **quam celerrimē,** as quickly as possible.
*****cēnsus, –ūs,** *m.,* 4, registration, census; **cēnsum habēre,** take a census.
**centum,** *num. adj., indecl.,* one hundred.
**certāmen, –inis,** *n.,* 3, contest, match.
**certē,** *adv.,* at least, certainly.
**certus, –a, –um,** *m/f/n.,* 1, 2, fixed, certain, sure; **certiōrem facere,** make more sure, inform; **certior fierī,** to be informed.
*****cervus, –ī,** *m.,* 2, stag, deer.
**cēterī, –ae, –a,** *m/f/n., pl.,* 1, 2, the rest of, the others, all the rest.
*****Chrīstiānus, –ī,** *m.,* 2, Christian.
*****Chrīstus, –ī,** *m.,* 2, Christ.
**cibus, –ī,** *m.,* 2, food.
**circum,** *prep. + acc.,* around, about.
**circumdō, –are, –dedī, –datus,** 1, *irreg.,* place around, surround.
**citrā,** *prep. + acc.,* on this side of.
*****cīvīlis, –e,** *mf/n.,* 3, civil, civic.
**cīvis, –is,** *mf.,* 3 (–ium), citizen.

cīvitās, –tātis, *f.*, 3, citizenship, state.

clam, *adv.*, secretly.

clāmō, –āre, –āvī, –ātūrus, 1, call out, shout.

*clāmor, –ōris, *m.*, 3, shouting, noise, clamor.

clārē, *adv.*, clearly, famously.

clārus, –a, –um, *m/f/n.*, 1, 2, clear, bright, famous.

classis, –is, *f.*, 3 (–ium), division, fleet.

claudō, –ere, clausī, clausus, 3, close, shut, shut in.

*clēmentia, –ae, *f.*, 1, clemency, mercy.

cōgitō, –āre, –āvī, –ātus, 1, think, think about, ponder.

cōgnōscō, –ere, –nōvī, –nitus, 3, begin to know, find out, learn; *perf. tense*, know.

cōgō, –ere, coēgī, coāctus, 3, collect, drive together; *with inf.*, compel, force.

cohors, cohortis, *f.*, 3 (–ium), cohort (the tenth part of a legion).

collis, –is, *m.*, 3 (–ium), hill; **ab summō colle**, from the top of the hill; **(in) mediō colle**, halfway up the hill.

*colloquium, –ī, *n.*, 2, conversation.

colō, –ere, coluī, cultus, 3, till, cultivate, worship.

colōnia, –ae, *f.*, 1, colony.

*color, –ōris, *m.*, 3, color.

*columna, –ae, *f.*, 1, column, pillar.

committō, –ere, –mīsī, –missus, 3, send together, commit (a crime), entrust; **proelium committere**, begin a battle.

commoveō, –ēre, –mōvī, –mōtus, 2, alarm, startle.

comparō, –āre, –āvī, –ātus, 1, prepare, make ready.

*competitor, –ōris, *m.*, 3, competitor.

complūrēs, –a, *mf/n. pl.*, 3, very many, several.

comprehendō, –ere, –prehendī, –prehēnsus, 3, seize, catch, grasp, comprehend.

*concēdō, –ere, –cessī, –cessūrus, 3, yield, grant, permit.

*concordia, –ae, *f.*, 1, concord.

*condemnō, –āre, –āvī, –ātus, 1, condemn.

condiciō, –ōnis, *f.*, 3, terms, agreement, condition.

cōnferō, –ferre, –tulī, collātus, *irreg.*, bring together, collect.

cōnficiō, –ere, –fēcī, –fectus, 3 (–io), accomplish, complete, finish.

*cōnfidentia, –ae, *f.*, 1, confidence.

cōnfirmō, –āre, –āvī, –ātus, 1, make firm, confirm, declare, establish.

*congregō, –āre, –āvī, –ātus, 1, gather, congregate.

conjiciō, –ere, –jēcī, –jectus, 3 (–io), throw, hurl.

conjūnx, –jugis, *mf.*, 3, husband wife.

conjūrātiō, –ōnis, *f.*, 3, conspiracy.

conjūrō, –āre, –āvī, –ātus, 1, swear together, conspire.

cōnor, –ārī, –ātus sum, 1, *dep.*, try, attempt (*used with inf.*).

cōnscrībō, –ere, –scrīpsī, –scrīptus, 3, enroll, enlist.

cōnsequor, –sequī, –secūtus sum, 3, *dep.*, pursue, overtake, gain.

cōnsīdō, –ere, –sēdī, —, 3, sit down, settle.

cōnsilium, –ī, *n.*, 2, plan, advice; **cōnsilium capere**, to form a plan, adopt a plan.

cōnspectus, –ūs, *m.*, 4, sight, view, presence.

cōnspiciō, –ere, –spēxī, –spectus, 3 (–io), catch sight of, perceive.

cōnstituō, –ere, –stituī, –stitūtus, 3, decide, determine.

cōnsul, –sulis, *m.*, 3, consul.

cōnsulātus, –ūs, *m.*, 4, consulship, consulate.

cōnsultum, –ī, *n.*, 2, decree, order.

contendō, –ere, –tendī, –tentus, 3, struggle, hasten, contend.

*continenter, *adv.*, continually, continuously.

contineō, –ēre, –uī, –tentus, 2, hold together, hem in

contrā, *prep.* + *acc.*, opposite, against.

*contrōversia, –ae, *f.*, 1, dispute, controversy.

conveniō, –īre, –vēnī, –ventūrus, 4, come together, assemble.

convertō, –ere, –vertī, –versus, 3, turn about, change, convert.

convocō, –āre, –āvī, –ātus, 1, call together, summon, convoke.

**402**

cōpia, –ae, *f.*, 1, abundance, supply; *pl.*,
forces, troops.

cor, cordis, *n.*, 3, heart.

cornū, –ūs, *n.*, 4, horn, wing (of an army).

corpus, –oris, *n.*, 3, body.

cotīdiē, *adv.*, daily, every day.

crās, *adv.*, tomorrow.

*creātor, –ōris, *m.*, 3, creator, maker,
founder.

*creātūra, –ae, *f.*, 1, creature.

crēdō, –ere, –didi, –ditūrus, 3, *with dat.*,
trust, believe.

creō, –āre, –āvī, –ātus, 1, make, create,
elect, choose.

*crucifīxit, he crucified.

crūdēlis, –e, *mf/n.*, 3, cruel.

crūdēliter, *adv.*, cruelly.

culpa, –ae, *f.*, 1, fault, blame.

cum, *prep.* + *abl.*, with, along with.

cūnctus, –a, –um, *m/f/n.*, 1, 2, all, the
whole.

cupiditās, –tātis, *f.*, 3, *with gen.*, desire
for, eagerness for, greed for.

cupidus, –a, –um, *m/f/n.*, 1, 2, *with gen.*,
desirous of, eager for.

cupiō, –ere, –īvī, –ītus, 3 (–io), desire,
wish, long for, be eager.

cūr, *adv.*, why? wherefore?

cūra, –ae, *f.*, 1, care, anxiety.

*cūriōsitās, –tātis, *f.*, 3, curiosity.

cūrō, –āre, –āvī, –ātus, 1, take care of,
care for, cure.

currō, –ere, cucurrī, cursūrus, 3, run.

*currus, –ūs, *m.*, 4, chariot.

*cursus, –ūs, *m.*, 4, running, course.

cūstōdia, –ae, *f.*, 1, guard, custody.

cūstōdiō, –īre, –īvī, –ītus, 4, watch,
guard.

*cūstōs, cūstōdis, *m.*, 3, guard.

## D

dē, *prep.* + *abl.*, down from, from, about,
concerning.

dea, –ae, *f.*, 1, *dat./abl. pl.*, deābus, goddess.

dēbeō, –ēre, –uī, –itus, 2, owe; *with
infin.*, ought, must.

decem, *num. adj.*, *indecl.*, ten.

*decemvirī, –ōrum, *m. pl.*, 2, board of
ten commissioners at Rome.

decimus, –a, –um, *m/f/n.*, 1, 2, tenth.

dēditiō, –ōnis, *f.*, 3, surrender.

dēdō, –ere, –didī, –ditus, 3, give over,
surrender.

dēfendō, –ere, –fendī, –fēnsus, 3, defend, protect, strike off.

dēfessus, –a, –um, *m/f/n.*, 1, 2, tired out,
exhausted.

deinde, *adv.*, thence, from there, then,
next.

dējiciō, –ere, –jēcī, –jectus, 3 (–io),
throw down, disappoint.

dēlectō, –āre, –āvī, –ātus, 1, delight.

dēleō, –ēre, –ēvī, –ētus, 2, destroy, wipe
out, delete.

*dēlīberō, –āre, –āvī, –ātus, 1, think
about, consider.

dēligō, –ere, –lēgī, –lēctus, 3, choose,
select.

dēmōnstrō, –āre, –āvī, –ātus, 1, show,
point out, demonstrate.

dēnique, *adv.*, finally, at last.

*dēns, dentis, *m.*, 3 (–ium), tooth.

dēpōnō, –ere, –posuī, –positus, 3, lay
aside, put down, resign.

*dēportō, –āre, –āvī, –ātus, 1, carry off,
carry down, banish.

*dērīdeō, –ēre, –rīsī, –rīsus, 2, mock,
deride.

*dēscendō, –ere, –scendī, –scēnsus, 3,
descend, climb down.

*dēsertus, –a, –um, *m/f/n.*, 1, 2, de-
serted.

dēsīderō, –āre, –āvī, –ātus, 1, desire,
long for, want, wish.

*dēstinō, –āre, –āvī, –ātus, 1, determine,
destine.

dēsum, dēesse, dēfuī, —, *irreg.*, be lacking, fail.

dētrahō, –ere, –trāxī, –trāctus, 3, draw
off, remove.

Deus, –ī, *m.*, 2, God.

deus, –ī, *m.*, 2, god.

dexter, –tra, –trum, *m/f/n.*, 1, 2, right;
dextra, –ae, *f.*, right hand.

dīcō, –ere, dīxī, dictus, 3, say, tell, speak;
diem dīcere, appoint a day.

*dictātor, –ōris, *m.*, 3, dictator.

diēs, –ēī, *m.*, *sometimes fem. in sing.*, 5,
day; multō diē, late in the day; diem

**ex diē,** day after day; **ad diem,** on time, promptly.

**difficilis, -e,** *mf/n.,* 3, difficult, hard; *superl.,* **difficillimus.**

**dīligēns, -entis,** *mfn.,* 3, careful, diligent.

**dīligenter,** *adv.,* carefully, diligently.

**dīligentia, -ae,** *f.,* 1, care, industry, diligence.

**dīmittō, -ere, -mīsī, -missus,** 3, send away, dismiss, lose.

**discēdō, -ere, -cessī, -cessūrus,** 3, go away, depart.

*****discipulus, -ī,** *m.,* 2, pupil, disciple; **discipula, -ae,** *f.,* 1, pupil.

*****discordia, -ae,** *f.,* 1, discord.

**dissimilis, -e,** *mf/n.,* 3, unlike, unlike to; *superl.,* **dissimillimus.**

**diū,** *adv.,* for a long time, **quam diū,** as long as; **quam diū?** how long?

**dīvidō, -ere, -vīsī, -vīsus,** 3, divide.

*****dīvīnus, -a, -um,** *m/f/n.,* 1, 2, divine, sacred.

**dīvitiae, -ārum,** *f., pl.,* 1, riches.

**dō, dare, dedī, datus,** 1, *irreg.,* give; **inter sē dare,** exchange; **in fugam dare,** put to flight; **poenās dare,** pay the penalty.

**doceō, -ēre, -uī, doctus,** 2, *with two accusatives,* teach, explain.

*****doctrīna, -ae,** *f.,* 1, teaching, instruction, doctrine.

**doctus, -a, -um,** *m/f/n.,* 1, 2, learned.

**dolor, -ōris,** *m.,* 3, grief, pain, sorrow.

**dolus, -ī,** *m.,* 2, device, trickery, deceit.

**domicilium, -ī,** *n.,* 2, dwelling, house, home.

**domina, -ae,** *f.,* 1, mistress (of slaves), lady.

**dominus, -ī,** *m.,* 2, master (of slaves), lord.

**domus, -ūs,** *f.,* 4, house, home; **domī,** *loc.,* at home; **domum,** *acc.,* homeward, home; **domō,** *abl.,* from home, out of the house.

**dōnum, -ī,** *n.,* 2, gift, present.

**dubitō, -āre, -āvī, -ātus,** 1, doubt; *with infin.,* hesitate.

**dūcō, -ere, dūxī, ductus,** 3, lead, guide; **in mātrimōnium dūcere,** marry.

**dum,** *conj., usually with pres. indic.,* while.

**duo, duae, duo,** *m/f/n.,* two.

*****duodecim,** *num. adj., indecl.,* twelve.

**dux, ducis,** *m.,* 3, leader, general, guide.

# E

**ē** *or* **ex,** *prep. + abl.,* out of, out, from, out from.

**ēdūcō, -ere, -dūxī, -ductus,** 3, lead out.

**efficiō, -ere, -fēcī, -fectus,** 3 (-io), bring about, accomplish.

**ego, meī,** *mf., pers. pron.,* I; **ego ipse,** I myself.

**ēgredior, -gredī, -gressus,** 3 (-io), *dep.,* step forth, go out, leave.

*****elephantus, -ī,** *m.,* 2, elephant.

*****ēmittō, -ere, -mīsī, -missus,** 3, emit, let out.

**emō, -ere, ēmī, ēmptus,** 3, buy.

**eō,** *adv.,* there, thither, to that place.

**eō, īre, iī (īvī), itūrus,** *irreg.,* go.

*****epistula, -ae,** *f.,* 1, letter, epistle.

**eques, -itis,** *m.,* 3, horseman, knight; *pl.,* cavalry; **Equitēs,** the knights (one of the three orders of Roman society).

**equitātus, -ūs,** *m.,* 4, riders, body of horsemen, cavalry.

**equus, -ī,** *m.,* 2, horse.

**ēripiō, -ere, -ripuī, -reptus,** 3 (-io), snatch away, rescue.

**et,** *conj.,* and; **et . . . et,** both . . . and.

**etiam,** *adv.,* also, even, still.

**etsī,** *conj.,* even if, although.

**ēveniō, -īre, -vēnī, -ventūrus,** 4, come out, result; **ēvenit,** *impers.,* the outcome is.

**ēventus, -ūs,** *m.,* 4, outcome, result.

**excēdō, -ere, -cessī, -cessūrus,** 3, go out, withdraw, depart.

**excipiō, -ere, -cēpī, -ceptus,** 3 (-io), receive, welcome.

*****excitō, -āre, -āvī, -ātus,** 1, excite, rouse up.

*****exclāmō, -āre, -āvī, -ātūrus,** 1, shout out, exclaim.

*****exemplum, -ī,** *n.,* 2, example.

exeō, –īre, –iī (–īvī), –itūrus, *irreg.*, go forth, go out.

exercitus, –ūs, *m.*, 4, army.

exīstimō, –āre, –āvī, –ātus, 1, think, suppose, reckon.

expellō, –ere, –pulī, –pulsus, 3, drive out, expel.

*explānō, –āre, –āvī, –ātus, 1, smooth out, explain.

explōrātor, –ōris, *m.*, 3, scout.

expūgnō, –āre, –āvī, –ātus, 1, take by storm, capture by assault.

exspectō, –āre, –āvī, –ātus, 1, wait, wait for, expect.

*exspīrō, –āre, –āvī, –ātus, 1, exhale, expire.

*extendō, –ere, –tendī, –tentus, 3, extend.

exterior, –ius, *mf/n.*, 3, exterior, outer.

*extrā, *prep.* + *acc.*, outside, beyond.

*extrahō, –ere, –trāxī, –trāctus, 3, draw out, extract.

extrēmus, –a, –um, *m/f/n.*, 1, 2, outermost, end of, extreme.

## F

fābula, –ae, *f.*, 1, story, conversation, play.

facile, *adv.*, easily; *superl.*, facillimē.

facilis, –e, *mf/n.*, 3, easy; *superl.*, facillimus.

faciō, –ere, fēcī, factus, 3 (–io), make, do; certiōrem facere, inform; iter facere, march, make a march; vim facere, use force.

*factiō, –ōnis, *f.*, 3, a making, doing, political party, faction.

factum, –ī, *n.*, 2, deed, act.

*falsus, –a, –um, *m/f/n.*, 1, 2, mistaken, false.

fāma, –ae, *f.*, 1, report, rumor, fame.

*familia, –ae, *f.*, 1, household, family.

*fātālis, –e, *mf/n.*, 3, fated, deadly, fatal.

fātum, –ī, *n.*, 2, fate, destiny.

fēlīx, –īcis, *mfn.*, 3, happy, successful.

fēmina, –ae, *f.*, 1, woman.

*fenestra, –ae, *f.*, 1, window.

ferē, *adv.*, almost.

ferō, ferre, tulī, lātus, *irreg.*, bear, carry, bring.

fīdē, *adv.*, faithfully.

fidēs, –eī, *f.*, 5, faith, pledge.

fīdus, –a, –um, *m/f/n.*, 1, 2, faithful.

fīlia, –ae, *f.*, 1, *dat./abl. pl.*, fīliābus, daughter.

fīlius, –ī, *m.*, 2, son.

fīniō, –īre, –īvī, –ītus, 4, end, finish.

fīnis, –is, *m.*, 3 (–ium), end, limit; *pl.*, territory, boundary.

fīnitimus, –a, –um, *m/f/n.*, 1, 2, neighboring; *m. pl.*, neighbors.

fīō, –fierī, factus sum, *irreg.*, become, be made, be done, happen.

fīrmus, –a, –um, *m/f/n.*, 1, 2, firm, strong.

*flamma, –ae, *f.*, 1, flame.

flūmen, –inis, *n.*, 3, river.

fluō, –ere, flūxī, flūxūrus, 3, flow.

focus, –ī, *m.*, 2, hearth.

*fōrma, –ae, *f.*, 1, form.

*fōrmō, –āre, –āvī, –ātus, 1, form.

*fortasse, *adv.*, perhaps.

forte, *adv.*, by chance.

fortis, –e, *mf/n.*, 3, brave, strong.

fortiter, *adv.*, bravely.

fortitūdō, –inis, *f.*, 3, bravery, courage, fortitude.

fortūna, –ae, *f.*, 1, fortune, chance, luck.

*fortūnātus, –a, –um, *m/f/n.*, 1, 2, fortunate.

*forum, –ī, *n.*, 2, forum, market place.

fossa, –ae, *f.*, 1, ditch.

frāter, –tris, *m.*, 3, brother.

frūmentum, –ī, *n.*, 2, grain.

frūstrā, *adv.*, in vain.

fuga, –ae, *f.*, 1, flight; sē in fugam dare, flee; in fugam dare, put to flight.

fugiō, –ere, fūgī, —, 3 (–io), escape, flee.

*fugitīvus, –ī, *m.*, 2, fugitive.

fulmen, –inis, *n.*, 3, thunderbolt.

furtim, *adv.*, by stealth.

## G

gaudium, –ī, *n.*, 2, joy, gladness.

gēns, gentis, *f.*, 3 (–ium), tribe, clan, nation, race.

genus, –eris, *n.*, 3, race, kind, class.

gerō, –ere, gessī, gestus, 3, bear, carry

carry on, conduct, direct; **bellum gerere**, wage war.

*gladiātor, –ōris, *m.*, 3, gladiator, swordsman.

**gladius, –ī,** *m.*, 2, sword.

**glōria, –ae,** *f.*, 1, glory.

**grātia, –ae,** *f.*, 1, favor, grace; **grātiās agere**, give thanks.

**grātus, –a, –um,** *m/f/n.*, 1, 2, pleasing, pleasant, acceptable.

**gravis, –e,** *mf/n.*, 3, heavy, serious, grave.

**graviter,** *adv.*, heavily, severely, seriously.

**grex, gregis,** *m.*, 3, herd, flock.

# H

**habeō, –ēre, –uī, –itus,** 2, have, hold, consider; **cēnsum habēre**, take a census; **ōrātiōnem habēre**, deliver a speech.

**habitō, –āre, –āvī, –ātus,** 1, live, dwell, inhabit.

**herī,** *adv.*, yesterday.

**hīberna, –ōrum,** *n. pl.*, winter quarters.

**hīc,** *adv.*, here, in this place.

**hic, haec, hoc,** *m/f/n.*, *dem. pron./adj.*; *as pronoun:* he, she, it, *pl.*, they; *as adjective:* this, *pl.*, these; the latter.

**hiems, hiemis,** *f.*, 3, winter.

**hinc,** *adv.*, from this place, hence.

*historia, –ae, *f.*, 1, story, history.

**hodiē,** *adv.*, today.

**homō, –inis,** *m.*, 3, human being, man.

**honor, –ōris,** *m.*, 3, distinction, esteem, honor.

**hōra, –ae,** *f.*, 1, hour.

*horribilis, –e, *mf/n.*, 3, dreadful, horrible.

*hostīlis, –e, *mf/n.*, 3, hostile.

**hostis, –is,** *m.*, 3 (–ium), enemy, public enemy; *pl.*, the enemy.

**hūc,** *adv.*, hither, to this place, here.

*hūmānus, –a, –um, *m/f/n.*, 1, 2, human.

*humerus (umerus), –ī, *m.*, 2, shoulder.

**humilis, –e,** *mf/n.*, 3, low, humble.

# I

**ibi,** *adv.*, there, in that place.

**ibidem,** *adv.*, in the same place, in the same matter.

**īdem, eadem, idem,** *m/f/n.*, *dem. pron./ adj.*, the same.

**idōneus, –a, –um,** *m/f/n.*, 1, 2, suitable, fit.

**Īdūs, –uum,** *f. pl.*, the Ides (the 15th of March, May, July, October, and the 13th of the other months.

**igitur,** *conj.*, *always postpositive*, therefore.

**īgnis, –is,** *m.*, 3 (–ium), fire.

*īgnōminia, –ae, *f.*, 1, disgrace, ignominy.

**īgnōtus, –a, –um,** *m/f/n.*, 1, 2, unknown, strange.

**ille, illa, illud,** *m/f/n.*, *dem. pron./adj.*; *as pronoun:* he, she, it, *pl.*, they; *as adjective:* that, *pl.*, those; the former.

*imāgō, –inis, *f.*, 3, image, likeness.

*immolō, –āre, –āvī, –ātus, 1, sacrifice.

**immortālis, –e,** *mf/n.*, 3, undying, immortal.

**impedīmentum, –ī,** *n.*, 2, hindrance, impediment; *pl.*, heavy baggage.

**impediō, –īre, –īvī, –ītus,** 4, hinder, entangle, impede.

**imperātor, –ōris,** *m.*, 3, commander-in-chief, general, emperor.

**imperium, –ī,** *n.*, 2, command, military power, empire, power, rule.

**imperō, –āre, –āvī, –ātus,** 1, *with dat.*, order, command; levy (soldiers).

**impetus, –ūs,** *m.*, 4, attack.

*implōrō, –āre, –āvī, –ātus, 1, beseech, implore.

**impōnō, –ere, –posuī, –positus,** 3, put upon, lay upon.

**in,** *prep.*; *with abl.*, in, on; *with acc.*, into, against, upon.

**incendō, –ere, –cendī, –cēnsus,** 3, set on fire, kindle.

**incipiō, –ere, –cēpī, –ceptūrus,** 3 (–io), *used only in pres. system*, begin, undertake.

**incitō, –āre, –āvī, –ātus,** 1, urge on, arouse, spur on, incite.

**incola, –ae,** *mf.*, 1, inhabitant.

**inde,** *adv.*, from that place, thence, from there.

*indīvīsibilis, –e, *mf/n.*, 3, indivisible.

**indūcō, –ere, –dūxī, –ductus,** 3, lean on, influence, induce.

industriē, *adv.*, industriously.

industrius, -a, -um, *m/f/n.*, 1, 2, industrious.

ineō, -īre, -iī (-īvī), -itus, *irreg.*, go into, enter, begin.

*īnfāns, -antis, *mfn.*, 3, not talking; īnfāns, -antis, *mf.*, 3, infant.

*īnfantia, -ae, *f.*, 1, infancy.

īnferō, -ferre, -tulī, illātus, *irreg.*, bring in, inflict; bellum īnferre, wage war on.

īnferus, -a, -um, *m/f/n.*, 1, 2, below, lower; *superl.*, īnfimus.

*īnfestō, -āre, -āvī, -ātus, 1, make dangerous, infest.

*īnfidēlitās, -tātis, *f.*, 3, faithlessness, infidelity.

*īnflammō, -āre, -āvī, -ātus, 1, set fire to, inflame.

ingēns, ingentis, *mfn.*, 3, huge, enormous.

ingredior, -gredī, -gressus sum, 3, *dep.*, enter, step into.

inimīcus, -a, -um, *m/f/n.*, 1, 2, *with dat.*, unfriendly, hostile; inimīcus, -ī, *m.*, 2, a personal enemy.

inīquus, -a, -um, *m/f/n.*, 1, 2, unequal, unjust.

initium, -ī, *n.*, 2, beginning.

injūria, -ae, *f.*, 1, wrong, harm, injury.

injūstitia, -ae, *f.*, 1, injustice.

inopia, -ae, *f.*, 1, lack, need.

*inquam, inquis, inquit, *defective*, say.

īnsidiae, -ārum, *f. pl.* 1, treachery, plot, ambush.

īnsīgnis, -e, *mf/n.*, 3, marked, distinguished.

īnstruō, -ere, -strūxī, -strūctus, 3, arrange, build, construct, draw up (a battle line).

īnsula, -ae, *f.*, 1, island.

integer, -gra, -grum, *m/f/n.*, 1, 2, whole, untouched, honest.

*integritās, -tātis, *f.*, 3, soundness, integrity.

intellegō, -ere, -lēxī, -lēctus, 3, understand, find out, learn.

inter, *prep.* + *acc.*, between, among; inter sē, with one another.

interdum, *adv.*, sometimes.

intereā, *adv.*, in the meantime, meanwhile.

interficiō, -ere, -fēcī, -fectus, 3 (-io), kill.

interim, *adv.*, meanwhile, in the meantime.

intermittō, -ere, -mīsī, -missus, 3, interrupt.

*interrēgnum, -ī, *n.*, 2, interregnum, an interval between two reigns.

*intervallum, -ī, *n.*, 2, distance, interval.

intrā, *adv.*, *prep.* + *acc.*, within.

intrō, -āre, -āvī, -ātus, 1, enter.

inveniō, -īre, -vēnī, -ventus, 4, come upon, find.

invidia, -ae, *f.*, 1, envy, jealousy.

invidus, -a, -um, *m/f/n.*, 1, 2, envious, jealous.

*invītō, -āre, -āvī, -ātus, 1, invite.

invītus, -a, -um, *m/f/n.*, 1, 2, unwilling.

ipse, ipsa, ipsum, *m/f/n.*, *dem. pron./ adj.*, self, himself, herself, itself, very; *pl.*, themselves.

īra, -ae, *f.*, 1, anger.

īrātus, -a, -um, *m/f/n.*, 1, 2, angered, angry, irate.

is, ea, id, *m/f/n.*, *dem. pron./adj.*; *as pronoun:* he, she, it, *pl.*, they; *as adj.*: this, that, *pl.*, these, those.

iste, ista, istud, *m/f/n.*, *dem. pron./adj.*, that, that of yours; *pl.*, those, those of yours.

ita, *adv.*, so (manner), thus, in such a way.

itaque, *adv.*, and so, therefore.

item, *adv.*, likewise, in like manner.

iter, itineris, *n.*, 3, journey, route; iter facere, march; māgnum (māximum) iter, forced march.

iterum, *adv.*, a second time, again.

# J

jaciō, -ere, jēcī, jactus, 3 (-io), throw, hurl.

jam, *adv.*, now, already; nōn jam, no longer.

*jānua, -ae, *f.*, 1, front door, door, gate.

jubeō, -ēre, jūssī, jūssus, 2, *with acc. and inf.*, order, command.

jūdex, -icis, *m.*, 3, judge, juryman.

jūdicium, -ī, *n.*, 2, trial (in court), judgment, decision.

*jūdicō, -āre, -āvī, -ātus, 1, judge.
jugum, -ī, n., 2, yoke, ridge; **sub jugum mittere**, send under the yoke.
jungo, -ere, jūnxī, jūnctus, 3, join, unite.
*jūrō, -āre, -āvī, -ātus, 1, swear, take an oath.
jūs, jūris, n., 3, right, law, justice.
*jūstitia, -ae, f., 1, justice.
*jūstus, -a, -um, m/f/n., 1, 2, just.
juvenis, -e, mf/n., 3, young; **juvenis, -is**, m., 3 (-ium), young man, a youth.
juventūs, -tūtis, f., 3, youth, young men.
juvō, -āre, jūvī, jūtus, 1, irreg., help, aid.

# L

labor, -ōris, m., 3, labor, work.
labōrō, -āre, -āvī, -ātus, 1, labor, work, suffer.
*labyrinthus, -ī, m., 2, labyrinth.
lacus, -ūs, m., 4, lake.
laetitia, -ae, f., 1, joy, merriment.
laetus, -a, -um, m/f/n., 1, 2, happy, glad, joyful.
largior, -īrī, -ītus sum, 4, dep., bestow.
lātē, adv., widely.
*lātitūdō, -inis, f., 3, width, latitude.
*lātrō, -ōnis, m., 3, robber.
latus, -eris, n., 3, side, flank, wing of an army.
lātus, -a, -um, m/f/n., 1, 2, wide, broad.
laudō, -āre, -āvī, -ātus, 1, praise.
laus, laudis, 3, praise.
*lavō, -āre, -āvī, -ātus, 1, wash.
*lēgātiō, -ōnis, f., 3, legation, embassy.
lēgātus, -ī, m., 2, lieutenant (second in command to a general), envoy, ambassador.
legiō, -ōnis, f., 3, legion.
legō, -ere, lēgī, lēctus, 3, read, choose.
*leō, -ōnis, m., 3, lion.
levis, -e, mf/n., 3, light (in weight).
levō, -āre, -āvī, -ātus, 1, raise, lift.
lēx, lēgis, f., 3, law.
liber, librī, m., 2, book.
līber, -era, -erum, m/f/n., 1, 2, free.
līberī, -ōrum, m. pl., 2, children.
līberō, -āre, -āvī, -ātus, 1, set free, free.
lībertās, -tātis, f., 3, liberty, freedom.

ligneus, -a, -um, m/f/n., 1, 2, wooden.
ligō, -āre, -āvī, -ātus, 1, bind, tie; **alligō**, bind to.
lingua, -ae, f., 1, tongue, language.
littera, -ae, f., 1, letter (of the alphabet); pl., letter, epistle.
locō, -āre, -āvī, -ātus, 1, place, put.
locus, -ī, m., 2, place, region, location; pl., **loca, -ōrum**, n.
longē, adv., by far, far; **quam longē**, how far?
*longitūdō, -inis, f., 3, longitude.
longus, -a, -um, m/f/n., 1, 2, long, tall.
loquor, loquī, locūtus sum, 3, dep., speak, say, talk.
lūdō, -ere, lūsī, lūsus, 3, play, frolic, mock.
lūdus, -ī, m., 2, game, play, school.
lūmen, -inis, n., 3, light.
lūna, -ae, f., 1, moon.
*lupa, -ae, f., 1, she-wolf.
lūx, lūcis, f., 3, light; **prīmā lūce**, at daybreak.

# M

magis, adv., more.
magister, -strī, m., 2, teacher; **magistra, -ae**, f., 1, teacher.
magistrātus, -ūs, m., 4, public office, magistrate, magistracy.
*māgnitūdō, -inis, f., 3, magnitude.
māgnopere, adv., greatly, very much; comp., **magis**; superl., **māximē**.
māgnus, -a, -um, m/f/n., 1, 2, large, great, much (money); comp., **mājor**; superl., **māximus**.
mājor, mājus, mf/n., 3, comp. of **māgnus**, greater, larger.
male, adv., badly.
maleficium, -ī, n., 2, evil-doing, evil, harm.
malus, -a, -um, m/f/n., 1, 2, bad; comp., **pējor**; superl., **pessimus**.
mandātum, -ī, n., 2, order, command; pl., instructions, directions.
mane, adv., in the morning.
maneō, -ēre, mānsī, mānsūrus, 2, remain, stay.
manus, -ūs, f., 4, hand, arm, band (of men).

mare, –is, n., 3 (–ium), sea.

*marīnus, –a, –um, m/f/n., 1, 2, of the sea, marine.

maritimus, –a, –um, m/f/n., 1, 2, pertaining to the sea; maritime.

*martyr, –yris, m., 3, martyr.

māter, –tris, f., 3, mother.

*mātrimōnium, –i, n., 2, marriage; in mātrimōnium dūcere, marry; in mātrimōnium dare, give in marriage.

māximē, adv., superl. of māgnopere, very greatly, very much, especially.

māximus, –a, –um, m/f/n., 1, 2, superl. of māgnus, greatest, very large.

medius, –a, –um, m/f/n., 1, 2, middle, the middle of; (in) mediō colle (monte), halfway up the hill (mountain); mediā nocte, midnight.

melior, melius, mf/n., 3, comp. of bonus, better.

memoria, –ae, f., 1, memory; memoriā tenēre, remember.

mēns, mentis, f., 3, mind.

*mēnsa, –ae, f., 1, table.

mēnsis, –is, m., 3 (–ium), month.

*mereō, –ēre, –uī, –itus, 2, deserve, merit.

metus, –ūs, m., 4, fear, dread.

meus, –a, –um, m/f/n., 1, 2, poss. adj./ pron., my, mine.

*migrō, –āre, –āvī, –ātus, 1, migrate.

mīles, –itis, m., 3, soldier.

mīlitāris, –e, mf/n., 3, military; rēs mīlitāris, art of war, warfare.

mīlle, num. adj., indecl., one thousand; mīlia, –ium, n. pl., 3, with gen., thousands.

minimē, adv., superl. of parum, least of all, not at all, no.

minimus, –a, –um, m/f/n., 1, 2, superl. of parvus, smallest, least.

minor, minus, mf/n., 3, comp. of parvus, smaller, less.

miser, –era, –erum, m/f/n., 1, 2, wretched, unhappy, unfortunate.

mittō, –ere, mīsī, missus, 3, send.

modus, –ī, m., 2, manner, measure, mode.

moneō, –ēre, –uī, –itus, 2, warn, advise.

mōns, montis, m., 3 (–ium), mountain; (in) mediō monte, halfway up the

mountain; sub monte, at the foot of the mountain.

*mōnstrum, –ī, n., 2, monster.

*monumentum, –ī, n., 2, monument.

mora, –ae, f., 1, delay.

mors, mortis, f., 3 (–ium), death.

*mortālis, –e, mf/n., 3, mortal, deadly.

mortuus, –a, –um, m/f/n., 1, 2, dead.

mōs, mōris, m., 3, custom, habit; pl., manners.

moveō, –ēre, mōvī, mōtus, 2, move; castra movēre, break camp.

mox, adv., soon, presently.

multitūdō, –inis, f., 3, large number, multitude.

multō, adv., much, greatly.

multum, adv., much.

multus, –a, –um, m/f/n., 1, 2, much; pl., many.

mundus, –ī, m., 2, universe, world.

mūniō, –īre, –īvī, –ītus, 4, fortify.

*mūnitiō, –ōnis, f., 3, fortification.

mūnus, –eris, n., 3, duty, service, task, gift.

mūrus, –ī, m., 2, wall.

*mūsica, –ae, f., 1, music.

mūtō, –āre, –āvī, –ātus, 1, change.

*mystēria, –ōrum, n. pl., 2, mysteries.

# N

nam, conj., for, because.

*narrātiō, –ōnis, f., 3, narration.

narrō, –āre, –āvī, –ātus, 1, tell, narrate.

*nātiō, –ōnis, f., 3, nation, tribe, people.

nātūra, –ae, f., 1, nature, character.

nauta, –ae, m., 1, sailor.

*nāvālis, –e, mf/n., 3, naval.

*nāvigātiō, –ōnis, f., 3, voyage, navigation.

nāvigō, –āre, –āvī, –ātus, 1, sail, set sail, navigate.

nāvis, –is f., 3 (–ium), ship; nāvis longa, war galley, warship.

nē, conj., in order that not, that not, lest.

nē, adv., not.

–ne, interrog. particle, enclitic.

nec, conj., see neque.

*necessārius, –a, –um, m/f/n., 1, 2, necessary.

necesse, *indecl. adj.*, necessary; **necesse est**, *impers.*, *with inf.*, it is necessary, must.

necō, −āre, −āvī, −ātus, 1, put to death, kill.

negō, −āre, −āvī, −ātus, 1, say no, deny, say that . . . not.

negōtium, −ī, *n.*, 2, business, difficulty.

nēmō, —, *mf.*, *dat.*, nēminī, *acc.*, nēminem, *no gen. or abl.*, no one, nobody.

neque (nec), *conj.*, and . . . not, nor, neither; **neque (nec) . . . neque (nec)**, neither . . . nor.

neuter, −tra, −trum, *m/f/n.*, 1, 2, *gen.*, −īus, *dat.*, −ī, neither (of two).

*niger, −gra, −grum, *m/f/n.*, 1, 2, black.

nihil, *indecl. noun*, *n.*, nothing; *as adv.*, not at all.

nisi, *conj.*, if not, unless.

nōbilis, −e, *mf/n.*, 3, famous, noble; *m. pl.*, nobles.

noceō, −ēre, −uī, —, 2, *with dat.*, do harm, injure.

nōmen, −inis, *n.*, 3, name.

nōminō, −āre, −āvī, −ātus, 1, name, call by name, appoint.

nōn, *adv.*, not.

nōndum, *adv.*, not yet.

nōnne, *interrog. particle, in questions expecting the answer "Yes."*

nōnus, −a, −um, *m/f/n.*, 1, 2, ninth.

nōs, nostrum, *mf.*, *pron.*, *pl. of* ego, we.

nōscō, −ere, nōvī, nōtus, 3, begin to know, learn; *in perf.*, know.

noster, −tra, −trum, *m/f/n.*, 1, 2, *poss. adj./pron.*, our, ours.

nostrī, −ōrum, *m. pl.*, 2, our men, our troops.

nōtus, −a, −um, *m/f/n.*, 1, 2, well-known, familiar.

novem, *num. adj.*, *indecl.*, nine.

novus, −a, −um, *m/f/n.*, 1, 2, new, strange.

nox, noctis, *f.*, 3 (−ium), night; **mediā nocte**, at midnight.

*nūdus, −a, −um, *m/f/n.*, 1, 2, bare, naked, unprotected.

nūllus, −a, −um, *m/f/n.*, 1, 2, *gen.*, −īus, *dat.*, −ī, no, not any, none; *as noun*, no one.

num, *interrog. particle, in questions expecting the answer "No."*

numerus, −ī, *m.*, 2, number, account, amount.

numquam, *adv.*, never.

nunc, *adv.*, now, at this present moment.

nūntiō, −āre, −āvī, −ātus, 1, announce, report.

nūntius, −ī, *m.*, 2, messenger, message, news.

nūptiae, −ārum, *f. pl.*, 1, nuptials, marriage.

*nympha, −ae, *f.*, 1, nymph.

# O

Ō, *interj.*, O!, Oh!

ob, *prep.* + *acc.*, on account of, against.

objiciō, −ere, −jēcī, −jectus, 3 (−io), throw against, oppose, object.

oblongus, −a, −um, *m/f/n.*, 1, 2, oblong.

obses, −idis, *mf.*, 3, hostage, pledge.

*observō, −āre, −āvī, −ātus, 1, watch, observe, keep.

obtineō, −ēre, −uī, −tentus, 2, hold fast, get a hold on, occupy, obtain, acquire.

occīdō, −ere, −cīdī, −cīsus, 3, cut down, kill, put to death.

occupō, −āre, −āvī, −ātus, 1, seize, capture, occupy.

octāvus, −a, −um, *m/f/n.*, 1, 2, eighth.

octō, *num. adj.*, *indecl.*, eight.

oculus, −ī, *m.*, 2, eye.

*offerō, −ferre, obtulī, oblātus, *irreg.*, offer.

officium, −ī, *n.*, 2, service, duty, employment.

ōlim, *adv.*, once on a time, formerly, once.

*ōmen, −inis, *n.*, 3, omen.

omnīnō, *adv.*, in all, altogether.

omnis, −e, *mf/n.*, 3, every; *pl.*, all.

*opīniō, −ōnis, *f.*, 3, opinion, idea.

oportet, −ēre, −uit, 2, *impers.*, *with acc. and inf.*, it is fitting, ought.

oppidum, −ī, *n.*, 2, town.

opprimō, −ere, −pressī, −pressus, 3, overwhelm, crush.

oppūgnō, −āre, −āvī, −ātus, 1, attack, assault.

optimē, *adv., superl. of* bene, best.

optimus, –a, –um, *m/f/n.*, 1, 2, *superl. of* bonus, best, very good, excellent.

opus, –eris, *n.*, 3, work, task, labor.

ōra, –ae, *f.*, 1, coast, shore; ōra maritima, sea coast.

*ōrāculum, –ī, *n.*, 2, oracle.

ōrātiō, –ōnis, *f.*, 3, speech, oration; ōrātiōnem habēre, deliver a speech.

ōrātor, –ōris, *m.*, 3, speaker, orator.

ōrdō, –inis, *m.*, 3, row, order, rank.

orior, –īrī, ortus sum, 4, rise.

*ōrnāmentum, –ī, *n.*, 2, ornament.

ōrō, –āre, –āvī, –ātus, 1, beg, plead, pray, ask.

ōs, ōris, *n.*, 3, mouth, face.

ostendō, –ere, –tendī, –tentus, 3, point out, show.

ōtium, –ī, *n.*, 2, free time, leisure.

ovis, –is, *f.*, 3 (–ium), sheep.

# P

paene, *adv.*, almost.

paenīnsula, –ae, *f.*, 1, peninsula.

*pāgus, –ī, *m.*, 2, district.

pār, paris, *mfn.*, 3, equal, equal to.

parcō, –ere, pepercī, parsūrus, 3, *with dat.*, spare.

parēns, –entis, *mf.*, 3, parent, father, mother.

paro, –āre, –āvī, –ātus, 1, prepare, get ready, make ready.

pars, partis, *f.*, 3 (–ium), part, side; ex omnibus partibus, from all sides.

parvus, –a, –um, *m/f/n.*, 1, 2, small, little; *comp.*, minor; *superl.*, minimus.

passus, –ūs, *m.*, 4, step, stride, pace; mīlle passūs, mile; mīlia passuum, miles.

*pastor, –ōris, *m.*, 3, shepherd.

pater, –tris, *m.*, 3, father; *pl.*, forefathers, senators.

*patientia, –ae, *f.*, 1, patience.

patior, patī, passus sum, 3, *dep.*, suffer, permit.

patria, –ae, *f.*, 1, fatherland, native country, native land.

*patricius, –a, –um, *m/f/n.*, 1, 2, noble, patrician.

patriciī, –ōrum, *m. pl.*, 2, the patricians.

paucī, –ae, –a, *m/f/n., pl.*, 1, 2, few.

paulō, *adv.*, by a little, a little; paulō ante, a little while before, a short time ago; paulō posteā, a little while afterward (later).

paulum, *adv.*, a little.

pauper, –eris, *mfn.*, 3, poor; *as noun*, the poor (person, people).

pāx, pācis, *f.*, 3, peace.

peccātum, –ī, *n.*, 2, sin, crime, offense.

pecūnia, –ae, *f.*, 1, money, wealth, property.

pedes, –itis, *m.*, 3, footsoldier; *pl.*, infantrymen, infantry.

pējor, pējus, *mf/n.*, 3, *comp. of* malus, worse.

pellō, –ere, pepulī, pulsus, 3, drive out, expel, strike.

per, *prep. + acc.*, through, by.

percutiō, –ere, –cussī, –cussus, 3 (–io), strike, strike through, pierce.

perficiō, –ere, –fēcī, –fectus, 3 (–io), accomplish, finish, do thoroughly.

perfidia, –ae, 1, treachery, perfidy.

perfidus, –a, –um, *m/f/n.*, 1, 2, faithless, treacherous.

perīculum, –ī, *n.*, 2, danger, peril.

perītus, –a, –um, *m/f/n.*, 1, 2, skilled; *with gen.*, skilled in.

*permittō, –ere, –mīsī, –missus, 3, *with dat.*, intrust, permit.

permoveō, –ēre, –mōvī, –mōtus, 2, influence, disturb, alarm.

perpetuus, –a, –um, *m/f/n.*, 1, 2, unbroken, lasting, perpetual; in perpetuum, forever.

persuādeō, –ēre, –suāsī, –suāsūrus, 2, *with dat.*, persuade.

perterreō, –ēre, –uī, –itus, 2, frighten thoroughly, terrify, alarm.

pertineō, –ēre, –uī, —, 2, extend to, relate to, pertain to.

*perturbō, –āre, –āvī, –ātus, 1, disturb, perturb.

perveniō, –īre, –vēnī, –ventūrus, 4, arrive at, reach.

pēs, pedis, *m.*, 3, foot.

pessimus, –a, –um, *m/f/n.*, 1, 2, *superl. of* malus, worst.

*pestis, –is, *f.*, 3 (–ium), pest, plague.

**petō, –ere, -īvī (iī), –ītus,** 3, *with acc. of the thing, and* **ā** *or* **ab** *with abl. of the person,* seek, beg, ask.

*** phalanx, –angis,** *f.,* 3, array of soldiers in close order, phalanx.

*** philosophicus, –a, –um,** *m/f/n.,* 1, 2, philosophical.

*** pictūra, –ae,** *f.,* 1, picture.

*** pilleus, –ī,** *m.,* 2, cap.

**pīlum, –ī,** *n.,* 2, javelin, spear.

*** pīrāta, –ae,** *m.,* 1, pirate.

*** placeō, –ēre, –uī, –itūrus,** 2, *with dat.,* please; **si placet,** if you please.

*** planēta, –ae,** *f.,* 1, planet.

*** plēbēius, –a, –um,** *m/f/n.,* 1, 2, plebeian; of the people.

**plēbs, plēbis,** *f.,* 3, common people, the plebeians.

*** plūrālis, –e,** *mf/n.,* 3, plural.

**plūrimus, –a, –um,** *m/f/n.,* 1, 2, *superl. of* **multus,** most, very many.

**plūs, plūris,** *comp. of* **multus,** *sing. as noun, n.,* more; *pl. as adj.,* **plūrēs, plūra,** *mf/n.,* 3, several.

**plūs,** *adv., comp. of* **multum,** more.

**poena, –ae,** *f.,* 1, punishment, penalty; **poenās dare,** pay the penalty.

**poēta, –ae,** *m.,* 1, poet.

*** pompa, –ae,** *f.,* 1, procession, parade.

*** pōmum, –ī,** *n.,* 2, apple, fruit.

**pōnō, –ere, posuī, positus,** 3, place, put; **castra pōnere,** pitch camp.

**pōns, pontis,** *m.,* 3 (–ium), bridge.

**populus, –ī,** *m.,* 2, people, nation.

**porta, –ae,** *f.,* 1, gate.

*** portentum, –ī,** *n.,* 2, marvel, portent.

**portō, –āre, –āvī, –ātus,** 1, carry.

**possum, posse, potuī, —,** *irreg.,* can, be able.

**post,** *prep. + acc.,* after, behind; *adv.,* after, later.

**posteā,** *adv.,* afterward, later.

**posterus, –a, –um,** *m/f/n.,* 1, 2, following, next; *superl.,* **postrēmus.**

**postquam,** *conj.,* after.

**postrīdiē,** *adv.,* on the following day, next day.

**postulō, –āre, –āvī, –ātus,** 1, *with acc. of the thing and* **ā** *or* **ab** *with abl. of the person,* demand.

**potēns, –entis,** *mfn.,* 3, powerful, mighty, able.

**potestās, –tātis,** *f.,* 3, power, control.

**praeda, –ae,** *f.,* 1, booty.

**praeficiō, –ere, –fēcī, –fectus,** 3 (–io), *with acc. and dat.,* place in charge of, place in command of.

**praemittō, –ere, –mīsī, –missus,** 3, send ahead.

**praemium, –ī,** *n.,* 2, reward, prize, premium.

*** praeparō, –āre, –āvī, –ātus,** 3, prepare.

**praesidium, –ī,** *n.,* 2, protection, guard, garrison.

**praesum, –esse, –fuī, —,** *irreg., with dat.,* be in command of, be in charge of.

**praeter,** *prep. + acc.,* besides, except.

**praetereā,** *adv.,* besides.

*** praetor, –ōris,** *m.,* 3, praetor.

**premō, –ere, pressī, pressus,** 3, press, press hard, crush.

**prex, precis,** *f.,* 3, prayer, entreaty.

**prīmō,** *adv.,* at first, at the beginning.

**prīmum,** *adv.,* for the first time, first; **quam prīmum,** as soon as possible.

**prīmus, –a, –um,** *m/f/n.,* 1, 2, first, chief; **prīmā lūce,** at daybreak.

**prīnceps, –cipis,** *m.,* 3, chief, leader, first, leading man.

*** prīncipātus, –ūs,** *m.,* 4, leadership, first place.

**prior, prius,** *mf/n.,* 3, former, first; *superl.,* **prīmus.**

**prīvātus, –a, –um,** *m/f/n.,* 1, 2, personal, private.

**prō,** *prep. + abl.,* for, for the sake of, instead of, in behalf of, in defence of.

**probō, –āre, –āvī, –ātus,** 1, prove, approve.

**prōcēdō, –ere, –cessī, –cessūrus,** 3, go forward, advance, proceed.

*** prōclāmō, –āre, –āvī, –ātus,** 1, proclaim.

*** prōcōnsul, –sulis,** *m.,* 3, proconsul.

**prōdūcō, –ere, –dūxī, –ductus,** 3, lead out, lead forth, produce.

**proelium, –ī,** *n.,* 2, battle; **proelium committere,** begin battle.

**proficīscor, –ficīscī, –fectus sum,** 3, *dep.,* set out, set forth, start out.

**412**

**prōgredior, –gredī, –gressus sum,** 3 (–io), *dep.*, advance, proceed, go forward.

**prohibeō, –ēre, –uī, –itus,** 2, keep off, keep out, keep away, hinder, restrain, prohibit.

**prōjiciō, –ere, –jēcī, –jectus,** 3 (–io), throw forth, throw away, cast, betray.

*****prōmissum, –ī,** *n.,* 2, promise.

*****prōmittō, –ere, –mīsī, –missus,** 3, promise.

**prope,** *adv.,* near, nearly, almost; *prep.* + *acc.,* near.

**properō, –āre, –āvī, –ātus,** 1, hasten, hurry.

**propinquus, –a, –um,** *m/f/n.,* 1, 2, near; *with dat.,* near to.

**propter,** *prep.* + *acc.,* on account of.

**proptereā,** *adv.,* on that account; **proptereā quod,** because.

**prōscrībō, –ere, –scrīpsī, –scrīptus,** 3, outlaw, list publicly for death, proscribe.

*****prōtector, –ōris,** *m.,* 3, protector.

**prōvincia, –ae,** *f.,* 1, province.

*****prōvocātiō, –ōnis,** *f.,* 3, challenge.

**proximus, –a, –um,** *m/f/n.,* 1, 2, *superl. of* **prope,** nearest, next, last.

*****prūdēns, –entis,** *mfn.,* 3, prudent, wise.

*****prūdenter,** *adv.,* prudently.

**pūblicus, –a, –um,** *m/f/n.,* 1, 2, of the people, public.

**puella, –ae,** *f.,* 1, girl.

**puer, –puerī,** *m.,* 2, boy.

*****puerīlis, –e,** *mf/n.,* 3, youthful, boyish, puerile.

**pūgna, –ae,** *f.,* 1, fight, battle.

**pūgnō, –āre, –āvī, –ātūrus,** 1, fight.

**pulcher, –chra, –chrum,** *m/f/n.,* 1, 2, beautiful, pretty, handsome.

*****pulchritūdō, –inis,** *f.,* 3, beauty, pulchritude.

*****pūniō, –īre, –īvī, –ītus,** 4, punish.

**putō, –āre, –āvī, –ātus,** 1, think, suppose, believe.

## Q

*****quadrīgae, –ārum,** *f. pl.,* 1, four-horse chariot, chariot.

**quaerō, –ere, –sīvī, –sītus,** 3, *with acc. of the thing and* **ab, dē** *or* **ex** *with abl. of the person,* inquire, seek, ask.

*****quaestor, –ōris,** *m.,* 3, quaestor (a Roman official).

**quālis, –e,** *mf/n.,* 3, of what kind (sort)?

**quam,** *adv., after comparatives,* than; *with superl.,* as . . . as possible; *interrog. adv.,* how? **quam ob rem,** why? **quam diū,** how long? **quam diū,** as long as.

**quandō,** *interrog. adv.,* when?

**quantus, –a, –um,** *m/f/n.,* 1, 2, how great? how large?

**quārtus, –a, –um,** *m/f/n.,* 1, 2, fourth.

**quattuor,** *num. adj., indecl.,* four.

**–que,** *conj., enclitic attached to second word,* and.

**quī, quae, quod,** *m/f/n., rel. pron.,* who, which, that; *interrog. adj.,* what? which?

**quīdam, quaedam, quoddam (quid-dam),** *m/f/n., indef. adj./pron.,* certain, a certain one (thing.)

**quīnque,** *num. adj., indecl.,* five.

**quīntus, –a, –um,** *m/f/n.,* 1, 2, fifth.

**quīque, quaeque, quodquae,** *m/f/n., indef. adj.,* each.

**quis, quid,** *interrog. pron.,* who? what?

**quisque, quidque,** *mf/n., indef. pron.,* each one, every one.

**quō,** *interrog. adv.,* whither? where?

**quod,** *conj.,* because.

*****quōmodo,** *interrog. adv.,* how?

**quoque,** *adv., postpositive,* also.

**quot,** *interrog. adj., indecl.,* how many?

## R

**rapiō, –ere, –uī, raptus,** 3 (–io), snatch, seize, carry off.

*****raptō, –āre, –āvī, –ātus,** 1, seize and carry away.

**recipiō, –ere, –cēpī, –ceptus,** 3 (–io), take back; receive; **sē recipere,** withdraw, retreat.

*****recitō, –āre, –āvī, –ātus,** 1, say aloud, recite.

**reddō, –ere, –didī, –ditus,** 3, give back, pay back.

**redeō, –īre, –iī (–īvī), –itūrus,** *irreg.,* go back, return.

*****reditus, –ūs,** *m.,* 4, return.

**redūcō, –ere, –dūxī, –ductus,** 3, lead back, bring back.

**rēgīna, –ae,** *f.,* 1, queen.

regiō, –ōnis, f., 3, region.

rēgnō, –āre, –āvī, –ātūrus, 1, reign, rule.

rēgnum, –ī, n., 2, royal power, kingdom, throne.

regō, –ere, rēxī, rēctus, 3, guide, rule, direct, control, manage.

relinquō, –ere, –līquī, –lictus, 3, leave behind, abandon.

reliquus, –a, –um, m/f/n., 1, 2, remaining, the rest of.

remaneō, –ēre, –mānsī, –mānsūrus, 2, remain, stay behind.

*removeō, –ēre, –mōvī, –mōtus, 2, move away, remove.

repellō, –ere, reppulī, repulsus, 3, drive back, repel, repulse.

rēs, reī, f., 5, thing, matter, fact, affair; rēs pūblica, the state, commonwealth; rēs mīlitāris, art of war; rēs novae, revolution.

resistō, –ere, –stitī, —, 3, with dat., withstand, resist.

respondeō, –ēre, –spondī, –spōnsus, 2, answer, reply, respond.

*resurrēxit, he rose again.

retineō, –ēre, –uī, –tentus, 2, hold back, detain, retain.

reveniō, –īre, –vēnī, –ventūrus, 4, come back, return.

*reverentia, –ae, f., 1, reverence.

revocō, –āre, –āvī, –ātus, 1, call back, recall, revoke.

rēx, rēgis, m., 3, king.

*rhētoricus, –a, –um, m/f/n., 1, 2, rhetorical.

rīpa, –ae, f., 1, bank.

rogo, –āre, –āvī, –ātus, 1, with two accusatives, one of the person, one of the thing, ask, ask for.

*rosa, –ae, f., 1, rose.

*rōstrum, –ī, n., 2, beak of a bird or of a ship; pl., the rostra, speaker's platform.

rota, –ae, f., 1, wheel.

*ruīna, –ae, f., 1, downfall, collapse; pl., ruins.

rūrsus, adv., again, back again, anew.

*rūsticus, –a, –um, m/f/n., 1, 2, rustic, rural.

**S**

*saccus, –ī, m., 2, sack, bag.

sacer, –cra, –crum, m/f/n., 1, 2, sacred.

sacrificium, –ī, n., 2, sacrifice.

saeculum, –ī, n., 2, age, century.

saepe, adv., often.

salūs, –ūtis, f., 3, safety.

salūtō, –āre, –āvī, –ātus, 1, greet, salute.

*salvē, salvēte, imperative, 2, Hail! Good morning! Good day!

*sānctitās, –tātis, f., 3, sanctity.

sānctus, –a, –um, m/f/n., 1, 2, holy.

*sapientia, –ae, f., 1, wisdom.

scelus, –eris, n., 3, crime, wicked deed.

*sceptrum, –ī, n., 2, scepter.

*schola, –ae, f., 1, school.

scientia, –ae, f., 1, knowledge, science.

sciō, –īre, –īvī, –ītus, 4, know, know how.

scrībō, –ere, scrīpsī, scrīptus, 3, write.

*scrīptor, –ōris, m., 3, a writer.

*scrīptūra, –ae, f., 1, writing, scripture.

scūtum, –ī, n., 2, shield.

*sēcēdō, –ere, –cessī, –cessūrus, 3, withdraw, secede.

*sēcrētus, –a, –um, m/f/n., 1, 2, set apart, hidden, secret.

secundus, –a, –um, m/f/n., 1, 2, second, following, favorable.

sed, conj., but.

sedeō, –ēre, sēdī, sessūrus, 2, sit.

*sēditiōsus, –a, –um, m/f/n., 1, 2, quarrelsome, seditious.

*sella, –ae, f., 1, seat, chair, stool.

semper, adv., always.

*senātor, –ōris, m., 3, senator.

senātus, –ūs, m., 4, senate.

sentiō, –īre, sēnsī, sēnsus, 4, feel, perceive, think.

*sēparō, –āre, –āvī, –ātus, 1, put apart, set apart, separate.

septem, num. adj., indecl., seven.

septimus, –a, –um, m/f/n., 1, 2, seventh.

*sepulchrum, –ī, n., 2, sepulcher, burial place.

sequor, sequī, secūtus sum, 3, dep., follow.

*serēnus, –a, –um, m/f/n., 1, 2, clear, serene.

*serpēns, –entis, f., 3 (–ium), serpent.

serva, −ae, *f.*, 1, slave (female), handmaid, maidservant.

servitūs, −ūtis, *f.*, 3, slavery, servitude.

servō, −āre, −āvī, −ātus, 1, keep safe, save, guard.

servus, −ī, *m.*, 2, slave (male).

sex, *num. adj., indecl.*, six.

sextus, −a, −um, *m/f/n.*, 1, 2, sixth.

sī, *conj.*, if.

sīc, *adv.*, so (manner), in this way.

sīgnum, −ī, *n.*, 2, signal, sign, military standard.

*silentium, −ī, *n.*, 2, silence.

silva, −ae, *f.*, 1, forest, woods.

similis, −e, *mf/n.*, 3, like, similar; like to.

similiter, *adv.*, in like manner, similarly.

simulācrum, −ī, *n.*, 2, likeness, image, simulacrum.

simulō, −āre, −āvī, −ātus, 1, to make like, pretend.

sine, *prep.* + *abl.*, without.

*singulāris, −e, *mf/n.*, 3, one by one, single, singular.

sinister, −tra, −trum, *m/f/n.*, 1, 2, left; sinistra, −ae, *f.*, left hand.

*sociālis, −e, *mf/n.*, 3, sociable.

*societās, −tātis, *f.*, 3, alliance, society.

socius, −ī, *m.*, 2, ally, comrade.

sōl, sōlis, *m.*, 3, sun.

*solidus, −a, −um, *m/f/n.*, 1, 2, firm, solid, dense.

sōlus, −a, −um, *m/f/n.*, 1, 2, *gen.*, −īus, *dat.*, −ī, only, sole, alone.

*somnus, −ī, *m.*, 2, sleep.

*sordidus, −a, −um, *m/f/n.*, 1, 2, dirty, sordid.

soror, −ōris, *f.*, 3, sister.

spatium, −ī, *n.*, 2, space.

*spectāculum, −ī, *n.*, 2, spectacle.

*spectātor, −ōris, *m.*, 3, spectator.

spectō, −āre, −āvī, −ātus, 1, look at, watch.

spērō, −āre, −āvī, −ātus, 1, hope; *with acc.*, hope for.

spēs, speī, *f.*, 5, hope.

*spīna, −ae, *f.*, 1, thorn, backbone, central low wall of Roman racecourse.

*spīritus, −ūs, *m.*, 4, spirit.

*splendidus, −a, −um, *m/f/n.*, 1, 2, brilliant, shining, splendid.

*stadium, −ī, *n.*, 2, racecourse, stadium.

statim, *adv.*, immediately, at once.

*statua, −ae, *f.*, 1, statue.

statuō, −ere, −uī, −ūtus, 3, place, establish, determine.

stella, −ae, *f.*, 1, star.

*stimulō, −āre, −āvī, −ātus, 1, stimulate, stir up.

stō, stāre, stetī, stātūrus, 1, *irreg.*, stand.

studeō, −ēre, −uī, —, 2, *with dat.*, be eager for, desire; novīs rēbus studēre, desire a change of government.

studium, −ī, *n.*, 2, eagerness, zeal, study.

sub, *prep.* + *acc.*, *after verbs of motion to*, under, close up to; *with expressions of time*, toward, about; *prep.* + *abl.*, *place at which*, at the foot of, under, close to.

subitō, *adv.*, suddenly.

suī, *genitive, reflex. pron.*, of himself, herself, itself, themselves.

sum, esse, fuī, futūrus, *irreg.*, be, am, exist.

summus, −a, −um, *m/f/n.*, 1, 2, *superl. of* superus, greatest, highest, top of.

sūmō, −ere, sūmpsī, sūmptus, 3, take, put on, assume.

*super, *prep.* + *acc.*, over, above.

superbē, *adv.*, proudly.

superbia, −ae, *f.*, 1, pride.

superbus, −a, −um, *m/f/n.*, 1, 2, proud.

*superī, −ōrum, *m. pl.*, 2, the inhabitants of the upper world, the gods above.

superō, −āre, −āvī, −ātus, 1, conquer, overcome, win, defeat, surpass.

superus, −a, −um, *m/f/n.*, 1, 2, high, above; *superl.*, suprēmus/summus.

suprā, *adv.*, above.

suscipiō, −ere, −cēpī, −ceptus, 3 (−io), undertake, assume.

*suspendō, −ere, −pendī, −pēnsus, 3, hang up, suspend.

suspiciō, −ere, −spēxī, −spectus, 3 (−io), suspect.

sustineō, −ēre, −uī, −tentus, 2, hold out, withstand, sustain.

suus, −a, −um, *m/f/n.*, 1, 2, *poss. adj./ pron.*, his, her, hers, their, theirs, its; *m. pl.*, his (their) own friends (followers).

# T

*tabella, –ae, f., 1, tablet.

taberna, –ae, f., 1, shop.

tabula, –ae, f., 1, record, list, tablet.

tālis, –e, mf/n., 3, of such a kind, such.

tam, adv., with adj./adv., so, to such a degree.

tamen, conj., however, nevertheless.

tandem, adv., finally, at last, at length.

tantus, –a, –um, m/f/n., 1, 2, so great, so big, so fine.

taurus, –ī, m., 2, bull.

tēlum, –ī, n., 2, weapon, missile, dart.

*temperantia, –ae, f., 1, temperance.

*tempestās, –tātis, f., 3, storm, tempest.

templum, –ī, n., 2, temple.

temptō, –āre, –āvī, –ātus, 1, try, test, attempt.

tempus, –oris, n., 3, time.

teneō, –ēre, –uī, tentus, 2, hold, keep, occupy; memoriā tenēre, remember.

terminus, –ī, m., 2, limit, end, terminus.

terra, –ae, f., 1, earth, land, country.

terreō, –ēre, –uī, –itus, 2, frighten, terrify.

*terror, –ōris, m., 3, terror.

tertius, –a, –um, m/f/n., 1, 2, third.

*thronum, –ī, n., 2, throne.

timeō, –ēre, –uī, —, 2, fear, be afraid of.

*timidus, –a, –um, m/f/n., 1, 2, timid.

timor, –ōris, m., 3, fear, terror.

toga, –ae, f., 1, toga (robe worn by Romans in time of peace).

*torrēns, –entis, m., 3, torrent.

tōtus, –a, –um, m/f/n., 1, 2, gen., –īus, dat., –ī, whole, entire, all.

trādō, –ere, –didī, –ditus, 3, hand over, give up, surrender.

trādūcō, –ere, –dūxī, –ductus, 3, lead across, lead over, transport.

trahō, –ere, trāxī, trāctus, 3, draw, drag.

*tranquillitās, –tātis, f., 3, tranquillity.

trāns, prep. + acc., across, over.

trānseō, –īre, –iī (–īvī), –itus, irreg., cross over, go across, cross, pass through.

*trānsmarīnus, –a, –um, m/f/n., 1, 2, transmarine, from across the sea, foreign.

trānsportō, –āre, –āvī, –ātus, 1, carry over, transport.

trēs, tria, mf/n., three.

*tribūnal, –ālis, n., 3 (–ium), tribunal.

tribūnus, –ī, m., 2, tribune.

tribus, –us, f., tribe.

*tridēns, –entis, m., 3 (–ium), three-pronged spear, trident.

*triste, adv., sadly.

tristis, –e, mf/n., 3, sad.

*triumphālis, –e, mf/n., 3, of a triumph, triumphal.

*triumphus, –ī, m., 2, triumphal procession, triumph.

triumvirī, –ōrum, m. pl., 2, a board or commission of three men.

tū, tuī, mf., pers. pron., you.

tuba, –ae, f., 1, trumpet.

tum, adv., then, at that time.

*tunica, –ae, f., 1, tunic (a sleeveless garment worn by Romans).

turba, –ae, f., 1, crowd, uproar.

*tūtor, –ōris, m., 3, guardian, tutor.

tūtus, –a, –um, m/f/n., 1, 2, safe.

tuus, –a, –um, m/f/n., 1, 2, poss. adj./pron., your, yours (of one person).

# U

ubi, interrog. adv., where?; rel. adv., where, when.

ubīque, adv., everywhere.

ūllus, –a, –um, m/f/n., 1, 2, gen., –īus, dat., –ī, used in negative expressions, any at all.

*ūlterior, –ius, mf/n., 3, comp. adj., ulterior, farther.

ūltimus, –a, –um, m/f/n., 1, 2, last, farthest, remotest.

umquam, adv., ever.

ūnā, adv., along with.

unda, –ae, f., 1, wave.

unde, adv., whence; interrog. adv., whence?

undique, adv., from all sides, on all sides, everywhere.

ūnus, –a, –um, m/f/n., 1, 2, gen., –īus, dat., –ī, one; pl., alone, only.

*urbānus, –a, –um, m/f/n., 1, 2, pertaining to a city, urban.

urbs, urbis, f., 3 (–ium), city.

ut, conj., with subjunctive clause of purpose, that, in order that; with subjunctive clause *of result,* so that; *with indicative,* as, just as.

**uter, utra, utrum,** *m/f/n.,* 1, 2, *gen.,* –**ius,** *dat.,* –**ī,** *interrog. pron./adj.,* which (of two)? whichever?

**uterque, utraque, utrumque,** *m/f/n.,* 1, 2, *gen.* –**ius,** *dat.,* –**ī,** each (of two); *pl.,* both.

**ūtilis, –e,** *mf/n.,* 3, useful, usable.

**uxor, –ōris,** *f.,* 3, wife.

## V

*****vacuus, –a, –um,** *m/f/n.,* 1, 2, empty, vacant.

*****valē, valēte,** *imperative,* 2, Farewell! Good-by!

**validus, –a, –um,** *m/f/n.,* 1, 2, powerful, strong.

**vallēs, –is,** *f.,* 3 (–**ium**), valley.

**vallum, –ī,** *n.,* 2, rampart, wall.

*****varius, –a, –um,** *m/f/n.,* 1, 2, various.

**vāstō, –āre, –āvī, –ātus,** 1, lay waste, ravage, devastate.

*****vātēs, –is,** *mf.,* 3 (–**ium**), soothsayer, prophet, seer, poet.

**venia, –ae,** *f.,* 1, favor, pardon.

**veniō, –īre, vēnī, ventūrus,** 4, come.

**ventus, –ī,** *m.,* 2, wind.

**verbum, –ī,** *n.,* 2, word.

**vērē,** *adv.,* truly, really.

**vēreor, –ērī, veritus sum,** 2, *dep.,* fear, revere.

**vērō,** *adv.,* in truth, indeed, really, but.

*****vertex, –icis,** *m.,* 3, summit, vertex.

**vertō, –ere, vertī, versus,** 3, turn.

**vērum, –ī,** *n.,* 2, truth; *adv.,* truly, but.

**vērus, –a, –um,** *m/f/n.,* 1, 2, true.

**vesper, –erī,** *m.,* 2, evening.

**vester, –tra, –trum,** *m/f/n.,* 1, 2, *poss. adj./pron.,* your, yours (of more than one person).

*****veterānus, –a, –um,** *m/f/n.,* 1, 2, old, veteran.

**vetō, –āre, vetuī, vetitus,** 1, *irreg.,* forbid, veto.

**via, –ae,** *f.,* 1, road, street, way.

*****victima, –ae,** *f.,* 1, victim.

**victor, –ōris,** *m.,* 3, victor, conqueror.

**victōria, –ae,** *f.,* 1, victory.

**vīcus, –ī,** *m.,* 2, village.

**videō, –ēre, vīdī, vīsus,** 2, see.

**videor, –ērī, vīsus sum,** 2, *passive of* **videō,** seem, appear.

**vigilia, –ae,** *f.,* 1, watch, night watch (one fourth of the night).

**vigilō, –āre, –āvī, –ātūrus,** 1, be awake, watch.

**vīgintī,** *num. adj., indecl.,* twenty.

**villa, –ae,** *f.,* 1, farmhouse, country house, farm, villa.

**vincō, –ere, vīcī, victus,** 3, conquer, defeat, win.

*****violentia, –ae,** *f.,* 1, violence.

**vir, virī,** *m.,* 2, man.

**virgō, –inis,** *f.,* 3, maiden, virgin.

*****virīlis, –e,** *mf/n.,* 3, manly, virile.

**virtūs, –ūtis,** *f.,* 3, courage, manliness, virtue.

**vīs, vīs,** *f., irreg.,* force, power, violence; *pl.,* **vīrēs, vīrium,** strength, might; **vim facere,** use force.

*****vīsitō, –āre, –āvī, –ātus,** 1, visit.

**vīta, –ae,** *f.,* 1, life.

**vītō, –āre, –āvī, –ātus,** 1, avoid, shun.

**vīvō, –ere, vīxī, vīctus,** 3, live, be alive.

**vīvus, –a, –um,** *m/f/n.,* 1, 2, alive, living.

**vix,** *adv.,* barely, scarcely, hardly.

**vocō, –āre, –āvī, –ātus,** 1, call, summon.

**volō, –āre, –āvī, –ātūrus,** 1, fly.

**volō, velle, voluī, —,** *irreg.,* wish, be willing, desire.

**voluntās, –tātis,** *f.,* 3, wish, good will.

**vōs, vestrum,** *mf., pers. pron., pl. of* **tū,** you.

**vōx, vōcis,** *f.,* 3, voice; *pl.,* words; **magnā vōce,** in a loud voice.

**vulnerō, –āre, –āvī, –ātus,** 1, wound.

**vulnus, –eris,** *n.,* 3, wound.

*****vultur, –uris,** *m.,* 3, vulture.

# English-Latin

## A

**able, be able,** possum, posse, potuī, —.
**about,** dē + *abl.;* ad, circum + *acc.*
**about to** —, *use fut. part.*
**above,** *adv.,* suprā; *prep.,* super + *acc.*
**absent, be,** absum, –esse, āfuī, āfutūrus.
**accept,** accipiō, –ere, –cēpī, –ceptus.
**accident,** cāsus, –ūs, *m.*
**accomplish,** cōnficiō, –ere, –fēcī, –fectus;
 efficiō, –ere, –fēcī, –fectus.
**account, on account of,** ob, propter
 + *acc.*
**across,** trāns + *acc.;* (**a bridge**) in + *abl.*
**act,** *noun,* factum, –ī, *n.; verb,* agō, agere,
 ēgī, āctus.
**active,** ācer, ācris, ācre.
**adore,** adōrō, 1.
**advance,** prōcēdō, –ere, –cessī, –cessūrus;
 prōgredior, –ī, –gressus sum.
**advise,** moneō, –ēre, –uī, –itus.
**affair,** rēs, reī, *f.*
**after,** *adv.,* post; *prep.,* post + *acc.; conj.,*
 postquam.
**afterward,** posteā.
**again,** rūrsus; iterum (**a second time**).
**against,** in, contrā + *acc.*
**age,** aetās, –tātis, *f.;* saeculum, –ī, *n.*
**ago,** ante.
**aid,** *noun,* auxilium, –ī, *n.; verb,* adjuvō
 (juvō), 1.
**alive,** vīvus, –a, –um.
**all,** omnis, –e (*in pl.*); tōtus, –a, –um (**the
 whole**); cūnctus, –a, –um (**all together**).
**ally,** socius, –ī, *m.*
**almost,** paene; ferē.
**alone,** sōlus, –a, –um; ūnus, –a, –um.
**already,** jam.
**also,** etiam (*with verbs*); quoque, (*with
 nouns and pronouns; postpositive*).
**altar,** āra, –ae, *f.*
**although,** quamquam; etsī.
**altogether,** omnīnō.
**always,** semper.
**among,** inter, apud + *acc.*
**ancient,** antīquus, –a, –um.

**and,** et; ac, atque; –que.
**anger,** īra, –ae, *f.*
**announce,** nūntiō, 1.
**another,** alius, alia, aliud.
**answer,** respondeō, –ēre, –spondī, –spōnsus.
**any,** ūllus, –a, –um (*in negative expressions*).
**apple,** pōmum, –ī, *n.*
**appearance,** aspectus, –ūs, *m.*
**approach,** *noun,* adventus, –ūs, *m.; verb,*
 appropinquō, 1 (*with dat.,* or ad + *acc.*).
**approve,** probō, 1.
**arena,** arēna, –ae, *f.*
**arise,** orior, –īrī, ortus sum.
**armed,** armātus, –a, –um.
**arms,** arma, –ōrum, *n. pl.*
**army,** exercitus, –ūs, *m.*
**around,** circum + *acc.*
**arrival,** adventus, –ūs, *m.*
**arrive,** perveniō, –īre, –vēnī, –ventūrus
 (*with* ad + *acc.*).
**as,** ut; **as . . . as possible,** quam + *superl. adj. or adv.*
**ask,** rogō, 1; petō, –ere, –īvī, –ītus; quaerō,
 –ere, –sīvī, –sītus; ōrō, 1.
**at,** *use abl. of time or place, or locative.*
**at first,** prīmō; prīmum.
**at last,** tandem.
**at once,** statim.
**attack,** *noun,* impetus, –ūs, *m.; verb,* oppūgnō, 1.
**authority,** auctōritās, –tātis, *f.*
**avoid,** vītō, 1.
**await,** exspectō, 1.
**away from,** ā, ab + *abl.*

## B

**bad,** malus, –a, –um.
**baggage, heavy,** impedīmenta, –ōrum,
 *n. pl.*
**band (of men),** manus, –ūs, *f.*
**bank,** rīpa, –ae, *f.*
**battle,** proelium, –ī, *n.;* pūgna, –ae, *f.;*
 **begin battle,** proelium committere.
**battle line,** aciēs, –ēī, *f.*
**be,** sum, esse, fuī, futūrus.

**be able,** possum, posse, potuī, —.

**be absent,** absum, –esse, āfuī, āfutūrus.

**be afraid,** timeō, –ēre, –uī, —.

**be in command (charge) of,** praesum, –esse, –fuī, –futūrus (*with dat.*).

**be near (be present),** adsum, –esse, –fuī, –futūrus.

**be willing,** volō, velle, voluī, —.

**bear,** ferō, ferre, tulī, lātus; portō, 1.

**beautiful,** pulcher, –chra, –chrum.

**because,** quod; proptereā quod; nam.

**become, be done, be made,** fīō, fierī, factus sum.

**before,** *adv.,* anteā, ante; *prep.,* ante + *acc.*

**begin,** incipiō, –ere; *for tenses in perf. system use* coepī, –isse; **begin battle,** proelium committere.

**beginning,** initium, –ī, *n.*

**behalf, on behalf of,** prō + *abl.*

**behind,** post + *acc.*

**believe,** crēdō, –ere, –didī, –ditūrus (*with dat.*).

**besides,** *adv.,* praetereā; *prep.,* praeter + *acc.*

**best,** optimus, –a, –um.

**better,** *adj.,* melior, –ius; *adv.,* melius.

**between,** inter + *acc.*

**bind,** ligō, 1.

**blame,** accūsō, 1.

**body,** corpus, –oris, *n.*

**bold,** audāx, –ācis.

**boldly,** audācter.

**boldness,** audācia, –ae, *f.*

**book,** liber, –brī, *m.*

**booty,** praeda, –ae, *f.*

**both,** uterque, utraque, utrumque.

**both . . . and,** et . . . et.

**boy,** puer, puerī, *m.*

**brave,** fortis, –e.

**bravely,** fortiter.

**bravery,** fortitūdō, –inis, *f.*; virtūs, –tū-tis, *f.*

**break camp,** castra movēre.

**bridge,** pōns, pontis, *m.*

**brief,** brevis, –e.

**bring,** ferō, ferre, tulī, lātus; portō, 1; **bring aid,** auxilium ferre.

**bring back,** redūcō, –ere, –dūxī, –ductus; referō, –ferre, rettulī, –lātus.

**bring in, bring upon,** īnferō, –ferre, –tulī, illātus.

**broad,** lātus, –a, –um.

**brother,** frāter, –tris, *m.*

**build,** aedificō, 1; faciō, –ere, fēcī, factus.

**building,** aedificium, –ī, *n.*

**bull,** taurus, –ī, *m.*

**business,** negōtium, –ī, *n.*

**but,** sed.

**by,** ā, ab + *abl.*

## C

**call,** vocō, 1.

**call by name,** appellō, 1.

**camp,** castra, –ōrum, *n. pl.;* **break camp,** castra movēre; **pitch camp,** castra pōnere.

**can,** possum, posse, potuī, —.

**captive,** captīvus, –ī, *m.*

**care,** cūra, –ae, *f.*; dīligentia, –ae, *f.*

**care for (take care of),** cūrō, 1.

**carefully,** dīligenter.

**carry,** ferō, ferre, tulī, lātus; portō, 1; gerō, –ere, gessī, gestus; **carry on war,** bellum gerere.

**carry across, carry over,** trānsportō, 1.

**cart,** carrus, –ī, *m.*

**cause,** causa, –ae, *f.*

**cavalry,** equitēs, –um, *m. pl.;* equitātus, –ūs, *m.*

**century,** saeculum, –ī, *n.*

**certain,** certus, –a, –um; **make more certain,** certiōrem facere.

**certain, certain one,** *adj./pron.,* quīdam, quaedam, quoddam (quiddam).

**certainly,** certē.

**change,** mūtō, 1.

**chief,** prīnceps, –ipis, *m.*

**children,** līberī, –ōrum, *m. pl.*

**choose,** dēligō, –ere, –lēgī, –lēctus.

**citizen,** cīvis, –is, *mf.*

**city,** urbs, –is, *f.*

**clear,** clārus, –a, –um.

**climb,** ascendō, –ere, –scendī, –scēnsus.

**close,** claudō, –ere, clausī, clausus.

**close to,** prope + *acc.*

**come,** veniō, –īre, vēnī, ventūrus.

**coming,** adventus, –ūs, *m.*

**command,** *noun,* imperium, –ī, *n.;* man-dātum, –ī, *n.;* *verb,* imperō, 1 (*with dat.*

*of persons*); jubeō, –ēre, jūssī, jūssus (*with acc. of person + inf.*).

**command of, be in,** praesum, –esse, –fuī, –futūrus (*with dat.*).

**command of, place in,** praeficiō, –ere, –fēcī, –fectus (*with acc. and dat.*).

**commandment,** mandātum, –ī, *n.*; imperium, –ī, *n.*

**commit,** committō, –ere, –mīsī, –missus.

**common people,** plēbs, –is, *f.*

**commonwealth,** rēs pūblica, reī pūblicae, *f.*

**companion,** socius, –ī, *m.*

**compel,** cōgō, –ere, coēgī, coāctus.

**concerning,** dē + *abl.*

**condition,** condiciō, –ōnis, *f.*

**conquer,** superō, 1; vincō, –ere, vīcī, victus.

**conspiracy,** conjūrātiō, –ōnis, *f.*

**consul,** cōnsul, –ulis, *m.*

**contest,** certāmen, –inis, *n.*

**cottage,** casa, –ae, *f.*

**country,** patria, –ae, *f.*; terra, –ae, *f.*

**country house,** villa, –ae, *f.*

**courage,** virtūs, –tūtis, *f.*; animus, –ī, *m.*

**crime,** scelus, –eris, *n.*; maleficium, –ī, *n.*

**cross,** trānseō, –īre, –iī (–īvī), –itus.

**cruel,** crūdēlis, –e.

**cruelly,** crūdēliter.

**crush,** opprimō, –ere, –pressī, –pressus.

**custom,** mōs, mōris, *m.*

## D

**daily,** cotīdiē.

**danger,** perīculum, –ī, *n.*

**daring,** audācia, –ae, *f.*

**daughter,** fīlia, –ae, *f.*

**day,** diēs, –ēī, *mf.*; **every day,** cotīdiē; **following day, next day,** postrīdiē.

**daybreak, at,** prīmā lūce.

**dear,** cārus, –a, –um.

**death,** mors, mortis, *f.*

**decide,** cōnstituō, –ere, –stituī, –stitūtus; statuō, –ere, –uī, –ūtus.

**deed,** factum, –ī, *n.*

**deep,** altus, –a, –um.

**defeat,** superō, 1; vincō, –ere, vīcī, victus.

**defend,** dēfendō, –ere, –fendī, –fēnsus.

**delay,** mora, –ae, *f.*

**delight,** dēlectō, 1.

**deliver,** trādō, –ere, –didī, –ditus; **deliver a speech,** ōrātiōnem habēre.

**demand,** postulō, 1 (*with ā, ab + abl.*).

**deny,** negō, 1.

**depart,** discēdō, –ere, –cessī, –cessūrus; excēdō, –ere, –cessī, –cessūrus.

**desire,** *noun,* cupiditās, –tātis, *f.*; *verb,* cupiō, –ere, –īvī, –ītus; dēsīderō, 1; volō, velle, voluī, —.

**desirous,** cupidus, –a, –um.

**destroy,** dēleō, –ēre, –ēvī, –ētus.

**determine,** cōnstituō, –ere, –stituī, –stitūtus; statuō, –ere, –uī, –ūtus.

**device,** dolus, –ī, *m.*

**difficult,** difficilis, –e.

**diligence,** dīligentia, –ae, *f.*

**diligently,** dīligenter.

**directions,** mandāta, –ōrum, *n. pl.*

**discover,** inveniō, –īre, –vēnī, –ventus.

**distance,** spatium, –ī, *n.*

**distinguished,** īnsīgnis, –e.

**disturb,** permoveō, –ēre, –mōvī, –mōtus.

**ditch,** fossa, –ae, *f.*

**divide,** dīvidō, –ere, –vīsī, –vīsus.

**do,** agō, –ere, –ēgī, āctus; faciō, –ere, fēcī, factus.

**down from,** dē + *abl.*

**draw off,** dētrahō, –ere, –trāxī, –trāctus.

**draw up,** īnstruō, –ere, –strūxī, –strūctus.

**drive,** agō, –ere, ēgī, āctus; agitō, 1; pellō, –ere, pepulī, pulsus.

**drive back,** repellō, –ere, reppulī, –pulsus.

**drive out,** expellō, –ere, –pulī, –pulsus.

**duty,** officium, –ī, *n.*

**dwell,** habitō, 1.

**dwelling,** domicilium, –ī, *n.*

## E

**each,** *adj.,* quīque, quaeque, quodque; omnis, –e; *pron.,* quisque, quidque.

**each of two,** uterque, utraque, utrumque.

**eager,** alacer, –cris, –cre.

**eager for,** cupidus, –a, –um.

**eagerness,** studium, –ī, *n.*

**eagle,** aquila, –ae, *f.*

**earth,** terra, –ae, *f.*

**easily,** facile.

**easy,** facilis, –e.

**eight,** octō (*indecl.*).

**eighth,** octāvus, –a, –um.

either . . . or, aut . . . aut.
elapse, intermittō, –ere, –mīsī, –missus (*passive*).
elect, creō, 1.
empire, imperium, –ī, *n.*
end, fīnis, –is, *m.*; terminus, –ī, *m.*
enemy (of one's country), hostis, –is, *m.*; the enemy, hostēs, –ium, *m. pl.*; (personal) enemy, inimīcus, –ī, *m.*
enlist, cōnscrībō, –ere, –scrīpsī, –scrīptus.
enter, intrō, 1; ineō, –īre, –iī (–īvī), –itus.
entire, integer, –gra, –grum; tōtus, –a, –um.
entrust, committō, –ere, –mīsī, –missus.
envy, invidia, –ae, *f.*
equal, pār, paris; aequus, –a, –um.
escape, fugiō, –ere, fūgī, —.
establish, cōnfirmō, 1.
eternal, aeturnus, –a, –um.
even, etiam.
evening, nox, noctis, *f.*
ever, umquam.
every, omnis, –e; every day, cotīdiē.
evil, malus, –a, –um.
evil deed, maleficium, –ī, *n.*
exhausted, dēfessus, –a, –um.
expel, pellō, –ere, pepulī, pulsus.
extend, pertineō, –ere, –uī, —.
eye, oculus, –ī, *m.*

# F

faith, fidēs, –eī, *f.*
faithful, fīdus, –a, –um.
fall, cadō, –ere, cecidī, cāsūrus.
fame, fāma, –ae, *f.*
family, familia, –ae, *f.*
famous, clārus, –a, –um.
far, by far, longē.
farmer, agricola, –ae, *m.*
farm, farmhouse, villa, –ae, *f.*
fate, fātum, –ī, *n.*
father, pater, –tris, *m.*
fatherland, patria, –ae, *f.*
fault, culpa, –ae, *f.*
favor, grātia, –ae, *f.*
fear, *noun,* timor, –ōris, *m.*; metus, –ūs, *m.*; *verb,* timeō, –ēre, –uī, —.
feel, sentiō, –īre, sēnsī, sēnsus.
few, paucī, –ae, –a, *pl.*
field, ager, agrī, *m.*

fierce, ācer, ācris, ācre.
fiercely, ācriter.
fifth, quīntus, –a, –um.
fight, *noun,* pūgna, –ae, *f.*; *verb,* pūgnō, 1.
finally, tandem.
find, inveniō, –īre, –vēnī, –ventus.
find out, cōgnōscō, –ere, –nōvī, –nitus; intellegō, –ere, –lēxī, –lēctus.
finish, fīniō, –īre, –īvī (–iī), –ītus; cōnficiō, –ere, –fēcī, –fectus; perficiō, –ere, –fēcī, –fectus.
fire, īgnis, –is, *m.*
fireplace, focus, –ī, *m.*
first, first part of, prīmus, –a, –um; at first, prīmō; for the first time, in the first place, prīmum.
fitting, it is, oportet, oportēre, oportuit.
five, quīnque (*indecl.*).
flee, fugiō, –ere, fūgī, —; sē in fugam dare.
flight, fuga, –ae, *f.*
flock, grex, gregis, *m.*
flow, fluō, –ere, flūxī, flūxūrus.
fly, volō, 1.
follow, sequor, sequī, secūtus sum.
following, posterus, –a, –um; secundus, –a, –um; following day, postrīdiē.
food, cibus, –ī, *m.*
foot, pēs, pedis, *m.*; at the foot of, sub + *abl.*
foot soldier, pedes, –itis, *m.*
for, *prep.* (in behalf of, in defense of), prō + *abl.*; *conj.* (because), enim, nam, quod.
force, cōgō, –ere, coēgī, coāctus.
forces, cōpiae, –ārum, *f. pl.*
foreign, aliēnus, –a, –um.
forest, silva, –ae, *f.*
former, prior, –ius.
formerly, ōlim.
fortify, mūniō, –īre, –īvī, –ītus.
fortitude, fortitūdō, –inis, *f.*; virtūs, –tūtis, *f.*
forum, forum, –ī, *n.*
Forum, Forum, –ī, *n.*
four, quattuor (*indecl.*).
fourth, quārtus, –a, –um.
free, *adj.,* līber, –era, –erum; *verb* (set free), līberō, 1.
friend, amīcus, –ī, *m.*; amīca, –ae, *f.*

**friendly,** amīcus, –a, –um.
**friendship,** amīcitia, –ae, *f.*
**frighten,** terreō, –ēre, –uī, –itus; **frighten thoroughly,** perterreō, –ēre, –uī, –itus.
**from,** ā, ab, dē, ē, ex + *abl.*

## G

**game,** lūdus, –ī, *m.*
**gate,** porta, –ae, *f.*
**general,** imperātor, –ōris, *m.*
**gift,** dōnum, –ī, *n.*
**girl,** puella, –ae, *f.*
**give,** dō, dare, dedī, datus, 1.
**give back,** reddō, –ere, didī, –ditus.
**give up,** dēdō, –ere, –didī, –ditus; trādō, –ere, –didī, –ditus.
**glory,** glōria, –ae, *f.*
**go,** eō, īre, iī (īvī), itūrus.
**go out,** exeō, –īre, –iī (–īvī), –itūrus.
**god,** deus, –ī, *m.*; **God,** Deus, –ī, *m.*
**goddess,** dea, –ae, *f.*
**gold,** aurum, –ī, *n.*
**good,** bonus, –a, –um.
**grace,** grātia, –ae, *f.*
**grain,** frūmentum, –ī, *n.*
**great,** māgnus, –a, –um; **how great,** quantus, –a, –um; **so great,** tantus, –a, –um.
**greatly,** māgnopere.
**guard,** *noun,* cūstōs, –ōdis, *m.*; cūstōdia, –ae, *f.*; praesidium, –ī, *n.*; *verb,* cūstōdiō, –īre, –īvī, –ītus.

## H

**hand,** manus, –ūs, *f.*
**handmaid,** serva, –ae, *f.*
**happen,** fīō, fierī, factus sum.
**happy,** fēlīx, –īcis; laetus, –a, –um.
**harm,** *noun,* injūria, –ae, *f.*; *verb,* noceō, –ēre, –uī, — (*with dat.*).
**hasten,** properō, 1; contendō, –ere, –tendī, –tentus.
**have,** habeō, –ēre, –uī, –itus.
**he,** is, hic, ille, iste; **he himself,** ipse.
**head,** caput, –itis, *n.*
**hear,** audiō, –īre, –īvī, –ītus.
**heavy,** gravis, –e.
**heart,** cor, cordis, *n.*
**help,** *noun,* auxilium –ī, *n.*; *verb,* adjuvō, 1.

**her, hers,** ējus (*nonreflexive*); suus, –a, –um (*reflexive*).
**here,** hīc.
**hero,** vir, virī, *m.*
**herself,** suī (*reflexive*); ipsa (*intensive*).
**hesitate,** dubitō, 1 (*with inf.*).
**hide,** (sē) abdō, –ere, –didī, –ditus.
**high,** altus, –a, –um.
**hill,** collis, –is, *m.*
**himself,** suī (*reflexive*); ipse (*intensive*).
**his,** ējus (*nonreflexive*); suus, –a, –um (*reflexive*).
**hither,** hūc.
**hold,** habeō, –ēre, –uī, itus; teneō, –ēre, –uī, —.
**holy,** sānctus, –a, –um; sacer, –cra, –crum.
**home,** domicilium, –ī, *n.*; domus, –ūs, *f.*; **at home,** domī (*locative*).
**honor,** honor, –ōris, *m.*
**hope,** *noun,* spēs, –eī, *f.*; *verb,* spērō, 1.
**horse,** equus, –ī, *m.*
**hostage,** obses, –idis, *mf.*
**hostile,** inimīcus, –a, –um; hostīlis, –e.
**hour,** hōra, –ae, *f.*
**house,** domus, –ūs, *f.*; domicilium, –ī, *n.*; casa, –ae, *f.* (**hut**).
**household,** familia, –ae, *f.*
**how,** quam; quōmodo.
**however,** autem; tamen.
**how great,** quantus, –ā, –um.
**how long,** quam diū.
**how many,** quot.
**how much.** quantus, –a, –um.
**huge,** ingēns, ingentis.
**humble,** humilis, –e.
**hundred,** centum (*indecl.*).
**hurl,** jaciō, –ere, jēcī, jactus.
**hurry,** properō, 1; contendō, –ere, –tendī, –tentus.
**hut,** casa, –ae, *f.*

## I

**I,** ego, meī; **I myself,** ego ipse.
**Ides,** Īdūs, –uum, *f.*
**if,** sī; **if not,** nisi.
**image,** simulācrum, –ī, *n.*; imāgō, –inis, *f.*
**immediately,** statim.
**immortal,** immortālis, –e.
**in,** in + *abl.*
**in all,** omnīnō.

**in order that,** ut + *subjunctive;* **in order that . . . not,** nē + *subjunctive.*

**incite,** incitō, 1.

**increase,** augeō, –ēre, auxī, auctus.

**induce,** indūcō, –ere, –dūxī, –ductus.

**industrious,** industrius, –a, –um.

**industriously,** industriē.

**infantry,** peditēs, –um, *m. pl.*

**influence,** *noun,* auctōritās, –tātis, *f.; verb,* addūcō, –ere, –dūxī, –ductus; indūcō, –ere, –dūxī, –ductus.

**inform,** certiōrem faciō, facere, fēcī, factus; **be informed,** certior fīō, fierī, factus sum.

**inhabitant,** incola, –ae, *mf.*

**injure,** noceō, –ēre, –uī, — (*with dat.*).

**injury,** injūria, –ae, *f.*

**into,** in + *acc.*

**island,** īnsula, –ae, *f.*

**it,** id, hoc, illud, istud.

## J

**join,** jungō, –ere, jūnxī, jūnctus.

**journey,** iter, itineris, *n.*

**joy,** laetitia, –ae, *f.;* gaudium, –ī, *n.*

**joyfully,** laetē; *often translated by the adjective* laetus.

**judgment,** jūdicium, –ī, *n.*

**just,** aequus, –a, –um; jūstus, –a, –um.

## K

**keen,** ācer, ācris, ācre.

**keep,** servō, 1.

**keep away from, keep out,** prohibeō, –ēre, –uī, –itus.

**kill,** necō, 1; interficiō, –ere, –fēcī, –fectus; occīdō, –ere, –cīdī, –cīsus.

**kind,** benīgnus, –a, –um.

**kind, what kind of,** quālis, –e.

**kindness,** beneficium, –ī, *n.*

**king,** rēx, rēgis, *m.*

**kingdom,** rēgnum, –ī, *n.*

**know,** sciō, –īre, –īvī, –ītus; *in perfect system of* cōgnōscō, –ere, –nōvī, –nitus.

**knowledge,** scientia, –ae, *f.*

**known, well-known,** nōtus, –a, –um.

## L

**labor,** *noun,* labor, –ōris, *m.; verb,* labōrō, 1.

**lack,** inopia, –ae, *f.*

**lacking, be,** dēsum, –esse, –fuī, —.

**lady,** domina, –ae, *f.*

**lake,** lacus, –ūs, *m.*

**land,** terra, –ae, *f.;* **fatherland, native land,** patria, –ae, *f.*

**language,** lingua, –ae, *f.*

**large,** māgnus, –a, –um; **larger,** mājor, mājus; **largest,** māximus, –a, –um.

**last,** extrēmus, –a, –um; ūltimus, –a, –um.

**later,** post, posteā.

**law,** lēx, lēgis, *f.*

**lay aside,** dēpōnō, –ere, –posuī, –positus.

**lay waste,** vāstō, 1.

**lead,** dūcō, –ere, dūxī, ductus.

**lead across,** trādūcō, –ere, –dūxī, –ductus.

**lead back,** redūcō, –ere, –dūxī, –ductus.

**lead forth, lead out,** ēdūcō, –ere, –dūxī, –ductus; prōdūcō, 3.

**leader,** dux, ducis, *m.*

**leading man,** prīnceps, –ipis, *m.*

**learn,** cōgnōscō, –ere, –nōvī, –nitus.

**learned,** doctus, –a, –um.

**least,** *adj.,* minimus, –a, –um; *adv.,* minimē.

**leave, leave behind,** relinquō, –ere, –liquī, –lictus; **leave (depart),** discēdō, –ere, –cessī, –cessūrus; excēdō, –ere, cessī, –cessūrus.

**left,** sinister, –tra, –trum.

**left hand,** sinistra, –ae, *f.*

**legion,** legiō, –ōnis, *f.*

**less,** *adj.,* minor, minus; *adv.,* minus.

**lest,** nē + *subjunctive.*

**letter** (of alphabet), littera, –ae, *f.;* **letter** (epistle), litterae, –ārum, *f. pl.;* epistula, –ae, *f.*

**levy,** imperō, 1; cōnscrībō, –ere, –scrīpsī, –scrīptus.

**liberty,** lībertās, –tātis, *f.*

**life,** vīta, –ae, *f.*

**light,** levis, –e.

**light,** lūx, lūcis, *f.;* lūmen, –inis, *n.*

**like,** amō, 1.

**like,** similis, –e.

**likewise,** item; īdem.

limit, terminus, -ī, *m.*; fīnis, -is, *m.*
line of battle, aciēs, -ēī, *f.*
line of march, agmen, -inis, *n.*
little, *adj.*, parvus, -a, -um; *adv.*, paulum; a little while ago, paulō ante.
live, habitō, 1; vīvō, -ere, vīxī, vīctus; vītam agō, -ere, ēgī, āctus.
living, vīvus, -a, -um.
long, *adj.*, longus, -a, -um; *adv.*, long, for a long time, diū.
look, look at, spectō, 1.
lord, dominus, -ī, *m.*
lose, āmittō, -ere, -mīsī, -missus.
loud voice, māgna vōx, māgnae vōcis, *f.*
love, amō, 1.

# M

magistrate, magistrātus, -ūs, *m.*
maiden, virgō, -inis, *f.*
maidservant, serva, -ae, *f.*
make, faciō, -ere, fēcī, factus.
man, vir, virī, *m.*; homō, hominis, *m.*
manage, administrō, 1; regō, -ere, rēxī, rēctus.
many, multī, -ae, -a, *pl.*; very many, plūrimī, -ae, -a; how many, quot, *indecl.*
march, *noun*, iter, itineris, *n.*; *verb*, iter faciō, -ere, fēcī, factus; ambulō, 1.
marry, in mātrimōnium dūcō, -ere, dūxī, ductus.
master, dominus, -ī, *m.*; magister, -trī, *m.*
me, *use form of* ego.
meantime, meanwhile, intereā; interim.
memory, memoria, -ae, *f.*
message, nūntius, -ī, *m.*
messenger, nūntius, -ī, *m.*
middle, middle (part) of, medius, -a, -um.
mile, mīlle passūs; miles, mīlia passuum.
military affairs, rēs mīlitāris, reī mīlitāris, *f.*
mind, mēns, mentis, *f.*
mistress, domina, -ae, *f.*
money, pecūnia, -ae, *f.*
month, mēnsis, -is, *m.*
moon, lūna, -ae, *f.*
more, *noun*, plūs, plūris, *n.*; *adj.*, *pl.*, plūrēs, plūra; *adv.*, plūs; magis.

mother, māter, -tris, *f.*
mountain, mōns, montis, *m.*
mouth, ōs, ōris, *n.*; ōstium, -ī, *n.*
move, moveō, -ēre, mōvī, mōtus.
much, multus, -a, -um; (of money) māgnus, -a, -um.
multitude, multitūdō, -inis, *f.*
my, mine, meus, -a, -um.
myself, meī (*reflexive*); ipse, -a (*intensive*).

# N

name, *noun*, nōmen, -inis, *n.*; *verb*, nōminō, 1; appellō, 1.
narrow, angustus, -a, -um.
narrowly, angustē.
nation, gēns, gentis, *f.*; populus, -ī, *m.*; nātiō, -ōnis, *f.*
native land, patria, -ae, *f.*
nature, nātūra, -ae, *f.*
near, *prep.*, ad, prope + *acc.*; *adj.*, propinquus, -a, -um; fīnitimus, -a, -um.
necessary, necessārius, -a, -um; it is necessary, necesse est; oportet.
neighboring, fīnitimus, -a, -um.
neighbors, fīnitimī, -ōrum, *m. pl.*
neither, neque (nec); neither . . . nor, neque (nec) . . . neque (nec).
neither, neuter, -tra, -trum.
never, numquam.
nevertheless, tamen.
new, novus, -a, -um.
next, proximus, -a, -um.
next day, postrīdiē.
night, nox, noctis, *f.*
night watch, vigilia, -ae, *f.*
nine, novem (*indecl.*).
ninth, nōnus, -a, -um.
no longer, nōn jam.
no, none, nūllus, -a, -um.
no one, nūllus, -a, -um; nēmō (*no genitive*).
nor, neque (nec).
not, nōn.
not yet, nōndum.
nothing, nihil (*indecl.*).
now, nunc.
number, numerus, -ī, *m.*
nuptials, nūptiae, -ārum, *f. pl.*

## O

**obtain,** obtineō, –ēre, –uī, -tentus.

**often,** saepe.

**old,** antīquus, –a, –um.

**on,** in + *abl.*

**on account of,** ob, propter + *acc.*

**on all sides,** undique; omnibus ex partibus.

**once, once upon a time,** ōlim.

**one,** ūnus, –a, –um.

**one hundred,** centum (*indecl.*).

**only,** sōlus, –a, –um; ūnus, –a, –um.

**or,** aut; **either . . . or,** aut . . . aut.

**oration,** ōrātiō, –ōnis, *f.*; **deliver an oration,** ōrātiōnem habēre.

**orator,** ōrātor, –ōris, *m.*

**order (arrangement),** ōrdō, –inis, *m.*

**order (command),** *noun,* mandātum, –ī, *n.*; imperium, –ī, *n.*; *verb,* jubeō, –ēre, jūssī, jūssus (*with acc.* + *inf.*); imperō, 1 (*with dat. of the person*).

**other,** alius, –a, –ud; **the other (of two),** alter, –era, –erum; **(all) the others,** cēterī, –ae, –a.

**ought,** dēbeō, –ēre, –uī, –itus (*with inf.*); oportet (*with acc.* + *inf.*).

**our, ours,** noster, –tra, –trum; **our men,** nostrī, –ōrum, *m.*

**ourselves,** nostrī (*reflexive*), ipsī, –ae (*intensive*).

**out of, out from,** ē, ex + *abl.*

**outside,** extrā + acc.

**overcome,** superō, 1; vincō, –ere, vīcī, victus.

**overwhelm,** opprimō, –ere, –pressī, –pressus.

## P

**pace,** passus, –ūs, *m.*

**part,** pars, partis, *f.*

**pass over, pass through,** trānseō, –īre, –iī (–īvī), –itus.

**patrician,** *adj.,* patricius, –a, –um; *noun,* **the patricians,** patriciī, –ōrum, *m. pl.*

**peace,** pāx, pācis, *f.*

**penalty,** poena, –ae, *f.*

**peninsula,** paenīnsula, –ae, *f.*

**people,** populus, –ī, *m.*; **common people,** plēbs, plēbis, *f.*

**perceive,** sentiō, –īre, sēnsī, sēnsus.

**perpetual,** perpetuus, –a, –um; aeternus, –a, –um.

**persuade,** persuādeō, –ēre, –suāsī, –suāsūrus.

**pertain,** pertineō, –ēre, –uī, —.

**picture,** pictūra, –ae, *f.*

**pitch camp,** castra pōnō, –ere, posuī, positus.

**place,** *noun,* locus, –ī, *m.*; loca, –ōrum, *n. pl.*; *verb,* locō, 1; pōnō, –ere, posuī, positus.

**place in command (charge) of,** praeficiō, –ere, –fēcī, –fectus (*with acc. and dat.*).

**place upon,** impōnō, –ere, –posuī, –positus.

**plan,** cōnsilium –ī, *n.*; **to adopt a plan,** cōnsilium capere.

**play,** lūdō, –ere, lūsī, lūsus.

**please (if you please),** sī placet; sī tibi (vōbīs) placet.

**pleasant, pleasing,** grātus, –a, –um.

**plow,** arō, 1.

**poet,** poēta, –ae, *m.*

**ponder,** cōgitō, 1.

**poor,** pauper, –eris; **poor man,** pauper, –eris, *m.*

**possible, as . . . as possible,** quam + *superl. adj. or adv.*

**power,** potestās, –tātis, *f.*; imperium, –ī, *n.*

**powerful,** potēns, potentis.

**praise,** *noun,* laus, laudis, *f.*; *verb,* laudō, 1.

**pray,** ōrō, 1.

**prayer,** prex, precis, *f.*

**prepare,** parō, 1.

**present, be,** adsum, –esse, –fuī, –futūrus.

**pretty,** pulcher, –chra, –chrum.

**pretend,** simulō, 1.

**prisoner,** captīvus, –ī, *m.*

**private,** prīvātus, –a, –um; **private citizen,** prīvātus, –ī, *m.*

**proud,** superbus, –a, –um.

**proudly,** superbē.

**prove,** probō, 1.

**province,** prōvincia, –ae, *f.*

**public,** pūblicus, –a, –um.

**put to death,** necō, 1; interficiō, –ere, –fēcī, –fectus.

**put to flight,** in fugam dō, dare, dedī, datus.

## Q

**queen,** rēgīna, –ae, *f.*
**quick,** celer, celeris, celere.
**quickly,** celeriter.

## R ·

**race (tribe),** gēns, gentis, *f.*; genus, –eris, *n.*
**race,** certāmen, –inis, *n.*
**raise,** levō, 1.
**rampart,** vallum, –ī, *n.*
**rank,** ōrdō, –inis, *m.*
**rather,** *expressed by the comparative.*
**read,** legō, –ere, lēgī, lēctus.
**reason,** causa, –ae, *f.*
**recall,** revocō, 1.
**receive,** accipiō, –ere, –cēpī, –ceptus.
**refrain,** abstineō, –ēre, –uī, –tentus.
**region,** regiō, –ōnis, *f.*
**reign,** rēgnō, 1.
**remain,** maneō, –ēre, mānsī, mānsūrus.
**remember,** memoriā teneō, –ēre, –uī, tentus.
**reply,** respondeō, –ēre, –spondī, –spōnsus.
**rescue,** ēripiō, –ere, –uī, –reptus.
**resist,** resistō, –ere, restitī, — (*with dat.*).
**rest, rest of,** reliquus, –a, –um; cēterī, –ae, –a.
**restrain,** prohibeō, –ēre, –uī, –itus.
**return,** redeō, –īre, –iī (īvī), –itūrus.
**reward,** praemium, –ī, *n.*
**riches,** dīvitiae, –ārum, *f.*
**right (privilege),** jūs, jūris, *n.*
**right** (*opp. to* **left**)**,** dexter, –tra, –trum.
**right hand,** dextra, –ae, *f.*
**river,** flūmen, –inis, *n.*
**road,** via, –ae, *f.*
**rose,** rosa, –ae, *f.*
**route,** iter, itineris, *n.*
**row,** ōrdō, –inis, *m.*
**ruin,** ruīna, –ae, *f.*
**rule,** regō, –ere, rēxī, rēctus; rēgnō, 1.
**run,** currō, –ere, cucurrī, cursūrus.
**rush,** volō, 1.

## S

**sacred,** sacer, –cra, –crum.
**sacrifice,** sacrificium, –ī, *n.*

**sad,** tristis, –e.
**safety,** salūs, –ūtis, *f.*
**sail,** nāvigō, 1.
**sailor,** nauta, –ae, *m.*
**same,** īdem, eadem, idem.
**save,** servō, 1.
**say,** dīcō, –ere, dīxī, dictus; loquor, –ī, locūtus sum.
**say no,** negō, 1.
**scarcely,** vix.
**school,** lūdus, –ī, *m.*; schola, –ae, *f.*
**scout,** explōrātor, –ōris, *m.*
**sea,** mare, maris, *n.*
**second,** secundus, –a, –um.
**see,** videō, –ēre, vīdī, vīsus.
**seek,** petō, –ere, –īvī, –ītus; quaerō, –ere, quaesīvī, quaesītus
**seem,** videor, –ērī, vīsus sum.
**seize,** capiō, –ere, cēpī, captus; occupō, 1; rapiō, –ere, –uī, raptus.
**senate,** senātus, –ūs, *m.*
**senator,** senātor, –ōris, *m.*
**send,** mittō, –ere, mīsī, missus.
**send ahead,** praemittō, –ere, –mīsī, –missus.
**serious,** gravis, –e.
**service,** officium, –ī, *n.*; mūnus, –eris, *n.*
**set forth, set out,** proficīscor, –ī, –fectus sum.
**seven,** septem (*indecl.*).
**seventh,** septimus, –a, –um.
**several,** plūrēs, –a, *pl.*; complūrēs, –a, *pl.*
**sharp,** ācer, ācris, ācre.
**sheep,** ovis, –is, *f.*
**shield,** scūtum, –ī, *n.*
**ship,** nāvis, –is, *f.*
**shop,** taberna, –ae, *f.*
**shore,** ōra, –ae, *f.*
**short,** brevis, –e.
**shout,** *noun,* clāmor, –ōris, *m.*; *verb,* clāmō, 1.
**show,** dēmōnstrō, 1.
**side,** latus, –eris, *n.*; **on all sides,** omnibus ex partibus; undique.
**sign, signal,** sīgnum, –ī, *n.*
**sin,** peccātum, –ī, *n.*
**sister,** soror, –ōris, *f.*
**sit,** sedeō, –ēre, sēdī, sessūrus.
**six,** sex (*indecl.*).
**sixth,** sextus, –a, –um.

skilled, perītus, –a, –um (with gen.).

sky, caelum, –ī, n.

slave, servus, –ī, m.; serva, –ae, f.

small, parvus, –a, –um; smaller, minor, minus; smallest, minimus, –a, –um.

snatch, snatch away, ēripiō, –ere, –uī, –reptus.

so, ita, sīc (manner; used with verbs); tam (degree; used with adj./adv.).

so great, tantus, –a, –um.

soldier, mīles, –itis, m.

some, alius, alia, aliud; some . . . others, aliī . . . aliī.

sometimes, interdum.

son, fīlius, –ī, m.

soon, mox; as soon as possible, quam prīmum.

sorrow, dolor, –ōris, m.

space, spatium, –ī, n.

spare, parcō, –ere, pepercī, parsūrus (with dat.).

speak, loquor, –ī, locūtus sum; dīcō, –ere, dīxī, dictus.

speech, ōrātiō, –ōnis, f.

speed, celeritās, –tātis, f.

spirit, animus, –ī, m.

stand, stō, stāre, stetī, statūrus.

star, stella, –ae, f.

state, cīvitās, –tātis, f.; rēs pūblica, reī pūblicae, f.

still, etiam.

storm, tempestās, –tātis, f.

story, fābula, –ae, f.

street, via, –ae, f.

strengthen, cōnfīrmō, 1.

strike, strike through, percutiō, –ere, –cussī, –cussus.

strong, validus, –a, –um.

successful, fēlīx, –īcis.

suddenly, subitō.

suffer, patior, –ī, passus sum (with acc. + inf.).

suitable, idōneus, –a, –um.

summer, aestās, –tātis, f.

summon, convocō, 1.

sun, sōl, sōlis, m.

supply, cōpia, –ae, f.

supreme, suprēmus, –a, –um; summus, –a, –um.

sure, certus, –a, –um.

surpass, superō, 1.

surrender, dēdō, –ere, –didī, –ditus; trādō, –ere, –didī, –ditus.

surround, circumdō, –are, –dedī, –datus, 1.

suspect, suspiciō, –ere, –spēxī, –spectus.

swift, celer, celeris, celere.

swiftness, celeritās, –tātis, f.

sword, gladius, –ī, m.

# T

take, capiō, –ere, cēpī, captus; sūmō, –ere, sūmpsī, sūmptus.

take care of, cūrō, 1.

tall, altus, –a, –um; longus, –a, –um.

teach, doceō, –ēre, –uī, doctus.

teacher, magister, –trī, m.; magistra, –ae, f.

tell, narrō, 1.

ten, decem (indecl.).

tenth, decimus, –a, –um.

terrify, perterreō, –ēre, –uī, –itus.

territory, fīnēs, –ium, m. pl.

terror, terror, –ōris.

than, quam.

thanks, give thanks, grātiās agō, –ere, ēgī, āctus.

that, dem. pron./adj., is, ea, id; ille, illa, illud; that (of yours), iste, ista, istud.

that, rel. pron., quī, quae, quod.

that, conj. (not expressed in Latin after verbs of mental action).

that, in order that, conj., ut + subjunctive.

their, theirs, eōrum, eārum (nonreflexive); suus, –a, –um (reflexive).

them, use form of eī, illī, hī, istī.

themselves, suī (reflexive); ipsī, –ae (intensive).

then, at that time, tum; eō tempore.

thence, inde; deinde.

there, ibi; thither, eō; from there, inde; there is, est.

therefore, itaque; igitur (postpositive).

they, eī, illī, hī, istī.

thing, rēs, reī, f.

think, putō, 1; exīstimō, 1; arbitror, –ārī, –ātus sum, 1; think about, cōgitō, 1.

third, tertius, –a, –um.

this, dem. pron./adj., is, ea, id; hic, haec, hoc.

thither, eō.

thousand, mīlle (*indecl.*); thousands, mīlia, mīlium, *n.*

three, trēs, tria.

through, per + *acc.*

throw, jaciō, –ere, jēcī, jactus.

thunderbolt, fulmen, –inis, *n.*

thus, sīc.

time, tempus, –oris, *n.*; at that time, tum; eō tempore; for a long time, diū.

to, ad, in + *acc.*

today, hodiē.

toga, toga, –ae, *f.*

tomorrow, crās.

tongue, lingua, –ae, *f.*

toward, ad + *acc.*

town, oppidum, –ī, *n.*

transport, trānsportō, 1.

treacherous, perfidus, –a, –um.

treachery, īnsidiae, –arum, *f. pl.*; perfidia, –ae, *f.*

tribe, gēns, gentis, *f.*

tribune, tribūnus, –ī, *m.*

trickery, dolus, –ī, *m.*

troops, cōpiae, –ārum, *f. pl.*

true, vērus, –a, –um.

truly, vērē.

trumpet, tuba, –ae, *f.*

trust, crēdō, –ere, –didī, –ditūrus (*with dat.*).

try, cōnor, –ārī, –ātus sum, 1; temptō, 1.

turn, vertō, –ere, vertī, versus.

twenty, vīgintī (*indecl.*).

two, duo, duae, duo.

# U

under, sub + *acc.* (*with verbs that express motion to*); sub + *abl.* (*with verbs that express place where*).

understand, intellegō, –ere, –lēxī, –lēctus; sentiō, –īre, sēnsī, sēnsus.

undertake, suscipiō, –ere, –cēpī, –ceptus.

unfortunate, miser, –era, –erum.

unhappy, miser, –era, –erum.

unjust, inīquus, –a, –um.

unless, nisi.

unlike, dissimilis, –e.

unwilling, invītus, –a, –um.

urge on, incitō, 1.

us, *use form of* nōs.

use force, vim faciō, –ere, fēcī, factus.

used to, *imperfect tense of the indicative.*

# V

valley, vallēs, –is, *f.*

very, ipse, ipsa, ipsum; *also expressed by the superlative.*

victory, victōria, –ae, *f.*

view, cōnspectus, –ūs, *m.*

villa, villa, –ae, *f.*

village, vīcus, –ī, *m.*

virgin, virgō, –inis, *f.*

voice, vōx, vōcis, *f.*

# W

wage, gerō, –ere, gessī, gestus.

wagon, carrus, –ī, *m.*

wait, wait for, exspectō, 1.

walk, ambulō, –āre, –āvī, –ātūrus, 1.

wall, mūrus, –ī, *m.*

want, dēsīderō, 1; volō, velle, voluī, —; cupiō, –ere, –īvī, –ītus.

war, bellum, –ī, *n.*; make war on, bellum īnferre; wage war, bellum gerere.

war galley, nāvis longa, nāvis longae, *f.*

warn, moneō, –ēre, –uī, –itus.

watch, *noun* (night watch), vigilia, –ae, *f.*; *verb*, spectō, 1; (keep watch) vigilō, 1.

water, aqua, –ae, *f.*

wave, unda, –ae, *f.*

way, via, –ae, *f.*; iter, itineris, *n.*

we, nōs.

weapon, tēlum, –ī, *n.*; weapons, arma, –ōrum, *n. pl.*

well, bene.

well-known, nōtus, –a, –um.

what, *interrog. pron.*, quis, quid; *interrog. adj.*, quī, quae, quod.

what kind of, quālis, –e.

wheel, rota, –ae, *f.*

when, ubi; quandō.

whence, unde.

where, ubi; where from, unde.

which, *interrog. adj./relative pron.*, quī, quae, quod; *interrog. pron.*, quis, quid.

which (of two), uter, utra, utrum.

while, dum.

white, albus, –a, –um.

whither, quō.

who, *relative pron.*, quī, quae, quod; *interrog. pron.*, quis, quid.

**whole,** tōtus, –a, –um; integer, –gra, –grum; omnis, –e; cūnctus, –a, –um.

**why,** cūr, quam ob rem.

**wicked,** malus, –a, –um.

**wicked deed,** maleficium, –ī, *n.*

**wide,** lātus, –a, –um.

**width,** lātitūdō, –inis, *f.*

**wife,** uxor, –ōris, *f.*

**win,** superō, 1.

**wind,** ventus, –ī.

**wing,** āla, –ae, *f.*

**wing (of an army),** cornū, –ūs, *n.*

**winter,** hiems, hiemis, *f.*

**wish,** cupiō, –ere, –īvī, –ītus; volō, velle, voluī, —; dēsīderō, 1.

**with,** cum + *abl.*

**within,** *in expressions of time use abl. without prep.*

**without,** sine + *abl.*

**woman,** fēmina, –ae, *f.*

**wooden,** līgneus, –a, –um.

**woods,** silva, –ae, *f.*

**word,** verbum, –ī, *n.*

**work,** *noun,* opus, –eris, *n.*; labor, –ōris, *m.*; *verb,* labōrō, 1.

**worse,** pējor, pējus.

**worst,** pessimus, –a, –um.

**wound,** *noun,* vulnus, –eris, *n.*; *verb,* vulnerō, 1.

**wretched,** miser, –era, –erum.

**write,** scrībō, –ere, scrīpsī, scrīptus.

**wrong,** injūria, –ae, *f.*

# Y

**year,** annus, –ī, *m.*

**yesterday,** herī.

**yield,** cēdō, –ere, cessī, cessūrus.

**yoke,** jugum, –ī, *n.*

**you,** *sing.,* tū, tuī; *pl.,* vōs, vestrum.

**young,** juvenis, –e.

**young man, a youth,** juvenis –is, *m.*; adulēscēns, –entis, *m.*

**your, yours,** *sing.,* tuus, –a, –um; *pl.,* vester, –tra, –trum.

**yourself,** tuī (*reflexive*); ipse, ipsa (*intensive*).

**yourselves,** vestrī (*reflexive*); ipsī, ipsae (*intensive*).

**youth (state of being young),** adulēscentia, –ae, *f.*; juventūs, –tūtis, *f.*

# Grammatical Index

complementary infinitive, 60, 99, 103
conjugation, definition, 14, 19 • first, second, *etc.*, *see* **first conjugation**, *etc.* • irregular verbs, *see* **eō, ferō, fīō, possum, sum, volō**
consonant stems, 115, 116, 121, 122
consonants, pronunciation, 2, 358
*cum*, enclitic, 93, 145, 146, 211 • with ablative of accompaniment, 74, 75 • with ablative of manner, 75

dative case, definition, 24 • indirect object, 24 • review of uses, 347 • with adjectives, 99 • with compound verbs, 303 • with special verbs, 302
*dē*, with ablative of place from which, 192 • with ablative of separation, 192 • with cardinal numbers, 161 • with partitive genitive, 242 • with *quīdam*, 242
*dea*, dative and ablative plural, 25, 45
declension, definition, 24 • first, 25 • second, 40, 41, 45, 51, 52 • third, 115, 116, 121, 122, 126, 131 • fourth, 226, 227 • fifth, 265
demonstrative, adjectives and pronouns, 155, 156, 165, 166, 172
denominative verbs, formation, 342
deponent verbs, 307, 308, 320, 329, 340, 346
derivatives, *see* **word studies**
description, ablative, 314 • genitive, 314
difference, ablative of degree of, 259
diphthongs, 357, 358
direct object, accusative used for, 21 • position, 21, 33
direct question, 46, 341
*domus*, use, 227
*dum*, with temporal clauses, 246
*duo*, declension, 160
duration of time, accusative, 173

*ego*, declension, 144
emphasis, word order, 33 • personal pronouns, 13, 144, 156 • possessive adjectives, 9, 145
emphatic, present time, 19
enclitic, *–cum*, 93, 145, 146, 211 • *–ne*, 46 • *–que*, 11

*eō*, indicative, 303, 304 • subjunctive, 320, 329, 340, 346
*ex* (*ē*), ablative of place from which, 192 • ablative of separation, 192 • with numerals, 161 • with *quīdam*, 242
expletive, there, 14
expressions of place, 108
expressions of time, 108
extent of space, accusative, 228

*ferō*, indicative: active, 313; passive, 313 • subjunctive: active, 320, 329, 340, 346; passive, 313, 320, 329, 378
fifth declension, 265
*fīlia*, dative and ablative plural, 25, 45
*fīlius*, vocative, 52
finite verb, definition, 3
*fīō*, indicative, 205, 314, 315 • subjunctive, 320, 329, 340, 346
first conjugation, indicative: active, 19, 20, 34, 58, 64, 69, 73, 79; passive, 179, 205 • subjunctive: active, 319, 328, 339, 346; passive, 319, 328, 374, 375 • principal parts, 65
first declension, summary, 25
fourth conjugation, indicative: active, 19, 195, 196; passive, 195, 196, 205 • subjunctive: active, 319, 329, 340, 346; passive, 319, 329, 374, 375
fourth declension, 226, 227
frequentative verbs, 347
future active infinitive, 277
future active participle, as principal part of verbs, 65 • formation, 277 • with *sum*, 289
future perfect tense, active, 79, 191, 196 • passive, 204
future tense, active, 58, 185, 190, 196 • passive, 179, 185, 190, 196

gender, definition, 10 • first declension, 25 • second, 40, 41, 52 • third, 115 • fourth, 226 • fifth, 265 • grammatical, 10 • natural 10
genitive case, 9 • description, 314 • partitive (of the whole), 242 • position, 33 • possession, 9 • review of uses, 335

parsing, 107

participles, deponent verbs, 308 • equivalents for, 246, 282, 288 • forms: present active, 282, perfect passive, 205, 282, 288; future active, 277, 289 • tenses, 283, 288, 289, 296, 297 • translation, 278, 282, 288, 290, 295, 296

partitive genitive, 242

parts of speech, in Latin and English, 107

passive voice, 19, 178, 195, 196, 204, 205, 206, 320, 329, 372, 374, 378

penult, 2, 359

perfect infinitives, 271

perfect passive participle, 205, 282, 288

perfect stem, 69, 87

perfect system, 87, 191, 196, 205

perfect tense, indicative: active, 69, 191, 196; passive, 204 • subjunctive: active, 339, 340; passive, 374, 375 • vs. imperfect, 70

person, definition, 10 • indicators: active, 13, 14, 69, 79, 87; passive, 180 • relative pronoun, 210 • verb, 13

personal pronouns, first person, 144 • second, 144 • third, 146, 156, 165 • not expressed, 13, 144, 156 • with enclitic –cum, 145, 146

phrases with " to, " 24

place, adverbs of, 254 • expressions of, 108 • from which, 109, 192 • from which, with names of cities, etc., 109, 192 • in which, 15 • locative, 15, 109, 192 • to which, 109 • to which, with names of cities, etc., 109 • where, 15

pluperfect tense, indicative: active, 73, 74, 182, 183, 184, 191, 196; passive, 205 • subjunctive: active, 345; passive, 375

plūs, genitive with, 253

positive degree, 234

possession, genitive of, 9, 145, 156

possessive adjectives, 9, 145, 149

possum, indicative, 98, 99 • subjunctive, 320, 329, 340, 346

potēns, declension, 133

predicate, definition, 3 • accusative, 221 • adjective, 4, 14, 60, 103, 221, 278 • nominative, 3, 14, 102, 221, 278 • noun, 3, 14, 60, 103, 221, 278

prefixes, 5, 389

prepositions, review, 109 • with ablative, 110 • with accusative, 110

present infinitive, active, 20, 31, 33, 34, 35, 184, 195 • passive, 206

present participle, 282, 283

present stem, 20, 87, 184, 189, 195

present system, verbs, 87

present tense, indicative: active, 19, 20, 31, 184, 189, 195; passive, 179, 185 • subjunctive: active, 319; passive, 319 • use in dum-clauses, 246

primary, sequence, 340 • tenses, 340

principal (independent) clauses, 246

principal parts, 64, 184, 190, 195

progressive verb forms, 19, 35

pronouns, demonstrative, 155, 156, 180 • intensive, 150 • interrogative, 92 • personal, 144 • reflexive, 145 • relative, 210, 211

pronunciation, 2, 357–360

purpose clauses, with ut or nē, 321 • with relative pronoun, 321 • vs. result clauses, 334

quam, as adverb, 258 • with comparatives, 236 • with superlatives, 258

questions, direct, 46, 341 • indirect, 341

quī, as interrogative adjective, 93 • as relative pronoun, 210

quīdam, with dē, ex, 242

quis, as interrogative pronoun, 92

quod, with causal clauses, 246

reflexive, adjective, 149 • pronoun, 145, 146, 150, 151, 156, 157, 279 • with enclitic –cum, 146 • vs. ējus, 156

relative clause, 211, 246, 283, 288, 296, 321

relative pronoun, agreement, 211 • declension, 211 • definition, 210 • vs. interrogative adjective, 211 • vs. interrogative pronoun, 211 • with enclitic –cum, 211

respect (specification), ablative, 138

result clauses, with ut or ut nōn, 333, 334 • vs. purpose clauses, 334

F
G
H
I
J